Novels
for Students

National Advisory Board

Novels
for Students

**Presenting Analysis, Context, and Criticism on
Commonly Studied Novels**

Volume 14

Jennifer Smith, Editor

Foreword by Anne Devereaux Jordan

GALE GROUP

★

THOMSON LEARNING™

*Detroit • New York • San Diego • San Francisco
Boston • New Haven, Conn. • Waterville, Maine
London • Munich*

Novels for Students

Staff

Editor: Jennifer Smith.

Contributing Editors: Anne Marie Hacht, Michael L. LaBlanc, Ira Mark Milne, Daniel Toronto, Carol Ullmann.

Managing Editor, Content: Dwayne D. Hayes.

Managing Editor, Product: David Galens.

Publisher, Literature Product: Mark Scott.

Literature Content Capture: Joyce Nakamura, *Managing Editor*. Sara Constantakis, *Editor*.

Research: Victoria B. Cariappa, *Research Manager*. Sarah Genik, Ron Morelli, Tamara Nott, Tracie A. Richardson, *Research Associates*. Nicodemus Ford, *Research Assistant*.

Permissions: Maria L. Franklin, *Permissions Manager*. Shalice Shah-Caldwell, *Permissions Associate*. Deborah Freitas, *IC Coordinator/Permissions Associate*.

Manufacturing: Mary Beth Trimper, *Manager, Composition and Electronic Prepress*. Evi Seoud, *Assistant Manager, Composition Purchasing and Electronic Prepress*. Stacy Melson, *Buyer*.

Imaging and Multimedia Content Team: Barbara Yarrow, *Manager*. Randy Bassett, *Imaging Supervisor*. Robert Duncan, Dan Newell, Luke Rademacher, *Imaging Specialists*. Pamela A. Reed, *Imaging Coordinator*. Leitha Etheridge-Sims, Mary Grimes, David G. Oblender, *Image Catalogers*. Robyn V. Young, *Project Manager*. Dean Dauphinais, *Senior Image Editor*. Kelly A. Quin, *Image Editor*.

Product Design Team: Pamela A. E. Galbreath, *Senior Art Director*. Michael Logusz, *Graphic Artist*.

ISBN 0-7876-4897-3
ISSN 1094-3552

Printed in the United States of America.

10 9 8 7 6 5 4 3 2 1

Table of Contents

The Informed Dialogue: Interacting with Literature

When we pick up a book, we usually do so with the anticipation of pleasure. We hope that by entering the time and place of the novel and sharing the thoughts and actions of the characters, we will find enjoyment. Unfortunately, this is often not the case; we are disappointed. But we should ask, has the author failed us, or have we failed the author?

We establish a dialogue with the author, the book, and with ourselves when we read. Consciously and unconsciously, we ask questions: "Why did the author write this book?" "Why did the author choose that time, place, or character?" "How did the author achieve that effect?" "Why did the character act that way?" "Would I act in the same way?" The answers we receive depend upon how much information about literature in general and about that book specifically we ourselves bring to our reading.

Young children have limited life and literary experiences. Being young, children frequently do not know how to go about exploring a book, nor sometimes, even know the questions to ask of a book. The books they read help them answer questions, the author often coming right out and *telling* young readers the things they are learning or are expected to learn. The perennial classic, *The Little Engine That Could, tells* its readers that, among other things, it is good to help others and brings happiness:

"Hurray, hurray," cried the funny little clown and all the dolls and toys. "The good little boys and girls in the city will be happy because you helped us, kind, Little Blue Engine."

In picture books, messages are often blatant and simple, the dialogue between the author and reader one-sided. Young children are concerned with the end result of a book—the enjoyment gained, the lesson learned—rather than with how that result was obtained. As we grow older and read further, however, we question more. We come to expect that the world within the book will closely mirror the concerns of our world, and that the author will *show* these through the events, descriptions, and conversations within the story, rather than *telling* of them. We are now expected to do the interpreting, carry on our share of the dialogue with the book and author, and glean not only the author's message, but comprehend how that message and the overall affect of the book were achieved. Sometimes, however, we need help to do these things. *Novels for Students* provides that help.

A novel is made up of many parts interacting to create a coherent whole. In reading a novel, the more obvious features can be easily spotted—theme, characters, plot—but we may overlook the more subtle elements that greatly influence how the novel is perceived by the reader: viewpoint, mood and tone, symbolism, or the use of humor. By focusing on both the obvious and more subtle literary elements within a novel, *Novels for Students* aids readers in both analyzing for message and in determining how and why that message is communicated. In the discussion on Harper Lee's *To Kill a Mockingbird* (Vol. 2), for example, the mockingbird as a symbol of innocence is dealt with, among other things, as is the importance of Lee's use of humor which "enlivens a serious plot, adds depth to the characterization, and creates a sense of familiarity and universality." The reader comes to understand the internal elements of each novel discussed—as well as the external influences that help shape it.

"The desire to write greatly," Harold Bloom of Yale University says, "is the desire to be elsewhere, in a time and place of one's own, in an originality that must compound with inheritance, with an anxiety of influence." A writer seeks to create a unique world within a story, but although it is unique, it is not disconnected from our own world. It speaks to us *because* of what the writer brings to the writing from our world: how he or she was raised and educated; his or her likes and dislikes; the events occurring in the real world at the time of the writing, and while the author was growing up. When we know what an author has brought to his or her work, we gain a greater insight into both the "originality" (the world of the book), and the things that "compound" it. This insight enables us to question that created world and find answers more readily. By informing ourselves, we are able to establish a more effective dialogue with both book and author.

Novels for Students, in addition to providing a plot summary and descriptive list of characters— to remind readers of what they have read—also explores the external influences that shaped each book. Each entry includes a discussion of the author's background, and the historical context in which the novel was written. It is vital to know, for instance, that when Ray Bradbury was writing *Fahrenheit 451* (Vol. 1), the threat of Nazi domination had recently ended in Europe, and the McCarthy hearings were taking place in Washington, D.C. This information goes far in answering the question, "Why did he write a story of oppressive government control and book burning?" Similarly,

it is important to know that Harper Lee, author of *To Kill a Mockingbird,* was born and raised in Monroeville, Alabama, and that her father was a lawyer. Readers can now see why she chose the south as a setting for her novel—it is the place with which she was most familiar—and start to comprehend her characters and their actions.

Novels for Students helps readers find the answers they seek when they establish a dialogue with a particular novel. It also aids in the posing of questions by providing the opinions and interpretations of various critics and reviewers, broadening that dialogue. Some reviewers of *To Kill A Mockingbird,* for example, "faulted the novel's climax as melodramatic." This statement leads readers to ask, "Is it, indeed, melodramatic?" "If not, why did some reviewers see it as such?" "If it is, why did Lee choose to make it melodramatic?" "Is melodrama ever justified?" By being spurred to ask these questions, readers not only learn more about the book and its writer, but about the nature of writing itself.

The literature included for discussion in *Novels for Students* has been chosen because it has something vital to say to us. *Of Mice and Men, Catch-22, The Joy Luck Club, My Antonia, A Separate Peace* and the other novels here speak of life and modern sensibility. In addition to their individual, specific messages of prejudice, power, love or hate, living and dying, however, they and all great literature also share a common intent. They force us to *think*—about life, literature, and about others, not just about ourselves. They pry us from the narrow confines of our minds and thrust us outward to confront the world of books and the larger, real world we all share. *Novels for Students* helps us in this confrontation by providing the means of enriching our conversation with literature and the world, by creating an *informed* dialogue, one that brings true pleasure to the personal act of reading.

Sources

Harold Bloom, *The Western Canon, The Books and School of the Ages,* Riverhead Books, 1994.

Watty Piper, *The Little Engine That Could,* Platt & Munk, 1930.

Anne Devereaux Jordan
Senior Editor, TALL
(Teaching and Learning Literature).

Introduction

Purpose of the Book

The purpose of *Novels for Students (NfS)* is to provide readers with a guide to understanding, enjoying, and studying novels by giving them easy access to information about the work. Part of Gale's "For Students" Literature line, *NfS* is specifically designed to meet the curricular needs of high school and undergraduate college students and their teachers, as well as the interests of general readers and researchers considering specific novels. While each volume contains entries on "classic" novels frequently studied in classrooms, there are also entries containing hard-to-find information on contemporary novels, including works by multicultural, international, and women novelists.

The information covered in each entry includes an introduction to the novel and the novel's author; a plot summary, to help readers unravel and understand the events in a novel; descriptions of important characters, including explanation of a given character's role in the novel as well as discussion about that character's relationship to other characters in the novel; analysis of important themes in the novel; and an explanation of important literary techniques and movements as they are demonstrated in the novel.

In addition to this material, which helps the readers analyze the novel itself, students are also provided with important information on the literary and historical background informing each work. This includes a historical context essay, a box comparing the time or place the novel was written to modern Western culture, a critical overview essay, and excerpts from critical essays on the novel. A unique feature of *NfS* is a specially commissioned critical essay on each novel, targeted toward the student reader.

To further aid the student in studying and enjoying each novel, information on media adaptations is provided, as well as reading suggestions for works of fiction and nonfiction on similar themes and topics. Classroom aids include ideas for research papers and lists of critical sources that provide additional material on the novel.

Selection Criteria

The titles for each volume of *NfS* were selected by surveying numerous sources on teaching literature and analyzing course curricula for various school districts. Some of the sources surveyed included: literature anthologies; *Reading Lists for College-Bound Students: The Books Most Recommended by America's Top Colleges;* textbooks on teaching the novel; a College Board survey of novels commonly studied in high schools; a National Council of Teachers of English (NCTE) survey of novels commonly studied in high schools; the NCTE's *Teaching Literature in High School: The Novel;* and the Young Adult Library Services Association (YALSA) list of best books for young adults of the past twenty-five years.

Input was also solicited from our advisory board, as well as educators from various areas.

From these discussions, it was determined that each volume should have a mix of "classic" novels (those works commonly taught in literature classes) and contemporary novels for which information is often hard to find. Because of the interest in expanding the canon of literature, an emphasis was also placed on including works by international, multicultural, and women authors. Our advisory board members—educational professionals—helped pare down the list for each volume. If a work was not selected for the present volume, it was often noted as a possibility for a future volume. As always, the editor welcomes suggestions for titles to be included in future volumes.

How Each Entry Is Organized

Each entry, or chapter, in *NfS* focuses on one novel. Each entry heading lists the full name of the novel, the author's name, and the date of the novel's publication. The following elements are contained in each entry:

- **Introduction:** a brief overview of the novel which provides information about its first appearance, its literary standing, any controversies surrounding the work, and major conflicts or themes within the work.

- **Author Biography:** this section includes basic facts about the author's life, and focuses on events and times in the author's life that inspired the novel in question.

- **Plot Summary:** a factual description of the major events in the novel. Lengthy summaries are broken down with subheads.

- **Characters:** an alphabetical listing of major characters in the novel. Each character name is followed by a brief to an extensive description of the character's role in the novel, as well as discussion of the character's actions, relationships, and possible motivation.

  Characters are listed alphabetically by last name. If a character is unnamed—for instance, the narrator in *Invisible Man*–the character is listed as "The Narrator" and alphabetized as "Narrator." If a character's first name is the only one given, the name will appear alphabetically by that name.

- Variant names are also included for each character. Thus, the full name "Jean Louise Finch" would head the listing for the narrator of *To Kill a Mockingbird,* but listed in a separate cross-reference would be the nickname "Scout Finch."

- **Themes:** a thorough overview of how the major topics, themes, and issues are addressed within the novel. Each theme discussed appears in a separate subhead, and is easily accessed through the boldface entries in the Subject/Theme Index.

- **Style:** this section addresses important style elements of the novel, such as setting, point of view, and narration; important literary devices used, such as imagery, foreshadowing, symbolism; and, if applicable, genres to which the work might have belonged, such as Gothicism or Romanticism. Literary terms are explained within the entry, but can also be found in the Glossary.

- **Historical Context:** This section outlines the social, political, and cultural climate *in which the author lived and the novel was created.* This section may include descriptions of related historical events, pertinent aspects of daily life in the culture, and the artistic and literary sensibilities of the time in which the work was written. If the novel is a historical work, information regarding the time in which the novel is set is also included. Each section is broken down with helpful subheads.

- **Critical Overview:** this section provides background on the critical reputation of the novel, including bannings or any other public controversies surrounding the work. For older works, this section includes a history of how the novel was first received and how perceptions of it may have changed over the years; for more recent novels, direct quotes from early reviews may also be included.

- **Criticism:** an essay commissioned by *NfS* which specifically deals with the novel and is written specifically for the student audience, as well as excerpts from previously published criticism on the work (if available).

- **Sources:** an alphabetical list of critical material quoted in the entry, with full bibliographical information.

- **Further Reading:** an alphabetical list of other critical sources which may prove useful for the student. Includes full bibliographical information and a brief annotation.

In addition, each entry contains the following highlighted sections, set apart from the main text as sidebars:

- **Media Adaptations:** a list of important film and television adaptations of the novel, including source information. The list also includes stage adaptations, audio recordings, musical adaptations, etc.

- **Topics for Further Study:** a list of potential study questions or research topics dealing with the novel. This section includes questions related to other disciplines the student may be studying, such as American history, world history, science, math, government, business, geography, economics, psychology, etc.

- **Compare and Contrast Box:** an "at-a-glance" comparison of the cultural and historical differences between the author's time and culture and late twentieth century/early twenty-first century Western culture. This box includes pertinent parallels between the major scientific, political, and cultural movements of the time or place the novel was written, the time or place the novel was set (if a historical work), and modern Western culture. Works written after 1990 may not have this box.

- **What Do I Read Next?:** a list of works that might complement the featured novel or serve as a contrast to it. This includes works by the same author and others, works of fiction and nonfiction, and works from various genres, cultures, and eras.

Other Features

NfS includes "The Informed Dialogue: Interacting with Literature," a foreword by Anne Devereaux Jordan, Senior Editor for *Teaching and Learning Literature* (*TALL*), and a founder of the Children's Literature Association. This essay provides an enlightening look at how readers interact with literature and how *Novels for Students* can help teachers show students how to enrich their own reading experiences.

A Cumulative Author/Title Index lists the authors and titles covered in each volume of the *NfS* series.

A Cumulative Nationality/Ethnicity Index breaks down the authors and titles covered in each volume of the *NfS* series by nationality and ethnicity.

A Subject/Theme Index, specific to each volume, provides easy reference for users who may be studying a particular subject or theme rather than a single work. Significant subjects from events to broad themes are included, and the entries pointing to the specific theme discussions in each entry are indicated in **boldface**.

Each entry has several illustrations, including photos of the author, stills from film adaptations (if available), maps, and/or photos of key historical events.

Citing Novels for Students

When writing papers, students who quote directly from any volume of *Novels for Students* may use the following general forms. These examples are based on MLA style; teachers may request that students adhere to a different style, so the following examples may be adapted as needed.

When citing text from *NfS* that is not attributed to a particular author (i.e., the Themes, Style, Historical Context sections, etc.), the following format should be used in the bibliography section:

"Night." *Novels for Students.* Ed. Marie Rose Napierkowski. Vol. 4. Detroit: Gale, 1998. 234–35.

When quoting the specially commissioned essay from *NfS* (usually the first piece under the "Criticism" subhead), the following format should be used:

Miller, Tyrus. Critical Essay on "Winesburg, Ohio." *Novels for Students.* Ed. Marie Rose Napierkowski. Vol. 4. Detroit: Gale, 1998. 335–39.

When quoting a journal or newspaper essay that is reprinted in a volume of *NfS,* the following form may be used:

Malak, Amin. "Margaret Atwood's "*The Handmaid's Tale* and the Dystopian Tradition," *Canadian Literature* No. 112 (Spring, 1987), 9–16; excerpted and reprinted in *Novels for Students,* Vol. 4, ed. Marie Rose Napierkowski (Detroit: Gale, 1998), pp. 133–36.

When quoting material reprinted from a book that appears in a volume of *NfS,* the following form may be used:

Adams, Timothy Dow. "Richard Wright: "Wearing the Mask," in *Telling Lies in Modern American Autobiography* (University of North Carolina Press, 1990), 69–83; excerpted and reprinted in *Novels for Students,* Vol. 1, ed. Diane Telgen (Detroit: Gale, 1997), pp. 59–61.

We Welcome Your Suggestions

The editor of *Novels for Students* welcomes your comments and ideas. Readers who wish to suggest novels to appear in future volumes, or who have other suggestions, are cordially invited to contact the editor. You may contact the editor via e-mail at: **ForStudentsEditors@gale.com.** Or write to the editor at:

Editor, *Novels for Students*
Gale Group
27500 Drake Road
Farmington Hills, MI 48331-3535

Literary Chronology

1775: Jane Austen is born on December 16 in England.

1802: Alexandre Dumas is born on July 24 in Villers-Coterêts, north of Paris.

1812: Charles Dickens is born on February 7 in Portsea, England.

1817: Jane Austen dies, most likely of Addison's disease, on July 18.

1818: Jane Austen's *Persuasion* is published.

1821: Gustave Flaubert is born on December 12 in Rouen, France.

1831: Rebecca Harding Davis is born Rebecca Harding on June 24 at her aunt's home in Washington, Pennsylvania.

1838: Charles Dickens's *Oliver Twist* is published to popular acclaim.

1844: Alexandre Dumas's *The Three Musketeers* is published.

1857: Gustave Flaubert's *Madame Bovary* is published in two volumes in April. The novel immediately gains a wide readership, due not only to its notoriety but also to its artistry.

1862: Rebecca Harding Davis's *Margret Howth: A Story of To-Day* is published.

1870: Charles Dickens dies on June 8, while working on his last book, *The Mystery of Edwin Drood*.

1870: Alexandre Dumas dies in Puy, near Dieppe on the coast of France, on December 5.

1880: Gustave Flaubert dies on May 8 in Croisset, France.

1890: Katherine Anne Porter is born Callie Russell Porter on May 15 in Indian Creek, Texas.

1896: John Dos Passos is born on January 14 in Chicago, Illinois.

1899: Ernest Hemingway is born on July 21 in Oak Park, Illinois.

1910: Rebecca Harding Davis dies on September 29 in Mount Kisco, New York, of edema of the lungs caused by heart disease.

1915: Saul Bellow is born in Lachine, Quebec, Canada.

1931: Marilyn Harris is born on June 4 in Oklahoma City, Oklahoma.

1931: Nobel laureate Toni Morrison is born Chloe Anthony Wofford on February 18 in Lorain, Ohio.

1936: Paul Zindel is born on May 15 in Staten Island, New York.

1938: John Dos Passos's *U.S.A.* is published.

1939: Margaret Eleanor Atwood is born on November 18 in Ottawa, Canada.

1940: Ernest Hemingway's *For Whom the Bell Tolls* is published. Hemingway's reputation as one of America's most important writers is already well established, and the new novel receives overwhelmingly positive reviews from critics and the public alike.

1942: John Winslow Irving is born on March 2 in Exeter, New Hampshire.

1944: Buchi Emecheta is born as Florence Onye Buchi Emecheta on July 21 near Lagos, Nigeria. Her parents are from the Igbo village of Ibuza in southeastern Nigeria.

1953: Ernest Hemingway wins the Pulitzer Prize for *The Old Man and the Sea*. In the following year, he wins the Nobel Prize for literature and the Award of Merit from the American Academy of Arts & Letters.

1961: Ernest Hemingway commits suicide in Ketchum, Idaho.

1962: Katherine Anne Porter's *Ship of Fools* is published, and becomes a huge success commercially—it is number one on the best-seller list within weeks of its publication in April, but, after a few months, there is a backlash from critics who regard the novel in a less than favorable light.

1964: Saul Bellow's *Herzog* is published, gaining popular and critical acclaim for its examination of Western intellectual traditions, its colorful characterizations, and its innovative narrative structure.

1966: Katherine Anne Porter receives a Pulitzer Prize and National Book Award for *The Collected Stories of Katherine Anne Porter*, published in 1965.

1968: Paul Zindel's *The Pigman* is published. The book is listed as one of the Child Study Association of America's Children's Books of the Year for 1968, and wins the Boston Globe-Horn Book Award in 1969. It is also listed as one of the American Library Association's Best Young Adult Books in 1975.

1970: John Dos Passos dies.

1971: Paul Zindel's first play, *The Effect of Gamma Rays on Man-in-the-Moon Marigolds*, published in 1964, wins the Pulitzer Prize for Drama.

1973: Marilyn Harris's *Hatter Fox* is published.

1973: Toni Morrison's *Sula* is published and is nominated for a National Book Award in 1974.

1975: Saul Bellow is awarded the Pulitzer Prize for his novel *Humboldt's Gift*.

1976: Saul Bellow wins the Nobel Prize for Literature.

1980: Katherine Anne Porter dies on September 18 in Silver Springs, Maryland.

1983: Buchi Emecheta's *The Wrestling Match* is published.

1988: Margaret Atwood's *Cat's Eye* is published.

1989: John Irving's *A Prayer for Owen Meany* is published.

1993: Toni Morrison wins the Nobel Prize for Literature, and thus becomes the first African American and only the eighth woman ever to win the award.

Acknowledgments

The editors wish to thank the copyright holders of the excerpted criticism included in this volume and the permissions managers of many book and magazine publishing companies for assisting us in securing reproduction rights. We are also grateful to the staffs of the Detroit Public Library, the Library of Congress, the University of Detroit Mercy Library, Wayne State University Purdy/Kresge Library Complex, and the University of Michigan Libraries for making their resources available to us. Following is a list of the copyright holders who have granted us permission to reproduce material in this volume of *Novels for Students (PfS)*. Every effort has been made to trace copyright, but if omissions have been made, please let us know.

COPYRIGHTED MATERIALS IN NfS, VOLUME 14, WERE REPRODUCED FROM THE FOLLOWING PERIODICALS:

ANQ, v. 94, Winter, 1996. Copyright © 1996 Helen Dwight Reid Educational Foundation. Reproduced with permission of the Helen Dwight Reid Educational Foundation, published by Heldref Publications, 1319 18th Street, N.W., Washington, D.C. 20036-1802.—*ARIEL*, v. 22, October, 1991 for "Margaret Atwood's 'Cat's Eye': Reviewing Women in a Postmodern World," by Earl G. Ingersoll. Copyright © 1991 The Board of Governors, The University of Calgary. Reproduced by permission of the publisher and the author.—*Critique*, v. 37, Fall, 1995. Copyright © 1995 Helen Dwight Reid Educational Foundation. Reproduced with permission of the Helen Dwight Reid Educa-tional Foundation, published by Heldref Publications, 1319 18th Street, N.W., Washington, D.C. 20036-1802.—*The Hemingway Review*, v. 17, Fall, 1997. Copyright © 1997 by The Ernest Hemingway Foundation. Reproduced by permission.—*Interracial Books for Children Bulletin*, v. 15, 1984. Reproduced by permission.—*Romance Quarterly*, v. 37, May, 1990. Copyright © 1990 Helen Dwight Reid Educational Foundation. Reproduced with permission of the Helen Dwight Reid Educational Foundation, published by Heldref Publications, 1319 18th Street, N.W., Washington, D.C. 20036-1802. Reproduced by permission.—*Studies in the Novel*, v. 32, Fall, 2000. Copyright © 2000 by North Texas State University. Reproduced by permission.—*Teacher Librarian*, v. 27, December, 1999. Reproduced by permission.—*Victorian Newsletter*, v. 83, Spring, 1993 for "Oliver Twist and the Contours of Early Victorian England" by David Paroissie. Reproduced by permission of *The Victorian Newsletter* and the author.

COPYRIGHTED MATERIALS IN NfS, VOLUME 14, WERE REPRODUCED FROM THE FOLLOWING BOOKS:

Becker, George J. From *John Dos Passos*. Frederick Ungar, 1974. Copyright © 1974 by Frederick Ungar Publishing Co., Inc. Reproduced by permission.—Duckworth, Alistair M. From *Critical Essays on Jane Austen*. Edited by Laura Mooneyham White. G. K. Hall & Company, 1982. Copyright © 1998 by G. K. Hall & Company. Reproduced with the permission of Macmillan Library Reference

USA, a division of Ahsuog, Inc.—Dutton, Robert R. From *Saul Bellow*. Edited by Warren French. G. K. Hall & Company, 1982. Copyright © 1992 by G. K. Hall & Company. Reproduced with the permission of Macmillan Library Reference USA, a division of Ahsuog, Inc.—Gissing, George. From *The Immortal Dickens*. Kraus Printing Company, 1969. Reproduced by permission.—Heilman, Robert F. From *Critical Essays on Katherine Anne Porter*. Edited by Darlene Harbour Unrue. G. K. Hall & Company, 1997. Reproduced with the permission of Macmillan Library Reference USA, a division of Ahsuog, Inc.—Kirkpatrick, Smith. From *Critical Essays on Katherine Anne Porter*. Edited by Darlene Harbour Unrue. G. K. Hall & Company, 1997. Reproduced with the permission of Macmillan Library Reference USA, a division of Ahsuog, Inc.—McKee, Patricia. From *Producing American Races*. Duke University Press, 1999. Copyright © 1999 by Duke University Press, Durham, NC. All rights reserved. Reproduced by permission.—Moss, Howard. From *Katherine Anne Porter: Modern Critical Views*. Edited with an introduction by Harold Bloom. Chelsea House Publishers, 1986. Copyright © 1986 by Chelsea House Publishers, a division of Chelsea House Educational Communications, Inc. Introduction Copyright © 1986 by Harold Bloom. All rights reserved. Reproduced by permission.—Pfaelzer, Jean. From *Parlor Radical: Rebecca Harding Davis and the Origins of American Social Realism*. University of Pittsburgh Press, 1996. Copyright © 1996, University of Pittsburgh Press. All rights reserved. Reproduced by permission.—Reilly, Edward C. From *Understanding John Irving*. University of South Carolina Press, 1991. Copyright © 1991, University of South Carolina. Reproduced by permission.—Waldron, Mary. From *Jane Austen and the Fiction of Her Time*. Cambridge University Press, 1999. © Mary Waldron, 1999. Reproduced by the permission of Cambridge University Press and the author.—Wrenn, John H. From *John Dos Passos*. Twayne Publishers, 1999. Copyright © 1999 by Twayne Publishers. Reproduced with the permission.

PHOTOGRAPHS AND ILLUSTRATIONS APPEARING IN *NfS*, VOLUME 14, WERE RECEIVED FROM THE FOLLOWING SOURCES:

Adolf Hitler (saluting) and Heinrich Himmler, Nuremberg, Germany, 1938. USHMM Photo Archives.—African American soldiers, returning home from Europe after World War I, photograph. Hulton/Archive. Reproduced by permission.—Anti-Vietnam War protest (sitdown, MPs with rifles up at right, building in distance), Pentagon, Washington, D.C., photograph. National Archives and Records Administration.—Atwood, Margaret, 1986, photograph. AP/Wide World Photos, Inc. Reproduced by permission.—Austen, Jane, photograph. Reproduced by permission.—Bellow, Saul, photograph. Archive Photos, Inc. Reproduced by permission.—Biafran War soldier, Nigeria, 1968, photograph. (c) Hulton-Deutsch Collection/Corbis. Reproduced by permission.—Cat's-eye marbles, photograph by Kelly A. Quin. Copyright © 2001 Kelly A. Quin. Reproduced by permission of photographer.—Civil rights movement, a crowd of picketers and a single man standing in front of them with arms outstretched.—Cooper, Gary, and Ingrid Bergman, in the movie "For Whom the Bell Tolls," 1943, photograph. The Kobal Collection. Reproduced by permission.—Cruikshank, George, illustrator. From an illustration in "Oliver Twist" by Charles Dickens. The Reader's Digest Association, Inc., 1987.—Dickens, Charles, photograph. The Library of Congress.—Dos Passos, John, photograph. The Library of Congress.—Drawing by Hernan Roundtree for "Madame Bovary" by Gustave Flaubert, of Emma Bovary, photograph. Corbis-Bettmann. Reproduced by permission.—Drummers beating drum, as Navajo people look on, photograph by Buddy Mays. Corbis. Reproduced by permission.—Dumas, Alexandre, photograph.—Emecheta, Buchi, photograph by Jerry Bauer. Reproduced by permission.—Factory workers dividing combed wool, photograh. (c) Hulton/Archive Photos, Inc. Reproduced by permission.—Flaubert, Gustave, photograph. Library of Congress.—Friedan, Betty, with Yoko Ono, photograph. (c) Bettmann/Corbis. Reproduced by permission.—Hemingway, Ernest, photograph. Corbis-Bettmann. Reproduced by permission.—Hinds, Ciaran, 1995, photograph. The Kobal Collection. Reproduced by permission.—Irving, John, photograph. AP/Wide World Photos. Reproduced by permission.—Jourdan, Louis, gazing into the eyes of Jennifer Jones, from a scene of "Madame Bovary," by Vincente Minnelli. The Kobal Collection/MGM. Reproduced by permission.—Kierkegaard, Soren (left profile), sketch.—Kramer, Stanley, conversing with Elizabeth Ashley, Vivien Leigh, and Gertrude Hartley on the set of "Ship of Fools," photograph. The Kobal Collection. Reproduced by permission.—Lester, Mark, in the film "Oliver!," 1968, photograph. The Kobal Collection. Reproduced by permission.—Mazzello, Joseph, and Ian Michael Smith, in the film "Simon Birch," 1998, photograph by Alan Markfield. The Kobal Collection. Reproduced by permission.—Morrison, Toni (bandanna on head), 1993, photograph. AP/Wide World Photos. Reproduced by permission.—Musketeers sword fighting, with a fortress behind them, illustration by Norman Price and E. C. Van Swearingen. From "The Three Musketeers," by Alexandre Dumas. Grosset & Dunlap Publishers, 1953. Copyright, 1953, by Grosset & Dunlap, Inc. All rights reserved.—Nietzsche, Friedrich, photograph. Archive Photo/DPA. Reproduced by permission.—Nigerian women, carrying baskets, photograph. © Bettmann/Corbis. Reproduced by permission.—Nine American Indians, standing in front of Alcatraz, photograph. AP/Wide Photo. Reproduced by permission.—North, Oliver, photograph. AP/Wide World Photos. Reproduced by permission.—Porter, Katherine Anne, photograph by Paul Porter. AP/Wide World Photos. Reproduced by permission.—Sheen, Charlie, standing with Kiefer Sutherland, from a scene of "The Three Musketeers," directed by Stephen Herek. The Kobal Collection/Walt Disney. Reproduced by permission.—Spanish loyalist riflemen firing from truck ruins, 1936, Spain, photograph. UPI/Corbis-Bettmann. Reproduced by permission.—Springer, Marilyn Harris, photograph. Reproduced by permission.—Title page from "Persuasion" written by Jane Austen, photograph. Special Collections Library, University of Michigan. Reproduced by permission.—Two young boys working the textile mills, photograph. The Library of Congress.—Union Soldiers, photograph. The Library of Congress.—Zindel, Paul, 1971, photograph. AP/Wide World Photos. Reproduced by permission.

Contributors

Bryan Aubrey: Aubrey holds a Ph.D. in English and has published many articles on twentieth-century literature. Entries on *Cat's Eye, Hatter Fox, A Prayer for Owen Meany,* and *Ship of Fools.* Original essays on *Cat's Eye, Hatter Fox, A Prayer for Owen Meany,* and *Ship of Fools.*

Wendy Perkins: Perkins is an associate professor of English and American literature and film at Prince George's Community College and has published several articles on British and American authors. Entries on *For Whom the Bell Tolls, Herzog, Madame Bovary,* and *Persuasion.* Original essays on *For Whom the Bell Tolls, Herzog, Madame Bovary,* and *Persuasion.*

Kelly Winters: Winters is a freelance writer and has written for a wide variety of educational publishers. Entries on *Margret Howth: A Story of To-Day, Oliver Twist, The Pigman, Sula, The Three Musketeers, U.S.A.,* and *The Wrestling Match.* Original essays on *Margret Howth: A Story of To-Day, Oliver Twist, The Pigman, Sula, The Three Musketeers, U.S.A.,* and *The Wrestling Match.*

Cat's Eye

Margaret Atwood
1988

Cat's Eye was published in Toronto in 1988 and was the ninth novel by Margaret Atwood, one of Canada's most acclaimed writers of fiction and poetry. It is about a successful painter, Elaine Risley, who returns to Toronto, the city where she grew up, for a retrospective of her work at a gallery named Sub-Versions. Risley is trying to come to terms with being fifty. She must also grapple with disturbing memories from her childhood, and much of the novel consists of Risley's narration of this period in her life. At the core of Risley's story is the cruelty she suffered as a young girl at the hands of her three best friends, particularly a girl named Cordelia. This teasing shatters Risley's self-esteem and leads her to adopt neurotic habits, such as peeling her skin, biting her nails, and chewing her hair. She also develops fainting fits and has suicidal impulses.

In exploring the world of childhood female friendships, Atwood broke new ground. Never before had the world of eight- to twelve-year-old girls been examined so thoroughly and with such unflinching insight.

The novel also explores the nature of memory and identity, since Risley is aware of how unreliable memory can be, and how our experience of the present is colored by past events. The nature of artistic creativity is another theme, as Risley discovers her vocation as a painter. Finally, the novel provides a vivid picture of Toronto in the 1940s and 1950s, and shows how dramatically the city had changed by the 1980s.

Margaret Atwood

Author Biography

Margaret Eleanor Atwood was born on November 18, 1939, in Ottawa, Canada. Her father, Carl Edmund Atwood, was a forest entomologist; her mother, Margaret Dorothy (Killam) was a graduate in home economics from the University of Toronto.

Atwood spent her earliest years in Ottawa during the winters and the rest of the year in northern Quebec and Ontario. In 1946, her father took up a position as professor at the University of Toronto, and the family moved to Toronto.

In 1957, Atwood became a student of English at Victoria College, University of Toronto. In 1961, after graduation, she studied English at Radcliffe College, Harvard University, and was awarded a master's degree in 1962. She then went on to doctoral studies at Harvard until 1963. The following year she taught English literature at the University of British Columbia. Her first collection of poetry, *The Circle Game* (1966), won the Governor General's Award.

Since then, Atwood has published poetry, novels, short stories, children's literature, and nonfiction and has taught in many Canadian and American universities. Her poetry includes *The Animals in That Country* (1968), *The Journals of Susanna Moodie* (1970), *You Are Happy* (1975), *Two-Headed Poems* (1978), *Interlunar* (1984), and *Morning in the Burned House* (1995). Her novels are *The Edible Woman* (1969); *Surfacing* (1972); *Lady Oracle* (1976); *Life before Man* (1979); *Bodily Harm* (1981); *Encounters with the Element Man* (1982); *Unearthing Suite* (1983); *The Handmaid's Tale* (1985), which was a bestseller and won the Governor General's Award, the *Los Angeles Times Award*, and the Arthur C. Clarke science fiction award; *Cat's Eye* (1988); *The Robber Bride* (1993), which won the Canadian Authors Association Novel of the Year Award; *Alias Grace* (1996), which won the Giller Prize; and *The Blind Assassin* (2000). Atwood's short story collections include *Dancing Girls and Other Stories* (1977) and *Bluebeard's Egg and Other Stories* (1983); her nonfiction includes *Survival: A Thematic Guide to Canadian Literature* (1972).

Atwood has worked and traveled extensively in Europe, and she has received honorary degrees from many institutions, including Trent University, Smith College, and the University of Toronto. She was president of the Writers Union of Canada from 1982 to 1983, and president of P.E.N. International's Anglo-Canadian branch from 1984 to 1985.

Atwood married James Polk, a novelist, in 1967. They divorced in 1973. Atwood now lives with Canadian writer Graeme Gibson. They have a daughter, Jess, who was born in 1977.

Plot Summary

Part One: Iron Lung

Cat's Eye begins with an observation about the nature of time, attributed by Elaine Risley, the narrator, to her brother Stephen. This leads her to announce that nothing in life is ever lost; it is just a matter of what one remembers at any given moment. She then flashes back to a memory of her childhood friend, Cordelia, when they were teenagers. Risley is haunted by the memory of Cordelia, whom she has not seen for many years.

Part Two: Silver Paper

Risley reflects on how much Toronto has changed, and how much the city has meant to her. She reveals that she is married with two daughters, and is a successful painter. She is returning to

Toronto for a retrospective of her work at a gallery called Sub-Versions. Her memories of her childhood take up the remainder of this part. Her father was a field entomologist, which meant that the family traveled a lot. But when she was eight, her father became a university professor and they moved to Toronto.

Part Three: Empire Bloomers

After a chapter in which present-day Risley shops in Toronto for a new dress for the gallery opening, the narrative returns to her childhood. She describes the school she attended. The school has a heavily British atmosphere, and Risley learns from her intimidating teacher, Miss Lumley, about the British Empire. Risley makes friends with three girls, Carol Campbell, Grace Smeath, and Cordelia, all of whom come from families more affluent than Risley's.

Part Four: Deadly Nightshade

Present-day Risley, full of anxiety about the retrospective, reaches the gallery and meets Charna, who is organizing the show. Risley is interviewed by Andrea, a reporter, and is uncooperative. The narrative returns to eight-year-old Risley and the developing friendships between the four girls. One November day when Risley is nearly nine, Cordelia, Grace, and Carol play a game that involves burying Risley in a hole in Cordelia's backyard. They put boards on top of the hole and shovel dirt on, then go away, leaving Risley buried. After a while, they return and get her out.

Part Five: Wringer

Risley enters Simpsons, a department store, observing all the changes since she was last there many years ago. The narrative returns to her childhood, to a period when Risley was victimized by her friends, especially Cordelia. They criticize her frequently and arrange various punishments, telling her she has done something wrong. Risley lives in fear of offending them and develops nervous habits. She only gains relief when the family leaves Toronto for summer vacation.

Part Six: Cat's Eye

In Simpsons, Risley drinks a cappuccino and thinks back over her past. She helps a drunken woman in the street. Then, the story returns to her childhood. Risley is in fifth grade and has a new teacher, Miss Stuart, whom she likes. But Cordelia's malicious treatment of Risley gets worse. Risley, desperate, does not know what to do. Her mother notices something is wrong and tells Risley she must stand up for herself. In response to her troubles, Risley discovers that by fainting she can remove herself from unpleasant situations.

Part Seven: Our Lady of Perpetual Help

Risley leaves the department store, goes back to the studio, and looks up her old friends in a telephone directory. She finds no one she knows. Back as a child, Risley overhears a conversation in which Mrs. Smeath is denigrating (denying the importance of) her, and even labeling her a heathen. She begins to hate the woman. One March day, Cordelia throws Risley's hat into a ravine; Risley tries to retrieve it from the icy creek. She gets soaked, and then lies beside the creek, numb from the cold, until a vision of the Virgin Mary frees her. Risley finds the strength to reject her friends and find new ones.

Part Eight: Half a Face

The adult Risley recalls how on a trip to Mexico she was deeply affected by a statue of the Virgin Mary; then the story once more returns to Risley's childhood. Risley is in sixth grade with Carol, but Cordelia and Grace have skipped a grade. Cordelia and Grace graduate from middle school, and eventually Carol moves away, too. When Risley enters high school, Cordelia returns. She has been expelled from her private high school, and has taken to stealing. Risley is younger than the other girls, who have entered puberty and are more interested in boys. The two girls resume their friendship, but now they are on a more equal footing.

Part Nine: Leprosy

Risley reads an article about herself and the upcoming exhibit opening in the Toronto newspaper; the narrative then returns to her life in the tenth grade. She has gotten her period, and her body has started to develop. She now feels like she is "among the knowing," no longer separate from the other girls. She and Cordelia spend time together, exchanging what they think are witty remarks, and they mock their former friend Grace, although Risley has repressed many of her negative memories from that time in her life. Risley teases Cordelia, and gets a feeling of power from it; Risley is now the stronger of the two. In eleventh grade, Risley becomes known for her sharp tongue, and she uses it most frequently on Cordelia. Risley also starts to go out with boys. Risley and Cordelia take a zoology class, and Risley finds she loves dissecting animals. Soon she starts to avoid Cordelia; Cordelia's family moves, and Cordelia attends a different

school. Risley takes her grade thirteen final exams and suddenly realizes that she is going to be a painter, not a biologist as she thought. Risley visits Cordelia and finds that she has dropped out of school and has no purpose in life.

Part Ten: Life Drawing

Risley has lunch with Jon, her former husband. In the continuation of the story of her earlier life, Risley takes a Life Drawing course taught by Josef Hrbik, a refugee from Eastern Europe. She also wins a scholarship to the University of Toronto and studies Art and Archeology. At the drawing class she meets fellow student Jon; she also has an affair with Hrbik, who is concurrently having an affair with Susie, another one of his students. Risley meets Cordelia again, who now works at the Stratford Shakespeare Festival and has found a purpose in her life. Risley and Jon become lovers.

Part Eleven: Falling Women

Risley walks around her old Toronto haunts, reflecting on her past. Her earlier story resumes with Risley having two lovers, Jon and Josef. She discovers Susie bleeding from an abortion she performed on herself, and this leads Risley to end her affair with Josef. She graduates and gets a job in an advertising agency, then designs book covers for a publisher. She attends a lecture where her brother speaks about the beginning of the universe. After she becomes pregnant, she and Jon marry, but they soon quarrel. Risley continues painting and exhibits her art in a feminist group show, where one irate woman throws ink over one of Risley's paintings. Risley visits Cordelia, who is in a private home for the mentally ill because she tried to commit suicide.

Part Twelve: One Wing

Risley continues to walk around Toronto, reliving her memories. In the evening, she has dinner with Jon. They go back to his studio and make love. The narrative returns to her disintegrating marriage to Jon, many years earlier. Risley tries to kill herself by slitting her wrist with an Exacto knife, but Jon finds her and takes her to the hospital. Risley leaves him, taking her daughter Sarah with her to Vancouver. She acquires a reputation as a painter, and marries her second husband, Ben.

Part Thirteen: Picoseconds

After more of Risley's walking around Toronto, the narrative flashes back five years, and Risley describes how her brother was killed by hijackers on an airplane. She also recalls her parents' deaths, especially her mother's final illness, during which her mother brought up Risley's past with Cordelia. The narrative then returns to the present, as she discovers that her old school has been pulled down and a new one stands in its place. Her memories of herself as a child almost overwhelm her.

Part Fourteen: Unified Field Theory

Risley arrives at the gallery an hour before the exhibition opens, and walks around, looking at her paintings and remembering what inspired her to paint each one. She describes her own paintings, ironically juxtaposing her own explanations with those written in high-flown language in the catalog. The exhibition opens to the public; Risley half-expects Cordelia to appear.

Part Fifteen: Bridge

Late the next afternoon, Risley goes back to the bridge from where Cordelia threw her hat into the ravine. She thinks she sees Cordelia there and prepares to forgive her for the injuries the older girl inflicted on her. But the woman she sees is not Cordelia. The novel ends as Risley flies back home from Toronto, observing two old women chatting easily together in the plane, and regretting that she and Cordelia will never be able to do that together.

Characters

Andrea

Andrea is a young newspaper reporter in her twenties who interviews Risley about the painter's retrospective.

Mr. Banerji

Mr. Banerji is an Indian student of Risley's father. He comes to Christmas dinner with the family when Risley is a child. Later, he marries and becomes a professor at the University of Toronto.

Ben

Ben is Risley's second husband. He is practical and efficient, the opposite of Risley's first husband, Jon. He has a son by a previous marriage, and he runs a travel agency specializing in Mexican destinations.

Carol Campbell

Carol Campbell is one of Risley's childhood friends. She comes from a wealthier family than Risley and enjoys showing Risley all her posses-sions. Her parents are strict, and Carol regularly receives corporal (physical) punishment. She is more delicate than Risley, who regards Carol as a sissy. Although she is not the ringleader, Carol joins with Grace and Cordelia in tormenting Risley. Because she and Risley are in the same class, she takes on the responsibility of reporting all of Risley's faults and failings to Grace and Cordelia, who are older and in a different class.

Charna

Charna is the woman who organizes Risley's retrospective at the Sub-Versions gallery in Toronto. She writes a catalogue that uses scholarly and trendy language to interpret the paintings, and her analyses sometimes conflict with Risley's own descriptions.

Cordelia

Cordelia is one of Risley's school friends. Cordelia is a year older than Risley; she is the tallest of the group of four friends, which also includes Grace and Carol. Cordelia has a dominant personality, and the others tend to follow her lead. She is the ringleader in the girls' abusive behavior towards Risley, but Cordelia claims that she does this out of friendship; she says the only reason she criticizes Risley is so that Risley can improve herself.

It is Cordelia's idea to play a game in which the girls bury Risley in a big hole she has dug in her back garden. It is also Cordelia who throws Risley's hat into the ravine and, with the others, abandons her, wet and cold, in the snow. After this incident, Risley rejects Cordelia, Grace, and Carol and finds new friends.

Cordelia attends a private school but is expelled for making an obscene drawing. She becomes friends again with Risley in high school, although this time it is Risley who has the power. Cordelia pays little attention to her schoolwork and takes to shoplifting small items, such as tubes of lipstick, from stores. She does not have as much success with the boys as Risley does, lacking the self-confidence to behave naturally.

Cordelia changes schools again but soon drops out. She has no aim or purpose in life. She recovers for a while, finding a job as a bit-part player at the Stratford Shakespeare Festival in Stratford, Canada, but then she loses direction again. The last time she appears in the novel is when Risley visits her in a home for the mentally ill. Cordelia is under heavy medication.

Although this is the last time Risley sees Cordelia, memories of Cordelia haunt Risley well into adulthood. It is only at the end of the novel, when the middle-aged Risley returns to Toronto for her retrospective, that she is finally able to forgive Cordelia for her abusive treatment.

Josef Hrbik

Josef Hrbik is Risley's teacher in her Life Drawing class. Josef is a refugee from Eastern Europe, in his mid-thirties, with dark curly hair. He has a melancholy, serious manner and he is authoritarian in his opinions. The male students make fun of him, calling him Uncle Joe. Josef has affairs with two of his students, Risley and Susie, simultaneously. Risley eventually decides that she can never make him happy and feels inadequate because of her failure. She ends the relationship.

Jon

Jon is Risley's first husband, a fellow student of art in Toronto. As a young man, Jon cultivates a Bohemian lifestyle. His apartment is always messy, and Risley never knows whom she may find staying there. Jon is immature but fun to be with. He and Risley have violent quarrels soon after they marry. They divorce and Jon remarries. Risley meets him again when she returns to Toronto, and they make love once more. He makes a living by creating special effects for movies.

Miss Lumley

Miss Lumley is Risley's schoolteacher when Risley is eight. She is elderly and strict and rules the class by fear. She uses a rubber strap to inflict punishment.

Elaine Risley

Elaine Risley is a successful, fifty-year-old painter, and the narrator of the story. Growing up in a family that moves frequently because of her father's work, Risley is an inquisitive and observant child. She is happy up to the age of eight, when the family moves to Toronto and she has to get used to living permanently in a city. She makes friends with three girls, Carol Campbell, Grace Smeath, and Cordelia. Unfortunately, Risley is different from them, in the sense that she comes from a less affluent and privileged background, and they soon begin to pick on her.

Led by Cordelia, the girls criticize her for her behavior and her appearance. The criticisms are usually presented as friendly attempts to help Risley improve, so that she can stop doing and saying the wrong things. But most of the time Risley has no idea of what she has done wrong. The abuse is devastating to her self-esteem, and causes her to develop a number of neurotic habits, such as peeling the skin from her feet and biting her fingers. Although she eventually finds the strength to reject her friends, she does not easily recover from the emotional wounds they inflicted.

In high school, Risley becomes known for her caustic tongue, and she enjoys making remarks to other girls that she knows will hurt. When she is in college, she has an affair with her drawing instructor, Josef Hrbik, and then marries Jon in haste when she finds she is pregnant. Neither she nor Jon has the maturity to make the marriage work. Risley becomes depressed and attempts suicide. She leaves Toronto with her child, Sarah, and moves to Vancouver, where some years later she meets and marries Ben. She has another daughter, Anne.

Risley succeeds as a painter, becoming well-known for her feminist themes. Her flourishing career brings her back to Toronto at the age of fifty, for a retrospective. She has by then developed a prickly personality. When she is interviewed by a reporter who asks questions she thinks are silly, she gives unhelpful answers tinged with hostility. She still has times when she thinks her life is worthless. But as a former victim, she is willing to help others who are in bad situations, as when she assists a drunken woman in the streets of Toronto. But she is under no illusions that this makes her a good person, telling herself: "I know myself to be vengeful, greedy, secretive and sly."

Mr. Risley

Mr. Risley is Elaine's father. He is an entomologist, and when Elaine is very young, he travels around a lot with his family, carrying out field research on forest insects. Mr. Risley is a self-made, practical man. He grew up on a farm in Nova Scotia without running water or electricity. After taking all his high school courses by correspondence, he put himself through university by doing menial jobs. When Elaine is eight, her father becomes a professor at the University of Toronto. He has a pessimistic view of the future of humanity and often gives impromptu lectures at the family dinner table about the environmental horrors that will soon afflict the world. Some of these views are expressed only half-seriously; Mr. Risley is a man who likes to follow chains of thought to their logical conclusions.

Mrs. Risley

Mrs. Risley is Elaine's mother. Like most women in the 1940s and 1950s, she does not work outside the home. She is unlike the conventional housewife, however, and Elaine notices as a child that her mother is different from the mothers of her friends. Mrs. Risley does not like housework, and prefers to do things like going out skating, or walking on her own in the ravine. She also dresses informally, wearing slacks when others might wear skirts or dresses. Her favorite hobby is gardening. As a mother she is not strict, and she does not know what to do when she discovers that Elaine's friends torment her. When Elaine is ten, Mrs. Risley suffers a miscarriage.

Stephen Risley

Stephen is Risley's older brother. He is a prodigy, and as a child, he develops an interest in physics and astronomy. As a teenager, he attends a private school for the gifted and tells Risley about the problems of two-dimensional universes and the nature of time. He finishes his undergraduate degree in two years rather than four and takes a graduate degree in astrophysics in California. Soon he becomes well-known in his field, and Risley attends one of his lectures in Toronto. His speculations on unified field theory intrigue her. Stephen dies in his forties when the airplane on which he is traveling to Frankfurt for a conference is hijacked by terrorists and he is shot. His memory lives on with Elaine, however, and she commemorates him and his ideas through two paintings, "One Wing," and "Unified Field Theory."

Grace Smeath

Grace Smeath is one of Risley's friends as a child. A year older than Risley, she has pale skin and wears glasses. Grace is bossy and likes to have her own way. If Risley and Carol try to play anything she does not like, Grace says she has a headache and goes home. When the girls play school, Grace is the teacher, the others are the students. Risley and Carol put up with this because they like to be with Grace—Risley worships her. When Cordelia becomes part of their group, Grace follows Cordelia's lead and criticizes Risley, reporting on Risley's failings at the Sunday school they both attend.

Mrs. Smeath

Mrs. Smeath is the mother of Grace Smeath. She is ill, with a heart condition, and rests on the sofa every afternoon. Mrs. Smeath is pious, dislikes vulgarity, and is snobbish. She believes that the church she and her family attend is better than other churches because everyone there wears hats. She despises Risley's family because they do not go to church. Mrs. Smeath is aware of the fact that the other girls are tormenting Risley but she says it is God's punishment and Risley deserves it. Risley overhears this and develops a hatred for Mrs. Smeath, which she later expresses by painting Mrs. Smeath "naked, exposed and desecrated" in a number of her paintings.

Miss Stuart

Miss Stuart is Risley's teacher in grade five. She is Scottish, and the opposite of Miss Lumley. She is popular with the children, loves art, and knows how to keep discipline in a firm but fair way.

Susie

Susie is a student in Mr. Hrbik's Life Drawing class. She wears tight jeans and heavy makeup; Risley thinks of her as silly and unintelligent. Susie has an affair with Hrbik, becomes pregnant, and tries to abort the baby herself. Risley discovers her unconscious and bleeding from the botched abortion, and she is rushed to the hospital.

Themes

Memory and Identity

Although she is a successful middle-aged painter, Risley does not have a secure sense of identity or self-worth. In Jon's studio in Toronto, she confesses that sometimes it is all she can do to drag herself out of bed in the morning. On such occasions she feels worthless, and this reminds her of how Cordelia's relentless criticisms used to make her feel as if she was nothing. Only the previous day, Risley saw a poster advertising her retrospective, with a picture of herself on it, and this gave her some satisfaction that she had at least achieved a "public face." But what of the private one? Risley's private self is buried under the weight of repressed memories, and yet memory is the only tool she has to reconstruct who she is and how she came to be that way.

But memory, as she continually reminds the reader, is unreliable. Although the past extends its hold over the present—Risley's relationship with Cordelia still haunts her—who can accurately remember the past? Risley draws attention to the fact

Topics for Further Study

- To what extent is Elaine Risley a feminist? How is she also critical of feminism? Do some research on the topic of feminism to support your conclusions.

- Problems in adult life are often explained by reference to a difficult family environment or social conditions such as poverty. Atwood suggests that the cruelties small children inflict on each other may be an equal cause of adult dysfunction. Find cases that support each theory and report on how prevalent each is.

- When Risley is asked to draw what she does after school, her drawing reveals her troubled state of mind. (It shows her lying in bed and is almost entirely colored black). If you were given a similar assignment, what would the drawing look like and how might it reflect your own mental condition or mood?

- How are boys' relationships with each other described in the novel, and how do they differ from the relationships between girls? Are boys less cruel to each other than girls are, or are they cruel in different ways? Use examples from the novel to support your claims.

- How does Risley's upbringing and family background differ from those of her friends Grace and Cordelia? How do the roles played by their parents differ?

---

that there are gaps in her memory. When she tries to recall her ninth birthday party, for example:

> I close my eyes, wait for pictures. I need to fill in the black square of time, go back to see what's in it. It's as if I vanish at that moment and reappear later, but different, not knowing why I have been changed.

At one point, Risley speculates on what future diseases of the memory may affect her; there are so many different ways of losing and reclaiming the past. And it is not only as an adult that memory is fragile. Even as a child, Risley sometimes cannot recall events, even though she knows they happened. She has even forgotten that she has forgotten things. In particular, she forgets the bad things that have happened to her, sometimes only a few months after they have occurred. She has a gift for burying the past.

By the time she reaches her twenties she does not even want to remember, and she finds that "The past has become discontinuous, like stones skipped across water, like postcards: I catch an image of myself, a dark blank, an image, a blank."

Later, when she is in her forties, Risley does not even remember the traumatic incident when she nearly froze to death in the ravine: "My memory is tremulous, like water breathed on." The image is suggestive. Still, calm water reflects the face of the observer; water disturbed presents only a jagged, distorted image, like a broken mirror. Somehow Risley must try to connect all the fragments to create a self that is whole.

Coming of Age

Because there are two distinct narrative threads in the novel, there are also two coming-of-age themes. One is when young Risley enters adolescence and early adulthood. She attends college, discovers her talent for painting, has her first lover, and establishes her place in adult society. However, Atwood treats this part of Risley's story in much less detail than her childhood world, which is the main focus of interest. The main coming-of-age story is of Risley as a fifty-year-old painter trying to come to terms with being middle-aged. This is an almost constant theme in the present-day narrative sections. Risley draws attention to the fact that she is aging: she should get bifocals, but thinks they would make her look old; she walks but does not jog because jogging is bad for the knees; she searches for a dress in the department store that will transform her, but notes that this is less possible with the advancing years. She surveys the range of wares in the cosmetics section and is not put off by the strangeness of some of the ingredients: "I'd use anything if it worked—slug juice, toad spit, eye of newt, anything at all to mummify myself, stop the drip-drip of time, stay more or less the way I am."

In addition to these concerns, Risley has little confidence that in middle age she has attained the kind of wisdom that would compensate for the discomforts of aging. Hence her mental restlessness and obsession with the figure of Cordelia from her past. And although her career is successful, that also reminds her of the fact that she is no longer young.

She is concerned when she sees herself described in a newspaper article as "eminent": "the mausoleum word. I might as well climb onto the marble slab right now and pull the bedsheet over my head." She feels the same about having a retrospective: "first the retrospective, then the morgue."

Art and Science

In addition to being a coming-of-age novel, *Cat's Eye* is also a *künstlerroman* ("artist novel"), about the growth of an artist—her discovery of her vocation and development of mastery of her craft. The pivotal moment in this respect is when Risley first realizes that her destiny is to be an artist. This occurs during her grade thirteen biology exams (in certain places in Canada, students who are bound for university go through an extra grade). She knows already that she can draw anything, "the insides of crayfish ears, the human eye, frogs' genitalia, the blossom of the snapdragon . . . in cross section." This seems to be an innate ability. But at that moment she has a revelation, "like a sudden epileptic fit," and knows with absolute certainty that she is not going to be a biologist, but a painter.

Later passages describe Risley's artistic education: the Life Drawing class; the development of her taste through art history courses; her experiments in the technique of egg tempera; and then her emergence as a painter in her own right. A vital moment comes when she is in her twenties and makes a change in her artistic subjects: "Until now I've always painted things that were actually there, in front of me. Now I begin to paint things that aren't there." This helps her to develop a surreal, visionary quality in her work, and she also begins to emerge as a painter with a feminist sensibility, as when she paints the Virgin Mary as a fierce lioness, for example.

Risley's career as a painter is in contrast to the vocations of her father and brother, both of whom are scientists. As an entomologist, her father examines the world in microscopic, objective detail; her physicist brother is drawn to speculations, couched in the language of mathematics, about the origins of creation and the laws that govern it. His interest is in the search for a unified field theory— a single theory that would explain all the diverse laws of physics and how they manifest in the physical world. Although Risley's art is personal and subjective, concerned with her inner world of feelings rather than the objective world of things, she and Stephen do have something in common, in that she, too, searches for a "unified field theory" (the title of one of her paintings). For Risley, this is a way of creating wholeness, understanding, and healing through art.

Style

Point of View and Organization

The novel is told in the first person by the narrator, Elaine Risley. All of the events in the novel are told from her point of view, although the perspective within that point of view shifts considerably—from the young child just discovering the world, to the young woman coming of age, to the middle-aged painter coming to terms with being fifty.

Each of the novel's fifteen parts is named after one of Risley's paintings. The title of the painting is a clue to what happens in the section named after it. In the section entitled "Wringer," for example, which takes its name from Risley's observations of the wringer washing machine in her childhood home, Risley experiences the cruelty of her friends for the first time. She is metaphorically "put through the wringer." The section "Cat's Eye" covers the period when Risley retreats from the painful feelings caused by Cordelia's cruelty and tries to become as cold and unfeeling as her cat's eye marble. The section "Our Lady of Perpetual Help" refers to the pivotal moment when Risley believes she has been helped out of the ravine by the Virgin Mary.

The story is not chronological in organization. Each section begins with Risley in the present, revisiting Toronto, and then switches to long, very detailed flashbacks to her childhood. There are also sections in the present-day narrative when Risley recalls memories from the past. Past and present are thus closely interwoven, and the entire novel is told in the present tense, which has the effect of emphasizing that the past remains very much alive with Risley.

Symbol and Metaphor

A central symbol is the cat's eye marble that Risley keeps as a child. She treasures it, putting it in her purse for safekeeping, not risking losing it in a game. The marble is clear glass with a bloom of blue petals in the center. It resembles not cats' eyes but "something that isn't known but exists anyway," and she compares it to the eyes of aliens from outer space. She feels it protects her, and she longs to see like the cat's eye. In other words, to be an eye only—to experience the world only through her vision, with all other senses and feelings switched off. Then she will not experience any pain. This fantasy is her defense against the abusive treatment she is receiving from her friends.

Although Risley feels that the cat's eye protects her, the image also has a negative connotation. The crystal sphere in the marble is so blue and so pure it looks like "something frozen in the ice." Being frozen in ice is a metaphor for Risley's emotional condition after the trauma inflicted by Cordelia and the other little girls. Risley walls off a place inside herself where she thinks she can be safe, but the result is that she cannot go through normal emotional development. Like the cat's eye, she is "frozen."

Simile

Atwood's style is marked by striking figurative language, including much use of the simile. A simile is an explicit comparison between two distinctly different things. Risley shows her ability to make these kinds of comparisons early in her life. When traveling in the back seat of the family car, she observes the backs of her parents' ears. Her father's are "like the ears of gnomes, or those of the flesh-colored, doglike minor characters in Mickey Mouse comic books." Her mother's are narrow and fragile, "like the handles of china cups," and her brother's are round, "like dried apricots." It is easy to see how Risley would become an artist, since the ability to see relationships between disparate things is part of the artist's sensibilities, whether the artist is a painter, like Risley, or a writer, like Atwood.

Similes recur frequently in Atwood's atmospheric descriptions. The evening air coagulates "like a custard thickening"; the warm, humid air is "like invisible mist"; in a Toronto August, "Haze hangs over the city like wet smoke."

Perhaps the most memorable simile in the entire novel is this one, as Risley and Cordelia listen to Frank Sinatra records in the 1950s: "A disembodied voice, sliding around on the tune like someone slipping on a muddy sidewalk. He slithers up to a note, flails, recovers, oozes in the direction of another note."

Setting

The novel is set in Toronto. It gives a vivid and detailed portrait of the city during the 1940s and 1950s, during Risley's childhood and youth, and in the 1980s, when she returns and observes how drastically the city has changed. A typical ex-

ample is when Risley walks through the side street where her art teacher, Josef Hbrik, used to live. In those days the street was sordid and broken-down, but now it has been renovated and is lined with a double row of expensive boutiques. Transformations like this have changed Toronto from a place renowned for its provincial dullness to its status in the 1980s as a "world class" city—"New York without the garbage and the muggings." Risley mentions this, however, in a mocking tone. Her picture of Toronto is colored by her dislike of it.

Risley's chronicle of her early years gives a series of snapshots illustrating what day-to-day life was like for young girls during this period. Risley and her friends amuse themselves by playing with movie star coloring books featuring 1940s stars such as Veronica Lake; they spend their allowances on "penny gumballs, red licorice whips, orange Popsicles." Little by little, the adult world creeps into their awareness: Risley hears the square dance music that plays on the radio; the girls discover the gusseted corsets, known as foundation garments, in the pages of the Eaton's Catalogues that are strewn around the Smeath home. And at school they learn to observe some of the rituals of the fading British Empire, such as wearing poppies on Remembrance Day and waving Union Jack flags when Princess Elizabeth visits the city.

Historical Context

Feminism

Although she resists attempts to fit her into a narrow definition of the term, Atwood is known as a feminist writer. Her formative years in Toronto in the late 1950s and 1960s coincided with the emergence of what is often referred to as the "second wave" of modern feminism. This was marked, among other things, by the publication of Betty Friedan's *The Feminine Mystique* in 1963, a book that Atwood acknowledges had a large influence on her own thinking. During the 1960s, women in North America began to challenge stereotypical definitions of how women should behave, and to question the traditional roles assigned to them. A political movement emerged, spearheaded in the United States by the National Organization of Women (NOW), demanding equal employment opportunities and equal pay for women, as well as an end to sexual harassment and the exploitation of women in pornography.

Compare & Contrast

- **1950s:** Atwood decides to be a writer. While Canadian literature is domestically robust, international appreciation is sporadic.

  1980s: Canadian writers such as Atwood and Alice Munro are internationally renowned figures. Canadian literature is studied extensively in Canadian and American universities.

  Today: The bibliography of international literature issued by the Modern Language Association lists more than seven hundred books and articles by and about Canadian authors written in 1998 alone.

- **1950s:** Only a limited number of occupations, such as nurse, teacher, secretary, or airline stewardess, are open to women, who are encouraged to be happy in their traditional roles as wives and mothers.

1970s: In Canada in 1971, nearly 40 percent of women aged 15 and older are part of the labor force. They account for almost one-third of the total labor force. However, average annual earnings of women working full-time is only 59.7 percent of those of men. Women attend university in greater numbers (accounting for 37 percent of all university students in 1971), and professions formerly dominated by men, such as medicine and law, gradually become more open to women.

Today: In Canada in 1999, 58.9 percent of women aged 15 years and older are part of the labor force, representing 45.8 percent of the total workforce. However, the average wage of a woman working full-time is still equivalent to only 72.5 percent of a man's wages. In education, women's participation continues to rise. In 1997–1998, women represent 55.7 percent of the student population at the university undergraduate level.

In Canada, the Voice of Women was founded in 1960 to lobby the provincial and federal governments concerning women's rights. Many grassroots women's groups sprang up, with the goal of changing women's attitudes about themselves and their relations with men.

A glimpse of the early feminist movement in Toronto can be found in *Cat's Eye*. In the 1960s, Elaine Risley attends "consciousness raising" meetings of women, in which issues are raised that Risley has never consciously thought about before: "Things are being overthrown. Why, for instance, do we shave our legs? Wear lipstick? Dress up in slinky clothing? Alter our shapes? What is wrong with us the way we are?"

The purpose of the meeting is to empower women, and there is a lot of anger expressed against men. (Risley feels ambivalent about the meeting, however; she is more comfortable with men than with women.) Later, Risley exhibits her work in an all-female group show, at which most of the art has

a radical feminist slant more extreme than anything Risley paints.

The Canadian women's movement bore fruit in 1967, when a Royal Commission on the Status of Women in Canada was created. Its final report, issued in 1970, contained 167 recommendations. This Commission has been described as the single most important event in advancing the status of women in Canada at that time.

Abortion Rights

Another social issue relevant to the novel is abortion rights. Susie, the art student, performs an abortion on herself, botches the job and has to be taken to the hospital. At the time of this incident, in the 1960s, abortion in Canada, as well as the United States, was illegal. Incidents such as that involving Susie were not uncommon. Risley says, "Everyone my age knows about it. Nobody discusses it. Rumors are down there, kitchen tables, money exchanged in secret; evil old women; illegal doctors, disgrace and butchery."

But pressure to legalize abortion was mounting in North America, partly due to activism by women's groups. Canada's abortion laws were first liberalized in 1969. In Canada in 1970, feminist groups from all over the country organized two days of protests. Thirty-five women chained themselves to the parliamentary gallery in the House of Commons, closing Parliament for the first time in Canadian history. The Canadian Alliance to Repeal the Abortion Law formed in 1974. In 1988, the Canadian Supreme Court declared Canada's abortion law unconstitutional. This meant that Canadian women could legally have abortions. Interestingly, when Risley, the emerging feminist painter, unexpectedly becomes pregnant, she refuses to seek an abortion, nor does she wish to become a single mother. She and Jon take the more socially acceptable, as well as traditional, route and marry.

Critical Overview

Cat's Eye was received with enthusiasm by reviewers, many of whom considered it to be Atwood's finest work to date. Alice McDermott, in the *New York Times Book Review*, praised the novel's "precise and devastating detail, the sense of the ordinary transformed into nightmare," and also commented that "It is a novel of images, nightmarish, evocative, heartbreaking and mundane . . . Atwood's most emotionally engaging fiction thus far."

Stefan Kanfer, in *Time*, commented on Atwood's understanding that the humiliations of childhood have deeper effects than anything that happens in adulthood: "The cruelties done to the narrator become sources of a melancholia that affects the rest of her days.... Risley's emotional life is effectively over at puberty."

Like a number of reviewers, Hermoine Lee in *New Republic* noted the parallels between *Cat's Eye* and Atwood's own life, referring to the novel as "fictive autobiography." Lee found the most gripping part of the novel to be the sections where young Risley suffers at the hands of her friends: "Atwood's account of this torture is horrifyingly brilliant, and will strike home to anyone who was ever involved in childhood gang warfare, whether as bullier or bullied."

In the 1990s, critics found plenty of themes in the novel to discuss, and its reputation remains high in the canon of Atwood's work. For example, in 1995, Coral Ann Howells, in *Margaret Atwood*, examined the novel from the point of view of the "crucial importance of retrospective art in the female protagonist's construction of her self." In 1999, Karen F. Stein, in *Margaret Atwood Revisited,* noted that the novel introduces "typical Atwood motifs of mirrors, twinning, and doubling." She also observed that the note of forgiveness and compassion on which the novel ends is ambiguous. Howells again, in a later essay, "Transgressing Genre: A Generic Approach to Margaret Atwood's Novels," described *Cat's Eye* as a *künstlerroman*, concerned with the construction of the subject's identity, but one that resists more precise classification. This resistance is a "distinctive characteristic of life-writing in the feminine."

Criticism

Bryan Aubrey

Aubrey holds a Ph.D. in English and has published many articles on twentieth-century literature. In this essay, he considers the role played by the figure of the Virgin Mary in the life and art of the painter Elaine Risley.

An important motif in *Cat's Eye* is the figure of the Virgin Mary. As a child, Risley first encounters the visual representation of the Virgin, and the Virgin enters her imagination and plays a role in her tormented childhood, her development as an artist, and her later search for release from haunting memories. As a mature artist, Risley transforms Catholic iconography and theology into a personal vision of wholeness and redemption.

Because Risley is not raised in a religious home, she must discover the symbolic and healing power of the Virgin for herself. Her father is against religion. He believes it is a form of brainwashing that has been responsible for wars, massacres, bigotry, and intolerance. Risley's mother also has a negative view of religion. For these reasons the family does not attend church, something Risley does for the first time when she accompanies the Smeath family to their Sunday worship at a Protestant church. From the Smeath family she hears only negative appraisals of Catholics. One of their complaints is that Catholics worship the Virgin Mary.

Risley becomes familiar with depictions of the Virgin from the Sunday school that she attends with Grace. But these are Protestant representations that show the Virgin subordinate to Jesus. Only when Risley happens to pick up a piece of paper in the street—printed by the local Catholic school—does she discover traditional Catholic iconography of the Virgin. In this picture the Virgin wears a dark blue robe and a crown and has a halo. Her red heart is shown outside her chest, with seven arrows (to Risley they look like spears) piercing it. These arrows represent the Seven Sorrows of Mary, and in Catholic thought they refer to trials that Mary endured in her earthly life, including Christ lost on the way to Jerusalem, the betrayal of Christ, the Crucifixion, and the Entombment.

Risley stores all these details in her acute visual memory. The picture acts as a seed for her artistic imagination to grow. Later, the exposed heart of the Virgin becomes part of the inspiration behind Risley's series of satirical paintings, "White Gift," where it reappears as the bad heart of Mrs. Smeath.

Nine-year-old Risley is so affected by the portrait of the Virgin that not long afterwards she begins praying to her. Risley sees this as an act of rebellion, since she understands that normally a person should pray to God. This incident might be seen as the earliest moment when Risley's feminist sensibility begins to form, since she is implicitly rejecting the patriarchal version of God in favor of a female icon.

Shortly after this incident Risley has what she believes is a direct encounter with the Virgin. When she is lying freezing in the snow, abandoned by her friends, a lady with rays shooting from her head comes to her, walking as if on air. She is wearing a dark hood, and inside her cloak Risley sees a glimpse of red. She assumes this is the red heart of the Virgin, glowing like a coal outside her chest. The Virgin tells Risley, *"You can go home now . . . It will be all right. Go home."* This gives Risley the strength she needs to haul herself out of the ravine. It is a pivotal moment, important both for Risley's mature art and for her later adult quest to lay to sleep the ghost of her childhood memories associated with Cordelia.

Risley's next encounter with the Virgin comes when she is in her twenties, but the fact that it is recalled in the section that immediately follows Risley's childhood rescue by the Virgin suggests its thematic importance. This time Risley sees a statue of the Virgin in a church in Mexico. It is the only statue of the Virgin she has seen that attracts her. The statue has a number of small items pinned

> **In light of the important role the Virgin has played in Risley's life and art, it is not surprising that she should also play a part in a crucial moment at the end of the novel."**

to it by believers who were grateful to the Virgin for having saved something of theirs. Risley realizes the statue represents the Virgin in her role as Our Lady of Lost Things. In other words, the Virgin restores what has been lost. At the time, Risley has repressed so much from her childhood that she does not consciously know what she has lost, and so she does not know what to pray to the Virgin for.

Only later, on her return to Toronto in middle age, does her quest become urgent. The wounds she suffered in childhood still deeply affect her responses to life, and she must resolve in her mind why those things happened and find a way of reconciling with Cordelia.

The image of the Virgin as Our Lady of Lost Things links closely with another recurring metaphor in *Cat's Eye*, drawn not from the world of religion but from the discoveries of quantum physics. In the opening paragraph of the novel Risley recalls her physicist brother once telling her that:

> Time is not a line but a dimension, like the dimensions of space. If you can bend space you can bend time also, and if you knew enough and could move faster than light you could travel backward in time and exist in two places at once.

Risley interprets this to mean that time is like a series of liquid transparencies, one laid on top of another. A person looks down through time, like water, not back into it, and time is a layered vessel that still contains everything that has happened in the past. As Risley puts it, "Nothing goes away"; everything that appears to have been forgotten or buried waits to be rediscovered and reclaimed, whether one delves deeply into the quantum fields of creation or prays to Our Lady of Lost Things. Later, Risley will paint "Unified Field Theory," a painting that brilliantly synthesizes these two per-

Feminist leader Betty Friedan meets with followers at her home

spectives, one from the objective world of matter as revealed through physics, the other from the subjective realm of religion.

But before she can produce "Unified Field Theory," Risley has a lot of artistic development to do. Several years after she observes the statue Our Lady of Lost Things, she paints her own version of the Virgin Mary. Risley paints a witty, down-to-earth feminist revision of the Catholic icon. Risley's Virgin is nothing like the traditionally meek, Catholic Mother of God. The painter gives her the head of a lioness and an expression designed to startle the observer: "My Virgin Mary is fierce, alert to danger, wild. She stares levelly out at the viewer with her yellow lion's eyes. A gnawed bone lies at her feet." This Virgin resembles the fierce Indian goddess Kali, a dark figure often depicted dancing on skulls, more than anything in the Western Catholic tradition.

The remainder of Risley's painting is satirical. "Our Lady of Perpetual Help" is shown in a winter coat with a purse over her shoulder, carrying grocery bags and looking tired. She is more like an overworked Everywoman, a suburban 1950s housewife—being perpetually helpful is wearing her out—than the divine Virgin who is the object of veneration.

Risley cleverly subverts some traditional iconography in this painting. In Christian art the Virgin is sometimes shown with an apple, to emphasize her status as the second Eve. (In the book of Genesis, Eve brought trouble into the world by eating the forbidden apple; in contrast, Mary, although she may hold an apple, is never shown eating it.) In Risley's painting, the apple becomes just a mundane item, something that might well fall from an overstuffed grocery bag.

Elaine also makes another interesting twist on tradition when she paints an egg—another item that has fallen from the grocery bag. In Christian art, an egg is a symbol of fertility; it is not associated with the Virgin, who represents chastity. Fertility is associated with the many pagan fertility goddesses that Christianity rejected.

Elaine's visual meditations on the Virgin reach their fullness in "Unified Field Theory," which is the final painting in her retrospective. It is at once a highly personal and an all-encompassing cosmic vision. The title is taken from a lecture given by Risley's brother Stephen that Risley attended. Stephen speculated about the quest for a unified field theory that would encompass all the diverse laws of matter and explain how creation came about. Speaking of creation, he says:

But what of the moment beyond the first moment? Or does it even make sense to use the word *before*, since time cannot exist without space and space-time without events and events without matter-energy? But there is something that must have existed before. That something is the theoretical framework, the parameters within which the laws of energy must operate.

Stephen concludes that the language of this unified field from which everything emerges must be the universal language of mathematics.

In her painting, Risley, who knows nothing of mathematics, recasts this theory in terms of a visual image of the Virgin as a unified field of compassion, a feminine deity who is the font of all things and a divine help in time of need.

Risley's Virgin hovers over a bridge, on either side of which are the tops of snow-covered trees. This is clearly the bridge where little Risley, freezing in the snow in the ravine, saw a vision of the Virgin and was saved by her. In place of the red heart that had so impressed the young Risley, this Virgin holds at the level of her heart an outsized cat's eye marble. This is a very personal symbol for Risley since it was the cat's eye that acted as her talisman, protecting her when she was a child. When she rediscovered it in middle age as she was sorting through her belongings with her dying mother, it triggered a moment of revelation in which all her forgotten past became clear to her. This explains why Risley's Virgin of Lost Things holds a cat's eye marble.

Behind the Virgin, the sun (a masculine symbol) has set, and the moon, symbol of the feminine, is rising. The pinpoints of light on the Virgin's dress suggest the stars against a night sky, and also the light that makes the stars possible. This Virgin seems to give rise to the entire space-time universe, while not being bound by it (she hovers over, but does not touch, the bridge, which is also symbolically the point of manifestation through which the timeless streams into time). Risley's Virgin of Lost Things is the home of everything that has been scattered and lost throughout the universe—the same universe that in the painting is depicted, as seen through a telescope, swirling around below the Virgin. Thus the Virgin is Risley's attempt to create through art a vision of wholeness that would leave nothing out, present, past, or future, and would also embody the universal, compassionate heart.

In light of the important role the Virgin has played in Risley's life and art, it is not surprising that she should also play a part in a crucial moment at the end of the novel. This is after Risley has looked at the painting of "Unified Field Theory" at the gallery, at a time when her need to put the past to rest becomes critical. Risley returns to the bridge and the ravine where Cordelia's cruelty reached its climax and the Virgin saved her. This time, however, although she can recall every detail of the vision she had of the Virgin, Risley convinces herself that the vision never really happened.

Be that as it may, the Virgin remains embedded in Risley's imagination. When she sees a woman whom she believes to be Cordelia approaching (just as the Virgin approached her all those years ago), she reaches out to her childhood nemesis and says, "*It's all right . . . You can go home now.*" These simple words of forgiveness and reassurance are exactly the words spoken by the Virgin to liberate Risley as a child. At the vital moment, the adult Risley manages to transcend the revenge fantasies that she has harbored, even as an adult, against Cordelia. Risley has long realized that all the faults Cordelia found in her, and which so drastically affected her self-esteem, were actually projections of Cordelia's own feelings of inadequacy. She knows that she and Cordelia are like twins; it is hard to know where one begins and the other ends. Both need healing, and in that one moment of forgiveness—whatever new regrets may later arise—Risley has raised herself to the level of the divine figure that has resonated in her artistic imagination since she was a child. She has herself become, just for that moment, just for Cordelia, Our Lady of Perpetual Help.

Source: Bryan Aubrey, Critical Essay on *Cat's Eye*, in *Novels for Students*, The Gale Group, 2002.

Earl G. Ingersoll

In the following essay, Ingersoll explores the growth and transformation of Elaine in Cat's Eye.

Although one finds evidence of postmodernism in the manipulation of popular forms such as the Gothic in *Lady Oracle* and science fiction in *The Handmaid's Tale, Cat's Eye* is Margaret Atwood's first full-fledged "postmodern" work. Always the wily evader of critics' pigeonholes, Atwood, in a recent interview, has denied the classification of her work as "postmodern." She expresses her own amused disdain towards the critical-academic world for its attraction to "isms" in the discourse of *Cat's Eye* when Elaine Risley visits the gallery where her retrospective show is to be mounted. Risley dismisses the paintings still on display: "I don't give a glance to what's still on the walls, I hate those neo-expressionist dirty greens and putrid oranges, post this, post that. Everything is post these days, as if we're just a footnote to something earlier that was real enough to have a name of its own." At the same time, this novel is clearly Atwood's most postmodern in its play with form—the fictional autobiography—and in its continual self-referentiality as a text.

At the centre of this postmodern text is Atwood's complex use of her own past. Few writers have spoken out so vehemently against readings of their work as autobiography. As her interviews indicate, she is very aware that her audience is bent upon biographical readings of her fiction. With obvious amusement she tells how in question-and-answer sessions following her public readings she has often just finished disclaiming autobiographical roots for her characters when someone in her audience asks if she was overweight as a child like Joan in *Lady Oracle* or anorexic as a young woman like the unnamed narrator of *The Edible Woman.* For Atwood, there are clearly gender implications here since, as she has argued, women have traditionally been thought so imaginatively impoverished that all they could write about was themselves.

At the same time, although there is no Atwood biography—and she would be one of the last writers to authorize one—she is among the most interviewed contemporary writers. Thus, as she herself must know, serious readers of her work are familiar enough with the outlines of her family and her early life to be enticed into seeing the painter Elaine Risley—that stereotyped persona of modernist fiction—as at least partly her own reflection. Obviously she is not; and yet she *is*, despite the curious warning on the copyright page which reads in part as follows:

> This is a work of fiction. Although its form is that of an autobiography, it is not one . . . with the exception of public figures, any resemblance to persons living or dead is purely coincidental. The opinions expressed are those of the characters and should not be confused with the author's.

It is easy enough to see that Atwood is attempting to protect herself from potential legal action generated by former friends or associates who might choose to see themselves as models for the less appealing characters in *Cat's Eye.* However, the attempt to deny *any* connection with Elaine Risley must encourage the reader to suspect that the lady doth protest too much. In this way, part of the enjoyment of this text involves a shifting back and forth between invention and the facts of the inventor's past.

Atwood has provided her audience with so many of those facts of her early life that it is next to impossible for the informed reader to dismiss as coincidental the roots of Elaine's childhood in Atwood's. She has told her interviewers, for example, about the summers she spent as a child living in tents and motels while the family accompanied her father, an entomologist, doing research in the Canadian north. On more than one occasion she has described to her interviewers how she and her brother would help their father collect insects he shook from trees. In this context, given the writer's having gone on record as frustrated with her audience's misguided autobiographical readings of her earlier work, it is difficult not to conclude that *Cat's Eye* is, among many things, a highly sophisticated expression of play with her audience's expectations. Atwood may plead ignorance of contemporary critical theory, but she is undercutting the conventional notion that autobiography privileges an autobiographical fiction as more truthful than other forms of fiction. She shows us in Elaine Risley, a painter/writer who may seem in a conventional sense to be exploring the truth of her past but who in a truer sense is creating, or writing, a past as she chooses now to see it, rather than as it might have once existed.

The novel begins with a definition of time, justified perhaps by Risley's having returned to Toronto, her home, for a retrospective exhibition of her art. She dismisses linear time in favor of "time as having a shape . . ., like a series of liquid transparencies . . . You don't look back along time but down through it, like water. Sometimes this comes to the surface, sometimes that, sometimes nothing. Nothing goes away." In the story she tells of her youth, Elaine offers a retrospective of the woman she has been and the women who have been important to her as she now sees herself and them. That past is very much seen through the cat's eye marble into which Elaine looked at eight and saw her future as an artist. The image of the cat's eye is central, since it represents a world into which she has been allowed access; at the same time, it is a world of inevitably distorted vision. Thus, the truth is not an entity to which we struggle to gain access so much as a way of looking and, in the process, creating the text of that truth.

Elaine Risley's retrospective allows her to review the people and relationships that have been important to the first fifty years of her life. In reconstructing her past—or the critical years from age eight to young womanhood—Elaine Risley is in large part deconstructing that past. The consequences of that deconstruction—what turns out to be the novel itself—is a complicated series of transformations through which the persona discovers that the past is only what we continue to reconstruct for the purposes of the present. And perhaps beyond that, Elaine Risley discovers that of all her relationships—with the opposite sex and with her own—the most important may have been the strange friendship with her tormentor/double Cordelia. By the end of the narrative, the persona will have finally exorcised the spirit of an alter ego who was perhaps primarily *that*, another self whom she no longer needs to fear, hate, or even love.

The focus of the early chapters is the very young Elaine Risley's struggle to find models in the two women who are crucial to her formative years. She begins her retrospective with her eighth birthday, a not surprising age for the onset of consciousness. For Risley, like Atwood, this was the time of her move to Toronto, and for Risley at least the end of happiness. Through the move to Toronto, a backwater of civilization in the 1940s, but still civilization, Elaine as a child is suddenly forced to confront "femininity." Having lived in tents and motels, she and her mother must don the costumes and the roles appropriate to their gender and put away their unfeminine clothes and ungendered roles until the warm weather when they return to the North. Overnight Elaine feels like an alien from another planet. The future of painful socialization is represented by the doorway in her new school marked "GIRLS," the doorway which makes her wonder what the other one marked "BOYS" has behind it from which she has been shut out.

We might expect Elaine to cherish the memory of a paradise lost of relatively ungendered life as a child in nature. Instead, she feels guilty for being unprepared to operate in a world of mothers who are housekeepers preoccupied with clothes and labour-saving devices. Although the mature Elaine mutes the resentment, the child Elaine suspects that her mother has failed her as the role model needed to help her find her way in a world of "twin sets" and wearing hats to church. The young Elaine's inability to fault the mother she loves forces her to internalize as guilt her sense of inadequacy. If she is suffering the pain of being out of place, it must be something that is wrong with *her*; certainly it cannot be anything wrong with the definition of womanhood embodied in the mothers of her friends, Cordelia, Carol, but especially Grace Smeath.

Clearly Mrs. Smeath is the Bad Mother that Elaine suspects her own mother of being for not

"It is Elaine's victimization at the hands of other little girls, not those mysteriously dangerous men, which leads her to the nervous reaction of peeling the skin off her feet and hands."

having prepared her for socialization. In the Smeath household, Elaine and her friends are involved in that socialization; they study to be future housewives by cutting out pictures of "frying pans and washing machines" to paste into scrapbooks for their "ladies." A more important aspect of that socialization is represented by regular attendance at church. When the Smeaths invite Elaine to join them for the first of what eventually seems an endless series of Sundays, Atwood describes the interior of the church through the eyes of the young Elaine who might as well be a creature from Mars. One feature that becomes crucially important to Elaine are the inscriptions under the stained-glass pictures of Jesus—"SUFFER·THE·LITTLE·CHILDREN"—and of Mary—"THE·GREATEST·OF·THESE·IS·CHARITY."

Because she feels radically incapable of fitting into the world outside her home, Elaine becomes the victim of Cordelia's sadistic punishments for her incompetence as a student of womanhood. These punishments, which range from reprimands and shunnings to being buried alive, culminate in the scene of Elaine's almost freezing to death in a nearby ravine where Cordelia has thrown her hat. This is a ravine where "*men*" lurk to molest careless little girls. It is Elaine's victimization at the hands of other little girls, not those mysteriously dangerous men, which leads her to the nervous reaction of peeling the skin off her feet and hands, almost as though she is studying to become a child martyr by flaying herself alive. She is saved, she convinces herself, not so much by her own mother as by the apparition of the ultimate Good Mother, the Virgin Mary.

Mrs. Risley and Mrs. Smeath function then as variants of the Good Mother and the Bad Mother. Elaine's mother suspects that Cordelia and the other girls are tormenting her daughter, but she assumes

What Do I Read Next?

- Atwood's bestselling novel *The Handmaid's Tale* (1985) is set in a future in which reproductive ability has dwindled to the point where only a small minority are capable of having children. In a repressive, male-dominated oligarchy, women are divided into classes, the lowest of which, the handmaids, are used solely for procreation.

- The autobiographical novel *Portrait of the Artist as a Young Man* (1916), by James Joyce, is a classic *künstlerroman*. It shows the intellectual and emotional growth of the character Stephen Dedalus, and how the development of his artistic awareness involves a rejection of the values of the society in which he was raised.

- Alice Munro is one of Canada's leading writers. Her novel *Lives of Girls and Women* (1971), set in a small town in southwest Ontario in the 1950s and 1960s, is a *künstlerroman* about the coming of age of a writer.

- *The Diviners* (1974), by Margaret Laurence, is a *künstlerroman* set in various locations in Canada. With the use of many flashbacks to childhood, it tells the life story of Morag Gunn, a middle-aged female novelist.

- Annie Dillard's *An American Childhood* (1987) is an autobiography that explores the development of Dillard's artistic, spiritual, and naturalist interests up to the end of her high school years.

- In *Differencing the Canon: Feminist Desire and the Writing of Art's Histories* (1999), art historian Griselda Pollock discusses feminist approaches to art history, re-reads artists such as Van Gogh, Toulouse-Lautrec, and Manet from a feminist perspective, and assesses the work of feminist painters such as Artemisia Gentileschi and Mary Cassatt.

- Stephen W. Hawking's bestselling *A Brief History of Time* (1988), which Atwood acknowledges as an influence for *Cat's Eye*, provides a fascinating overview of the quest for a unified field theory.

---

that Elaine can tell her the truth and she never notices the marks of Elaine's flaying herself. Mrs. Smeath, on the other hand, *knows* that Elaine is being tormented but does nothing. In fact, Mrs. Smeath even *knows* that Elaine has overheard her saying that Elaine *deserves* to be punished for being at heart a graceless heathen. It is not until Elaine almost dies that Mrs. Risley acts. Somewhere down in the pool of the past lurks the monster of resentment against this Good Mother who should have known and acted sooner. Mrs. Risley becomes the representation, like her husband, of the well-intentioned, virtuous, but not terribly effective liberal humanists who *sense* that evil exists but refuse to acknowledge it, since a knowledge of evil would force them to find a place for it in their world.

Mrs. Smeath, on the other hand, is much easier for Elaine to deal with. Even as a child, Elaine can clearly see Mrs. Smeath's evil in the transparent world of that cat's eye which will be the emblem of her insight as an artist. She comes to see the crucial difference *within* Mrs. Smeath as a woman who professes to being a Christian—"SUFFER·THE·LITTLE·CHILDREN" and "THE·GREATEST·OF·THESE·IS·CHARITY"—yet believes that the greatest charity to little children who happen to be "heathens" is to make them indeed suffer. And, it is very much to the point that the individual who functions as Elaine's Muse is Mrs. Smeath, *not* Mrs. Risley. This variety of the Bad Mother, more in line with Freud's reality principle, generates a whole series of paintings through which Elaine vents her anger, hatred, and malice. Mrs. Smeath as the bad mother may very well represent much of what she finds most despicable in the conventional notion of Woman. At the same time, it is an evil which generates art and it is that art which liberates her from a self enslaved in anger towards and hatred of that image of "Woman."

That same indeterminacy is evident in Elaine's bizarre relationship with Cordelia. When she declares her independence, following Cordelia's move to another school, Elaine becomes powerful, assertive, verbally aggressive, and Cordelia fades into powerlessness, into the kind of silence which was Elaine's position early on in this power struggle veiled as a friendship. Elaine's enjoyment of a new facility with words, as though her tongue has been empowered by her earlier victimization, makes it clear how important the element of the retrospective is in this text. Told in a traditionally chronological fashion, Elaine's empowerment through language would have led the reader to anticipate that she would become a writer, rather than a painter.

In this symbiotic relationship, Elaine's friend/persecutor is given the name Cordelia. Most readers sense the irony in Atwood's borrowing the name of one of Shakespeare's innocent tragic heroines, but there are also implications of a transfer being transacted here. In the years following the Second World War, *King Lear* became one of our most attractive cultural myths in part because Cordelia reminds us how the innocent are swept up in the destruction of war and civil disorder and perhaps also that the innocent embody the redemptive power of love. At the same time, it is the refusal of Lear's single faithful daughter to speak, just as much as her sisters' hypocritical flattery, which sets in motion the machinery of conflict and destruction by which she and her family are overwhelmed. In this sense, Elaine, perhaps following her mother's example, is somewhat like Cordelia, choosing silence and martyrdom rather than risk the anxiety and guilt of self-assertion. Eventually, anger and resentment find their sublimated or socialized modes of expression, first in her verbal assaults on the imperfections of others and finally in her art, so often a visualization of her anguish at the hands of her tormentors.

More than anyone else, Cordelia is the one from whom she must free herself by acknowledging not only difference but kinship. Cordelia *is* a "secret sharer." Like her readers, Elaine keeps expecting her former tormentor to show up at the gallery, the most appropriate ghost to appear in this retrospective. Cordelia, however, does not need to appear: Elaine has already exorcized much of the guilt, hatred, and anger generated in her relationships with Mrs. Smeath and Cordelia through her art, conveniently brought together so that the artist, like her audience, can read this retrospective as a testimony to the transformative power of art. When

Elaine returns to the bridge, the power of her creative consciousness calls up an apparition of Cordelia from the deeps of that pool of time with which we began. She tells us:

> I know she's looking at me, the lopsided mouth smiling a little, the face closed and defiant. There is the same shame, the sick feeling in my body, the same knowledge of my own wrongness, awkwardness, weakness; the same wish to be loved; the same loneliness; the same fear. But these are not my own emotions any more. They are Cordelia's; as they always were.

> I am the older now, I'm the stronger. If she stays here any longer she will freeze to death; she will be left behind, in the wrong time. It's almost too late.

> I reach out my arms to her, bend down, hands open to show I have no weapon. *It's all right*, I say to her. *You can go home now.*

In a strange and unexpected sense, Cordelia has become her name. Just as Elaine earlier was rescued from physical death in the icy stream below this bridge, this time she acknowledges another variety of rescue. She confirms what this retrospective has been moving toward all along—the recognition that her art has rescued her from the spiritual death of a lifetime wasted in anger and resentment. Having recognized the power of Cordelia within herself, Elaine can at last release the Cordelia she has made to appear in the final hours before she prepares to leave home again. Perhaps she recognizes also that she and Cordelia had identities less distinct from each other than it seemed in childhood, that each had been fashioning the other in the image of a self she could not otherwise confront. Now Elaine herself can be a variety of the "Good Mother" and simply send Cordelia home before she freezes to death in "the wrong time."

In the end, *Cat's Eye* is postmodern in several interrelated ways. Atwood offers the informed reader the lure of a few well-known features of her own childhood and then proceeds to invent an autobiography which is the experience of Elaine Risley, a character who may bear only the most superficial similarities. Autobiography, even when intended, is obviously enough only another form of fiction. By offering us, in the words of the novel's preliminary note, a work of fiction whose form is that of an autobiography, she gives us a text which confirms that truth by showing how Elaine Risley has invented herself, constructed an autobiography, through her art. Elaine is even allowed to be amused by her critics' (mis)readings of her painting, one of whom writes of Risley's "disconcerting deconstruction of perceived gender and its re-

Elaine carries her cat's eye as a token of protection, but the marble's frozen center is also a metaphor for her emotional state after enduring Cordelia's cruelties

lationship to perceived power, especially in respect to numinous imagery."

In addition, this text raises questions about the representation of women, about writing as a woman, about autobiography, and about mothers and daughters. As Barbara Johnson has argued, autobiography and its reflection in autobiographical fiction are a supplanting of the mother, a kind of giving birth to oneself through the creation of the text. Using the classic text of Mary Shelley's *Frankenstein,* Johnson argues that what a woman writer (the very term "woman writer" has traditionally been conceived of as a "freak of nature") creates has conventionally seemed a "monster." Johnson asks: "Is autobiography somehow always in the process of symbolically killing the mother off by telling her the lie that we have given birth to ourselves?". In telling us the story of her life, Elaine Risley foregrounds Cordelia as a monster only to show how she freed herself from Cordelia to become as a young woman monstrous in her own way, and appropriately through *language*, with her "mean mouth." She offers us in Mrs. Smeath, the Bad Mother, whom she subsumes psychologically in her art, a kind of monstrosity which exorcizes the monstrous complicity of Mrs. Smeath in her per-

secution by Cordelia and the other girls. And she offers us in Mrs. Risley, the Good Mother, a failed guide to the intricacies of femininity in the outside world and, therefore, a mother who must be killed off before Elaine can achieve selfhood at fifty.

Why, we might ask, has it taken Elaine so long to give birth to herself, the sort of act managed by the Paul Morels and the Stephen Dedaluses of modernist fiction by their twenty-fifth birthdays? Part of the answer is obvious in the question. Elaine Risley is a female rather than a male character. In this context, a good analogue is Virginia Woolf who was well aware that she could not begin work on *To the Lighthouse*, dealing in part with the loss of her mother, until she was in her forties. As we have learned from sociologists like Nancy Chodorow, women must struggle to achieve a sense of self separate from others, in part because they are "mothered" or nurtured primarily by women. In this vein, Chodorow argues, mothers see themselves as continuous with their daughters:

> Because they are the same gender as their daughters and have been girls, mothers of daughters tend not to experience these infant daughters as separate from them in the same way as mothers of infant sons. In both cases, a mother is likely to experience a sense of

oneness and continuity with her infant. However, this sense is stronger, and lasts longer, vis-à-vis daughters.

In these ways, the retrospective of her art is partly an invention to allow Elaine to achieve a sense of self, distinct from both Mrs. Risley and Mrs. Smeath. It is also a belated recognition of her mothering herself as the child and the young woman Elaine as well as her mothering of Cordelia whom she now can release from her hatred and her love. Having completed this retrospective of her life and given birth to herself, Elaine can acknowledge the separateness of her "daughters"— both the girl she was and Cordelia as her "other." At the risk of increasing Atwood's anxiety with yet another autobiographical reading of her fiction, it might be recalled that *Cat's Eye* is the revision and completion of a manuscript she began in her mid-twenties and finished as she approached her fiftieth birthday. Despite Margaret Atwood's disclaimer that the novel is not autobiographical, it is a text performing itself as a text, a text of the author's own struggle to achieve selfhood as a woman and as an artist.

Source: Earl G. Ingersoll, "Margaret Atwood's *Cat's Eye*: Re-Viewing Women in a Postmodern World," in *ARIEL*, Vol. 22, No. 6, October 1991, pp. 17–27.

Sources

Howells, Coral Ann, *Margaret Atwood*, St. Martin's, 1995, pp. 148–60.

———, "Transgressing Genre," in *Margaret Atwood, Works and Impact*, edited by Reingard M. Nischik, Camden House, 2000, pp. 143–47.

Kanfer, Stefan, Review, in *Time*, Vol. 133, No. 6, February 6, 1989, p. 70.

Lee, Hermoine, Review, in *New Republic*, Vol. 200, No. 15, April 10, 1989, p. 38.

McDermott, Alice, "What Little Girls Are Really Made Of," in *New York Times Book Review*, February 5, 1989, p. 1.

Stein, Karen F., *Margaret Atwood Revisited*, Twayne, 1999, pp. 87–95.

For Further Reading

Bloom, Harold, ed., *Margaret Atwood*, Modern Critical Views series, Chelsea House, 2000.

This is a collection of some of the best recent criticism on Atwood's work.

Bouson, J. Brooks, *Brutal Choreographies: Oppositional Strategies and Narrative Design in the Novels of Margaret Atwood*, University of Massachusetts Press, 1993.

An examination of Atwood's first seven novels from the perspective of feminist and psychoanalytic theory.

Cooke, Nathalie, *Margaret Atwood: A Biography*, E. C. W. Press, 1998.

This biography follows the details of Atwood's personal life and also shows how she emerged as such a significant figure in Canadian literature and culture and an internationally renowned writer.

Ingersoll, Earl G., ed., *Margaret Atwood: Conversations*, Ontario Review Press, 1990.

This is a collection of twenty-one interviews with Atwood, conducted in the 1970s and 1980s, in which Atwood talks extensively about her work and her views.

Sullivan, Rosemary, *The Red Shoes: Margaret Atwood Starting Out*, HarperCollins Canada, 1998.

This is a well-researched, engaging biography of Atwood's early life, covering the period from the 1940s to the 1970s.

For Whom the Bell Tolls

Ernest Hemingway
1940

When *For Whom the Bell Tolls* was published in 1940, it immediately became a resounding critical and popular success and helped cement Ernest Hemingway's reputation as one of America's foremost writers. Readers praised its realistic portrait of not only the political tensions in Europe that would soon erupt into World War II but also the complexities of the entire experience of war for the individual who found him or herself fighting for a cause. Hemingway had previously explored this theme, most notably in his short story collection, *In Our Time* (1924), and in his novels *The Sun Also Rises* (1926) and *A Farewell to Arms* (1929). Yet his attitude toward his subject in *For Whom the Bell Tolls* reveals a subtle shift. While his previous works focused more on the meaninglessness of war, this novel ends with a reaffirmation of community.

For Whom the Bell Tolls chronicles the experiences of American college professor Robert Jordan, who has volunteered to fight for the Loyalist cause in the Spanish Civil War. His initial idealism is quickly tempered by the realities of war. Yet his courage enables him to remain devoted to the cause, even as he faces death. Hemingway's compassionate and authentic portrait of his characters as they struggle to retain their idealistic beliefs has helped earn the novel its reputation as one of Hemingway's finest.

Ernest Hemingway

Author Biography

Ernest Hemingway was born on July 21, 1899, in Oak Park, Illinois, to Clarence Edmunds (physician) and Grace (music teacher) Hemingway, both strict Congregationalists. He started writing when he was a teenager, penning a weekly column for his high school newspaper. During this period, he also began to write poems and stories, some of which were published in his school's literary magazine. After graduating high school in 1917, Hemingway started his career as a reporter for the *Kansas City Star*, covering city crime and writing feature stories. The position helped him develop a journalistic style, which would later become one of the most identifiable characteristics of his fiction.

When World War I broke out, he volunteered as a Red Cross ambulance driver in Italy. After suffering severe leg injuries, Hemingway met and fell in love with a nurse who would eventually break off their relationship. Disillusioned with the war and with romantic relationships, Hemingway returned home and turned his attention to fiction writing. To support himself, however, he returned to reporting, accepting a position at the *Toronto Star*.

Like many of his compatriots of the Lost Generation, Hemingway left America for Europe, where he joined the group of literary expatriates in Paris, including Gertrude Stein and F. Scott Fitzgerald. He lived in Paris for the next seven years, working on his fiction and serving as a European correspondent for American newspapers. From 1937 to 1938, he covered the Spanish Civil War, and from 1944 to 1945, he reported on the battles of World War II.

Edward J. O'Brien named Hemingway's short story "My Old Man," which appeared in his first publication, *Three Stories and Ten Poems*, in his list of the best stories of 1923. Hemingway's next publication, a series of short stories interspersed with vignettes, entitled *In Our Time* (1924), was well received, and he began to earn a reputation as an astute chronicler of the Lost Generation. This reputation was solidified after the publication of his next story collection, *Men Without Women* (1927), and the novels *The Sun Also Rises* (1926) and *A Farewell to Arms* (1929). When *For Whom the Bell Tolls* was published in 1940, it was regarded by the public and the critics as one of his best works.

Along with his growing reputation as one of the most important contemporary American writers, Hemingway developed a mythic persona that he helped perpetuate. During the middle of the century, the public began to envision Hemingway as the personification of his heroes—a hard drinking, forceful American, who could stand his ground on the battlefield, in the boxing ring, and on safari. Several American magazines, such as *Life* and *Esquire*, chronicled his adventures. Yet, during this period, he also devoted himself to his craft, which he considered of paramount importance in his life and his time.

During the 1950s, a life of alcohol abuse and rough living took a toll on his health. His health problems, compounded by his three failed marriages and periods of creative stagnation, resulted in a mental breakdown in 1960, and the following year on July 2, Hemingway committed suicide in Ketchum, Idaho.

Hemingway has retained his reputation as one of America's most significant and influential writers. During his long literary career, he earned several accolades, including the Pulitzer Prize in 1953 for *The Old Man and the Sea*, the Nobel Prize for literature in 1954, and the Award of Merit from the American Academy of Arts & Letters in 1954.

Plot Summary

The novel chronicles the experiences of American professor Robert Jordan from Saturday afternoon to Tuesday noon during the last week of May 1937. Jordan has volunteered to fight with the Loyalist guerrilla army in the Spanish Civil War. His mission is to blow up a bridge near Segovia prior to a Loyalist offensive in that area, scheduled to occur in three days. When the novel opens, he is behind enemy lines, ready to meet up with Pablo and his wife Pilar, his contacts, and the leaders of one of the guerrilla factions.

Jordan studies the bridge as he determines how he will blow it up at the necessary moment. He has previously blown up bridges and trains, but he never has had to time a demolition so carefully. Pablo and Pilar have been set to help Jordan plan and execute the mission, gathering together other guerrilla bands if necessary.

Jordan finds Pablo and Pilar and travels with them to their hideout in a mountain cave where he meets Maria, a beautiful young woman. Maria has escaped the Fascists after being tortured and raped. Jordan also meets Anselmo at the hideout, an elderly guerrilla fighter who is determined to die, if need be, for the Loyalist cause. Even though he recognizes that the Loyalists have committed atrocities during the war, Jordan has aligned himself with them, blaming their poverty and oppression for their cruel actions. He hates the Fascists as much as the others do, noting that their cruelty stems not from a desire for freedom but from naked ambition and a lust for power. After hearing Maria's shocking tales of abuse, Jordan redoubles his determination to kill as many Fascists as he can, even if he sacrifices his own life as a result.

That evening, however, he begins to fall in love with Maria, after spending most of the night with her, and considers a future with her. As a result, for the first time, Jordan becomes fearful about the mission since he now has something to live for other than stopping the Fascist occupation. He knows, though, that fear will prevent him from keeping a cool head as he plans his operation.

Jordan is able to suppress his fears, and he carefully plans the destruction of the bridge, drawing several sketches to familiarize himself and the other guerrillas with the area and to determine the best course of action. The operation, however, is almost destroyed by Pablo, who, fearing for his safety, deserts the camp after stealing the explosives.

Pablo returns on the third morning after having a change of heart, accompanied by more Loyalists with horses. The explosives and detonators, however, have been damaged so severely that Jordan has no other choice than to try to blow up the bridge with hand grenades, which would be a much more dangerous task.

The group begins to carry out their mission, unaware that the anticipated Loyalist advance has failed. First, Jordan and Anselmo kill the guards while Pablo and the others attack the Fascists who are approaching the bridge, in order to slow their movement. After Jordan blows up the bridge, he scrambles to safety. Anselmo, however, has been hit by falling debris and dies. Jordan blames Pablo for the death of the old man, determining that if they had used the explosives, they all would have been safe.

Jordan reunites with Pablo, Pilar, Maria, and two of the men Pablo had brought with him. Pablo insists that the others had been killed in the battle, but Jordan determines that Pablo had killed them for their horses. Pablo acknowledges the murders with a shrug, noting that the men had not been part of his group.

Jordan plans their escape away from the front. He insists that Pablo should go first, since he knows the territory, accompanied by Maria. Jordan knows that those in front will have the best chance of reaching safety before the Fascists discover them. He then sends Pilar and the two guerillas on and follows them. The others make it safely across the open road, but Jordan is injured when his horse, wounded by the Fascists' bullets, falls on him. The others pull him out of the line of fire, but he insists that they go on ahead and leave him there, knowing that his injuries would slow them down and place them all in danger. Despondent, Maria tries to convince him to allow her to stay with him, but he refuses, insisting that he will live through her. The others have to carry her away.

After the others leave, Jordan sits against a tree with his gun propped up in his lap and waits for the Fascists, hoping to slow them down as the others escape. As he waits, he thinks about what has brought him to this point and determines that he has done the best that he could and thus his death will not be in vain. The novel ends as Jordan sees a Fascist lieutenant coming into view and prepares to fire.

Media Adaptations

- *For Whom the Bell Tolls* was adapted as a film by Sam Wood, with a screenplay by Dudley Nichols, starring Gary Cooper and Ingrid Bergman, from Paramount, 1943. It is available on video and DVD.

- An audio version, read by Alexander Adams, has been published by Books on Tape.

Characters

Anselmo

Anselmo is an elderly member of Pablo's band. Anselmo lacks education but reveals a moral and compassionate nature. He supplies the human element to the struggle that Jordan and Pablo so often ignore, as he embodies the Loyalist ideals to which the two men had originally devoted their lives. Each time he witnesses or participates in a killing, the event profoundly troubles him. He is killed as he helps Jordan blow up the bridge.

General Golz

General Golz is one of the Russians who have been sent to help the Loyalist army. He oversees the upcoming planned attack against the Fascists.

Robert Jordan

Before the Spanish Civil War, Robert Jordan had been a college Spanish instructor with a deep love of Spain and its people. His liberal political leanings prompted him to join the Loyalists in their fight against the Fascists. Initially, he idealized the Loyalist cause and the character of its devotees, but as the novel begins, with Jordan embroiled in the realities of war, he experiences a profound disillusionment. He notes that his devotion to the cause had been almost like a religious experience, likening it to "the feeling you expected to have but did not have when you made your first communion." That "purity of feeling," however, soon dissipated. He has observed atrocities on both sides of the conflict and has been chided for his naivete and "slight political development." At Gaylord's Hotel in Madrid, where he heard the callousness of the Russian officers, he concluded that they could "corrupt very easily" but then wondered "was it corruption or was it merely that you lost the naivete that you started with?"

He has come to the realization that most of the people of Spain have, like him, become disillusioned about their noble cause and so are not as willing to sacrifice themselves to it. As a result, he no longer defines himself as a communist; now he insists instead that he is an "anti-fascist," not a firm supporter of a cause but at least a dissenter to a movement he finds abhorrent.

His sense of duty compels him to complete the task he has taken on—the blowing up of a bridge in Fascist territory in an effort to aid the Loyalists' advance—even when he understands the probability of failure and the danger to himself and others. His courage, evident throughout the novel as he carries out his perilous mission, faces its greatest test after the mission fails to impede the Fascist movements and he suffers a severe injury when his horse stumbles. Understanding that his injuries will slow the others' escape, he convinces them to go on ahead to safety without him. He quickly overcomes his desire to kill himself and determines to face the oncoming Fascist forces in a last effort to help his comrades escape.

Maria

Jordan meets the young and beautiful Maria at Pablo's hideout. She has been brutalized by the Fascists after they murdered her father, a Loyalist mayor. Fascist sympathizers shaved her head as punishment for her association with the enemy, and, as a result, she is tagged with the nickname "Rabbit," which also suggests her timid demeanor. She gains strength, however, through her intense and short-lived love affair with Jordan.

Several critics, including Leslie Fiedler, have noted that Maria, like many of Hemingway's women, lacks development. She appears in the novel as an idealized image of a devoted woman who enjoys extreme sexual pleasure in her relationship with the protagonist. She seems to exist in the novel as tool to help reveal Jordan's character and to provide him with a sense of meaning. By the end of the novel, he must decide between his love for her and his duty to his compatriots.

Maria's immediate sexual attraction to Jordan seems unlikely given the sexual abuse she has repeatedly experienced at the hands of the Fascists. Yet her romantic insistence on staying with the injured Jordan at the end of the novel inspires readers' sympathy.

Pablo

Pablo serves as a foil to Jordan. He is the leader of the central guerrilla band and Pilar's husband. Prior to Jordan's appearance, he had earned the group's fearful respect. Yet, when Jordan challenges his authority and outlines the dangerous plan to blow up the bridge, Pablo's cowardice and self-absorption emerge. He tries to cover his fear by insisting that the mission is too dangerous, claiming that the lives of his men would be put at risk and their headquarters would most likely be discovered, since it is close to the bridge. His men, however, determine that they will follow Jordan's plan of action in an effort to ensure a Loyalist victory.

Pablo's vicious battle with Jordan for supremacy over the group, coupled with the fear that he will endanger the mission, prompts the band to consider killing him, but Pablo escapes with the explosives before they can act. Pablo's return to the group the next morning appears to be generated by his feelings of remorse over his actions; yet his primary motive may be his jealously over Maria's love for Jordan. When he returns, he insists that he now wholeheartedly supports the mission.

Hemingway suggests that, like Jordan, Pablo has lost his idealism by witnessing the brutalities of war on both sides. His acknowledgment of these atrocities has weakened his resolve to fight for the cause and has made him fearful for his own safety. Yet, though Jordan also at some points in the story becomes afraid for his life, he eventually exhibits the strength of character necessary to help ensure the safety of the others in the group. Pablo too often gives in to fears for his own safety and to jealousy over Jordan's power and his relationship with Maria.

Yet his character is contradictory. When Pilar asks him why he did not kill Jordan when he had the opportunity, Pablo replies that Jordan is "a good boy." Pablo appears to redeem himself at the end of the novel when he admits that he returned to the camp because, as he describes his desertion, "having done such a thing, there is a loneliness that cannot be borne." Ironically, Jordan must depend on Pablo for the group's survival. After Jordan is severely wounded, Pablo leads the rest of them to safety.

Pilar

Pilar is married to Pablo, the leader of the central guerrilla band. Unlike many of Hemingway's other women, Pilar is a complex, strong woman who does not allow her husband to dominate her. When Pablo's actions threaten to subvert their mission, Pilar promptly takes over as leader of the guerrillas. Hemingway suggests that Jordan could not have carried out his mission without her. She comes to represent in the novel the ideals and dedication of the Spanish Loyalists.

She also helps engineer Jordan and Maria's relationship, giving her as a gift to him. Pilar tells Maria that she supports and encourages her union with Jordan but admits that their relationship will make her jealous. Pilar insists that she is "no *tortillera* (lesbian) but a woman made for men": "I do not make perversions," she claims, yet she refuses to explain her jealousy.

Michael Reynolds, in his article "Ringing the Changes: Hemingway's 'Bell' Tolls Fifty," writes that this scene, more than any other, reveals her complexity. Hemingway, he notes, "who would become increasingly fascinated with such triangles, realized the androgynous side of men and women earlier than most have given him credit." Pilar has insisted elsewhere, "I would have made a good man, but I am all woman and ugly. Yet many men have loved me and I have loved many men." However, as Reynolds notes, Hemingway has characterized her as androgynous, juxtaposing her insistence of her attraction to men with her tenderly holding Maria at the end of the novel, as the band leaves Jordan behind, waiting to die.

Her strength of character also emerges in her supernatural powers. When she reads Jordan's palm, she foresees his death, yet she stays devoted to the mission even at the risk of her own life. Her powers of perception allow her to recognize the depths of Jordan's and Maria's suffering, which prompts her to help them come together.

Pilar serves as the group's storyteller, spinning her stories as appropriate thematic backdrops to the action. As the group prepares for their mission, she tells the story of Finito, a bullfighter overcome by fear in the bullring, and of Pablo and his men murdering Fascist sympathizers by throwing them over a cliff.

El Sordo

El Sordo is the leader of a neighboring guerrilla band. Jordan asks him and his men to join Pablo's band to help blow up the bridge.

Themes

Idealism

The elderly peasant Anselmo most fully represents the Loyalist ideals in the novel. Hemingway suggests that his lack of education and his compassionate nature allow him to believe in the cause and to fight for it to the end of his life. Through his idealism, he supplies the human element to the struggle that Jordan and Pablo so often ignore.

Pablo has largely forgotten the ideals of the cause to which he had originally devoted his life. He has seen too much of the reality of war and so participates now more out of self-interest than out of patriotism. As a result, he can take pleasure in his brutal murder of the Fascists. And when he considers the plan to blow up the bridge too dangerous, he flees with the explosives. Yet he appears to retain some of the ideals to which he once dedicated himself. When Pilar asks him why he did not kill Jordan when he had the opportunity, Pablo replies that Jordan is "a good boy," since his motives are noble. He also notes the camaraderie that results from devotion to the cause when, as he describes his desertion, he notes, "having done such a thing, there is a loneliness that cannot be borne."

Jordan struggles to retain his sense of idealism throughout the novel. Initially, he volunteers to serve with the Loyalists because of his liberal attitudes toward politics and his deep love of the Spanish people. However, he quickly gets a taste of the reality of war when he sees atrocities committed on both sides. He notes that his education on the true politics of war came as he listened to the cynical attitude of the Russian officers at Gaylord's in Madrid as they discussed their intentions to pervert the Loyalists' devotion to their cause for their own ends. This attitude is reflected in the opening chapter as Jordan discusses the mission with Golz, who focuses only on the military aspect of the plan.

Courage

Jordan's courage emerges in the face of his growing disillusionment. James Nagel, in his article on Hemingway for the *Dictionary of Literary Biography*, notes that Jordan "has a realistic skepticism about what the war will actually accomplish, but he dedicates himself fully to the cause nonetheless." Even though he suspects the mission will fail, he carefully plans and executes it, accepting the fact that failure most likely will result in death. His relationship with Maria helps provide him with the

Topics for Further Study

- Watch the film version of *For Whom the Bell Tolls*. Do you think the film is dated? What scenes would you update for today's audience?

- Compare the portrait of war in *A Farewell to Arms* to that of *For Whom the Bell Tolls*. How are they simliar? What differences do you see? Which resonates the most for you as the reader, and why?

- Research the Loyalist sympathizers during the Spanish Civil War. Do Hemingway's guerrilla bands in *For Whom the Bell Tolls* represent an accurate portrayal of the Loyalist faction during this war? Explain your answer.

- Some critics find the relationship between Jordan and Maria to be overly romantic and unrealistic. Support or refute this conclusion.

strength to continue as he allows himself to envision a future with her. His final act of courage appears at the end of the novel, as he faces imminent death at the hands of the Fascists. His fear initially prompts him to consider suicide. However, his strength of character returns when he recognizes that he can help ensure the safety of the rest of the group by staying alive to delay the advance of the Fascists.

Style

Point of View

The novel presents the narrative through an omniscient point of view that continually shifts back and forth between the characters. In this way, Hemingway can effectively chronicle the effect of the war on the men and women involved. The narrator shifts from Anselmo's struggles in the snow during his watch to Pilar's story about Pablo's execution of Fascists and El Sordo's lonely death to help readers more clearly visualize their experiences.

In "Ringing the Changes: Hemingway's 'Bell' Tolls Fifty," Michael Reynolds writes, "Without drawing undue attention to his artistry, Hemingway has written a collection of short stories embedded in a framing novel." Against the backdrop of the group's attempt to blow up the bridge, each character tells his or her own story: Maria tells of her parents' murder and her rape; Jordan shares what he learned about the true politics of war at Gaylord's in Madrid. Pilar provides the most compelling and comprehensive stories of Finito's fears in the bullfighting ring and of Pablo and his men as they beat the Fascists to death in a drunken rage.

Hemingway employs flashbacks and flashforwards to enhance thematic focus. Pilar's stories of struggle and heroism make their mission all the more poignant and place it in an historical context. Jordan's flashbacks to a time when his ideals were not tempered by the reality of war highlight his growing sense of disillusionment. His dreams of a future with Maria in Madrid add a bittersweet touch to his present predicament and his final death scene.

Style

One of Hemingway's most distinct and celebrated characteristics is his deliberate writing style. Trained as a newspaper reporter, Hemingway used a journalistic style in his fiction, honed down to economical, abrupt descriptions of characters and events. His goal was to ensure that his words accurately described reality. The best example of his economical style comes at the end of the novel, as Jordan faces death. Hemingway's spare, direct description of Jordan's final moments as he considers suicide and then determines to survive long enough to help the group escape reflects Jordan's stoicism and his acceptance of the inevitable.

Historical Context

The Spanish Civil War

Civil war broke out in Spain in 1936, but the underlying causes can be traced back several years prior to that date. In the 1930s Spain experienced continuous political upheavals. In 1931, after years of civil conflict in the country, King Alfonso XIII voluntarily placed himself in exile, and on April 13 of that year, a new republic emerged. The Leftist government, however, faced similar civil unrest, and by 1933, the conservatives regained control. By 1936 the people voted the leftists back in.

Compare & Contrast

- **1930s–1940s:** The world experiences a decade of aggression in the 1930s that culminates in World War II. This second world war results from the rise of totalitarian regimes in Germany, Italy, and Japan. One week after Nazi Germany and the USSR sign the Treaty of Nonaggression, Germany invades Poland, and World War II begins.

  Today: The world is threatened by Islamic fundamentalist groups who have declared a holy war against the West. These radical groups have committed terrorist acts in several countries including the United States. On September 11, 2001, the most devastating acts of terror to date worldwide are delivered as terrorists fly planes into the World Trade Center Towers in New York City and into the Pentagon and are responsible for the crash of another plane in Pennsylvania.

- **1930s–1940s:** Civil war breaks out in Spain in 1936 between the Fascists, backed by Germany and Italy, and the Loyalists, backed by the USSR.

  Today: Spain has been established as a social and democratic country that is governed by a parliamentary monarchy. National sovereignty is vested in the Spanish people.

- **1930s–1940s:** American women gain a measure of independence in the workplace as they labor in the factories, replacing men who have gone to war. By 1945, the peak of the war production, approximately 19 million women hold jobs. Independence is difficult to relinquish when, at the end of the war, the men come home and demand their jobs back, and their wives return to their traditional roles in the home.

  Today: American women have made major gains in their fight for equality even without the 1972 Equal Rights Amendment Bill. Discrimination against women is now against the law.

After the assassination of Jose Calvas Otelo, an influential Monarchist, the army led a revolt against the government and sponsored the return of General Francisco Franco, who had been exiled because of his politics.

As a result, civil war broke out across the country between the Loyalist-leftists and the Monarchist-rightists. Russia backed the leftists while Germany and Italy supported the rightists. The war continued until 1939 with each side committing atrocities: the leftists slaughtered religious and political figures while the rightists bombed civilian targets. At the beginning of 1936, the Loyalists were suffering from an effective blockade as Franco's troops gained control. On March 28, the war ended as the rightists took the city of Madrid.

Hemingway, siding with the Loyalists, first lent his support to their cause by raising money for ambulances and medical supplies. In 1937, he ran the Ambulances Committee of the American Friends of Spanish Democracy. During the war, he often returned to Spain as a journalist, penning articles for the *North American Newspaper Alliance* and *Esquire*. When the Fascist army won control of Spain in 1939, Hemingway had just started writing *For Whom the Bell Tolls*.

The Lost Generation

This term became associated with a group of American writers in the 1920s who felt a growing sense of disillusionment after World War I. As a result, many left America for Europe. T. S. Eliot and Ezra Pound initially relocated to London, while F. Scott Fitzgerald and Hemingway traveled to Paris, which appeared to offer them a much freer society than America or England did. During this period, Paris became a mecca for these expatriates, who congregated in literary salons, restaurants, and bars to discuss their work in the context of the new age. One such salon was dominated by Gertrude Stein, who at one gathering insisted "you are all a lost generation," a quote immortalized by Hemingway in the preface to *The Sun Also Rises*. That novel, like *For Whom the Bell Tolls* and Fitzgerald's *The Great Gatsby*, presents a penetrating portrait of this Lost Generation.

The characters in works by these authors reflected the authors' growing sense of disillusionment along with the new ideas in psychology, anthropology, and philosophy that had become popular in the early part of the century. Freudianism, for example, which had caused a loosening of sexual morality during the Jazz Age, began to be studied by these writers as they explored the psyches of their characters and recorded their often subjective points of view of themselves and their world. Hemingway's men and women faced a meaningless world with courage and dignity, exhibiting "grace under pressure," while Fitzgerald's sought the redemptive power of love in a world driven by materialism.

This age of confusion, redefinition, and experimentation produced one of the most fruitful periods in American letters. These writers helped create a new form of literature, later called modernism, which repudiated traditional literary conventions. Prior to the twentieth century, writers structured their works to reflect their belief in the stability of character and the intelligibility of experience. Traditionally, novels and stories ended with a clear sense of closure, as conflicts were resolved and characters gained knowledge about themselves and their world. The authors of the Lost Generation challenged these assumptions as they expanded the genre's traditional form to accommodate their characters' questions about the individual's place in the world.

Critical Overview

When *For Whom the Bell Tolls* was published in 1940, Hemingway's reputation as one of America's most important writers was already well established. The new novel received overwhelmingly positive reviews from critics and the public alike, with many insisting that it was Hemingway's best novel to date. It quickly became a bestseller, as the first printing's 210,000 copies immediately sold out. In less than six months, that figure jumped to over 491,000. Michael Reynolds, in his assessment of the novel for the *Virginia Quarterly Review*, notes that a reviewer in the *New York Times* insisted that it was "the best book Ernest Hemingway has written, the fullest, the deepest, the truest. It will be one of the major novels in American

literature." Reynolds adds that Dorothy Parker claimed that it was "beyond all comparison, Ernest Hemingway's finest book," and an article in the *Nation* proclaimed that it set "a new standard for Hemingway in characterization, dialogue, suspense and compassion."

These and other critics praised Hemingway's thematic focus on idealism and responsibility, especially as a reflection of the mood of the times, as the world braced for the devastation of the impending world war. Reynolds writes, though, that the novel "transcends the historical context that bore it, becoming a parable rather than a paradigm."

Later, however, some critics found fault with the novel's politics. Hemingway's inclusion of Loyalist as well as Fascist atrocities drew criticism from liberal sympathizers. Other critics have complained about the idealized relationship between Jordan and Maria. Leslie A. Fiedler, for example, in his *Love and Death in the American Novel*, finds fault in all of Hemingway's characterizations of love. He comments that if, in *For Whom the Bell Tolls*, Hemingway "has written the most absurd love scene in the history of the American novel, this is not because he lost momentarily his skill and authority." Fiedler suggests that the love affair between Jordan and Maria "illuminates the whole erotic content of his fiction."

While the novel has never regained the critical status it enjoyed when it was first published, the novel is currently regarded, as James Nagel notes in his article on Hemingway for *Dictionary of Literary Biography*, as "nearly perfect." Philip Young in *American Writers* comments, "none of his books had evoked more richly the life of the senses, had shown a surer sense of plotting, or provided more fully living secondary characters, or livelier dialogue." Reynolds concludes his review with the following assessment: "And thus, softly, across time, *For Whom the Bell Tolls* continues in muted tones to toll for us."

Criticism

Wendy Perkins

Perkins is an associate professor of English and American literature and film at Prince George's Community College and has published several articles on British and American authors.

Spanish Loyalists fighting in the Spanish Civil War

In this essay, she defines Robert Jordan as one of Hemingway's "code heroes."

Several of Hemingway's protagonists share qualities that define them as a specific type of character that has come to be known as Hemingway's "code hero." The world in which Hemingway's code heroes find themselves helps to define them. Often the setting is war or some other dangerous arena, like the plains of Africa or a boxing ring, where the hero faces the ultimate test of courage. The protagonist must face fear along with a growing sense of despair over the meaninglessness of experience. Fear results not only from physical danger and impending death but also from the gradual disintegration of the self in a world of "nothingness," a world stripped of consoling ideals. He reveals his courage as he stoically faces his inevitable defeat and accepts it with dignity.

In his early work, Hemingway's heroes find dignity through purely personal moments of fulfillment. For example, the protagonist in his short story "The Short Happy Life of Francis Macomber" becomes a code hero when he stands his ground as a buffalo charges at him on an open plain in Africa. Previously, he had shown himself to be a coward when he had run from a lion, an action his wife

uses to humiliate him and thus gain power over him. Yet, by the end of the story, Macomber has found his courage and so experiences a perfect moment of transcendence when he faces the buffalo without fear. His perfect moment is a purely personal one, based on his own desperate need to prove himself a man. Robert Jordan, the protagonist in *For Whom the Bell Tolls*, presents another example of Hemingway's code hero. However, Hemingway alters his traditional type in his characterization of Jordan. Instead of defining him as a hero through a personal moment of dignity, as he does with Macomber, Hemingway presents a man who becomes a hero through an expression of communal responsibility.

Robert Jordan volunteers to help the Loyalists in their war with the Fascists during the Spanish Civil War because of his liberal politics and his great love for the Spanish people. Initially, he is devoted to their cause; however, he soon becomes disillusioned about the reality of war. He sees atrocities committed on both sides and listens to Loyalist sympathizers plot, not for the good of the cause, but for their own personal gain. During his frequent internal debates, Jordan comes to the conclusion that he distrusts the politics and practices of those he has sworn to support. He has heard Russian of-

> Even though he suspects that their plan to blow up the bridge and thus check the Fascist advance will fail and even though he recognizes that many of his compatriots have lost their belief in the cause, he refuses to turn his back on them."

ficers, who in theory have come to aid the Loyalists, discuss their intentions to gain personal advantages during the war. He has also heard of how the Spanish people, for whom he is ultimately fighting, can take enjoyment from the brutal slaughter of the enemy.

The world of *For Whom the Bell Tolls* appears to lack meaning like the God-abandoned world of Macomber on an African safari or of Frederick Henry on the battlefield of *A Farewell to Arms* (1929). Both Macomber and Henry eventually exhibit a strong sense of dignity in the face of their meaningless existence in very personal moments. Both men are alone at the end of their stories, revealing a certain "grace under pressure," a courageous standing of their ground as they confront their fear of the unknown. Jordan, however, stands his ground not for a purely personal sense of dignity and self-worth but for the common good. Even though he suspects that their plan to blow up the bridge and thus check the Fascist advance will fail and even though he recognizes that many of his compatriots have lost their belief in the cause, he refuses to turn his back on them.

In *Death in the Afternoon*, Hemingway expressed one of the tenets of his code heroes: "What is moral is what you feel good after and what is immoral is what you feel bad after." As Pablo notes, Jordan is a "good boy" whose sense of morality is tied to the protection of his community. This moral code frames the novel. On the first page, Hemingway quotes from a poem by John Donne. The poem opens with the statement "No man is an island, entire of itself; every man is a piece of the Continent" and closes with an insistence that, as a

result, "never send to know for whom the bell tolls; it tolls for thee." This opening suggests that Jordan's experience will inevitably be a common one—that his test will be to find the courage to work toward the good of the community. He can only fulfill his personal destiny if he fulfills that of the group.

Jordan struggles with this philosophy throughout the novel as he plans the destruction of the bridge, assuming that the mission will fail, and as he considers suicide while facing death at the hands of the Fascists. At one point, near the end of the novel, he tries to convince himself, "why wouldn't it be all right to just do it now and then the whole thing would be over with?" Yet, finally, he recognizes that he must resist the urge to end his suffering and must, instead, stand his ground, because, he notes, "there is something you can do yet." He forces himself to retain consciousness so that he can stall the Fascists and so give the others a few more minutes to get to safety.

Thus while Jordan is certainly a member of the Lost Generation, facing a world bereft of meaning and sense, he ends his life in a community of the lost, insisting to his comrades that he will remain with them, even after death. One of his final images is of the group making their way to safety, to a place where they can continue to fight for the cause. The ultimate dignity that Jordan achieves in the novel is through his determination not to give up his hope for the future, even though he knows that he cannot be a part of it. Thus he achieves the status of a true hero, one who not only honors his own sense of responsibility but also, ultimately, that of his community.

Source: Wendy Perkins, Critical Essay on *For Whom the Bell Tolls*, in *Novels for Students*, The Gale Group, 2002.

Ramón Buckley

In the following essay, Buckley examines the historical background of Ronda in order to understand Hemingway's fictional depiction of revolution staged there in For Whom the Bell Tolls.

Ronda sits perched in the hills of southern Spain, halfway between Seville and Malaga. Its dramatic setting, hanging on the cliffs above a river splitting the town in two, has inspired poets and artists for generations, most notably Rainier Maria Rilke. It is therefore not surprising that Hemingway should have chosen Ronda as a destination during his first visit to Spain in 1923. Carlos Baker tells the story:

The night life of Seville was boring to Hemingway. They watched a few flamenco dances, where broad-beamed women snapped their fingers to the music of guitars. . . "Oh for Christ's sake" he kept saying, "more flamingos!" He could not rest until Bird and McAlmon agreed to go on to Ronda. It was even better than Mike had predicted—a spectacular village with an ancient bullring, high in the mountains above Malaga.

His love affair with Ronda did not diminish. In *Death in the Afternoon* (1932) Hemingway wrote:

> There is one town that would be better than Aranjuez to see your first bullfight in if you are only going to see one and that is Ronda. That is where you should go if you ever go to Spain on a honeymoon or if you ever bolt with anyone. The entire town and as far as you can see in any direction is romantic background. . . if a honeymoon or an elopement is not a success in Ronda, it would be as well to start for Paris and commence making your own friends.

Later on in his life, when Hemingway returned to Spain in the mid-1950s, Ronda again became a favorite destination, especially when he befriended bullfighter Antonio Ordóñez, who is from Ronda. Like fellow expatriate Orson Welles, Hemingway spent long sojourns at Ordóñez's "cortijo" (country house) near Ronda.

When Hemingway arrived in Spain in February 1937 to cover the Spanish Civil War, most of the south, including Ronda, had already fallen to Franco. He was therefore unable to go to Andalusia during the war, but there is little doubt that, even before reaching Spain, he had heard innumerable stories about the peasant uprisings that took place in the south following the July 1936 military coup. Chapter 10 of *For Whom the Bell Tolls* is Pilar's painfully graphic account of one such uprising. More than any other chapter in the novel, it has stirred readers' imaginations with its gruesome realism, sparing no detail in recounting the massacre of fascist landlords by Andalusian peasants.

Although Hemingway does not mention the location of the massacre in *For Whom the Bell Tolls*, scholars have traditionally assumed that Ronda was the site of the peasant uprising. This assumption, however, has not gone uncontested. Angel Capellán has argued that because both Pilar and Pablo (the peasant leaders) say they come from Castilla (central Spain) we should look for an appropriate town in this area. Capellán suggests Cuenca, like Ronda dramatically perched on the ledge of a cliff. Hemingway himself, however, put the matter to rest when he told Hotchner: "When Pilar remem-

> "... it seems to me that there is a need to examine the real history of Ronda—the actual events that took place in this town in July 1936—in order to understand Hemingway's fictional rendering."

bers back to what happened in their village when the fascists came, that's Ronda, and the details of the town are exact."

The details of the town may be "exact" in *For Whom the Bell Tolls*, but not necessarily the details of the events that took place in Ronda in 1936. Writing to Bernard Berenson in 1954, Hemingway stated that the fascist massacre in the novel was a thing that he had "invented completely." However, he hastened to add that a writer has "the obligation to invent truer than things can be true." This would seem to indicate that Hemingway was trying to reach beyond actual events in a small Spanish town to a "higher reality," a description of the July peasant revolution which would reveal its "inner truth," to paraphrase Hemingway himself.

Because Pilar's description of the massacre is generally considered a highlight of the novel, Chapter 10 has attracted a fair amount of critical attention. Robert Gajdusek analyzes the revolution in terms of Jungian archetypes and points to the myth of Dionysus to explain the peasant revolution. Gajdusek also points out that when Hemingway compares Pilar's skill as a narrator to that of the Spanish writer Francisco de Quevedo, he is shining his own boots, so to speak, for all to see.

As if to balance Gajdusek's approach to the chapter through pagan myth, H. R. Stoneback has argued that it possesses an undercurrent of Catholic doctrine which he claims runs throughout the novel as a whole. Stoneback argues that the priest who is finally slaughtered is the real protagonist of Pilar's tale, and that the priest points to one of the novel's central themes, the need for atonement.

As engaging as these two readings of Chapter 10 may be, it seems to me that there is a need to

What Do I Read Next?

- Hemingway's *A Farewell to Arms* (1929) chronicles a doomed love affair between an American lieutenant and a British nurse during World War I.

- F. Scott Fitzgerald's *The Great Gatsby* (1925) is considered, along with *The Sun Also Rises*, to be one of the seminal works of the Lost Generation.

- Antony Beevor's *The Spanish Civil War*, published in 2001, presents a comprehensive account of the conflict that served as a bloody precursor to World War II.

- Hemingway's *The Sun Also Rises* (1926) focuses on the aftermath of World War I, especially on how the war affected the lives of displaced Americans.

examine the real history of Ronda—the actual events that took place in this town in July 1936—in order to understand Hemingway's fictional rendering. In 1996 I was invited to Ronda for a conference on Hemingway and Orson Welles, a perfect opportunity to do research in the local archives and to browse through the records of the Town Hall, and above all, to talk with senior citizens who could still remember those days of passion and death. Oddly enough, no book has been written on the subject, and those books that mention the massacre of Ronda do so from a partisan perspective. This, then, is a brief—and certainly incomplete—narration, pieced together from different written and oral accounts of the revolution.

On 19 July 1936 the commander of the small army garrison in Ronda, upon reports of a military uprising in Morocco, went to the Town Hall with a small platoon and demanded that the mayor submit to his authority and publicly announce that the city was under martial law and the army was taking control. The mayor belonged to the left-wing coalition known as the Popular Front. He refused

to follow the commander's orders and swiftly disarmed him and his small band of soldiers, heavily outnumbered by the peasant groups beginning to assemble on the plaza outside the town hall. Thus, Ronda remained loyal to the Republican government of Madrid, and did not fall to the fascists until 18 September 1936.

However, it would be would be wrong to assume that during these two months the Republican government in Madrid had any control over the town or its inhabitants. As soon as the reports of a military rising in Africa began to spread, the peasants from neighboring villages poured into Ronda and in effect took control. Although the mayor was nominally in charge, the real power belonged to a "Comité" formed by the peasants themselves, most of whom belonged to CNT (*Conferación Nacional del Trabajo*), the Anarchist Labor Union.

The task of this committee was three-fold: first, to arrest all persons suspected of having fascist sympathies; second, to insure that food was evenly distributed to all inhabitants (money was outlawed and vouchers with the CNT rubber-stamp were issued); third, to prepare to defend Ronda from a probable attack by fascist troops stationed in Seville.

The word "revolution" immediately comes to mind when we attempt to describe the situation in Ronda in summer 1936. The Secretary's "Record of Proceedings" for 28 July 1936, preserved in Ronda's Town Hall, displays revolutionary rhetoric: "[W]e are living through a moment of historic transcendence . . . the fascist coup has spurred the populace to rise to the last man and to demand social justice . . . a new society is being born, based upon liberty, justice and equality . . . justice has now become 'revolutionary justice' designed to cleanse the state of all fascist elements as well as to establish the basis for a new social order etc."

Ronda—like so many other towns and villages in Andalusia—was living through a revolution characterized, according to Pitt-Rivers, by "its moralism, its naturalism, its millenarian belief, its insistence upon justice and order in the organization of social relations, its refusal to tolerate authority not vested in the community, to admit any social organization other than the pueblo." The Andalusian anarchists had been waiting for generations for the right moment to strike. In July 1936 a weak government in Madrid, together with a coup by the fascist generals in Morocco produced the ideal situation for such a rising. The Anarchists realized the vacuum of power affecting great parts of Spain and moved quickly to take control.

There is no official record of how many people were killed during the summer 1936 peasant revolution of Ronda. Estimates range from 200 to 600. Hugh Thomas remarks: "Hemingway's account is near to reality of what happened in the Andalusian town of Ronda. . . 512 were murdered in the first month of the war." Thomas took this figure from the Catholic writer José María de Peman, so he is not necessarily accurate. Still, the figure is staggering considering that the town's population in 1935 was 15,000 people.

The summer 1936 massacre in Ronda did not take place quite in the way Hemingway described it. Normal procedure would be for the Anarchists' Committee to draw up a list of people who were either fascist or had fascist sympathies and to order their arrest. Some were arrested, but others were taken to a lonely location out of town (sometimes the cemetery itself) and shot dead. I was told that the truck which carried this doomed cargo came to be known as "Dracula," and that the sight of this truck entering a neighborhood, usually at night, was not a welcome one for those fearing arrest.

No mass carnage occurred in front of the Town Hall—as Hemingway describes—but several massacres did occur, the most notorious involving the killing of a number of local priests: "On the twenty-third of July two hundred armed peasants entered the castle, where the local Salesian priests have their residence, in order to search for machine guns, which, they said were stored secretly in the basement. . . On the following day, they returned and took the priests under arrest. . . In the evening, a number of these priests were taken from the prison where they were being kept and driven to an out-of-town location known as El Tajo, where they were shot dead . . . They were the first victims of the red terror in Ronda."

No fascists were thrown over the cliff, as Hemingway would have it. One person did commit suicide by throwing himself over the cliff, according to an eyewitness report. Edward Stanton has drawn my attention to a passage in *Death in the Afternoon* that seems to foreshadow the fascist massacre in *For Whom the Bell Tolls*:

> The bull ring at Ronda was built at the end of the eighteenth century and is of wood. It stands at the edge of the cliff and after the bullfight when the bulls have been skinned and dressed and their meat sent out for sale on carts they drag the dead horses over the edge of the cliff and the buzzards that have cir-

cled over the edge of the town and high in the air over the ring all day, drop to feed on the rocks below the town.

It is hardly surprising that the dramatic cliffs of Hemingway's beloved Ronda should come to mind as a setting for the portrayal of revolution in a small Spanish town.

One key element in Hemingway's description was apparently absent in the Ronda revolution of 1936: the practice of ritual. There is nothing haphazard or disorganized—as one would expect in a mob action—in Hemingway's fictional massacre. Everything follows Pablo's carefully established plan and unfolds in three stages. First, the fascists are arrested in their homes, taken to the Town Hall, and imprisoned. Second, Pablo's men besiege the small local garrison of the Guardia Civil until it is finally conquered and its defenders shot. The final stage of Pablo's plan is the most surprising and (for some critics) the most shocking: "While the priest was [hearing confession,] Pablo organized those in the plaza into two lines. He placed them in two lines as you would place men in a rope pulling contest, or as they stand in a city to watch the ending of a bicycle road race with just enough room for the cyclists to pass between or as men stood to allow the passage of a holy image in a procession." The ritual of death is about to begin.

According to Blackey and Paynton, ritual in a revolutionary process serves two important functions: it reaffirms individual loyalties and brings mob violence under control by curbing the destructive instincts which any revolutionary process inevitably arouses. There is therefore nothing "morbid" or "gruesome" about the organized lynching of the fascist prisoners. Only by so doing—Blackey and Paynton would argue—does the peasant community become truly "revolutionary." Only through this "communion of blood" are revolutionary loyalties firmly established.

The ritual of death—the sacrifice of the landlords—will bring about the regeneration of the peasant community. "'We thresh fascists today' said one [peasant], 'and out of this chaff comes the freedom of this pueblo'." The peasants themselves understand that the revolution—like other rituals they have participated in (harvest fiestas, bullfights, the Catholic mass)—should bring about a catharsis, a spiritual cleansing.

Pilar explains both the nature of revolutionary ritual and the reasons for its failure: "Certainly if the fascists were to be executed by the people, it was better for all the people to have a part in it, and I wished to share the guilt as much as any, just as I hoped to share in the benefits when the town should be ours. But after Don Guillermo ['s death] I felt a feeling of shame and distaste, and with the coming of the drunkards and the worthless ones into the lines . . . I wished I might disassociate myself altogether. . ." The exemplary punishment of a few fascist landlords became a bloodbath by a mob totally out of control, as Hemingway so vividly portrays in his novel.

He does not, however, condemn the revolution itself, but rather the way it is mishandled when the drunkards take over. Pilar puts the blame squarely on the CNT for the bloodbath: "It would have been better for the town if they had thrown over [the cliff] twenty or thirty of the drunkards, especially those of the red-and-black scarves, and if we ever have another revolution, I believe they should be destroyed at the start." While it is true that CNT members ("red and black scarves") got out of hand and turned "revolution" into "bloodbath," it is also true that without the CNT there would hardly have been a revolution in Spain at all. The Anarchists in general should be credited both for the early success of the revolution in most of Andalusia as well as for their failure to control it. As we noted earlier, it was precisely through "ritual" that Pablo—a true anarchist—attempted to control his own revolutionary coup. The fact that he failed in no way discredits the ritual he engaged in.

But was this "ritual-of-death" a Hemingway invention or a common practice amongst Anarchists? Although I found no evidence of such ritual in the massacre at Ronda, I did locate several instances in the records of neighboring towns and villages. Here are but a few examples—In Almeria, a bullfight took place in which six fascists were shot dead for each of the six bulls in the fight. In Huercanal (Cordoba), the whole village lined the streets to stab, with their own kitchen knives, a sexton reported to have received as many as two hundred wounds before he was finally put to death (the report is strikingly similar to Hemingway's own story). In the village of Grazalema, close to Ronda, a local peasant being questioned about the fascists he murdered during the uprising first refused to answer, and then finally stated that "he" did nothing . . . that "Grazalema" did it (this recalls the medieval story of Fuenteovejuna—a town that rose in arms against its Governor and then refused to apportion individual responsibility for the deed—"Fuenteovejuna did it").

Stories such as these—which Hemingway must have heard in plenty as soon as he arrived in Spain in February 1937—ultimately inspired him to write his own account of the July 1936 peasants' uprising. Pilar's long and detailed story of this revolt becomes the cornerstone of the whole novel. The revolution failed not simply because "three days . . . later the fascists took the town", but because, the peasant revolt of Andalusia drowned in its own blood. The failure of the Anarchist revolution of July was the perfect justification—nine months later—for the May 1937 Communist takeover of the Republican government. It is no idle coincidence that Hemingway begins the narration of his story at precisely this moment. Robert Jordan receives his orders from a Soviet commander, General Golz, and although Jordan is not affiliated with the Communist Party, he strongly believes (as did Hemingway himself) that only the Communists could win the war for the Republic.

Thus Hemingway takes us from the beginnings of the war (the Anarchist revolution of July 1936), to its midpoint (the Communist takeover in May 1937) and then points to the end of the war with the death of Robert Jordan and his reflections on what the war has meant for him and his reasons for fighting "the good fight." Although the main action of *For Whom the Bell Tolls* takes place in May 1937, the novel should be read as a "total" commentary on the war, spanning its commencement and its final moments.

Much has been written about Hemingway's political position during the Spanish Civil War. William Watson has shown the close ties, mediated by Joris Ivens, between Hemingway and the Communist Party. It was Hemingway's deep conviction—while the war lasted—that only the Communist Party could possibly bring final victory to the Republic. But as soon as the war was over and Hemingway began to write *For Whom the Bell Tolls*, he "detached himself politically," as Allen Josephs puts it, and contemplated the war from a broader perspective. It is from this politically detached position that Hemingway narrates, through Pilar, the Anarchist rising of 1936. It is no accident that he chose Pilar to tell the tale of revolution, for only Pilar, as Stanton has suggested, has the epic grandeur, the tragic feeling, and the *duende* to tell such a story. Her tale echoes Yeats' of the Irish Easter Rising: "a terrible beauty is born!".

Source: Ramón Buckley, "Revolution in Ronda: The Facts in Hemingway's *For Whom the Bell Tolls*," in *Hemingway Review,* Vol. 17, No. 1, Fall 1997, pp. 49–56.

Gary Cooper (far right) as Robert Jordan and Ingrid Bergman (second from right) as Maria in the 1943 film version of the novel

Wolfgang E. H. Rudat

In the following essay, Rudat briefly explores Hemingway's satirization of macho posturing in For Whom the Bell Tolls.

In *For Whom the Bell Tolls*, Hemingway presents us with a strange dialogue between Fernando and the gypsy woman Pilar, whose praise of melons from the Valencia region draws this reply:

"The melon of Castile is better," Fernando said. "*Qué va*," said [Pilar]. "*The melon of Castile is for self abuse. The melon of Valencia is for eating.*" (85, italics, except for the Spanish, added)

Why does Hemingway have Pilar recommend the melon of Castile as an object for self abuse for the male Fernando and thus as an object of vaginal signification? Is this one of the numerous seemingly meaningless obscenities in Hemingway's Spanish Civil War novel, some of which appear to serve no other purpose than providing comic relief? Hemingway offered an explanation when he remarked in his famous interview with the *Paris Review* in 1958 that

it is very bad for a writer to talk about how he writes. He writes to be read by the eye and no explanations or dissertations should be necessary. *You can be sure that there is much more than will be read at any first*

reading and having made this it is not the writer's province to explain it or run guided tours through the more difficult country of his work. (Plimpton 29–30, italics added)

I approach *For Whom the Bell Tolls* as a text where not only do earlier parts determine the meanings of later parts as is customary, but where the meanings of earlier parts are retroactively informed by later passages: phrases, passages, or scenes *palimpsestically* interact with those that come later in the novel. How, then, does Hemingway retroactively endow with thematic significance the foulmouthed Pilar's remark about certain melons being vaginal objects? In a novel that seems to celebrate the bravery of a few good men. "Andrés Lopez of Villaconejos," as he identifies himself to guards he encounters while trying to deliver a message from Robert Jordan to a Loyalist headquarters, replies, when asked where he was born:

"Villaconejos," Andrés said. "And what do they raise there?" "*Melons*," Andrés said. "As all the world knows." (375, italics added)

What the ironist Hemingway wants to communicate to the reader is that, according to Pilar's and even Andrés's own pronouncement, in Señor Lopez's home town they raise something which

> **" And we as readers might do well to consider the possibility that Hemingway actually may have used *For Whom the Bell Tolls* to satirize, however subtly, macho posturing—including the macho posturing that he himself had been guilty of in his own writings."**

males can employ for the purpose of "self abuse"— "As all the world knows."

That Hemingway could expect the reader to discover a palimpsestic intertextuality between Andrés's mention of melons from Villaconejos on page 375 and Pilar's obscene pronouncement almost 300 pages earlier concerning the proper use of the "melon of Castile" results from his writing a linguistic-game novel that centers around the nickname the protagonist gives to his lover—"Rabbit"—the Spanish word for which is *conejo*. Andrés Lopez comes from a place named "Village of Rabbits." But then, *conejo* is also a slang term for the female pudendum, comparable to English "[p———]." Therefore an association between Pilar's "melon of Castile" and the melons of "Villaconejos" indeed makes sense—*if* Hemingway is presenting Andrés's home town as a "Village of [P———s]." But is this what Hemingway is doing?

Señor Lopez had gained quite a reputation among the men in the village he grew up in when, during a bullbaiting, he had the animal's "ear clenched tight in his teeth" as he was driving "his knife again and again and again" into the bull's neck. "And every year after that he had to repeat it. They called him the bulldog of Villaconejos and joked about him eating cattle raw." "Or they would say. 'That's what it is to have at pair of *cojones*! Year after year!'."

But Andrés isn't happy about having to live up to his reputation, and he feels relieved every time he doesn't have to go through with it:

Surely. He was the Bulldog of Villaconejos and not for anything would he have missed doing it each year

in his village. But he knew there was no better feeling than the one the sound of the rain gave when he knew he would not have to do it.

The reader perceives the irony that, whereas Andrés is afraid of repeating his performance, his fellow villagers extol his courage. However, Hemingway also may be satirizing the concept that underlies the use of the word *cojones* in the meaning of courage: he ridicules and perhaps even questions the appropriateness of such a male-sexist concept by presenting Andrés's hometown as a "Village of Pussies."

Hemingway thus poetically transmogrifies those men who would restrict a universal character trait, courage, to those humans who possess male genitalia into *conejos*/ "pussies" / "wimps" / cowards. The change in my word selection suggests my belief that Hemingway was more interested in exposing macho posturing by "wimps" than actually "vaginifying" those men. But then we must not forget that the palimpsestic interaction of the novel does transform a paragon of "what it is to have a pair of *cojones*" into what Pilar views as sexually symbolized by a melon. A middle ground would be that without necessarily meaning any physiological references, Hemingway *spiritually* unmans or "melonifies" the would-be bullfighters of Villaconejos.

It is important to note that Hemingway does not tell us of Andrés's boyhood adventures and adolescent fears until his cowardice *as a soldier* has been revealed. Andrés is ordered to deliver a message that might prevent his returning for the dangerous bridge-blowing, and it is that order that prompts Andrés to remember his bullbaiting days:

[Andrés] wanted to get this message-taking over and be back for the attack on the posts in the morning. *Did he really want to get back though or did he only pretend he wanted to be back?* He knew the reprieved feeling he had felt when the *Inglés* had told him he was to go with the message ... when the *Inglés* had spoken to him of the message he had felt the way he used to feel when he was a boy and he had wakened in the morning of the festival of his village and heard it raining hard so that he knew that it would be too wet and that the bullbaiting in the square would be cancelled. (363–64, italics added)

Hemingway carefully sets Andrés up for his eventual exposure during adulthood. We know from pages 363–64 that Andrés has the "reprieved feeling": that having been given an opportunity to escape the dangers of the bridge-blowing mission he is reminded of the reprieve rain afforded him when bullbaitings in his boyhood village were cancelled. It is therefore appropriate that Hemingway has Andrés mention the melons of Villaconejos when he is on a journey that he knows will grant him a "reprieve" from the deadly fighting at the bridge.

It is through having Andrés relive his adolescent bullbaiting reprieves during his military reprieve that Hemingway performs a "melonification" of this extolled paragon of manhood. When the guerilla group meets on the morning of the bridge-blowing mission, Agustin makes a seemingly strange remark to Andrés's brother about his brother's absence: "And thy brother? . . . Thy famous brother has mucked off?." Why does Hemingway have Agustin refer to Andrés as a "famous" brother, and why is that famous brother's name conspicuously absent from this context? While Agustin presumably is referring to the "Bulldog of Villaconejos" and his famous "pair of *cojones*," the author actually is calling on the reader to take a closer look at the absentee's name. Hemingway is making a hilarious pun in his satiric portrayal of the cowardly Señor Lopez: the name of Andrés's Biblical predecessor, Andrew, literally means "manly."

Once we discover that Hemingway actually uses Señor Lopez's first name for a linguistic pun, we see how Pilar's pronouncement on the usefulness of melons fits into the linguistic games the author plays in the "Andrés Lopez of Villaconejos" context: Hemingway poetically un-Andrews Señor Lopez not only into a *conejo*, but also into a "melon"—into something that "All the world knows . . . they raise in Villaconejos." And we as readers might do well to consider the possibility that Hemingway actually may have used *For Whom the Bell Tolls* to satirize, however subtly, macho posturing—including the macho posturing that he himself had been guilty of in his own writings.

Source: Wolfgang E. H. Rudat, "Macho Posturing in *For Whom the Bell Tolls*: The Role of Andrés of Villaconejos," in *ANQ*, Vol. 94, No. 1, Winter 1996, pp. 27–30.

Sources

Fiedler, Leslie A., *Love and Death in the American Novel*, Dell, 1960.

Nagel, James, "Ernest Hemingway," in *Dictionary of Literary Biography*, Volume 9: *American Novelists, 1910–1945*, Gale Research, 1981, pp. 100–20.

Reynolds, Michael, "Ringing the Changes: Hemingway's *Bell* Tolls Fifty," in *Virginia Quarterly Review*, Vol. 67, No. 1, Winter 1991, pp. 1–18.

Young, Philip, "Ernest Hemingway," in *American Writers*, Vol. 2, 1974, pp. 247–70.

For Further Reading

Buckley, Ramon, "Revolution in Ronda: The Facts in Hemingway's *For Whom the Bell Tolls*," in *Hemingway Review*, Vol. 17, No 1, Fall 1997, pp. 49–57.
    Buckley places the novel in its historical context.

Martin, Robert A., "Robert Jordan and the Spanish Country: Learning to Live in It 'Truly and Well,'" in *Hemingway Review*, Vol. 16, No. 1, Fall 1996, pp. 56–64.
    Martin presents a close analysis of the character of Robert Jordan and his relationship to Spanish culture.

Meyers, Jeffrey, "*For Whom the Bell Tolls* as Contemporary History," in *The Spanish Civil War in Literature*, edited by Janet Perez and Wendell Aycock, Texas Tech University Press, 1990, pp. 85–107.
    This essay explores the political implications of the novel.

Wylder, Delbert E., "*For Whom the Bell Tolls*: The Mythic Hero in the Contemporary World," in *Hemingway's Heroes*, University of New Mexico Press, 1969, pp. 127–64.
    Wylder presents an analysis of Robert Jordan who, he writes, "follows the mythical journey of the hero in a modern setting."

Hatter Fox

Marilyn Harris
1973

Hatter Fox, published in New York in 1973, was Marilyn Harris's fourth novel. Tapping into an emerging public interest in Native American history and culture, Harris created a story about Hatter Fox, a rebellious, angry seventeen-year-old Navajo girl who is despised by white society in New Mexico. Locked up in a reformatory and on a path of self-destruction, Hatter meets Teague Summer, an idealistic young white doctor from the Bureau of Indian Affairs who is determined to save her from herself. Eventually, after many false starts, Hatter begins to make progress. Summer takes on more and more responsibility for her welfare, and an unlikely friendship takes root before the novel reaches its tragic conclusion.

The novel raises many important social issues that are as relevant today as they were in 1973. For example, how should society deal with young offenders and those who simply do not fit into the way society operates? How should society treat minorities, in this case Native Americans? Should Native Americans assimilate into the dominant culture or retain their own distinct cultural identity? As these issues unfold in the novel, it becomes clear that *Hatter Fox* is about a deep racism in society that creates individual victims and victimizers. Although there are some good, well-meaning characters in the novel, and the relationship between Hatter and Summer shows that goodness can triumph, the novel clearly shows the negative consequences for both groups when one culture oppresses and tries to change another.

Author Biography

Marilyn Harris was born on June 4, 1931, in Oklahoma City, Oklahoma, the daughter of John P., an oil executive, and Dora (Veal) Harris. Harris was educated in her home state, attending Cottey College from 1945 to 1951, then transferring to the University of Oklahoma, where she received a bachelor of arts degree in 1953 and a master of arts degree in 1955.

Harris's first collection of short stories, *King's Ex*, was published by Doubleday in 1967. After that Harris proved a prolific author, publishing seventeen books, including novels, short stories, romance/historical fiction and children's fiction in a twenty-year period from 1970 to 1989. These works included *In the Midst of Earth* (1969), *The Peppersalt Land* (1970), *The Runaway's Diary* (1971), *Hatter Fox* (1973), *The Conjurers* (1974), *Bleeding Sorrow* (1976), *The Portent* (1980), *The Last Great Love* (1981), *Warrick* (1985), *Night Games* (1987), and *Lost and Found* (1991).

Harris also wrote the widely known, seven-novel "Eden" series, a historical saga about the Eden family of England. The series contains *This Other Eden* (1977); *The Prince of Eden* (1978); *The Eden Passion* (1979); *The Women of Eden* (1980); *Eden Rising* (1982); *American Eden* (1987); and *Eden and Honor* (1989).

Harris's work has received a wide readership; in 1983, nine million of her books were in print, and her work has been translated into many languages, including French, German, Spanish, Portuguese, Polish, and Japanese. She has been an author in residence at Oklahoma's Central State University, and has also received numerous awards for her writing, including the University of Oklahoma Literary Award, in 1970; Lewis Carroll Shelf Award, 1973, for *The Runaway's Diary*; Oklahoma Federation of Writers Teepee Award, 1974; Women in Communications By-Liner Award, 1975; Oklahoma Writers Hall of Fame Award, 1980; and Cottey College Distinguished Alumna Award, 1981. Harris is also an O. Henry Award winner.

Harris married Edgar V. Springer, Jr., a professor, in 1953; the couple have two children: John P. and Karen Louise.

Marilyn Harris

Plot Summary

Summer Attacked by Hatter

Hatter Fox is set in New Mexico in 1973. Teague Summer, a young doctor who works for the Bureau of Indian Affairs, is summoned to a crowded jail cell in Santa Fe to attend to a wounded Navajo boy. He notices that among the group of about twenty imprisoned youths there is a Navajo girl of about seventeen who appears to be their leader. When he enters the cell, the girl, whose name is Hatter Fox, looks at him with a terrified expression on her face. Then she attacks him, stabbing him in the shoulder with a knife.

Summer Seeks Out Hatter

After Summer recovers, he is curious about Hatter, who is still at the jail. He visits her and observes her in an isolation cell chanting to herself. Within a few days, he receives a request from a social worker from the State Reformatory for Girls outside Albuquerque, asking if he has any information on Hatter Fox. He ignores the request, still haunted by the image of Hatter chanting in the jail cell. Two weeks later, Dr. Thomas Levering, head psychiatrist at the reformatory, sends Summer another letter, begging him to come down to the reformatory and give them whatever information he

Media Adaptations

- *Hatter Fox* was made into a CBS-TV movie-of-the-week entitled *The Girl Called Hatter Fox* and was broadcast in October, 1978. It was directed by George Schaefer and starred Ronny Cox as Dr. Teague Summer and Joannelle Nadine Romero as Hatter Fox.

has about Hatter. She is unmanageable, having destroyed property, tried to escape, and attacked another girl. No one knows anything about her or her background, including the local Navajos.

On his initial visits, Summer is shocked by what he finds. First, he discovers that as a punishment, Hatter is sometimes confined in a dog pen outside in the freezing cold. Then he finds her in solitary confinement in a basement isolation cell, strapped down on a cot so she cannot move. She has also been subjected to force-feeding. Summer asks to be left alone with her, and Dr. Levering reluctantly agrees. Summer removes the straps from Hatter, and tells her that he is here to help her, but Hatter refuses to speak, and again looks terrified. Then, when he turns his back, she attacks Summer again, jumping on his back and clawing at his face and eyes.

Summer is determined to have nothing more to do with her, but a snowstorm prevents him from returning to Santa Fe. Levering persuades him to try once more to help Hatter. He meets the administrator of the reformatory, Dr. George Winton, who tells him that in seventeen years at the reformatory he has never had a failure and does not want one now. Though Summer dislikes the bureaucratic attitudes exhibited by Levering and Winton, he agrees that he will do what he can—but before he makes any decision, he wants to see Hatter once more.

Back in the basement again, Summer meets Clito and Claude, the two huge guards in charge of the cells. Summer takes Hatter a cup of coffee and talks to her, but still she refuses to respond. Then

finally, she looks directly at him and drinks the now-cold coffee. Summer finds this an encouraging sign, and thinks that at last Hatter may be willing to let him help her. He arranges to stay at the reformatory for a few weeks.

Summer Moves into the Reformatory

The following morning he finds Hatter back in the restraining bed. Claude tells him that she has refused to sleep on her cot, insisting on the floor instead. This is against the reformatory rules. Summer again tries to get through to Hatter, worried by her condition. She is half-starved, and her struggles against the restraints have cut her flesh. He believes she will die if she continues in this way. He feels compassion for her, persuades Claude to release the restraints, and bandages her wounds. A lewd remark by Claude suggests to Summer that Claude may have raped Hatter at some point.

Summer has no proof, but he shares his suspicions with Levering. Angered by Levering's bureaucratic, unresponsive attitude, he declares that he is quitting and returning to Santa Fe. But in a bar in Albuquerque he quickly changes his mind, and decides to spend three days in the cell adjoining Hatter's. On the first day, Hatter refuses to eat. Summer physically struggles with her and forces the food down her throat; she bites his finger in the process.

The next day, Hatter begins to speak to Summer, but she is still fearful and resentful. She says she is sick and tells him to go away. Realizing that Hatter has developed a fever, Summer transfers her to the infirmary. Once there, the efficient but overbearing nurse, Rhinehart, takes over.

Rhinehart understands Indian beliefs, and she tries to convince Hatter that Claude, not Summer, is the "witch" who has been tormenting her. She then performs a traditional ritual to destroy the hold the witch has over Hatter. Although Hatter claims that she does not believe in witches, she does becomes more cooperative. However, she is still subject to violent and unpredictable moods, and a screaming fit lands her in a straitjacket once more. This time she pleads with Summer to help her by killing her. After the outburst, Rhinehart convinces Dr. Winton, the administrator, to let Summer stay and work in the infirmary to keep a close eye on Hatter.

During a late-night dinner in Rhinehart's apartment, the nurse relates her history to Summer; they begin to repeat these dinners each evening.

Hatter Begins to Make Progress

Days pass, and Summer works in the infirmary tending to various girls and watching Hatter, who is cooperative but silent. Christmas approaches. Summer returns to Santa Fe on Christmas Eve for some fresh clothes and a break from the monotony, and contemplates not going back to the reformatory.

He returns that evening, surprised to see that Rhinehart is throwing a private Christmas party for Summer and Hatter, who is charming and well-behaved. She even gives Summer a gift of hand-kerchiefs. But when Hatter retires to her room and Summer follows, she starts to tell him about the abuse that she has suffered at other institutions like this. Summer apologizes for these events, but tells her that if she behaves herself she can be out of the reformatory by spring. As he leaves that night, she asks him, "When it's all over, will I be white or Indian?" Summer doesn't know how to answer her.

He arranges for her to work in the infirmary where he can keep an eye on her. Some tranquil days follow, as Hatter works hard and well, and opens up more to Summer about her past. She seems to have become reasonably calm and productive.

But the calm is shattered when Hatter becomes jealous of Mango, one of the girls at the reformatory, whom Summer also befriends. Hatter tries to attack Mango with a knife as she sleeps, but Summer stops her. Summer is the only one who witnesses the incident, but he doesn't say anything.

Trying to overcome this setback, Summer gets permission to take Hatter on a trip to Albuquerque. She is nervous in the city, but seems to come alive when she guides Summer to a rocky ledge high on the side of a mountain, with a spectacular view of the surrounding area. She tells Summer she used to go there as a child, then tells him that the reason she was nervous in the city was because she had worked as a prostitute there the previous year, to make enough money to survive. She remains silent for an hour, lost in the beauty of nature.

But soon there is another setback. Back in the reformatory, Hatter is attacked by a gang of girls, who give her a merciless beating. Summer is angry that Winton will not hold an investigation to find out the culprits.

Hatter Leaves the Reformatory

Hatter recovers, and March passes uneventfully. But during April, Summer realizes that Hatter is expecting to go with him to Santa Fe when she is released. He is not prepared to take on this responsibility, and so raises no protest when the reformatory arranges for Hatter to be taken in by the Good Hope orphanage, even though the orphanage has a bad reputation. But when Summer sees her being dragged off roughly to the orphanage, he intervenes. Agreeing to become her guardian, he drives her to Santa Fe, arranges for her to stay in a rooming house, and tries to find her a job. She works briefly at a mock Indian trading post, where she has to dress in an Indian outfit and be photographed with tourists. She soon walks out and finds herself a better job, working at a grocery store owned by a Navajo man.

Hatter seems happy, and for several weeks Summer's friendship with her blossoms. But one day, Summer becomes angry with her and insists that before they go for a day out she must return to find a paycheck that she has lost. Returning with the check, Hatter is focused only on Summer and carelessly crosses the road, where she is run over by a bus and killed. Summer is grief-stricken and blames himself for her death.

Characters

Claude

Claude is the guard in charge of the solitary confinement cells at the reformatory. He is in his late twenties, and built like a football player. He insists that all the rules of the institution be carried out, but he is not very intelligent and does not know when to be flexible. He is sometimes crude in his manner, and Summer suspects that he may have abused Hatter sexually.

Clito

Clito is an assistant guard at the reformatory. He helps Claude deal with Hatter, and has the responsibility of force-feeding her. He is large and his face suggests he may be Mexican.

Hatter Fox

Hatter Fox is a seventeen-year-old Navajo girl. She is slender, with long straight black hair and delicate features. Her life has been characterized by abuse, neglect and abandonment. She does not know who her parents are, and she was raised in several different environments. As a young child, she was abandoned and taken in by an old woman, whom she called grandmother, but who was not her real grandmother. The old woman told Hatter that Changing Woman had given Hatter to her. Hatter was fond of the old woman, but she died before Hatter was five. Hatter was then taken in by a Navajo Indian family who were also caring for about a hundred other children. But Hatter was soon falsely accused of killing one of them, and the family cruelly abused and abandoned her. She was sent to a Christian mission school, where she was abused again, enduring many beatings and other abuse from the cruel couple who ran the school. She remained at the mission school until she was thirteen.

After this, Hatter appears to have just drifted for several years, and no details are given. Her story resumes when she is about sixteen. For a while she attended classes at the university in Albuquerque, but was kicked out because she was not registered. Then she lived for a year amongst the students in Albuquerque as a prostitute. This episode came to an end when the Indian students on campus told her to leave. Hatter interpreted this as another betrayal from her own people. Hatter then moved to Santa Fe, living in a commune before her arrest with a group of other teenagers. The kids were high on drugs and armed with explosives, which they were apparently going to use to blow up a building called the Palace of Governors. (It is never made clear the extent to which Hatter was involved in this plot.) Hatter's arrest lands her in the jail cell where Teague Summer first encounters her.

Hatter is so traumatized by her painful experiences in life that she can bring herself to trust no one. She is strong-willed, highly intelligent and stands out from the crowd. She is also violent and uncontrollable. She attacks Summer twice, as well as Mango, a girl at the reformatory to which she is sent. Hatter has no friends, and lashes out even at those who try to help her. The girls at the reformatory dislike her and give her a severe beating when they get the chance. Filled with self-destructive tendencies, Hatter has no interest in going on living.

However, Summer is fascinated by Hatter and slowly wins her trust. Gradually, she begins to cooperate with him and prepare herself for a life outside the reformatory. She shows that when she wants to be, she can be charming, graceful and outgoing. But she is still subject to violent moods and fits of despair and confusion. It is hard for such an unusual, high-strung Indian girl to fit tidily into white society, and she is aware of this. But Summer persuades her to make the necessary effort, and she seems to be succeeding, before a tragic accident ends her life.

Dr. Thomas Levering

Thomas Levering is the head psychiatrist at the State Reformatory. In his fifties, Levering is tall, with a gaunt appearance, as if he is about to succumb to an illness or has just recovered from one. He seems weighed down by dealing with all the problems in the reformatory. Levering invites Summer to help in dealing with Hatter, but then angers him by proposing that Hatter be sent to the state mental hospital. Summer dismisses Levering as a bureaucrat, concerned only with relieving himself of the responsibility for an unsolvable problem. However, Levering does care about the welfare of the girls in the reformatory, and he is well-liked and respected by them, and by everyone else in the institution.

Mango

Mango is an inmate of the State Reformatory. She is a big Mexican girl from El Paso who has been imprisoned for attempting to kill her father. Mango does well in the reformatory, however, despite being stabbed in the arm by Hatter, and she is due for release within a month. The staff of the reformatory trust her and she is given responsible tasks to perform. This is because Mango has shown she is willing to learn the rules and abide by them. Summer befriends her and buys her a carton of cigarettes as a gift, then comforts her when she has to delay her departure from the reformatory because she becomes sick. This arouses Hatter's jealousy, and she almost attacks Mango for a second time, although Summer stops her.

Rhinehart

Rhinehart is the nurse in charge of the reformatory's infirmary, and is Summer's guide at the reformatory, letting him know about events that have gone on in the past and assisting him in rehabilitating Hatter, both physically and mentally. In her sixties, small and overweight (Summer thinks she looks like a woman wrestler), she has a strong personality. She quickly takes charge of the situation when Hatter is brought to the infirmary, and knows enough about Indian beliefs to concoct a ritual to free Hatter from the spell the girl believes she is under. Summer regards her as a good person, "a colorful, brusque, eccentric." Originally from Australia, Rhinehart came to New York when she was nineteen, and worked as a waitress at nights while putting herself through nursing school. She is lonely and regards the girls at the reformatory as her family; they are all she has.

Dr. Teague Summer

Teague Summer is a twenty-eight-year-old doctor, originally from Lowell, Massachusetts, who works for the Bureau of Indian Affairs in Santa Fe, New Mexico. He first meets Hatter Fox when he is called to a jail cell to attend to a wounded Indian boy. Hatter stabs him in the shoulder with a knife. From that point on, Summer can't forget Hatter. He accepts a request from the authorities to visit her in the state reformatory, and tries to explain to her that he wants to help her. Although sometimes he wants to wash his hands of the troublesome girl, he shows considerable persistence and resourcefulness in trying to get through to her, even though she continues to ignore him almost completely. He even comes up with the idea of going into solitary confinement in the cell next to her so he can observe her. He tells himself he must try to understand her on her terms rather than his. He must learn how to interpret her silences and understand her nonactions as well as her actions. Eventually, Hatter begins to respond to him. Their progress is like a slow dance, one step forward, three steps back.

Summer sticks to his task because he is idealistic. "I have an absolute and childlike faith in the goodness of man," he states, and he is deeply shocked by what he sees as the cruel and inhuman treatment of Hatter in the reformatory. Summer also shows himself to be levelheaded, usually able to evaluate situations calmly, although he is also subject to fits of anger and indignation when things do not go his way. He can be assertive, and is willing to stand up to the authorities at the reformatory when he thinks they are wrong. He dislikes the rule-bound institution and sympathizes with those who are imprisoned in it.

Summer is a modest man who does not have a high opinion of himself. He admits to having a lackluster childhood, with no achievements to speak of. He joined the Peace Corps and went to Bolivia full of idealism but returned disillusioned, for what reason he does not say. He became a doctor in order to please his parents, even though it was against his better judgment. "I'm just a plain, second-rate M.D.," he says. He is also honest enough to admit that nothing in his medical training prepared him for dealing with a person in Hatter's situation.

Summer shows some development during the course of the novel. At the beginning he has a smug attitude about how much white people in Santa Fe have done for the benefit of the Indians. He thinks Indians should learn to adjust, as everyone else has to do. But later, when he has formed an attachment

to Hatter, and she mentions Alcatraz, he points out that the Indians no longer occupy the island. Then he adds, "We had denied them even that," which suggests that he has become more sympathetic to the Indian cause. It is Summer's request for Hatter to find her lost paycheck that leads directly to her accidental death, for which he feels responsible.

George Winton

George Winton is the administrator in charge of the State Reformatory. He is in his sixties, and gives the impression of being "everybody's young-at-heart grandfather." With his ruddy cheeks he looks as if he could play Santa Claus. Winton has been at the reformatory for seventeen years, and believes that he has never had a failure; all the girls in his charge are eventually returned to society to lead productive lives. Although Summer accepts that Winton is well-trained and professional, he thinks Winton is concerned about Hatter more because he does not want his perfect record spoiled than from any real interest in her welfare. Summer wonders whether Winton has ever seen the solitary confinement cells or is aware of the brutal things that go on in the reformatory. But it is Winton who insists that Summer take on the task of Hatter's rehabilitation, so he shares some of the credit for the progress she makes.

Themes

Racism

Racism pervades the novel. Harris creates a picture of a society imbued with extreme prejudice against Indians. This is apparent from the very first page, in which Summer notes that "someone who should know better" referred to Hatter as "the worst of all possible bitches, an intelligent Navajo." Then when Summer first sees Hatter in the jail cell, he overhears someone cursing, "Goddamn Indian kook."

At the reformatory, Levering and Winton do not exhibit racist attitudes, but the otherwise admirable Rhinehart does, offering the comment that Indians "aren't long on gratitude" and telling Hatter, supposedly as a joke, that she looks "almost human." Mango, another girl at the reformatory, believes that Hatter is "crazy in the head, like all Indians," and a matron offers the opinion: "Nothing but trouble, that one. What can you expect?" She suggests there is nothing wrong with Hatter that a beating cannot cure. Later, when Summer is trying to find work for Hatter, Mr. Duncan, who

Topics for Further Study

- Form an argument for why Native Americans should either assimilate into the general population or retain their own distinct cultural identity.

- Is Hatter's death an appropriate end to the story or is it too tragic? What message, if any, does Hatter's death convey? Write a possible alternate ending to the story.

- Research the history of some Indian tribes in the American Southwest, including the Pueblos, the Hopi, and the Navajo. What problems do Native Americans face when they leave their reservations to live and work in cities?

- Research the history of the "red power" movement in the late 1960s and 1970s. What did Native Americans gain from this movement?

- Do some research to find out what current conditions are like on Native American reservations. How has life changed on the reservations in the past fifty years? What are some of the main issues facing Native Americans living on reservations today?

- Pick two Native American tribes and research the principal tenets of their worldviews as they relate to religion and the natural world. How do these tribes' belief systems differ from both Christianity and modern secular views? How do the tribal tenets, religious systems, or worldviews differ from each other?

owns a mock Indian trading post, says, "I'm glad to see one of them who wants to work."

All these comments reflect attitudes based on stereotypes of the American Indian. Hatter herself is well aware of these stereotypes, sardonically commenting, "Navajos use buttons for money. And sheep. They're stupid."

There are also signs of more overt racism in the society, in the form of discrimination against Indians: the gallery owner in Santa Fe who does not want an Indian for a receptionist; the white police officers who arrest Hatter for panhandling but ignore the white teenagers who are doing the same thing.

Victim and Victimization

The theme of Hatter as victim is prominent throughout the novel. Summer notices her downtrodden status early on when he remarks, "If ever the Creator had wittingly or unwittingly created a victim, she was it."

Hatter is a classic example of a vicious circle: those who are victims of hatred will hate in return. Hatter's tales of her childhood reveal constant abuse. She was cruelly beaten at the Christian mission school. Then when she was taken in by an Indian family who cared for about a hundred children, she was falsely accused of killing one of them. She was tied up and made to lie next to the girl's bloody corpse. Even Hatter's own people reject her, as when Indian students on the college campus in Albuquerque tell her that she must get out of town because, as a prostitute, she is giving them a bad name.

When Hatter is sent to the reformatory, the pattern of abuse and victimization continues. Summer suspects that she has been raped by a guard, and he personally witnesses her undergo acts of cruelty and sadism such as being confined to a dog pen and being strapped down on a restraining bed.

Faced with this abuse, Hatter trusts no one. All she can do is hate in return, which can only create more victims and potential victims. She attacks Summer twice, stabs Mango once, and later stands over her, knife in hand, as Mango sleeps. (Only Summer's intervention saves Mango from harm, although Hatter later claims that she would not have hurt the girl.)

Hatter's hatred, born of her victimization, also manifests as self-hatred. Single-mindedly she pursues a course of self-destruction, refusing to eat, refusing to cooperate in any way with the authorities at the reformatory. Summer knows that if something is not done, she will soon be dead. On two occasions also, Hatter begs others (first Mango and then Summer) to kill her. Even at the end, Hatter cannot escape her victimhood, although this time she suffers not at the hand of humans but as the plaything of a cruel fate. It appears that however hard she and Summer try, destiny will not permit her to rise above her allotted role as victim.

Culture Clash

The clash between Indian and white culture is apparent at many points in the novel. There is a clash of Indian beliefs, customs, and attitudes with white civilization. It is clear that white people do not understand the way Indians do things. Hatter relates that when the old woman who cared for her died, the Indians held a four-day "Sing," which is a ceremony or chant. Hatter characterizes the contemptuous reaction of whites: "Thought they could sing away her dying."

Hatter is not well-versed in the Navajo beliefs embodied in such mythological figures as Changing Woman, Monster Slayer, and Child of the Water. She only knows the names that the old woman told her. But she is sufficiently imbued with Indian views and customs to conduct her own "Sing" while in her cell at the reformatory, to see the ghost of the old woman returning, and then to walk with her through the night. Hatter is Indian to the core in the way she responds to the ritual conducted by Rhinehart, the only person in the novel who appears to understand Indian beliefs, which frees her from the spell of a witch. Mystified by the procedure, Summer can find only this explanation for the transformation Hatter has undergone: "A child, lost in the twentieth century, has slipped effortlessly back to the roots of her origin."

For her part, Hatter has as little understanding of Christianity as the whites have of Indian beliefs. In the rooming house where she stays after leaving the reformatory, she removes the picture of Christ from the wall and puts it in a drawer. "Is that one of your gods?" she asks Summer.

The difference between the two cultures is seen again when Hatter leads Summer up to a mountain ledge, where she sits for an hour in a kind of mystical communion with nature. Summer tries to explain what he feels has happened to her: "a release, a relaxation, a return to absolutes—sun, wind, space." It is as if Hatter has become part of the natural world. The implicit contrast is with the oppressive atmosphere of the city, in which Hatter is uncomfortable. The passage illustrates the difference between the Indian reverence for nature, the sense that human life is intimately connected to the natural world, and the materialist white culture that experiences human life as separate from nature. In the latter view, nature is something to be exploited and dominated by technology, one result of which is that cities spring up in the deserts and large numbers of people crowd together in unhealthy conditions. Sensing this, Hatter wishes that the city of Albuquerque below them could simply go away, taking "all their bricks and smoke and keys and locks with them."

The culture clash is also discernible in Hatter's refusal to conform to the rules of the dominant society. One of the reasons that she remains a victim is that she does not acknowledge the validity of what Summer describes ironically as the rules of the "white civilized world." These are rules such as punctuality, obedience, conformity, "fitting in," working for pay, managing money carefully, pursuing a career. In the end, it is Hatter's failure to conform to what to her is an alien paradigm that literally kills her. Summer insists that she act responsibly and deposit her paycheck before she can take the day off. But to Hatter, the paycheck is "just a piece of paper." Doing what the white world demands, for the princely sum of $41.28, leads directly to her deadly encounter with the tourist bus.

Style

Point of View

The novel is told in the first person ("I") by the character Teague Summer. The use of this technique means that the reader gains insight into the minds of the other characters only through Summer's direct interactions with them and the thoughts and opinions he expresses. No scene can take place in the novel unless Summer participates in it or observes it.

Often in a first-person narrative, the narrator is the principal character and main focus of interest for the reader, in which case he or she is sometimes referred to as a central narrator. But this is not always the case. The narrator's purpose may be to tell the story of another character, not himself, in which case he is sometimes called a peripheral narrator. Which kind of narrator is telling the story is often apparent at the beginning of the novel. In *Hatter Fox*, the first sentence makes it clear that the principal interest is not Summer but Hatter: "I had heard of Hatter Fox, but I had never seen her." In the following few paragraphs the reader learns more about Hatter but nothing of Summer. Although Summer does emerge as an important character in his own right (so that the term peripheral narrator may not be appropriate in this case), the focus of the story is clearly on Hatter Fox.

Setting

The novel is set in several different locations. The main setting is the State Reformatory for Girls, and Harris spends considerable time creating a picture of a very uninviting state-run institution. Summer's very first sight of the reformatory is a grim one: "a barren complex of red-brick buildings surrounded entirely by high barbed-wire fences; at the gate were two guardhouses, and chained outside, four dogs." It would be hard to imagine a more ominous or dispiriting sight. The interior of the administration building is described in similarly depressing terms: "All institutions have the same odor. . . . they all smell the same, a curious blend of floor wax and old coffee, and strong detergents, a necessary odor when dealing with humanity en masse." When Summer accompanies Levering to the basement, he encounters the "all-too-familiar smells of jail cells: old urine and older sickness. The steps were very narrow, lit only by bare bulbs hung from single cords." By the time they reach the subbasement, the air has become clammy and chilly. Thus, by the time Summer first encounters Hatter in the reformatory, the bleak, intimidating atmosphere of the place has been fully established. By way of contrast, there are some scenes set in or around the cities of Santa Fe and Albuquerque, and for the most part (Hatter's discomfort there notwithstanding) these come like a breath of fresh air after the oppressive nature of the institution.

Structure

Although the novel is not divided into chapters, its structure is fairly simple. Events unfold in linear sequence, covering a period of about five months. There are no flashbacks. Nor are there any subplots to complicate the action, and the cast of characters is not large. The effect of this is to keep the focus consistently on Hatter Fox and the slowly developing relationship between her and Summer.

Given the straightforward structure, Harris makes effective use of rhythm and pacing in the plot. Scenes involving much action or tension, such as when Hatter stabs or attacks Summer, or when she is involved in other, less violent confrontations with him, are alternated with quieter scenes of reflection, when Summer gives voice to his thoughts about his own situation and what he proposes to do about Hatter.

Historical Context

Native Americans in the 1960s and 1970s

When Hatter Fox is trying to convince Summer that she knows where she can go once she leaves the reformatory, she mentions one word: Alcatraz. She is referring to an incident that began in November, 1969. Seventy-eight members of the group Indians of All Tribes, many of whom were college students from San Francisco, took over Alcatraz Island in San Francisco Bay. They demanded that the site of the former federal penitentiary be turned into an Indian cultural center. They offered to purchase the island for twenty-four dollars in beads and cloth. The group said they were following a precedent set by the white man's purchase of Manhattan Island several hundred years earlier.

The occupation lasted until June, 1971. It was a sign of the increasing militancy of Indian activist groups in the late 1960s as they sought to preserve their heritage and rights of self-determination. Encouraged by the gains made by African Americans during the civil rights movement and the militancy of the "black power" movement, Indian activists proclaimed the advent of "red power."

There were more radical incidents in the early 1970s. In November 1972, members of the American Indian Movement (AIM) occupied the Bureau of Indian Affairs (BIA) building in Washington, D.C., demanding reform of relations between Indians and the federal government. They called the building the Native American Embassy. (The BIA is a government agency that comes under the jurisdiction of the department of the Interior. In the novel, Teague Summer is an employee of the BIA.) Then, for ten weeks in 1973, AIM occupied the hamlet of Wounded Knee on the Pine Ridge Indian Reservation in South Dakota, demanding reform of tribal government.

In *Hatter Fox*, Hatter has encountered some of these young Indian activists on college campuses in Albuquerque. Summer is aware of them, too, but has a negative impression of them, commenting on their "futile intensity . . . the suicidal zeal with which they approached their lost cause of salvaging a dead past."

Lost cause or not, *Hatter Fox* implies that many Indians were on the margins of society in New Mexico in the 1970s. They were the poor, the unemployed, the rootless and culturally marginalized, who migrated from Indian reservations to

Compare & Contrast

- **1960–1970s:** Many sports teams, such as the Atlanta Braves and the Washington Redskins, have names that refer to Indians, and many sports teams have Indian mascots. Few people question whether this is appropriate.

  Today: Many sports teams throughout the nation have dropped names and nicknames that refer to Native Americans. The decade-long movement to abolish "Chief Illiniwek," the Indian mascot of the University of Illinois, continues to gather momentum.

- **1968:** The Navajo Community College is founded; it is the first tribally-controlled college in the United States. During the 1970s, eighteen Indian-controlled colleges are founded as part of the movement toward Indian self-determination.

  Today: With campuses at Tsaile, Arizona, and Shiprock, New Mexico, Diné College (formerly Navajo Community College) has an enrollment of more than 4,500 students. There are now thirty-two Indian colleges; a 2001 report by the American Indian Higher Education Consortium and the Institute for Higher Education Policy describes tribal colleges as a critical factor in improving the lives of impoverished Indians.

- **1973:** Members of the American Indian Movement seize control of the village of Wounded Knee, on the Pine Ridge Sioux reservation in South Dakota. The takeover lasts for seventy-two days; it is a highly visible sign of Indian militancy.

  1999: President Bill Clinton visits Pine Ridge reservation, becoming the first United States president for more than sixty years to visit an Indian reservation. The visit is intended to bring attention to the poverty suffered by Native Americans. At the same time, the Clinton Administration announces a $1.5 billion package to help those living on reservations.

---

cities such as Santa Fe and Albuquerque in search of work.

This portrait has some basis in fact. Historically, the movement away from the reservations began for the Navajo in World War II, when the war economy created job opportunities in copper mines, on the railroads, in shipyards, and in agriculture. For many Navajos, it was the first time they had experienced life outside of the reservation. Many moved to cities such as Flagstaff, Arizona, and Albuquerque. Some succeeded in adjusting to city life; others became trapped in a cycle of poverty.

The same pattern occurred nationally. During a twenty-year period from approximately 1960 to 1980, more than two hundred thousand Indians left their reservations and moved to large cities. Many of them were reluctant to assimilate to the values of the dominant culture, and social problems resulted. Research in one large city, Denver, showed that the arrest record for Indians was twenty times the rate for whites and eight times the Hispanic rate. This conflict with the authorities is reflected in *Hatter Fox*: Hatter gets arrested twice, and on the second occasion she is clearly discriminated against, since a group of nearby whites who are committing the same offense of panhandling are not apprehended.

Socio-economic statistics from the period show the difficult conditions endured by Indians nationally. In 1973, the unemployment rate on Indian reservations averaged 37 percent. If underemployment caused by seasonal work was taken into account, the figure rose to 55 percent. In 1970, the median income of Indians was only half that of whites. In the same year, one-third of all Indian families lived below the official poverty level. A *Reader's Digest* article in 1970 (quoted in *Native Americans in the News*) pointed out that life expectancy for Indians was only forty-four years, compared to an average of sixty-six years nationwide; infant mortality was three times the national average; school dropout rates were twice the national average; and teen suicide was five times the national average. The last two statistics are relevant for *Hatter Fox*: Hatter has had little formal schooling, and more than once she expresses a wish to die.

Although the situation of Indians during the period was often bleak, some progress was made in the early 1970s. Under the administration of President Richard Nixon, the federal government was more responsive to Indian aspirations. In some cases Indian land illegally taken by the government was returned to Indians. One such case resulted in the return of Blue Lake in New Mexico, an Indian religious shrine, to the Pueblo Indians.

Critical Overview

As a "popular" rather than a literary novel, *Hatter Fox* did not attract many reviews. The reviews it did receive, however, were generally favorable, although with some sharp dissenting views. A reviewer for *Newsweek* declared it to be a "touching, skillful melodrama," adding that "Fate conveniently glues a 'Love Story' ending onto this romantic fantasy." (The allusion is to the tragic love story that was made into a movie in the 1960s, starring Ali MacGraw.) High praise came from Pamela Marsh in *Christian Science Monitor*, who described *Hatter Fox* as "a steel trap of a book. Advance a few pages and you'll be stuck fast until [Harris] sees fit to let you go." Marsh offered this interpretation of the novel's theme:

> Perhaps . . . Hatter Fox stands for the whole Indian nation, puzzling whites by violent reaction to mistreatment, puzzled in their turn by violent suppression of that violence, and constantly suspicious of muddled men of good will who attempt to help.

James Brockway, in *Books and Bookmen*, wondered how much of the material in the novel was authentic and how much the product of the author's imagination: "how much . . . is an accurate picture of what really happens in such 'reformatories?'" He continued, "The novel raises issues, moral, psychological and social, which are really quite frightening." His overall evaluation of the novel was largely positive, although he argued that the first part of the novel, "engrossingly told," was superior to the second part, which "tends to become a report on [Summer's] efforts to save [Hatter], with various incidents inserted, sometimes a little artificially, to maintain the interest, while the dénouement is not free from sentimentality."

A negative review came from the *Listener's* Sara Maitland, who complained of the book's "sentimental idealism, sloppy writing and generally inadequate characterisation." J. K. Yenser, the *Library Journal* reviewer, expressed a similar highly critical view: "However well intentioned, the themes of social injustice and institutional mistreatment are handled in a heavy-handed fashion. Both plot and character fail to convince."

Criticism

Bryan Aubrey

Aubrey holds a Ph.D. in English and has published many articles on twentieth-century literature. In this essay, he considers Harris's novel in terms of the cultural climate in which it was written.

Harris's *Hatter Fox*, a popular novel that contains many different perspectives on Native Americans, reflects the cultural climate in which it was written. The early 1970s was a time when old perceptions, stereotypes, and prejudices about Native Americans were starting to give way to a new understanding. This was fueled by several factors. In the late 1960s the rise of the "red power" movement made the general public more aware of Native American grievances and aspirations. New attitudes in the reporting of Native American affairs emerged in newspapers and on television. A number of books, including Dee Brown's *Bury My Heart at Wounded Knee* (1971), a sympathetic account of Indian history, helped to create for the general public a romantic ideal of the vanishing Native American culture. Finally, literature created by emerging Native American writers, such as N. Scott Momaday in his novel, *House Made of Dawn* (1968), presented the Native American experience from the inside, opening up new ways of understanding a culture that had long been seen only through the distorting lens of white culture. Even the term "Native American" was a part of this new awareness. Up until this time, the usual term, and the one used throughout *Hatter Fox*, was "Indian."

Much of the range of attitudes towards Native Americans, both positive and negative, the old as well as the new, can be found in *Hatter Fox*. The most obvious is the blatant racism with which whites view Indians. The novel is awash with negative stereotypes. An assembly of minor characters, present in the novel to demonstrate the general societal attitude to Indians in New Mexico, make it clear that to whites the Indian is crazy, lazy, untrustworthy, ungrateful, stupid, primitive, and a troublemaker. The comment of a police officer about Hatter, "Her kind spells nothing but trouble," sums up this attitude. And the presentation of Hatter as wild, violent and uncontrollable—at least in the eyes of the white world—is another stereotype, a variant of the way Indians were often identified in the early American imagination as savage, hateful and debased. In this view, Hatter can only be "tamed" by being defeated, having her will broken and being forced to learn the rules of "civilized" society.

The racism depicted in the novel manifests itself in more subtle ways, too, as when Hatter is in a restaurant with Summer. She notices that the waiter is looking at her in a strange way, "Like he didn't like me, but he'd like me for a while as long as I was with you." In other words, the price of her acceptance in polite white society is her association with a white man. As long as that continues, she becomes almost like an honorary white person.

Such negative views and racial stereotyping have their roots deep in American history. They are the result of the persistent tendency to judge Indians in terms of white standards, rather than to try to understand them on their own terms. Because Indians differed from whites, they were seen as not measuring up to white standards. Little attempt was made to understand Indian values and the Indian worldview. This attitude is known as ethnocentrism.

One consequence of ethnocentrism is the belief that minorities should assimilate, or integrate, with the dominant community. Historically in the United States this idea has been known as the "melting pot." It has been applied generally to immigrants, who are encouraged to submerge their ethnicity and become part of mainstream America.

Assimilation as applied to Native Americans has had a long history. Assimilationists have been active since about 1880, and rapid assimilation of Native Americans was the goal of United States government policy in the 1920s. The idea was that Native Americans could only survive by becoming more like whites. They had to become "civilized." However, historians James S. Olson and Raymond Wilson argue that assimilationist policies had a "negative effect on Native American life.... In the name of assimilation, European Americans demanded conformity, but even then Native Ameri-

The novel portrays the mistreatment of Native Americans like these, members of the group Indians of All Tribes, who in protest took over Alcatraz Island in November 1969

cans knew that European American society would never accept them."

In the novel, Summer encounters assimilation when he meets a man named Chief Sitting Bull who owns a convenience store that sells Indian souvenirs just outside Albuquerque. Although he has no connection with the original Sitting Bull, the man is of Indian blood and often dons a feathered headdress to be photographed with gullible tourists. In addition to exploiting the Indian heritage (for which he is disliked by his own people), Chief Sitting Bull, who drives a Cadillac, embraces superficial American materialist values. To Summer, the man's face is "alive with profit" and shows no trace of his Indian heritage. He shuns native crafts and sells plastic tomahawks instead, as well as beads made in Japan. When a tourist asks him what tribe he belongs to, he replies, "No tribe. Just the American tribe." Then he points behind him to a large American flag and a faded photograph of President Richard Nixon.

Ironically, only a few minutes before he meets this unsavory product of assimilation, Summer has been musing on the plight of the Indian, observing

> Hatter puts her finger on the problem of what it means to be caught between two worlds when she inquires of Summer at the reformatory, 'When it's all over, will I be white or Indian?'"

smugly that it is not his fault, and that Indians should adjust: "Others had learned to adjust. 'Adapt or perish'—that applied to all of us." But his encounter with Chief Sitting Bull suddenly makes him see the wild and rebellious Hatter in a more favorable light. She has not sold out her heritage; she is the genuine article.

The truth, however, is that even Hatter, for all her pride and rebelliousness, has also felt the siren call of assimilation. Much later in the novel she confesses to Summer that she used to wear "real white powder," as a result of which she "didn't look Indian at all." She adds that when she acts like an Indian, she gets into trouble, but "When I act like a white person, I'm okay." It is clear that the pressure to assimilate is great.

Hatter puts her finger on the problem of what it means to be caught between two worlds when she inquires of Summer at the reformatory, "When it's all over, will I be white or Indian?" Her confusion over her self-identity is understandable, but she receives little support from Summer. He replies by lapsing back into the complacent views he expressed earlier, that Indians should just adapt: "Acculturation took place every day. Completely painless. Survival for anyone was a matter of adjustment, of flexibility.... White or Indian? What the hell difference did it make?" Considering that Summer has spent an entire month doing his best to get Hatter to assimilate and seeing firsthand the problems that raises, his attitude here seems astonishingly ignorant. He seems to have forgotten all about his earlier disturbing encounter with Chief Sitting Bull.

Summer is a well-meaning man, and the fact that he has chosen to work for the Bureau of Indian Affairs suggests that he harbors no prejudice against Indians. But like many white people, he has to struggle with a subtle racism of his own, although he is sufficiently perceptive to be at least half-aware of it. This can be seen from a telling observation he makes about Hatter's appearance and his own reaction to it. As he watches her sleeping in the infirmary, he thinks, "She doesn't look Indian—as though it were wrong for an Indian to look Indian. The delicate oriental features pleased me more than ever, the non-Indian look." In other words, Summer is happiest when Hatter looks least like an Indian.

Another problematic aspect of Summer's reaction to Hatter is that when he first observes her he seems to fall victim to another stereotype, that of the "exotic" Indian who possesses mystical, other-worldly powers beyond those of the white man. This is a perception that developed largely in the 1960s. The movement known as the counter-culture saw in Indian beliefs about the connection between man and nature a way of countering the destructive materialism of Western culture.

At the same time, as Michael Dorris put it in his article "The Grass Still Grows, the Rivers Still Flow: Contemporary Native Americans," "the quasi-mystical writings of Carlos Castaneda convinced sundry hippies, romantics, and Californians-of-all-regions that Indians were somehow genetically endowed with extrasensory powers." (Castaneda wrote a series of books alledgedly based on the teachings of an ancient Mexican Indian shaman named don Juan.)

Something of this romanticizing of the Indian finds its way into Summer's perceptions of Hatter. When he first sees her, she seems to have a unique, inexplicable power that enables her to control the other young people in the cell with her. Her flowing movements and ritualistic gestures mark her out as special. On Summer's next visit, he hears her chanting in her cell and is captivated not only by the beauty of the melody but also by its power: "Only an American Indian can take a minor key and make it sound victorious." Hatter also, in Summer's observation, possesses unusual mental powers of concentration that enable her to resist the harsh conditions of her incarceration. She can stare at a spot on the ceiling and completely shut out everything else around her. She can lie completely still for long periods. Even when she is half-starved, lying in the punishment cell, he sees about her a "strange, almost primal mystical beauty. . . she dominated that grim cell, just as she had dominated the cell back in Santa Fe, occupied it and conquered the ugliness somehow."

Just as Summer gives expression to the countercultural stereotype of the Indian whose beliefs, knowledge and unusual abilities make her somehow "special," he also voices some of the attitudes that characterized the militant aspect of Indian activism in the 1960s and 1970s. During this period the goal of assimilation was replaced by the goal of self-determination for Native Americans. Olson and Wilson observe that "Assimilation, by definition a celebration of non-Native American values, became a bad word in the 1970s, a reminder of three centuries of cultural imperialism."

Summer's complacent attitudes expressed elsewhere notwithstanding, this is the sentiment that lies behind his comments about "Christian genocide," "the plague of Christianity," and "old injustices [to the Indian] ... carefully omitted from the history books." Here he sounds rather like a left-wing radical of the 1970s (although this is hardly consistent with his character elsewhere in the novel).

Finally, it is Summer who discovers through Hatter the lure of the Native American worldview as the antidote to the excesses of Western materialism—another belief of the counterculture of the sixties. This occurs when Hatter takes him up the mountains outside of Albuquerque. He notices how she immediately seems to enter into deep communion with nature, with rocks and wind and sky. It is as if she has become a part of eternity, part of the things that never change, in contrast to the ugliness of the smoky city below, the home only of things that have a beginning and an end. As Hertha D. Wong puts it in "Nature in Native American Literatures":

> European Americans have seen Nature as a potent force to be subdued and as a valuable resource to be used, whereas Native Americans have viewed nature as a powerful force to be respected and as a nurturing Mother to be honored.

Hatter Fox, then, gives voice to a whole range of attitudes toward Native Americans and their culture that were part of the cultural atmosphere of the United States in the late 1960s and early 1970s. It should be pointed out, however, that since Harris, the author, is not herself Native American, the novel is not classified as Native American literature. It is essentially a view of Native Americans from the outside. This marks the book as different from another cultural phenomenon of the period, the increased interest in and publication of Native American writers such as Momaday and later writers such as Louise Erdrich and Leslie Marmon Silko, who wrote from within their own traditions.

Source: Bryan Aubrey, Critical Essay on *Hatter Fox*, in *Novels for Students*, The Gale Group, 2002.

Doris Seale

In the following review-essay, Seale questions whether Hatter Fox *is acceptable reading material for the classroom, asserting that the novel's message is one of hopelessness for Native Americans.*

Native survivors of public education, of the generation now into the middle years, learned to keep a low profile in the classroom. Most years, there were the Conquistadors and Westward Expansion; every year, we got the Pilgrim Fathers. If you were lucky and quiet, you might get through all of it without being asked to be Indian-show-and-tell for Thanksgiving. (There was, at least, no assigned reading on Indians.) Well, we are all long grown, with children, young relatives and friends coming up behind us, and every year they still get Conquistadors, Westward Expansion, Pilgrim Fathers and Thanksgiving. But now history units frequently do include an "Indians" reading assignment.

These reading assignments are given with good intentions. Sometimes, the teacher is sensitive and concerned, with some knowledge of what she/he is talking about. More usually, teachers themselves know very little about the subject, and seem to expect the whole class to come back with a book on Pocahontas or Squanto and how they helped the Pilgrims. Sometimes the assignment takes the form of pick-a-tribe-and-here-is-what-I-want-you-to-find-about-it. This is a slight improvement, but does not take into consideration the fact that there are some Nations on which very little information is available. (And I will not soon forget the day an entire fifth grade class came into the library for material on the "Chippoo a" Indians.) On the upper elementary and secondary levels, fiction titles are often assigned.

All of this brings me to one of the more unusual manifestations of the assigned-reading-on-Indians phenomenon—a Teacher's Guide on *Hatter Fox*, a novel by Marilyn Harris, which has been prepared and distributed by Ballantine Books, publishers of the paperback edition of that title. The Teacher's Guide is included in Ballantine's 1984 catalog for "Junior-Senior High Classrooms and Libraries." Such publisher-supplied lesson plans are a marketing device to increase sales by tapping the vast school market, in this case, high schools. It is a marketing strategy that—in this case at least—is highly questionable.

> " Marilyn Harris may have intended to write an exposé of white cruelty to Native people, but the book's message is that, for Indians, there is no hope—they do not have a place in white America."

Hatter Fox is a novel about a young Navajo girl of that name, told from the point of view of an Anglo Bureau of Indian Affairs doctor, Teague Summer. Hatter had been badly mistreated by her own people and by whites; at seventeen, she has become "Hatter, the renegade, the prostitute, the drug addict, the thief," called by "[s]omeone who should have known better ... 'that worst of all possible bitches, an intelligent Navajo.'" Summer first encounters Hatter when he is called to a jail cell in Santa Fe where a group of young people are being held on drug charges; one of them, a young Indian, has slashed his wrists. When Summer enters the cell, Hatter stabs him with a knife.

The next time he sees her, Hatter is in a cage at the State Reformatory for Girls; she has proved so intractable that she has been confined to the "doghouse," a cage too small for standing up in, in the yard, in the snow. In a move that must seem at least unlikely to anyone acquainted with the penal system, Summer is given special dispensation to come and "live in" and try to reach Hatter. When, after some indecision, he arrives to take up his new post, he finds that she has been relegated to a sub-sub dungeon, where she is strapped to a thing euphemistically called a "bed" and is being force-fed and sexually abused by her two keepers. She will neither speak nor indicate in any other way that she is a rational, human creature.

After many encounters, some of them violent, Summer manages to break down Hatter's resistance; he then has her moved to the infirmary, where a "kindly" nurse is of great help to him with his "problem." Here, also, Hatter begins to talk of her past, and a horrifying one it is; abandonment by her people and sadistic treatment by a boarding school headmaster are among the least of it. An attempt to integrate her into the rest of the prison population fails when the other girls attack her and beat her unconscious.

After several months, Hatter is released into Summer's custody. The idea of turning her into a solid citizen has by now become an obsession for Summer, and he insists that she take a job at a "mock Indian trading post," wearing an Indian dress and headband and serving as part of the decor. After she runs from this, a second, more congenial job, with a Navajo grocery store owner, leads to her first paycheck, a milestone of *great* importance to Summer. Promised a day off, Hatter, in her excitement, forgets the check. Summer rages at her; she goes back to the store for the check; on the way back, crossing the street without looking, Hatter is struck by a bus and killed instantly. End of tale.

The Message? There's No Hope

Marilyn Harris may have intended to write an exposé of white cruelty to Native people, but the book's message is that, for Indians, there is no hope—they do not have a place in white America. Over and over again, the point is made that the fate of Hatter Fox is a metaphor for the fate of her people, and "Hatter Fox was an unworkable genetic formula."

For Indians, Harris sees no options. If they will not—or cannot—assimilate, they are doomed. On the other hand, assimilation can only corrupt the noble savages:

> The Indian with the bogus name who owns the trading post is a pudgy little man with an enormous beer belly and liver spots on his hands and sellout on his face... he is not liked or trusted by his own people but he drives a Cadillac, so who cares? ... I ... looked into his face ... for even a single vestige of his heritage, and found nothing, not even the dead look of a survivor.

Those individuals misguided enough to attempt to combine both Indian and white worlds in their lives are portrayed as those "Indian bastards on campus," with the "futile intensity of the young Indian militants," who approach "their lost cause of salvaging a dead past" with "suicidal zeal."

There is, in fact, not one positive non-white character in this book, but since none of the characters are very savory, perhaps I shouldn't complain. The Native and Hispanic people are never spoken of simply as human beings. They are always stereotypes—a "sullen-faced Mexican guard," a "fat, bored-looking Mexican woman with a mouth full of gold teeth," a "strong, rather blank-looking Mexican face." A young woman is "not pretty in the conventional sense, but [has] the strong, almost masculine, sultry beauty of certain Mexican women." There is even a gratuitous reference to "good savage aborigines" from an Australian-born character.

To give her the benefit of the doubt—which, I own, I find very difficult to do, I do not believe that Marilyn Harris intended to write a racist book. Nevertheless, at a time when "life as we know it" seems to be threatened all over the world by the demands of people of color, I would not underestimate the appeal of this sort of writing.

There is, as well, a nearly prurient quality to the descriptions of the abuse inflicted upon Hatter that is very unpleasant. Whether this was unintentional or an attempt to make a statement about Summer's motivation, is impossible to say. Certainly, Summer frequently expresses his satisfaction at the degradation to which Hatter is subjected: "The sight of her totally restrained body now had a curiously pleasing effect on me"; ". . . [T]he moment was a good one, holding her, sharing her defeat..."; "I wanted to punish her, to bring her into line"; and, "I had to be certain she knew that now I literally controlled her destiny."

The sensationalism of the writing, if nothing else, would seem to make *Hatter Fox* unsuitable reading for secondary English classes. Still, there is the undeniable attraction, for some teachers, of having a prepared lesson plan, so that the work of teaching the novel is already done. Added to this is the fact that when *Hatter Fox* was first published in 1973, the reviews were generally good. *The Christian Science Monitor* thought it "a steel trap of a book" and found it moving. *Newsweek* called it a "touching, skillful . . . romantic fantasy," and referred to Hatter as "this emotional Helen Keller." The first paperback edition, from Bantam, came out in 1974; it was followed, in 1983, by the Ballantine edition. *Paperback Review* welcomed the newest edition; their reviewer thought that the book would help "readers understand some of the problems of being an American Indian in contemporary society," and stated that it deserved "serious attention by high school students and teachers who may have missed it during its first appearance." In addition, *Hatter Fox* was a made-for-TV-movie about two years ago, which may have been a factor in Ballantine's decision to push the book to high school teachers since students are more likely to read something they have already seen on television.

What Do I Read Next?

- *This Other Eden* (1977) is the first of Harris's seven-novel family saga. It is set in eighteenth-century England against a background of the French Revolution and follows the fortunes of the noble Eden family.

- N. Scott Momaday's Pulitzer Prize–winning novel *House Made of Dawn* (1968) tells the story of Abel, a Native American who grew up on a reservation in New Mexico, fought in World War II, and then returned to the United States and moved to Los Angeles. In Los Angeles, Abel slips away from the Native American culture of his upbringing as he tries to deal with the harshness of modern industrial America.

- *Bury My Heart at Wounded Knee: An Indian History of the American West* (1970), by Dee Alexander Brown, made a huge impact on the American public when it was first published. For the first time it told the story of the Indian wars of 1860–1890 from the Native American point of view—a chronicle of ruthless white settlers, stolen land, and a people destroyed.

- *Unsung Heroes of World War II: The Story of the Navajo Code Talkers* (1998), by Deanne Durrett, tells the fascinating story of how the complex Navajo language was used to create the Navajo Code in World War II. The code baffled the Japanese and provided secure communication for American forces in the Pacific.

There is another aspect of the book that some may find appealing—or at least comfortable—and that is the character of Hatter Fox herself. She reflects an image that is familiar to white Americans from a thousand B movies and bad books. Hatter is not too Indian-looking and therefore beautiful: "She had long straight black hair and the delicate lips, nose, face, and large slanted Oriental eyes of the more unusual type of Navajo." She is the classic, inexplicable, savage-but-noble pagan princess. The reader can feel sorry for her without feeling threatened, because Hatter is clearly at the mercy of the establishment. The Indians are going to lose again.

Bad books, even very racist books, *can be* excellent teaching tools if handled sensitively. Unfortunately Ballantine's Teacher's Guide provides little to assist any teacher hoping to use *Hatter Fox* in a positive way. It was written by a "writer, poet and teacher of writing and literature," but not, I think, a person very familiar with Native American history, culture and current circumstances.

The major fault of the Guide is that it tends to reinforce, rather than counter, the distorted images of the book, because it dredges up so many negative associations that are not sufficiently explored in the follow-up exercises. The Introduction, for instance, describes Hatter as a "character who embodies the spirit of her race and whose personal history encapsulates the history of her people... [T]he ultimate truth ... is that there is, in fact, 'no room in the world' for what Hatter is." The idea is reinforced in a composition suggestion: "Write an essay proving that Hatter Fox's death is an inevitable consequence of who and what she is. Use evidence from the novel to show that there is 'no place in the world for Hatter Fox.'"

The lesson plan does not note that Hatter's death is in fact an "inevitable consequence" of Summer's involvement in her life. As with most do-gooders, his behavior toward her is at least as much motivated by his own needs as by a concern for her well-being. A refugee from "Lowell, Massachusetts" and his own mediocrity, Summer states that if he can manage to "save" Hatter, it will give him some justification for his own existence. (It does seem appropriate that Summer should be an employee of the B.I.A., although in the interests of accuracy, it should be pointed out that the B.I.A. has not been responsible for Indian health care since 1955.)

The lesson plan—like the book—presents the demise of the Native American as a *fait accompli*:

> There exists a great deal of historical material that details precisely how this destruction was accomplished. I would suggest drawing upon this material ... to reinforce the idea of Hatter Fox as a character who embodies much of the history of her race...

> ... Many of the books have photographs... The changes in the faces and bodies of a people recorded over time dramatize powerfully and sadly all that has been lost within them.

There is also a great deal of material, historical and otherwise and including photographs, that

demonstrates the strength, endurance and survival of a People, but the Teacher's Guide does not suggest obtaining it. Such materials are not all that difficult to find; they are in fact quite likely to be found in most good public library collections (see the box on suggested reading).

The Guide's first suggestion for "examining the stereotypes of the American Indian" is to be done before the book is read. The teacher is to ask students to "write down the words and images that come to mind when they hear the names 'Indian' and 'Navajo.' . . . You want to bring out all the negative associations you can." The Guide goes on to say:

> Hatter Fox exhibits many of the negative characteristics we have come to associate with Indians... At times ... she is violent, cunning, uncannily strong, dangerous, full of hate for all white people, wild in appearance and a believer of witchcraft... Harris has given the reader plenty of material in support of the stereotyped image of the American Indian.

Unfortunately, there is nothing here to counteract the book's negative images. The Guide *does* suggest that "Conversely, you *might* [emphasis added] also explore ... the positive aspects of Hatter's character and of the culture she comes from," but no attempt is made to list any of *these*. The final exercise in this section—a repeat of the list-making activity—offers no clue as to what a teacher is to do if the second list has as many "negative associations" as the first.

Suggestions Largely Useless

What might initially seem suggestions for countering the stereotypes are likely to be useless. The Guide asks, for instance, "What are the positive aspects of Navajo culture that the author suggests have been lost to us?" How are students to answer this? "Navajo culture" can hardly be said to have been dealt with positively—let alone accurately—in the book. (The book's references to the Indian world of "empty space" and Hatter's silence have more to do with the stereotypic Indian-as-a-child-of-nature image than with anything else.)

Consider the messages the book gives about Hatter's upbringing, which is one of the few things that could conceivably be considered about "Navajo culture." As a little girl, she lived with "the old woman," who was not her grandmother ("I didn't have any parents... The old woman used to tell me that Changing Woman had given me to her."). Before she dies, the old woman tells Hatter to wait at the hogan and someone will come for her, but no one does. Reports Hatter, "One day a couple of men rode by on horses, and I got ready to go, and they stopped and looked at me, but they rode off." Why is this child ostracized, let go, as though she were less than nothing? There would have to be a reason, a strong reason. One is never given.

Eventually Hatter leaves the hogan and is finally taken in by a man and woman (apparently Indian) who have "about a hundred kids there already." One day, one of the older boys pushes a little girl off a cliff, because she wouldn't give him his ball. The boy accuses Hatter and everyone believes him—"[T]hey said I did it. . . The woman said I was a witch, said people died when I came around." (On what grounds this statement is made is unclear, since the only previous death was of an old person come to the end of her time, for which Hatter could hardly be blamed.) Says Hatter:

> They had a sing then, and they all took me out to that canyon at the bottom of the cliff where the kid's body was and tied me up and made me lie down next to her. Her head was broken in, and they made me lie down in the blood, and they said her ghost would come back and kill me. . . And they left me there.

This incident seems intended to horrify, to create an impression of superstitious savagery consonant with the "unworkable genetic formula" business, but what basis is there for it in reality? A sing is not held for the purposes of murder and revenge, but for healing, for Hózhó. If you thought you had been witched, a sing might be held to determine who was doing the witching. If you were sure you knew who it was, you could have an Enemy Way done over you, but if the witch died, it would be as the result of their own evil turned back against them, and not from any such performance as the above. Another thing: being a Navajo witch is a *conscious* choice of disharmony, and the likelihood of a child being considered a witch is therefore pretty small.

And yet another point regarding this incident: I cannot say that Indians are never mean to their children. We are as human in our weaknesses as in our strengths. And, as tribal structure has crumbled under the various pressures to which a conquered people is subject, the changes in customary behaviors have been great. By and large, however, Native Americans remain people who treasure their children. For one thing, we've had to fight too hard to keep them. Navajo society is not so demoralized, nor so lacking in a sense of justice, that an accusation like the one made against Hatter would be accepted without any further investigation. That a child would be treated in this fashion, at all, is beyond anything I have ever experienced, read about

or heard tell of; it is the absolute antithesis of adult-to-child behavior among *all* Native peoples.

It does seem evident that what the Teacher's Guide means by "culture" is material such as this and the "witchcraft" episode, which occurs about halfway through the book. After Hatter has been transferred to the infirmary, she begins to communicate on a rudimentary level, but she still displays great fear of Summer. The nurse discovers that Hatter thinks he is a witch. "You'd better believe it," she tells Summer. "It's real enough to her. . . She's a full blood." (Are these the only people primitive enough to believe in things like the power of evil—which is one of the things Navajo witchcraft is about, whether you consider it as reality or as metaphor.) In a scene remarkable for the fertility of the author's imagination if nothing else, the nurse, aided by Summer, sets out to get rid of "the witch" (not Summer, of course). After making an object to stand for the witch, they proceed to burn it. Says Summer:

> I did as I was told, although it seemed to me that the objects over my head fought the descent to the basin. Glad to be rid of the thing, I struck a match and threw it down. . . At the first sight of flame, Hatter gave a scream the size and dimension of which I had never heard before. . . For as long as the objects burned, Hatter seemed to be in the worst sort of human agony imaginable. . . I turned away at last and . . . smelled, I swear it, burning flesh.

The Teacher's Guide deals with the episode in this fashion:

> Describe a ritual activity you have participated in, something in which you observe a set form of actions, with no deviations. What purpose does this ritual serve? . . . Research the purpose and form of a Navajo ritual and discuss it with the class.

The equation of witchcraft with Navajo ritual reduces Native religious practices and beliefs to the level of primitive superstitions. Navajo witchcraft is not a matter to be taken lightly, but it is *not* identical with Navajo religion, either. A discussion of the difference between superstition and religion—and of the differences between the actuality of Native religious beliefs and how they have been perceived by whites—would have been a valuable contribution, but no such material is provided—unless one accepts the Bibliography inclusion of Hyemeyohsts Storm's *Seven Arrows* (also published by Ballantine). Unfortunately, this title, by a person who claims to be a Cheyenne Shield Maker, has been cited by a committee of the Northern Cheyenne for its "irreligious and irreverent inaccuracies." And in any case, it has nothing at all to do with Navajo religion.

At the time the novel was written, Native-American activist groups, like the one shown here protesting the Vietnam War, were becoming increasingly more engaged in the political scene

The Guide's entire Bibliography is in fact problematic. It lists 11 titles, not one of which is devoted to the Navajo nation, even though at least as much—good, bad and indifferent—has been written about the Navajo as about any other Native people. Why was none of this included? (Five of the 11 books listed are "Ballantine Books I'm sure you'll want to include.") Even if a teacher was actually to do the suggested background reading, these books could give only an overview of Native history, with little basis for evaluating the specifically Navajo *Hatter Fox*.

It is not just that *Hatter Fox* is a bad book, although I think it is. Both *Hatter Fox* and the Teacher's Guide reduce the whole complex reality of Native peoples, past and present, to a level not far above *Love Story*. From neither the novel nor the lesson plan is it possible to learn anything of value about Native American history and culture— nor very much that is even true. It is true that the Native peoples of America have suffered in the past, and do still, at the hands of the dominant society, but it is by no means the whole story. The Indian population as a whole is on the increase, despite the deliberate government policies to insure otherwise, the worst health care in the country, and now, close to 80 percent unemployment on the

reservations. Our young people, often against impossible odds, do manage to get education. Just like other normal human beings, Indians are lawyers, plumbers, airline pilots, doctors, hockey players, teachers, musicians, librarians, actors and writers of every sort. Many of today's most gifted artists and craftspeople, both young and old, are Indian. Native people frequently live in two worlds, not always easily, but still, they do. The obstacles to achievement and a decent life are large, and a discussion of them outside the scope of this article, but, always, the worst obstacle, the one that makes it possible for all the others to exist, is the racism of white society.

Myths Stay Intact

Hatred can take more subtle form than bumper stickers saying, "Save a Salmon, Shoot an Indian." Whether the stereotyped thinking and implicit racism of *Hatter Fox* and the Teacher's Guide are the result of invincible ignorance, or of something even less attractive, does not matter very much; the end is the same. The myths stay intact, the lies and distortions of American history are perpetuated. Since Indians are already doomed, it will not matter very much if they lose their remaining lands— and thus what life ways they have managed to preserve—to the land consortia, agribusinesses, energy companies, "sports" fishermen and lumber interests that are eyeing them so hungrily.

The use of racist materials in classrooms is hardly so new as to be shocking. However, if education is to serve the needs of all our peoples, sooner or later we are going to have to start telling kids the truth. Or do we want to raise another generation to hate and distrust or hold in contempt all who differ from themselves? Isn't it enough yet?

Source: Doris Seale, "Indians without Hope, Indians without Options—The Problematic Theme of *Hatter Fox*," in *Interracial Books for Children Bulletin*, Vol. 15, No. 3, 1984, pp. 7, 10, 22.

Sources

Brockway, James, Review, in *Books and Bookmen*, August 1975, p. 58.

Dorris, Michael A., "The Grass Still Grows, the Rivers Still Flow: Contemporary Native Americans," in *Daedalus*, Journal of the American Academy of Arts and Sciences, Vol. 110, Spring 1981.

"Mad Hatter," in *Newsweek*, September 17, 1973, pp. 98–99.

Maitland, Sara, Review, in *Listener*, February 13, 1975.

Marsh, Pamela, Review, in *Christian Science Monitor*, August 22, 1973, p. 22.

Olson, James S., and Raymond Wilson, *Native Americans in the Twentieth Century*, Brigham Young University Press, 1984, pp. 157–77.

Weston, Mary Ann, *Native Americans in the News: Images of Indians in the Twentieth Century Press*, Greenwood Press, 1996, pp. 1–18, 127–66.

Wong, Hertha D., "Nature in Native American Literatures," in *American Nature Writers*, Vol. 2, Scribner, 1996, pp. 1141–56.

Yenser, J. K., Review, in *Library Journal*, August, 1973.

For Further Reading

Griffin-Pierce, Trudy, *Native Peoples of the Southwest*, University of New Mexico Press, 2000.
> This book approaches the southwestern Indian cultures in terms of their cultural vitality and evolution. There are detailed sections on each culture's language, territory, history, material culture, social organization, political organization, religion, and worldview.

Locke, Raymond Friday, *Book of the Navajo*, 5th ed., Holloway House, 1992.
> This is a comprehensive and readable account of Navajo history and culture.

Young, Robert W., *A Political History of the Navajo Tribe*, Navajo Community College Press, 1978, pp. 15–52.
> The first chapter contains a concise summary of Navajo history and culture.

Herzog

Saul Bellow
1964

After its publication in 1964, *Herzog* became a best-seller, cementing Saul Bellow's reputation with the public—as well as the critics—as one of the most important American writers of the twentieth century. The novel won the National Book Award for fiction and earned Bellow the International Literary Prize, honoring him as the first American recipient. The novel has won praise for its penetrating, sometimes humorous, portrait of a middle-aged man searching for meaning and selfhood in the anxiety-ridden America of the 1960s.

The novel is a series of fragmented reflections, often revealed in an epistolary, or letter, format. Moses Herzog, the main character, becomes obsessed with writing letters to "everyone under the sun," living or deceased, including his family, friends, enemies, and historical figures. Over the past few months, he has experienced a spiritual and emotional paralysis, triggered by the breakup of his marriage and his contemplation of the wasteland of modern life, "down in the mire of post-Renaissance, post-humanistic, post-Cartesian dissolution, next door to the void." In the letters, Herzog examines and evaluates various philosophical theories, recalls fond images of his childhood, apologizes to ignored friends and lovers, and especially berates those, like his wife and her lover, who have caused his suffering. Seymour Epstein, in his article on Bellow for *The Denver Quarterly*, notes that the letters reflect a need "to feel a passionate faith in some higher order, intelligence, or idea that will do as medium through which one can seek transcendence."

During the course of the novel, Herzog is forced to cope with his sense of alienation and displacement as he analyzes his past and tries to determine his future. By the end of the novel, his search has resulted in a tenuous, but nevertheless satisfying, restoration of his faith in himself and in humanity.

Author Biography

Saul Bellow was born in Lachine, Quebec, Canada, in 1915, the youngest of four children, to Russian immigrant parents. He and his family later moved to the Rachel Market section of Montreal and then to Chicago. The feelings of dislocation he would experience in his youth emerged as a dominant theme in *Herzog* and in many of his other works. Another theme that would surface in his works was a questioning of religion. Bellow was raised as an orthodox Jew but rejected that background during his college years. In 1937, he earned a degree with honors in anthropology and sociology from Northwestern University. During World War II, he served in the merchant Marines. His first novel, *Dangling Man*, was critically acclaimed when it was published in 1944, as was his next novel, *The Victim*, which was published in 1947.

After winning a Guggenheim Fellowship in 1948, Bellow lived in Europe for two years, where he wrote *The Adventures of Augie March*, which along with his later novels, *Herzog* and *Mr. Sammler's Planet* (1970), won the National Book Award for fiction. *The Adventures of Augie March*, along with the novels that followed, earned him popular as well as critical acclaim. In 1965, he became the first American recipient of the International Literary Prize, for *Herzog*—which became a bestseller in America. In 1968, France awarded him the Croix de Chevalier des Arts et Lettres. Bellow was awarded the Pulitzer Prize for his novel *Humboldt's Gift*, published in 1975. His highest award came in October of 1976, when he received the Nobel Prize for literature.

Bellow has taught at Boston University, New York University, Princeton, University of Chicago, Oxford, and Yale. He continues his literary endeavors, including his highly praised novel, *Ravelstein*, published in 2000.

Saul Bellow

Plot Summary

Part I

Herzog opens with Moses Herzog at his country house in Ludeyville, Massachusetts, in the Berkshires, in midsummer. He is described by the narrator as having "fallen under a spell," and as a result has been writing letters to "everyone under the sun," including family—dead and alive—friends, ex-friends, and historical figures. While there, he thinks back over his life, focusing especially on the past few months. His memories of this short period make up the narrative of the rest of the novel until the story returns, at the end, to the present time, with Herzog in Ludeyville. He has recently learned that his ex-wife, Madeleine, is living with his friend Valentine Gersbach and that the two had been lovers while she and Herzog were still married. Herzog writes the letters because of his overwhelming need "to explain, to have it out, to justify, to put in perspective, to clarify, to make amends."

The first line of the novel is given to Herzog, as he admits, "If I am out of my mind, it's all right with me." The narrator notes that some people thought he was "cracked" and "though he still behaved oddly, he felt confident, cheerful, clairvoyant, and strong." He soon goes back in time to the beginning of his "trouble" a few months ago, when he had been teaching classes in New York City. Gradually he noticed his mind starting to wander during class. He then shifts back further into his past, reviewing his life and the choices he has made. In the past, he was considered to be a noted scholar, but "his ambitious projects had dried up," including a study on romanticism.

His memory then turns to his relationship with Madeleine. He claims that he quit his teaching position to write, after encouragement from her, and so he buys the house in the country. There they meet Valentine and his wife, Phoebe. Herzog claims that soon, "Madeleine considered herself too young, too intelligent, too vital, too sociable to be buried in the remote Berkshires" and so convinced Herzog to move to Chicago, where she could finish her graduate studies in Slavonic languages. In Chicago, Herzog returns to teaching. One year later, Madeleine announces that she wants a divorce.

Feeling that he is "going to pieces" after the divorce, Herzog first moves to Europe for six months and then returns to New York. There he meets and begins a relationship with Ramona, an attractive businesswoman, who is a student in one of his classes. Although Herzog considers her to be "full of charm," "problems" soon develop. She quickly becomes serious about him, but Herzog is annoyed by her frequent lectures on his sterling capabilities and his future.

Part II

Herzog decides to take a break from Ramona and his thoughts about Madeleine and spend some time with friends in Martha's Vineyard. However, his depression throws him into an agitated state, and he immediately returns to New York. There, he receives a letter from a former student who is now working as a babysitter for Madeleine. The student writes that one night she found Junie, his daughter, locked in a car outside Madeleine's house while she and Valentine were arguing inside. Crying and shaking, Junie explained that Valentine had put her there.

Deeply concerned for his daughter's welfare, Herzog asks Simkin, his lawyer, to help him gain custody of her. Simkin, however, warns him that he would most likely fail in his attempts to get his daughter away from her mother. Herzog's frustration turns into a rage against Madeleine and Valentine "so great and deep, so murderous, bloody, positively rapturous, that his arms and fingers ache to strangle them."

When Herzog appears at the city courthouse where he is scheduled to meet Simkin, he sits in on a few court cases that are being tried that day. As he watches testimony about a mother who beat her son to death, he becomes incensed and runs out of the courtroom. He determines that "New York could not hold him now," and so flies to Chicago to see his daughter and to confront Madeleine and Gersbach.

As soon as he arrives in Chicago, he goes to his father's house, where he reminisces with his stepmother, Tante Taube. He remembers that at one point his father had wanted to shoot Herzog because of his "look of conceit or proud trouble. The elite look." He soon leaves with his father's pistol in his pocket.

At Madeleine's house, he watches Gersbach tenderly giving his daughter a bath. As a result, his anger dissipates, and he insists, "firing this pistol was nothing but a thought." At this point, he realizes "only self hatred could lead him to ruin himself because his heart was 'broken.'" Not yet giving up on his plans to get custody of Junie, he tries to convince Phoebe to sue her husband for a divorce, offering evidence of his adulterous relationship with Madeleine. He insists that together "we could nail them." Phoebe, however, refuses to help him, and suggests he "get away from this now."

After leaving Phoebe, Herzog picks up his daughter and spends the afternoon with her. Their time together is cut short, however, when they get into a car accident. At the scene, the police find his father's gun in his shirt and take him to the police station, where they book him for a misdemeanor. When they call Madeleine down to the station to pick up Junie, the police ask her whether Herzog has given her any trouble. Madeleine replies that while he has never physically harmed her, he has a terrible temper and his psychiatrist has warned her about him.

Part III

After the police determine that Herzog poses no threat to Madeleine, they put him in a cell until his brother, Will, comes to bail him out. He then decides to leave Chicago and go to his house in the Berkshires, which he considers fixing up and selling. There, he begins to experience a measure of contentment as he determines that he has freed himself of his "servitude to Madeleine." Beginning his final week of letter writing, Herzog writes to his son, Marco, asking him to come for a visit. When Will arrives, he tries to convince Herzog to spend some time in a mental hospital, but Herzog assures him that he is finally finding some peace.

Ramona soon arrives in a neighboring town looking for Herzog. When she calls, he invites her for dinner, even though it "troubled him slightly." As he waits for her, he determines, "I am pretty well satisfied to be ... just as it is willed," for "whatever had come over him during these last months, the spell, really seemed to be passing, really going." The novel concludes on the note that "at this time he had no messages for anyone. Nothing. Not a single word."

Characters

Luke Asphalter

Herzog's zoologist friend, who takes him in during his trouble with Madeleine, is "a good soul, with real heartaches." Luke is devastated by the death of his monkey, with whom he had formed a strong bond.

Phoebe Gersbach

Phoebe is Valentine's estranged and mousy wife. Herzog notes she lacks self-confidence, which suggests why she accepts her husband's adulterous behavior. She has been a passive wife to Valentine, feeling "her dowdiness and insufficiency." The narrator notes that she is a weak woman with limited energy, with only "enough feeling for the conduct of her own life." Unwilling to accept any responsibility for her failed marriage or the reality of her husband's shortcomings, she blames Herzog for aggravating Gersbach's ambitions. Her critical nature emerges in the guise of a disciplinary "head nurse."

Valentine Gersbach

Herzog's previous best friend and Madeleine's current lover, Valentine is a charismatic charmer—yet Herzog notes his overwhelming nature. Dealing with Valentine was like dealing with "an emotional king, and the depth of his heart was his kingdom." Herzog explains that Valentine "appropriated all the emotions about him, as if by divine or spiritual right" because he felt he could "do more with them, and therefore he simply took them over." Valentine experienced tragedy in his childhood. He lost his leg and his father died of sclerosis, which he was sure he would also contract. As a result, he "spoke as a man who had risen from terrible defeat, the survivor of sufferings few could comprehend." Valentine suggests that he feels su-

perior to others because he has suffered more and that his own trying experiences have enabled him to feel others' suffering more intently.

Herzog notes that he often took control of conversations with his booming voice and aggressive manner. Valentine was "so emphatic in style, so impressive in his glances, looked so clever that you forgot to inquire whether he was making sense." As a result of his commanding personality, Herzog allows him to practically run his life when they are all living in the Berkshires.

Daisy Herzog

Daisy is Moses's first wife and the mother of his son Marco. He deserts her after he enters into an affair with Madeleine. Moses acknowledges her loyalty to him as she endured freezing winters in their isolated home in eastern Connecticut while he was writing his book. He admits that his preoccupation with his work and his incessant playing of melancholy pieces on his oboe must have been difficult for Daisy to endure, even more so than Connecticut's inclement weather. Daisy is a conventional Jewish woman whose manner is "shy but also rather stubborn." He claims she is stable and organized, which are her strengths, yet sometimes her desire for order would prompt her to be overly systematic. Herzog admits that his impulsiveness and emotionalism encouraged her negative qualities when he claims, "I was behind those rigid curtains and underneath the square carpets."

Jonah Herzog

Jonah is Moses's Russian immigrant father, who has died before the novel begins. Herzog periodically reminisces about his father, who, although he "did everything quickly, neatly, with skillful Eastern European flourishes," failed at every business he attempted. Moses admits that his father had a bad temper and was often "nervy, hasty, obstinate, and rebellious." According to his son, Jonah's failures resulted from his lack of "the cheating imagination of a successful businessman." One day, incensed by his son's "Christianized smirk of the long suffering son," Jonah threatens to shoot Moses, who concludes that he caused his father a great deal of heartache.

Junie Herzog

Junie is Moses's adored and affectionate young daughter. He becomes obsessed with gaining custody of her when he thinks Madeleine is not properly taking care of her.

Madeleine Herzog

Madeleine is Herzog's second wife. We never get a clear picture of her since she is seen through Herzog's subjective vision of her, which may be distorted by his rage over her affair with Gersbach and the destruction of their marriage. Readers only glimpse fragments of his bitter memories about her and the pain that she caused him. From all the characters' responses to her, it appears as if she had great charm, beauty, and a brilliant mind. Herzog apparently felt overwhelmed by these qualities, admitting, "Compared with her he felt static, without temperament." At one point, he confesses that as was the case with himself, "everyone close to Madeleine, everyone drawn into the drama of her life became exceptional, deeply gifted, brilliant."

Yet, most of his descriptions of her are extremely negative. He describes her egotism when he insists, "The satisfaction she took in herself was positively plural—imperial." He suggests that she has an enormous capacity for hatred when he claims that she had a strong desire that he die, or at least be nonexistent in her life. This sense of her personality is reinforced by his assessment of her reasons for marrying him. He argues that what she had been looking for was an ambitious man, and that she had found one in him, "in order to trip him, bring him low, knock him sprawling and kick out his brains with a murderous . . . foot."

Marco Herzog

Moses's son is at the present time "entering an age of silence and restraint" with his father. Yet during his visits, Marco offers his father sympathy and patience. Moses notes that Marco has a good, strong character and is "one of the more stable breed of Herzogs."

Moses Herzog

Middle-aged scholar and educator Moses Herzog is at the point of mental collapse for most of the novel. His inability to accept his failed relationship with his wife Madeleine has triggered a sort of spiritual paralysis. In his book on Bellow, Dutton writes that Herzog "feels an alienation and, even worse, a uselessness, as if his life were an activity of wasted and misplaced effort." This uselessness prompts his search for fulfillment through scholarly activity, self examination, and relationships with others, especially women.

The novel's narrator characterizes Herzog as a complex narcissist with masochistic and depressive tendencies. Herzog himself admits to many of these same faults as he continually indulges in an obsessive self-examination to the point where he feels he cannot function as a scholar, educator, or father. He admits that he has failed as a husband, father, son, sibling, friend, and citizen and also has often failed to be truthful to himself about his and others' characters.

As he continually reassesses himself and his life, he incorporates into his worldview his judgments of the morality of his and others' actions. He inevitably finds everyone unable to measure up to his high standards. Ironically, however, this process provides him with a measure of satisfaction as he praises himself for his ability to take an honest and painful look at his own shortcomings.

Ultimately, it is difficult for us to get a clear picture of his interactions with other characters since all the events recounted in the novel have been filtered through Herzog's subjective viewpoint. In his descriptions, he appears to be a passive bystander to the collapse of his marriages, but others suggest that he may have had a more active role. Madeleine notes his frequent rages, and the narrator suggests that his first wife Daisy suffered from his ambitious nature.

Herzog finally finds a sense of peace at the end of the novel when he declares himself to be free of his obsessive pursuit of Madeleine. Although he has not come up with any firm answers to the questions he has been raising throughout the novel in his letters, he determines "I am pretty well satisfied to be . . . just as it is willed."

Mother Herzog

As Moses idolized his father, he also idolized his long-suffering mother. He remembers that she "had a way of meeting the present with a partly averted face" and a "dreaming look." Even in her Old World melancholy, she found the resources to spoil her children.

Shura Herzog

Moses's wealthy brother is generous yet misanthropic. Moses claims that toward him, his brother's "contempt was softened by family feeling."

Will Herzog

Moses's brother Will bails him out of jail when he is arrested for carrying their father's loaded gun. He describes Will as undemonstrative and reticent, yet also substantial and shrewd. In his support of Herzog, he proves himself to be "a balanced, reasonable person" who is pained by his brother's suffering.

Sandor Himmelstein

Sandor is a Chicago lawyer who had looked after Herzog when he split with Madeleine. He sympathizes with Herzog through his raging sexism. Sandor continually refers to women, including his daughters and his wife, in pejorative terms. In an effort to console Herzog, Sandor announces, "so you were a sucker! Big deal! Every man is a sucker for some type of broad." While Herzog insists that at times Sandor could be "generous, convivial, even witty," his recreation of this scene provides no evidence of those qualities.

Fitz Pontritter

Madeleine's father, a powerful, intelligent man, was a famous acting teacher and theatre director in New York. He had "many of the peculiar and grotesque vanities of theatrical New York in him." Madeleine hints that he might have abused her as a child.

Tennie Pontritter

Tennie, Madeleine's mother, sacrificed her life to her husband's ambitions. Herzog notes her long-suffering expression when he meets her. Madeleine is determined not to end up like her mother.

Ramona

Ramona is a woman Herzog becomes involved with in New York after his divorce from Madeleine. Thirty-year-old Ramona, who owns a flower shop, enrolls in one of his evening courses. Herzog describes her as well educated, "slightly foreign" looking, and charming. She loves to talk and engage in philosophical discussions about his behavior and character, and she is an excellent cook. Her interest in Herzog quickly becomes serious, and he suspects that she wants him to marry her. She becomes convinced that she could repair some of the damage Madeleine has done to his psyche, and thus, he would be better off if he married her.

He admits that she would make a good wife for several reasons: she is understanding, well-educated, and enjoys living in New York, where she is financially independent. Her most important quality, from his point of view, is her expertise in the bedroom. In her selflessness, she contains "an enormous desire to help him," to build him up, and so tries to renew his spirit through sexual pleasure. She offers him "asylum, shrimp, wine, music, flowers, sympathy, gave him room, so to speak, in her soul, and finally the embrace of her body." Yet, he continually resists becoming actively involved in a relationship with her. While he appreciates her ability to articulate her ideas and point of view on a number of topics, he feels that her discussions with him often deteriorate into lectures about his capabilities and his future, which annoys him. At one point he tells her, "I think your wisdom gets me. Because you have the complete wisdom. Perhaps to excess." He notes that she is good for him but that he "evidently can't believe in victories."

Throughout the novel, Herzog keeps Ramona at arm's length, yet he occasionally admits that she is "a great comfort" to him. While a night with Ramona invigorates him, he concludes that his new-found strength "revived his fears ... that he might break down, that these strong feelings might disorganize him utterly." By the end of the novel, Herzog has reached an uneasy acceptance of her.

Shapiro

Shapiro has been Herzog's friend since school days. Herzog agreed to write a review of his analysis of modern history but delayed it because of his problems with Madeleine. He eventually reviews the work in one of his letters. Shapiro is polite yet high-strung, pompous, and ill-humored.

Simkin

A lawyer Moses turns to for help in gaining custody of his daughter, Simkin is clever, yet has "a weakness for confused, high-minded people, for people with moral impulses" like Herzog. Simkin is a practical realist with "a certain amount of malice" that keeps him "in condition." Moses became "irresistible to a man like Simkin who loved to pity and to poke fun at the same time." After Simkin explains the realities of the legal system, Moses considers Simkin to be, along with Madeleine and Gersbach, one of his "Reality-Instructors."

Themes

Search for Meaning

At the beginning of the novel, Herzog admits he has been engaged in a desperate search for meaning—for insight into his own troubled existence and human existence in general. As he writes his letters, he conducts that search, entering into dialogues with people who have made an impact on his life and others–philosophers and thinkers who he trusts will give him guidance. Through this process, he hopes to gain knowledge and acceptance of self.

Topics for Further Study

- Using the historical section in this entry and other research sources, determine whether Herzog has followed an existentialist philosophy in the novel. Report on what you find and provide examples to support your conclusion.

- Research one of the historical figures Herzog writes a letter to, and answer it as you think that person would—or write Herzog a letter from a fictional character, expressing that person's point of view about Herzog and his actions.

- The novel has never been adapted to film, probably because of its complex narrative structure. Try to think of ways that Herzog's story could be made into a film. Take one scene and write a storyboard for it.

- Note the different things about contemporary American society that upset Herzog, as reflected in his letters. Investigate whether these subjects bothered other Americans during this period and whether they made any effort to voice their complaints.

One of the dialogues he engages in concerns religion. As he searches for answers to the questions he raises, he contemplates the Orthodox Jewish religion in which he was instructed as a child. When Madeleine decides to convert to Catholicism, Herzog is again forced to reexamine his beliefs. During this process, he writes letters to philosophers who have written on the subject. In a letter to Nietzsche, for example, he considers the philosophy that God is dead, but ultimately rejects it, insisting that the philosopher's ideas "are no better than those of the Christianity [he] condemns." By the end of the novel, he discards traditional theology and embraces humanism. Earl Rovit notes in his article on Bellow for *American Writers* that Herzog, like Bellow's other characters, ultimately concerns himself with "defining what is viably *human* in modern life— what is creatively and morally possible for the displaced person that modern man feels himself to be."

Anxiety

Throughout most of the novel, Herzog makes no progress in his search for meaning. His confusion and acknowledgement of the disorder that defines his life produce a mental and spiritual paralysis that leads him to the brink of collapse. His personal anxiety is compounded by historical reality. His is an "Age of Anxiety," where tensions boiled beneath the prosperous surface of America. Studies like John K. Galbraith's *The Affluent Society* noted that the rapid changes Americans were experiencing often left them confused and anxious. David Riesman, a sociologist at the University of Chicago, and a colleague, Nathan Glazer, argued in *The Lonely Crowd* that Americans had been coerced into conforming to social dictates set by politicians, religious leaders, and the media and, as a result, had difficulty maintaining individual values and beliefs. Although this often resulted in surface unity and serenity, it could also produce underlying feelings of alienation and frustration, thus creating the sense of being alone in a crowd. Many of Herzog's letters deal with the frustrations that resulted from living in his cultural moment.

One historical factor that caused Herzog grief was the emergence of the women's movement. Part of the problem in his relationship with Madeleine is that she is a strong woman who wants to be commended for her intelligence rather than her domestic skills. Herzog notes that when they were living in the country, he became angry when she did not clean the house, expecting her to fulfill her "duties" as a wife. He admits that in response, Madeleine accused him of "criticizing her mind and forcing her back into housework," and being "disrespectful of her rights as a person."

A related issue that causes Herzog anxiety is sexuality. He confesses that Madeleine's displays of independence and strength often left him feeling inadequate sexually. Most likely as a result of these emotions, he suggests that while he was married to her, he had sexual relationships with other women. Herzog's anxiety is compounded when he discovers that his best friend, Valentine Gersbach, was having an affair with Madeleine while she was still married to him.

His suffering is increased by the fact that he cannot seem to finish his second volume of a study on romanticism. Once a noted scholar who gained critical acclaim for his early work, Herzog feels he has not lived up to his academic, or personal, promise. These feelings of failure contribute to the paralysis he feels throughout most of the novel.

Madeleine's rejection of Herzog is the primary cause of his suffering. He concludes that he is "going to pieces" after she asks him for a divorce. His discovery of Madeleine's affair with Gersbach, carried on while Herzog was still married to her, compounds his despondency. His acknowledgement of her betrayal leads to feelings of rivalry with Gersbach. All of these emotions prompt Herzog to create verbal portraits of Madeleine and Gersbach that justify his hatred of them. As he struggles to "explain, to have it out, to justify, to put in perspective" his feelings about the two, he tries to determine what role he has in this mix.

Madeleine's rejection, coupled with his feelings of failure, causes Herzog to consider himself to be a victim and to engage in self-pity. Rovit argues that Herzog is "a victim of his own moral sense of right and wrong—his own accepted obligation to evaluate himself by standards that will inevitably find him lacking." He notes that Herzog suffers "intensely and rehearse[s] [his] agonies at operatic volume for all to hear."

Toward the end of the novel, Herzog transfers his feelings of victimization into an intense anger directed toward Madeleine and Gersbach. He finds an outlet for this anger after he receives a letter from a former student, informing him that she saw his daughter Junie being mistreated by the two. In response, Herzog departs in a rage for Chicago, and a confrontation with both of them. At this point, he admits that his anger is "so great and deep, so murderous, bloody, positively rapturous, that his arms and fingers ache to strangle them." After obtaining his father's loaded gun, Herzog goes to Madeleine's house, with the intent of shooting one or both of his nemeses. Yet, his anger is partially dissuaded when he faces the reality of the situation as he watches a tender moment between Gersbach and Junie.

Peace

Herzog finally finds a measure of peace when he is able to free himself from his obsession with Madeleine. Rovit argues that by the end of the novel, Herzog has climbed out of "the craters of the spirit," ridiculing "[his] defeats with a merciless irony, resolved to be prepared with a stronger defense against the next assault that is sure to come." Daniel B. Marin, in his article on Bellow for the *Dictionary of Literary Biography*, suggests that Herzog's "final silence expresses his trust in the intuitions that motivate him, even though they lie ultimately beyond his understanding."

Style

Structure

Herzog contains a unique narrative structure that helps illuminate its themes. Part of the novel is composed in an epistolary form, the narrative strung together by the series of letters Herzog writes to various people, deceased and living. The remainder consists of brief sections of narrative introduced by an omniscient narrator, who quickly turns things over to Herzog, expressing in the first person his observations and analyses of his world, either through his letters or in recreations of events that have occurred in the last few months. The resulting fragmented form illustrates Herzog's feelings of alienation and disconnection throughout the novel. The structure also reinforces his need to find some kind of order for his life.

Chester E. Eisinger, in his overview of Bellow for the *Reference Guide to American Literature*, argues that the structure of the novel provides "a vehicle beautifully appropriate for the self-communing protagonist in a book which is largely a meditation." He concludes that "the story of an alienated intellectual imprisoned in the self needs a medium that promises privacy and turns in upon itself."

Epstein, in his article on Bellow for *The Denver Quarterly*, praises Bellow's successful structuring of the novel, noting that "the true fictional function of the first-person form is to give the creating mind the instantaneous freedom to turn on itself and reveal the mockery in every posture." Bellow creates this string of monologues compiled in Herzog's letters and remembrances to illustrate how his main character has created, in large part, his own world. The structure allows his voice to control the entire narrative. Every now and then, in a self-reflective moment, Herzog recognizes his tendency to focus inward and pokes fun at himself, which provides delightful moments of irony and humor in the book.

Historical Context

Sexuality in the 1950s and 1960s

Most Americans in the 1950s retained conservative attitudes towards sexuality: they did not openly discuss sexual behavior, and promiscuity—especially for women—was not tolerated. However, traditional attitudes about sex began to change during this era. Dr. Alfred Kinsey's reports on the

Compare & Contrast

- **1963:** *The Feminine Mystique,* by Betty Friedan, is published. The book chronicles the growing sense of dissatisfaction American women feel about the unequal treatment they receive in the home, the workplace, and other institutions.

  Today: Women have made major gains in their fight for equality. Discrimination against women is now against the law.

- **1960s:** Divorce rates steadily increase during the decade. The Census Bureau reports that in 1970 there are 4.3 million divorced adults in America. Sociologists link the high divorce rate to what they consider to be the breakdown of the American family.

  Today: The growing divorce rate has prompted a redefinition of the American family that in-

cludes the nuclear unit—two parents and their children—as well as new family units including those headed by single-parents, foster parents, and step-parents.

- **1960s:** Developments concerning the rights of individuals and of groups generate conversations on the "Death of God," compulsory prayer or Bible reading in the public schools, and birth control.

  Today: These conversations continue and have become more prominent as Republicans gain control of the Senate and the presidency. A number of conservative Christian groups, usually referred to as the "religious right," are lobbying for a return of prayer in the classroom and are urging schools to promote sexual abstinence.

---

sexual behavior of men and women (1948, 1953) helped bring discussions of this subject out in the open. Although many Americans clung to puritanical ideas about sexuality, they could not suppress questions that began to be raised about what constituted normal or abnormal sexual behavior. Movie stars like Marilyn Monroe and Brigitte Bardot, who openly flaunted their sexuality, intrigued the public, and *Playboy* magazine, begun in 1953, gained a wide audience. Many regarded the magazine's pictures of naked women to be symbols of the end of Puritanism in America. *Playboy* itself promoted a new attitude towards sexuality with its "playboy philosophy" articles and its centerfolds of naked "girls next door." In the 1960s, relaxed moral standards would result in an age of sexual freedom. Herzog reflects these new attitudes towards sexuality as he seeks relationships with several different women, often while he is married.

Redefinition of Family

Divorce rates began to rise dramatically in the 1960s, which led to a redefinition of the American family. As the nuclear (sometimes called "tradi-

tional") family unit broke down, new family structures emerged and a more flexible definition of family was created. Families now could consist of two parents and their children, a couple who decided to have no children, a single parent and his or her children, a parent and stepparent and their children, or grandparents and their grandchildren. Children and their foster parents were also considered to be a family unit. Herzog's frequent absences from his children and their acclimation to new family units causes him much angst in the novel. He slowly comes to terms with his childrens' new living arrangements by the end of the novel, when he accepts the fact that they are content in their redefined families.

Existentialism

Existentialism was a popular element in literary works in the 1960s. The theories of this movement emerged from the writings of nineteenth-century Danish theologian Soren Kierkegaard and German philosophers Martin Heidegger and Friedrich Nietzsche. Existentialist themes can be found most prominently in literary works by Franz Kafka, Fyodor Dostoevsky, Albert Camus, Jean-Paul Sartre, and Samuel Beckett.

The philosophy of existentialism presents a specific vision of the condition and existence of men and women and an examination of their place and function in life. Existentialism after World War II came to be defined by its main argument, that existence precedes essence. According to this philosophy, men and women are responsible for their own existence and how they choose to behave gives essence or meaning to their existence. Existentialists believe we are all born into a meaningless void with no hope of spiritual salvation. Humans have the choice to remain passively in this void, which would cause intense moral anguish, or to exercise their power of choice and become engaged, through some form of action, in social and political life. These types of commitments will, according to this philosophy, provide us with a sense of accomplishment and meaning.

Throughout *Herzog*, the main character struggles with his "void" and his response to it. For most of the novel, Herzog remains passive in his condition, except for his letter writing, which has brought him to the point of near madness. By the end of the novel, he must make a decision to remain passive or to become more actively engaged with his world.

Herzog writes one of his letters to the Danish theologian Soren Kierkegaard, whose writings spawned the theories of existentialism reflected in the novel and many other literary works of the time

Critical Overview

Herzog gained popular and critical success after its publication in 1964. Critics praised its examination of Western intellectual traditions, its colorful characterizations, and its innovative narrative structure. Keith M. Opdahl, in an article on Bellow for the *Dictionary of Literary Biography*, notes the novel's historical relevance when he writes, "The prose is charged, rich, full of the specifics and precisely defined impressions that create the feel of mid-1960s American life." Opdahl argues that *Herzog* "is perhaps most notable for the style, which represents Bellow at his very best." He concludes, "Herzog's double remove permits Bellow to dote on detail, to slow the action when necessary to make the scenes live."

Eisinger finds *Herzog* to be "one of the finest novels of ideas written by a 20th-century American." Eisinger also praises the structure of the book, claiming that Bellow's adaptation of the epistolary novel provides "a vehicle beautifully appropriate for the self-communing protagonist in a book which is largely a meditation." Eisinger notes that

while the novel is "deficient in action," Bellow has written it in a "flexible, breathless, lively, energetic style which at the same time is restrained by the wry, skeptical, sometimes bitter expression with which [he] endows Herzog."

Criticism

Wendy Perkins

Perkins is an associate professor of English and American literature and film at Prince George's Community College and has published several articles on British and American authors. In this essay, she examines images of women in Bellow's novel.

"Nobody truly occupies a station in life any more. There are mostly people who feel that they occupy the place that belongs to another by rights. There are displaced persons everywhere." Earl Rovit, in his article on Saul Bellow in *American Writers*, determines that these words spoken by Eugene Henderson in Bellow's highly acclaimed

> Women are the enemy to Herzog, always ready to 'kick out his brains.' He concludes that he will 'never understand what women want. . . . They eat green salad and drink human blood.'"

novel *Henderson the Rain King* "could have been spoken by almost any of Bellow's characters or, for that matter, by Bellow himself." Rovit finds that a major theme in Bellow's fiction is how we cope with a sense of alienation and displacement.

This is also the case with Moses Herzog, the hero of Bellow's award-winning novel *Herzog*. Throughout the novel, Herzog experiences overwhelming feelings of disconnection that have resulted in a kind of spiritual and emotional paralysis, which has brought him to the brink of mental collapse. As he searches for insight into his troubled existence, he often resorts to blaming the women in his life for his suffering. As tries to understand and cope with his predicament, he composes selective and subjective portraits of these women, ignoring, to a great degree, his contribution to his own depressive state.

Bellow has employed an innovative structure in the novel to illustrate Herzog's limited view of his life. Part of the novel is composed in an epistolary form, the narrative strung together by the series of letters Herzog writes to various people, deceased and living. The remainder consists of brief sections of narrative introduced by an omniscient narrator, who quickly turns things over to Herzog, expressing in first person his observations and analyses of his experiences, either through his letters or in recreations of events that have occurred in the last few months. Thus, most of the narrative presents Herzog's subjective point of view. Bellow creates this string of monologues compiled in Herzog's letters and remembrances to illustrate how his main character has created, in large part, his own world.

Herzog's world is peopled with harshly stereotypical women. The three main female characters in the novel represent clear types: Daisy is the loyal, mousy wife; Madeleine is the aggressive "goddess"; and Ramona is the complete hedonist or pleasure-seeker. Herzog's portraits of these women illustrate distinct stages in his life. Martin Corner, in his article on Bellow in *Studies in the Novel*, argues that Herzog perceives these women as "instances in an argument, as exemplifications of moments in the history of freedom and self-awareness." As such, they become part of his subjective view of his world. Corner concludes that they are, for Herzog, "voices in an argument that he is passionate to refute."

Initially Herzog was comfortable with his marriage to Daisy, his first wife, because she enabled him to live the typical, ordinary life of an assistant professor. He describes her as a loyal wife who endured freezing winters in their isolated home in eastern Connecticut while he was writing his book on romanticism. He notes Daisy's loyalty when he comments, "Of course a wife's duty was to stand by this puzzling and often disagreeable Herzog. She did so with heavy neutrality, recording her objections each time—once but not more."

Herzog suggests that his uncontrollable infatuation with Madeline caused his final split with Daisy, which, although not commendable, could not be helped. However, his portrait of his relationship with Daisy has not been complete. The narrator suggests another reason for the destruction of Herzog's union with Daisy in descriptions of the trouble Herzog had writing his second volume on romanticism. The narrator notes that he was "becoming tougher, more assertive, more ambitious." His marriage to Madeleine and subsequent resignation from the university "showed a taste and talent . . . for danger and extremism, for heterodoxy, for ordeals, a fatal attraction to the 'City of Destruction.'" Madeleine proved a better partner for the more ambitious Herzog, a fact he himself never acknowledges.

Herzog paints Madeline as a complete monster, concerned only with her own gratification. Her treatment of him, he claims, has no justification. He insists that she revels in her supremacy over him, claiming at one point, "she had beaten him so badly, her pride was so fully satisfied, that there was an overflow of strength into her intelligence . . . one of the very greatest moments of her life." Her greatest goal in life, according to Herzog, is to "strike a blow." He is convinced that when Madeleine had been looking for an ambitious man "in order to trip him, bring him low, knock him sprawling and kick out his brains with a murderous . . . foot."

Herzog's view of Madeleine as an aggressive, not very nice woman is reflected in his reaction to a woman he sees at the train station while on his way to Martha's Vineyard. There he sees a "soft-faced," "independent" woman, whom he claims has "b——ch eyes." Women are the enemy to Herzog, always ready to "kick out his brains." He concludes that he will "never understand what women want. . . . They eat green salad and drink human blood." Referring to Madeleine's affair with Gersbach, Herzog argues "female deceit . . . is a deep subject" involving "sexual complicity, conspiracy." Yet he conveniently ignores his own infidelities when he was married to Madeleine and to Daisy.

Herzog's vision of Madeleine leaves out any clear motives for her seemingly demonic behavior. In his article on Bellow for *The Denver Quarterly*, Seymour Epstein notes that she "turns on Herzog with such hatred that one is prompted to go back and pick up the overlooked reasons for all that venom." There are passages in the novel that do, in fact, suggest that Herzog may have triggered some of Madeleine's outbursts, and that she might have had grounds for some of her actions. Aunt Zelda, Madeleine's aunt, informs him that he is "overbearing" and "gloomy" and "very demanding." She insists that he has to have his own way and that he "wore [Madeleine] out asking for help, support." She tells him, "you've been reckless about women." When she gets him to admit he was unfaithful to his wife, he tries to shift the blame back on Madeleine, claiming, "she made it tough for me, too. Sexually." Tired of hearing Zelda's support of her niece, he concludes "what crooks they were—Madeleine, Zelda . . . others. Some women didn't care how badly they damaged you." Zelda finally gets him to acknowledge that he could not satisfy Madeline because she did not love him, suggesting that she did not have an inherent desire to torture him.

Another criticism Herzog hurls at Madeleine has to do with her ambitions. He concludes that her desire was to take his "place in the learned world," to "overcome" him. While they were married, he insists, "she was reaching her final elevation, as queen of the intellectuals, the castiron bluestocking." Yet Herzog never acknowledges her right to be "in the learned world" and drops hints that he has tried to prevent her by constantly nagging her about attending to housework and leaving her books scattered around the house. At one point, he acknowledges, "she thinks I'm criticizing her mind and forcing her back into housework" and being "disrespectful of her rights as a person," which he

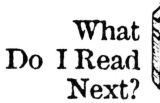

What Do I Read Next?

- Bellow's *The Adventures of Augie March* (1953) follows the hero's coming of age as he tries to make sense of his life in the middle part of the twentieth century in America.

- Bellow's *Mr. Sammler's Planet* (1970), which won the National Book Award for fiction, tells the life story of Artur Sammler, a Holocaust survivor living in New York, and his penetrating observations on the human condition and contemporary American culture.

- Walter Kaufmann's *Existentialism: From Dostoevsky to Sartre* (1984) anthologizes existentialist thinkers, and includes the arguments between Kierkegaard and Nietzsche on the subject of Christianity, a topic Herzog writes about in his letters.

- Stuart A. Kallen's *Life in America During the 1960s (The Way People Live)* (2001) presents a comprehensive overview of the history and culture of the period in which Bellow's novel takes place.

- Albert Camus's *The Stranger*, published in 1942, is a widely known novel dealing with existentialist themes.

appears to be guilty of but will not admit. The narrator reveals Herzog's overwhelming ambitions and ego, noting his attitude that "the progress of civilization—indeed, the survival of civilization—depended on the successes of Moses E. Herzog. And in treating him as she did, Madeleine injured a great project."

Herzog claims that her hatred for him causes her to banish him from the house. However, the narrator notes that "his behavior was so strange and to her mind so menacing, that she warned him through Gersbach not to come near" her. Herzog validates Madeleine's fears about his violent temper when he comes to her house with the intention of shooting her and/or Gersbach, claiming that the two have "opened the way to justifiable murder." Herzog soon learns, however, that both have been good parents to Junie.

Herzog presents Ramona as another distinct stereotype: the complete hedonist. Robert R. Dutton, in his article on Bellow for *Twayne's United States Authors Series Online*, argues, "Ramona, the object of Herzog's final pursuit, represents another retreat, this time from the ego-shattering experience with Madeleine." In Herzog's portrait of her, Ramona's goal is to provide him with a complete "life of pleasure," without asking anything in return. She becomes the perfect woman to him, fulfilling his every desire and making no demands on him. Yet he blames her, rather than his own inability to commit to her, for damaging their relationship. With Ramona, he admits that "this asylum was his for the asking" but will not commit to a relationship with her "because today's asylum might be the dungeon of tomorrow."

During his stay at Ludeyville, Herzog begins to free himself from his "servitude to Madeleine" and so finds a measure of peace and contentment. Whether or not he will be able to establish a lasting relationship with a woman remains a question, however. He does invite Ramona to dinner at the end of the book, but this still "troubles him slightly." Herzog has not come to any clear vision of his relationship with the women in his life, which suggests that he will continue to have problems in that area. Corner argues that "the condition of his moral recovery . . . is not some abstract choice for community over individualism, but the ability to see the world beyond his own interpretations." Herzog appears to be more open to the possibilities of a relationship with Ramona, but his subjective view of her still defines her as problematic by the end of the novel. His failure to fully "see the world beyond his own interpretations" provides an ambiguous conclusion to the book.

Source: Wendy Perkins, Critical Essay on *Herzog*, in *Novels for Students*, The Gale Group, 2002.

Martin Corner

In the following essay excerpt, Corner analyzes how, in the character of Herzog, Bellow dramatizes "the overcoming of the pathology of discursive consciousness through memory and acts of attention."

A Contrast

Consider the following passages from the first chapter of Saul Bellow's *Herzog*. Moses Herzog is riding in a cab through the streets of New York on his way to catch the train to Vineyard Haven:

> They made a sweeping turn into Park Avenue and Herzog clutched the broken window handle. It wouldn't open. But if it opened dust would pour in. They were demolishing and raising buildings. The Avenue was filled with concrete-mixing trucks, smells of wet sand and powdery gray cement. Crashing, stamping pile-driving below, and, higher, structural steel, interminably and hungrily going up into cooler, more delicate blue. Orange beams hung from the cranes like straws. But down in the street where the buses were spurting the poisonous exhaust of cheap fuel, and the cars were crammed together, it was stifling, grinding, horrible!

What we see here is as much Herzog as it is New York. Everything becomes a symbol of his inner state: the noise and violence of the streets, the derelict condition of the cab, the pressure, congestion and confinement. Even the girders of the new building, "interminably and hungrily going up into cooler, more delicate blue," are Herzog's desperate search for some zone of resolved consciousness and his sense of oppression at the city's greedy appetite for the projection of its life to the utmost possibility.

But as he rides to Grand Central, Herzog recalls family departures of his childhood from the Grand Trunk Station in Montreal: "The locomotive cried and the iron-studded cars began to move. Sun and girders divided the soot geometrically. By the factory walls the grimy weeds grew. A smell of malt came from the breweries. The train crossed the St Lawrence. Moses pressed the pedal and through the stained funnel of the toilet he saw the river frothing. Then he stood at the window. The water shone and curved on great slabs of rock, spinning into foam at the Lachine Rapids, where it sucked and rumbled." Here the child is looking outwards; everything is allowed simply to be itself. In the first passage, the world is drawn inwards, to become a symbolic confirmation of one man's consciousness. In the second, everything is held delicately free of the assimilating pull of symbolism; the world resists incorporation, remains itself. The first assimilates the world to character; the second moves outwards in attention to the world itself.

These distinct modes of representation offer a starting-point for a fresh look at the two principal tendencies within Bellow criticism. On the one hand, there are those who see his fiction as the record of an inward journey, from outer to inner truth, from the confusions of discourse to the truth of the heart. For such critics, Bellow is one kind of romantic: the romantic of inner, immanent truth, of direct illumination, of the ascetic inward journey to self-knowledge. On the other hand, those who have argued against this view tend to see Bellow as a different kind of romantic, a devotee of inclusion, brotherhood and community. For them, the important journey that he describes is that from the separateness of individual life to the morally sustaining connectedness of a shared humanity.

It will become clear that my broad sympathy is with the second position; Bellow does, in the end, insist that full humanity is found in the acceptance of a contract that links us to others in ethical mutuality. But the power of his work does not lie in what, so stated, is a familiar and unexceptionable position. The sharpness of Bellow's insight emerges in his dissection of what is involved in mutuality as against individualism, and of what, in extreme conditions, the precursors of such a shift might turn out to be. To move to community rather than individuality, commitment rather than separation, is for him an act neither of pure freedom nor of simple moral illumination; it is the product of a history which begins in the pre-ethical, at a stage in which consciousness is hardly aware of acting morally, but out of which moral action is born.

Bellow, in his mature fiction, offers two precious things: a pathology of average twentieth-century consciousness as it is formed within discourse, and a rooting of moral action in the pre-ethical category of attention. The first part is particularly evident in *Herzog* (1964); the second in *Mr Sammler's Planet* (1970). Between them they compose a history of the ethical, which begins with a recognition of how average discursive consciousness defeats the moral, and continues through a painful and not fully resolved account of the conditions of moral awareness and human interconnection. It will be my argument that the important journey for his central characters is outwards from a confining inwardness, away from the terms of discourse which give this inwardness its form; and that this involves an act of attention away from the self.

The Pathology of Inwardness: Herzog

Bellow's characteristic fiction is, in Bakhtin's terms, a representation of discourse. His Herzogs, Sammlers, and Cordes are images of distinct ways of talking and thinking about the world. Each is a life-position, a structure of valuation; each is also a formal construction of reality, directed toward a

> " Herzog's deepest inward vision is inseparable from the attention that moves outwards, from that looking-away which his experience has taught him."

particular shaping of the world. But it is here, also, that the self begins; Bellow understands the modern self as formed in discursive consciousness. We know ourselves as a specific discursive practice, and we know the world as that practice forms it for us. That, for his central characters, is where they find themselves at the start of their narratives. For Bellow, this is the inwardness of modern Western humanity, within a specific discursive practice. It is for that reason that Bellow's novels start from thought, discourse, and self-reflection, rather than from event or social relationships.

But with this inwardness there goes, unavoidably, self-enclosure. As Levinas would have recognized, Bellow's main characters use the characteristic thematizations of their discourse as a way of attaching the world to themselves; so described, the world becomes an extension of themselves, of what they already know. The pathology of discursive consciousness is, for Bellow, the difficulty that it has in looking beyond itself, in moving beyond the order of its own formulations. This is where the main characters of *Herzog* and *Mr Sammler's Planet* live: within their accounts of the world, within an unceasing discursive effort to describe the world coherently to themselves. True, each distrusts his description: Moses Herzog believes that he may be going mad, and Artur Sammler is almost persuaded that he has spent his whole life with the wrong books and the wrong explanations. But the fiction holds them within the discursive frame they have made for themselves; it is thus that they, and we, know who they are.

In this, Herzog and Sammler are alike. But it is important to recognize that each central character attempts a different discursive construction in his effort to make sense of the world. Herzog gropes toward the inclusive pattern of intellectual history; his mind works sequentially; he looks for a narrative that will set the history of developing human consciousness in clear order. Sammler, on the other hand, is overwhelmed by a simultaneity of memories and impressions; he looks for some unique key or cipher, some Kabbalistic node that will reveal the hidden coherence of the world, resolve all particulars into a simultaneous pattern.

Herzog's project is the more classically intellectual; he approaches the world as a historian of ideas (he has written a major work on Romanticism and Christianity). His mind is predominantly verbal; because he experiences the world as a text, he seeks to represent it as a text. The project fails, as the fragmentary nature of his letters shows. But it is important not to see this as Bellow's rejection of the intellectual project, not to go on to conclude that he is systematically anti-intellectual, a devotee of immediate illumination. He places Herzog in a distinguished tradition of understanding, which is adumbrated through the unsent letters, and he makes Herzog see that the future of humanity may well depend on the success of understanding. As one of the letters says, an intolerable flood of explanations may indeed be overwhelming the world, but this is no reason for giving up the attempt to understand: *"And these explanations are unbearable, but they have to be made. In the seventeenth century the passionate search for absolute truth stopped so that mankind might transform the world. Something practical was done with thought . . . But our revolutions, including nuclear terror, return the metaphysical dimension to us."* The project of understanding cannot be abandoned; the crisis of modern civilization is as much its withdrawal from certain efforts of understanding as it is the proliferation of explanations.

Nevertheless, even a necessary discursive tradition can, on the level of the individual life, become a pathology, a prison. Thought can be no liberation from the confusions of life if it gives in to "the delusion of total *explanations*", the idiocy of having an answer for everything: "readiness to answer all questions is the infallible sign of stupidity." Truth, even the absolute truth of metaphysics, is not a claim to explain everything, to have all the answers. Such a claim would represent the ultimate absorption of reality into thought, and Herzog, though engaged on an inclusive project of his own, is made to sense that total explanation is the defeat, not the fulfilment, of understanding. Nevertheless, for the time being, he continues with his effort to draw reality into the forms of his own argument.

This reality has two aspects, and between them Herzog is constantly searching for the explanatory links. On the one hand, there is his private world of failed relationships, peopled by such as Gersbach and Madeleine. On the other, there is public-historical reality, inhabited by the makers of thought and of history, the Heideggers and Eisenhowers. As a historian of human consciousness it is Herzog's necessary conviction that the two are connected, that one may even serve as an instance of the other. Herzog is Hegelian in his view of the world; he sees the same historical processes reaching self-awareness in the lives of individuals and in historical events. Thus his primary perception of people is as instances in an argument, as exemplifications of moments in the history of freedom and self-awareness. They become for him essentially ideological positions, embodiments of general truths. In this way he assimilates them to his understanding and makes them part of the construction of his world. He experiences them first of all as varieties of discourse. Himmelstein is the voice of the brutal-realist understanding of the world; Ramona, that of a spiritualized hedonism. They are, for him, voices in an argument that he is passionate to refute.

For Herzog, Madeleine and Gersbach are exemplifications of the demand for freedom in self-expression which has, in the later twentieth century, become irresistible, ceased to acknowledge any limits. He sees them as embodiments of the unrestrained conative self, trying all available stances (of love, friendship, faith, intellect, betrayal); they understand themselves in terms of that enterprise, and that is their selfhood. As an ideological position, Gersbach is defined by Herzog as a greedy, omnicompetent, but essentially fraudulent self-production; he is Hegelian modern man playing all the roles which come to consciousness in a high and articulate intelligence. Gersbach writes poetry, lectures on Buber, is a television intellectual; he is the modern equivalent of "a prophet, a *Shofat*, yes, a judge in Israel, a king." He is one version of the impulse to leave no possible life unlived. His speech embodies all that; it mixes worldly knowingness with intellect, clumsy Yiddish with a blunt psychosexual analysis. All this Herzog detests, with an added intensity because Gersbach has stolen Madeleine from him. But Madeleine herself is, for Herzog, also a false discourse, a vacuous statement of what it means to be human. She is intellect as style, the sham life of the mind that changes its cut and color as often as a Fifth Avenue couturier. Her intellectual and spiritual commitments are tedious because they are rootless; apart from her sexuality, Madeleine is seen by Herzog as no more than a false position in the argument of twentieth-century history.

The consequence of seeing others primarily as discursive positions is that Herzog cannot act morally toward either Madeleine or Gersbach, or indeed toward any others, such as Himmelstein, whom he sees in the same way. The condition of his moral recovery (which is a large part of the interest of the novel) is not some abstract choice for community over individualism, but the ability to see the world beyond his own interpretations. To read the world as one's own text is part of the pathology of discursive consciousness; believing that it sees, even understands, the world, such a consciousness sees only its own inscription. Herzog's moments of freedom from this are few, and most powerfully they include his memories of childhood. Then he could see without the itch to describe, to interpret, to explain. The model, for Bellow as for Herzog, is that moment on the train leaving Montreal, when the world still held its vivid separateness: "sun and girders divided the soot geometrically. By the factory walls the grimy weeds grew."

Because, for Bellow, childhood can supply a model of pure attention, it is not surprising that Herzog's journey away from the pathology of discursive consciousness begins in memory. Though he sees the present world as a symbolization of his own inner pressures and conflicts, and in that sense does not see the world at all, he can recall a time when the world was real for him, when its existence was hard, unassimilable and distinct. Besides his memory of riding the train across the St. Lawrence from Grand Trunk Station, another such moment is his recollection of the family home in Napoleon Street: "No dawn, the foggy winters. In darkness, the bulb was lit. The stove was cold. Papa shook the grates, and raised an ashen dust. The grates grumbled and squealed. The puny shovel clinked underneath. The Caporals gave Papa a bad cough. The chimneys in their helmets sucked in the wind. Then the milkman came in his sleigh. The snow was spoiled and rotten with manure and litter, dead rats, dogs." Here the syntax of Bellow's sentences, their primal predicative form, reflects the directness of the child's experience; this is a world revealed in its otherness by a simple attention that does not yet seek to read the world as text. When, as here, Herzog remembers himself as a child, he is remembering someone who could still see the world apart from himself, and who for that reason could love what he saw: "what was wrong

with Napoleon Street? thought Herzog. All he ever wanted was there." An important part of Herzog's ethical incapacity—and this is, for the most part, a novel of vengeance—comes from his inability to love his world. The more he stitches it to himself through his discursive accounts, the more paradoxically distant and unlovable it becomes. His childhood memories show him that the ability to love the world (ugly as it may have been) has its root in an attending to otherness, to the world apart from himself. This is the pointer to the outward journey that he must make.

Memories of childhood may indicate the direction, but they cannot replace the journey itself. Herzog's movement advances as he notices aspects of people that he cannot inscribe into his own text. Valentine Gersbach is a striking example. Of all the characters in the novel, he attracts the largest share of Herzog's antipathy; yet even here Herzog is compelled to see more than a false and vicious ideology of life. As well as discourse, Gersbach is also a physical presence. Herzog is confronted by something that cannot be assimilated, a strangeness, a remainder, something resistant. He feels this when Gersbach tells of how as a child he lost his leg under a railway car:

> Gersbach almost always cried, and it was strange, because his long curling coppery lashes stuck together; he was tender but he looked rough, his face broad and rugged, heavy-bristled, and his chin positively brutal. And Moses recognized that under his own rules the man who had suffered more was more special, and he conceded willingly that Gersbach had suffered harder, that his agony under the wheels of the boxcar must have been far deeper than anything Moses had ever suffered. Gersbach's tormented face was stony white, pierced by the radiant bristles of his red beard. His lower lip had almost disappeared beneath the upper. His great, his hot sorrow! Molten sorrow!

Under Herzog's rules of interpretation, Gersbach counts for something because he has suffered greatly; he embodies the cultural claims of suffering as a category, its authority as intellectual currency in the later twentieth century. But the man that he sees before him escapes this emblematic reduction through his physical presence and oddity. The particularity of the description, its attentive and defamiliarizing gaze, recovers a Gersbach outside Herzog's discursive identifications.

This recognition is at the heart of Herzog's change of mind when, looking through the bathroom window as Gersbach bathes Junie, he gives up the idea of shooting him. This is not simply a concession to Gersbach's fondness for the child, though that has its effect; when Herzog is forced to attend to the actuality of the man in front of him he can distinguish between what is generated inside his own head and an outward reality. "To shoot him!—an absurd thought. As soon as Herzog saw the actual person giving an actual bath, the reality of it, the tenderness of such a buffoon to a little child, his intended violence turned into *theater*, into something ludicrous." The theater, he recognizes, is of his own making; once again, as in his memories of childhood, Herzog feels the world pull away into a tangible otherness, and Gersbach, for the first time, becomes more than a construction of his own resentment. With this, moral action becomes a possibility.

In a parallel way Madeleine eludes Herzog's reduction of her to a false discursive position, a willed and fraudulent statement about the possibilities of life; and again it is her physicality, in her case her sexuality, that stands as a remainder outside all his descriptions of her. Bellow's way of creating character parallels the two modes of descriptive representation in the passages compared at the outset of this discussion. On the one hand, characters exist as terms in the internal argument of the novel's central consciousness, just as the streets of New York are absorbed into Herzog's inner turmoil. On the other hand, some aspects of these figures are left to be what they are; they stand independent of the central character's drive for comprehension and coherence. The details are trivial: Gersbach's chin, Madeleine's nose. But for a moment Herzog is prepared simply to attend to the resistant particularity of things, to notice the inexplicable as a remainder outside the bounds of discourse. This at least opens the possibility of moral action.

Attention and Understanding

These remainders strike Herzog as surds, as unaccommodatable particulars, evoking attention and troubling his attempt to shape a world continuous with himself. But his project of understanding is not defeated. If the escape through attention from the pathology of discursive consciousness is the condition of moral awareness (something that will emerge more fully in *Mr Sammler's Planet*), it is also for Bellow the condition of true comprehension. The resistant otherness of people changes Herzog's understanding and brings him closer to a true statement about the world.

Again, the most telling examples occur in Herzog's memories of childhood. He recalls his mother just before her death, when he was sixteen years old. His first memory is once again an act of intellectual assimilation; he thinks of her as a type of Jewishness, as an instance (like Gersbach) in the history of consciousness:

> Though he recalled his mother's sad face with love, he couldn't say, in his soul, that he wanted to see such sadness perpetuated. Yes, it reflected the deep experience of a race, its attitude toward happiness and toward mortality. This somber human case, this dark husk, these indurated lines of submission to the fate of being human, this splendid face showed the responses of his mother's finest nerves to the greatness of life, rich in sorrow, in death. All right, she was beautiful. But he hoped that things would change. When we have come to better terms with death, we'll wear a different expression, we human beings. Our looks will change. *When* we come to terms!

But even as he intellectualizes this memory of his mother, Herzog is struck by his failure to engage with the reality of her living and dying. He can see her face only as a text to be read, one that is inscribed with an outdated understanding of death. As that understanding changes, other faces, other texts, will appear. But to "come to better terms with death"? He finds the phrase on his lips, but what could it conceivably mean? Self-mockingly, he realizes that he has missed what was in front of him, his mother's death; that the discursive gesture has deflected his attention.

It is not further interpretation that takes him forward; it is what his mother was able to show him of death. In memory his mother takes the initiative; instead of being one instance of Jewishness that Herzog can dispose of in his categories of historical understanding, she steps forward as one who exists beyond all those categories and whose own act of explanation mocks, but also transcends, all explanatory discourse. Herzog recalls the moment when, six years old, he asked his mother about Adam's creation from the dust of the ground:

> She was about to give me the proof. Her dress was brown and gray-thrush-colored. Her hair was thick and black, the gray already streaming through it. She had something to show me at the window. The light came up from the snow in the street, otherwise the day was dark. Each of the windows had colored borders—yellow, amber, red—and flaws and whorls in the cold panes. At the curbs were the thick brown poles of that time, many-barred at the top, with green glass insulators, and brown sparrows clustered on the crossbars that held up the iced, bowed wires. Sarah Herzog opened her hand and said, "Look carefully, now, and you'll see what Adam was made of." She rubbed the palm of her hand with a finger, rubbed until something dark appeared on the deep-lined skin,

a particle of what certainly looked to him like earth. "You see? It's true."

Now his mother is no instance of anything; she belongs with the hard particularity of the 1930s street, a world of resistant objects not yet converted into symbol. When she rubs the skin of her palm into a semblance of earth she confronts Moses with the ungeneralizable particularity of death; she prepares him for the moment ten years later when she will show him her dying hand. "As he stared, she slowly began to nod her head up and down as if to say, 'That's right, Moses, I am dying now.' ... Her fingers had lost their flexibility. Under the nails they seemed to him to be turning already into the blue loam of graves."

The resistance and recalcitrance of such memories compel Herzog's attention and defy his attempt to absorb experience into the familiar terms of interpretation. But his sense of understanding is not diminished. It is at these moments that he has the sharpest feeling of having understood what is most important to him. Perhaps the trick with the palm of the hand was his mother's joke, a way of protecting him; but he finds truth in its comedy, honesty in its wit. "Maybe she offered me this proof partly in a spirit of comedy. The wit you can have only when you consider death very plainly, when you consider what a human being really is." At such moments Herzog's thought has the greatest solidity, is least the gyration of an overful brain; they are moments of contact with what resists inclusion within the project of comprehension, moments when he turns outwards.

The importance of such moments in the novel makes it clear that Herzog's career is a discipline of attention. Through memory, through his encounters with the unmanageable otherness of such as Gersbach, the interpretive itch begins to subside, and he can begin to look beyond it to the world. Toward the end of the novel, when he is back at Ludeyville, his mind continues to chase speculative possibilities and he launches on a few last letters. But he now knows that there is more help in the simple externality of objects around him. It is that, he feels, which enables him to turn away from madness: "I have wanted to be cared for. I devoutly hoped Emmerich would find me sick. But I have no intention of doing that—I am responsible, responsible to reason. This is simply temporary excitement. Responsible to the children. He walked quietly into the woods, the many leaves, living and fallen, green and tan, going between rotted stumps, moss, fungus disks; he found a hunter's path, also

a deer trail. He felt quite well here, and calmer. The silence sustained him, and the brilliant weather, the feeling that he was easily contained by everything about him." Instead of seeking to contain the world within himself, now he allows the world to contain him. What Herzog experiences here is not the defeat or reason and understanding, but their restoration, a restoration that is marked by a new awareness of his responsibility to what exists apart from himself. The pathology of discursive consciousness is being overcome.

Again it is attention to objects in their separate existence that gives Herzog's thought its solidity and firmness. This is apparent in the opening of his last letter of all, his letter to God, in which he is able at last to see the nature of his project and the terms under which it should be conducted: "*How my mind has struggled to make coherent sense. I have not been too good at it. But have desired to do your unknowable will, taking it, and you, without symbols. Everything of intensest significance. Especially if divested of me.*" The conditions for understanding are that he turn away from himself, that he resist symbolizing the world into an extension of his own mind; that he acknowledge a reality absolutely not himself. "Intensest significance" requires him to move outwards.

Herzorg's journey is not from an outer to an inner reality, but from his self-awareness as discursive consciousness outwards to the otherness of the world. Yet, paradoxically, it is in this movement that he is restored to himself. Instead of knowing himself as a nexus of discourse, he becomes aware of a stability and substantiality in his being that before had been hidden from him. "*I look at myself and see chest, thighs, feet—a head. This strange organization, I know it will die. And inside—something, something, happiness ... 'Thou movest me.' That leaves no choice.*" The form of this recognition is address: "*Thou* movest me." Herzog's deepest inward vision is inseparable from the attention that moves outwards, from that looking-away which his experience has taught him.

Herzog dramatizes, in one man, the overcoming of the pathology of discursive consciousness through memory and acts of attention. Moses Herzog begins to recover the gift that he had as a child, to see the world apart from himself; and with that, the possibility of moral action is re-opened to him. Though attention, in itself, is not a moral category, it is, nevertheless, the condition of the moral, and in *Mr Sammler's Planet* Bellow explores the consciousness of a man for whom attention is far less of a problem, but who still has to make terms with the ethical...

Conclusion

These two novels trace different stages in a history of outward movement away from the self-enclosure of discursively contructed consciousness to the otherness of the world. In this movement his main characters return to at least the possibility of moral action. But the movement itself may confront them with the reductive and negating otherness of evil, an otherness that calls the whole ethical project into question. The impulse that drives this movement is an attention that does not seek to assimilate others and the world to self-securing discursive structures. It may be a recollection of the benign attention of childhood that moves a character forward, as it does Herzog, or it may be the brutally inescapable attention of a Sammler on the brink of a mass grave. Bellow is in no doubt about the course that his characters need to follow. But he can offer no guarantees; this course may destroy them. All he can say is that, for all its risks, this is the only course that can lead to the possibility of moral action, to the realization of ethical community. Bellow is far from sentimentality in the conclusions of these novels. The possible good that he adumbrates in their conclusions is offered in full awareness of its slightness, a slender bridge thrown across the gulf which opens when the security of self-enclosure is left behind and attention looks across to what is not itself. It does not assure us of everything; but if we refuse the outward movement, we shall have nothing at all.

Source: Martin Corner, "Moving Outwards: Consciousness, Discourse and Attention in Saul Bellow's Fiction," in *Studies in the Novel*, Vol. 32, No. 3, Fall 2000, pp. 369–85.

Robert R. Dutton

In the following essay excerpt, Dutton examines Herzog's pursuit of "earthly salvation."

Symbols of the Mind

In the first chapter of the novel, Herzog goes to see Dr. Emmerich for a physical examination. Dr. Emmerich says, "I heard of your divorce—who told me? I am sorry about it." Herzog replies aphoristically in a quick note, "looking for happiness—ought to be prepared for bad results." Then the narrator states, "Emmerich put on his Ben Franklin eyeglasses and wrote a few words on the file card." So Poor Herzog's Almanac takes shape. Herzog leaves his "orderly, purposeful, lawful existence" to look for the synthesis that will bring him happi-

ness; in so doing, he is confronted by events that lead him to his sofa in his New York apartment, feeling much the same, no doubt, as Johnson's Rasselas feels at the end of his journey: to look for happiness is to chase the horizon. And Herzog does chase—Wanda, Sono, Zinka, Madeleine, Ramona. "(What a lot of romances! thought Herzog. One after another. Were those my real career?)." "A strange heart," he scribbles of himself. "I myself can't account for it." "Winning as he weeps, weeping as he wins. Evidently can't believe in victories."

Herzog's life after he has left the university is intended by Bellow to reflect the twisting and turning search of man as he seeks a higher self, a synthesis. Each of his confrontations with other characters represents a segment of that search. But we must remember that Herzog's mind is being examined and that each of these characters may be properly thought of as extensions of that mind. Daisy is therefore a reflection of his academic life; in this sense, she is a part of Herzog's condition:

> His early book ... was now on many reading lists, and the younger generation of historians accepted it as a model of the new sort of history ... [it] looks at the past with an intense need for contemporary relevance. *As long as Moses was married to Daisy, he had led the perfectly ordinary life of an assistant professor, respected and stable* [italics mine]. His first work showed by objective research what Christianity was to Romanticism.

The line italicized that describes Herzog's domestic life seems to be out of context, placed as it is within an account of Herzog the scholar. But with this strategic juxtapositioning the author encompasses his intentions that Herzog's relationship to Daisy and Herzog's intellectual endeavors are to be regarded as pieces of a whole, a state of mind. And, if we read closely in the following passage, it is possible to recognize in the description of Daisy the characteristics from which Herzog is escaping:

> She was childishly systematic about things. It sometimes amused Moses to recall that she had a file card ... to cover every situation ... When they were married she put his pocket money in an envelope, in a green metal file bought for budgeting. Daily reminders, bills, concert tickets were pinned by thumbtacks to the bulletin board. Calendars were marked well in advance. Stability, symmetry, order, containment were Daisy's strength ... By my irregularity and turbulence of spirit I brought out the very worst in Daisy. *I* caused the seams of her stockings to be so straight, and the buttons to be buttoned symmetrically. *I* was behind those rigid curtains and underneath the square carpets ... Of course a wife's duty was to stand by this puzzling and often disagreeable

Herzog. She did so with heavy neutrality, recording her objections each time—once but not more. The rest was silence—such heavy silence as he felt in Connecticut when he was finishing *Romanticism and Christianity*.

"Stability, symmetry, order, containment" are not only Daisy's strength but the elements of the protected and orderly existence that stir Herzog to rebellion. Then, when he states that it was he who was behind her idiosyncrasies, Bellow intends just that. Daisy and all she stands for are a part of Herzog's mind; and Bellow depicts in this relationship the thesis that man can stand only so much reason and order; that he longs for subjective research, to stretch himself, to flee from a world cold with intellect alone. After all, man is also a creature of the heart—certainly Herzog is.

After Herzog's escape from old barren reason, a meaningful pattern develops. He turns to Sono (he had been seeing the Japanese girl even before his divorce), who is the precise antithesis to Daisy: she is warm, loving, subservient, admiring ("T'es philosophe. O mon Philosophe, mon professeur d'amour. T'es tres important. Je le sais"); and she caters to all of his moods: "But often he sat morose, depressed, in the Morris chair. Well, curse such sadness! But she liked even that. She saw me with the eyes of love, and she said, 'Ah! T'es melancolique c'est tres beau'."

But Sono takes care especially of his sensory needs: "She loved massages, believed in them. She had often massaged Moses, and he had massaged her . . . She had a tender heart . . ." Bellow's implications are varied, but they are centered around a retreat into romantic melancholy and sensualism. The massages are direct appeals to the senses. As Herzog recalls Sono, he writes, "To tell the truth, I never had it so good. But I lacked the strength of character to bear such joy." And then he reflects: "That was hardly a joke. When a man's breast feels like a cage from which all the dark birds have flown—he is free, he is light. And he longs to have his vultures back again. He wants his customary struggles, his nameless, empty works, his anger, his afflictions and his sins." Sono, symbolic of Herzog's sensual nature, fails to content Herzog, the man. Happiness, the great synthesis, is not to be found in the indulgence of the senses. By nature, man is restless, and must push on from the lotus eaters: "she didn't answer my purpose. Not serious enough."

With Madeleine, Herzog moves in another direction to look for happiness; and, as he says, he ought to have been prepared for bad results.

Herzog writes a letter to the German philosopher Friedrich Nietzsche, also an existentialist scholar

Madeleine serves a complex function in Bellow's work, but her central purpose is to represent the object of man's pursuit and adoration of what is nebulously called "success." In fact, she is described as a bitch so often and by so many various people in the novel that we can only conclude that Bellow has in mind the proverbial "bitch-goddess" of success. Certainly her personality supports the idea. Everyone admires her great beauty; she is vain, demanding everyone's admiration and attention; she insists on dominating every situation. Deceitful and nasty to those in her power, she is always looking for new recruits to her standard. She is especially anxious to attract those who are ambitious: "Should he have been a plain unambitious Herzog? No. And Madeleine would never have married such a type. What she had been looking for, high and low, was precisely an ambitious Herzog. In order to trip him, bring him low, knock him sprawling and kick out his brains with a murderous bitch foot." Indeed, this "bitch" has made her mark on most of the people around Herzog. Dr. Edvig the psychiatrist is taken with her, as are Sandor Himmelstein, the Monsignor, Gersbach, and even Herzog's student Geraldine Portnoy, who speaks favorably of Madeleine even as she tells Herzog of his wife's infidelity.

> Daisy and all she stands for are a part of Herzog's mind; and Bellow depicts in this relationship the thesis that man can stand only so much reason and order. . . ."

Like success, Madeleine moves from object to object, and from interest to interest: "But when all was said and done, Madeleine didn't marry in the Church, nor did she baptize her daughter. Catholicism went the way of zithers and tarot cards, breadbaking and Russian civilization. And life in the country." For, as she angrily asks Herzog, "What makes you think I intend to have a life-long affair with you?" Her complete irresponsibility with money also bears mentioning; she spends outrageous sums on everything, from maternity clothes to cigarette boxes.

Appropriately enough, Madeleine takes everything that Herzog can give her—his name, money, reputation, and even his learning; and, when he can give nothing more, she moves to Gersbach, that "public figure" of a man, "that loud, flamboyant, ass-clutching brute . . ." "He started out in educational radio, and now he's all over the place. On committees, in the papers. He gives lectures to the Hadassah . . . readings of his poems." But Gersbach, too, will go the way of all flesh. As Herzog tells Phoebe, Gersbach's wife, toward the end of the novel, "He'll lose his value to Madeleine as soon as you withdraw. After the victory, she'll have to throw him out."

Through the sequence of Daisy, Sono, and Madeleine, Bellow intends that with man's disillusion in his intellect and emotions, he turns to the pursuit of worldly success—fame, money, position—only to find that its achievement is barren. Happiness is not here, and the lesson is long, costly, and painful, one not too easily survived.

Ramona, the object of Herzog's final pursuit, represents another retreat, this time from the ego-shattering experience with Madeleine. Ramona is an earth-goddess (she runs a floral shop) who "had made herself into a sort of sexual professional (or

priestess)." She is more than willing to salve all of Herzog's wounds, to reassure him of his intelligence and masculinity, his virility and value: "Nonsense—why talk like that! You know you're a good-looking man. And you even take pride in being one. In Argentina they'd call you *macho*—masculine."

Under Ramona's tutelage Herzog goes shopping for new clothes, a coat of crimson and white stripes and a straw hat, reminiscent of the 1920s and reflective of Herzog's retreat. Ramona does take good care of this sick Herzog, offering him "asylum, shrimp, wine, music, flowers, sympathy, gave him room, so to speak, in her soul, and finally the embrace of her body." Her sexual antics attract him, but they also bewilder him: "It was odd that Ramona should sometimes carry on like one of those broads in a girlie magazine. For which she advanced the most high-minded reasons. An educated woman, she quoted him Catullus and the great love poets of all times. And the classics of psychology. And finally the Mystical Body. And so she was in the next room, joyously preparing, stripping, perfuming. She wanted to please."

Ramona, Bellow intends, is another aberration of Herzog's mind. As such, the similarity in the attitudes of these two life-beaten people should be noted: "She was thirty-seven or thirty-eight years old, he shrewdly reckoned, and this meant that she was looking for a husband . . . She wanted to give her heart once and for all, and level with a good man, become Herzog's wife and quit being an easy lay." Herzog writes in his imaginary letters to her: "Dear Ramona, you mustn't think because I've taken a powder, briefly, that I don't care for you. I do! I feel you close about me, much of the time. And last week, at that party, when I saw you across the room in your hat with flowers, your hair crowded down close to your bright cheeks, I had a glimpse of what it might be like to love you." Herzog shows signs of Ramona's desperate resignations: "He exclaimed mentally, Marry me! Be my wife! End my troubles!" but then he catches himself "and was staggered by his rashness, his weakness, and by the characteristic nature of such an outburst, for he saw how very neurotic and typical it was."

What Herzog comes to discover through all of these experiences—his love affairs, which Bellow intends to be reflective and subjective, inclinations of personal gratification—is that he will never be content or at ease with himself through his misguided efforts to exploit a part of his nature, nor will he find a viable life through a denial of any other part of his nature. On one level he is trying to do the impossible—to find happiness through outer sources—to supplement himself, so to speak, through these love affairs. But on a deeper, universal level, these attachments and attractions are symbolic of elements to be found in all men, and all men will find that their ease of heart will come from within themselves if it comes at all.

A Definition

This lonely truth is brought home to Herzog when he dashes to Chicago to protect, he tells himself, his daughter from Gersbach and Madeleine, who are living together. As Herzog sneaks up to the house and looks through the bathroom window, he is greeted by a scene that goes far to dispel his mistaken pretensions of self and his misinformed idea of his relation to others. When he sees the hated pretender Gersbach tenderly and affectionately giving his daughter a bath and little Junie delighting in the scrubbing, Herzog looks at Gersbach and thinks:

> The hated traits were all there. But see how he was with June, scooping water on her playfully, kindly . . . The child jumped up and down with delight . . . Moses might have killed him now . . . There were two bullets in the chamber . . . But they would stay there. Herzog clearly recognized that . . . Firing this pistol was nothing but a thought. [Herzog writes a quick note] The human soul is an amphibian, and I have touched its sides. [And then he thinks] Amphibian! It lives in more elements than I will ever know; . . . I seem to think because June looks like a Herzog, she is nearer to me than to them. But how is she near to me if I have no share in her life? Those two grotesque love-actors have it all. And I apparently believe that if the child does not have a life resembling mine, educated according to the Herzog standards of "heart," and all the rest of it, she will fail to become a human being . . . As soon as Herzog saw the actual person giving an actual bath, the reality of it, the tenderness of such a buffoon to a little child, his intended violence turned into theater, into something ludicrous . . . Lingering in the alley awhile, he congratulated himself on his luck. His breath came back to him; and how good it felt to breathe! It was worth the trip.

Herzog realizes that he has been using his daughter in much the same way he has been using his affairs with women—as an imagined source of happiness. He had thought that little June needed him, that she was even a part of him. Obviously he is mistaken. It is even more important that he loses his intense hate of Gersbach and Madeleine; hence, as Bellow intends, Herzog no longer hates in himself those elements for which these two actors stand. Herzog is released from a self-imprisoning self-hatred of elements in his own nature.

But Herzog, since he still wants custody of his daughter, goes straight to the house of Phoebe Gersbach and urges her to divorce her husband; for the consequence may be that any scandal revealing Gersbach's infidelity may yet bring June back to him. But he is bluntly told the direction he must take when Phoebe refuses to do anything about Gersbach's affair with Madeleine: "'Why do you come to me [Phoebe asks], if you want custody of your daughter? *Either do something by yourself or forget it* [italics mine]. Let me alone, now Moses.' [Herzog admits] This too, was perfectly just . . . 'You're right. This was an unnecessary visit'."

With this last effort that is so obviously ill-conceived, Herzog returns to his house in Ludeyville, where he faces himself, finds his synthesis, and writes: "Why must I be such a throb-hearted character . . . But I am. I am, and you can't teach old dogs. Myself is thus and so, and will continue thus and so. And why fight it? My balance comes from instability. Not organization, or courage, as with other people. It's tough, but that's how it is. On these terms I, too—even I!—apprehend certain things. Perhaps the only way I'm able to do it. Must play the instrument I've got."

All men must come to terms with their nature. Herzog realizes that in the past he has been victimized by that nature because of his inability to define it and accept it for what it is. He is beginning to understand himself as man: "And terrible forces in me, including the force of admiration or praise, powers, including loving powers, very damaging, making me almost an idiot because I lacked the capacity to manage them." Herzog, who now puts all of the blame for his problem squarely on himself, faces the fact that he is a human being subject to "terrible forces"; but he also realizes that he is only at their mercy if he fails to understand them.

It is little wonder that, as the story opens with Herzog back in Ludeyville, he states in the first line, "If I am out of my mind, it's all right with me." And, at the end of the novel, the line is repeated. The importance of this remark far exceeds its seeming casualness, for Bellow intends it to be interpreted literally, at least in a sense: for Herzog's mind has failed to manage these "terrible forces." Furthermore, with the concluding scene, which finds Herzog closely involved with nature, Bellow intends that Herzog is *out of his mind* [italics mine]: he is no longer subject to the "terrible forces" of the mind, and he has found his place in the natural order of things:

> Then he thought he'd light candles at dinner ... But now it was time to get those bottles from the spring ... He took pleasure in the vivid cold of the water ... Coming back from the woods, he picked some flowers for the table. He wondered whether there was a corkscrew in the drawer ... A nail could be used, if it came to that ... Meanwhile, he filled his hat from the rambler vine, the one that clutched the rainpipe ... By the cistern there were yellow day lilies. He took some of these, too, but they wilted instantly. And, back in the darker garden, he looked for peonies; perhaps some had survived. But then it struck him that he might be making a mistake, and he stopped ... Picking flowers? He was being thoughtful, being lovable. How would it be interpreted? (He smiled slightly.) Still, he need only know his own mind, and the flowers couldn't be used; no, they couldn't be turned against him. So he did not throw them away ... Walking over notes and papers, he lay down on his Recamier couch ... At this time he had no messages for anyone. Nothing. Not a single word.

Significantly, this is the first time in the novel that Herzog has left his position as an observer of nature, which he is throughout the book, to become a participant. And then there is the observation on the part of Herzog—not a knowledgeable conclusion, but an illumination—that he too must remain in nature, like the flowers, if he is to prosper. The novel ends as the backward action begins, with Herzog's lying on a couch. Only this time it is the couch of reason, a "Recamier couch," much like the one, no doubt, upon which Madame Recamier reclined when the French classicist David painted her likeness. Bellow implies that his protagonist is recovering his balance and is entering a world of the reasonable.

And perhaps Bellow's entire novel is to be interpreted in the light of the classic dictum, *know thyself*. At least Moses E. Herzog, "a solid figure of a man", has learned its importance. In any case, "at this time" there will be no more attempts to define himself through communication with the world, no more insistent intellectualization of the world or of his relationship to it. For now he is content to be—Moses E. Herzog. He writes his last letter: "But what do you want, Herzog? But that's just it—not a solitary thing. I am pretty well satisfied to be, to be just as it is willed, and for as long as I may remain in occupancy." We might even say that Herzog has attained a state of *sweet* reasonableness.

The Faust Legend

Bellow often uses the images of actors and theaters in order to convey the idea that "all the world's a stage, and all the men and women merely players." In *Herzog*, Bellow casts his protagonist into the dramatic tradition of Faust, which allows us to interpret Herzog's experiences and dilemmas through the Faustian myth, and further, to see Herzog as representative of the intellectual development of man since the Renaissance.

Bellow provides an endless variety of hints that point to his protagonist as Faust. For example, Herzog writes a letter to himself: "Dear Moses E. Herzog, Since when have you taken such an interest in social questions, in the external world? Until lately, you led a life of innocent sloth. But suddenly a Faustian spirit of discontent and universal reform descends on you. Scolding, Invective."

Within the first few pages, he is describing his studies: "His first work showed by objective research what Christianity was to Romanticism. In the second he was becoming tougher, more assertive, more ambitious ... He had a strong will and a talent for polemics, a taste for the philosophy of history ... digging in at Ludeyville, he showed a taste and talent also for danger and extremism, for heterodoxy, for ordeals, a fatal attraction to the 'City of Destruction'." Here is Faust with his ambition, polemics, philosophy, and tastes, and certainly his "fatal attraction" to Bunyan's "City of Destruction." Herzog is a university professor who is, in his words, as "bored" as Faust was. The flight that Herzog takes while in Poland is reminiscent of Faust's travels under the will of Mephistopheles: "They flew through angry spinning snow clouds over white Polish forests, fields, pits, factories, rivers dogging their banks, in, out, in and a terrain of white and brown diagrams." And the geography of Herzog's trip is significant because it encompasses the area in which Faust was operative, the Eastern European area, where Herzog lectures "in Copenhagen, Warsaw, Cracow, Berlin, Belgrade, Istanbul, and Jerusalem", and specifically in Cracow, where there "was a frightening moment ... when the symptom appeared", just a "little infection he had caught in Poland." In Goethe's work, Cracow is the precise setting for Faust's teaching and for his bargain with Mephistopheles. And Herzog feels Mephistopheles inside himself when he writes, "There is someone inside me. I am in his grip. When I speak of him I feel him in my head, pounding for order. He will ruin me."

Bellow intends that, as in the case of Faust, Mephistopheles be seen as a creature of Herzog's imagination; and, when Herzog says, "I do seem to be a broken-down monarch of some kind", it is with the idea that this spirit is a part of Herzog. And then, keeping in mind the view that the other characters in the novel are symbolic of forces within Herzog, Bellow has his protagonist say:

> Take me, for instance. I've been writing letters helter-skelter in all directions. More words. I go after reality with language. Perhaps I'd like to change it all into language, to force Madeleine and Gersbach to have a *Conscience* [italics in original] . . . If they don't suffer, they've gotten away from me. And I've filled the world with letters to prevent their escape. I want them in human form, and so I *conjure up a whole environment and catch them in the middle. I put my whole heart into these constructions. But they are constructions* [italics mine].

This passage contains the clear indication that Bellow would have the reader see his work as an exposition of a psychological condition. This condition, he intends figuratively and dramatically, is the result of diabolic forces. It will be remembered that Herzog decides Madeleine would never have married an unambitious person: "What she had been looking for, *high and low* [italics mine], was precisely an ambitious Herzog." She had "the will of a demon," he says. So Madeleine is an extension of the Mephistophelean spirit in Herzog, as is Gersbach: "He's a ringmaster, popularizer, liaison for the elites. He grabs up celebrities and brings them before the public. And he makes all sorts of people feel that he has exactly what they've been looking for." And, even as Mephistopheles suggests to Faust that he could peacefully lead a sensuous existence, so does Ramona try to convince Herzog that life with her would be ideal.

In addition to the aptness of the Faust legend as a description of the mental condition of Herzog, Bellow intends that the myth be seen as part of the resolution to his novel. Herzog states the case when he tries to explain his work to Zelda: "Herzog tried to explain what it was about—that his study was supposed to have ended with a new angle on the modern condition, showing how life could be lived by renewing universal connections . . . revising the old Western, Faustian ideology . . ."

In Goethe's drama, Faust finds his contentment in social usefulness. He creates a vast area of productive land out of the swamps, where people can live in freedom and in pragmatic activities. Through this achievement he finds peace and harmony. At one time Herzog has similar ideas. He thinks about giving his land and house in Ludeyville to a utopian group. The idea remains with him, but he finally decides against it.

This house, "an old ruin of a place but with enormous possibilities", suggests the condition of Herzog, as Bellow implies when his protagonist sees "the shadow of his face in a gray, webby window." And when Herzog tells his brother Will at the end of the story that "I could go to work and become rich. Make a ton of money, just to keep this house", he does so with the illumination that he himself is worth saving, that the first and most important step is to work with himself, which means knowing and enjoying himself in his human condition. Although this condition is admittedly beset with many limitations and countless liabilities, it is also one with "enormous possibilities." Through his hero, Bellow seems to be saying that man's earthly salvation is not to be gained in social movements, utopian visions, political nostrums, scientific investigations (and this compulsive activity is what Herzog's letters are all about), but in learning to live with himself as he exists in the subangelic position of man.

Source: Robert R. Dutton, "*Herzog*," in *Saul Bellow*, edited by Warren French, G. K. Hall & Co., 1982, pp. 124–34.

Sources

Corner, Martin, "Moving Outwards: Consciousness, Discourse and Attention in Saul Bellow's Fiction," in *Studies in the Novel*, Vol. 32, No. 3, Fall 2000, p. 369.

Dutton, Robert R., "Saul Bellow," in *Twayne's United States Authors Series Online*, G. K. Hall & Co., 1999.

Eisinger, Chester E., "Herzog: Overview," in *Reference Guide to American Literature*, 3d ed., edited by Jim Kamp, St. James Press, 1994.

Epstein, Seymour, "Bellow's Gift," in *Denver Quarterly*, Winter 1976, pp. 35–50, 423.

Marin, Daniel B., "Saul Bellow," in *Dictionary of Literary Biography*, Volume 2: *American Novelists Since World War II, First Series*, Gale Research, 1978, pp. 39–50.

Opdahl, Keith M., "Saul Bellow," in *Dictionary of Literary Biography*, Volume 28: *Twentieth-Century American-Jewish Fiction Writers*, Gale Research, 1984, pp. 8–25.

Rovit, Earl, "Saul Bellow," in *American Writers*, Vol. 1, Scribner's Sons, 1974, pp. 144–66.

For Further Reading

Dutton, Robert R., *Saul Bellow*, Twayne Publishers, 1982.
  Dutton presents a thoughtful study of the themes in Bellow's novels.

Fuchs, Daniel, *Saul Bellow: Vision and Revision*, Duke University Press, 1984.

The first two chapters provide informative background information on Bellow's place in the modern tradition and his relationship to Dostoevsky. The remaining chapters offer penetrating analyses of his novels, including studies of his manuscripts.

Kiernan, Robert F., *Saul Bellow*, Continuum, 1989.

The first chapter of this book presents valuable information on Bellow's life and career. The remainder of the work critiques one novel per chapter. Kiernan draws interesting comparisons between Bellow and William Faulkner.

Malin, Irving, ed., *Saul Bellow and the Critics*, New York University Press, 1967.

This collection of critical essays considers the general trends in critiquing Bellow's fiction, including concentrations on themes, characterizations, imagery, style, and sources. The last chapter, written by Bellow, considers the author's view of the future of the novel.

Madame Bovary

Gustave Flaubert
1857

After *Revue de Paris* published several installments of Gustave Flaubert's *Madame Bovary*, the editor decided to remove from the novel several passages he determined would be offensive to France's conservative Second Empire (1852–1870), ruled by Emperor Napoleon Bonaparte III. Flaubert was understandably furious over the loss of control over his work. Yet, even after the offending passages were edited, the government soon banned the novel and charged Flaubert with obscenity due to its detailed depiction of the heroine's adulterous relationships. Charges were soon dropped, however, and the novel was published in two volumes in April 1857. *Madame Bovary* immediately gained a wide readership, due not only to its notoriety but also to its celebrated artistry.

Flaubert worked on the novel from September 1851 to April 1856, during which time he rewrote the manuscript several times, often spending days perfecting a single page or paragraph. The result of his painstaking creativity was a penetrating psychological study of its heroine, Emma Bovary, as she struggles to find fulfillment through a realization of her romantic fantasies of love and wealth. Flaubert's realistic portrait of the tragic fate of this complex woman has earned him the reputation as one of the most celebrated and influential novelists of the nineteenth century.

Gustave Flaubert

After graduation, Flaubert entered law school in Paris, prodded by his parents. In 1844, he had what was most likely an episode of epilepsy. As a result, he gave up the law and turned to a literary career. The best of his early work, the novel *Novembre* (1885; translated [1934] as *November*) is a fictional account of Flaubert's sexual relationship with an older woman he had met in 1836 in Trouville.

Flaubert worked on his most famous and celebrated novel, *Madame Bovary*, from September 1851 until April 1856. The novel gained notoriety after the French government charged Flaubert with obscenity and stopped its publication, determining the work to be a challenge to moral decency. The charges and the ban, however, were soon dropped, and *Madame Bovary* would become one of the most celebrated novels of the nineteenth century. Ironically, Flaubert came to resent the attention paid to the novel, especially since, as a result, few of his other works received the consideration he thought they deserved. Yet, through his body of work, Flaubert has come to be regarded as one of the finest novelists of the nineteenth century. Flaubert died on May 8, 1880, in Croisset, France, ending a long and successful literary career.

Author Biography

Gustave Flaubert was born on December 12, 1821, in Rouen, France, to Achille Cleophas (a physician) and Caroline (Fleuriot) Flaubert. Flaubert lived with his family in an apartment in the hospital where his father served as chief surgeon and professor. Stirling Haig, in his article on Flaubert in *Dictionary of Literary Biography*, suggests that Flaubert, who was exposed to pain and suffering at the hospital throughout his childhood, developed a "gloomy perspective on life and death" that he would later weave into the fabric of his works.

Flaubert began writing in his childhood. By 1832, he had completed two texts: the serious-minded *Eloge de Corneille* (Tribute to Pierre Corneille, the seventeenth-century playwright) and the juvenile *La Belle Explication de la Fameuse Constipation* (The Fine Explanation of the Famous Constipation). While a student at the Collège Royal de Rouen, Flaubert devoured the classics and staged plays by Victor Hugo, Alexandre Dumas, and Jean Baptiste Poquelin Molière. He started writing historical fiction (for school assignments) and psychological mysteries, elements of which foreshadow the characterizations in his novels.

Plot Summary

The narrative begins from the perspective of a French schoolboy, who records Charles Bovary's first day in his class. Everyone stares at Charles, the fifteen-year-old "new boy" from the country, who enters with an exceedingly embarrassed manner. His classmates soon begin to tease him, ostracizing him for his country manner and dress. The teacher also ridicules him when he can't understand Charles's pronunciation of his name and makes him sit on a dunce stool near him.

Charles is an average student, but others note that "he had not the least elegance of style." After his parents determine that he would make a fine doctor, he enrolls in medical school, where he becomes a mediocre student. He soon begins to enjoy his freedom at college, frequenting the tavern and playing dominos, which develops into "an initiation into the world, the introduction to forbidden pleasures." As a result, he fails his medical examinations. Later, he returns to school and, through careful memorization of the questions, retakes the exams and passes. Soon after, he moves to Tostes to begin his practice. When his mother decides he must marry, she finds him a forty-five-year-old wealthy widow. Charles finds Héloïse ugly and thin. After they marry, she takes control of the household and complains incessantly of health problems.

One night Charles is called away to a farm-house to set a farmer's broken leg. The farmer, Monsieur Rouault, is a widower with one daugh-ter, Emma. Charles is struck by her beauty and re-turns to the farmhouse as often as he can, ostensi-bly to check on her father but in reality because he is drawn to the farm and especially to her. When Héloïse finds out that Rouault has a beautiful daughter, she forbids Charles's return to the farm. After Héloïse loses her inheritance, Charles's par-ents accuse her of lying about her wealth and cause a scene. Héloïse becomes so upset that she falls ill and suddenly dies.

Charles returns to the farm and soon asks Rouault for his permission to marry Emma. Al-though he finds Charles rather dull, Rouault agrees, since he determines that Emma is not much use to him around the farm. After a suitable period, Emma and Charles marry at the farmhouse and then go on to Tostes. Charles clearly adores his wife and so becomes supremely happy and contented. Emma, however, is not satisfied. She had thought herself in love with Charles before they married, but those feelings failed to materialize. She finds none of the passion in her marriage that she has read about in books and dreamt about for herself. Although Charles is supremely content, their life together soon falls into monotony for her.

One evening she and Charles attend a ball at La Vaubyessard, the home of the Marquis d'An-dervilliers, one of Charles's patients. This first ex-perience with "the complexion of wealth" enthralls Emma, who desperately wants to become a part of this world. The memory of the ball and the lifestyle it represents develops into an obsession with her, reinforcing her sense of the meaninglessness and monotony of her life. A viscount, with whom she danced that evening, becomes the personification of all the romantic heroes she finds in the senti-mental novels she reads.

When the dramatic event she hopes will trans-form her life fails to materialize, she begins to slip into depression, abandoning all her hobbies and do-mestic duties. Soon, her health suffers, and Charles decides they will move to Yonville-l'Abbaye, hop-ing that a change of scenery will improve her con-dition.

After they move, Emma finds herself pregnant; however, when she realizes that she cannot afford

Media Adaptations

- There have been eight film versions of *Madame Bovary*, and five television versions. The most famous adaptation was directed by Vincente Minnelli in 1949 for MGM. Jennifer Jones starred as Emma and Van Heflin as Charles.

an elegant layette, she loses all interest in the up-coming birth and pays little attention to her daugh-ter, Berthe, after she is born. In Yonville, Emma meets Léon Dupuis, a lawyer's clerk, who has her same romantic temperament. As the two spend a good deal of time together, they fall in love with each other. Refusing to declare her feelings for Léon, Emma turns her attentions to her family, showing new interest in her daughter. Her pride in remaining virtuous, however, clashes with her frus-tration over not being able to admit her love for Léon. When she tries to get advice and comfort from the local priest, he cannot understand her dilemma. Weary of not being able to express his love for Emma, or of not having it reciprocated, Léon decides to move to Rouen. His farewell to Emma is strained, as both suppress their feelings for each other and their pain over their separation.

After Léon leaves, Emma upbraids herself for not acknowledging her love for him and falls back into a deep depression, alleviated temporarily by extravagant spending sprees. One day, she meets Rodolphe Boulanger, a country squire, who comes to Charles for medical advice. He finds Emma quite attractive and so plans to seduce her, determining that "she's gaping for love like a carp on the kitchen table for water." They meet at the Agricultural Ex-position, where Boulanger tries to convince her that men and women should give in to their desires. Weeks later, during a horseback ride in the woods, he seduces her.

The two enter into an affair, seeing and writ-ing each other often. Their relationship fills Emma with a happiness she has never known. She often sneaks out in the early morning to Boulanger's bed. One morning as she returns home, she runs into

Monsieur Binet and gives him a clumsy excuse for being there. Binet and others in the town begin to suspect that Emma is having an affair. Soon Boulanger's affections for her begin to wane.

Emma tries to shift her attentions back to Charles and so is encouraged when he plans to try out a new method for treating clubfoot. Emma and Charles are convinced that the success of the operation will make him famous. Charles, however, botches the operation on Hippolyte, a handyman at the inn, and as a result, the patient's gangrenous leg must be amputated. Emma becomes humiliated at the thought that such a man as her husband "could amount to anything, as if she had not already had sufficient evidence of his mediocrity twenty times over."

Emma's and Boulanger's love for each other becomes reinvigorated. When Monsieur Lherueux, the merchant, begins to press her for payment of her outstanding bills, she convinces Boulanger to run off with her to Italy. On the night they are to leave, however, he has second thoughts and abandons her. As a result, Emma falls into a deep depression and her health suffers. In an effort to cheer her up, Charles takes her to the opera at Rouen, where she sees Léon. The two soon begin a passionate affair, and Emma borrows more money to support their extravagances. Yet, their passion cannot live up to their romantic imaginations, and as a result, it inevitably fades. Emma's bills mount up to the point at which she and Charles are threatened with financial ruin. When she cannot pay back the loans and can find no one, including Léon, to give her financial assistance, she becomes desperate. In an attempt to prostitute herself, she goes to Boulanger to plead for his help. He does not have the money to help her, however, and the bailiff comes to seize all of her and Charles's property.

Finding no way out of her dilemma, Emma takes arsenic and suffers an agonizing death. When Charles finds her love letters to Rodolphe, he blames fate rather than Emma and soon dies. Berthe moves in with an aunt and lives in poverty. The novel ends with Monsieur Homais winning the Legion of Honor.

Characters

Monsieur Binet

Monsieur Binet, Yonville's tax collector, does not often participate in the social life of the town. Monsieur Homais claims he is "a dead fish" with "no imagination, no wit, nothing of what makes a man a social light." He serves as a foil to Emma when she runs into him one morning as she is returning from Boulanger's estate. Emma turns to him for help when she is about to lose her home, but he refuses to help her. Two of the village women watch through the window, suspecting that Emma is "making advances to him," which appears to be confirmed when he immediately jumps back exclaiming, "What are you thinking of, Madame?" The women see this as evidence of Binet's courage.

Monsieur Rodolphe Boulanger

Rodolphe Boulanger, a thirty-four-year-old country squire, is "cynical in temperament and keen of intellect." He seduces Emma during a horseback ride in the woods after a careful manipulation of her feelings. When he first meets her, he immediately comprehends the problems in her relationship with Charles and so determines that she will be vulnerable to him. He notes that she has been starved for passion and eloquent words of love and so tells her that some force beyond his control drove him to her. His ability to understand her predicament and provide her with the romantic words and the attention she craves causes her to fall in love with him.

His callous and shallow nature become apparent in his decision to discard her after their affair begins to bore him. He decides that Emma is like all mistresses: "the charm of newness, slipping down little by little like a garment, revealed unclothed the eternal monotony of passion."

Abbé Bournisien

Abbé Bournisien, Yonville's priest, suggests his lack of perception when Emma comes to him, trying to explain her unhappiness and looking for strength to resist her feelings for Léon. He insists to Emma that any woman who has enough to eat and a fire in winter should be perfectly happy. As a result of his lack of understanding, she does not confide in him and turns her back on religion as a source of comfort.

Berthe Bovary

Berthe Bovary is the daughter of Charles and Emma Bovary.

Charles Bovary

From the beginning of the novel, Flaubert characterizes Charles as dull, dim, and graceless. The narrator notes that his conversation was "flat as the sidewalk of the street and the ideas of everyone he spoke to passed through it without exciting emotion, laughter, or contemplation." Charles has few interests besides his family. He does not care about the theater or books and has never learned any skills like swimming or fencing that would make him an interesting companion or husband. His name suggests his "bovine," cud-chewing personality.

Many of Charles's patients in both Tostes and Yonville, however, appreciate his lack of airs. They also admire his sense of responsibility. Yet his inability to develop a firm grasp of the intricacies of his profession results in his botching of a clubfoot operation, and his patient subsequently suffers the amputation of his leg.

Charles adores Emma, which, combined with his weak will, allows her to control his life. He turns a blind eye to her financial extravagances and her attentions to other men, which Emma usually does not take great pains to hide. His lack of perception extends to his relationship with her. Often, Charles has no idea what Emma is thinking or feeling, unless her health obviously begins to deteriorate. His lack of ambition and his country habits, coupled with his weak nature, irritate and depress Emma. Yet Charles is ever loyal to her, even after he discovers that she has been having affairs with Rodolphe Boulanger and Léon Dupuis. His intense love for her ultimately destroys him, however. Soon after she commits suicide, Charles wastes away and dies.

Monsieur Charles-Denis-Bartholomé Bovary

Monsieur Bovary, Charles's father, was a former assistant surgeon-major. After he was forced to leave the service, Bovary found a wife with a large dowry so he could live comfortably. He failed, however, at farming, since he drank and ate up his profits. Eventually, Charles's vain, braggart father became a bitter drunk, "disgusted with humanity" in his later years.

Madame Emma Bovary

Emma's sensuality becomes apparent as soon as Charles meets her. While she is sewing, she pricks her fingers and raises them up to her mouth to suck them. Later, she licks every drop of liquor from the bottom of a glass with her tongue. Charles does not encourage this quality in her. Soon after they are married, she becomes bored by the monotony of their life together.

Discontented with her life on the farm, she agrees to marry Charles, confusing her desire for a better, more comfortable life with feelings of love for him. She had thought herself in love with Charles before they married, but those feelings failed to materialize. Soon after their marriage, she

waits for a dramatic event to transform her life. When none occurs and she finds no fulfillment in her relationship with him, she develops an appreciation for the things money can buy. The narrator notes that she "confused, in her longing, the sensual appeals of luxury with the joys of the heart, elegance of manners with delicacy of sentiment." Her desire to live a life full of luxury leads to her destruction.

Frustrated by her inability to afford the lifestyle she feels she deserves, Emma turns to other men to satisfy her passionate nature. Her romantic vision of love, however, destroys her relationships, not only with her husband but also with her lovers. When Charles fails to live up to her expectations of what a man should be, she dreams about finding lovers like those she reads about in sentimental novels. When her marriage provides none of the passion she finds in these books, she wonders "just what was meant, in real life, by the words felicity, passion and intoxication, which had seemed so beautiful" on the page.

She falls in love with Léon and Rodolphe when they compare favorably to Charles. However, neither can live up to her romantic vision of love. As a result, she alienates both men. Inevitably, she rediscovers in adultery all the uniformity of marriage. As she drains "every pleasure by wishing it to be too intense," she succumbs to a "universal numbness" that, coupled with her financial troubles, prompts her to commit suicide.

Madame Héloïse Bovary

Héloïse Bovary, Charles's first wife, is a forty-five-year-old wealthy widow when Charles marries her. Charles is not content with this woman, whom his mother determined he should marry, finding her ugly and thin. She takes control of the household and complains incessantly of her health, which turns out to be actually quite frail. When her family loses its fortune, and Charles's parents angrily accuse her of fraud, she falls ill and dies.

Madame Bovary

Mrs. Bovary, Charles's mother, had once adored her husband, which irritated him. When she was first married, she was a happy and affectionate woman, but as she was forced to face her husband's infidelities and overindulgences, she became difficult, irritable, and nervous. She swallowed her frustration "in a mute stoicism." Unhappy with her marriage, she spoiled Charles, transferring to him all of her lost ambitions.

She tries to extend her control over Charles after he becomes an adult by choosing his wife. Her control slips, however, when Charles marries Emma, whom Madame Bovary considers "too refined in her airs for their financial position." She also becomes jealous of Charles's love for Emma. In an effort to reassert her dominance, she makes frequent visits to the couple and continually corrects Emma's housekeeping.

Monsieur Léon Dupuis

Emma meets Léon Dupuis, a lawyer's clerk, soon after she and Charles move to Yonville. Léon has the same romantic sensibility as does Emma; his thoughts, like hers, are constantly "interweaving with fiction." He admits to her that his heart "becomes involved" with the characters he reads about, as it "beats underneath their costumes." Emma and Léon feed off each other's romantic imagination as they consummate their relationship. When they link hands, "the past, the future, reminiscences and dreams, all were blended in the charm" of the moment.

Eventually Léon tries to revolt against Emma's absorption of his personality. Yet his timid nature allows her to dominate him, even as his affection for her wanes. Even after he becomes bored by her demands, he is indecisive about their future, allowing her to dictate when and where they meet.

Félicité

Fourteen years old when she comes to work as Emma's maid, Félicité is an orphan "with a sweet face." Emma tries to make a ladies' maid of her and Félicité obeys without question. However, after Emma dies, she steals most of her clothes.

Monsieur Homais

Monsieur Homais, the pharmacist, is the Bovarys' neighbor. The pompous Homais pontificates about religion, society, and human nature, which does not earn him many friends. He tries to hide his illegal medical activities and treats Charles with exceptional kindness in order to ensure that Charles will not turn him in to the authorities. Charles, however, is too unobservant to notice.

Justin

Justin, a boy who works in the pharmacy, falls in love with Emma—so much so that he cannot refuse her when she asks him to let her into the cabinet where Monsieur Homais keeps arsenic.

Madame Lefrançois

Madame Lefrançois, the widowed innkeeper at Yonville, complains and gossips a great deal about her customers.

Monsieur Lheureux

Monsieur Lheureux, Yonville's linen draper, encourages Emma's extravagant spending habits through clever sales tactics. Initially "polite to the point of obsequiousness," Lheureux grovels in front of his customers until he makes a sale. He convinces Emma to purchase expensive items that she cannot afford by preying on her desire for elegance and allowing her to buy on credit. When Emma's bills mount, he demands payment and shows no remorse or consideration for her dilemma.

Themes

Search for Self

When Emma first marries Charles, she does not have a clear sense of identity. However, she knows that she does not want to be stuck on the farm for the rest of her life. Initially, she assumes that what she feels for Charles will develop into love and that she will become content to be a doctor's wife. Soon, though, when her feelings for Charles fail to materialize, she enters into a severe depression, feeling herself to be displaced and unable to endure the monotony of her life and marriage.

Passion

In an effort to alleviate her depression, she turns to sentimental novels, imagining herself as the heroine who falls passionately in love with a dashing man who rescues her from a life of poverty and desperation. Her imagination re-creates these fictional figures into two men, with whom she enters into passionate affairs. Her sexual relations with these men give her a sense of identity, at least for a time.

Class Consciousness

Emma's search for identity and fulfillment also centers on issues of class. Soon after she marries Charles and realizes that she cannot find contentment in her relationship with him, she begins to buy things for the house and for herself. Emma's spending, however, soon puts the family in debt. When she attends the ball at La Vaubyessard, Emma sees for the first time, "the complexion of wealth" that characterizes the upper class. From that point on, Emma desperately tries to become a part of that world through her relationship with Rodolphe and through extravagant purchases.

Emma's desire to move up in class leads to disaster for those around her as well as herself. She transfers her ambitions to Charles, who determines that he can perform a new surgery on clubfoots. However, when he performs the untested operation on a local man, he botches the procedure, which results in the amputation of the patient's leg.

When she realizes that Charles will never help them move above their station, her extravagant spending increases to the point of financial ruin. In a desperate attempt to acquire money and thus to save herself from the public humiliation of the auctioning off of her property, she tries to prostitute herself. When that tactic fails, Emma finds suicide her only recourse. Her death devastates Charles, who dies soon after, and Berthe, their child, becomes orphaned and impoverished.

Style

Structure

Flaubert often illustrates Emma's character and situation through a juxtaposition of scenes in the novel. Most of these instances involve Emma's mingling of past memories with present reality. One occurs when Emma is at the ball. As she looks out the windows and observes the servants on the lawn, separated from the evening's glamour and festivities, she envisions herself "as she had been once" on her father's farm. The juxtaposition of past and present reinforces Emma's obsession with "this luxurious life" that she witnesses at the ball. Another instance occurs when she is looking at Léon one day. As she gazes at him, she conjures an image of Charles as she has seen him so many times in the past. The juxtaposition of her image of Charles with her gaze on Léon prompts her to compare the two. Deciding that Charles is infinitely inferior, she promptly falls in love with Léon.

Flaubert uses a different kind of juxtaposition during the scene at the agricultural fair. Here he jumps back and forth between two simultaneous events: Rodolphe's initial seduction of Emma and the awarding of prizes at the fair. As a result, Flaubert highlights Rodolphe's calculated, self-serving attempt to lure Emma into his bed.

Topics for Further Study

- Watch the 1949 MGM film version of *Madame Bovary*, especially the scene at the ball when Emma is dancing. Choose another scene in the novel that focuses on Emma's passionate nature and describe how you would film it.

- Compare Tolstoy's *Anna Karenina* to Emma, analyzing their motivations and their fate.

- Research the rights of women in France during the mid-nineteenth century. How much freedom and opportunity would a woman like Emma have in that culture?

- Investigate the lives of the French middle class during the nineteenth century. How strict was their class system? What moral standards did they follow?

Symbol

Flaubert also uses symbolization to reinforce his themes. He adds a note of foreshadowing at the ball when Emma sees a guest rumored to have been Marie Antoinette's lover. The description of the slovenly man with bloodshot eyes and "drops of gravy falling from his lips" reinforces the fact that he has "led a life wild with debauch" and forecasts Emma's own decline. In another scene, at the close of the agricultural exposition, the crowd enjoys a display of fireworks. In an effort to allay fears that they might start fires, Monsieur Binet notes that no sparks have fallen. Yet, destruction is eminent for Emma, as her affair with Rodolphe has been sparked.

Historical Context

Realism

The term realism first appeared in a Parisian periodical of 1826, as noted by Haig in his article on Flaubert in the *Dictionary of Literary Biography*. The journalist defines the term as a movement

Compare
&
Contrast

- **Mid-nineteenth century:** In 1835, French philosopher Victor Cousin first uses the phrase "l'Art pour l'Art" ("Art for Art's sake") to define a new literary movement that promotes style over other literary elements. Flaubert is greatly influenced by this movement.

  Today: The confessional narrative gains a prominent position in the literary world.

- **Mid-nineteenth century:** In 1848, the first American convention concerning women's rights is held in Seneca Falls, New York.

  Today: Women have made major gains in their fight for equality and although some bills—like the 1972 Equal Rights Amendment Bill—still have not passed to this day, discrimination against women is now against the law.

- **Mid-nineteenth century:** The Second Empire begins in France in 1852. French social mores, under the leadership of Bonaparte III, include a devotion to a strict moral code, at least in public.

  Today: Some see the election of George W. Bush to the office of president as the result of America's desire to return to a more conservative sense of morality.

---

that would "lead to the imitation not of artistic masterpieces but of the originals that nature offers us." Later in the article, the writer determines that realist works could in the future be considered "the literature of truth." Realism became a popular form of painting, especially in works by Gustave Courbet, and literature in the mid-nineteenth century. Novelists in this movement turned away from what they considered the artificiality of romanticism to a focus on the commonplace in the context of everyday contemporary life. They rejected the idealism and celebration of the imagination typical of romantic novels and instead took a serious look at believable characters and their often problematic interactions with society. In order to accomplish this goal, realistic novels focus on the commonplace and eliminate the unlikely coincidences and excessive emotionalism of romanticism. Novelists like Samuel Clemens discard traditional sentimental novelistic forms as they chronicle the strengths and weaknesses of ordinary people confronting difficult social problems, like the restrictive conventions nineteenth-century African Americans suffered under. Writers who embraced realism use settings and plots details that reflect their characters' daily lives and realistic dialogue that replicates natural speech patterns.

Realism in *Madame Bovary* emerges in Flaubert's discarding of the idealism of traditional romantic literature in his exploration of the day-to-day life of Emma Bovary. Other writers like Honoré Balzac and Stendhal had also focused on the daily life of their characters; however, those characters lead exciting lives and can not be considered "ordinary." Flaubert was one of the first to chronicle in his fiction the often monotonous and sordid life of the middle class.

Censorship in Nineteenth-Century France

France's Second Empire (1852–1870), ruled by Emperor Napoleon Bonaparte III, set a moral tone by repressing challenges to traditional codes of conduct. The government allowed authors to write about characters who threatened the accepted tenets of society; however, they expected the characters to be justly punished for such actions. They supported didactic literature that encouraged readers to condemn immoral behavior, such as adultery. However, when Flaubert refused to denounce Emma in *Madame Bovary* for her actions and Emma herself did not ask for forgiveness, Flaubert was charged with pornography and blasphemy, and the book was banned. All charges against him were eventually dropped and the ban lifted. However, Haig notes that the judge who discharged the case did so with a warning of the excesses of realism, a novelistic form that he considered both "vulgaire et souvent choquant" (vulgar and often shocking). Although Flaubert did not consider himself a realist, critics have placed the novel in this literary school.

Critical Overview

When *Madame Bovary* was published in installments in *Revue de Paris* in 1857, its realistic subject matter earned the novel immediate notoriety, which was enhanced when the French government soon banned it and charged Flaubert with obscenity. Its initial reception was mixed. Many readers were shocked by the novel's "immoral" characterizations but praised Flaubert's undeniable artistry. Others were offended more by the novel's obvious link to realism, as noted by Lennard J. Davis, in his article on Flaubert for *European Writers*. Davis cites one critic who insisted that *Madame Bovary* "represents an obsession with description. Details are counted one by one, all are given equal value" and that, as a result, "there is neither emotion nor feeling for life in this novel." Davis notes another reviewer who claimed that Flaubert was an "unwavering analyst . . . a describer of the minutest subtlety" but that a machine made "in Birmingham or Manchester out of good English steel" could have written a comparable novel. Most scholars, however, have celebrated the work as one of the finest of its age. F. W. J. Hemmings in *The Age of Realism* insists, "this finely balanced mixture, where Emma is concerned of empathy and critical objectivity . . . has earned the novel its celebrity as the first masterpiece of the realist esthetic."

Criticism

Wendy Perkins

Perkins is an associate professor of English and American literature and film at Prince George's Community College and has published several articles on British and American authors. In this essay, she examines Flaubert's exploration of naturalistic themes in Flaubert's novel.

> [The wind-tower] was a giant, standing with its back to the plight of the ants. It represented in a degree . . . the serenity of nature amid the struggles of the individual—nature in the wind, and nature in the vision of men. She did not seem cruel to him then, not benef-

Illustration by Hernan Roundtree from Madame Bovary

icent, not treacherous, not wise. But she was indifferent, flatly indifferent."

This famous passage from Stephen Crane's short story "The Open Boat," which focuses on four men in a small dinghy struggling against the current to make it to shore, is often quoted as an apt expression of the tenets of naturalism, a literary movement that emerged in the late-nineteenth and early-twentieth centuries in France, America, and England. Writers included in this group, such as Crane, Emile Zola, and Theodore Dreiser, expressed in their works a biological and/or environmental determinism that prevented their characters from exercising their free will and thus controlling their fates. Crane often focused on the social and economic factors that overpowered his characters. Zola's and Dreiser's works include this type of environmental determinism, coupled with an exploration of the influences of heredity, in their portraits of the animalistic nature of men and women engaged in the endless and brutal struggle for survival. In *Madame Bovary*, completed in 1856, Gustave Flaubert's treatment of the main character in *Madame Bovary*, proves the novel to be an important precursor of the naturalist movement. As Flaubert explores the environmental and biological

"

Flaubert's compelling portrait of a desperately unfulfilled woman in *Madame Bovary* places the novel firmly in the naturalist tradition as it engages readers in a tragic study of free will and determinism."

forces that shape Emma Bovary's character and experience, he raises important questions about how much influence we have over our destinies.

Two biological factors help determine Emma's fate: her innate sensuality and her romantic imagination. Her sensuality becomes apparent as soon as Charles meets her. As he watches her sew, she pricks her fingers on the needle. Immediately she raises them up to her mouth and sucks them. Later, when they are drinking liquor, she drains her glass and licks, with the tip of her tongue, the final drops. Her passionate nature could have been allowed full expression in marriage and thus resulted in a satisfying relationship and a contented life for Emma. However, Charles's "placid dullness" quickly dampens her passion. She notes that if Charles had been receptive to her spirited nature, "a sudden overflow would have poured from her heart as the ripe fruit falls from a tree when one lays hand to it." She expects him to "initiate [her] into the forces of passion . . . but he taught nothing . . . knew nothing, desired nothing." As a result, Emma could only wonder "just what was meant, in real life, by the words felicity, passion and intoxication, which had seemed so beautiful to her in books."

Emma turns to sentimental novels, with their dashing heroes, in an attempt to imaginatively live the passionate life she desires. Her imagination recreates these fictional figures into two men, with whom she enters into adulterous affairs. Her attraction for Léon turns to love one afternoon as she gazes at him and at the same time conjures an image of Charles as she has seen him so many times in the past. When the juxtaposition of the images of these two men causes her to compare them, Léon emerges as the superior. Thereafter, Léon becomes the focal point for her marital boredom as he reap-

pears in her imagination "taller, more handsome, more polished, more indistinct" than he actually is. Thus, by the time the two are reunited, Emma is primed to fulfill her romantic dream of a passionate relationship with him.

Her imaginative vision of the opera singer becomes the final determining force that propels her into an affair with Léon. As she listens to the singer, his voice "seemed to her no more than the echo of her own consciousness and the illusion which cast its spell over her, something out of her own life." When she sees Léon at the opera, she transfers her feelings for the singer to him, making their union inevitable.

Emma's affair with Rodolphe is sparked by her evening at La Vaubyeeard, where, for the first time, she experiences the intoxicating world of the upper class, a world she wants desperately to make her own. The evening is capped by her waltz with a viscount, which embodies for her the "luxurious life which she must soon abandon." Later, as Rodolphe tries to convince her to give in to her desires, she recalls images of the viscount and of Léon. The juxtaposition of these images with the presence of Rodolphe and his amorous words causes an imaginative fusion for Emma, who is now ready to allow herself to be seduced.

Emma's fate is determined not only by her nature and her vivid imagination. These biological forces combine with environmental factors that help propel Emma to her tragic end. Flaubert notes the social reality of the world Emma is so desperate to enter as he describes the gentlemen seated at the dinner table at La Vaubyeeard: "in their indifferent glances was the serenity of passions daily gratified." Their "brutality" emerges "in fairly unexacting matters where force is employed and in which vanity takes pleasure: the handling of blooded horses and the society of abandoned women."

Rodolphe recognizes Emma as one such "abandoned woman." He callously manipulates her feelings after he determines that she is "gaping for love like a carp on the kitchen table for water." Thus he knows that he will be able to seduce her with loving words and attention. Revealing his self-serving nature, he worries about "how to get rid of her afterwards." Her affair with Rodolphe initially brings her the fulfillment she lacked in her relationship with Charles. However, soon Rodolphe decides that "Emma was like all mistresses; the charm of newness, slipping down little by little like a garment, revealed unclothed the eternal monotony of passion." As a result, he abandons her, leaving her more despondent than she had been before the affair.

Emma's financial situation exacerbates her depression, causing her to spend more extravagantly and thus increasing her debt. Her vision of herself enjoying the comforts of the upper class prompts her to surround herself with artifacts from that world. She notes the lack of control she has over their financial situation and over her romantic imagination when she decides that she would rather have a boy than a girl, since "a man, at least is free . . . but a woman is continually restrained." She insists that a woman is governed by "the fragilities of the flesh and the restrictions of the law. Her will . . . flutters in every wind; there is always some desire urging her on, some convention restraining her."

As in the situation that the men in Crane's open boat discover for themselves, no benevolent force comes to Emma's aid. She feels a sense of abandonment after she tries to talk to the local priest but cannot make him understand her desperate plight. When she tries to explain her unfulfilled needs to him, he insists that all one requires is to be warm and well fed. After Rodolphe leaves her, she again searches for spiritual solace "but no sensation of rapture descended to her from heaven, and she would rise, her legs wearied, with a vague consciousness of having been vastly cheated." Susanna Lee, in her article on the novel for *Symposium*, writes that "God's absence or indifference . . . is a foundational event in *Madame Bovary*, the explicit reason for Emma's contaminated existence."

Emma's passionate nature and her vivid imagination combine with the social forces of her age to determine her fate. As Emma faces the disintegration of her love affair with Léon and the humiliation of her financial situation, she desperately searches for some form of salvation, but can find none. As a result, she determines that her only escape can be through death. Flaubert's compelling portrait of a desperately unfulfilled woman in *Madame Bovary* places the novel firmly in the naturalist tradition as it engages readers in a tragic study of free will and determinism.

Source: Wendy Perkins, Critical Essay on *Madame Bovary*, in *Novels for Students*, The Gale Group, 2002.

William C. VanderWolk

In the following essay, VanderWolk examines the "considerations of gender" in Madame Bovary

What Do I Read Next?

- Flaubert's heartwarming short story "Un coeur simple," collected in *Trois Contes* (1977), has been celebrated for its realistic portrait of human dignity and compassion.

- In *L'Education sentimentale*, published in 1869, Flaubert presents his assessment of his generation in the story of Frédéric Moreau and his friends in Paris during the 1840s.

- *Politics, Culture, and Class in the French Revolution* (1984), written by Lynn Hunt, offers a comprehensive overview of French culture during and after the Revolution.

- In *Anna Karenina*, published in 1877, Leo Tolstoy chronicles the passion and tragic fate of his married heroine as she enters into an affair with a dashing officer.

---

to identify Flaubert's views on masculine versus feminine writing.

Questions of gender in recent French literary criticism have generally been posed by feminist critics. Writers such as Hélène Cixous, Julia Kristeva, and Luce Irigaray have pointed out that men do not need to pose such questions, as they are already in possession of the dominant language system. "What does it mean to write as a woman or to read as a woman?" has been a common question in feminist criticism whether one speaks of a feminist critique, a *Female Aesthetic*, gynocritics, or gynesis. Male critics have indeed rarely felt the need to formally pose such a question, but with the rise of gender theory, the comparative study of sexual difference, men have felt empowered to ask: "What does it mean to write as a man or to read as a man?" All of this is complicated by the question of essentialism and the debate over whether or not critics should distinguish between male and female modes of writing and reading. All anti-essentialist feeling rejects biological sex as the determining factor in writing or reading. Yet even after one eliminates biological sex as a consideration, the masculine/feminine opposition does not disappear. Feminists in particular continue to struggle with the question of whether it is best to assimilate or differentiate feminist views from the mainstream, whether to identify an "écriture féminine" or aspire to an "écriture" that would be equally accessible to women. The most fruitful avenue of exploration seems to be to raise questions of gender, both biological and non-biological, and asking such questions may, after all, be the most significant contribution of feminist criticism to the study of literature.

Writers as diverse as Jean de Meung, Christine de Pisan, Marguerite de Navarre, Rousseau, Stendhal, and Balzac have debated various influences—positive and negative—of women writers and readers in particular. The twentieth century has expanded and heightened the discussion, in both intellectual and emotional terms. In this paper, I will examine Gustave Flaubert's thinking about the problem of masculine versus feminine writing to show that many of the questions pertinent today were being asked over a century ago by an author whose misogyny today's feminists would find reprehensible. While Flaubert was concerned with maintaining a "masculine" style, a stylistic study of his writing yields less than a thematic one. It is in the very threads of Flaubert's story that we find categories of sexual difference which give rise to the questions we are highlighting here. A brief examination of considerations of gender in *Madame Bovary* will show how Flaubert attempted to put his views into literary practice and will underline the importance of the questions raised for twentieth-century gender criticism.

In a letter to his longtime lover, Louise Colet, Flaubert declares: "Je suis un homme-plume. Je sens par elle, à cause d'elle, par rapport à elle et beaucoup plus avec elle." "Homme and "plume" are key words in the formulation of Flaubert's aesthetic, for they represent the author in his entirety. The man—and I think we must read the masculine into this term rather than the generic "man"—would not exist without the pen—this is a common thread throughout Flaubert's correspondence. But just as importantly, the pen's existence depends on the man, the essentially masculine man who controls the language system. Flaubert was keenly aware of the role of gender in writing, and he used male images to describe the writing process: "Cet homme qui se dit si calme est plein de doutes sur lui-même. Il voudrait savoir jusqu'à quel cran il peut monter et la puissance exacte de ses muscles. Mais demander cela, c'est être bien ambitieux, car la connaissance précise de sa force n'est peut-être autre que le génie." This notion of strength is seen in Flaubert's development of an impersonal style: "Rappelons-nous toujours que l'impersonnalité est le signe de la Force." "Homme" and "plume" thus become inextricable forces in an aesthetic based on the assumption of male ownership of the pen.

Flaubert's correspondence reveals him to be a misogynist, his reflections on women and sex consisting mainly of vulgarities transmitted to male friends and condescending homilies sent to Louise Colet. Sartre points out that for Flaubert, "comme pour ses amis, la copulation est éminemment publique; les filles sont propriété collective, on partouse, on se raconte grossièrement les parties de jambes en l'air, on se communique les bonnes adresses." Despite such stereotypical male attitudes, however, and perhaps because of them, Flaubert was deeply concerned with questions of gender difference when it came to literary creation. He writes, "j'aime les phrases mâles et non les phrases femelles comme celles de Lamartine", and though we can imagine what he means, Flaubert never specifically spells it out.

Ironically, the most powerful character to emerge from this fundamentally masculine enterprise was a female, Emma Bovary. In creating his heroine, Flaubert was forced to examine how a male creates a female character and how much transference took place between himself and Emma. Baudelaire immediately recognized the male in Emma, calling her androgyny her greatest strength as a literary character, "une âme virile dans un charmant corps féminin." While Emma is indeed androgynous, we can say the same for her creator. While he has infused his character with a masculine part of himself, he has in turn assumed a certain female sensibility in his characterization and even his most sacredly impersonal language. Paradoxically, then, Flaubert would seem to be the kind of androgynous writer feminist theorists have idealized yet without any of the sensibilities feminists attach to their notion of such a writer.

Flaubert was acutely aware of his emotional involvement with his character, and he occasionally found himself almost physically ill after a difficult passage. He writes to Louise Colet:

> Il faut t'aimer pour t'écrire ce soir, car je suis épuisé. J'ai un casque de fer sur le crâne. Depuis deux heures de l'après-midi, j'écris de la "Bovary." Je suis à la

Baisade, en plein, au milieu. On sue et on a la gorge serrée. Voilà une des rares journées de ma vie que j'ai passée dans l'Illusion, complètement, et depuis un bout jusqu'à l'autre. Tantôt à six heures, au moment où j'écrivais le mot "attaque de nerfs," j'étais si emporté, je gueulais si fort, et sentais si profondément ce que ma petite femme éprouvait, que j'ai eu peur moi-mâme d'en avoir une.

Flaubert has invested himself in the novel through identification with Emma. He is polymorphic as well as androgynous. The fictive illusion captures him as do the fictive illusions of Emma's reading. Yet the misogyny remains very much in evidence in a term such as "ma petite femme." There exists at once sameness and difference, and the feminine Other Flaubert finds within himself bears no resemblance to the other woman Hélène Cixous describes: "There always remains in woman that force which produces/is produced by the other—in particular, the other woman . . . Text: my body—shot through with streams of song; I don't mean the overbearing, clutchy "mother" but, rather, what touches you, the equivoice that affects you, fills your breast with an urge to come to language and launches your force . . . that part of you that leaves a space between yourself and urges you to inscribe in language your woman's style." Everything is different/difference here between Flaubert's Other and Cixous's as well as between their conception of "force" in writing. And the difference does not stem solely from biological considerations but is seated in the fabric of writing itself. Flaubert is concerned with the preservation of the dominance of male over female, whether in the conception of a Romantic heroine or the formulation of a writing style. Cixous, on the other hand, proposes that a woman can write with a force equal to the male's. Flaubert's "androgyny," then, is a false one, as his incorporation in his character remains incomplete. Yet we must be careful not to dismiss the emotional input of the author, for it is significantly sexually inflected, and it raises questions of gender in our minds as well as Flaubert's.

Emma's well-documented projection into the literary characters she envies is not accompanied by any of the defenses Flaubert provides for himself when he projects himself into his character. In her utter reliance on the validity of literature, she loses herself in the illusions of metaphor, what René Girard calls "external mediation." Despite Flaubert's complete dispersal of self into every element—human and natural—of his scene, he is still conscious of the fiction: "Mais je redoute le réveil, les désillusions des pages recopiées." Taken

> **Flaubert was acutely aware of his emotional involvement with his character, and he occasionally found himself almost physically ill after a difficult passage."**

into the seduction scene during the act of creation, Flaubert the artist still realizes he must go through the work of revision. After allowing the restraints of self to be broken, Flaubert returns to assert his mastery over the written word. The illusion of immediacy and immersion is broken. Fiction is no longer authentic life; he is no longer seduced by the metaphor. This is the ultimate masculine act, the immersion in language, the realm of the Father.

Emma, whose lack of gender definition has been noted, finds her downfall in her inability to leave fiction, especially a fiction she has entered after the very seduction scene Flaubert has just described writing. Lucette Czyba has noted this dichotomy between Flaubert's and Emma's relation to fiction. Czyba sees the writing of *Madame Bovary* as a "dépassement" of Flaubert's romantic youth. "Le texte ne reproduit pas en effet passivement les thèmes anesthésiants de l'idéologie dont l'héroïne est victime mais les présente de façon à produire activement les conditions d'une lecture démystificatrice." Emma's attitude, however, is "'romantique' car elle conserve l'illusion d'éprouver des désirs spontanés alors qu'ils sont en fait médiatisés." Emma's incorporation into fantasy is a complete metamorphosis. Her present and her past are part of the metaphor. Yet her fictive world eventually disintegrates. The very scene in which her mental illusions are destroyed is also, like the seduction scene, one which demonstrates Flaubert's dispersal into the novel.

Rejected by Rodolphe, ignored by Léon, all Emma has left is the memory of her loves. Forced into recognizing that her literary models have failed her, she experiences an *attaque de nerfs* that resembles Flaubert's own nervous attacks which began in early 1844. In a letter to Hippolyte Taine,

Flaubert described those attacks as "une maladie de la mémoire, un relâchement de ce qu'elle recèle. On sent les images s'échapper de vous comme des flots de sang." Flaubert's description of Emma's attack echoes his own: "elle ne souffrait que de son amour, et sentait son âme l'abandonner par ce souvenir, comme les blessés, en agonisant, sentent l'existence qui s'en va par leur plaie qui saigne."

Association between the open wounds and death is deliberate on Flaubert's part; if Flaubert's own attacks signaled a possibility of literal death, Emma's attacks correspond to the death of her fictional self. The distinct images of Emma's memory explode "à la fois, d'un seul bond, comme les mille pièces d'un feu d'artifice." She is fragmented, a disassociated body. Her memory has become divorced from herself, and without her fictive models or her memory, she no longer has the assurance of identity. Emma's body is divorced from the body's experience and from language. Lacan's theory of the fragmented body describes this process at separation: "This experience (when the body senses its split from the Real) can neither be included in the Imaginary, the realm of illusory wholeness, nor can it be part of the Symbolic, the domain which grants a conditional identity. The traumatic moment can thus return in psychosis as the experience of the 'fragmented body', unique for every subject, remainder and reminder of this fracture, appearing in art as images of grotesque dismemberment." Emma feels herself fragmenting, and language fails to prevent it from happening. Without the prerogative of the masculine, i.e., writing, Emma is condemned to fragmentation.

Critics such as Michal Peled Ginsburg see Emma's downfall more in her inability to narrate than in her immersion in literary reverie. If Emma were able to tell her story as other Flaubertian characters have (*Mémoires d'un fou*, *Novembre*, *La Tentation de Saint Antoine*), she would be conscious of the repetitive nature of her experience and would then have the power to escape the complete immobility in which she finds herself. Ginsburg writes: "Emma dreams not too much but too little—too little not in terms of the practical welfare of a provincial woman but in terms of the possibility of creating fiction, of coming into being as a narrator." Flaubert thus keeps Emma in a woman's place, in silence.

Marguerite Duras generalizes this idea of men imposing silence on women: "The silence in women is such that anything that falls into it has an enor-

mous reverberation. Whereas in men, this silence no longer exists . . . Because men have established the principle of virile force. And everything that emerged from this virile force—including words, unilateral words—reinforced the silence of women. In my opinion, women have never expressed themselves." Yet Emma's silence has repercussions that go beyond the simple recognition of women's silence. Emma is not simply a woman who does not write; she is a fictional character whose creator does not permit her to do so. By looking at some of her attempts to write, we may better understand Flaubert's motives.

Emma, while dreaming of becoming a famous novelist, writes only letters to her lovers. As Naomi Schor has pointed out, Emma's letter writing goes through three stages. At first, Emma writes letters in order to receive letters from her lovers. She takes "pleasure in the communication forbidden, impossible on the speech plane." Emma later uses her correspondence in an attempt to revive a waning passion: ". . . dans les lettres qu'Emma lui envoyait, il était question de fleurs, de vers, de la lune et des étoiles, ressources naïves d'une passion affaiblie, qui essayait de s'aviver à tous les secours extérieurs." Finally, when Emma sees in Léon only the same emptiness she found in her husband, she attempts to remystify him in writing: ". . . en écrivant, elle percevait un autre homme, un fantôme fait de ses plus ardents souvenirs, de ses lectures les plus belles, de ses convoitises les plus fortes." Emma the writer thus remains as ineffectual as the women Hélène Cixous describes who write in secret because they are ashamed, because writing is "reserved for the great—that is for 'great men'." By the end of this third stage, Emma no longer writes in hopes of having a letter in return; she writes to purge herself of the monotony of her life.

Schor concludes her analysis of Emma's writing by claiming that on one level, at least, Emma triumphs over Homais and comes to represent Flaubert's view that writing has a feminine sex:

> It is not by chance that the writing apprenticeship and the 'virility apprenticeship,' if I may call it that, follow paths which ultimately converge at the time of Emma's affair with Léon, for their affair marks the triumph of the imaginary over the real, this being the precondition of all writing. If, insofar as the effect *on* the real is concerned, Homais' writing surpasses Emma's; considered in terms of the 'reality effect,' it is without any doubt Emma's (Flaubert's) writing that surpasses Homais' for the 'reality effect' can only be achieved through a total renunciation of any real satisfaction, can only be the just reward of sub-

limation, i.e., castration. For Flaubert writing thus has a sex, the sex of an assumed lack, the feminine sex."

If we reconsider "the triumph of the imaginary over the real" as an essential precondition of writing, Schor's conclusion can be brought into question. It the imaginary is seen as stemming from the collection of experiences each author has in his or her memory, then we could say that the triumph of memory over the real is the essential precondition of writing. And since Emma's memories focus largely on works of literature, for her—and I submit for Flaubert—writing retains the masculine-coded connotation it has traditionally had. Writing thus does not represent a lack, but a fulfillment in the transformation of memory into language. Flaubert's desire to write "des phrases mâles" is representative of his desire to translate his memories into writing.

Flaubert, unlike Emma, captures his memories and activates them in his literary creation. According to Charles Bernheimer, Flaubert creates "with the blood issuing from the wound of memory, be it Emma's, his own, or the accumulated archival memory of the nineteenth century." Flaubert thus escapes the fate he has prepared for his main character. By dispersing himself throughout his fiction, Flaubert becomes an integral part of each work. He becomes his own reader as he grapples with his memories, and in a sense becomes the hero of his own work. Victor Brombert surely speaks for many readers when he writes: "A curious symbiotic relationship exists between Flaubert and his heroine. The novelist . . . draws his fictional creature toward himself, and discovers himself in Emma even more than he projects himself into her . . . [Flaubert] is to some extent playing hide and seek with himself." This relationship between author and character is not as curious as it seems when one takes gender into account. Flaubert is fascinated by Emma's femaleness, just as he endows her with a certain maleness. As we have seen, he does not allow Emma to win the game of hide and seek that he is playing not only with himself but with her, but if he did not let her play, she would lose much of her force as a character.

If Flaubert is the hero of his own work, then he must necessarily be a reader of himself, creating a new relationship between author and reader. Marcel Proust's observation "En réalité chaque lecteur est quand il lit le propre lecteur de soi-même" remains true, but the author has added himself to our numbers. By doing so, he allows the reader to share his memories, and in a sense to become a collaborator of the work. Fusion of author and character results in a fraternity between author and reader which allows the reader to find truth and beauty in the universal. For Flaubert, this universal is decidedly masculine-tinted for it can be attained only through the strength of masculine prose (presumably, Lamartine would be excluded).

Reader/writer/participant/reader once again—these are all facets of the man who was in constant pursuit of truth, beauty, and self-understanding. Flaubert never allowed his character to escape her *bovarysme* because he never allowed her to discover the unifying process of the artist. In 1852 he sent this very Baudelairian statement to Louise Colet: "Ne faut-il pas pour être artiste, voir tout d'une façon différente à celle des autres hommes?". Flaubert's characters were among the "autres hommes" whose view of the world and whose goals were often different from the artist's. Their search for self-understanding was invariably derailed by an equally strong desire for happiness, a goal of second rank in Flaubert's hierarchy: "Ne sens-tu pas qu'il y a quelque chose de plus élevé que le bonheur? que l'amour et que la Religion, parce qu'il prend sa source dans un ordre plus impersonnel? . . . Je veux dire l'idée." The artist is able to accomplish what his characters cannot: he can transfer his memories and personal preoccupations into writing, and by reading the idea of himself which he has created, he can better understand himself.

This last statement must, however, be viewed in the context of Flaubert's own terminology as it pertains to gender, for otherwise it would be incomplete. He writes of these "autres hommes," a group into which I have placed his characters, including Emma Bovary. Although I have attributed to her certain masculine traits, she is decidedly female. Going one step further, if we ignore the physical sex of these "autres hommes" for a moment, is Flaubert not indeed referring to those who are not artists and therefore not controllers of language, i.e., females? Is not the list of things that Flaubert disdains—happiness, love, and religion—an enumeration of interests that nineteenth-century French society assigned primarily to women? And finally, in distancing himself from anything personal, is Flaubert not trying to eliminate the feminine from his writing? Flaubert was a man writing with the force of a man for an audience of men who presumably would best understand his work. (He always had his male friends, Alfred Le Poittevin or Louis Bouilhet, critique his work, rather than Louise Colet. He preferred to critique hers.) Yet his

Louis Jourdan as Rodolphe Boulanger and Jennifer Jones as Emma Bovary in the 1949 film version of the novel

encounter with Emma Bovary clouded the waters somewhat for him, and he was forced to reexamine his position, even though he did not fundamentally change it.

Flaubert's notion of the idea ("Idée") is clearly linked to his fascination with the power ("Force") of writing, the strength so closely gender-identified with the masculine. His correspondence describes this "Idée" not as an idea, for Flaubert even writes that he is not much interested in ideas, but rather as an integral part of style: ". . . l'âme courbée se déploie dans cet azur, qui ne s'arrête qu'aux frontières du Vrai. Où la Forme, en effet, manque, l'Idée n'est plus." The composing of *Madame Bovary* was Flaubert's conscious attempt to eliminate all but "la Forme," to write his "livre sur rien." Even though he is unable to succeed in such an undertaking, it is important that he was always conscious of his stated goal. Even if Emma Bovary shares some of herself with Flaubert, and even if the text writes its author as much as the author writes it, Flaubert never ceased to write the masculine, attempting to eliminate "les phrases femelles" and all attachment to anything outside the cherished "Idée."

Flaubert's concept of writing presents a direct contrast to modern-day feminist theories of feminine writing. For Hélène Cixous, for example, "l'écriture féminine" is located in a realm where all difference has been abolished. There are no rigid boundaries of style because writing is a never-ending process:

> The book—I could reread it with the help of memory and forgetting. Start over again. From another perspective, from another and yet another. Reading, I discovered that writing is endless. Everlasting. Eternal.

> Writing or God. God the writing. The writing God.

Although there is no difference here, it is still the realm of the omnipotent, represented for Cixous by the omnipotent mother. Thus it is that writing, while emanating from a sexless world, can, for Cixous, be gender-identified as feminine; hence the appellation "l'écriture féminine."

In light of definitions of "l'écriture féminine," what then is the place of Flaubert's "écriture masculine" in the history of literary criticism? Certainly, since the rise of feminist criticism, style based solely on a masculine conception of strength has been roundly condemned. And yet some of the more forceful proponents of a new writing that might be considered genderless call for just such a strong language, but one that will not be limited to males. Kristeva speaks of a "spasmodic force" of the unconscious which disrupts women's language because of their strong links with the pre-Oedipal mother-figure. Yet it is actually disrupting the traditional male-dominated system of language and, far from weakening feminine writing, strengthens it from within the system. "For Kristeva . . . there is a *specific practice of writing* that is itself 'revolutionary', analogous to sexual and political transformation, and that by its very existence testifies to the possibility of transforming the symbolic order from the inside." An author's biological sex is thus secondary to the subject position she or he takes up in determining revolutionary potential.

Certain patterns appear throughout the feminist aesthetic which help shed light on our discussion of Flaubert's view of language in relation to twentieth-century critics. First, we see as a given of feminist theory a rejection of the appropriation of language. The goal is to carve out a place for women's writing, inside or outside of the established order. Second, women's writing squarely places itself in the sociopolitical arena. One cannot discuss women's writing without examining its revolutionary effects outside the world of literature.

Finally, for Kristeva and others, gender distinctions disappear. There is no longer any "écriture féminine" or "écriture masculine," only "écriture."

We seem to have come full circle here. For it could be argued that before feminist criticism there was only "écriture." The radical difference, of course, is that this previous writing was generally written by males for a public subsumed in a male-dominant society. Literature by and for females could not be taken quite as seriously. Flaubert wrote according to that essentially male model, but he was not totally comfortable with the assumption of the masculine in his writing. He had to prove constantly to himself that his language was sufficiently "male," so that he would not fall into the trap of Romanticism, into the "female" phrases of Lamartine. Flaubert would certainly have been aghast at the feminine writing proposed by Cixous, for he was fighting to conserve and perfect the traditional Symbolic order.

It would be an injustice to see Flaubert as simply a proponent of male dominance. While he stands for the system feminists are resisting, he was open to questions of gender in the creative process. From a non-gender-identified writing came a style that was consciously male. At the same time, he became aware of the dangers of such a fundamental strategy. Emma Bovary taught him the power of the feminine and allowed him to see himself as he never had before. Flaubert opened a debate that would soon be taken up by Zola in his criticism of Hugo and would continue throughout the Naturalist and Symbolist periods.

Flaubert's world, a world of men, by men, and for men, is not likely to return, precisely because male ownership of language can no longer be taken for granted. Yet through his struggle to preserve that domain, Flaubert necessarily gained consciousness of its arbitrariness. By posing questions concerning gender, Flaubert unwittingly contributed to the evolution of viable alternatives to writing the masculine.

Source: William C. VanderWolk, "Writing the Masculine: Gender and Creativity in *Madame Bovary*," in *Romance Quarterly*, Vol. 37, No. 2, May 1990, pp. 147–56.

Sources

Davis, Lennard J., "Gustave Flaubert," in *European Writers*, Vol. 7, Scribner's, 1985, pp. 1373–94.

Haig, Stirling, "Gustave Flaubert," in *Dictionary of Literary Biography*, Volume 119: *Nineteenth-Century French Fiction Writers: Romanticism and Realism, 1800–1860*, Gale Research, 1992, pp. 120–51.

Hemmings, F. W. J., ed., *The Age of Realism*, Penguin, 1974.

Lee, Susanna, "Flaubert's Blague Supérieure: The Secular World of *Madame Bovary*," in *Symposium*, Vol. 54, No. 4, Winter 2001, pp. 203–17.

For Further Reading

Ginsburg, Michal Peled, *Flaubert Writing: A Study in Narrative Strategies*, Stanford University Press, 1986.
    Ginsburg presents a penetrating analysis of the structure and style of Flaubert's work.

Green, Anne, *Flaubert and the Historical Novel*, Cambridge University Press, 1982.
    Green places the novel into its historical and cultural context.

Knight, Diana, *Flaubert and the Historical Novel*, Cambridge University Press, 1985.
    Knight presents a comprehensive psychological study of Emma Bovary and compares her to Flaubert's other characters.

Levin, Harry, *The Gates of Horn: A Study of Five French Realists*, Oxford University Press, 1963.
    Levin places the novel in the realist tradition and compares it to other works in this movement.

Margret Howth:
A Story of To-Day

Rebecca Harding Davis

1862

Margret Howth: A Story of To-Day, published in 1862 in Boston, was Rebecca Harding Davis's second widely acknowledged work, and her first novel. Set in an Indiana mill town during the fall and winter of 1860, it depicts the suffering of the working poor at a time when industrialization was growing across America.

During the time Davis wrote, the society she lived in was divided into areas of activity that were considered appropriate for men, or for women. Women were expected to take care of home and family; men were expected to attend to the world of ideas, politics, and money. Writing books was considered to be a male activity, and women who wanted to be authors, like Davis, were expected to write "moral" fiction: fiction that educated, elevated, and promoted religious values.

However, some writers, such as Davis, preferred to present uncouth, sinful, or "low" characters, who were generally ordinary, poor, and flawed people. This realistic fiction was intended to be the opposite of popular nineteenth-century fiction, which presented strong heroes, beautiful heroines, and romantic plots. Davis managed to fit her depiction of unattractive, sinful, and flawed people within the social ideal that women write moral fiction by using her stories to examine social and religious issues—and to bring up moral questions. She writes at the beginning of the book:

> "You want something . . . to lift you out of this crowded, tobacco-stained commonplace, to kindle and chafe and glow in you. I want you to dig into

this commonplace, this vulgar American life, and see what is in it. Sometimes I think it has a new and awful significance that we do not see."

Margret Howth was first published in six installments in the *Atlantic Monthly* beginning in October, 1861. At the request of her editor, James Fields, Davis rewrote the novel to make the ending happier. Although she was disappointed with the necessity of doing this to make the book more agreeable to the public, she had faith that Fields was probably right.

According to Jane Atteridge Rose in *Rebecca Harding Davis*, the book has been called "the earliest realistic depiction of an American woman as an individual and as ordinary." Jean Fagan Yellin, in her afterword to the Feminist Press edition of the novel, wrote that "readers immediately recognized" the significance of the book, and that critics commented on Davis's revealing "the fictional possibilities in people who had been presumed to be inarticulate, or whom economic or social oppression had submerged."

Author Biography

Rebecca Harding Davis was born Rebecca Harding on June 24, 1831, at her aunt's home in Washington, Pennsylvania, and soon was taken to the family home in Big Spring, Alabama (later renamed Huntsville), where she would become the oldest of five children. Although they only lived there until Davis was five, Davis later remembered her mother's description of "the mixed magnificence and squalor of the life on the plantations among which we lived; the great one-storied wooden houses built on piles; the pits of mud below them in which pigs wallowed," according to Jan Atteridge Rose in *Rebecca Harding Davis*.

In 1837, the Hardings moved to Wheeling, West Virginia, a steel-manufacturing town. Wheeling was a prosperous, diverse place, a center for new immigrants looking for work and for those who wanted to migrate farther west. Her experiences in Wheeling would provide characters and incidents that would recur, with little alteration, in much of her fiction.

Davis was educated at home by her mother. She was an avid reader, although her reading was limited, for the most part, to the Bible and works by John Bunyan, Sir Walter Scott, and Miss Edgeworth. She also read several stories by Hawthorne, which impressed her deeply because instead of

writing about knights, fairies, and magical events, he took ordinary people and events and made them seem magical. Many years later, she realized how deeply his vision and sensibility affected her.

She attended Washington Female Seminary in Pennsylvania, where she was exposed to antislavery lectures and radical reformers. After she had attended for three years, her education was over; more education was unthinkable for a young woman of her time. Although she did not marry, she remained in her parents' house, taking care of younger siblings and doing the housework. She continued to read widely, using her father's library and the textbooks her brother, Wilson, brought home from college. In the late 1850s she began publishing reviews, poetry, stories, and editorials in the *Wheeling Intelligencer*, and in 1859, she briefly worked as its editor.

During this time she also took long walks, keenly observing everyone she saw—a range of people that apparently included "thieves, convicts, prostitutes, drunks, addicts, and suicides," according to Rose.

In 1861, her first work, "Life in the Iron Mills," was published in the *Atlantic Monthly*. Noted for the "bold authority" in its description of impoverished iron workers, according to Rose, the book "exploded with a force that shook America's Eastern intellectual community to its foundation" with its realistic treatment of unpleasant subjects and situations.

James T. Fields, co-owner of Ticknor and Fields publishers, as well as editor of the *Atlantic*, asked Davis to write another piece, but requested that this one be less depressing than "Life in the Iron Mills." He rejected *Margret Howth* at first because it was still too sad, and Davis rewrote it to satisfy him, with what Rose described as a "happy ending in which the ambitious and egoistic male becomes domesticated and the self-sacrificing female is fulfilled through marriage." According to Rose, the book has been described as "the earliest realistic description of an American woman as an individual and as ordinary."

Because of the book's success, Davis was invited to Fields's home in Boston to meet other well-known writers of the time. After this visit, she stopped in Philadelphia to meet Lemuel Clarke Davis, a lawyer who had written to her about her work "Life in the Iron Mills." The two fell in love and were engaged during her visit. On March 5, 1863, they were married. They had three children, Richard Harding, Charles Belmont, and Nora. Eventually, Richard Harding Davis's career as a journalist and writer would overshadow his mother's.

Davis went on to write several novels and story collections, which are regarded as a form of "spiritual activism," according to Michele L. Mock in *NWSA Journal*, and as a form of pioneer American realistic fiction. She died on September 29, 1910, in Mount Kisco, New York, of edema of the lungs caused by heart disease.

Plot Summary

Chapters I–II

Margret Howth: A Story of To-Day opens as Margret Howth begins her new job working on the ledgers at Knowles & Company woolen mill, owned by Dr. Knowles. The job is dreary, lonely, and depressing; she works alone, in a dirty room high in the mill; on the floors below, workers slave in suffocating heat and deafening noise, amid the caustic fumes of dyes. She has taken the job to make money to take care of her impoverished parents; her father, a former schoolteacher, has gone blind and can no longer support the family. At the end of the day she returns to the family home, a formerly comfortable place that is now spare, since she and her mother have sold everything valuable in order to buy food.

Dr. Knowles, the owner of the mill, follows her. He has a grand scheme in mind, and he has been watching Margret to see how she will fit into it. He is also friends with her father, and spends time with him, arguing politics. Margret notices that the doctor is watching her, as he has watched her for her whole life, "with a kind of savage scorn," but doesn't know why he does so. His grand plan is to sell the mill and use the money to found a commune, where he will take ex-slaves, alcoholics, and all other downtrodden people, and teach them self-reliance and self-worth. All will live on an even footing with the others, and the community will be based on "perpetual celibacy, mutual trust, honour," and individuals will "rise according to the stuff that's in them." And, he hopes, Margret will work on this plan with him.

Lois Yare, a mixed-race woman who is deformed from rickets—a disease caused by malnutrition—and who has suffered brain damage, comes to the door. She began working at the mill when she was seven years old, but because of her condition couldn't keep up with the work. She left the mill, planning never to go back, and became a peddler of fruits and vegetables. She is a kind, optimistic, and loving person, and everyone she meets can't help but be kind to her; she believes that everything will be right someday—if not here, then in heaven—and that even among the poorest people, there are some who are "the Master's people," meaning children of Christ. Her mother was an alcoholic and her father, Joe Yare, is a thief, but she has never let her poor origins, or her physical suffering, affect her outlook. She tells the Howths that her father has just gotten out of jail, news that she's delighted about. He will be working as a stoker in the mill.

Chapters III–VII

The next day, Margret goes to work again. She thinks about her lost love, Stephen Holmes, an entrepreneur. She was once engaged to him, but the wedding was called off when she had to begin taking care of her aging and impoverished parents. She hears him walk past the room where she sits reconciling the mill's books, but he doesn't stop, and she thinks he doesn't know she's inside. He is now engaged to Miss Herne, the intelligent but unpleasant daughter of the man who is co-owner of the mill with Dr. Knowles. He admits that he doesn't love her, but without her money he can't realize his ambition of owning his own factory some day. When he walks past the room where Margret is working, he does know she's inside, and he misses her, but he thinks it's better if he doesn't speak to her anymore, because it will be too painful for both of them.

Holmes plans to buy Dr. Knowles's share in the mill, using money his future father-in-law will give him. One of the workers at the mill, a coaldigger, meets Holmes and asks him if he will do a favor for Lois's father, Joe. Holmes and the worker are the only two people who know Yare was involved in a forgery. If Holmes keeps quiet about it, Yare won't go back to jail and can clean up his life and move on. Holmes, however, says it's not up to him: Yare broke the law, so he must pay the consequences.

While Holmes is riding in a carriage with Miss Herne, they see Margret, and he decides that before he marries Miss Herne, he will talk to Margret one more time. He goes to her and tells her he always loved her, but that love kept him from realizing his ambition in life. As he talks, he realizes that ambition is nothing, and begs her to take him back. She is disgusted by that fact that he put power before love, and refuses. He tells her "I will wait for you yonder [in Heaven] if I die first," and she admits that she loves him too, despite her refusal.

Dr. Knowles finds Margret and tells her he wants to show her "a bit of hell: outskirt." He takes her to a mission house, where prostitutes, gamblers, vagabonds, runaway slaves, ragged children, and other poor and forgotten people live, and tells her ironically, "it's a glimpse of the under-life of America—God help us!—where all men are born free and equal." He asks if she will join him in working for them, and tells her that God is calling her to this work. This is why he has been watching her all her life—to assess her fitness and see if she can fit into his grand plan. She doesn't give him an answer, however.

Chapters VIII–XI

Holmes goes to the mill, where Joe Yare begs him not to tell anyone about the forgery. Holmes, again, refuses to keep the secret. That night, while Holmes is sleeping in the mill, Yare sets it on fire. Yare's daughter, Lois, knowing Holmes is upstairs, runs into the burning building and saves him, but not before she inhales a deadly dose of toxic fumes from the burning dye vats.

Holmes lives, but his dream of wealth and power is destroyed. So is Dr. Knowles's dream, since the mill burned down before they could conclude the sale, and now he has no money to build his commune and achieve his grand scheme of becoming a famous reformer. He devotes himself to simpler acts of charity at the mission house.

Holmes recuperates in bed. His body heals, but his spirit feels sick as he thinks about how materialistic he was, how ready he was to deny love and marry a woman he despised just to get money. He is inspired by Lois's pure faith to reconsider his life and how he has wasted it, but realizes it's not too late to make amends. He asks Margret to marry him, and she accepts. Knowles is deeply disappointed, since he thought she was going to work with him at the mission, but in the end, Margret's life as Holmes's wife fills her with such happiness that she is completely fulfilled. In a surprising event that ties up the one remaining loose end, the poverty Margret's family has endured is suddenly ended when oil is discovered on the Howth property.

Characters

Miss Herne

Miss Herne is the daughter of the man who is co-owner (with Dr. Knowles) of the weaving mill. She is engaged to Stephen Holmes, who plans to marry her to get her father's money. She is attractive, with light blue eyes and blond hair, but has what Davis describes as a "cheap, tawdry intellect," and a sharp, sarcastic tongue that has given her a reputation of being "brilliant" and a "fine talker." She is shallow, and wears a great deal of perfume, which Holmes is disgusted by; he compares it to the stench of the mill. Her fine dress and educated talk only thinly mask the fact that she has no substance—no depth. She has had an easy life and is not reflective by nature; when she sees people, she doesn't think of them as real people with troubles and joys, but only as good-looking or ugly, well-dressed or badly dressed. She isn't interested in love, but believes Holmes is infatuated with her, and enjoys the sense of power over him that this gives her. She views him as her future slave, but on the surface, acts feminine and fluttery. Holmes, reflecting on his engagement to her, thinks, "That nerveless, spongy hand,—what a death-grip it had on his life!"

Stephen Holmes

Stephen Holmes is young, good-looking, on his way up in the world, and talented. He is a self-made entrepreneur, and although he is capable of acts of kindness, such as giving Lois Yare a cart so that she can start up her own business, he is cynical about love. When he is told that "God is love," he responds, "Was He? No wonder, then, He was the God of women, and children and unsuccessful men." He believes he can be his own savior and that people should be responsible for themselves, not rely on God to make things right. His plan is to make a lot of money and eventually move back East, where he feels more comfortable.

Holmes is a quiet man, and perhaps because of this, others seek him out to tell him their troubles; Davis describes him as "one of those men who are unwillingly masters among men," a born leader. However, Davis implies that this popularity is largely because he's perceived as a "go-getter" and people are impressed by this, and by the fact that he is expected to become rich. Tellingly, she notes that beggars don't bother to ask him for anything, because they know he won't help them.

Holmes was once betrothed to Margret Howth, but gives up his betrothal when her father goes blind and she has to stay home and take care of him. Holmes plans instead to marry Miss Herne, whose father is co-owner of the mill with Dr. Knowles. If he marries her, he will get her father's money, which he can then use to fund his ambition to own his own factory someday. He doesn't love Miss Herne, but feels that dealing with her will be a small problem, far overshadowed by the wealth he could have. Because of his "coarse" interest in money, he is an unusual hero for literature of Davis's time, which featured more idealistically depicted heroes; Davis was aware of this, and asks the reader, "How can I help it . . . if it made his fingers thrill with pleasure to touch a full pocket-book as well as his mistress's hand?"

When Holmes is about to marry Miss Herne, however, the mill is destroyed by a fire, which almost kills him. He is saved by Lois Yare, and slowly nursed back to health. In watching Lois and the nurses who take care of him, he finally sees the value of selfless love over greed and ambition. He realizes that he has spent his life chasing spiritually empty dreams, and as his body heals, his soul sickens. He goes to Margret on Christmas Eve and tells her he loves her; the two are reunited, and will be married.

Margret Howth

Margret Howth is a plain woman, unlike the conventionally beautiful heroines of most nineteenth-century fiction. Davis describes her as having "no reflected lights about her; no gloss on her skin, no glitter in her eyes, no varnish on her soul." She dreamed of marrying Stephen Holmes, a prosperous businessman, but that dream was destroyed when he decided to marry someone else or, since the story is not clear on this point, when she decided she could not marry him. Her father, previously a schoolteacher, has become blind, and she believes her first duty is to him. Although she seems dutiful and accepting of her fate, inwardly, she is not. She is secretly tormented by the fact that she must take a dull, joyless job at a weaving mill, by the fact that now she can never be a wife and mother, and by the fact that she has lost her true love. As Davis writes, "Christ was a dim, ideal power, heaven far off. She doubted if it held anything as real as that which she had lost." In this, she is an unusual heroine for literature of the time; most readers would have been shocked by a woman who is not terribly religious, who is miserable about caring for her aging parents, and who does not meekly accept her duty and pretend to be glad about it.

Margret has low self-esteem—she doesn't believe she's worthy of love—but is also caught up in her own suffering to such an extent that at first, she has no time to think about the suffering of others, such as Lois Yare, a poor and deformed peddler, or the people at a rescue mission run by Dr. Knowles, whom she sees when he takes her to see "a bit of hell: outskirt." However, as the story progresses, her heart opens to these people through Knowles's appeals and through Lois Yare's example. Eventually, she realizes that she, like most people, is involved in creating the world's "gulf of pain and wrong," and joins the doctor in helping people who are ill, impoverished, and hopeless.

Mrs. Howth

Margret's mother is a long-suffering woman, devoted to her husband. She works long and hard simply to help the family survive. She never lets her husband see her fears about their possible starvation, but always acts pleasant and hopeful. Margret notices that her mother's eyes are "dim with crying . . . though she [Margret] never saw her shed a tear," and describes her as "always cheery, going placidly about the house . . . as if there were no such things in the world as debt or blindness." Her mother goes on long walks, foraging in the fields for unharvested peas or corn, and comes home hopeless and exhausted, but never discusses her pain with anyone.

Samuel Howth

Margret's father, a former schoolteacher, is now impoverished and blind. A royalist who is descended from people who fought on the British side during the American Revolution, he sneers at democracy and dreams of bygone eras when kings and queens ruled. One of his greatest pleasures is debating politics with Dr. Knowles; since going blind, he has increased the vehemence of his arguments, and looks forward to the doctor's visits. He is convinced that Knowles's commune scheme to elevate the poor and downtrodden will fail, because "any plan . . . founded on self-government, is based on a sham, the tawdriest of shams." In all this debating, he seems to live in a world of political fantasy, and is removed from his own poverty. In fact, because he is blind, his wife and Margret have been able to conceal from him the fact that they had to sell many of their old belongings in order to have money for food.

Joel

The Howth family servant, Joel is a rough, uneducated man who nevertheless reads the newspaper and is avidly political, despite his ignorance. Unlike Mr. Howth, he believes fervently in the power of democracy, and keeps up with current affairs to see whether the government is truly "carryin' out the views of the people." He has little role in the story until the end of the book, when he discovers oil on the Howth property, thus restoring wealth and good times to the Howth family.

Dr. Knowles

Dr. Knowles, principal owner of the weaving mill where Margret works, is old and obese, "overgrown, looking like a huge misshapen mass of flesh," and has a face that "repelled most men: dominant, restless, flushing into red gusts of passion, a small intolerant eye, half hidden in folds of yellow fat." He is part Creek Indian on his mother's side, and thus carries what others consider "the blood of a despised race." However, because he has this blood, he has an innate sympathy with outcasts, the poor, and those who suffer from prejudice. This sympathy is an obsession for him: nothing in the world could be as important as social work, work for the poor. When he first appears in the book, the author hints that he is involved in some sort of obsessive scheme, which the other characters comment on incredulously. He has also been observing Margret for many years, secretly assessing her character to see if she will be suitable for his plans. He believes that her dream of becoming a wife and mother has been shattered for one reason: so that she can participate in his plan. "It was his part to put her work into her hands," Davis remarks.

Knowles takes Margret to his mission house and forces her to see that other people in the world are suffering far more than she is. Her loss of a selfish man is nothing compared to what others have to face: sickness, starvation, slavery, prejudice, ignorance.

Knowles is arrogant about his plan, believing that he, and he alone, can be a savior of many people, and dreaming about the praise he will earn. Knowles's plan is to sell the mill and use the money to create a communal farm, where poor, oppressed, and downtrodden people can live clean, simple lives of dignity and self-worth. However, his commitment to this cause is tested when a fire, set by Joe Yare, burns the mill to the ground before he can sell it. At first Knowles is deeply bitter about this, but gradually realizes the value of small acts of kindness, which can be as helpful as any grand scheme in helping those who are less fortunate. He works at his House of Refuge near the railroad tracks, and instead of being filled with the desire to be praised for his grand scheme, he accepts that the work he now does may not bear fruit until after his death, and he may never be personally rewarded for it.

Mr. Pike

The manager at the weaving mill, Pike is a cunning, sly man, who embezzles money from the mill, but reveals another side of his character when his little daughter is nearby: he is proud of her and kind to her, and brings her to the mill so she won't be lonely at home. His wife has died, and Pike explains, "I'm father and mother, both, to Sophy now." He has two sons, much older, to whom he gave a good education; they are now out West, seeking their fortunes, and he's proud of them. Davis comments, "Even this man could spare time out of his hard, stingy life to love, and be loved, and to be generous!"

Joe Yare

Lois Yare's father, a former slave, has spent time in jail for stealing. He also once committed forgery, a fact that only Stephen Holmes and a coal-digger at the mill know about. If Holmes told about this, Yare could be sent back to jail. When the coal-digger asks Holmes to give Yare a chance and not inform on him, telling Holmes that Yare is trying to reform and start a new life without crime, Holmes says that he didn't make the law; Yare broke it, and he must pay the consequences.

Yare goes to Holmes and begs him not to tell of the forgery, saying of prison, "what good'll it doe me to go back there? I was goin' down, down, an' bringin' th' others with me." Holmes refuses, so that night, knowing Holmes is sleeping in the factory, Yare torches it and burns it to the ground. His daughter, Lois, runs in and saves Holmes, and ultimately she dies because of exposure to toxic fumes. In the end, Holmes, who has undergone a change of heart, tells Yare he won't report him for the arson, either, although he is still disgusted by this "vicious, cringing wretch." Davis does not make it clear whether Holmes thinks Yare is wretched simply because he is black, or because he has lived through slavery and has never had a chance to improve himself. However, she remarks that his sad eyes may have seemed dishonest to other people, but when he looks at his daughter, Lois, he has nothing but kindness for her, and he worries about what she thinks of his past.

Lois Yare

Lois Yare is a mixed-race woman, the daughter of an alcoholic mother and a criminal father. She is also deformed and stunted from a bout of rickets, and apparently also has brain damage. She started working at Knowles's weaving mill when she was seven years old, but because of her handicaps she couldn't keep up with the work, and the overseer was getting ready to send her to the poorhouse. She left the mill when she was sixteen, but still remembers the horror of working there—the stench of the dye vats, the toxic fumes, the noise and heat—and swears she will never set foot inside again. Her eyes, despite her deformed appearance, are "singularly soft, brooding brown." Everyone she meets is attracted to her because of her kindness and happiness.

She works as a wandering peddler, driving her cart from farm to farm, buying and selling produce. She was given the cart by Stephen Holmes, who knew she could not return to the mill. Her cart reveals that she has the soul of an artist: the vegetables are arranged with care for their color, texture, and shapes, and the cart itself, though patched and old, has "a snug, cosey look." Whenever she can, she gives to people, even if it's only a piece of fruit. Davis writes, "She thought that unknown Joy linked all earth and heaven together, and made it plain."

Although Lois suffers more than any other major character in the book, she is the most filled with love and kindness. Instead of being bitter about her experiences, she believes that "things allus do come right, some time," because "The Master," or Christ, will make it so, and that everyone will have a chance, even if they have to wait until they're in heaven to get it. A true Christian, she knows that many of the starved, drunk, criminal, ex-slave, and downtrodden people she sees are really "the Master's people," even though they are despised by white, wealthy people. Her faith never wavers, no matter what happens, and she teaches all the other characters about the true nature of faith, Christianity, and love.

When her father sets the mill on fire, Lois realizes that Stephen Holmes is inside, and although the mill terrifies her, she runs in and saves his life. Later, it turns out that this heroic act will kill her: she has inhaled deadly fumes from the burning dye vats.

Themes

Role of Women in the Nineteenth Century

In the nineteenth century, a woman was expected to find a husband, raise a family, and run a clean and orderly household. In addition, a woman was not supposed to have a career or to be highly educated; her life was limited to her home and her family.

In the novel, Margret Howth deviates from these expectations, because she has lost, or given up, her chance to find a husband—at least throughout most of the book. She has let Stephen Holmes go because she is now burdened with the care of her blind and poor father, as well as her mother, because her mother was dependent on her father's income. She's a working girl, quite a descent in social class from her upbringing as a schoolteacher's daughter.

In another sense, however, Margret is still traditional in that she's fulfilling the only other acceptable role for a woman; if a woman couldn't or wouldn't get married, it was socially acceptable for her to live with and care for her parents, particularly if one or both of them was ill. Davis portrays Margret as loving her parents but chafing under this restricted life; she feels guilty for resenting the lot that has fallen on her, but this doesn't stop her from feeling her resentment. This honest attitude seems very modern, similar to that of many women who are caretakers of children or parents and who give up their careers outside the home to provide these services.

Effects of the Industrial Revolution

During the mid-nineteenth century, the Industrial Revolution brought dramatic changes to workers' lives. Before the Industrial Revolution, goods were manufactured by craftspeople who brought their individual attention and particular talents to each piece they produced, leading to pride and a feeling of mastery, creativity, and self-worth. For example, before the textile mills developed, cloth was woven and spun by people working in their own homes or in small shops. After the use of large mechanized looms became widespread, looms were run by large numbers of relatively untrained people—often women and children—who served the machine by inserting bobbins and shuttles of thread, clearing lint, and doing other menial and repetitive tasks for many hours each day. These working conditions gave workers little sense of

pride or control over their fate. In addition, wages
were low, the work was exhausting, and there were
no provisions to take care of workers who became
ill or injured on the job. The need for large numbers of unskilled laborers to run these kinds of machines led to the growth of the poor working class,
made up of ex-slaves, immigrants, and rural poor
who were displaced from their farms by the growth
of industry. These people often "fell through the
cracks" of the new system, as Davis shows in *Margret Howth* with her depictions of the immigrant
laborers in the mill, and the ex-slaves, alcoholics,
and other down-and-out people whom Dr. Knowles
wants to save.

Breakdown of Old Social Orders

With the Civil War and the rise of industrialism, American society became more fluid as old
patterns of society broke apart and changed. In the
early nineteenth century, society was relatively stable. People "knew their place" in an order governed
by economic status, gender, race, and family name.
By the middle of the nineteenth century the numbers of the working poor were growing as immigrants and poor rural people moved to the cities in
search of work, and found only menial labor available. Americans became more mobile, moving
from one social class to another and from one state
to another. In *Margret Howth*, Margret's own father moves from being a highly respected schoolteacher to being blind and poor, dependent on his
daughter's efforts and his wife's meager scaveng-
ing in the fields. Stephen Holmes is on his way to
being highly respected as part-owner of the textile
mill, and as son-in-law of the owner. Lois Yare
moves from being a crippled ex-textile worker to
an independent entrepreneur, with her own produce
cart. In previous decades, this kind of social movement would not have been nearly as easy.

Utopian Reform Movements in the Nineteenth Century

The nineteenth century saw a proliferation of
experimental utopian communities, like the one Dr.
Knowles wants to establish in the novel. These
communities were typically based either on religious views, like those of the Mormons, Amish,
Hutterites, and Shakers, or on social and political
theory, like those of the Owenites and Brook Farm.

All of these communities included people who
wanted to establish a new social order, usually
communal, and some included nontraditional marital arrangements, such as polygamy or group
marriage.

Topics for Further Study

- Research the life of a worker in a large industry in the 1860s, such as a steel mill worker, textile mill worker, or railroad builder. Write a diary of a week in the worker's life, describing
your work, daily routine, and problems you face.

- Davis believed that religion was the answer to
some of our social problems. Do you agree or
disagree? Why? How do you think social problems, such as poverty, drugs, and widespread
unemployment, should be dealt with?

- In *Margret Howth*, Davis mentions that many
of the workers in the mill were immigrants or
African Americans. Did you have ancestors who
were in the United States in the 1860s? If so, do
you know what types of work they did? Write
about their lives; if you don't know the facts of
their lives, write about what you would have
done for work if you had lived during that time.

- Research the rise of labor unions and write about
the changes they created in working conditions.
Do you think we still need unions to protect
workers? Why or why not?

Most of the colonies did not survive past the
beginning of the twentieth century. Some were dependent on the charisma and strength of their leaders, and when the leaders died, the groups disinte-
grated; others were affected by the widespread
social change from an emphasis on rural life to
more industrialized, urban, secular, and scientific
values. In addition, those with more nontraditional
social arrangements, such as group marriage, suffered increasing hostility from the outside world.

However, some of the groups, such as the Mormons, Amish, and Hutterites, flourished and still
exist today. Other groups, not directly linked to the
nineteenth-century movements but based upon
many of the same principles of communal ownership, self-sufficiency, and decision making by con-
sensus, have sprung up in recent decades; some of
the longest-lived and most well-known of these "in-

tentional communities" are The Farm in Tennessee and the Findhorn Community in Scotland.

Style

Author Intrusions

Throughout the book, Davis often refers to herself, the author, as "I," and addresses the reader as "you," as if she's having a conversation with the reader about the book. For example, the book begins, "Let me tell you a story of To-Day,—very homely and narrow in its scope and aim." Chapter V begins, "Now that I have come to the love part of my story." In addition to these short descriptions of what she's about to tell the reader, she also makes assumptions about the reader and embarks on sermons about what she thinks the reader wants, and what the reader should want, should believe, and should do. The first five pages of the novel consist of one of these sermons, in which Davis refers to the Civil War, slavery, patriotism, and chivalry, and notes that she will write about other truths "that do not speak to us in bayonets and victories—Mercy and Love. Let us not neglect them, unpopular angels though they be." Thus, she tells readers that this will not be a war story or a story of slavery; it will not be stirring and patriotic; it will tell about "common things" and common people. After this five-page discussion, the action of the novel begins with the narrator finding an old ledger, which reminds her of the story she wants to tell. Throughout the book, she interrupts to address the reader about religion, society, and other topics, or to warn of her intentions: "I am going to end my story now."

To the modern reader, these author comments may seem intrusive and distracting. Often, a modern reader may not know what Davis is referring to, because society has changed, or because she comments about events current at the time, but no longer remembered. For example, of Christmas 1860, she writes, "Do you remember how Christmas came that year? how there was a waiting pause, when the States stood still, and from the peoples came the first awful murmurs of the storm that was to shake the earth?" She's referring to the coming Civil War, and this reference would have been deeply meaningful to people who lived then, though modern readers might find it confusing if they are not versed in Civil War history.

References to Social, Literary, and Biblical Figures

Davis's style is typical of the nineteenth century, with author intrusions, references to social, literary, and Biblical figures, and short quotations in foreign languages sprinkled liberally throughout the text. Davis often refers to Biblical stories and characters, literary figures, religious thinkers, philosophers, political leaders, and social reformers, but modern readers may not know who these people were or what their significance is. For example, she compares Margret's hair to "Bysshe Shelley"—a reference to Percy Bysshe Shelley, an English romantic poet. In the following few pages, in a political, social, and religious debate between Dr. Knowles and Mr. Howth, the two men refer to Cornwallis, a British general; Auguste Comte, a French mathematician and philosopher; Jeffersonian democracy versus Federalism; a biblical verse from the Book of Luke; abolitionists and Fourierites (followers of the French reformer Francois Marie Charles Fourier); and the philosophers Baruch Spinoza, Johann Gottlieb Fichte, and Comte de Claude Henri Sant-Simon, a French socialist reformer. When Davis wrote the book, these references would have been understood by most educated people, but modern readers may not follow the substance of the argument unless they are similarly educated or do some research.

Foreign Language Quotes

Davis occasionally inserts phrases or quotations in Italian, Latin, French, and German, which also would have been familiar to educated people of her time. These are typically drawn from widely read books such as Dante Alighieri's *Inferno*, John Bunyan's *Pilgrim's Progress*, and the works of Johann Wolfgang von Goethe.

Historical Context

Margret Howth: A Story of To-Day is set in an Indiana textile mill, but the town Davis describes is her own home town of Wheeling, Virginia—later to become Wheeling, West Virginia, as a result of the Civil War.

Civil War

At the time Davis wrote her book, the Civil War had already started, but the book is set in the months just before it begins. In the decades before the war, the North and South had become increas-

Union soldiers at an encampment during the Civil War

ingly different from each other in terms of politics, economy, and society. The North was more heavily industrialized and commercial, employing great numbers of immigrants, whereas the South was still an agricultural society, based on slave labor. Although tensions between North and South arose largely because of their different economic and political situations, the institution of slavery became a focal point of the war.

The war began in April of 1861, when Fort Sumter was fired upon and Virginia seceded from the Union. Other states followed, leading to years of bloody combat. Few places were as divided as Wheeling, where Davis lived. Some people there chose to fight for the North, and others, often from the same families, chose to fight for the South. Still others, not wanting to risk their lives, simply fled into the mountains. In the summer of 1861, Wheeling was occupied by federal troops and put under martial law; by July, Wheeling was the center of "loyal Virginia," the part of Virginia (later called West Virginia) that did not secede. In August of 1861, Davis wrote in a letter: "Just now 'New Virginia' and its capital are in a state of panic and preparation not to be described," according to Jean

Fagan Yellin in her afterword to the Feminist Press edition of the book.

The Civil War was a bloody conflict: almost as many Americans were killed during the war as were killed in all the other wars the United States has been involved in.

Industrialization and Technological Changes

Although Davis refers indirectly to the coming war, the main intent of the book is to consider the increasing effects of industrialization on American society. During the 1800s, the American economy, particularly in the North, shifted from an agricultural base to an industrial one. Railroads, petroleum refining, electrical power, steel manufacturing, textile mills, and other industries appeared or expanded. The growth of industry resulted in a new social class of rich industrialists and a prosperous middle class. It also led to vast growth in the working-class labor force, made up largely of immigrants and people who migrated to the cities from farms.

In the new industries, there were no laws to prevent children from working, to limit the hours anyone worked, or to provide for time off. Workers, including children, often worked twelve or

Compare & Contrast

- **1860s:** The Civil War begins in 1861, and its four-year conflict is one of the bloodiest periods in American history.

  Today: Although the United States has since been involved in numerous wars and conflicts all over the world, none has been as bloody as the Civil War.

- **1860s:** Most women in America are not educated beyond grade school; those women who do receive an education usually are sent to a women's school for a few years, while their brothers go on to college.

  Today: Both men and women in the United States have equal opportunities for education and college.

- **1860s:** Slavery is legal throughout the American South.

  Today: Slavery has long since been abolished in the United States, and there have been ongoing efforts to increase civil rights for minorities; however, prejudice and oppression still linger.

- **1860s:** Widespread industrialization results in a great need for cheap labor, and there are no laws protecting workers from exploitation and dangerous working conditions, no laws preventing child labor, and no laws regulating how many hours people may work.

  Today: Laws regulate workplace safety, provide for a minimum wage, prevent child labor, and determine how many hours employers may ask employees to work each day.

---

more hours a day, seven days a week, often in sweltering heat, suffocating fumes, and deafening noise—for very low wages. If they complained, they were fired, because there were always more hungry people looking for work who would take their places. If workers became injured or were unable to keep up with the work, as Lois was in the book, they were simply fired, with no compensation. No work meant no pay, and starvation was often the result.

Because the growth of technology and increasing farm production led to lowered prices for farm produce, many farmers also went through hard times. Young people often simply left their family farms and went to the cities to look for work, adding to the swelling number of laborers seeking employment. Often, the work they found was seasonal, and they, like other workers, were unemployed for part of the year.

Americans who were born in the 1860s would see huge changes in their lifetime: a shift from candles to kerosene lamps to electricity; a shift from walking and horseback riding to steam-powered trains to electric trolley cars to gasoline-powered automobiles.

Critical Overview

Margret Howth: A Story of To-Day, is widely acknowledged as a pioneering work in American realism; Rose, in *Rebecca Harding Davis*, noted that the book "has been cited as the earliest realistic depiction of an American woman as an individual and as ordinary."

The book was originally titled *The Deaf and the Dumb*; As Rose notes, Davis was referring not to deaf people who are disabled, but to those who are deaf to everything that is not superficial, and the dumb refers to those who comprehend profound spiritual truths but are unable to express them. At the request of her editor, James T. Fields, Davis changed the title to *Margret Howth: A Story of To-Day*. "To-Day" in the title refers to the fact that the story took place in current time (at the time when it was written) but also refers to the mundane,

Laborers in a woolen mill like the one in which Margret works

material world, as opposed to the spiritual realm, heaven, or "To-Morrow," where Davis believed that all people go when they die.

This emphasis on the mundane, commonplace elements of life and on common people was relatively new in fiction, which until then had focused on wealthy, beautiful people. Davis deliberately turned against this and made her heroine, Margret Howth, plain looking, with "no gloss to her skin, no glitter to her eyes"; the other characters are all ordinary looking or actually ugly, and she writes about "vulgar American life," as she tells the reader near the beginning of the book. Rose remarked that

readers of the time, used to softer, more idealistic fiction, would have been shocked by "a heroine who is miserable caring for her parents, an egocentric, superficial hero, and an antagonist who expresses the moral attitudes of the author."

Davis was aware that readers might find her approach unusual, and she explains it in an aside to the reader in the middle of the book:

> I live in the commonplace. Once or twice I have rashly tried my hand at dark conspiracies, and women rare and radiant in Italian bowers; but I have a friend who is sure to say, "try and tell us about the butcher next door, my dear, . . . I must show men and women

as they are in that especial State of the Union where I live."

James T. Fields rejected Davis's first draft of the book; according to Rose, he objected to its narrative tone, which he found too depressing, and which he believed wouldn't sell. Davis responded that she had originally intended the story to end "in full sunshine," and that the negativity he perceived had crept in through her eagerness to tell the truth about her characters, but that she would change the book back to conform to her original idea. Rose remarks that the new, happy ending seems contrived and that it is "inconsistent with Davis's vision," and writes, "regrettably, similarly contrived happy endings compromise many of Davis's later works as well." Davis herself did not like the new ending; according to Rose, she compared it to "giving people broken bits of apple-rind to chew."

The novel's success led Davis to meet several famed nineteenth-century authors, including Nathaniel Hawthorne, Oliver Wendell Holmes, Ralph Waldo Emerson, Louisa May Alcott, and Bronson Alcott. She felt a creative and spiritual kinship with Hawthorne and Holmes, but was unimpressed by Emerson and Bronson Alcott because of their idealistic reactions to the advent of the Civil War.

In the 1930s, critic Arthur Hobson Quinn remarked in *American Fiction: An Historical and Critical Survey* that Davis had revealed the "fictional possibilities inherent in people who had been presumed to be inarticulate, or whom economic and social oppression had submerged," and Fred L. Pattee wrote in the *Dictionary of American Biography* that "Russian-like in their grim and sordid realism," her books were "distinct landmarks in the evolution of American fiction."

In 1951, Bernard R. Bowron, Jr., remarked in *Comparative Literature* that Davis was a pioneer in "the literature of industrialism, critically concerned with contemporary social problems," which led to the development of American naturalism.

The American writer Tillie Olsen brought increased attention to Davis and her work in 1985 with her homage in the afterword to the 1972 Feminist Press edition of Davis's "Life in the Iron Mills".

In *Publishers Weekly*, Penny Kaganoff wrote that although she didn't recommend the book for "the general reader," she thought it was "important for feminist literary scholars and libraries."

Criticism

Kelly Winters

Winters is a freelance writer and has written for a wide variety of educational publishers. In this essay she considers themes of blood and race in Davis's book.

Rebecca Harding Davis's novel *Margret Howth* is a novel of social reform, as Davis brings up questions about the fate of the poor, relationships among people of different races, and the effects of industrialization. An interesting aspect of the book, however, is that although Davis urges social reform through Christianity, she seems to believe in theories of race and "blood" that imply that some people are destined to live among the "dregs" of humanity no matter what assistance they are given.

In the nineteenth century, two pseudosciences were in vogue—ethnology and phrenology. Both of these purported to link physical traits with nonphysical ones, and to link biological sex and race with particular physical traits. These "sciences" often led to biased, inaccurate conclusions about some physical traits and the supposed mental, moral, or spiritual capacity of people with these traits.

Early ethnologists studied hereditary traits, as well as blood, of different people, in order to determine how these traits were linked to race. Their underlying assumptions were racist, as they attempted to determine what characteristics belonged to each race of people, and which race was "naturally" superior. Of course, whites were determined to be superior, and Native Americans, African-Americans, Asians, Hispanics, and other groups were considered inferior. The term "blood" was used to refer to inherited racial characteristics—not simply physical characteristics, but the intellectual, emotional, and, particularly, moral traits that were supposedly linked to race.

In addition, another popular pseudoscience was phrenology, in which the different shapes and sizes of individuals' heads and their different facial features were believed to correspond to particular intellectual, spiritual, or moral traits. Because these traits were considered to be as inborn and as genetically determined as the physical traits, they were considered unchangeable—one was doomed by birth to a particular place in society, to a life of crime, or to a religious life. Naturally, features considered typically "white," such as a high forehead, long narrow nose, and thin lips, were believed to show intelligence, whereas features more typical of other groups had negative connotations.

Because these theories were widely discussed as part of the popular culture during the nineteenth century, references to these theories are frequent in writing of the time, including Davis's *Margret Howth*. Characters are defined and their actions are explained by their "blood" or by their inherited appearance. A well-known example of these theories appearing in fiction occurs in the Sherlock Holmes stories by Sir Arthur Conan Doyle; when Holmes meets his archrival, the villain Moriarty, Moriarty says to Holmes, "you have less frontal development than I should have expected," referring to the shape of Holmes's head.

"Blood" is frequently mentioned in the book—not referring to the red fluid that leaks out after wounds but to heredity and even fate. Margret, despite her parents' poverty, is of "Virginia" blood, "cool, high-bred"; in one scene, Davis writes, "she looked at the big blue-corded veins in her wrist, full of untainted blood." She is like her mother, who has "hospitable Virginian blood," and like her father, who is descended from British Loyalists and thus carries his royalist tendencies in his blood, as his wife tells Dr. Knowles.

Dr. Knowles, in comparison, is the son of a white father and a mother who was half Cree Indian and half-white. Another character notes that it's no wonder that he's drawn to work among the most desperately poor people—alcoholics, prostitutes, runaway slaves—because his mother was "a half-breed," and, thus, Knowles must have inherited her "redskin" tendencies to drink and steal, and that gives him sympathy with people who do likewise. Knowles is described as "coming out of the mire, his veins thick with the blood of a despised race," but it's clear that the other characters believe he's swimming against the tide, and that eventually, he will sink back to the level he came from.

Stephen Holmes, on the other hand, may be white, but he's just as much a prisoner of his blood and his genetic inheritance as anyone else in the book. In a discussion about religion, Holmes sees Dr. Knowles looking at Holmes's "massive head, with its overhanging brow, square development at the sides and lowered crown." Holmes sees what Knowles is looking at, puts his hand on top of his head, and says, "Exactly. Crippled there by my Yorkshire blood—my mother." He's referring to his own preference for making money over some of the more esoteric things in life—he chooses

> "Although Davis urges social reform through Christianity, she seems to believe in theories of race and 'blood' that imply that some people are destined to live among the 'dregs' of humanity no matter what assistance they are given."

money over love, and his main interest in life is having money and power. He is "crippled" by his Yorkshire blood, because people from that region of England are said to be interested mainly in money; this trait has been passed down to him and apparently there's nothing he can do about it.

Lois is the daughter of an ex-slave father, Joe Yare, and a white woman who died from the effects of alcoholism. Lois is deformed from rickets—a disease that results from a vitamin deficiency and is not genetic—and has also suffered some kind of brain damage. Despite the fact that she is the most kind and loving person in the book, she has one trait that sets her apart from even the poorest poor: "the taint in her veins of black blood." She is only "set apart" in the view of the wealthier characters, however; she is welcome at any home in the district and is loved by everyone because of her kindness. She is unconcerned with appearances; of all the characters in the book, she's the only true Christian. Like Jesus, she knows that even among "the very lowest" there are "the Master's people"—people who, though starved and beaten, would "scorn to be cowardly or mean"—who show God's kindness to everyone. Lois is one of these people, and this is why she's so loved.

Although Lois is the "lowest of the low," which is hinted at by her name, Lois, and her father's nickname, Lo, she is the only character in the book who truly lives by Christian principles. Other characters in the book, such as Dr. Knowles and Margret, may think they are doing God's will—and Knowles is positive that he is—but only Lois is truly spiritual, and she puts them all to

What Do I Read Next?

- Upton Sinclair's 1906 book *The Jungle*, a masterpiece of social realism, exposed conditions in a Chicago meatpacking plant and led to the passage of laws governing the purity of food and to the creation of the Food and Drug Administration.

- Harriet A. Jacobs's *Incidents in the Life of a Slave Girl* (1861), written in the same period as *Margret Howth*, tells of Jacobs's life in slavery and her escape from it.

- "Life in the Iron Mills" (1861) was Davis's first major published work, and examines the appalling conditions workers endured in an iron mill in the mid-nineteenth century.

- *Rebecca Harding Davis and American Realism* (1991), by Sharon M. Harris, surveys Davis's role in creating a new American genre.

shame, despite the harshness of her life and the prejudice she is daily exposed to.

The other characters, however, can't see past her race. Knowles, who seems like he should know better because of the social work he's involved in, says of Lois, "that girl's artist-sense is pure, and her religion, down under the perversion and ignorance of her brain. Curious, eh?" There's no evidence in the book that Lois is "perverted," and although she isn't educated, she's not "ignorant," and in fact seems wiser than many others. Holmes writes off her spiritual gifts, as well as her artistic gifts, by commenting that the shape of her head makes it apparent that she was simply born that way. He tells Dr. Knowles, "Look at the top of her head . . . It is necessity for such brains to worship."

The only person who is aware that Lois's life has been shaped not so much by heredity as by society is Margret, who eventually realizes that Lois's life has been warped, her potential has been wasted, and she has suffered not simply by "the fault of her blood" and her illness, but, more tellingly, by so-

cial attitudes towards her. "Society had finished the work [that heredity began]," Margret thinks.

Lois's father, Joe Yare, is a thief who has never had any opportunity to better himself. He is black, like the runaway slaves described in the book as "stolid, sensual wretches, with here and there a broad, melancholy brow, and desperate jaws." Fresh from two years in jail, he hopes to make a new start, but is initially thwarted by Stephen Holmes, who says he will report him for a forgery. Yare tries to kill Holmes by setting a fire in the mill, but Holmes survives, and the two eventually face each other. Davis writes of Holmes, "Did God make him of the same blood as this vicious, cringing wretch crouching to hide his black face at the other side of the bed?" One must wonder if Yare is characterized as a "vicious, cringing wretch" simply because he is black, or because of his crimes. Later, however, Davis writes, "what if he were black? what if he were born a thief? what if all the sullen revenge of his nature had made him an outcast from the poorest poor? Was there no latent good in this soul for which Christ died, that a kind hand might not have brought to life?"

In her afterword to the Feminist Press edition of the book, Jean Fagan Yellin asked, "Is Yare a criminal because he is black (that is, because he is somehow racially incapable of civilization)? Or because, when held in slavery, he was denied access to the Christianity and literacy essential to civilization?" *Margret Howth* doesn't answer this question, but as Yellin noted, it does ask how privileged, wealthy white people should respond to people like Yare. Should they punish them, as Holmes initially decides to punish Yare, or should they be compassionate, as Holmes is in the end?

Davis, of course, believed in compassion, and she was opposed to slavery, but the book makes plain that she, like other people of her time, tended to believe that there was some truth in the theories of blood and race. As Dale M. Bauer wrote in *Differences: A Journal of Feminist Cultural Studies*, "By the conclusion, Davis's thinking seems to be in line with the dominant theories of ethnology, reiterating the thesis that 'there's a good deal of an obstacle in blood' or that a 'vice of blood' overrules charity, sympathy, and social welfare work." The question the book brings up, however, is why would one try to help those who were poor and oppressed if their condition was supposedly hereditary? Wouldn't they sink back down into the "mire" they came from? Davis was, of course, a product of her own time and culture and like most people was not immune to popular ideas of her own time, particularly since they were presented as scientific. However, the book gives the impression that she personally was troubled by the conflict between these ideas of blood and race and her opposing Christian belief that oppressed people were as good as privileged people and that they should be regarded with compassion and given help in improving their lives. *Margret Howth: A Story of To-Day* magnifies this conflict, but does not provide any final answers regarding Davis's attitude towards it.

Source: Kelly Winters, Critical Essay on *Margret Howth: A Story of To-Day*, in *Novels for Students*, The Gale Group, 2002.

Jean Pfaelzer

In the following essay excerpt, Pfaelzer provides an overview of Margret Howth, *outlining the political, social, and personal issues the novel explores.*

Margret Howth is also the story of the breakup of rural social structures in an emerging industrial capitalist economy. The novel begins with an image of one of the most profound changes of industrialization, the painful and repressive adjustment of a young woman who leaves home and enters the workplace for the first time. It explores how new relationships of production surrounding the woolen mill—wages, contracts, and competition—are replacing the rural networks of family, barter, gossip, and charity. Thus Davis contrasts the atomized and defensive personalities spawned by the economy of the mill—Knowles, Holmes, and Joe Yare—to the caring and responsible relationships of dependency sustaining those who work and live in the surrounding countryside, outside the economic aura of the mill—the Howths, local farmers, and, in particular, the peddler Lois. In contrast to the sham utopianism embraced by Knowles, Lois unites the community by trading its garden produce, a role that links her to its preindustrial economy. By comparing the new manufacturing town with the rural life of the farms (the Howth farm is still just a long walk from the mill), Davis exposes the tensions in the early stages of capitalist development. Mercantile and farm ethics of hard work, thrift, attachment, honesty, and community are yielding to individualism, secularity, self-interest, competition, alcoholism, and petty crime.

The novel begins on Margret's first day of work, her twentieth birthday, when she enters the

> " In *Margret Howth*, it is as the vessel for men's salvation that women's essential nature takes on a transformative role in the ongoing social debate about American industrialism."

mill as a bookkeeper in order to "support a helpless father and mother; it was a common story." Clearly, her status has worsened. Margret's climb onto her stool on October 20, 1860, in a small "closet," a dark seventh-floor office, is mainstream American literature's first record of a young rural woman leaving home to work in a factory. The floors shake with the incessant thud of the looms, and the office is heavy with the smell of dye and copperas, a sulfate of copper, iron, and zinc used in woolen dyes. Seated uncomfortably on her stool which is, metaphorically, "too high for a small woman," the American heroine is no longer looking out a window, but finds herself fully occupied by the world of work within. As in "Life in the Iron-Mills," images of artistic repression define industrial work. Unwilling to "dramatiz[e] her soul in writing," she has taken up ledger work, the uncreative and monotonous copying from one book to another. With her steel pen "lining out her life, narrow and black," she soon wipes the ink from her pen in a "mechanical fashion"—reified by her task. Through the imagery of writing itself Davis replaces sentimental fiction's metaphoric and literal closet of the house with the realist's enclosed office: female confinement endures.

In contrast to her own anonymous "cramped quiet lines," Margret soon discovers a series of charcoal sketches drawn on the office walls by her predecessor, P. Teagarden, who has boldly emblazoned his name on the ceiling with the smoke of a candle—an interesting literary gesture from a woman novelist who is pleading with her publisher to keep her work anonymous. Teagarden has also left behind a doleful chicken pecking the floor of a wire cage, which, along with the drawings, prompts Margret to recall how, as an aspiring and imaginative young girl, she planned to "dig down into the middle of the world, and find the kingdom of the griffins, or . . . go after Mercy and Christiana in their pilgrimage." As Margret walks past soot-stained warehouses toward her home in the hills after her first day of work, the narrator observes, "One might have fancied her a slave putting on a mask, fearing to meet her master"—an image of alienation and self-disguise that fuses wage slavery, chattel slavery, and the repressions of domestic life. These images of mechanical confinement and artistic inhibition anticipate such images as the caged parrot of Kate Chopin's *The Awakening*, who incessantly chants, "Allez-vous en!" ("Go away!" "Get out!") and the wallpaper in Charlotte Perkins Gilman's "The Yellow Wallpaper," whose design becomes a frightening projection of female repression.

Despite Fields's title for her novel, Davis always saw Dr. Knowles as the center of the story. Influenced by his readings of early European socialists, Knowles, like Hollingsworth in Hawthorne's *Blithedale Romance*, plans to use the profits from the sale of the mill to launch a utopian community made up of the most degraded and impoverished residents of the town—alcoholics, prostitutes, and abandoned women—and he hopes to recruit Margret (suggesting Margaret Fuller, perhaps) as his aide. The relationship between Margret and Knowles, rather like that between Hollingsworth and Zenobia, distills the tensions between the telos of sentimentalism and the telos of romanticism. Knowles presumes that Margret "had been planned and kept by God for higher uses than daughter or wife or mother. It was his part to put her work into her hands." Like her mother, who thinks that "Margret never had any opinions to express," Knowles presumes that her desire is a species of his own, which he fantasizes as incestuous and repressed intimacy: "Between the two there lay that repellent resemblance which made them like close relations,—closer when they were silent."

While Margret views her office job as a consequence of her father's financial incompetence and of Holmes's rejection—"perhaps life had nothing better for her, so she did not care"—Knowles, who consistently misreads Margret, sees her work as a romantic test. Intending to "make use" of her in his utopian community, "he must know what stuff was in the weapon before he used it. He had been reading the slow, cold thing for years,—had not got into its secret yet. But there was power there, and it was the power he wanted." He is convinced that Margret is an emanation of his best self and that if he can control her it will assign them

both significance. To Knowles, Margret is a "Damascus blade which he was going to carry into battle." But only in his phallic projection is she dangerous; in fact, Margret's repression and plainness undercut Knowles's egoistic fantasies: "There were no reflected lights about her; no gloss on her skin, no glitter in her eyes."

In my view, a central problem with Davis's novel comes from a contradiction within transcendentalism itself: how to reconcile egoism with the dissolution of self that allows for political engagement. Like Bronson Alcott, Knowles tries to resolve this profound impasse by linking his ambitious quest to the universal good, a fusion of the personal and the public at the core of utopianism. In assigning political righteousness to his dominating fantasies of Margret, Knowles legitimizes her powerlessness at the same time that he blesses it with historical possibility. Margret's social vision, by contrast, derives from sentimentalism. Fred Kaplan explores how sentimentalism inherited the Enlightenment faith in the redemptive power of emotions over self-calculation. He cites David Hume, for example, who argues that "the ultimate ends of human actions can never . . . be accounted for by *reason*, but recommend themselves entirely to the sentiments and affections of mankind, without any dependence on the intellectual faculties." Kaplan thus distinguishes sentiment, an "access of feeling," from the romantic "excess of feeling," which, almost by definition, must deny the world. Furthermore, he suggests, while sentiment offers an optimistic vision overall, it nonetheless takes its force from a keen awareness of human nature that, paradoxically, jeopardizes its claims to an ideal world. Margret's dilemma is thus to find a way to defend the sentimental woman against the self-sufficient romantic imagination on the one hand, and the post-Calvinist forces of philosophical realism on the other. If sentimentalism sought to atrophy woman in her emotions and traditional social duties, realism sought to limit woman as the dubious product of her social conditions and biology. To Davis, neither race, gender, class, nor region should be prescriptive.

For Davis, the split between preindustrial and industrial values has a gendered valence. She believes that transcendentalism prompts patriarchal self-interest, which fits comfortably with the industrial breakup of rural and familial communities. In Knowles and Holmes, both mill owners, she portrays men who assert their self-reliance while they remain emotionally and financially dependent. The romantic man needs the sentimental woman, typified by Lois, as an enduring sign of the living gospel, and as an apostle of anti-egotistical and anticapitalistic values that can heal the culture as a whole. In *Margret Howth*, it is as the vessel for men's salvation that women's essential nature takes on a transformative role in the ongoing social debate about American industrialism. In this Davis again echoes Emerson, who holds that self-reliance is not a paradigm of freedom from duty, but rather a model of an internalized standard of duty.

Thus, rather than a protonaturalist text, *Margret Howth* belongs to a discursive category that Thomas Laqueur terms the "humanitarian narrative," a hybrid of sentimentalism and early realism in which details of suffering, particularly bodily suffering, prompt compassion—understood in its time as a moral imperative to undertake social change. "Sentiment thereby shapes Davis's vision of social goals. For example, Margret, despairing of her plight, agrees to accompany Knowles on a visit to a crowded railroad shack, a "haunt of the lowest vice," where he hopes to recruit members for his celibate community. In this passage Davis recalls the nighttime visit to the mill in "Life in the Iron-Mills," but this time the witness is female, as are the homeless Irish women and fugitive slaves who live in the shack; as an empathic female, the narrator repudiates Knowles's romantic appropriation of suffering.

True to the lineaments of sentimentalism, the suffering of the industrial poor is pictured as an imprisoning and confining female site where gender transcends class. Knowles views poverty as erotically female: "'Come here!' he said, fiercely, clutching [Margret's] hand. 'Women as fair and pure as you have come into dens like this,—and never gone away. Does it make your delicate breath faint?" Knowles and Margret stand over women who are prostrate and drunk, incompetent as mothers and incapable of taking action on their own behalf: "Women, idle trampers, whisky-bloated, filthy, lay half-asleep, or smoking on the floor, set up a chorus of whining and begging when they entered. Half-naked children crawled about in rags."

The destitute women are further distinguished by their Catholic faith, which, to Davis, marks them as recent immigrants: "On the damp mildewed walls, there was hung a picture of . . . Pio Nono, crook in hand, with the usual inscription, "Feed my sheep." This ironic reference to Pius IX (the pope who whose betrayal of the Italian revolution of 1848 was bitterly described by Margaret Fuller) points to Davis's lifelong hostility to Catholicism as well as to Protestant churches that were unwilling to engage in the Social Gospel. Davis conflates the Irish women with runaway slaves, who are mutually eroticized: "In the corner slept a heap of half-clothed blacks. Going on the underground railroad to Canada. Stolid, sensual wretches." The narrator's racial discourse is indistinguishable from that of Knowles, who, while viewing the slave women as his future utopians, is trapped in the rhetoric of human commerce, and who observes, "so much flesh and blood out of the market, unweighed!." When Margret, by contrast, picks up a slave child and kisses her face, Knowles responds, "Would you touch her? . . . Put it down." Locked in their own discursive systems, Margret and Knowles appropriate the poor in different ways.

Eventually Margret agrees to join the community, a reluctant choice that mainly stems from her plight as a lonely single woman who is tired of taking care of her pettish mother and her bigoted father. Margret is repulsed by Mr. Howth's dreams of secession, his admiration for Napoleon, and his tiresome investigations of the Middle Ages when commoners still believed in the "perfected manhood in the conqueror." Unlike Knowles, her father believes that now "the world's a failure. All the great dreams are dead." Even in a novel that prioritizes affectional bonds, Davis, like Susan Warner in *The Wide Wide World*, satirizes a father who is self-interested, unreliable—indeed, "blind." Margret's decision to enter Knowles's "House of Refuge," a parody of the idealized home, reflects the disempowerment of domesticity and frustrations at her parents' house, "in which her life was slowly to be worn out: working for those who did not comprehend her; thanked her little,—that was all."

Davis, herself a single woman taking care of her parents, is unromantic about the trials of housewifery on a meager income, the "white leprosy of poverty." She pictures how Mrs. Howth forages in the harvested fields for late peas or corn, until Margret "could see the swollen circle round the eyes, and hear her [mother's] breath like that of a child which has sobbed itself tired"—a role reversal that exposes the protective covenant of motherhood. Not only is the family vulnerable to economic pressures outside its moral sway; Davis's satiric representations of Margret's family as conflicted and inept—indeed, her very act of ironizing the family—destroys it as sentiment's utopian telos.

Thus, Margret's choice to follow Knowles is based not only on her poverty, but also on her own isolation as a woman whose lover has rejcted her, whose dog has run away, and whose mother prefers the company of her father. Compared to the House of Refuge, her parents' home offers neither Margret nor her mother female authority, emotional transcendence, or the moral significance of domestic work. Margret also turns to a life of social duty because Jesus (often shaped in sentiment as a consoling figure who protects women from isolation) also "had been alone."

Unlike Margret, but also unlike the romantic figure Mitchell in "Life in the Iron-Mills," Knowles has a political role: "Fanatics must make history for conservative men to learn from." Knowles is a follower of the French utopian socialists Fourier (1772–1827) and Saint-Simon (1760–1825) and of the German romantic and founder of "absolute idealism," Johann Gottlieb Fichte (1762–1814), whose works Davis probably read with her brother, Wilson, a student of European romanticism. From Fourier's design for phalansteries, Knowles planned a community that would work "like leaven through the festering mass under the country he loved so well." From Fichte, who was influenced by the "ethical activism" of Jean-Jacques Rousseau and Emmanuel Kant, Knowles inherited the view of a morally empowered ego. Unlike the solipsistic strain found in many transcendentalists, Fichte believed in a socially ethical self that could withstand pressures from the competitive and aggressive world of nature. History, once a prerogative of God, now belonged to the individual, who had a duty to create a rational, moral, egalitarian, and self-sufficient community free from the "anarchy of trade." Organized into guilds, the tightly organized community would provide each member with tools, the value of one's labor, and the right to a full creative life. While Davis never develops Knowles's utopian design, in his plans to "make use" of Margret, however, he also exhibits the authoritarianism of Hawthorne's Hollingsworth and of Saint-Simon, who argued that leadership belongs to the educated elite—scientists, physiologists, historians, and economists—who can best design and supervise a technocratic but providential state on behalf of the poorest and most numerous classes.

Unlike Margret, Knowles identifies with social as well as personal suffering. On the one hand, the details of the humanitarian narrative touch his Fichtean sense of moral empiricism: "All things were real to this man, this uncouth mass of flesh that his companion sneered at; most real of all, the unhelped pain of life, the great seething mire of dumb wretchedness in streets and alleys, the cry for aid from the starved souls of the world." On the other hand, still reiterating the word *real*, Davis locates Knowles's political drive in his own racial oppression. In her first reference to the plight of Native Americans, the narrator explains that Knowles's mother was a Creek Indian and notes: "You and I have other work to do than to listen,—pleasanter. But he, coming out of the mire, his veins thick with the blood of a despised race, had carried up their pain and hunger with him: it was the most real thing on earth to him,—more real than his own share in the unseen heaven or hell."

In contrast to the social egoism that compels Knowles is Stephen Holmes's "self-existent soul." Holmes, who has purchased the mill with his fiancée's dowry, is driven by economic self-interest. He has "turned his back on love and kindly happiness and warmth, on all that was weak and useless in the world," that is, everything he identifies with Margret. A representative of the emerging ideology of bourgeois individualism, Holmes views his new fiancée, the mill, its workers, and Margret as his property, which he will try to transform into an aspect of his self. Since purchasing the mill, he has become so mechanized that to Margret his familiar footsteps now sound like an "iron tread . . . so firm and measured that it sounded like the monotonous beatings of a clock." Now, "in the mill he was of the mill." Eventually he even decides to sleep in the mill, where his hard bed and chairs are made of iron—"here was discipline." Only money, he finds, is erotic: "it made his fingers thrill with pleasure to touch a full pocket-book as well as his mistress's hand."

Fusing his utilitarian belief that "all things were made for man" with a romantic vision of the self, Holmes seeks "a savage freedom . . . the freedom of the primitive man, the untamed animal man, self-reliant and self-assertant, having conquered Nature." As Margret realizes that she must leave Holmes to his "clear self-reliant life,—with his Self, dearer to him than she had ever been," Davis marks the dangers of romanticism through a character who has chosen solitary wholeness over communal fragmentation. Nonetheless, even in a sentimental narrative that values nurturance and concern, both Margret and Dr. Knowles are attracted to Holmes whose credo is *Ego sum*. Margret finds Holmes "a master among men: fit to be a master," and Knowles likewise observes "If there were such a reality as mastership, that man was born to rule."

Holmes rather than Knowles thus inherits the mantle from Mitchell in "Life in the Iron-Mills." Pictured, like Mitchell, through images of coolness and ice, Holmes is an exponent of the "great idea of American sociology,—that the object of life is *to grow*." Unlike the korl woman, however, who is "hungry to know," Holmes has a "savage hunger" that drives him to transcend his childhood in the slums and become a "merchant prince." In contrast to the statue, he believes that "endurance is enough" for the slaves and destitute factory workers who work at his mill. Images of slavery surround Holmes; he believes that he has been "bought and sold" by his fiancée, who "held him a slave to her fluttering hand." While she is "proud of her slave," he resents the fact that "there were no dark iron bars across her life." It is tempting to think that having promised Fields a perfect day in June, Davis was mocking her publisher when Miss Herne masquerades as June in a tableau vivant. Anticipating the tableaux vivants in Edith Wharton's *House of Mirth*, Miss Herne dresses as a seductive, dangerous, and serpentine figure who, in Holmes's view, glows with a "smothered heat beneath the snaring eyes" and whose "unclean sweetness of jasmine-flowers mixed with the . . . smells of the mill . . . Patchouli or copperas,—what was the difference? The mill and his future wife came to him together." Miss Herne's decadent sexuality, a form of promiscuity earlier associated with aristocratic excesses that threatened middle-class virtues, has in *Margret Howth* evolved into a female metaphor for the seductive power of industrial capitalism itself. Margret's chastity, by contrast, emerges as a trope for bourgeois morality, which, in the end, prevails.

In *Margret Howth*, true community arises through the understanding of shared suffering rather than through the design of any single individual. In the figure of Lois Yare, Davis's first African-American character, the politics of pathos bridge the discourses of sentimentalism and realism, mobilizing democratic sentiment through the values of domesticity. Lois embodies the tension between personal pain, inscribed in the language of sentimentality, and industrial oppression, inscribed in the language of vernacular realism. To signify the loss of preindustrial innocence, Davis invokes the racist stereotype of a childlike, physically handicapped, mentally retarded mulatto woman: "Her soul, being lower, it might be, than ours, lay closer to Nature." Nonetheless, when speaking for herself

Lois insists that it is the mill (where she had worked from the time she was seven until she turned sixteen), not her nature, that has ruined her mind and her health. Like Stephen Holmes, she was "of" the mill: "I kind o' grew into that place in them years; seemed to me like as I was part o' the' engines, somehow."

Countering the narrator's racist observation that Lois's "tainted blood" had "dragged her down" is Lois's own clear insistence on the erotic force and toxic ecology of the mill:

> Th' air used to be thick in my mouth, black wi' smoke 'n' wool 'n' smells. In them years I got dazed in my head . . . 'T got so that th' noise o' th' looms went on in my head night 'n' day,—allus thud, thud . . . th' black wheels 'n' rollers was alive, starin' down at me, 'n' th' shadders o' th' looms was like snakes creepin',—creepin' anear all th' time.

Lois's sense of defilement by the mill marks her passage to adulthood and affiliates her narrative with that of other girls in sentimental fiction (such as Ellen Montgomery in Susan Warner's *Wide Wide World*, 1850), who are initiated into a culture that has abused their bodies and repressed their emotions. Lois recalls that before she went to work on the looms she used to play house in the lumberyard at the mill; now she realizes that her "crushed brain and unawakened powers" were caused by the "mass of iron and work and impure smells" of those years.

But for Davis, writing from a slave state in 1861, the traditional midcentury fictional ending of marriage and home is historically and imaginatively unavailable for a black woman character—a tension that Davis seems to have understood. Initially Margret identifies with Lois, the disfigured and bitter survivor of years of slavery and brutal child labor, through their common female suffering, acknowledging that her own "higher life" was also "starved, thwarted." As Julie Elison observes, in the nineteenth century pain (which is always gendered) serves as the link between the body and power. However, Margret soon recognizes a crucial distinction: unlike Lois she "was free—and liberty . . . was the cure for all the soul's diseases." Thus Davis refuses to let slavery and blackness serve as a generic metaphor for many other sorts of pain.

Although permanently deformed, Lois recovers spiritually through her relationship to nature. In the figure of Lois we can trace the profound influence of Emerson on Davis. Lois is indeed a nature scholar who, in Emerson's sense, "can read God directly." In a series of passages that adhere rather closely to the prescriptions of "The American Scholar" and "Nature," Lois reveals what Emerson calls an "original relation to the universe," Emerson argues that a primal contact with nature allows one to experience God firsthand, unmediated by corrupt churches or biblical interpretation; able to be "read" by anyone, nature can replace the Bible as the greatest spiritual text. Further, a nature scholar is unalienated because he is infantile:

> Few adults can see nature. Most persons do not see the sun. At least they have a very superficial seeing. The sun illuminates only the eye of the man, but shines into the eye and heart of the child. The lover of nature is he whose inward and outward sense are still truly adjusted to each other; who has retained the spirit of infancy even into the era of his manhood ... In the presence of nature a wild delight runs through them, in spite of real sorrows.

In *Margret Howth* Lois is a child-artist who reads nature as a great spiritual text; she becomes the world's eye. For Davis, Lois's primal ability arises from the fact that she is black and female. Even though Lois is clearly a young adult, the narrator and various characters refer to her as a cheerful child. Unlike Knowles and Holmes, Lois has eyes quick to know the other light that "went into the fogs of the fetid dens from which the coarser light was barred." Like the scholar-artist, she has the simplicity of character to become an "interpreter" of nature who understands that nature is (in Emerson's phrase) a "remoter and inferior incarnation of God, a projection of God in the unconscious." Thus Lois, says the narrator, can see glimpses of the "heavenly clearness" of God's light: "Was it weakness and ignorance that made everything she saw or touched nearer, more human to her than to you or me?." Surrounded by Emersonian images of sunlight, Lois "liked clear, vital colours ... the crimsons and blues. They answered her somehow. They could speak. There were things in the world that like herself were marred,—did not understand—were hungry to know: the gray sky, the mud streets, the tawny lichens."

Emerson's scholar inevitably becomes a realist artist whose unmediated sensibility is shaped not by tradition or imagination but by the eye: "To the human eye that the primary forms, as the sky, the mountain, the tree, give us ... a pleasure arising from outline, color, motion, and grouping." Lois is such an artist, fulfilling Emerson's requirement that art should become an epitome of the real world, a "result or the expression of nature, in miniature." Lois instinctively composes her cart along such

lines: "Patched as it was, [it] had a snug, cosy look; the masses of vegetables, green and crimson and scarlet, were heaped with a certain reference to the glow of color ... What artist sense had she,—what could she know—this ignorant huckster—of the eternal laws of beauty or grandeur?." Davis frequently judges her characters by this transcendent artistic capacity. Like Hugh Wolfe, Lois, an "ignorant huckster," has built her sculpture from the materials of her work. By contrast, despite his humanitarian inclinations Knowles is "blind to the prophecy written on the earth," and, similarly, in his isolated myopia Holmes sees that "the windless gray, the stars, the stone under his feet, stood alone in the universe, each working out its own soul into deed. If there were any all embracing harmony, one soul through all, he did not see it."

While Davis masculinizes society, she feminizes nature which, as such, is vulnerable to male exploitation and definition. Viewed in relation to urban life and industrial control, nature in *Margret Howth* becomes a projection of woman's unconscious and an image of her recurrent need for mothering. Like Emerson, who sees nature as a "beautiful mother," Lois finds in nature a new mother who "longs to take her uncouth child home again." Onto this maternal sensibility Davis layers a feminized sense of erotic unity. While Holmes's impetus is toward separation, discontinuity, and self-denial, Lois moves toward a transcendent sense of nature that erases boundaries—"Why, sometimes, out in the hills, in the torrid quiet of summer noons, she had knelt by the shaded pools, and buried her hands in the great slumberous beds of water-lilies, her blood curdling in a feverish languor, a passioned trance, from which she roused herself, weak and tired"—a romantic and erotic erasure of the self and others, subject and object. The surrender to the romantic universal also removes the entranced child-woman from the inevitability of history, represented by the mill. Marianne Hirsch suggests that in female romanticism sleep not only signifies withdrawal into the symbolic landscape of the innermost self; it also suggests the one-dimensional nature of a woman's development. Excluded from social interaction, she is thrown back into herself, where she can explore her spiritual or emotional sides, but only at the expense of other aspects of her selfhood.

For Emerson, Lois's transcendent capacity would have had a social function: "The office of the scholar is to cheer, to raise, to guide men by showing them facts amidst appearances." In contrast to Knowles, who is ineffectually trying to forge a utopian society in his own image, Lois, the peddler, through her "Great Spirit of love and trust" and her romanticized trinity of "a faith in God, faith in her fellow-man, faith in herself," offers the enduring possibility of a true preindustrial community. One morning, for example, as Margret walks alongside Lois into town, they stop and visit at each farmhouse, collecting produce and butter and enjoying several breakfasts. Repudiating the imagery of mechanical time that surrounds Holmes, Lois's leisurely work connects Margret, the isolated bookkeeper, with her neighbors. For the first time "the two women were talking all the way. In all his life Dr. Knowles had never heard from this silent girl words as open and eager as she gave to the huckster about paltry, common things." As she shares "disjointed" womanly talk with Lois, Margret feels "keenly alive" for the first time. Even in the town, where Margret used to see the houses as closed and silent, she discovers through Lois a sisterhood of servants, housemaids, and news vendors.

In the end, rage generated by racism and poverty brings down the industrial house—a danger that Davis believed the North must heed. Lois rescues Holmes from a fire that her angry father, Joe, has started at the mill, and dies after inhaling the fumes of burning copperas. But her death does not represent the Christian martyrdom of Stowe's Uncle Tom or Little Eva. Lois's pre-oedipal attachments, her allegiance to childhood, her dissolution of boundaries, and her sense of the dangers of industrialism render her death an inevitable effect of the adult world of industrial and chattel slavery. Her death actualizes sentimental rage, reiterating the novel's choice between romance and self, community and ego. As Lois lies dying, the community, black and white, comes together and invests her death with the power of social redemption. In *Margret Howth* Davis revises the theme of much female fiction from the mid-nineteenth century—the endless attempt to achieve self-sacrifice—by viewing women's submission as a tragic consequence of masculine assertion and romantic egoism. Eventually Margret quits the House of Refuge and forgives Stephen Holmes, who has repented of his ambitious romance and returned to Margret, announcing, "I need warmth and freshness and light: my wife shall bring them to me. She shall be no strong-willed reformer, standing alone: a sovereign lady with kind words . . . only to that man whom she trusts." The narrator notes, however, that Margret "paid no heed" to this final comment.

Davis was quite disappointed with Margret, and wrote to James Fields that she did not want the novel named after its heroine because "she is the completest failure in the story, besides not being the nucleus of it." Whether Margret dissatisfied her author as a woman or as a literary achievement is tauntingly unclear. If Margret's betrothal and reentry into her family sanction what Davis took to be available forms of female adulthood for middle-class women, Lois's death from the brutality of child labor and the toxic waste of the mill suggests the sorrowful fate of mill girls and former slaves. Since Fields had vetoed Davis's plan to "kill Dr. Knowles at Manassas," "in the end, she leaves Knowles and Holmes mutually penniless from the fire. Knowles abandons his utopian plan and quietly builds the House of Refuge as a homeless shelter. The impoverished Howth family, however, is ironically rescued by their slave, Joel, who discovers oil on their farm—a portentous omen of industrial inevitability in a book that marks its risks.

Margret Howth critiques transcendentalism's investment of the egotistical imagination with social power. In this early novel Davis challenges literary and philosophical systems that, in their formal structures and social textures. divorce the reader from life in the commonplace. Midway through the novel, as Davis prepares to satisfy Fields and "come to the love part of [her] story," she speaks to her place in literary history: "I am suddenly conscious of dingy colors on the palette with which I have been painting." She compares her ambivalent characters, who must navigate difficult choices in their public and personal lives, to figures in "once upon a time" fiction, when readers "had no fancy for going through the world with half-and-half characters." Nature, she reminds herself, no longer turns out "complete specimens of each class." Refusing to write of a heroine who "glides into life full-charged with rank, virtues, a name three syllabled, and a white dress that never needs washing," she announces that her heroines will never be "ready to sail through dangers dire into a triumphant haven of matrimony." Thus, Davis introduces the reconciliation of Margret and Holmes with a manifesto on realism: "I live in the commonplace. Once or twice I have rashly tried my hand at dark conspiracies, and women rare and radiant in Italian bowers; but I have a friend who is sure to say, 'Try and tell us about the butcher next door, my dear'." This became her lifelong literary charge.

Young boys working barefoot in a textile mill

In *Margret Howth* Davis extends her discourse of realism and talks about "the butcher next door," seeking to challenge the restrictive tenets of sentimentalism—its illusion that domestic culture can transcend political culture, that the self can be divorced from social circumstances, and that domestic life can guarantee women status, autonomy, economic security, and moral redemption. Romanticism, she found, severed the individual from history just as the imperatives of slavery and industrialism were threatening the American illusion of community. Indeed, autonomy became a snare that threatened women's identity as social subjects. Exploring subjectivity in the history of slavery and early industrialization, Davis finds that her characters face aesthetic frustration and emotional repression. In fastening the emerging strategies of literary realism onto felt experience, Davis reclaims from sentimentalism its subjectivity and intensity of feeling. In *Margret Howth*, her first novel, the social practices of domesticity, female labor, free black labor, and nascent industrialization authorize emotional appeals, shaping American realism as an indigenous and heartfelt political narrative.

Source: Jean Pfaelzer, "The Common Story of *Margret Howth*," in *Parlor Radical: Rebecca Harding Davis and the*

Origins of American Social Realism, University of Pitts-burgh Press, 1996, pp. 62–75.

Sources

Bauer, Dale M., "In the Blood: Sentiment, Sex, and the Ugly Girl," in *Differences: A Journal of Feminist Cultural Studies*, Vol. 11, No. 3, Fall 1999, p. 57.

Bowron, Bernard R., Jr., "Realism in America," in *Comparative Literature*, Vol. 3, Summer 1951, p. 273.

Kaganoff, Penny, Review, in *Publishers Weekly*, Vol. 238, No. 18, April 19, 1991, p. 63.

Mock, Michele L., "A Message to Be Given: The Spiritual Activism of Rebecca Harding Davis," in *NWSA Journal*, Vol. 12, No. 1, Spring 2000, p. 44.

Pattee, Fred L., in *Dictionary of American Biography*, Vol. 5, edited by Allen Johnson and Dumas Malone, Charles Scribner's Sons, 1930, p. 143.

Quinn, Arthur Hobson, *American Fiction: An Historical and Critical Survey*, D. Appleton-Century, 1936.

Rose, Jane Atteridge, *Rebecca Harding Davis*, Twayne Publishers, 1993, pp. 1–32.

Yellin, Jean Fagan, "Afterword," in *Margret Howth: A Story of To-Day*, The Feminist Press, 1990, pp. 271–302.

For Further Reading

Baym, Nina, *Woman's Fiction: A Guide to Novels by and about Women in America, 1820–1870*, Cornell University Press, 1978.

Baym provides a critical guide to novels written by women or that feature women characters in the mid-nineteenth century.

Harris, Sharon M., *Rebecca Harding Davis and American Realism*, University of Pennsylvania Press, 1991.

Harris discusses Davis's influence on the literary movement of American realism.

Mock, Michele L., "A Message to Be Given: The Spiritual Activism of Rebecca Harding Davis," in *NWSA Journal*, Vol. 12, No. 1, Spring 2000, p. 44.

Mock explores Davis's beliefs and describes her as a forerunner of contemporary ecofeminism.

Pfaelzer, Jean, *Parlor Radical: Rebecca Harding Davis and the Origins of American Social Realism*, University of Pittsburgh Press, 1997.

Pfaelzer discusses Davis's place as a founder of the social realist movement.

Yellin, Jean Fagan, *Women and Sisters: The Antislavery Feminists in American Culture*, Yale University Press, 1990.

Fagan discusses several women writers who wrote works opposing slavery.

Oliver Twist

Charles Dickens

1838

Oliver Twist, published in 1838, is one of Charles Dickens's best-known and well-loved works. It was written after he had already attained success as the author of *The Pickwick Papers*. It has been adapted as a film and a long-running Broadway musical and has been considered a classic ever since it was first published. The book originally appeared as a "serial"; that is, each chapter was published separately, in order, in a magazine called *Bentley's Miscellany*, of which Dickens was editor. Each week, readers waited avidly for the next installment in the tale; this partly accounts for the fact that each chapter ends with a "cliff-hanger" that would hold the reader's interest until the following chapter was published.

Dickens uses the characters and situations in the book to make a pointed social commentary, attacking the hypocrisy and flaws of institutions, including his society's government, its laws and criminal system, and its methods of dealing with poor people. Interestingly, he doesn't suggest any solutions; he merely points out the suffering inflicted by these systems and their deep injustice. Dickens basically believed that most people were good at heart but that their good impulses could be distorted by social ills.

After publishing *Oliver Twist*, Dickens went on to write *Nicholas Nickelby*, *The Old Curiosity Shop*, *Barnaby Rudge*, *American Notes*, *Martin Chuzzlewit*, *Dombey and Son*, *David Copperfield*, *Bleak House*, *Hard Times*, *Little Dorrit*, *A Tale of Two Cities*, *Great Expectations*, *Our Mutual Friend*, and

The Mystery of Edwin Drood. After 1858 he often toured, reading out loud from his works to huge audiences; every new piece from his pen was eagerly awaited, and he was perhaps the most famous and best-loved author who has ever lived.

Author Biography

Charles Dickens was born on February 7, 1812, in Portsea, England. His father, John Dickens, was a navy clerk. In 1814, John Dickens was transferred to London, and in 1817, the whole family moved to Chatham, near the naval docks. Dickens's life during the next five years was stable and happy; he was tutored by his mother and later went to school in Chatham. His father had a small collection of books, and Dickens read them avidly.

In 1822, Dickens's father was transferred back to London, but he had gotten himself deeply in debt by then and was soon sent to a debtors' prison, or workhouse, along with his wife and Dickens's siblings. Dickens, who at twelve was considered old enough to work, had to work in a boot-blacking warehouse. Alone in a strange city, separated from his family, he endured harrowing experiences that marked him with a hatred for the social system and the desire to succeed so that he would never have to live this way again. After a few months, he was saved when his grandmother died and her small legacy allowed Dickens's father to get out of prison.

When he was fifteen, Dickens became a clerk in a solicitor's office, and at sixteen, he became a court reporter, a job that taught him much about London and all its people. In 1932, he became a journalist, and in 1834, he became a staff writer for the well-known *Morning Chronicle*. He was soon known as one of the best reporters in the city. He used these experiences to write anonymous pieces, titled "Sketches by Boz," for the *Monthly Magazine*. Gradually, however, his anonymity faded, and the name "Dickens" began attracting attention. In 1836, *Sketches by Boz, Illustrative of Everyday Life* was published, followed by a second series, and the complete sketches were published in 1839.

Also in 1836, the first number of *The Posthumous Papers of the Pickwick Club* was published. Eventually, printing of the stories rose from 400 to 40,000, a number that would be large for a new author even today.

Charles Dickens

Flushed with his success, Dickens married Catherine Hogarth, the daughter of a newspaper editor, in April of 1836. They had ten children and remained married for twenty-two years but eventually would become incompatible and separate.

After publishing *Oliver Twist* (1838), Dickens went on to write *Nicholas Nickelby* (1838–1839), *The Old Curiosity Shop* (1840–1841), *Barnaby Rudge* (1841), *American Notes* (1842), *Martin Chuzzlewit* (1843–1844), *Dombey and Son* (1846–1848), *David Copperfield* (1849–1850), *Bleak House* (1852–1853), *Hard Times* (1854), *Little Dorrit* (1855–1857), *A Tale of Two Cities* (1859), *Great Expectations* (1860–1861), *Our Mutual Friend* (1864–1865), and *The Mystery of Edwin Drood* (1870, unfinished).

Dickens also wrote short stories, travel pieces, and dramas. He was the editor of *Household Words* and *All the Year Round*, well-known periodicals of his day.

After 1858, he often toured, reading out loud from his works to huge audiences; every new piece from his pen was eagerly awaited, and he was perhaps the most famous and best-loved author who has ever lived. He died on June 8, 1870, while working on his last book, *The Mystery of Edwin*

Drood. He is buried in Westminster Abbey, one of the highest honors in England.

Plot Summary

Chapters One through Nine

The book opens with Oliver's birth in a workhouse, as his unmarried and nameless mother dies. He is soon transferred to an "infant farm," run by Mrs. Mann, who starves the children under her care and pockets the money given to her for their food. Although many of the children die, investigations always determine that the death was "accidental." Oliver lives with her until he is nine, when the parish beadle, Mr. Bumble, arrives to tell her that Oliver is supposed to return to the workhouse. At the workhouse, he gets in trouble for asking for more food. For this audacious behavior, he is locked up, and the workhouse board decides to give five pounds to anyone who will take Oliver as an apprentice and thus relieve the parish of his care.

A chimney sweep, Gamfield, offers to take Oliver but is rejected when a kindly magistrate finds that Oliver is terrified of Gamfield. He goes back to the workhouse until an undertaker, Mr. Sowerberry, agrees to take him. At Sowerberry's house he must sleep among the half-built coffins and eat leftovers even the dog won't touch. In addition, he is bullied by Noah Claypole, another charity boy who works for Sowerberry, and by Charlotte, Sowerberry's servant.

Sowerberry decides to have Oliver work as a hired mourner at children's funerals, because he looks so unhappy all the time. This promotion makes Claypole furiously jealous, and he attacks Oliver, who violently defends himself, hitting the much bigger Claypole to the floor. Sowerberry beats Oliver and then locks him up until bedtime.

The next morning, Oliver runs away to London. On his way out of town, he stops to say goodbye to Dick, a younger, frailer child who was his best friend at Mrs. Mann's.

On the road to London, Oliver is starving and exhausted. He begs for food and sleeps outside. He meets a strange boy, dressed in a large man's coat, who seems very street-smart. This boy, Jack Dawkins, otherwise known as the Artful Dodger, offers to introduce Oliver to a man who will give him free housing.

In London, they make their way to a dirty, dangerous street and enter a run-down house, where a filthy old man greets them. This is Fagin, the leader of a group of child criminals. Oliver falls asleep but wakes to see Fagin gloating over a treasure. Fagin explains that this is his life savings, but, in fact, it's stolen goods. Later, the Dodger comes in with another boy, Charley Bates, and they practice picking Fagin's pockets.

Chapters Ten through Nineteen

Oliver sometimes takes part in this game, but he doesn't realize yet that it is practice for stealing. He thinks Fagin is respectable and is simply teaching the boys good work ethics. He begs to be allowed to go out with Charley and the Dodger and gets into trouble when they pick a man's pocket and then run away. Oliver doesn't run, and he's immediately grabbed as the thief. He is shocked, having finally realized that his "friends" are all thieves.

He is taken to the police station, and the man who accused him, Mr. Brownlow, follows. This man has second thoughts about the accusation because Oliver doesn't look like a thief. Oliver also looks familiar to him, although he doesn't know why. In the courtroom, an evil magistrate, Mr. Fang, sentences him to three months of hard labor. Oliver faints. Another witness shoves into the courtroom and reports that he saw the whole crime and that Oliver is innocent. Oliver is released, but he is weak and disoriented. Mr. Brownlow takes Oliver home with him.

Oliver remains unconscious for several days. Mrs. Bedwin, Brownlow's housekeeper, takes care of him. At Brownlow's house, he is fascinated by a portrait of a kind-looking woman on the wall. Brownlow notices that Oliver resembles the woman.

Meanwhile, Dawkins and the Dodger have gone back to Fagin's and reported that they have lost Oliver to the police. Fagin is enraged.

More thieves show up: Bill Sikes and his dog; Nancy, Sikes's girlfriend; and Betsy. Fagin tells them that Oliver is a danger to them all because he may tell the police about them. Nancy poses as Oliver's sister and goes to the police station to find out what happened and where Oliver is.

Brownlow asks Oliver to tell him his life's story, but this is interrupted by a visit from Mr. Grimwig, an argumentative old man who often says, "I'll eat my head." He says that he will eat his head if Oliver is anything other than a common thief, and Brownlow decides to test Oliver by giving him some books to return to the bookseller's, with money to pay his bill.

Oliver heads out on the errand but is intercepted by Nancy and Sikes, who take him back to Fagin's lair. Meanwhile, Brownlow and Grimwig have come to the unsettling conclusion that the boy has taken off with the books, the money, and the new clothes Brownlow gave him and that he really is a thief.

At Fagin's, Fagin threatens Oliver, but Nancy unexpectedly defends him, saying that if Fagin hurts him, she will personally hurt Fagin. Oliver is dressed in his old rags and locked up.

Back in Oliver's birth town, Mr. Bumble visits Mrs. Mann and tells her that he is going to London to appear in court in a settlement for two paupers. She tells him all is well at her house, except for Dick, who, she says, has been making trouble. The trouble is that he wants someone to help him write a letter to Oliver Twist before he dies. Bumble is horrified by this request and urges Mrs. Mann to lock Dick in the coal cellar.

In London, Bumble sees an advertisement offering five guineas for any information about Oliver Twist. The ad was placed by Brownlow, and Bumble goes to his house and tells Brownlow about Oliver's poor origin and supposed bad behavior. This turns Brownlow against Oliver, and he forbids Mrs. Bedlow to mention him again.

At Fagin's, Oliver is told that if he continues to resist, he will be hanged for theft. Fagin keeps him locked up, and Bates and the Dodger try to convince him to become a thief. Fagin, who comes in with another thief named Tom Chitling, who has just gotten out of jail, agrees.

On a nasty night, Fagin creeps out and heads over to Sikes's place, where he tells Sikes that he has a plan for a burglary in Chertsey. Sikes says that it can't be done; another thief, Toby Crackit, has looked the place over and found that he can't entice any of the servants to come in on the plan. Sikes finally says that they can get into the house but only if they have a boy small enough to get through a tiny window and then unlock the door. Fagin likes this plan because, even if they get caught, Oliver's prospects for a normal life will be ruined and he will have to continue his life of crime.

Chapters Twenty through Thirty-One

Nancy shows up to take Oliver to Sikes's place and confesses to him that she wants to help him but can't do anything right now. She tells him it will

Media Adaptations

Oliver Twist was adapted as a silent film in 1909, directed by J. Stuart Blackton and starring William Humphrey and Elita Proctor Otis; in 1912, directed by Thomas Bentley; and in 1916, directed by James Young and starring Marie Doro and Tully Marshal.

- The book was adapted as a film in 1922, directed by Frank Lloyd and starring Jackie Coogan and Lon Chaney; in 1933, directed by William J. Cowen and starring Dicke Moore and Irving Pichel; and in 1948, directed by David Leon and starring John Howard Davies and Alec Guinness.

- Television versions were released in 1959, directed by Daniel Petrie and starring Richard Thomas and Eric Portman; in 1982, directed by Clive Donner and starring Richard Charles and George C. Scott; in 1985, directed by Gareth Davies and starring Ben Rodska and Eric Porter; in 1997, directed by Tony Bill and starring Alex Trench and Richard Dreyfuss; and in 1999 starring Sam Smith and Robert Lindsay, directed by Renny Rye.

- A long-running Broadway musical based on *Oliver Twist*, entitled *Oliver!*, was adapted as a feature film in 1968, directed by Carol Reed.

---

be good for them both if he keeps quiet about her being on his side.

Sikes and Oliver set out on the long journey to the house the gang will rob. At a deserted old house, they meet Barney, who is occasionally a waiter in a seedy bar in Saffron Hill, and Toby Crackit, the well-known burglar. In the middle of the night, they head out. Oliver is petrified and doesn't want to participate in the crime, but Sikes tells him he will kill him if he doesn't. Sikes opens a tiny window and tells Oliver to enter and open the door for the rest of the gang. Oliver goes in, planning to wake up the people inside and warn them, but they have already heard the break-in, and they shoot at Oliver and the other burglars. Toby and Sikes run off, with Oliver, who is bleeding.

Back in the workhouse, Mrs. Corney, the matron, is making tea. Mr. Bumble visits her and notices that she's doing very well from defrauding the poor; she has good food, silver teaspoons, and nice furniture. He decides it would be in his best interest to marry the widow, so he flirts with her.

They are interrupted by a pauper who says that another pauper, old Sally, is dying and wants to speak to Mrs. Corney. Sally tells Mrs. Corney that many years ago she nursed a poor unmarried woman who had a child and then died. Before she died, she gave something made of gold to Sally. Sally kept it instead of giving it to the child, who, if he had received it and had known something about his mother, could have been proud of his origins. Sally's last words are, "They called him Oliver. . . . The gold I stole was—" but she dies before she can finish the sentence.

Toby Crackit returns to Fagin's and tells Fagin that the burglary fell apart and they had to leave the wounded Oliver behind in a ditch. Fagin is enraged, even more so because Toby has no idea where Sikes is either.

Fagin goes to the Three Cripples, the public house where Barney works. The landlord says Barney hasn't been heard from either. Fagin asks for a man named Monks, and the landlord says Monks will show up soon.

Fagin goes to Sikes's, where Nancy is alone and upset. She says she would rather that Oliver be dead than that he return to Fagin's clutches. This angers Fagin, and he leaves. As he walks the dark streets, someone calls out to him. It's Monks. Fagin lets him into his house and they talk. Monks insists that Fagin could have made a thief out of the boy, and Fagin says he has done everything he could. They see a shadow and fear that a woman is eavesdropping on them, but they can't find anyone.

Back at Mrs. Corney's, Bumble proposes marriage to her, and she agrees, telling him that she will tell him the rest of Sally's story about the golden treasure after they're married.

At the scene of the robbery, Oliver wakes up in the ditch, injured and exhausted. He drags himself back to the house, where he is taken in and the servants gloat over capturing one of the burglars. The lady of the house, Mrs. Maylie, and her adopted niece Rose, are surprised to find that the dangerous burglar is only a small boy, and they feel sorry for him. The doctor, Mr. Losberne, agrees to question Oliver in the ladies' presence. The doctor also says he will get the servants, Giles and Brittles, who fired at Oliver, to cooperate. He then talks to them and confuses them about whether or not they can be sure Oliver was actually the boy who was involved in the robbery. This also confuses two London detectives, Blathers and Duff, and they return to London without arresting Oliver.

Chapters Thirty-Two through Forty-One

Oliver's broken arm heals under the care of Rose Maylie, Mrs. Maylie, and Mr. Losberne. They take a trip to London so that Oliver can see Mr. Brownlow, and Oliver points out the ruined house where the robber gang met. The doctor jumps out of the carriage and goes into the building, where he finds an ugly, deformed man who says he has lived alone there for twenty-five years.

At Brownlow's house, they find a "For Rent" sign in the window, and neighbors tell them Brownlow has gone to the West Indies with Mrs. Bedlow and Mr. Grimwig. Oliver is deeply disappointed because he knows that Brownlow must have decided that he really was a thief when he did not return when Brownlow sent him out on his errand to the bookseller's.

The group goes on to a rural cottage, where they spend the summer, and Oliver is healed and enchanted by the beautiful countryside.

During this peaceful time, Rose Maylie becomes ill with a dangerous fever. Mrs. Maylie writes to Mr. Losberne and to "Harry Maylie, Esquire." Oliver takes the letters to the nearest village to deliver them, and he runs into a tall man wearing a cloak, who swears at him and then falls down in a fit of convulsions.

Harry Maylie, who is Mrs. Maylie's son, arrives. He is deeply in love with Rose, but Mrs. Maylie tells him that Rose will probably refuse to marry him because there is some sort of scandal attached to her and that if she becomes his wife, she will ruin his future career.

One day soon after, Oliver has a nightmare about Fagin and wakes to see Fagin looking at him through the window. He tells the others, but they can't find any evidence that anyone has been outside the window.

Harry asks Rose to marry him, and, as predicted, she says that she does love him but can't marry him because it will attach scandal to his name. Disappointed, Harry leaves, but he makes

Oliver promise to write him regularly and tell him what is happening in the Maylie household.

At the workhouse, Mr. Bumble and Mrs. Corney (now Mrs. Bumble) have been married for eight weeks. They fight constantly. Mr. Bumble is now subservient to her wicked temper and physical abuse. As a result, he goes to a public house to drown his sorrows. At the pub, he meets a mysterious man in a cloak, who asks Mr. Bumble for information about Oliver Twist's birth. Mr. Bumble tells the man that his wife has this information and will give it up for money. They arrange a meeting the next day at an address in a seedy part of town. The man's name, he says, is Monks.

At the meeting, Mrs. Bumble tells Monks that Sally stole a locket and a wedding ring from Oliver's mother. It is inscribed with the name "Agnes" and a date that is a year before Oliver's birth. He gives her a payment of twenty-five pounds, takes the ring and locket, and throws them into the river, where they will be lost forever.

At Sikes's house Sikes is ill and wretched, but Fagin, the Artful Dodger, and Charley Bates show up with food, drink, and a little money. They go back to Fagin's to get the money, and everyone except Nancy leaves. Monks shows up, and Nancy eavesdrops on their conversation. The reader is not told what she hears.

When Fagin returns and gives her the money for Sikes, Nancy leaves. She's very upset and distraught, and Sikes notices that she's behaving strangely. He decides she must have a fever. She puts a sleeping potion in his drink, and when he falls asleep, she leaves and goes to a hotel, where Rose Maylie is staying. She tells Rose that she is the one who grabbed Oliver to take him back to the thieves but that she regrets it. She then asks Rose if she knows Monks. Rose doesn't, but Nancy tells her, "He knows you." She tells Rose that she learned of her and found out where she was staying by eavesdropping on Monks and Fagin.

Monks, she says, offered to pay Fagin for finding Oliver and to pay him more if Fagin could turn him into a thief. She later heard him say that all evidence of Oliver's true identity is gone and that Monks has his money. Despite this, he wanted Oliver to suffer, to be imprisoned and worse, and he would devote his life to ruining Oliver's. Monks also said that Mrs. Maylie and Rose would give a fortune to know where Oliver is.

Rose offers to protect Nancy if she will turn away from the thieves, but Nancy says it's too late. She tells Rose she will walk on London Bridge every Sunday night, in case Rose wants to talk to her again. Rose writes to Harry, asking him what to do about this situation.

Oliver enters, excited because he has seen Mr. Brownlow entering a house. Rose takes Oliver to the house, and they have a joyous reunion. Rose discusses Nancy's revelations with Mr. Brownlow, and Brownlow recruits Mr. Losberne and Harry Maylie.

Chapters Forty-Two through Fifty-One

On the same night that Rose and Nancy meet, Noah Claypole and Charlotte come to London. They have stolen a twenty-pound note, and, by chance, they stop at the Three Cripples, the thieves' pub. Fagin overhears them talking about their crime and the difficulty of cashing such a big note without arousing suspicion, and he offers to take them in and teach them. He tells them that one of his best thieves, the Artful Dodger, has been arrested and could end up a "lifer."

Charley Bates arrives and explains that there are witnesses to the crime, so the Dodger's fate is sealed. Shamefully enough, the stolen item was a small snuffbox, not even anything expensive or daring. Fagin tells him that Dawkins will perform well at the trial and will uphold his dignity as a daring thief. Claypole is sent to the police station to see how the hearing goes; the Dodger mocks everyone there.

The following Sunday night, Nancy tries to leave to go to London Bridge, in case the Maylies are there to meet her. Sikes senses something amiss and refuses to let her go. Fagin assumes she has another boyfriend and plots to convince her to turn against Sikes and perhaps poison him. This will be convenient for Fagin, who thinks Sikes knows too much. He decides to have her followed so he can find out where her real affections lie. Then he can use the information against her and convince her to do Sikes in. He assigns Claypole to this job.

A week later, Nancy goes to London Bridge, followed by Claypole. Brownlow tells Nancy that he wants to get the secret of Oliver's identity out of Monks and that he also wants her to turn Fagin over to him. She refuses to betray either of them but tells him that if he goes to the Three Cripples, he can see Monks there. She describes him, and it turns out that the description is familiar to Brownlow—it matches someone he already knows.

Fagin is furious that Nancy talked to Brownlow, and in his anger he recruits Sikes by telling him that Nancy did so and that Noah can prove it. Sikes runs home and locks Nancy in and then tells her everything she said was heard by Claypole. She begs him to spare her life, but he is unmoved and kills her.

He is horrified by what he's done and runs outside with his dog, wandering aimlessly, feeling pursued and haunted. He realizes that people may be on the hunt for a murderer with a dog, so he tries to drown the dog, but the dog escapes.

Meanwhile, Brownlow has abducted Monks from the Three Cripples and brought him to his house. Brownlow tells Monks he must cooperate or Brownlow will give him to the police and charge him with fraud and robbery.

It turns out that Monks's father and Brownlow were friends for many years. When Monks's father was a boy, his sister, who was going to marry Brownlow, died. Brownlow and Monks's father were always close after that.

Monks's father was forced by his parents to marry. They chose a woman ten years older, who was greedy and evil. They had one son, Monks. The couple eventually separated, and the woman went to Europe, taking the young Monks with her. Eventually, Monks's father met a new love, a girl of nineteen, and became engaged. Monks's father then inherited money from a relative in Rome, but while there, he contracted a fatal illness. When his ex-wife heard about this, she went to see him, and when he died, she and her son, Monks, inherited all the money.

Brownlow tells Monks that before Monks's father left England, he left a portrait of his new love with Brownlow. Brownlow was unable to find the girl or her family after Monks's father's death.

Brownlow tells Monks that he was startled by Oliver's resemblance to this portrait and that he knew Monks might know who Oliver was. Monks had gone to the West Indies, so Brownlow followed him there and then followed him back to London. Brownlow tells Monks that he knows Monks's father made a will that contained the secret of Oliver's identity but that Monks's mother destroyed it so that she and Monks could keep all the money.

Monks breaks down and says he will confess all the facts in front of witnesses and in writing. Brownlow says that he must also give back Oliver's share of the inheritance. Monks agrees.

Mr. Losberne enters and says that Sikes's dog has been found and a huge manhunt is on for him. Also, he says, Fagin will soon be arrested.

Meanwhile, Toby Crackit, Chitling, and Kags, a convict, have gathered in a decrepit old house on an island in the Thames. After dark, Sikes appears. They are horrified by him because, although they're thieves, they're not murderers, at least not of women. A crowd gathers outside, yelling that Sikes is inside. He tries to escape by shinning down a rope from the chimney of the house but slips into a loop he has made and inadvertently hangs himself.

Two days later, Mrs. Maylie, Rose, Mr. Losberne, and Mrs. Bedwin travel toward Oliver's birthplace. Behind them, Mr. Brownlow and Monks follow. In a meeting, Mr. Brownlow tells Monks, "This child is your half-brother; the illegitimate son of your father, my dear friend Edwin Leeford, by poor young Agnes Fleming, who died in giving him birth."

Monks agrees. Agnes Leeford was his father's young sweetheart, and he had planned to marry her, as shown by the ring he gave her and the locket with her name on it. He had written a will, which allotted an annual income of eight hundred pounds each to Monks and his mother and which gave the rest of the property to Agnes and her unborn child. If the child was a boy, he was to receive the money only if he had led a clean, honorable life. If he had not, his money was to go to Monks.

Monks says that his mother burned the will, and he swore to her that he would find the child, if it lived, and make its life a misery.

Mr. and Mrs. Bumble are then brought in and forced to confess that Mrs. Bumble stole the locket and ring that were once Agnes's.

Brownlow then says that Agnes had a much younger sister and that after her father died, she was adopted by some country people. Monks's mother tracked her down and told the new parents that she was illegitimate and thus tainted. This scandal marked her life, and she was treated poorly until Mrs. Maylie noticed her and took her away. Thus, Oliver is Rose's nephew. Also, Rose's previous reluctance to marry Harry, because of her belief that the scandal attached to her would taint him, is eliminated now that she has a respectable origin. They become engaged.

Chapters Fifty-Two and Fifty-Three

Fagin is in court, and the verdict is "Guilty." He is sentenced to death by hanging. He realizes that, of all the people in the courtroom, none care about him and all are glad he will die. Brownlow and Oliver visit him in his cell, and Brownlow asks about some papers that Monks gave to Fagin. Fagin tells him where the papers are. Oliver is so upset by this visit that he is unable to walk for some time afterward.

A few months later, Rose and Harry are married, and Harry gives up his plans for a political career in favor of life as a clergyman. Mrs. Maylie comes to live with them in their country parsonage. Oliver generously allows Monks to keep half of the inheritance, and Monks goes to the New World and eventually dies in prison. The rest of Fagin's gang are transported far from England and die overseas. Mr. Brownlow adopts Oliver as his son, and they live with Mrs. Bedwin, close to Rose and Harry's parsonage. Mr. Losberne and Mr. Grimwig also settle close by. Noah and Charlotte Claypole become police informers; they buy drinks on Sundays and then report on the pubs for being open, which is against the law on Sunday. The Bumbles lose their jobs and become so poverty-stricken that they must live in the workhouse they once ran. Charley Bates repents of his life of crime and becomes a wholesome farmer.

Characters

Artful Dodger

See Jack Dawkins.

Barney

Barney is a waiter at the Three Cripples, a pub where the thieves hang out. He has a nasal condition, so everything he says sounds like he has a cold.

Charley Bates

Charley Bates is a member of Fagin's gang and is most notable for his habit of laughing all the time, even when it's inappropriate.

Mrs. Bedwin

Mrs. Bedwin is a comforting, motherly old woman, very clean and neat. She is Mr. Brownlow's housekeeper and takes care of Oliver when Mr. Brownlow takes him in. Even when Mr. Brownlow becomes disillusioned about Oliver's true nature, her faith in Oliver never wavers.

Betsy

Betsy is a member of Fagin's gang; she is not really pretty but is healthy looking and loyal to the gang.

The Bookseller

The bookseller runs the book stall where Mr. Brownlow stands reading when the Artful Dodger and Charley Bates pick his pockets. They run away, and Oliver is accused of the crime, but the bookseller follows him to court and insists on testifying that he is innocent. He is "an elderly man with decent but poor appearance."

Brittles

Brittles is a servant of Mrs. Maylie's. Although he is over thirty years old, he is considered a "boy" by the others in the household, indicating that he may be a little slow.

Mr. Brownlow

Mr. Brownlow is a wealthy, respectable gentleman, well educated, moderate, and kind. At first he believes that Oliver has stolen from him but soon realizes this is wrong and takes Oliver in and has his housekeeper, Mrs. Bedwin, nurse him back to health. When Oliver disappears again, he believes Oliver truly was a thief, but he is ready to renounce this view when Oliver comes back into his life. He does all he can to help Oliver and to restore him to his relatives and a respectable life. Dickens describes him as having "a heart large enough for any six ordinary old gentlemen of humane disposition."

Mr. Bumble

Mr. Bumble is the parish beadle, a position of petty and pompous authority that fills him with a sense of his own importance. He is a bully and loves to abuse people whom he knows can't fight back, but when he is faced with anyone stronger, he's a coward. He's also greedy: he marries Mrs. Corney simply because she seems rich and receives his just reward of a bitterly unhappy marriage.

Charlotte

Charlotte is the Sowerberrys's maid; she is strong but slovenly and lazy. She later joins Noah Claypole in a life of crime.

Tom Chitling

Tom Chitling is one of Fagin's gang. He is about eighteen, not very bright, and has small eyes and a pock-marked face.

Noah Claypole

Noah is a charity boy who works for Mr. Sowerberry and who abuses Oliver simply because he can: Oliver is smaller than Noah, and lower in the social order. Noah is big, clumsy, greedy, cowardly, and lazy. He later joins Fagin's gang, using the alias "Morris Bolter," and asks Fagin for easy, safe jobs; he first specializes in taking money from children sent on errands and later becomes an informer, telling the police about pubs that are illegally open on Sunday.

Mrs. Corney

Mrs. Corney oversees the workhouse where Oliver was born. She is a widow but later marries Mr. Bumble, whom she terrorizes with her temper and her physical and verbal abuse. She hates the paupers and considers them an annoyance; she doesn't even see them as human and has no sympathy for them even when they are dying of starvation and disease.

Toby Crackit

Toby Crackit is a well-known burglar who works with Fagin and Sikes; unlike them, he is flamboyant.

Jack Dawkins

Also called the Artful Dodger, Dawkins is the best thief in Fagin's gang. He wears a man's coat with the sleeves turned up and is street-smart beyond his years. He is eventually caught for pickpocketing, but he swaggers and brags and is disrespectful to everyone in court.

Dick

Dick is Oliver's best friend at Mrs. Mann's "infant farm." The two of them have stuck together through their shared experiences of beatings, starvation, and neglect. Like Oliver, Dick has a pure soul and remains kind, sweet, and trusting until his early death from illness.

Fagin

Fagin is a master criminal, the head of a gang of child thieves, whom he trains and uses, taking half of their income. He is ugly and filthy, with red hair and a matted red beard, and he has no loyalty to anyone or anything but himself; he easily turns against Bill Sikes, for example, and tries to get Nancy, Sikes's girlfriend, to kill him. He is eventually caught and sentenced to death. He goes mad when he realizes that no one in the world cares about him and that the spectators are all happy that he will be hanged.

Mr. Fang

Mr. Fang is the magistrate who deals with Oliver when he is accused of stealing. He is notorious for his strictness and inflexibility, and he is completely uninterested in the facts of the matter, until a witness whose testimony can't be denied steps in and speaks in Oliver's favor.

Agnes Fleming

Agnes Fleming is the daughter of a retired naval officer. She appears at the workhouse to give birth to Oliver, but no one knows her name, where she came from, or who her relatives are until the end of the book. Her sister is Rose Maylie's mother, so Oliver and Rose are cousins.

Gamfield

Gamfield is a chimney sweep who sees an advertisement offering five pounds to anyone who will take Oliver off the parish's hands. He is eager to get the money and applies to be Oliver's master, but at the last minute he is refused when a kindly magistrate sees that Oliver is deeply afraid of him.

Mr. Giles

Mr. Giles is Mrs. Maylie's butler. When the gang of thieves puts Oliver through the window of Mrs. Maylie's house, Giles shoots at Oliver, unaware that he is just a boy. Even after he finds out, however, he enjoys the sense that he is a hero and doesn't tell those who are praising him that he has defended the house from a child. Despite his exalted sense of his own importance, he is basically good at heart, loyal, and agreeable.

Mr. Grimwig

Mr. Grimwig is a friend of Mr. Brownlow's. He is a retired lawyer and has a habitually argumentative personality, perhaps as a remnant of his law days. He is heavy, old, lame in one leg, and he carries a heavy stick, which he likes to pound on the ground to make his point. His favorite expression is "I'll eat my head," which he says when he doesn't believe something is true.

Kags

Kags is a robber who was transported overseas as punishment for his crime—presumably to Australia, although Dickens doesn't make this clear. He has returned to London, and his past has marked his face: he is "a robber of fifty years, whose nose had been almost beaten in."

Edward Leeford

See Monks.

Mr. Limbkins

Mr. Limbkins is the head of the parish board, which oversees the welfare of the poor. He is very fat and has a very red face; like many of the other functionaries in the book, he actually does little to help anyone other than himself.

Mr. Losberne

Mr. Losberne is a surgeon who is called when Oliver is found injured after the attempted burglary of Mrs. Maylie's house. He is good-humored and quick-witted, as is shown by the way he confuses Giles, Brittles, and the London detectives assigned to the burglary case. Like Mr. Brownlow, he believes in Oliver's essential goodness and is devoted to helping him.

Mrs. Mann

Mrs. Mann is a harsh old woman who runs a foster home; she takes in pauper children and raises them, and the parish gives her an allowance for the upkeep of each child. She pockets this money, starves the children, and otherwise abuses them. The corrupt system is revealed by the fact that whenever she is investigated after a child's death from starvation, illness, or neglect, the investigators blithely state that the death was "accidental" and continue sending children, and money, to her.

Harry Maylie

Harry is Mrs. Maylie's son. He is about twenty-five, good-looking, with an easy, pleasant demeanor. He is deeply in love with Rose and wants to marry her even if she has some scandal in her background.

Mrs. Maylie

Mrs. Maylie is Rose's adoptive aunt. She is a well-mannered, genteel, elderly woman. She is generous and loving, as shown by her adoption of Rose and her equal kindness to Oliver.

Rose Maylie

Rose, like Oliver, is a sweet, generous, loyal, and optimistic person. She is Agnes Fleming's younger sister and Oliver's aunt, although she doesn't know this until the end of the book. For most of the book, she and the others believe there is some sort of scandal attached to her origins; for this reason, she refuses to marry Harry Maylie, although she deeply loves him, because she doesn't want his career marred by her low origins. Later, when her name is cleared, they enjoy a happy marriage.

Monks

Toward the end of the book, the reader learns that Monks's true name is Edward Leeford. He is Oliver's half-brother and has sworn to spend his life ruining Oliver's, because if he does so, he can keep the money he illegally inherited from their father. He has spent his life in crime, and even when Oliver splits the inheritance with him to allow him the resources to lead an honest life, he continues as a criminal and eventually dies overseas.

Nancy

Nancy, like Betsy, might have been pretty once, but her rough life has made her untidy and ill mannered. However, she still has some nobility of soul left, as shown by the fact that she regrets bringing Oliver back to the gang and later tries to help him get free of them, despite the fact that she knows the gang will kill her if they find out.

Bill Sikes

Bill Sikes is the most notorious and ruthless member of Fagin's gang; he is strong, impulsive, and dangerous. Dickens remarks that he has the sort of legs that "always look in an unfinished and incomplete state without a set of fetters to garnish them." He later murders Nancy, his girlfriend, when he hears that she has turned against the gang, and he is pursued throughout London until he accidentally hangs himself while trying to escape. Dickens accentuates his inhumane personality when he has Sikes try to kill his own dog, lest the dog lead pursuers to him.

Mr. Sowerberry

Mr. Sowerberry is a tall, gaunt, mournful-looking man, befitting his profession as undertaker. He takes on Oliver as an apprentice and teaches him the trade.

Mrs. Sowerberry

Meaner than her husband, Mrs. Sowerberry is short and thin, with a sharp face and a nasty disposition. She becomes jealous of Oliver when she sees that her husband favors him and so treats Oliver badly.

Sally Thingummy

Sally is a withered old pauper who serves as a midwife at Oliver's birth, despite the fact that she is somewhat drunk. She later dies in the workhouse, but not before she reveals some secrets about Oliver's mother.

Oliver Twist

Oliver is born in a workhouse to an unknown woman whose name, the reader learns much later, is Agnes Fleming. He is sensitive, compassionate, kind, loyal, and gentle, and no matter how much he is abused and mistreated, he retains these qualities as well as his deep faith in the innate goodness of people. At times he seems rather naïve; for example, when he sees the members of Fagin's gang practicing picking Fagin's pockets and when he goes out with them to steal but has no idea they are thieves until they run off and he is apprehended for the deed. An example of his loyalty is his love for his childhood friend Dick; when he goes back to the workhouse, his first thought is to find Dick, and he is crushed to learn that Dick has since died. Although he is badly treated by many people in the book and comes to fear them, he never hates them. Similarly, although Monks has spent most of his life trying to ruin Oliver's, Oliver has no hard feelings against him and divides his own inheritance with Monks, although Monks is legally entitled to nothing.

Themes

Good and Evil

According to George Gissing in *Critical Study of the Works of Charles Dickens*, Dickens once wrote, "I wished to show, in little Oliver, the principle of good surviving through every adverse circumstance, and triumphing at last." The novel does this but perhaps at the cost of depicting Oliver as a realistic character. Although he runs away from Mr. and Mrs. Sowerberry, in the remainder of the novel Oliver has little initiative or drive. He is the tool of thieves or the protégé of kind Samaritans, but he never purposefully seeks his own life or decides, on his own, what he must do.

Nevertheless, the pattern of good versus evil runs throughout the book; generally, the good people, like Oliver, Mr. Brownlow, and the Maylies, are very good, and the bad people, such as Fagin, Monks, and Sikes, are thoroughly bad.

A rare exception is Nancy, who has led a corrupt life but who nevertheless yearns to protect Oliver and do some good. Despite these desires, however, she is so sunk in her own miserable life that she doesn't believe she can ever change; she feels she is doomed to die at the hands of the criminals, and she turns out to be right.

Other characters, such as Mr. Bumble and Mr. Fang, are presented as holders of positions of public trust who are nevertheless evil and untrustworthy. These characters, and the corrupt-but-good ones like Nancy, were intended to shock readers of Dickens's time out of their traditional class-based views, which held that the poor were often corrupt and criminal, whereas those who were wealthy or in high positions were automatically moral. One of the most corrupt and scheming people in the book is Monks's mother, a high-born and wealthy woman who proves to be an evil and selfish manipulator.

Satire of the Poor Laws

Throughout the book, Dickens shows, and comments on, the effects of the laws on the poor. Confined to workhouses, starved, and mistreated, the poor have no way of redeeming themselves from unending misery and death except by running away or turning criminal. Statistics show that crime soared after the Poor Laws of 1834, despite the government's exultation that much money would be saved on feeding, housing, and clothing them.

Dickens shows the effects of the Poor Laws in his depiction of the criminal underworld of London as well as through dark, mocking humor, as when Mr. Bumble and Mr. Sowerberry are discussing the low price the parish board will pay for coffins. When Sowerberry complains about the small prices, Mr. Bumble remarks with a laugh that the coffins are correspondingly small, so Sowerberry is not losing much. The coffins are small because they're made for children who died of neglect or starvation; the men's laughter only serves to show their callousness and the callousness of the public in allowing such things to happen. Dickens also mocks authority figures' fear of the poor, as when Oliver is locked up for the "crime" of asking for more food. In addition, he enlists the reader on his side by saying that unsympathetic people, who are not upset by the fact that Oliver had to eat food even the dog wouldn't touch, should be as hungry as Oliver was and have to eat such food themselves.

Topics For Further Study

- *Oliver Twist* attacks the nineteenth-century treatment of orphans by showing how they were abused. How are orphans treated in our society? Investigate and write about what happens to children whose parents are dead or unknown, and who don't have family members willing to take them.

- Fagin is sentenced to death for his crimes. Do you think this is justified? Why or why not?

- Oliver is remarkably "good," despite the starvation and abuse he receives during his childhood. Do you think this is realistic? Why or why not?

- Investigate what it was like to live in London during the middle of the nineteenth century. If you lived there, what job would you have done? What would your life have been like?

- Fagin is evil and cunning, and Dickens also frequently mentions that he is Jewish, leading critics to remark that Dickens was anti-Semitic, though this may not have been the case. How common was anti-Semitism in Dickens's time? Research and write about how Jewish people were viewed and treated in England during the nineteenth century.

Alienation

Many, if not most, of the characters in the book are alienated from their society and each other. Oliver is an orphan, the quintessential outcast, and with the exception of Dick, the people with whom he associates throughout his childhood are deeply selfish and mistrustful, interested in their own welfare and no one else's. Among the thieves, there is no camaraderie; they often spy on each other and are ready to turn on each other at a moment's notice if it will gain them more money or freedom from jail. The "good" characters in the book present a rare little community of trust and goodwill, but they are so good that at times they seem unrealistic: no quarrel or misunderstanding ever mars their pleasant society. In addition, they are a small minority compared to the vast number of other characters in the book, most of whom are solitary and cut off from their origins and families, or associate in rough, shifting, untrustworthy, and temporary alliances.

Style

Shifting Narrative Voice

Throughout the novel, Dickens employs a shifting narrative voice; as James R. Kincaid noted

in *Dickens and the Rhetoric of Laughter,* "It is impossible to define the characteristics or moral position of the narrators in this novel, for they are continually shifting." At times the narrator is detached and wordy, as in the opening paragraph in which he says abstractly that he will not name the town or workhouse where a certain "item of mortality" was born. At the same time, he is mocking the conventions of many novels of his time, which open with a lengthy and often smug description of the main character's birthplace and family.

The narrator doesn't consistently stay in this remote but sarcastic voice but sometimes shifts to remarking ironically on the supposedly wonderful way in which the poor are treated and on how kind it is; or sometimes the narrator appeals to the friendly feeling of the reader: "We all know how chilled and desolate the best of us will sometimes feel." As Kincaid noted, "We can never count on being in any single relationship with the narrative voice for long. Just as we relax. . . . We are pushed away."

Dark Humor

The novel is filled with dark humor, from Mr. Bumble and Mr. Sowerberry laughing about the abundance of small children's coffins to Dickens's mocking the seriousness and puffery of the members of the parish board, to his exposure of the cowardice and avarice of Noah and Charlotte, to the caperings of the Artful Dodger when he is put on trial. This humor only serves to sharpen the desperate sufferings of Oliver and the other characters, however, so that although readers may laugh while they are reading the book, when they're done, they tend to remember the sadness in it.

Characterization

Dickens uses "flat" characters; his people don't tend to grow or change over the course of the book. Oliver, who begins good, stays good, and he never wises up; never once does he show any awareness that the thieves are truly evil or any real disgust at Fagin's life. He is afraid of the thieves, but he is afraid because they may hurt him, not because he is aware that they're twisted and corrupted souls. Fagin, who begins evil, stays that way. Many of the characters are easily marked by certain "tags" of behavior or voice: Mr. Grimwig habitually thumps his cane on the ground and asserts, "I'll eat my head!"; Fagin is always out for money; Mr. Brownlow is steadfastly good; Monks is obsessively evil. Mr. Bumble is consistently pompous and shallow, and Noah Claypole remains a coward and a bully throughout the book.

In modern fiction, characters like these are considered a mark of poor writing, but in Dickens's time, readers were not bothered by such flat depictions. In addition, because the novel was written as a serial that required readers to remember all the characters for a long period of time, it was necessary for writers to make their characters easy to remember and categorize.

Historical Context

In the mid-nineteenth century, England was suffering from economic instability and widespread unemployment. The economic instability was a legacy of the Napoleonic era, which lasted until 1815. During this time, England was at war with France. The English government had imposed heavy taxes to pay for the war, and although these did not really affect the wealthy classes, they were a crushing burden on the poor. Prices rose, food became scarce, and inflation rose. Also because of the war, French and European markets for English goods were closed, leading to unemployment among workers.

Workers were also unemployed because the increasing use of machinery in manufacturing had made many of their jobs obsolete; for example, instead of employing many individual weavers, textile manufacturers began using mechanized looms, with only a few people needed to run them. The angry workers, known as Luddites, led movements to smash industrial machinery, a crime that was made punishable by death in 1811.

The Napoleonic War ended in 1815, but the misery did not. With the war over, England entered the worst depression it had ever seen. The number of poor people, never low, increased to crisis levels. Historically, each parish had been responsible for taking care of its poor by handing out money and food, and more and more people now chose to take these handouts. Others worked but took the assistance anyway, and when employers found out about this, they lowered their wages, making it impossible even for honest workers to survive on their wages. In addition, several thousand war veterans had returned to England, swelling the ranks of the jobless.

During this time, children often worked long hours, every day of the week, in dangerous factories. In 1833, child labor and working conditions began to be regulated and controlled.

In 1834, the "Poor Laws" were passed. They required that people needing public assistance live in workhouses, where they were poorly fed and badly treated. The object of this plan was to make public assistance unattractive to the poor and thus to decrease the number of people on assistance, as well as the associated costs. The plan did save money, but at a great cost in human suffering, as Dickens makes plain in *Oliver Twist*.

In 1837, Queen Victoria ascended the English throne and began her long rule and a relatively stable period in English history. This stability, and the increasing numbers of people in the middle classes who were educated enough to read books for leisure and had the money to buy them and the time to read them, would help the young Dickens to an illustrious future.

Critical Overview

In *Dickens and His Readers: Aspects of Novel Criticism Since 1836*, George H. Ford quoted George Borrow, who wrote in 1838 that "Everybody was in raptures over a certain *Oliver Twist* that had just come out." Readers of the time, far from being dismayed by the dark quality of the

Compare & Contrast

- **1838:** It is not yet known that every person in the world has different fingerprints, so the criminal justice system relies on eyewitness reports, confessions, and rough clues to determine who has committed crimes.

  Today: Fingerprinting, DNA analysis, and sophisticated analysis of microscopic clues left at crime scenes have made the criminal justice system much more precise than it was in Dickens's day.

- **1838:** Throughout the 1800s, a variety of crimes in England are punishable by death. In 1800, 200

types of crimes merited the death penalty. By 1837, reforms have diminished this number to 15 types of crimes.

Today: In England, there is no death penalty for any crime.

- **1838:** Laws control the movement and daily lives of poor people who are confined to "workhouses" or "debtor's prisons" where they are starved and mistreated.

  Today: England has an extensive social welfare system, which provides aid to unemployed, ill, and elderly people.

---

book, loved it. An exception was Thackeray, who mocked Dickens's portrayal of Nancy, saying she was sentimentally and unrealistically presented. Dickens was so upset by this comment that he wrote an angry reply to Thackeray in the preface to the book, according to Ford. Ford also noted that although most readers loved the book, some were indeed alienated: "the kind of reader who cannot bear to be ruffled by violent emotions."

Some of these readers were critics who were dismayed by its presentation of criminals, workhouse inmates, and illegitimacy. According to Ford, Henry Fox wrote that the book was "painful and revolting"; Fox quoted Lady Carlyle, who commented, "I know that there are such unfortunate beings as pick-pockets and street walkers . . . but I own I do not wish to hear what they say to one another." Fox also wrote that although the book seemed to be such a fad that few dared to speak against it, "I suspect, when the novelty and the fashion of admiring [it and other books] wear off, they will sink to their proper level."

For these readers, Dickens's attacks on the social institutions responsible for crime and poverty were not considered enough to make up for the fact that he was presenting indecent, wretched characters to his supposedly sheltered readers. However, in *Critical Studies of the Works of Charles Dick-*

ens, George Gissing noted that these views were not shared by most readers and wrote, "When criticism had said its say, the world did homage to a genial moralist, a keen satirist, and a leader in literature."

Gissing did remark on what he saw as the book's flaws: "Attempting a continued story, the author shows at once his weakest side, the defect which he will never outgrow. There is no coherency in the structure of the thing; the plotting is utterly without ingenuity; the mysteries are so artificial as to be altogether uninteresting." However, he did note that at the time Dickens wrote the book, fiction was in its infancy, and readers were not nearly as demanding as they are now. Tight, complex, and realistic plotting had yet to be developed, so modern readers cannot fault Dickens for not using it. If modern readers overlook the creaky plot mechanisms, what remains is "a very impressive picture of the wretched and the horrible," with realistic descriptions of the London streets and people, their daily habits, voices, food, and clothing.

Joseph Gold, in *Charles Dickens: Radical Moralist*, wrote that it was not surprising that critics in Dickens's day were upset by the book, because what Dickens did was to "humanize the criminal. This was not readily forgiven, for to humanize the criminal is to show his relationship to the reader, who would prefer to regard him as another

Illustration by George Cruikshank from the 1892 and 1897 editions of Oliver Twist

species." This was very different from previous novels, which either romanticized criminals as gallant outcasts or as complete monsters, utterly inhuman.

In *Modern Critical Views: Dickens*, J. Hillis Miller commented that the book was flawed mainly because of its depiction of Oliver, who from beginning to end is a tool of others. He does rebel against the thieves who try to mold him into one of them, but in the end he succumbs to the molding of Mr. Brownlow and friends; Mr. Brownlow adopts him, and he becomes what Brownlow wants him to be. He has not solved the dilemmas of his parentage and of determining on his own what he wants to be and to do. He lives happily ever after, but "only by living in a perpetual childhood of submission to protection and direction from without."

Geoffrey Thurley, in *The Dickens Myth*, remarked that of course the book's plot is absurd but that the book's enduring value stems from its "moral vision" and its depiction of the confrontation between good and evil.

In *Dickens: A Collection of Critical Essays*, John Bayley wrote that the book, unlike its predecessor, *The Pickwick Papers*, was "a modern novel," as shown by the fact that despite its flaws it can still touch the modern reader.

Criticism

Kelly Winters

Winters is a freelance writer and has written for a wide variety of educational publishers. In this essay, she considers themes of survival, the portrayal of criminals, and attitudes toward money and power in Dickens's Oliver Twist.

Oliver Twist is notable for its emphasis on the struggle to survive, its presentation of the poor and criminals as real people with their own stories and sufferings, and its emphasis on money and the hypocrisy it frequently breeds.

Both Oliver and the thieves are victims of the Poor Laws and other social institutions that prevent or discourage them from productive work. They all battle hunger, cold, and lack of decent living conditions, and society seems bent on rubbing them out—even Oliver's harmless and sweet friend Dick is viewed as a nuisance and a danger by the authorities. As Dickens wrote, children in the "infant farm" are often killed when they are "overlooked in turning up a bedstead, or inadvertently scalded to death" during clothes washing. When the workhouse board decides to get rid of Oliver so they won't have to pay for his food and lodging anymore, they consider sending him to sea, "the probability being, that the skipper would flog him to death, in a playful mood, some day after dinner, or would knock his brains out with an iron bar." This they regard as his rightful due, as if, being a pauper, he is therefore a criminal in need of punishment. He is almost apprenticed to Gamfield, a cruel chimney sweep who takes pleasure in torturing small boys, with the board's approval, until at the last minute he is saved from this horrible fate by a kind magistrate.

In addition, one of the board members, "the gentleman in the white waistcoat," repeatedly remarks, "I know that boy will be hung," as if he is already a criminal and the death penalty is his due. This comment is particularly chilling because Oliver is depicted as a kind, loving child who has done nothing wrong during his short life. However, because of social attitudes toward the poor, he is considered doomed or inherently evil, a born criminal.

Like a prisoner, Oliver is given very little food, is frequently beaten, and is often confined in a small, dark room. Throughout the novel, this imprisonment is repeated whenever Oliver offends someone who has more power than he does. He is variously imprisoned in a "coal cellar," a "dark and solitary room," "a little room by himself," a "cell," "a stone cell . . . the ante-room to the coal cellar," and the claustrophobic coffin workshop, as well as the dark, filthy, and labyrinthine rooms of Fagin's criminal gang.

The criminals themselves are shown as living in "dens" like those of animals: dirty "holes," houses boarded up and entered through tiny openings, with dark passages; at times Dickens uses the word "kennel" to describe these places and writes of the criminals as if they are predatory animals who must hunt to survive.

Before Dickens's novels, few writers had presented criminal life as physically, morally, and psychologically repellent, preferring instead to glorify criminal characters as fascinating, glamorous, or romantic outlaws, similar to Robin Hood; this tendency continues in modern fiction, with murder mysteries, gangster movies, Mafia mini-series, and prison escape tales in which the criminals are heroes. In *Oliver Twist*, Dickens shows the filth and degradation the thieves live in and their utter lack of faithfulness to each other; with rare exceptions, they are all ready to spy on each other and turn each other in if they can save themselves, make money, or gain new alliances by doing so. As Fagin says, they are all "looking out for Number One." This nerve-wracking, unstable, and dangerous world was new to readers and accounted for both the negative remarks of some critics as well as the fascination of many readers, who were able to see into a world of which they had no direct experience.

Dickens also showed the unglamorous end of some of the thieves' careers: Fagin is hanged; Monks dies in prison overseas, unmourned after a life of crime; and the Artful Dodger is arrested and jailed for life. None of the thieves, in fact, remains active in crime, as if Dickens did not want to show any of them achieving "success" as criminals.

Dickens's motive in portraying the criminals as ordinary and even pathetic people was to establish a sympathy between the reader and these degraded specimens of humanity. He links the poverty and suffering created by the Poor Laws with the growth of crime, saying through the story that the rich, wealthy, and complacent people who

> "Dickens frequently attacks the smugness and complacency of people whose place in society is secure and who have no sympathy for those who suffer."

don't care about the sufferings of the poor are in fact creating a huge underclass of criminals, who in turn prey on both rich and poor. By seeing the criminals as human, readers will be awakened to their sufferings and to the sufferings of the poor, instead of simply thinking (as many people did, and still do) that what happens to the poor is not their problem.

For example, until Rose Maylie meets and talks to Nancy, she has no idea that women like Nancy exist. Perhaps she knows of the existence of "bad women," but Nancy makes her see that some "bad women" may actually be "good," or, more realistically, a mix of the two—simply human, like herself. Once she realizes this, she is eager to help Nancy, although Nancy insists it's too late. This lesson of human kindness and compassion is not learned by the servants of the hotel where Rose is staying; they are bitterly rude to Nancy, seeing her only as an instrument of evil because she is not a respectable or wealthy woman.

Dickens frequently attacks the smugness and complacency of people whose place in society is secure and who have no sympathy for those who suffer. He mocks the parish board, Mr. Fang the magistrate, Mr. Bumble, Mrs. Corney, and others, and in the case of Mr. Bumble and Mrs. Corney, some of the worst offenders, he makes sure to put them in the very position of the people they previously abused and despised, as they end up in the very workhouse where they once tormented others.

Dickens vigorously attacks the Poor Laws of 1834, showing the resulting brutal treatment of the poor. The workhouse system was designed to save money; by making the workhouses repellent places of starvation and hard labor, the authorities intended to make hard work outside the workhouse seem like a better choice and thus prevent able-

What Do I Read Next?

- Dickens's *The Pickwick Papers* (1836–1837) is a humorous satire on pre-Victorian London.

- Dickens's *David Copperfield* (1849–1850), drawn from Dickens's own early experiences, tells the story of a young orphan.

- *Bleak House*, by Dickens (1852–1853), is a satirical tale set in the labyrinth of the English legal system.

- Dickens's *A Tale of Two Cities* (1859) is a dramatic narrative of the French Revolution.

- Charlotte Brönte's *Jane Eyre* (1847) tells another story about an orphan in nineteenth-century England.

bodied people from becoming what in modern times are called "welfare abusers." By lessening the number of people who took public assistance, the authorities could save a great deal of money. However, they went too far in their emphasis on money over humaneness, as Dickens shows. He also has venomous words for those in the system who see it as a form of "Christian charity," for as he shows, it is not spiritually or religiously based at all. Those who claim it is real "charity," as opposed to torment, are exposed as the most wicked of hypocrites. As Dickens ironically writes:

> [The system of starving the poor] was rather expensive at first, in consequence of the increase in the undertaker's bill, and the necessity of taking in the clothes of all the paupers, which fluttered loosely on their wasted, shrunken forms, after a week or two's gruel. But the number of workhouse inmates got thin as well as the paupers; and the board were in ecstasies.

When Oliver is born in the workhouse, he is regarded as yet another mouth to feed on a sort of assembly line of poor children. This dehumanization is shown by the way Mr. Bumble makes up names for the children, in alphabetical order, so that Oliver is randomly named "Twist" because he

comes after a child whom Bumble named "Swubble" and before one whom Bumble will name "Unwin." Bumble has devised a whole list of these alphabetic names, which he will apply to orphans in logical order. The babies are never seen as human but as a procession of burdens, and they are discussed as economic factors—how much money Mrs. Mann will get for him or other orphans and how much she can keep for herself by not feeding them. In addition, Oliver is considered to be such a financial liability on the parish that they are willing to pay five pounds to anyone who will take him away and teach him a trade—a job skill that will prevent him from returning to the parish as a pauper in adult life.

The thieves, of course, are obsessed with getting money, although bad at saving it. Later in the book, Oliver's entry into a loving surrogate family is made even more idyllic by the fact that he inherits a great deal of money. Dickens does not take the story far enough to tell us what becomes of Oliver as an adult and if he spends any of his considerable fortune to help the poor, but given his character as presented in the novel, it would be safe to assume that he would.

Source: Kelly Winters, Critical Essay on *Oliver Twist*, in *Novels for Students*, The Gale Group, 2002.

David Paroissien

In the following essay, Paroissien examines Oliver Twist *as a reflection of English society and its changing environment during Dickens's formative years.*

Readers familiar with literature about Britain written during the interval between Napoleon's defeat at Waterloo in 1815 and the coronation of Queen Victoria twenty-two years later know how rich it is in studies that map the distinctive features of the post-war period. Some writers, like Bulwer Lytton in his *England and the English* (1833), mixed sociology and history in order to analyze society in the manner of De Toqueville and Montesquieu. Others—David Ricardo, Sismondi, the Swiss economist and historian, and Patrick Colquhoun, are examples—focussed more specifically on the best ways to exploit the source of England's wealth. Some took the position that a free economy would promote social harmony and growth. Dissenters, like Sismondi, advocated government controls as the best way to ensure stability by regulating the production of goods and slowing the economy in order to counter the increasing gap between the rich and the poor. Other barometers of the period include its fiction, which provided commentary of a different sort, as readers discovered in their vicarious participation in the imagined settings of novels truths about the real world they inhabited. It is my contention that *Oliver Twist* (published serially from February 1837 to April 1839) can be read as a literary work that reveals a good deal about the period which shaped Dickens's early life, those years in which people faced, for the first time, some of the public and private challenges posed by the Industrial Revolution.

The distinctive features which characterize *Oliver Twist* as an imaginative instrument for the empirical exploration of early Victorian England require enumeration. Dickens uses the novel to explore two major concerns: first, the plight of children born into the early phase of the Industrial Revolution, and, second, the difficulty of reading "correctly" the external signs of the new urban culture, whose impact on the class system, to take one important instance, rendered unreliable previous assumptions about both the means by which one social group was distinguished from another and the underlying presumption of separateness. These two social realities form the novel's moral agenda and account for a determined effort by Dickens to create a new literary form in which to convey his vision. Prototypical features of *Oliver Twist* include the use of a child hero to convey the specific threats the young faced in their painful initiation into life, the suspenseful revelation of unsuspected connections between different social groups, and the employment of several characters and a narrator to assemble clues and solve mysteries in the manner of a detective.

I shall begin with the foundling hero, whose illegitimate birth in a workhouse many Victorians evidently read as a prelude to the boy's almost certain misfortune and descent into crime. Dickens plays on this likely response to Oliver's fate in several scenes early in the novel. Members of the managerial class who administered the New Poor Law of 1834, for example, are portrayed as taking pleasure in humiliating Oliver, and they aggressively predict his demise. "'I know that boy will be hung,'" warns one member of the Board of Guardians, a prophecy he and his companions do their best to assist by handing over Oliver to anyone willing to take him on as an apprentice.

Once parish overseers resigned juvenile paupers in their care to an employer, children were generally subject to further degradation, a point made clear by Oliver's apprenticeship to an un-

" I suggest that the novel's emphasis on Oliver's happy survival calls attention to the failure of government officials to offer a constructive response to the problem of juvenile delinquency."

dertaker. In the hands of cruel employers, typified in the novel by Gamfield and Sowerberry, children often ran away and drifted into crime. And when apprentices fled from the harsh conditions and brutal treatment commonly associated with menial jobs, adolescents often took to stealing, parliamentary investigators discovered, because they had no other way to survive. This development, in turn, had further destructive consequences. If they were caught, boys and girls were taken before police magistrates, who sentenced them to several months in jail. If they remained free, they might fall prey to villains like Fagin, who specialized in training boys to pick pockets. In return for the stolen goods, which the adults fenced for a profit, Fagin and his kind provided food and shelter for their young associates.

The sequence of events showing Oliver's journey from the workhouse in Mudfog to Fagin's den in London shapes the novel's narrative structure and gives it an almost epic scope. In Dickens's own words, the tale portrays a classic struggle of "little Oliver . . . surviving through every adverse circumstance" (1841 Preface). Because Oliver is "so jolly green," he is quickly spotted as a potential recruit by the alert young thief who finds him starving in Barnet High Street. And he is easily ensnared with the promise of help, the first kind word or gesture Oliver has ever received in his life. "'Don't fret your eyelids on that score,'" says the Artful Dodger, sympathetically, when Oliver confesses that he has no money and nowhere to stay. "'I've got to be in London to-night; and I know a 'spectable old genelman as lives there, wot'll give you lodgings for nothink, and never ask for the change'.''

Fagin's warm welcome and invitation to eat pointedly contrast with Oliver's earlier experiences concerning food and accommodation. In the workhouse he had been reviled for asking for more, a direct attack on the dietaries introduced by the government in 1836, which ignored the needs of growing children and simply stipulated that the young should be fed "at discretion." Later, on the evening of his arrival at the undertaker's, after he had been sold by the parish officials, Mrs. Sowerberry's preparations for the apprentice's first meal go no further than ordering her servant to "'give this boy some of the cold bits that were put by for Tip,'" the family dog. "'We are very glad to see you, Oliver—very,'" said Fagin, commanding the Dodger to remove some sausages from a skillet and draw up a tub "'near the fire for Oliver,'" making an offer no hungry boy could refuse.

The guiding principle of parsimony written into the Poor Law Amendment Act of 1834—I refer to the euphemistic notion of "less eligibility"—also meant that Union authorities were not encouraged to spend money educating children or providing vocational or industrial training for their charges. Instead, they were urged to reduce administrative expenses for the young as quickly as possible, a justification for the practice of offering a nominal premium to masters as an inducement to take on apprentices as a cheap supply of labor.

Children thus forced into the labor market were so commonly abused that the young "slaves" often ran away from their employers, preferring to fend for themselves in the streets and survive by stealing. And once on a course that doomed them to an outlaw existence, one of two possibilities usually prevailed. They might live relatively well while their luck held, like the boys in Fagin's gang, who drank heavily, gambled and enjoyed the sexual favors of their female companions. Or, if they were caught, they faced prosecution and certain imprisonment, thus completing a downward spiral from which there was almost no chance of escape.

Dickens drives this point home through the juxtaposition of the parallel court appearances of Oliver and the Artful Dodger in chapters 11 and 43. For the hero to escape, "a stronger hand than chance" must intervene to rescue Oliver from the Hatton Garden magistrate, Mr. Fang, and effect his miraculous delivery into middle class respectability and ease. Lacking Oliver's good fortune and help from wealthy friends, Fagin's "best hand" has no one to come to his aid when, later in the novel, he is arrested and tried at Bow Street police court.

Instead, the Artful Dodger is convicted and sent abroad to a penal colony in Australia, lagged as a lifer for stealing a twopenny sneeze-box, in the "flash" idiom of the thieves.

Modern readers sometimes object that Oliver's final removal from London and adoption by Mr. Brownlow "as his own son" conflict with Dickens's realistic treatment of poverty and its inevitable link with crime. On the contrary, I suggest that the novel's emphasis on Oliver's happy survival calls attention to the failure of government officials to offer a constructive response to the problem of juvenile delinquency. Orphans and abandoned children in early Victorian England, Dickens realized, constituted an entire class at risk, feral children of the slums destined either for the hangman's noose or transportation to a penal colony.

Finding a solution to the problem of juvenile crime assumed particular urgency in the 1830s when the commitment and conviction of those under sixteen rose more rapidly than ever before in English history. Public officials and members of Poor Law boards who sat "in solemn conclave," like the sadistic "white-waistcoated gentleman" and his fellows, often viewed young offenders as incorrigibles, "A distinct body of thieves whose life and business it is to follow up a determined warfare against the constituted authorities by living in idleness and on plunder." Sentiments life this pervaded government reports and oral testimony from prison governors, policemen and magistrates, witnesses united in a belief that the maintenance of law and order required tough penal measures.

Indifference to children's needs, the most pressing of which were voluminously documented in parliamentary papers published by the government from 1800 onwards, clearly angered Dickens. In novel after novel he aimed a series of sledgehammer blows at some of the instances of misery he saw around him. The defacto infanticide practiced in the country's baby farms, the sexual exploitation of girls on a scale surpassing any previously known and the absence of government regulations for promoting public health all receive careful attention in *Oliver Twist*. In Dickens's view, England's conduct deserved the severest censure. The country seemed willing to pay for its post-war prosperity by using its young as carelessly as we dispose of plastic cups and paper plates today.

Dickens's choice of a child hero to call attention to the plight of the nation's youth is closely related to the second part of his agenda. This aspect of *Oliver Twist* was equally unique, especially in the novel's emphasis on the care middle-class readers needed to take when they attempted to interpret the external signs of England's new urban culture. If urban reality made it easy to overlook the needs of infants and juveniles, as they were being generated in record numbers for almost certain destruction during the first three decades of the nineteenth century, that same new world also created, through the anonymity and multiplicity of city life, interpretative challenges unknown to earlier generations.

Reference to the novel's treatment of class and the apparent separateness of traditional social groups suggests that Dickens saw this phenomenon very clearly. In a society whose social structure remained relatively stable, customary markers of difference such as dress, vocabulary, accent and occupation served two general functions. They tended to limit opportunities for social mobility by confining individuals to the circumstances into which they were born. They also provided an aid to recognition most people were quick to assimilate. The way one spoke and dressed, together with one's occupation and source of income, offered reliable clues to status and position.

The four apparently distinct groups of characters in *Oliver Twist* illustrate how these notions of class and separateness were challenged by an urban culture, whose contours Dickens read and mastered perhaps more quickly than most of his contemporaries. One at first assumes that the novel's different groups have nothing in common, that beadles, criminals, businessmen and genteel members of the middle class are set apart on the opposite side of gulfs, destined never to meet. Only in fiction, runs one likely objection, do thieves rub shoulders with innocents and respectable upholders of the law, in turn, commit actions that, on a moral plane, reduce them to the level of criminals.

On the other side of this formulation are deserving individuals whose goodness and virtue are assessed negatively on the basis of misleading external appearances. Oliver's own birth in the workhouse furnishes the most obvious example of an infant who, initially, defied attempts by even "the haughtiest stranger" to assign him to "his proper station in society," until he was "badged and ticketed" as a parish child the minute he was wrapped up in old calico robes "which had grown yellow in the same service." The dilemmas of Rose Maylie and Nancy carry this theme even further. Nancy, thief and prostitute, can only be placed outside the law, despite her goodness and courage, while her

respectable "sister" Rose, the embodiment of every domestic virtue Dickens can summon from the culture, nevertheless remains under a "stain," forbidden to marry the man who loves her because she is thought to be illegitimate. Revelations at the end of the novel clear up the ambiguities surrounding Rose's birth, and Oliver's ancestry proves sufficiently worthy to justify his assumed middle-class status. But for Nancy heroic death and implied forgiveness in heaven must suffice.

The novel's mystification and literary devices drive home Dickens's point about class interconnectedness in other ways. Punctuating the narrative, for example, are a series of journeys, each presented with scrupulous care for accuracy and topographical detail. The expedition of Oliver and Sikes is perhaps the most dramatic instance, a twenty-five mile trip from Bethnal Green to Chertsey, a remote Thames-side village in Surrey, where Mrs. Maylie and Rose reside. Dickens devotes two chapters to their foray and the attempted robbery in order to warn readers about dangers many overlooked. Sitting in her "detached house surrounded by a wall," Mrs. Maylie has no idea that her home has been under surveillance by a member of Fagin's gang for two weeks, or that Sikes so covets her silver plate that he submits to Fagin's proposal to use Oliver as the means of breaking in through a small, unsecured lattice-window at the back of the house.

The linking of inhabitants from widely disparate locales is further reinforced by the sudden and mysterious appearance of Fagin and Monks outside Oliver's study one midsummer evening later in the story. Safe though Oliver is at Mrs. Maylie's summer cottage, goodness, Dickens appears to suggest, never remains completely invulnerable. In the new urban world of the 1830s, criminals and law-abiding citizens seemed to share the same ground, or to have access to it on nearly equal terms. Similar instances of this theme appear elsewhere in the novel. On one occasion Oliver runs into Monks as he leaves a country inn while on an errand for Mrs. Maylie; on another, Nancy, whose life had been squandered in the streets, makes her way to "a family hotel in a quiet but handsome street near Hyde Park," to meet Rose Maylie and provide information that Mr. Brownlow uses to solve the mystery of Oliver's identity.

Brownlow's role as a prototypical detective is reinforced by the narrator and by Rose and Nancy, all of whom patiently assemble clues and demonstrate a keen intelligence. This very quality, privi-

Mark Lester (front center) as Oliver in Oliver!*, the Academy Award-winning 1968 musical film version of the novel*

leged by its prominent role, seems to be one Dickens wants to propose for adoption by his readers. Extend your sympathies to those whose suffering deserves support. And sharpen your ability to decode the complicated social messages embedded in city life.

This summary makes mine a reductive reading on *Oliver Twist*, one that deliberately links the novel with its formative social and historical contexts. A more expansive inquiry would admit as evidence the literary features of the novel Dickens inherited from his predecessors. It would also take into account the compelling biographical aspects of Oliver's story, into which Dickens confessed to his publisher that he had thrown his "whole heart and soul." My account, nevertheless, accords with Dickens's deepest conviction that fiction always tells us something about the way readers thought and lived and how he, like his contemporaries, tried to make sense of the bafflement of existence. To this end, I have focussed on the experience of reading *Oliver Twist* as a novel dedicated to reading experience as it was shaped, for many readers, by the urban conditions of the 1830s.

Source: David Paroissien, "*Oliver Twist* and the Contours of Early Victorian England," in *Victorian Newsletter*, Vol. 83, Spring 1993, pp. 14–17.

George Gissing

In the following essay, Gissing discusses Dickens's motives for writing Oliver Twist, *as well as the political, social and economic climate in which it was written.*

I

It was a proof of Dickens's force and originality that, whilst still engaged upon *Pickwick*, with the laughter of a multitude flattering his joyous and eager temper, he chose for his new book such a subject as that of *Oliver Twist*. The profound seriousness of his genius, already suggesting itself in the course of Mr. Pickwick's adventures, was fully declared in "The Parish Boy's Progress." Doubts might well have been entertained as to the reception by the public of this squalid chronicle, this story of the workhouse, the thieves' den, and the condemned cell; as a matter of fact, voices were soon raised in protest, and many of *Pickwick's* admirers turned away in disgust. When the complete novel appeared, a *Quarterly* reviewer attacked it

vigorously, declaring the picture injurious to public morals, and the author's satire upon public institutions mere splenetic extravagance. For all this
Dickens was prepared. Consciously, deliberately,
he had begun the great work of his life, and he had
strength to carry with him the vast majority of English readers. His mistakes were those of a generous
purpose. When criticism had said its say, the world
did homage to a genial moralist, a keen satirist, and
a leader in literature.

In January, 1837, appeared the first number of
a magazine called *Bentley's Miscellany*, with Dickens for editor, and in its second number began
Oliver Twist, which ran from month to month until March of 1839. Long before the conclusion of
the story as a serial, it appeared (October, 1838) in
three volumes, illustrated by Cruikshank. Some of
these illustrations were admirable, some very poor,
and one was so bad that Dickens caused it to be removed before many copies of the book had been
issued. Years after, Cruikshank seems to have
hinted that his etchings were the origin of *Oliver
Twist*, Dickens having previously seen them and
founded his story upon them. The claim was base-
less, and it is not worth while discussing how
Cruikshank came to imagine such a thing.

There had fallen upon Dickens the first penalty
of success; he was tempted to undertake more work
than he could possibly do, and at the same time was
worried by discontent with the pecuniary results of
his hasty agreements. During the composition of
Oliver he wrote the latter portion of *Pickwick* and
the early chapters of *Nickleby*; moreover, he compiled an anonymous life of the clown Grimaldi, and
did other things which can only be considered hack-
work. That he had not also to work at *Barnaby
Rudge*, and thus be carrying on three novels at the
same time, was only due to his resolve to repudi-
ate an impossible engagement. Complications such
as these were inevitable at the opening of the most
brilliant literary career in the Victorian time.

How keenly Dickens felt the hardship of his
position, toiling for the benefit of a publisher, is
shown in Chapter XIV, where Oliver is summoned
to Mr. Brownlow's study, and, gazing about him
in wonder at the laden shelves, is asked by his bene-
factor whether he would like to be a writer of books.
"Oliver considered a little while and at last said he
should think it would be a much better thing to be
a bookseller; upon which the old gentleman
laughed heartily and declared he had said a very
good thing."—"Don't be afraid," added Mr.
Brownlow, "we won't make an author of you whilst

> " 'I wished to show, in
> little Oliver, the principle of
> good surviving through every
> adverse circumstance, and
> triumphing at last.' Think what
> we may of his perfectly sincere
> claim, the important thing, in our
> retrospect, is the spirit in which
> he made it."

there's an honest trade to be learnt, or brick-mak-
ing to turn to." An amusing passage, in the light of
Dickens's position only a year or two after it was
written.

II

Oliver Twist had a twofold moral purpose: to
exhibit the evil working of the Poor Law Act, and
to give a faithful picture of the life of thieves in
London. The motives hung well together, for in
Dickens's view the pauper system was directly responsible for a great deal of crime. It must be remembered that, by the new Act of 1834, outdoor
sustenance was as much as possible done away with,
paupers being henceforth relieved only on condition
of their entering a workhouse, while the workhouse
life was made thoroughly uninviting, among other
things by the separation of husbands and wives, and
parents and children. Against this seemingly harsh
treatment of a helpless class Dickens is very bitter;
he regards such legislation as the outcome of cold-
blooded theory, evolved by well-to-do persons of
the privileged caste, who neither perceive nor care
about the result of their system in individual suffering. "I wish some well-fed philosopher, whose meat
and drink turn to gall within him; whose blood is
ice, whose heart is iron, could have seen Oliver
Twist clutching at the dainty viands that the dog had
neglected. . . . There is only one thing I should like
better, and that would be to see the philosopher making the same sort of meal himself, with the same rel-
ish." (Chapter IV.) By "philosopher" Dickens meant

a political-economist; he uses the word frequently in this book, and always in the spirit which moved Carlyle when speaking of "the dismal science." He is the thorough-going advocate of the poor, the uncompromising Radical. Speaking with irony of the vices nourished in Noah Claypole by vicious training, he bids us note "how impartially the same amiable qualities are developed in the finest lord and the dirtiest charity boy." This partisanship lay in his genius; it was one of the sources of his strength; its entire sincerity enabled him to carry out the great task set before him, that of sweetening in some measure the Augean stable of English social life in the early half of our century.

That he was in error on the point immediately at issue mattered little. The horrible condition of the poor which so exasperated him resulted (in so far as it was due to any particular legislation) from the old Poor Law, which, by its system of granting relief in aid of insufficient wages had gone far towards pauperizing the whole of agricultural England. Not in a year or two could this evil be remedied. Dickens, seeing only the hardship of the inevitable reform, visited upon the authors of that reform indignation merited by the sluggishness and selfishness which had made it necessary. In good time the new Act justified itself; it helped to bring about increase of wages and to awaken self-respect, so far as self-respect is possible in the toilers perforce living from hand to mouth. But Dickens's quarrel with the "guardians of the poor" lay far too deep to be affected by such small changes; his demand was for justice and for mercy, in the largest sense, for a new spirit in social life. Now that his work is done, with that of Carlyle and Ruskin to aid its purpose, a later generation applauds him for throwing scorn upon mechanical "philosophy." Constitutional persons, such as Macaulay, might declare his views on social government beneath contempt; but those views have largely prevailed, and we see their influence ever extending. Readers of *Oliver Twist*, nowadays, do not concern themselves with the technical question; Oliver "asks for more," and has all our sympathies; be the law old or new, we are made to perceive that, more often than not, "the law is an ass," and its proceedings invalid in the court of conscience.

III

In a preface to *Oliver* (written in 1841) Dickens spoke at length of its second purpose, and defended himself against critics who had objected to his dealing with the lives of pickpockets and burglars. His aim, he tells us, was to discredit a school of fiction then popular, which glorified the thief in the guise of a gallant highwayman; the real thief, he declared, he had nowhere found portrayed, save in Hogarth, and his own intention was to show the real creature, vile and miserable, "for ever skulking uneasily through the dirtiest paths of life." From the category of evil examples in fiction of the day, he excepts "Sir Edward Bulwer's admirable and powerful novel of Paul Clifford," having for that author a singular weakness not easily explained. His own scenes lie in "the cold, wet, shelterless midnight streets of London," in "foul and frowsy dens," in "haunts of hunger and disease"; and "where"—he asks—"are the attractions of these things?"

This defence, no doubt, had in view (amongst other things) the censure upon *Oliver Twist* contained in Thackeray's story of *Catherine*, which was published in *Fraser's Magazine*, 1839–40, under the signature of "Ikey Solomons jun." Thackeray at this time was not the great novelist whom we know; seven years had still to elapse before the publication of *Vanity Fair*. His *Catherine* is a stinging satire upon the same popular fiction that Dickens had in view, but he throws a wider net, attacking with scornful vigour *Paul Clifford* and *Ernest Maltravers*, together with the Jack Sheppards and Dick Turpins and Duvals, and, in two instances, speaking contemptuously of *Oliver* itself. "To tread in the footsteps of the immortal Fagin requires a genius of inordinate stride," and he cannot present his readers with any "white-washed saints," like poor "Biss Dadsy" in *Oliver Twist*. Still, says the author, he has taken pains to choose a subject "agreeably low, delightfully disgusting, and at the same time eminently pleasing and pathetic." His heroine is a real person, one Catherine Hayes, whose history can be read in the Newgate Calendar; she was brought up in the workhouses, apprenticed to the landlady of a village inn, and, in the year 1726, was burned at Tyburn for the murder of her husband. Thackeray uses his lash on all novelists who show themselves indulgent to evil-doers. "Let your rogues act like rogues, and your honest men like honest men; don't let us have any juggling and thimblerigging with virtue and vice." In short, he writes very angrily, having, it is plain, Dickens often in mind. Nor is it hard to see the cause of this feeling. Thackeray was impatient with the current pictures of rascaldom simply because he was aware of his own supreme power to depict the rascal world; what thoughts may we surmise in the creator of Barry Lyndon when he read the novels of Bulwer and of Ainsworth, or the new production of the author of *Pickwick*? Only three years more, and we find him writing a heartfelt eulogy of the *Christmas Carol*, praise which proves him thoroughly to have appreciated the best of Dickens. But it must be avowed that very much of *Oliver* is far from Dickens's best, and Thackeray, with his native scorn of the untrue and the feeble, would often enough have his teeth set on edge as he perused those pages. *Catherine* itself, flung off in disdainful haste, is evidence of its author's peculiar power; it has dialogues, scenes, glimpses of character beyond the reach of any other English novelist. In certain directions Thackeray may be held the greatest "realist" who ever penned fiction. There is nothing to wonder at in his scoff at Fagin and Nancy; but we are glad of the speedy change to a friendlier point of view.

It was undoubtedly Dickens's conviction that, within limits imposed by decency, he had told the truth, and nothing but the truth, about his sordid and criminal characters. Imagine his preface to have been written fifty years later, and it would be all but appropriate to some representative of a daring school of "naturalism," asserting his right to deal with the most painful facts of life. "I will not abate one hole in the Dodger's coat, or one scrap of curl-paper in the girl's dishevelled hair." True, he feels obliged so to manipulate the speech of these persons that it shall not "offend the ear," but that seemed to him a matter of course. He appeals to the example of the eighteenth-century novelists, who were unembarrassed in their choice of subjects. He will stand or fall by his claim to have made a true picture. The little hero of the book is as real to him as Bill Sikes. "I wished to show, in little Oliver, the principle of good surviving through every adverse circumstance, and triumphing at last." Think what we may of his perfectly sincere claim, the important thing, in our retrospect, is the spirit in which he made it. After a long interval during which English fiction was represented by the tawdry unreal or the high imaginative (I do not forget the homely side of Scott, but herein Scott stood alone), a new writer demands attention for stories of obscure lives, and tells his tale so attractively that high and low give ear. It is a step in social and political history; it declares the democratic tendency of the new age. Here is the significance of Dickens's early success, and we do not at all understand his place in English literature if we lose sight of this historic point of view.

IV

By comparison with the book which preceded it, *Oliver Twist* seems immature. Putting aside the first chapter or two, *Pickwick* is an astonishingly ripe production, marvellous as the work of a man of five and twenty, who had previously published only a few haphazard sketches of contemporary life. *Oliver*, on the other hand, might well pass for a first effort. Attempting a continued story, the author shows at once his weakest side, the defect which he will never outgrow. There is no coherency in the structure of the thing; the plotting is utterly without ingenuity, the mysteries are so artificial as to be altogether uninteresting. Again, we must remember the time at which Dickens was writing. Our modern laws of fiction did not exist; a story was a story, not to be judged by the standard of actual experience. Moreover, it had always to be borne in mind how greatly Dickens was under the influence of the stage, which at one time he had seriously studied with a view to becoming an actor; all through his books the theatrical tendency is manifest, not a little to their detriment. Obviously he saw a good deal of *Oliver Twist* as if from before the footlights, and even in the language of his characters the traditional note of melodrama is occasionally sounded. When, long years after, he horrified a public audience by his "reading" of the murder of Nancy, it was a singular realization of hopes cherished in his early manhood. Not content with his fame as an author, he delighted in giving proof that he possessed in a high degree the actor's talent. In our own day the popularity of the stage is again exerting an influence on the methods of fiction; such intermingling of two very different arts must always be detrimental to both.

Put aside the two blemishes of the book—on the one hand, Monks with his insufferable (often ludicrous) rant, and his absurd machinations; on the other, the feeble idyllicism of the Maylie group—and there remains a very impressive picture of the wretched and the horrible. Oliver's childish miseries show well against a background of hopeless pauperdom; having regard to his origin, we grant the "gentle, attached, affectionate creature," who is so unlike a typical workhouse child, and are made to feel his sufferings among people who may be called inhuman, but who in truth are human enough, the circumstances considered. Be it noted that, whereas even Mr. Bumble is at moments touched by natural sympathy, and Mr. Sowerberry would be not unkind if he had his way, the women of this world—Mrs. Corney, Mrs. Sowerberry, and the workhouse hags—are fiercely cruel; in them, as in many future instances, Dickens draws strictly from his observation, giving us the very truth in despite of sentiment. Passing from the shadow of the workhouse to that of criminal London, we submit to the effect which Dickens alone can produce; London as a place of squalid mystery and terror, of the grimly grotesque, of labyrinthine obscurity and lurid fascination, is Dickens's own; he taught people a certain way of regarding the huge city, and to this day how common it is to see London with Dickens's eyes. The vile streets, accurately described and named; the bare, filthy rooms inhabited by Fagin and Sikes and the rest of them; the hideous public-house to which thieves resort are before us with a haunting reality. Innumerable scarcely noticed touches heighten the impression; we know, for instance, exactly what these people eat and drink, and can smell the dish of sheep's head, flanked with porter, which Nancy sets before her brutal companion. Fagin is as visible as Shylock; we hear the very voices of the Artful Dodger and of Charley Bates, whose characters are so admirably unlike in similarity; Nancy herself becomes credible by force of her surroundings and in certain scenes (for instance, that of her hysterical fury in Chapter XVI) is life itself. The culminating horrors have a wild picturesqueness unlike anything achieved by other novelists; one never forgets Sikes's wanderings after the murder (with that scene in the inn with the pedlar), nor his death in Jacob's Island, nor Fagin in the condemned cell. These things could not be more vividly presented. The novelist's first duty is to make us see what he has seen himself, whether with the actual eye or with that of imagination, and no one ever did this more successfully than Dickens in his best moments.

His allusion (in the Preface) to Hogarth suggests a comparison of these two great artists, each of whom did such noteworthy work in the same field. On the whole, one observes more of contrast than of likeness in the impressions they severally leave upon us; the men differed widely in their ways of regarding life and were subjected to very different influences. But the life of the English poor as seen by Dickens in his youth had undergone little outward change from that which was familiar to Hogarth, and it is *Oliver Twist* especially that reminds us of the other's stern moralities in black-and-white. Not improbably they influenced the young writer's treatment of his subject. He never again deals in such unsoftened horrors as those death-scenes in the workhouse, or draws a figure so peculiarly base as that of Noah Claypole; his hu-

mour at moments is grim, harsh, unlike the ordinary Dickens note, and sometimes seems resolved to show human nature at its worst, as in the passage when Oliver runs after the coach, induced by promise of a half penny, only to be scoffed at when he falls back in weariness and pain (Chapter VIII). Dickens is, as a rule, on better terms with his rascals and villains; they generally furnish matter for a laugh; but half-a-dozen faces in *Oliver* have the very Hogarth stamp, the lines of bestial ugliness which disgust and repel.

V

One is often inclined to marvel that, with such a world to draw upon for his material, the world of the lower classes in the England of sixty years ago, he was able to tone his work with so genial a humanity. The features of that time, as they impress our imagination, are for the most part either ignoble or hideous, and a Hogarth in literature would seem a more natural outcome of such conditions than the author of *Pickwick* and the *Christmas Carol*. Dickens's service to civilization by the liberality of his thought cannot be too much insisted upon. The atmosphere of that age was a stifling Puritanism. "I have been very happy for some years," says Mrs. Maylie; "too happy, perhaps. It may be time that I should meet with some misfortune." (Chapter XXXIII.) Against the state of mind declared in this amazing utterance, Dickens instinctively rebelled; he believed in happiness, in its moral effect, and in the right of all to have their share in it. Forced into contemplation of the gloomiest aspects of human existence, his buoyant spirit would not be held in darkness; as his art progressed, it dealt more gently with oppressive themes. Take, for instance, the mortuary topic, which has so large a place in the life of the poor, and compare Mr. Sowerberry's business, squalid and ghastly, with that of Mr. Mould in *Chuzzlewit*, where humour prevails over the repulsive, and that again with the picture of Messrs. Omer and Joram in *Copperfield*, which touches mortality with the homeliest kindness. The circumstances, to be sure, are very different, but their choice indicates the movement of the author's mind. It was by virtue of his ever-hopeful outlook that Dickens became such a force for good.

Disposing of those of his characters who remain alive at the end, he assures us, as in a fairy tale, that the good people lived happily ever after, and we are quite ready to believe it. Among the evildoers he distinguishes, Mr. Bumble falls to his appropriate doom; Noah Claypole disappears in the grime which is his native element—severity, in his case unmitigated by the reflection that he, too, was a parish-boy and a creature of circumstances. Charley Bates it is impossible to condemn; his jollity is after Dickens's own heart, and, as there is always hope for the boy who can laugh, one feels it natural enough that he is last heard of as "the merriest young grazier in all Northamptonshire." But what of his companion, Mr. Dawkins, the Dodger? Voices pleaded for him; the author was besought to give him a chance; but of the Dodger we have no word. His last appearance is in Chapter XLIII, perhaps the best in the book. We know how Dickens must have enjoyed the writing of that chapter; Mr. Dawkins before the Bench is a triumph of his most characteristic humour. What more is to be told of the Dodger after that?

We take philosophic leave of him, assured that he is "doing full justice to his bringing-up, and establishing for himself a glorious reputation."

Source: George Gissing, "Chapter IV: *Oliver Twist*," in *The Immortal Dickens*, Kraus Reprint Co., 1969, pp. 63–87.

Sources

Bayley, John, "Things As They Really Are," in *Dickens: A Collection of Critical Essays*, edited by Martin Price, Prentice-Hall, 1967, pp. 83–96.

Ford, George H., *Dickens and His Readers: Aspects of Novel Criticism since 1836*, W. W. Norton and Company, 1965, pp. 35–47.

Gissing, George, *Critical Studies of the Works of Charles Dickens*, Haskell House, 1965, pp. 43–57.

Gold, Joseph, *Charles Dickens: Radical Moralist*, University of Minnesota Press, 1972, pp. 25–65.

Kincaid, James R., *Dickens and the Rhetoric of Laughter*, Oxford University Press, 1971, pp. 50–75.

Miller, J. Hillis, "The Dark World of Oliver Twist," in *Charles Dickens*, edited by Harold Bloom, Modern Critical Views series, Chelsea House, 1987, pp. 29–69.

Thurley, Geoffrey, *The Dickens Myth: Its Genesis and Structure*, St. Martin's Press, 1976, pp. 43–50.

For Further Reading

Fido, Martin, *The World of Charles Dickens: The Life, Times and Work of the Great Victorian Novelist*, Carlton, 1999.
This book provides background information on Dickens's time, life, and work.

Hobsbaum, Philip, *A Reader's Guide to Charles Dickens*, Farrar, Straus and Giroux, 1972.
This work examines all of Dickens's work and provides a guide to readers.

Kaplan, Fred, *Dickens: A Biography*, Johns Hopkins University Press, 1998.
This biography of Dickens is written for high school students.

Pool, Daniel, *What Jane Austen Ate and Charles Dickens Knew: From Fox Hunting to Whist—The Facts of Daily Life in Nineteenth-Century England*, Touchstone Books, 1994.
This fascinating volume explains all the customs of daily life in Dickens's time.

Persuasion

Jane Austen
1818

When *Persuasion* was published posthumously in 1818, only a small circle of people knew of and admired Jane Austen's novels. Since that date, however, Austen has come to be one of the world's most widely read and most beloved authors. She claimed once to her nephew, who would later write her biography, "the little bit (two inches wide) of Ivory on which I work with so fine a Brush produces little effect after much labour." Scholars and readers, however, have overwhelmingly disagreed with her assessment that her work produces "little effect," finding her to be a conscious artist and astute social critic. In *Persuasion*, her last novel, Austen continues to present in minute detail the daily lives of her characters, upper-middle-class men and women living in England at the beginning of the nineteenth century. This novel perhaps is her most romantic, centering on postponed but enduring love. Anne Elliot, the story's heroine, suffers from a decision that was forced upon her several years ago—to break off a relationship with the man she deeply loved. As Austen examines the causes and consequences of this action, she offers a penetrating critique of the standards of the British class system and the narrow-mindedness of those who strictly subscribe to them. The novel's witty realism helped guarantee Austen's position as one of the finest novelists.

Author Biography

Jane Austen was born on December 16, 1775, in England, to George and Cassandra (Leigh) Austen. Her father was a clergyman in Steventon, a small town in Hampshire County. Her mother, whose ancestors were titled, was born into a higher social class. She and her husband settled into a comfortable but modest life, associating with the local gentry and raising eight children. Jane's close relationship with her siblings and her family's relationship with the local gentry would provide her with material for her plots and influence her creation of the settings and characterizations in her novels.

Austen received only five years of formal schooling; however, she continued her education at home. When she was in her teens, she wrote plays, verses, short novels, and other prose works, which were primarily parodies of sentimental fiction. Soon she began writing *Elinor and Marianne*, an early version of *Sense and Sensibility*, and after that, *First Impressions*, which later became *Pride and Prejudice*. Even though a London publishing house rejected the draft of the latter work after her father had submitted it, the novel was heartily enjoyed by her family and a wide circle of acquaintances.

Scholars divide Austen's literary career into an early and a late period separated by a writing hiatus of eight years. The first includes her early writings, *Sense and Sensibility* and *Pride and Prejudice* (both published in 1811), and *Northanger Abbey* (written in 1803 but published posthumously in 1818). Her late period includes *Mansfield Park* (1814), *Emma* (1816), and *Persuasion* (published posthumously along with *Northanger Abbey* in 1818. During the eight-year hiatus, Austen moved frequently with her family, staying in Bath, London, Clifton, Warwickshire, and Southampton, where they moved after her father died in 1805.

Austen started writing her last novel, which the family would later title *Sandition*, in 1817. She had not completed the novel when she died, most likely of Addison's disease, on July 18, 1817, in Winchester, England.

During her lifetime, Austen's works were well received, especially *Sense and Sensibility* and *Pride and Prejudice*, yet since all her works were published anonymously, she was not well known by the public. After her death, when her brother revealed her authorship, scholars began critiquing her work. By the end of the nineteenth century, she

Jane Austen

came to be regarded as one of the most important English novelists, a position she retains today.

Plot Summary

Volume I

The novel opens in the summer of 1814 with Sir Walter Elliot, widower and father of three daughters, Elizabeth, Anne, and Mary, in Kellynch Hall, his estate in Somersetshire, England. Sir Walter's greatest pleasure is to pick up the Baronetage, a book that documents his and his family's history and social standing. He is very close to his eldest daughter, Elizabeth, who shares his vanity and class consciousness, and who has been the mistress of Kellynch Hall for the past thirteen years since her mother died. Elizabeth has struck up a friendship with Mrs. Clay, the daughter of the family lawyer, which troubles Anne, who does not trust Mrs. Clay's motives.

Sir Walter's extravagant spending habits have placed the family into considerable debt. Neither he nor Elizabeth has been able to devise any means of easing their financial burdens without compromising their dignity or relinquishing the comforts they regard as necessities for anyone of their breeding

Media Adaptations

- *Persuasion* was adapted as a film by Roger Michell, starring Amanda Root and Ciaran Hinds, Columbia/Tristar Studios, 1995; available from Columbia Home Video.

- The novel was also adapted in an earlier film version by Howard Baker, starring Anne Firbank and Bryan Marshall, BBC Video, 1971.

and social position. As a result, Sir Walter begs their close family friend, Lady Russell, to advise them, along with Mr. Shepherd, their lawyer.

Kind-hearted and generally rational, Lady Russell draws up, with Anne's help, a plan for them to economize. However, her father can not approve the suggestions Lady Russell has made for changes in his lifestyle. He decides that he would rather leave his home than live in a manner that he considers undignified. As a result, he determines to find a smaller but comfortable house in Bath and rent out Kellynch Hall, even though he is bothered by the gossip the move might generate. Anne becomes distressed over the thought of leaving her home and moving to a city where she thinks she will not know anyone.

When Admiral Croft, a native of Somersetshire, shows interest in Kellynch Hall, Sir Walter notes his considerable wealth and determines that he and his wife would be suitable tenants. Anne also approves of the couple, especially since several years ago, she had fallen deeply in love with Mrs. Croft's brother, Captain Frederick Wentworth. She hopes that Wentworth might visit his sister, which would afford Anne the opportunity to see him again.

Several years before in the summer of 1806, Wentworth lived at his brother's home near Kellynch Hall and soon fell in love with Anne. Her father, however, did not approve of the match, considering it to be "a very degrading alliance." Lady Russell shared Sir Walter's disapproval, noting that Wentworth had no money. She also considered "his

sanguine temper, and fearlessness of mind," a dangerous combination and so strongly advised Anne against marrying him. Anne could not ignore the displeasure felt by her father and Lady Russell, who had become a surrogate mother to her. Lady Russell eventually convinced her that her engagement to Wentworth was improper for both Anne and Wentworth. After Anne broke off the engagement, Wentworth determined that he had been "ill-used" and left the country. The break caused Anne a great deal of suffering, clouding "every enjoyment of youth" and causing an "early loss of [her] bloom and spirits."

During the next seven years, Anne never found anyone to compare with Captain Wentworth "as he stood in her memory." Charles Musgrove, a well-respected local man, had asked Anne to marry him, but she turned him down, and eventually he married her sister Mary. Anne has come to regret her decision to break off her relationship with Wentworth, blaming it on her "over-anxious caution."

As the Elliots plan their move, Mary decides that she is in bad health and insists that Anne come to stay with her before relocating to Bath. Mary frequently complains of ill health, most often to gain the attention of her family. Anne gives in to her sister since she is not looking forward to the move to Bath. In addition, her sister lives near Kellynch Hall where she hopes Wentworth will visit. Her patience and good nature soon cure Mary's "illness."

While at Mary's, Anne becomes well acquainted with Charles's parents, Mr. and Mrs. Musgrove, who are considerably less elegant and orderly than the Elliots but whose hospitality and kindness soon endear them to Anne. The Musgroves' spirited and good-natured daughters, Henrietta and Louisa, also are welcome guests in Mary's home.

Anne soon runs into Wentworth through her association with the Musgroves and the Crofts. Although he and Anne are frequently in each other's company, they do not engage in any conversation and speak only to each other when it is necessary to be polite. His coldness toward her upsets Anne. All of the others are quite impressed with the captain, especially the Musgroves' daughters. Henrietta seems to have forgotten her attachment to Charles Hayter, a young man she had become close to before she was introduced to Wentworth. Henrietta's attentions, however, soon return to Charles, and the others now assume Wentworth and Louisa will make a match.

One day, as Anne plays with her young nephew, he jumps on her back and refuses to get off. When Wentworth immediately rescues her, she becomes speechless at his kindness. Through this incident, she comes to understand that while he has not been able to forgive her, "he could not be unfeeling" toward her. Though he resented what she had done to him, "he could not see her suffer without the desire of giving her relief . . . an impulse of pure, though unacknowledged friendship." This act becomes proof of his "warm and amiable heart," the acknowledgement of which fills Anne with strong feelings of both pleasure and pain.

Wentworth organizes a trip for all of them to Lyme to visit his friend Captain Harville. While there, they meet Captain Benwick, who has been mourning the death of his fiancée, Harville's sister. Right before they leave Lyme, they take a walk along the Cobb, a long stone pier at the water's edge. Louisa demands that Wentworth catch her as she jumps down the steps, but she moves before he has a chance to prepare and falls on the pavement, knocking herself unconscious. They take Louisa to the Harville's house where she stays to recuperate.

Volume II

After Anne moves to Bath, she becomes friendly with William Elliot, her cousin and the heir presumptive to the Elliot estate, who has been accepted back into the family after a period of estrangement. She also renews her friendship with Mrs. Smith, a widowed schoolmate of hers, who suffers from ill-health and financial problems.

A month later, Anne is thrilled over the news that Louisa and Benwick are engaged, which puts to rest her fears over her friend's attachment to Wentworth. Wentworth soon comes to Bath to visit the Crofts, who have come for a short stay. One evening, when they are all gathered together at a party, Anne begins to suspect that he still has feelings for her after he appears jealous over Mr. Elliot's attentions towards her. The next morning, Anne visits Mrs. Smith who tells her that Mr. Elliot is a man "without heart or conscience," who had led her husband into debt.

The next day Anne discusses with Harville the difference between men's and women's emotions, both claiming that their own sex retains feelings of love the longest. During this conversation, Wentworth writes a letter, which everyone assumes is to Captain Benwick. As they leave, Wentworth leaves the letter where only Anne will discover it. The letter reveals how much he still loves her and his

hopes that she returns his affections. Anne becomes overwhelmed with emotion. Later, when they meet on the street, they both declare their love for each other. Anne admits that although Lady Russell was not reasonable in her previous assessment of Wentworth, Anne felt that it was her duty to follow her father's and Lady Russell's wishes.

Lady Elliot and Sir Walter now accept Wentworth as a suitable match for Anne, due to his distinguished military career and his wealth. Wentworth helps Mrs. Smith get some of her husband's money back. The novel ends happily for all.

Characters

Captain Benwick

Benwick, "an excellent young man," had been engaged to Captain Harville's sister. Anne meets him when she and her group travel to Lyme to visit Harville, Wentworth's friend. Harville's sister died the preceding summer while Benwick was at sea, and he has been in mourning ever since. Anne notes his "melancholy air" and his withdrawal from conversation. When she strikes up a friendship with him, she finds that his need to be useful prompts him to keep busy, constructing toys for the children and fixing things for the Harvilles. He and Anne discuss poetry, but she warns him of its power to stir the emotions and so suggests that he read it sparingly.

Mrs. Clay

Elizabeth strikes up a friendship with Mrs. Clay, the daughter of Mr. Shepherd, the family's lawyer. Mrs. Clay has returned to her father's house with her children after an unprosperous marriage. She has a sharp mind and "understood the art of pleasing," which makes her untrustworthy to Anne and Lady Russell, who consider her friendship with Elizabeth "dangerous." They both believe that she would like to form a romantic relationship with Sir Walter.

Admiral Croft

Admiral Croft and his wife rent Kellynch Hall after the Elliots move to Bath. His "goodness of heart and simplicity of character" are "irresistible" to Anne.

Mrs. Croft

Mrs. Croft is a "well-spoken, genteel, shrewd lady," who appears older than her thirty-eight years, due to her spending so much time at sea with her husband. Anne admires her for her open and easy manners and her devotion to being with her husband, even under the harsh conditions at sea.

Anne Elliot

Anne Elliot, Sir Elliot's middle daughter, possesses an elegant mind and sweet character recognized by all but her father and sister, who regard her as ordinary and so do not pay her much attention. Years ago, during her relationship with Wentworth, Anne had been quite attractive, but the pain she suffered after their split caused her "bloom" to vanish early.

Anne's loyalty and sense of family duty emerged as she forced herself to follow her father's and Lady Russell's advice concerning her engagement to Wentworth. Her naïve and gentle nature could not stand up to these two powerful influences in her life. She especially trusted Lady Russell's good council and so was persuaded to admit that a marriage to Wentworth would be improper and imprudent. Her unselfishness extended to Wentworth, whom she was convinced would also benefit from the breaking of their engagement, a belief that helped her endure their painful split.

Years later, Anne displays her maturity and levelheadedness as she constructs a plan with Lady Russell to help her father economize. Mary and her friends recognize her responsible nature and her kind heart, which emerges as she nurses her sister and takes charge after Louisa falls from the Cobb. All, except her father and sister, look to Anne for direction when a problem arises.

Over the years, Anne develops a keen understanding of human nature and so recognizes her father's and sister's shallow class consciousness. As she meets and enjoys the company of the Crofts and the Musgroves, she comes to relax her own strict standards of behavior and situation. This change becomes apparent when everyone but Anne makes a fuss when her cousins, the Dowager Viscountess Dalrymple and her daughter, the Honorable Miss Carteret, come to Bath. Anne finds them boring, preferring "the company of clever, well-informed people who have a great deal of conversation." She ignores William's observation that the family's association with them would be good for their position in society. She feels that those whose sincerity sometimes caused them to be imprudent or to lack decorum should be trusted more than those whose guardedness never allowed them to make a social mistake.

Her maturity also contributes to her understanding that while she should not yield to another's persuasion, she must retain her loyalty to her friends and family, even at the expense of her own desires.

Elizabeth Elliot

Elizabeth, the eldest Elliot daughter, has been the mistress of Kellynch Hall for the past thirteen years since her mother died, "presiding and directing with a self-possession and decision." She shares her father's vanity and class snobbery and ignores Anne, for the most part, considering her not worthy of her time or attention.

Mary Elliot

Sir Walter and Elizabeth also did not think much of Mary, the youngest Elliot, but when she married Charles Musgrove, she acquired a measure of importance in their estimation. Exhibiting the same kind of self-involvement as does her sister and father, Mary often complains of being unwell and always insists that her needs take precedence over those of her family. She often turns to Anne to "nurse" her back to health. When she feels that she has been properly attended to, she has high spirits, but when left alone for too long a period, she inevitably comes down with a new series of complaints.

Just as Anne is planning her move to Bath, Mary contracts another aliment and insists that she "cannot possibly do without" Anne's care. While Mary shows none of Anne's compassion nor even temper, Anne frequently agrees to stay with her sister since she was "not so repulsive and unsisterly as Elizabeth, nor so inaccessible to all influence of hers."

Sir Walter Elliot

"Vanity was the beginning and the end" of Sir Walter's character. He spent his time perfecting his personal appearance and reviewing his position in society. His favorite pastime is to reread his entry in the Baronetage, a book that records his and his family's history and social standing. He is quite attached to his eldest daughter, Elizabeth, who shares his temperament, but considers his two other daughters to be of very inferior value. He has lost hope of Anne ever marrying well and so puts his faith in Elizabeth to uphold the honor of the family through a prosperous marriage.

Sir Walter's snobbery had previously prompted him to deny his blessing for Anne's plans to marry Wentworth. He considers a naval career undesirable, insisting that sailors work hard but do not deserve to be raised from an obscure birth into distinction that he considers unmerited. He also finds sailors rather unattractive, due to their weathered features. Sir Walter only appreciates people and things he finds aesthetically pleasing. He reveals his shallowness when, at the end of the novel, he welcomes Wentworth into the family since the captain has amassed over twenty-five thousand pounds and has moved as high in his profession as possible and thus is no longer "nobody." Wentworth is now esteemed "quite worthy to address the daughter of a foolish, spendthrift baronet."

William Elliot

William Elliot, Esq., Anne's cousin and the heir presumptive to the Elliot inheritance, had a falling out with the family after his relationship with Elizabeth failed to end in marriage. The family had also discovered that he had "spoken most disrespectfully of them," which they could not forgive. Soon after, he married a rich woman "of inferior birth." After she died, he tried to resume his relationship with Elizabeth, but she would not consider it.

Eventually, he reestablishes his relationship with the family by insisting that his treatment of them had been due to an unfortunate misunderstanding. Sir Walter forgives him, and the family now becomes "delighted" with him, influenced by his charm and the fortune he has amassed through marriage. William now turns his attentions to Anne, who initially is flattered. To all, he appears polished, agreeable, and sensible. His conversations with others reveal "correct opinions" about the world and family honor. He also displays a kind heart and a sense of moderation.

The family assumes that he will marry Anne. While she admits the thought of being able to move back to Kellynch is hard to resist, she decides there is something about his character that bothers her. She distrusts his past, due to rumors that he had indulged in bad habits. Also, although he appears to be rational and discreet, he is not open. Anne notices that he never displays his emotions—any "warmth of indignation or delight." She becomes suspicious of his guardedness.

Anne's suspicions of William are proven true when Mrs. Smith reveals to her his true character. Elliot is, in reality, "a designing, wary, cold-blooded being who thinks only of himself." Mrs. Smith has experienced firsthand his lack of feeling for others when she watched him lead her husband into overwhelming debt. She concludes that he is "black and hollow at heart." Mrs. Smith proves his true nature when she shows Anne a letter he had written, criticizing her family. At the end of the novel, Elliot runs off with Mrs. Clay.

Captain Harville

Anne considers Captain Harville, a good friend of Wentworth's, a perfect gentleman, "unaffected, warm, and obliging."

Mrs. Fanny Harville

Mrs. Harville is "a degree less polished than her husband," yet she displays the same good heart, warmly welcoming the group from Somersetshire to her home. She also insists that Louisa recuperate under her care after her accident.

Charles Hayter

Charles Hayter, a scholar "very superior in cultivation and manners" to the Musgroves, has been involved in a relationship with Henrietta. When Wentworth arrives, Henrietta's attentions and affection are temporarily transferred from Charles to him.

Charles Musgrove

Charles Musgrove, a well-respected local man, had asked Anne to marry him, but she turned him down, and eventually he married her sister Mary. Her marriage to Charles pleases Sir Walter, who appreciates that Charles's standing in society is second only to Sir Walter's.

Charles's good nature allows him to tolerate his wife's frequent bids for attention, a quality Anne admires. She admits that his temperament and common sense make him superior to her sister; however, he is not clever enough in conversation for her to regret turning him down. He spends much of his time involved in sport but in nothing else of consequence, a situation Anne decides would have been improved if he had married a woman of equal understanding who could have helped steer him in a more useful and rational direction.

Henrietta Musgrove

Henrietta and Louisa, Charles's sisters, are typical women of their time and station. They live "to be fashionable, happy and merry." They both are high spirited and open but have no time for the more cultivated pursuits that occupy much of Anne's time. Anne appreciates their mutual affection for each other, something she has not enjoyed with her own sisters. Henrietta and Louisa pay Wentworth a great deal of attention and develop a "fever of admiration" for him that Anne fears might turn into love. Henrietta had been in a romantic relationship with another man before she met Captain Wentworth. Her attention and affection, however, soon return to the former man.

Louisa Musgrove

Louisa Musgrove is more incautious than her sister is. Her desire to jump off the Cobb causes her serious injury. While she recuperates, she falls in love with Captain Benwick.

Mr. Musgrove

Mr. Musgrove and his wife live an unordered life. Anne notes that they, "like their houses," always seem to be "in a state of alteration." They are old English in style, whereas their children are devoted to the new, and whereas neither is educated nor elegant, their friendliness and hospitality ensure their popularity; they never lack invitations or visitors.

Mrs. Musgrove

Mrs. Musgrove shares her husband's easy manner.

Lady Russell

The Elliots have relied on Lady Russell's generous support and generally reasonable advice ever since Mrs. Elliot died. Though she possessed a winning combination of benevolence and strict integrity, she was prejudicial against those she deemed of lower rank and consequence. She shared Sir Walter's disapproval of Anne's early attachment to Wentworth, noting that the captain had no money. She also considered "his sanguine temper, and fearlessness of mind," a dangerous combination and so strongly advised Anne against marrying him. Wentworth's behavior had not suited Lady Russell's own ideas, and she was hasty in suspecting them to indicate a character of "dangerous impetuosity." When Anne and Wentworth reestablish their relationship, Lady Russell reveals her magnanimous nature, admitting that she was wrong about him.

Mr. Shepherd

Mr. Shepherd, the Elliot's lawyer and Mrs. Clay's father, presents himself to be "civil and cautious."

Mrs. Smith

Mrs. Smith, Anne's widowed schoolmate, had been kind to her after Anne's mother died. When Anne reestablishes their friendship in Bath, she finds Mrs. Smith in ill health and financial difficulty. Mrs. Smith displays "good sense and agreeable manners" even during her hard times. Anne admires her "elasticity of mind," her lack of self-pity, and her resourcefulness.

Captain Frederick Wentworth

In the summer of 1806, Captain Wentworth, Mrs. Croft's brother, lived near Kellynch Hall and soon fell in love with Anne, who noted his quick mind, fearlessness, and generous spirit. These qualities, however, prompted Lady Russell's disapproval, which led to her advising Anne not to marry him.

When he reappears in Somersetshire years later, however, Wentworth's sterling character again reveals itself to Anne. He shows his compassionate heart as he listens to Mrs. Musgrove's sorrow over her son's early death, and he takes full responsibility for Louisa's accident, even though her impetuosity had been the cause. His stirring conversation about his days at sea prompt all to feel a "warm admiration" for him. While his stubbornness will not allow him to forgive Anne's initial rejection of him, that same quality will not let him give up on her. His generous nature allows him to forgive Sir Walter's and Lady Russell's interference as he becomes a part of the family.

Themes

Class Consciousness

The predominant theme in *Persuasion* focuses on the consciousness of class. Austen defines one main social division—the landed gentry of the upper-middle class—through her realistic portrayals of the Elliot family and those who travel in their sphere. She notes the traditions of this structured social group as well as its restricted vision of those outside the group. The ladies and gentlemen of the landed gentry, as represented by Sir Walter, depend on social hierarchies to ensure their superiority over the lower classes. Sir Walter's favorite pastime is to pore over the Baronetage, reminding himself of his exalted social position. The pride he takes in this position has degenerated into an inflated vanity and aesthetic sense, as he can appreciate only things that, like his own visage, please his eye.

His sense of superiority translates into an arrogance directed at those in lower classes who are presumptuous enough to try to improve their social station. One such interloper is Captain Wentworth, who assumes that his deep love for Anne, coupled with his success as a naval officer, should be enough to earn Sir Walter's blessing of their union. However, Sir Walter, backed by Lady Russell, rejects the captain as a suitable son-in-law, due to his lack of money and his profession, which Sir Walter considers undesirable. He notes that sailors work hard, but he insists that they do not deserve to be raised from an obscure birth into the upper class.

Anne's sister Elizabeth reflects her father's strict rules of etiquette. She devotes her time to "doing the honours, and laying down the domestic law at home . . . opening every ball of credit which a scanty neighbourhood afforded." Mary, Anne's youngest sister, has turned her feelings of superiority of class into a form of hypochondria. When she feels that she has not been paid enough attention, she comes down with an "illness" that must be attended to, preferably by Anne, who displays none of the class snobbery of the rest of the family.

All of the Elliots except Anne illustrate the gentry's limited vision of the realities of the world. They live in comfortable isolation in a privileged community set apart from the unpleasant truths of the social stratification and political system that has enabled them to live an advantaged life. Their restricted view does not recognize women like Mrs. Smith who have fallen on hard times, even if one of their class (as was the case with Mrs. Smith) has been the cause.

Sir Walter's change of heart, when Anne asks for his blessing the second time Captain Wentworth asks her to marry him, is the result of several factors. Wentworth has amassed a small fortune and so can afford to provide an even more comfortable life for Anne than the one she enjoyed with her economically-challenged father. Wentworth has also risen to the top of his profession, which, in the early part of the nineteenth century, was becoming highly honored. Thus Sir Walter is able to welcome the captain into the family and proudly record his name in the Baronetage without suffering the shame of Anne marrying someone unworthy of her social position.

Courtship and Marriage

The rituals of courtship and marriage are determined and strictly enforced within each class. They are governed by a sense of order, decorum,

Topics for Further Study

- Observe and listen to a conversation that involves several people. Write a short sketch of the conversation, focusing on the perspective of one of the people involved. Describe not only what is said but also what you imagine the person is thinking during the conversation.

- Read Austen's *Pride and Prejudice*, written during her first phase, and compare the central character, Elizabeth Bennet, to Anne Elliot. What similarities and differences do you discover?

- Research the psychological foundations of the act of persuasion. In what ways could Anne have prevented her father's and Lady Russell's influence over her?

- Investigate the lives of the middle-class British at the beginning of the nineteenth century. Discuss how strictly social lines were drawn during that period.

and self-control according to the rigid roles that women are expected to fulfill. A young woman is duty bound to obey her father's authority in all matters, submitting without question to the restrictions placed on her. When fathers forbade their daughters from marrying unacceptable men, they expected and got obedience. Sir Walter made a similar decree, with Lady Russell's support, which Anne felt she must obey, even though she would suffer greatly over her break from Wentworth. The novel ends happily only after Sir Walter changes his opinion about Wentworth and so gives his permission for Anne to marry him.

Style

Domestic Comedy

Austen helped create the domestic comedy of middle-class manners, a genre that is concerned with family situations and problems. This type of novel focuses on the manners and conventions of the British middle class—in Austen's work, specifically the landed gentry. The plot is structured around problems that arise within the family concerning the particular fashions and outlook of this structured social group. The point of view is often satirical, as it illuminates and critiques the idiosyncrasies of its members. Although the plot can offer clever solutions to the family's conflicts, it is less important than the characterizations and the dialogue. In *Persuasion*, Austen's plot revolves around the conflicts within her family and their desire to keep those they deem undesirable out. Though some characters, such as Lady Russell and Mrs. Clay, are decidedly flat, most of the Elliot family is carefully drawn to reflect the realities of upper-middle-class life in England at the beginning of the nineteenth century. As the plot evolves, Austen critiques the snobbery and arrogance of the landed gentry in her depiction of Sir Walter. All conflicts are worked out by the end of the novel, signaled by Anne's happy marriage to Wentworth.

Historical Context

Sentimental Novel

The sentimental novel was a popular form of fiction in England at the end of the eighteenth century. This type of fiction focuses on the problems encountered by virtuous men and women as they strive to lead exemplary lives. By the end of the novel, characters who displayed a sense of honor and behaved in a moral fashion were able to solve their problems and regain a sense of order in their world. The didactic plot promoted accepted standards of morality, encouraging readers to believe that such behavior would be justly rewarded in time. Characters in these novels did not check their emotions, which suggested their benevolence and compassion. The most well-known example of this genre is Samuel Richardson's *Pamela, or Virtue Rewarded*, published in 1740, which chronicled the life of the title character, a servant girl who survived continuous assaults on her honor. Other novels in this genre include Goldsmith's *The Vicar of Wakefield* (1776), Mackenzie's *The Man of Feeling* (1771), and Edgeworth's *Castle Rackrent* (1800). Austen broke from this form in her novels, which concentrate on realistic depictions of the tensions between her heroines and their society.

A Woman's Place

During the late eighteenth and early nineteenth centuries, women were confined to the classes into which they were born, unless their fathers or husbands moved up or down in the social hierarchy. The strict rules for each social class defined the women and their lives. Women in the upper classes had the leisure to educate themselves; however, they, like their counterparts in the lower classes, were not expected to think for themselves and were not often listened to when they did. Urges for independence and self-determination were suppressed in women from all classes. The strict social morality of the period demanded that women exhibit the standards of polite femininity, culminating in the ideals of marriage and motherhood. Jane Austen's novels both reflect and challenge the period's attitudes toward women. Her heroines must operate within the confines of the middle class, yet their quick minds and independent spirits make them yearn for at least a measure of autonomy. Brian Southam, in his article on Austen for *British Writers*, comments that each of Austen's heroines must "practice the morality of compromise and discover her own way of accepting the demands of society while preserving the integrity of her own values and beliefs."

Social Revolution

Austen's novels describe how British society was divided at the end of the eighteenth century into three classes: the aristocracy, the gentry, and the yeoman class. Yet, the revolutionary fervor at the end of this century and the beginning of the next, exemplified by the American and French revolutions, was seeping into the social fabric of England. During this period, class distinctions began to relax and to be redefined. As the lower-middle classes became more prosperous, they began to emulate their social "betters," as did the landed gentry of the upper-middle class. The middle classes became absorbed with a cultivation of the "proper" manners, dress, and décor practiced by the aristocracy.

Critical Overview

By the time *Persuasion* was published in 1818, Austen's novels had gained a limited reading audience that was dramatically expanded in 1833, when her novels were republished in the Bentley's Standard Novels series. Scholars began to pay at-

Compare
&
Contrast

- **Late 1700s:** *Vindication of the Rights of Woman* by Mary Wollstonecraft is published in 1792. The book chronicles the growing sense of dissatisfaction women feel about the unequal treatment they receive in the home and in other institutions.

  Today: American women have made major gains in their fight for equality with the passage of many pieces of legislation. Although some notable pieces of legislation, including the 1972 Equal Rights Amendment bill, have not been passed, discrimination against women is now against the law.

- **Late 1700s:** One of the most popular forms of literature during this period is the sentimental novel—a didactic work that promotes and rewards its characters' "proper" moral behavior.

  Today: The most popular forms of literature for the general reading public are thrillers and memoirs.

- **Late 1700s:** The American War of Independence is waged from 1775 to 1783. As a result, British domination of America comes to an end.

  Today: Catholics in Northern Ireland, backed by the Irish Republican Army (IRA), continue their struggle to break free from English rule.

---

tention to *Persuasion* and Austen's other novels in 1870, after the publication of *Memoir of Jane Austen*, the first major biography of her, written by her nephew James Edward Austen-Leigh. The biography triggered several articles on her works, including some by critics Margaret Oliphant and Richard Simpson. Scholarly attention to her novels increased at the end of the century and continued into the twentieth, especially after the publication of Mary Lascelles's *Jane Austen and Her Art* in 1939.

Persuasion, like her other novels, was praised for its realistic depiction of character and society. In his article on Austen for *British Writers*, Brian Southam applauds the "semantic drama" of the novel, commenting that within the novel "we can follow the scheme of characterization that brings the meaning of [the title] to life in the complexities and contradictions of human nature." Margaret Drabble, in her introduction to the Signet publication of the novel, praises its "strong anti-romantic tendencies," its "unexpected generosities," and its "welcoming of the possibility of a new order." These scholars have helped cement the novel's reputation as a literary classic.

Criticism

Wendy Perkins

Perkins is an associate professor of English and American literature and film at Prince George's Community College and has published several articles on British and American authors. In this essay, she argues that Austen's novel is a reflection of its revolutionary age.

In an article in *British Writers*, Brian Southam presents an overview of Jane Austen's work and concludes that her fiction reveals a firm sense of time and place. He argues that Austen's novels "communicate a profound sense" of England at the beginning of the nineteenth century, "when the old Georgian world of the eighteenth century was being carried uneasily and reluctantly into the new world of Regency England, the Augustan world into the romantic." Gary Kelly, in his critique of Austen's works for *Dictionary of Literary Biography*, notes that British society was influenced by the revolutionary fervor surrounding the American and French battles for independence during this age and finds that zeitgeist was represented "as a progressive dialectic of gentry and professionals."

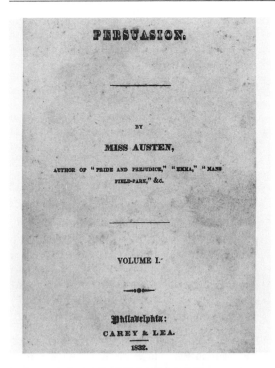

Title page from the 1832 edition of Persuasion

Austen's novels join this dialectical discussion, for they focus specifically on the changes in the country's social fabric as strict hierarchies of class were being challenged. The sense of this historical moment as a period of transition becomes most evident in her last novel, *Persuasion*. In her depiction of the members of the Elliot family and their circle, Austen not only chronicles the changes that were occurring in the British class system during this period, but she also appears to support them.

Austen begins the novel with a description of Sir Walter, the patriarch of the Elliot family, and his class obsession, evident in his constant perusal of the Baronetage, where he notes the description of the social standing and history of his family. Sir Walter is a traditional gentleman of the landed gentry, the upper-middle level of the British class system. Through his characterization, Austen records all that she finds pretentious and shallow in the most conservatively rigid members of this group. In her detailed depiction of Sir Walter's manners and fashionable pursuits, Austen lays the groundwork for her critique of the superficialities of the middle class.

In Sir Walter's structured society, the harmony of the group depends on each individual complying with its fixed rules. The appearance of wealth and propriety are sacrosanct in his world, and Sir Walter is a firm devotee of its conventions. As a result, when his extravagant spending habits threaten to bring him to the brink of financial ruin, he cannot come up with a plan to economize. He insists that he can endure no changes to his lifestyle that will compromise his dignity or comfort or that will place him in too close proximity to the lower classes. Fortunately, Lady Russell convinces him to find a less expensive dwelling in Bath, where he can appear to be enjoying a change of scenery and retain his social position.

The shallowness of the upper classes is reflected in the attitudes Sir Walter and his eldest daughter Elizabeth harbor regarding Anne. Unable to place value on her intellectual and moral merit, they find her loss of "bloom" after suffering through her break from Wentworth evidence of her inferiority.

Sir Walter's sense of superiority is epitomized in his overweening vanity, which is "the beginning and the end" of his character, and his arrogant dismissal of anyone from the lower classes who is presumptuous enough to try to gain entry into his circle. This attitude causes his daughter Anne to suffer greatly when it results in his refusal to approve of her marriage to Wentworth, who does not enjoy the benefits of a noble birth nor, initially, of the leisure class.

Austen's critique of this society develops a harder edge in her depiction of William Elliot, their self-serving cousin who reveals himself to be "black and hollow at heart." Austen illustrates the blindness of the middle class to the faults of its own privileged and "dignified" members when the Elliot family quickly allows him back into the family after a troubled past relationship with him. When they permit him to reestablish himself in their good graces, most find his character sterling. Anne, however, with her astute powers of perception that do not depend on social standing, suspects a duplicitous nature, which her friend Mrs. Smith confirms. The narrative soon reveals that he has come to Bath and reintegrated himself with the family only to insure his inheritance.

Austen's illustration of the age's spirit of change is centered in Anne. Her openness reflects the transitional nature of Regency England, when class distinctions began to blur. As the lower-middle classes became more prosperous, successful professionals were eager to share the privileges of the gentry and so began to imitate their manners and fashions. As a result, the traditional distinction between the two groups—a noble bloodline—began to ease. Anne embraces this change when she falls in love with Wentworth, a sailor who, when they first meet, is professionally but not economically successful. She also reveals her democratic spirit when she reestablishes her friendship with Mrs. Smith, an old schoolmate, who has fallen on hard times. Mrs. Smith represents the economic realities of the lower classes, which the gentry successfully ignored.

Anne has suffered from the strict code of manners and tightly defined roles thrust upon her by her social class. Her ties to her family must supersede her own desires, and as a result, they prevent her from marrying the man she loves. She believes, even at the end of the novel when she gains her family's approval for her marriage to Wentworth, that it is her duty to obey their wishes when they initially forbid her union with him. Her sense of duty springs from the moral obligation she feels to her family and to Lady Russell, who has become her surrogate mother. Austen juxtaposes this sense of duty with Anne's struggle for individuality and fulfillment, which she achieves in part, at the end of the novel, due to the changes that were beginning to occur in her world. She is finally able to marry Wentworth, not only because of his change in fortune but also as a result of the relaxed definition of a "gentleman." Wentworth has become socially acceptable through the new respect paid his profession. During the early part of the nineteenth century, England held its navy in high regard as a result of its victories at sea and its protection of trading routes.

Austen supports this transitional spirit through her depiction of other characters. While Mr. and Mrs. Musgrove have the breeding that insures their inclusion into Sir Walter's circle, their unconventional behavior strains the boundaries of their class. The Musgroves' unpretentious nature emerges in their encouragement of their daughters' independent spirits and in their lack of concern for traditionally proper mates for them. Anne notes that they live an unordered life and that, "like their houses," they always seemed to be "in a state of alteration."

At first Anne seems put off by their disorder. However, as she gains experience and maturity, she accepts and promotes the relaxation of social norms. When she discovers and comes to an appreciation of the Musgroves' warm hearts and openness, she embraces their differences and in-

> " Anne has suffered from the strict code of manners and tightly defined roles thrust upon her by her social class."

cludes them in her circle of friends. She welcomes them with open arms when they arrive in Bath, especially after having to suffer the company of her stuffy and dull cousins, Lady Dalrymple and Miss Carteret. Anne's new openness becomes apparent in her distrust of William Elliot and in her decision that she appreciates spontaneity over formality. She concludes that she could "so much more depend upon the sincerity of those who sometimes looked or said a careless or a hasty thing, than of those whose presence of mind never varied, whose tongue never slipped."

The Harvilles and the Crofts also help educate Anne about the possibilities of a world free from rigid class structures. Although they have cramped accommodations, the Harvilles warmly welcome Anne and her group to Lyme, and after the accident, they insist on nursing Louisa back to health. Anne also appreciates Mrs. Croft's unconventional behavior in her relationship with her husband. Mrs. Croft has redefined the limiting roles for women in her position, as noted when she responds to Captain Wentworth's assertion that naval vessels are no place for ladies. She corrects him sharply, noting, "But I hate to hear you talking so, like a fine gentleman, and as if we were all fine ladies, instead of rational creatures."

Austen promotes the concept of women being "rational creatures" as she emphasizes Anne's "strong, mature mind," qualities that become evident in her behavior throughout the novel. Through Anne, Austen challenges traditional notions that fashionable women should only concern themselves with learning to sing and play the piano and to memorize English verse and passages from novels. Women who could present this shallow display of the arts became perfect social ornaments and wives. As a counter to these limited women, Austen presents Anne as rational and witty, able to think for herself. She has developed an interior life independent of those in her class and strives to make

What Do I Read Next?

- Austen's *Sense and Sensibility*, published in 1811, chronicles the lives of Elinor and Marianne Dashwood as they learn to find a balance between the extremes of the two qualities noted in the title.

- *Pride and Prejudice*, published in 1813 and considered to be Austen's best novel, presents an intimate portrait of Elizabeth Bennet and her struggles with family, social, and romantic problems.

- *Emma*, published in 1816, focuses on one of Austen's most endearing and complex characters as she tries to influence the lives of those in her circle.

- Robert B. Cialdini's *Influence: The Psychology of Persuasion*, published in 1993, presents the science of persuasion as it helps readers understand the psychological foundations of this technique.

---

her own choices concerning her relationships and her destiny.

Austen reinforces her social critique and her support of change at the end of the novel. Even though Anne admits that she was right in following her father's and Lady Russell's advice in not marrying Wentworth, citing her sense of duty, Austen underlines the fact that Anne and Wentworth have lost several years of happiness due to the narrow-mindedness and overly cautious opinions of others. After Anne and Wentworth reunite, however, Lady Russell also shows signs that she has become more open to new social standards. She admits that because Wentworth's "manners had not suited her own ideas, she had been too quick in suspecting them to indicate a character of dangerous impetuosity." Now, she concedes that "she had been pretty completely wrong" and determines "to take up a new set of opinions and of hopes." Sir Walter, ever the symbol of the old world, remains at the end of the novel "a foolish, spendthrift baronet, who had not had principle or sense enough

to maintain himself in the situation in which Providence had placed him." Kelly notes Sir Walter's static nature in contrast to the transformations occurring around him when he comments that at the conclusion, his estate, "dangerously overextended morally, socially, and financially, is not so much reinvigorated as superseded by an estate acquired entirely on merit and able to take into itself the neglected best of the older estate."

Persuasion participates in the revolutionary spirit of its age through Austen's penetrating critique of the sacred ideals of the British class system and her documentation and support of the changes that were emerging at the end of the Age of Reason. Through her characterization of her heroine, Anne Elliot, she presents a wise and sympathetic portrait of one woman's shifting perspective of her relation to society and her understanding of herself.

Source: Wendy Perkins, Critical Essay on *Persuasion*, in *Novels for Students*, The Gale Group, 2002.

Mary Waldron

In the following essay excerpt, Waldron examines Austen's moral intentions in Persuasion.

Of all six completed novels *Persuasion* most resists a late twentieth-century reader's attempts to exonerate Austen from charges of prescriptiveness and didacticism. If Anne Elliot was 'almost too good' for the author, a reading based on an assumption of Austen's attachment to conventional contemporary wisdom will certainly leave her too good for us. Marilyn Butler, among others, avers that 'Anne comes near to being dangerously perfect' and much modern criticism finds her somewhat tediously fault-free. Curiously, though, it is the one work of Austen's which attracted prompt contemporary criticism on moral grounds; in 1818 the following was included in a review in *The British Critic*:

> [The novel] contains parts of very great merit; among them, however, we certainly should not number its *moral*, which seems to be, that young people should always marry according to their own inclinations and upon their own judgement; for that if in consequence of listening to grave counsels, they defer their marriage, till they have wherewith to live upon, they will be laying the foundation for years of misery, such as only the heroes and heroines of novels can reasonably hope ever to see the end of.

These two attitudes, nearly two hundred years apart, provide us with a bewildering paradox—is the novel supporting or rejecting contemporary rules of conduct? What was Austen up to in *Per-*

suasion? Various answers have been put forward; like *Mansfield Park* it continues to provoke explanations, if not apologies, for its moral stance—most often critics find something wrong with it, some failure of coherence or consistency. If we examine the novel within the framework of the present study, we should be able to come close to an answer to the questions surrounding *Persuasion* without implying that Austen somehow did not quite achieve her aim. The five other novels, and the fragments, have all manoeuvred among available stereotypes to find a new way of presenting in fiction the problems of human interaction in life as Austen perceived it, rather than life as it might, according to contemporary conduct-theory, desirably be lived. *Persuasion* is no exception, but it takes a somewhat different direction.

Emma had come in for a good deal of criticism on the grounds that its heroine was no compliment to the female sex. In 'Opinions of *Emma*', Miss Isabella Herries 'objected to my exposing the sex in the character of the Heroine', and Fanny Knight's current admirer, James Wildman, was apparently of the same opinion. Austen replies:

> Do not oblige him to read any more.—Have mercy on him, tell him the truth & make him an apology. He & I should not in the least agree of course, in our ideas of Novels and Heroines;—pictures of perfection as you know make me sick & wicked—but there is some good sense in what he says, & I particularly respect him for wishing to think well of all young Ladies; it shews an amiable & delicate Mind.—And he deserves better treatment than to be obliged to read any more of my Works.

There was very little likelihood that Austen would, at this stage, fulfil expectation by writing an exemplary novel or create a 'picture of perfection'. What she did was to invent a character with whom no one could find fault on the grounds of manners or behaviour ('with manners as consciously right as they were invariably gentle'), who fulfils outwardly all the ideals of the conduct books, and subject her to narrow and mindless interpretations of those ideals. This heroine is thereby forced into a pragmatism which throws her back on *feeling* as 'her spring of felicity' and the reference-point of her judgement. But this novel is not a new, late celebration of sensibility, a *'Woman of Feeling'*. Anne is deeply convinced that reason and feeling are not oppositional but complementary; what goes against feeling goes against reason also. She is more like Marianne than she is like Elinor. But she is not influenced by fashionable moral and social theory. She has come to her conclusions from experience—she has found out that inflexible ad-

> **What she did was to invent a character with whom no one could find fault on the grounds of manners or behaviour . . . who fulfils outwardly all the ideals of the conduct books, and subject her to narrow and mindless interpretations of those ideals."**

herence to rule and precept does not invariably increase the sum of human happiness and may well do the opposite. Who has gained by her sacrifice? As the result of the failure of traditional 'sensible' solutions to make sense of her life, Anne has to go back to first principles, and in the intolerable tension between what she feels is right and what is forced upon her by contemporary judgements, is nearly drained of energy; she almost fails to give her life back its meaning. The novel presents no single solution to any of her problems and the dénouement is a matter of luck rather than judgement. The best we can say of the ending is that time and chance are kind to Anne Elliot. Deserving as she may be, the reader must be aware that she could have remained disappointed and alone for the rest of her life.

In the *Plan of a Novel* of (circa) 1816, Austen postulates a heroine very like Anne: 'a faultless Character herself—perfectly good, with much tenderness & sentiment, & not the least Wit—very highly accomplished, understanding modern Languages & (generally speaking) everything that the most accomplished young Women learn, but particularly excelling in Music—her favourite pursuit—& playing equally well on the Piano Forte & Harp—& singing in the first stile'. Austen adds a modicum of 'Wit' and subtracts the harp and the singing (significantly, in emphasising the waste of Anne's real musical talents—'having no voice, no knowledge of the harp, and no fond parents to sit by and fancy themselves delighted'), but otherwise this is both Austen's rather contemptuous concept of the conventional heroine *and* Anne Elliot to the life. However, what happens to her is not according to that convention. The novel is essentially a critique of the common fictional adventures of such a girl, which were often only one degree removed from the ludicrous junketings described in the *Plan.* Fictional 'cant' is still the author's target.

As we have seen, Austen's admiration for the works of Fanny Burney was becoming a little detached and ironical even in 1796, just after the publication of *Camilla.* She remembers sending her love to 'Mary Harrison' hoping that when she is 'attached to a young Man, some *respectable* Dr. Marchmont may keep them apart for five volumes'. Anne and Captain Wentworth are kept apart for *two*—thus fulfilling a fictional expectation, but without the obsessive moralising of Marchmont and Edgar's most unlikely submission to his opinion and easy conviction of Camilla's guilt. But Burney's later publication, *The Wanderer*, which came out during Austen's confident period after the success of *Pride and Prejudice*, is clearly part of the immediate stimulus for *Plan of a Novel* and more seriously for *Persuasion*, Juliet Granville's adventures as she tries to earn a meagre living and later flies from her brutal pursuers through the English countryside are undeniably the source of the caricature heroine in *Plan:*

> often reduced to support herself . . . by her Talents & work for her Bread;—continually cheated & defrauded of her hire, worn down to a Skeleton, & now & then starved to death—.At last, hunted out of civilized society, denied the poor Shelter of the humblest Cottage . . . having at least 20 narrow escapes of falling into the hands of Anti-hero—& at last in the very nick of time . . . runs into the arms of the Hero himself . . .

Not an exact parallel, perhaps, but recognisable enough. Burney had many axes to grind in her novel—it is a complex examination of social attitudes which deserves a good deal of respect—but her serious purpose drives her to present thoroughly unlikely characters and situations and inflates her language, which often bears no resemblance to any recognisable human dialogue. The multiplicity and intensity of Juliet's tribulations, from which she surprisingly emerges sweet, modest and clean, producing alternately 'a torrent of tears' and 'mantling blushes', would come for Austen in the category of 'unnnatural conduct and forced difficulties' which she cites as her grounds for finding Sarah Burney's *Clarentine* 'foolish'. In *Persuasion* conduct is to be natural, the difficulties will derive predictably from common rather than extraordinary situations, and the outcome will be satisfactory, but quite independent of anyone's deserts.

At the opening of the novel, Anne has lost her moral bearings. That is not to say that she does not behave according to Christian principles of tolerance and endurance, but that she has no faith in the value of these things. She adopts approved virtues in a rather mechanical, joyless way because she has little alternative. This is due in great part to the chief difference between her and most of the other Austen heroines—her isolation. Not even Fanny Price is so deprived of a companion to whom she can speak. Unlike Elizabeth Bennet and Elinor Dashwood, Anne is caught between two selfish and uncongenial sisters; the only person who appears to care at all whether she lives or dies is Lady Russell, a good woman of limited intelligence who relies on a set of narrow and cautious precepts and rates reason above—not equal to—feeling. In context we can see her as a responsible woman reacting adversely to what she saw as dangerous new ideas. There is more than a hint in the text that she is familiar with the radical/conservative debate; she 'gets all the new publications' and Elizabeth is bored by her interest in 'new poems and states of the nation'. When Anne accepts her advice and breaks her engagement to Frederick Wentworth, she has literally no one else to turn to, no one else with whom to discuss her life-choices. During the eight years which elapse before she meets Wentworth again, her isolation becomes total, since she can no longer communicate even with Lady Russell. In her own mind she separates her duty to submit to the 'grave counsels' of her elders from *their* duty to make sure their advice will lead to certain good—a hopeless expectation. She forgives herself for her submission, but at the same time blames the system within which she lives for its chill caution and ungenerous prudence. She feels sure that given the chance she would never act according to its precepts—'she felt that were any young person, in similar circumstances, to apply to her for counsel, they would never receive any of such certain immediate wretchedness, such uncertain future good'. So far, she has not had the chance, for her family situation deprives her of all influence and her circle of acquaintance is too narrow. She has adopted a negative and passive view of life in which she allows herself to be either ignored or used for other people's convenience. There is a sense in which she is almost punishing Lady Russell by refusing either to recover or to discuss her situation: 'But in this case [that of Charles Musgrove's proposal], Anne had left nothing for advice to do; and though Lady

Russell, as satisfied as ever with her own discretion, never wished the past undone, she began now to have the anxiety which borders on hopelessness for Anne's being tempted, by some man of talents and independence'. Having initially accepted advice, Anne sees no reason to comfort her friend for its effects. She simply does not talk to her about it.

It is important for our understanding of the novel to examine the background to Lady Russell's advice and its impact on a contemporary reader. Few in 1818 would have argued against the general inadvisability of an almost penniless, though 'gently' reared, girl engaging herself to marry an actually penniless, if optimistic, young sailor on the off-chance that he might one day succeed in making enough money to keep them both—and their children. In general, Lady Russell would have been held to be right. The undesirability of long engagements was received opinion. Older and supposedly wiser heads would not depend on the first flush of love and commitment to last; suppose a girl or young man met someone they liked better? Better not to trust to the vicissitudes of time and change. After eight years, Anne no more believes this in her own case than she had done at nineteen, when she was persuaded that her love would only be a burden to him:

> She was persuaded that under every disadvantage of disapprobation at home, and every anxiety attending his profession, all their probable fears, delays and disappointments, she should yet have been a happier woman in maintaining the engagement, than she had been in the sacrifice of it; and this, she fully believed, had the usual share, had even more than a usual share of all such solicitudes and suspense been theirs

A little later, the authorial voice calls this 'romance', and this description, even in its pejorative sense, would have attracted a good deal of contemporary agreement. But we do not have to identify Anne's beliefs with the author's. Anne could have no means of knowing what the outcome would be; her prudence at nineteen may have been 'unnatural', but is it therefore to be rejected as useless? As usual with an Austen novel the narrative leaves questions open at the same time as appearing to answer them. We can imagine, if we choose, how Anne might have fared if the engagement had continued and Wentworth had not succeeded; had, perhaps, ended up like his friend Harville, disabled on half pay. Anne finds the Harvilles' efforts to be happy in inadequate seaside lodgings charming and cosy—a harder head would call this romance also. How might she have coped, in reality? We are told, significantly, that Mrs Harville is 'a de-

gree less polished than her husband'—hardened perhaps by material deprivations. Anne knows very little about such things, except that the warmth of the Harvilles' domestic life seems to contrast strongly with the coldness of her own family situation. Even a less cautious observer than Lady Russell might easily pronounce her in error. Austen's habit of driving the allegiances of readers against the grain of their convictions is very evident here. And we are not even quite sure that the narrative tilts *against* Anne, for the example of Benwick's engagement to Fanny Harville, undertaken before they had the means to marry, is given as an example of what might have happened in the case of Anne and Wentworth if Sir Walter had been less of a snob and Lady Russell less entrenched in principle. Admiral and Mrs Croft seem to have taken some risk in marrying without much attention to material considerations. No single situation is put forward for reader approval. Anything could have happened.

But Anne's particular situation is aggravated by the unhelpful personality of her lover. We are surely not expected to suppose that Wentworth is justified in demanding that Anne choose between himself and the only other person in the world who cares a fig for her. He compounds her misery by his version of a contemporary expectation of female conduct. Meekness combined with ignorance had long since been rejected by those promulgating the rules; moralists like Hannah More were now constructing even more improbable models like Lucilla Stanley, who were able to impress onlookers with their firmness of opinion in situations which those onlookers approved, while in general keeping a very low profile indeed. Wentworth demonstrates this double expectation—he loves Anne partly for her traditional womanly virtues (her 'gentleness, modesty, taste, and feeling') but expects her to rise up in revolt against those traditions when, and probably only when, it suits him. His confusions on this score are several times made clear; he states as his twin requirements in a wife 'a firm mind, with sweetness of manner'; he seems little interested in how that sweetness can be maintained while she defies the counsels of her family. He is a long time working out what Tony Tanner has called a combination of 'flexibility and firmness, the concessionary and the adamant' which is necessary in all human dealings, and does not recognise the complexity of his demands. His confusion is made specifically evident; he does not wish his putative wife's firmness of mind to extend to insisting on coming to sea with him; his argument with his sister at Uppercross makes this very clear, and his manner of extricating himself from this exchange is symptomatic of unease and uncertainty:

> 'Now I have done . . .—When once married people begin to attack me with, 'Oh! you will think very differently, when you are married.' I can only say, 'No, I shall not;' and then they say again, 'Yes, you will,' and there is an end of it.'

He got up and moved away.

Anne is constantly the overhearer of Wentworth's rather desperate attempts to make a consistent structure for his wishes and desires; his conversation about the hazelnut with Louisa contains the same kind of obstinate theorising. His analogy has no validity, for the nut that clings to the tree will rot, while those that fall will germinate. After eight years, he is still an angry man, emotionally confused and refusing to see reason. Much later he admits this.

The story requires the two to meet again, and Austen makes sure that the re-encounter is believable, though entirely the work of chance. Sudden and unpredictable meetings after years of inexplicable silence are legion in the fiction of the time; this one is different. Ironically, Sir Walter's financial difficulties lead directly to it, when the Crofts come to Kellynch as his tenants. To give ample space for further exploration of the couple's attitudes, Anne is typically rejected as a companion in Bath by her elder sister, Elizabeth, (who substitutes the ambitious gold-digger, Mrs Clay) and demanded as support by her discontented sister Mary Musgrove at Uppercross. The social mores of the time would make an exchange of visits between the Musgroves and Crofts inevitable; the shared profession of Admiral Croft and his brother-in-law and the 'peace [which was] turning all our rich Navy Officers ashore' would make a visit from Wentworth very likely.

He comes, and the event gives readers the opportunity to observe even more closely than the narrative has so far allowed, the nature of the relationship between him and Anne. Light is soon thrown on what might be supposed to be the root cause of Lady Russell's uneasiness all those years ago, however she might rationalise it into purely economic consideration. We have already been told that Wentworth and Anne 'were gradually acquainted, and when acquainted, rapidly and deeply in love'. Lady Russell would see this as a dangerous version of the Romeo-Juliet story—'too rash, too ill-advised, too sudden'. 'Rational esteem' may

be present, but the chief component of this love is something more basic, and Austen does not flinch from demonstrating it. The necessity for novel heroines (such as Burney's Camilla and Juliet) to be cool in their response to awkward suitors or rejected lovers is here ignored. Twice during this early phase of renewal Anne is shaken to the foundation of her being by his touch; once even through the body of the little child clinging to her back; it 'produced such a confusion of varying, but very painful agitation, as she could not recover from'; and again as he assists her into the carriage of his sister and brother-in-law: 'his will and his hands had done it . . . it was proof of his own warm and amiable heart, which she could not contemplate without emotions so compounded of pleasure and pain, that she knew not which prevailed'. All the time Anne is also aware of his continued 'high and unjust resentment', but this makes no difference. Indeed, the strength of her feeling overcomes what is clearly seen both by herself and by the reader as unscrupulousness and arrogant petulance in his flirtation with the Musgrove daughters. By all contemporary fictional standards Anne ought to disapprove enough to resolve to have nothing more to do with him. But it never crosses her mind. What we are seeing here is not the anxious internal debate about what is *right* which so often dominates the proceedings in Burney and Edgeworth, for instance, but the unstructured reactions of strong emotion. Without generalising, the narrative comes down heavily in favour of the 'single and constant attachment' which Elinor Dashwood tries so valiantly to reject when she thinks her hopes of Edward are gone forever; her words could easily be Lady Russell's, but they could never issue from the lips of Anne Elliot: 'And after all . . . that is bewitching in the idea . . . and all that can be said of one's happiness depending entirely on any particular person, it is not meant—it is not fit—it is not possible that it should be so'. Though Anne sees that a 'second attachment' is possible for others, even forsees Benwick's and is more tolerant of it than Wentworth is, for herself it is not on the agenda. It is not a moral question; she is not aiming at any '*beau idél*' of female conduct; her 'high-wrought love and eternal constancy' are the products of passion, not principle. She simply cannot help herself. But what she does not do for a time is revive within herself the energy to rekindle Wentworth's response. She almost hands him over to Louisa.

By many of Austen's contemporaries her failure to cure herself of this 'ill-placed attachment' might be interpreted as weakness—even obstinacy in thus clinging to the past. We might now rather describe it as a loss of moral energy and recognise it as a destructive form of sublimation; Austen appears in some sort to present it as such. Anne contents herself with defusing the petty disagreements between her sister and her husband and in-laws and indulging the often selfish demands of her more positive companions. She is aware that she is wasted, but tells herself that there is nothing she can do. Her attitude is summed up in her physical response to life—why has she abandoned dancing in order to accompany others? It cannot be that at twenty-seven her joints are too stiff for the exercise. Some of her dejection seems almost wilful—the creation of a desert called 'duty' in which to protect herself from the necessity for positive action.

A change of heart is necessary for the dynamics of the story—Anne must move from passive to active in order to regain a positive purpose in life. Perhaps the most remarkable feature of this novel is the way in which the author minutely charts the re-establishment of communication between Anne and Wentworth. It begins at Lyme. Still feeling marginalised, her first encounter with Benwick shows Anne indulging in self-pity and other negative feelings. If we read chapter 11 of the first volume with attention to the depth of reference of its free indirect style, we find her ignoring certain clues to Wentworth's state of mind as if she is afraid even to begin to hope. While contemplating the idea of Benwick, whom she is about to meet, and the tragedy of his loss, she thinks of herself as in worse case: "'he has not, perhaps, a more sorrowing heart than I have. I cannot believe his prospects to be so blighted forever'"; she has missed the purport of Wentworth's account—his acknowledgement of the strength of such a feeling as he supposes Benwick to have had: 'He considered his disposition as of the sort which must suffer heavily, uniting very strong feelings with quiet, serious, and retiring manners, and a decided taste for reading, and sedentary pursuits'. It is open to the reader to wonder whether he has almost inadvertently begun to speak once more to Anne. She begins to be more obviously the focus of his thought from the time when the as yet unrecognised Mr Elliot admires her during the pre-breakfast walk—'He [Wentworth] gave her a momentary glance,—a glance of brightness, which seemed to say, "That man is struck with you,—and even I, at this moment, see something like Anne Elliot again"'; this accelerates with the disaster on the Cobb and culminates with his overheard statement at Mrs Harville's: "'but, if Anne will stay, no one so proper, so capable as Anne!'"—an indication, if ever there was one, of his abandonment of his view of her as feeble. But Anne is by no means ready to interpret all this as anything but an effort to get the best nursing for Louisa—now, she teaches herself to suppose, the object of his affection. She cannot yet accept the idea of constancy in a man. (For different reasons, Emma has also shown this kind of obtuseness; perhaps Austen regarded it as more believable than the stoical determination to repress desire which is evident in many contemporary novels). Accustomed to pessimism, she protects herself from hope that she thinks is bound to be unjustified. While she swiftly recognises Benwick's melancholy as an indulgence in an *expected*, theoretical and literary, sensibility rather than real suffering, and wryly comments to herself that she could well do with the same advice as she proffers to him, she fails to notice the resurfacing of Wentworth's powerful attraction to her. She is too ready to accept his flirtation with Louisa as actual courtship. She misinterprets everything because with him she cannot be detached.

The reader should see Wentworth at first exasperated by his permanent emotional commitment to Anne, and gradually coming to perceive that he cannot and does not want to escape; this is invisible to Anne, and incidentally to everyone else, for Wentworth tells her later that he is almost 'entangled' in an engagement with Louisa at this point. The reader is, as so often with Austen, at the third point of the triangle, which shifts the attention outward from the main action and shows the protagonists to be deceived or deceiving, without the direct intervention of a narrator. (There is again a parallel here with Emma and Mr Knightley.) Though Anne's 'second spring' has already begun, some cautious fear in her refuses to believe it. Wentworth has clearly shown his appreciation of her judgement and his instinctive intimacy with her when he seeks her opinion about their encounter with Louisa's parents—("Do you think this a good plan?"'); but after they have all gone away to Lyme, leaving her to await the advent of Lady Russell, she takes refuge in brooding melancholy, injecting her situation with the poetry of tragic loss:

> A few months hence, and the room now so deserted, occupied but by her silent, pensive self, might be filled again with all that was happy and gay, all that was glowing and bright in prosperous love, all that was most unlike Anne Elliot!

An hour's complete leisure for such reflections as these, on a dark November day, a small thick rain almost blotting out the very few objects ever to be discerned from the windows, was enough to make the sound of Lady Russell's carriage exceedingly welcome; and yet, though desirous to be gone, she could not quit the mansion-house, or look an adieu to the cottage, with its black, dripping, and comfortless veranda, or even notice through the misty glasses the last humble tenements of the village, without a saddened heart.—Scenes had passed in Uppercross, which made it precious. It stood the record of many sensations of pain, once severe, but now softened; and of some instances of relenting feeling, some breathings of friendship and reconciliation, which could never be looked for again, and which could never cease to be dear. She left it all behind her; all but the recollection that such things had been.

In their way, these thoughts are as literary as Benwick's, who Anne has been so sure will revive to love again, and on whom she has enjoined a more positive effort to 'fortify the mind' by recourse to works other than poetry. Anne is not without a sense of humour, and is herself 'amused at the idea of her coming to Lyme, to preach patience and resignation to a young man whom she had never seen before; nor could she help fearing . . . that, like many other great moralists and preachers, she had been eloquent on a point in which her own conduct would ill bear examination'. But her self-criticism does not prevent her from now indulging in what must be described as a consolatory but also somewhat enjoyable wallow in romantic melancholy much like Benwick's. She too has been reading Byron. We are later informed that she can read Italian—the quotation from Dante which introduces *The Corsair*—'nessun maggior dolore, / Che ricordarsi del tempo felice / Nelle miseria' aptly sums up her state of mind. There are clear structural and narratorial reasons why the time-scale of the novel is the period 1806 to 1814—the absence and wholesale return of naval officers is necessary to the plot—but the fact that it coincides with the publication and frenzied popularity of Byron's Turkish tales is used here by Austen in a similar contrapuntal way to her use of contemporary novels; aware of her immediate readers' inevitable acquaintance with these works, she constantly refers to them in a way that is both ironic and revealing. In the three poems which are mentioned by Anne and Benwick in their conversation at Lyme—*The Giaour, The Bride of Abydos* and *The Corsair*—a male lover has lost the woman of his heart in sensational circumstances involving abduction, murder and sudden death; the heroes are as a consequence dedicated to lifelong desolation which

occasions their withdrawal from the scenes of action and their total resistance to consolation. That Benwick is *not* inconsolable very soon becomes evident—Anne is aware of 'some dawning of tenderness towards herself' and his need to replace Fanny Harville rather than mourn her forever is later proved by his engagement to Louisa. But Anne sees far more of a parallel with Byron's heroes in herself, and her thoughts constantly echo his lines—especially certain passages from *The Giaour*. Her internal monologue quoted above has much in common with his lament:

> The keenest pangs the wretched find
> Are raptures to the dreary void,
> The leafless desert of the mind
> The waste of feelings unemploy'd.
> Who would be doom'd to gaze upon
> A sky without a cloud or sun?

Echoes, more perhaps in the vocabulary than the sense, recur; the Friar muses of the Giaour: 'But sadder still it were to trace / What once were feelings in that face'; Anne notices Wentworth looking at her: '*Once* she felt that he was . . . observing her altered features, perhaps, trying to trace in them the ruins of the face which had once charmed him'. She is only too willing to interpret Mary's rather spiteful report that Wentworth 'should not have known her again' in the light of the Giaour's description of himself:

> The wither'd frame, the ruin'd mind,
> The wrack by passion left behind.
> A shrivell'd scroll, a scatter'd leaf,
> Sear'd by the autumn blast of grief!

Anne is often shown to identify herself with autumnal decay—once even as she notes the evidence that the farmer at Winthrop was 'counteracting the sweets of poetical despondence and meaning to have spring again', and we can be fairly sure that some of the quotations with which she toys on that walk were from Byron.

Source: Mary Waldron, "Rationality and Rebellion: *Persuasion* and the Model Girl," in *Jane Austen and the Fiction of Her Time*, Cambridge University Press, 1999, pp. 135–47.

Alistair M. Duckworth

In the following essay, Duckworth explores the "new direction" Austen takes in Persuasion *toward social status and heritage as compared to her earlier novels.*

The success with which *Emma* accommodates its imaginative heroine in a traditional community invites us to read Jane Austen's conservative commitment as a sincere response rather than a conventional cover or camouflage. Unlike *Emma*, however, *Persuasion* (1818) does not bring its heroine to a defined social place and role; and in the last novel the attitude to social heritage differs subtly, if not in the end radically, from that communicated in the earlier novels. Though Anne Elliot becomes the wife of Captain Wentworth and the delighted mistress of a "very pretty landaulette," she has (as her status-obsessed sister Mary observes with satisfaction) "no Uppercross-hall before her, no landed estate, no headship of a family," *Persuasion* marks a new direction in Jane Austen's search for accommodations. Her deliberate decision not to provide Anne with abbey, house, hall, place, park, or cottage on her marriage to a man who has gained a fortune of £25,000 from prize money does not indicate—as the failure to finish *The Watsons* did—an oppressed sense of insurmountable difficulties to be overcome. The nature of the problem has changed, as has the kind of accommodation sought.

One way to describe the new direction of *Persuasion* is to compare Anne Elliot's role with that of Fanny Price. Like Fanny, Anne is often made aware of her "own nothingness." Fanny, however, becomes involved despite herself in issues of social importance at Sotherton, Mansfield, and Thornton Lacey, defending traditional "grounds" from the injuries of selfish improvements, innovative behavior, and materialistic ways. When she becomes the mistress of the Mansfield parsonage, she redeems her society. In *Persuasion*, by contrast, "place" is no longer there to be defended, since Sir Walter Elliot, the "foolish spendthrift baronet, who had not had principle or sense enough to maintain himself in the situation in which Providence had placed him," has rented his ancestral home and moved to Bath, where, to Anne's sorrow, he feels "no degradation in his change." Kellynch Hall will never be Anne's to "improve," nor is she to find a home like Uppercross (of which she could have been mistress one day, had she accepted Charles Musgrove's proposal of marriage).

Uppercross mansion, with "its high walls, great gates, and old trees, substantial and unmodernized," exists at the heart of the kind of organic community Jane Austen had described in her positive pictures of places like Delaford and Thornton Lacey. But in *Persuasion* the viability of its "old English style" is put in some question. Charles Musgrove, heir to the estate, has introduced improvements in the community in the form of a farmhouse "elevated into a cottage," complete with "veranda, French windows, and other prettinesses."

Ciaran Hinds as Captain Wentworth in the 1995 film version of the novel

Meanwhile, within the great house the Musgrove girls have created an air of confusion in the old-fashioned, wainscoted parlor, by furnishing it with a pianoforte, harp, flower stands, and "little tables placed in every direction." The ancestral portraits seem "to be staring in astonishment" at "such an overthrow of all order and neatness." Yet despite her exposure of the selfishness of the younger generation, Jane Austen does not adopt a censorious attitude. In this respect, *Persuasion* differs from earlier works in which the desire of Mary Crawford to new-furnish Mansfield or of Marianne Dashwood to new-furnish Allenham were suspect signs of "modern manners" to be repudiated by the reader.

Anne's task in *Persuasion* is not, then, to reclaim Kellynch (debased beyond Anne's powers of recovery by her father's extravagance, otiosity, and absurd pride in rank) but to discover new possibilities of accommodation for herself. Thus in conversation with Mr. Elliot, her false suitor, she proclaims herself "too proud to enjoy a welcome which depends so entirely upon place" while later she assures Wentworth that "every fresh place would be interesting to me." The novel provides Anne with a number of "fresh" possibilities of accommoda-

> So consistent is the contrast between the landed and the naval characters in *Persuasion*, and so consistent the preference for the latter, that critics have been led to make excessive historical claims concerning the new directions of the novel."

tion, which are associated not with the stabilities of the land (Winthrop, the future home of Henrietta Musgrove, is significantly described as an "indifferent" place, "without beauty and without dignity") but with the risks and uncertainties of life at sea or among sailors. Mrs. Croft knows "nothing superior to the accommodations of a man of war," having lived with her husband Admiral Croft in no fewer than five ships, crossed the Atlantic four times, and been once to the East Indies. Ashore, the Crofts are tenants of Kellynch, where their improvements include the removal of a number of large looking glasses from Sir Walter's dressing room. They drive an unfashionable gig and, while in Bath, live in lodgings that are none the worse, as the Admiral tells Anne, "for putting us in mind of those we first had at North Yarmouth. The wind blows through one of the cupboards just in the same way." Described as "generally out of doors together ... dawdling about in a way not endurable to a third person," the Crofts are the most successful portrait of seasoned "connubial felicity" in Jane Austen's work. Their partnership in life, no less than in their style of driving the gig, provides Anne with a model of marriage, an exemplary way of responding to an existence in which the waters are not always smooth.

A second naval family, the Harvilles, provides another positive example. Anne meets Captain Harville in Lyme shortly before Louisa Musgrove's disastrous leap from the steps on the Cobb calls into question the nature of her "fortitude." Suffering from a severe wound, Harville reveals a more estimable form of fortitude in his modest house near the Cobb. Its rooms are so small that Anne is at first astonished that he can think them "capable of accommodating so many." But her astonishment gives way to pleasure deriving from "all the ingenious contrivances and nice arrangements of Captain Harville, to turn the actual space to the best possible account, to supply the deficiencies of lodging-house furniture, and defend the windows and doors against the winter storms to be expected." In his illness, Captain Harville has at least set his house in order; and we are surely asked to discover in his usefulness, active employment, and positive outlook an exemplary response to reduced social expectations. Like Mrs. Smith in her even worse circumstances in Westgate Buildings, Harville responds not only with resolution and independence but with "elasticity of mind." Without fortune or carriage or spacious accommodations, Harville extends an "uncommon" degree of hospitality to the visitors in Lyme, whereas the Elliots in Bath, in sycophantic pursuit of their aristocratic relations and guiltily aware of their own reduced style of living, have altogether abandoned "old fashioned notions" of "country hospitality."

So consistent is the contrast between the landed and the naval characters in *Persuasion*, and so consistent the preference for the latter, that critics (myself included) have been led to make excessive historical claims concerning the new directions of the novel. We should not see the renting of Kellynch Hall as a doom-laden portent of the decline of the landed order; nor should we see in the energy and initiative of the naval characters implications as to the arrival on the social scene of a new, perhaps "bourgeois," class. As Jane Austen's own family showed, a modest but well-connected gentry family could more than adequately fill both landed and naval roles in the period. Nor should we see *Persuasion*'s new directions as a contradiction of the traditional values embodied in the character of Mr. Knightley. It is true that in her last completed novel, Jane Austen reexamines both the idea of the gentleman and the role of manners. But in repudiating Sir Walter's definition of the gentleman—which excludes sailors on the grounds that they are without property, have to work, and are exposed to inclement weather that ravages their looks—she does not abandon her trust in gentlemanly behavior; and in consistently presenting the hypocritical Mr. Elliot as a man of "polished" manners, she does not renounce her faith in morally informed manners as a medium of social intercourse.

The contrast between land and sea in *Persuasion* works not to announce a new social leadership but rather to open new possibilities of accommodation for the marginal woman. What if our hopes of landed entitlement are disappointed—is this the end of the world? "Desire" is, of course, fulfilled in the marriage of Anne to Wentworth, but the dependence on marriage for the closure of the novel's plot is not escapist, in view of the positive examples of the Crofts, the Harvilles, Mrs. Smith, and Anne herself, who in the lonely period before her rapprochement with Wentworth showed stoicism, self-reliance, and above all "usefulness" in her social relations.

Even the most interesting of *Persuasion*'s new directions, its new attitude to nature, needs careful description. Sister of a great landowner, Jane Austen had always shown (like Fanny on her trip to Sotherton) a proprietary interest in "the appearance of the country, the bearings of the roads, the difference of soil, the state of the harvest, the cottages, the cattle." In her last works, however, nature begins to express states of consciousness, as her heroines respond to atmospheric conditions and seasonal moods. On the walk to Winthrop, for example, Anne's "autumnal" feelings of loss and loneliness find consolation in "the view of the last smiles of the year upon the tawny leaves and withered hedges." But such "romanticism" is closer to that expressed in the sonnets of Charlotte Smith (1784) and William Lisle Bowles (1789) than to that of Wordsworth or Coleridge, and unlike Captain Benwick's romantic attitudes, it is never allowed to become self-indulgent. Even so, Anne's feelings for the natural scene mark a new emphasis in Jane Austen's response to the land, which is no longer viewed mainly as a place to be inhabited by the heroine in a responsible social role but as a possible source of alternative emotional consolation.

Like *Persuasion*, Jane Austen's unfinished fragment *Sanditon*, written in the winter before her death on 18 July 1817, also shows signs of a more private interest in nature. *Sanditon* describes with remarkable brio the transformation of an old village into a seaside resort for valetudinarians. Mr. Parker and Lady Denham are partners in this speculative enterprise, which brilliantly captures aspects of the rootless, fashion-seeking Regency era. Mr. Parker makes of his inheritance "his Mine, his Lottery, his Speculation & his Hobby Horse." He moves from his old house—like Donwell Abbey, unfashionably low and sheltered but "rich in . . . Garden, Orchard & Meadows"—to a new house, to which he gives the topical name of Trafalgar House. Trafalgar House lacks a kitchen garden and

shade trees, is exposed to winter storms, and is built near a cliff "on the most elevated spot on the Down." Jane Austen's satire is in the eighteenth-century tradition of Horace Walpole, who, in a letter to Montagu (15 June 1768), wrote: "How our ancestors would laugh at us, who knew there was no being comfortable, unless you had a high hill before your nose, and a thick warm wood at your back! Taste is too freezing a commodity for us, and depend upon it will go out of fashion again." It seems clear that the lofty and precarious location of Mr. Parker's new house was intended to prefigure the crash of his speculative ventures, but what is remarkable about *Sanditon* is Jane Austen's *sang-froid* in face of the "improvements" she describes. Here, after all, is the theme of *Mansfield Park*, but *Sanditon*'s heroine is unlikely to play Fanny's role of social redeemer, or even of social conscience. Like Emma, she responds aesthetically to the external scene, finding "amusement enough in standing at her ample Venetian window, & looking over the miscellaneous foreground of unfinished Building, waving Linen, & tops of Houses, to the Sea, dancing & sparkling in Sunshine & Freshness." Charlotte Heywood is like previous heroines in terms of her emerging from a traditional rural home into the glare of a materialistic world, but her accommodation to this world is more detached, more self-contained; she finds the Sanditon scene "very striking—and very amusing—or very melancholy, just as Satire or Morality might prevail." And rather than being critical of Sanditon's "modern" developments, she views them "with the calmness of amused curiosity." *Sanditon* is a remarkable work by a woman about to move into her last accommodations in College Street, Winchester. In its satire of hypochondria, it announces itself to be on the side of life and health; and in its presentation of the heroine, it arouses our curiosity. Like Mr. Knightley in his early concern for Emma, we "wonder what will become of her." More than in her future husband, we are interested in the home she would have found.

Source: Alistair M. Duckworth, "Austen's Accommodations," in *Critical Essays on Jane Austen*, edited by Laura Mooneyham White, G. K. Hall & Co., 1998, pp. 190–94.

Sources

Drabble, Margaret, "Introduction" in *Persuasion*, by Jane Austen, Signet, 1989, pp. v–xx.

Kelly, Gary, "Jane Austen," in *Dictionary of Literary Biography*, Volume 116: *British Romantic Novelists, 1789–1832*, Gale Research, 1992, pp. 3–35.

Southam, Brian, "Jane Austen," in *British Writers*, Vol. 4, Scribner, 1981, pp. 101–24.

For Further Reading

Brown, Lloyd, W., *Bits of Ivory: Narrative Techniques in Jane Austen's Fiction*, Louisiana State University Press, 1973.

Brown presents a penetrating study of how Austen structures the realistic portraits of daily life in her novels.

Butler, Marilyn, *Jane Austen and the War of Ideas*, Clarendon Press, 1975.

This work explores Austen's dominant themes, including an analysis of class consciousness, a central theme in all of her novels.

Litz, A. Walton, *Jane Austen: A Study of Her Artistic Development*, Oxford University Press, 1965.

Walton places *Persuasion* in Austen's second phase and examines the structure and style of the novel.

Pinion, F. B., *A Jane Austen Companion: A Critical Survey and Reference Book*, Macmillan, 1973.

Pinion presents a comprehensive and useful introduction to the themes and structure of Austen's work.

The Pigman

Paul Zindel
1968

Paul Zindel's first novel, *The Pigman*, published in New York in 1968 by Harper & Row, is a story of two dispossessed young people who find a surrogate parent in Angelo Pignati, an Italian man who has never had children and whose wife is dead. He shares his humor and joy in life with them, and in his presence, they are allowed to be carefree and childlike in a way that they can't be with their own families.

The novel is considered by many critics to be the "first truly [young adult] book," according to Teri Lesesne in an interview with Zindel in *Teacher Librarian*. When Zindel wrote the book, he realized that few books depicted teenagers dealing with real problems in the modern world. He also talked to many teenagers who said they hated to read or had been branded as troublemakers, and he targeted his story to them. Zindel's honesty and humor "broke new ground, and prepared the soil" for many excellent young adult books to come, according to Lesesne.

In an interview with *Scholastic* students, Zindel said that he was inspired to write the book while he was house-sitting in a fifty-room "castle" on Staten Island. A teenage boy trespassed on the grounds, and when Zindel went out to yell at him, he found out that the boy was actually a very interesting person. The character of John Conlan in *The Pigman* was modeled on this young man. The character of Lorraine was modeled on a student in one of the chemistry classes Zindel taught. He told the interviewer, "I thought, what a wonderful ad-

Paul Zindel

venture it would be to team those two life models for me into a story in which they met an eccentric, old mentor figure."

Author Biography

Paul Zindel was born on May 15, 1936, in Staten Island, New York, and grew up on Staten Island with his mother and sister. His father, a police officer, abandoned the family when Zindel was very young, and Zindel rarely saw him. His mother struggled to make ends meet, and because of their poverty, the family moved often. Zindel felt like a misfit because he had no father and because the family moved so much, but later realized that this feeling of being different from others had fueled his imagination. He wrote his first play in high school, and enjoyed the praise he got from other students for his morbid sense of humor.

He attended Wagner College on Staten Island, where he studied chemistry, but also took a creative writing course with famed playwright Edward Albee, who encouraged Zindel to write more plays. He wrote his second original play during his last year of college.

After college, Zindel worked briefly as a technical writer for Allied Chemical, but he hated the job. After six months, he quit and became a high-school chemistry and physics teacher. While teaching, he continued to write plays; his first staged play was *The Effect of Gamma Rays on Man-in-the-Moon Marigolds*, loosely based on his own life. The play won several awards, including Best American Play and the Pulitzer Prize for Drama; it was produced on Broadway; and it was made into a film and a television drama.

Charlotte Zolotow, an editor for the publisher Harper & Row, was impressed by the play and asked Zindel if he had any novels in mind. She encouraged him to write *The Pigman*, his first novel, which was published in 1968. The novel was selected as one of the Notable Children's Books of 1940–1970 by the American Library Association and was named one of their Best of the Best Books for Young Adults in 1975. It was also one of the Child Study Association of America's Children's Books of the Year in 1968, and was given the Boston Globe-Horn Book Award for Text in 1969. The book was inspired by two teenagers Zindel met, a young man who had many of the adventures that later appeared in the book, and a young woman who was very much like Lorraine, one of the two main characters. The Pigman, an eccentric old Italian man, was based on an Italian grandfather who was a mentor to Zindel when he was young.

In 1969, Zindel quit teaching and became a full-time writer. In a profile published on the *Scholastic* Web site, he said, "I felt I could do more for teenagers by writing for them." He read several young adult books and felt that they had nothing to do with what teenagers were really like, and he resolved to write honestly from the teenagers' point of view. Since then, he has written many acclaimed books for young adults, including *My Darling, My Hamburger, I Never Loved Your Mind, Pardon Me, You're Stepping on My Eyeball!, The Undertaker's Gone Bananas, Confessions of a Teenage Baboon, Raptor, Loch, The Doom Stone, Reef of Death*, and most recently, *Rats*.

In 1973, Zindel married Bonnie Hildebrand. They have two children, David and Elizabeth.

In the *Scholastic* profile, Zindel wrote, "I like storytelling. We all have an active thing that we do that gives us self-esteem, that makes us proud; it's necessary. I have to tell stories because that's the way the wiring went in."

Plot Summary

Told in chapters alternating from Lorraine's and John's point of view, *The Pigman* opens with an "Oath," signed by both John and Lorraine, two high school sophomores, in which they swear to tell only the facts, in this "memorial epic" about their experiences with Angelo Pignati, whom they later refer to as the "Pigman."

Harmless Pranks Accelerate

John, one of two protagonists who act as narrator, explains that he hates school, in fact hates "everything," and tells about his past escapades, in which he set off firecrackers in the school bathroom and organized his whole class to roll damaged apples across the classroom floor when the substitute teacher had her back turned. Intelligent, charming, and bored, he's not a bad kid, but is pentup and restless, with parents who don't understand him and don't want to try.

Lorraine, the other protagonist and narrator of the book, is similarly alienated from her family, which consists only of her mother. Her father, who left when her mother was pregnant with her, is now dead, and her mother works as a private nurse to try and make ends meet. Like John, Lorraine is very intelligent; she wants to be a writer. A keen observer of people, she is compassionate and sensitive. She and her mother moved into John's neighborhood at the beginning of freshman year, and Lorraine and John, perhaps drawn by their mutual restlessness and alienation, have since become good friends.

Lorraine and John, with two other friends, play more pranks outside of school. They devise a game in which the challenge is to call strangers on the phone and keep them on the line for as long as possible by telling outlandish stories. Picking numbers at random from the phone book, Lorraine eventually calls Angelo Pignati, an old man who lives in their neighborhood. He's only too happy to talk to them, and when Lorraine tells him they're calling from a charity and asking for money, he unwittingly offers to give them ten dollars.

Lorraine thinks the joke has gone too far and wants to end the phone call, but John gets on the line and makes arrangements to pick up the money from Mr. Pignati at his house. John tells her Mr. Pignati is probably lonely and will welcome their company.

They Meet Mr. Pignati

Mr. Pignati is thrilled to see them. His house, though messy, smells warm and inviting, and he offers them wine and food, and invites them to come to the zoo with him. He explains that his wife, who usually goes with him, is out of town. He shows them his collection of porcelain pigs, plays a game with them, and gives them the ten dollars.

The next day, they go to the zoo with him and visit his "best friend," Bobo, a vicious baboon. Mr. Pignati seems oblivious to the baboon's nasty personality, and he talks lovingly to the animal and feeds him peanuts and other treats.

Lorraine and John continue visiting Mr. Pignati, lying to their families about where they are going. He tells them to make themselves at home and, while exploring his house, they find funeral documents that show that Mr. Pignati's wife, Conchetta, is actually dead, not on vacation. Her clothes are still in her closet, and Mr. Pignati misses her so much that he can't stand to admit she's really gone.

They Experience Joy in Life

Mr. Pignati takes them on a shopping spree for gourmet delicacies, which his wife loved, and buys roller skates for all three of them. Carefree, they eat the food, drink wine, and listen to his jokes. All of this is a sharp contrast to their own homes, which are depressing and humorless. In John's house, everything is so neat and clean that no one can relax, and his father is always lecturing him about responsibility and trying to force him to be someone he's not, urging him to get a job on Wall Street.

In Lorraine's house, her mother hassles her about hanging out with boys, asks her to stay home from school to clean the house, won't let her use the phone, makes derogatory comments about her appearance, and occasionally hits her. John and Lorraine end up going over to Mr. Pignati's house every day after school for wine and conversation, and become the children Mr. Pignati never had. Eventually they confess that they were never affiliated with any charity, and that they like him more than anyone else and want to be honest with him. In response, he tells them what they already know, that his wife is actually dead, not on vacation.

John begins roller-skating in Mr. Pignati's house, and soon Mr. Pignati and Lorraine join in, but the exercise is too much for Mr. Pignati, who has a heart attack. They call an ambulance and, at the hospital, pose as his children so they can get in to visit him. He tells them to make themselves at home at his place while he's in the hospital, and they do, but they begin overstepping boundaries: Lorraine dresses up in some of Conchetta's clothes, John wears some of Mr. Pignati's, and they pretend to be adults. The fancy evening clothes awaken their awareness of each other as sexual beings, and they tease each other and kiss, but this change in their relationship makes both of them uncomfortable, so they stop and put their own clothes back on. However, they can't take back what they've begun to feel for each other.

A Betrayal and Its Consequences

John decides that while Mr. Pignati is gone, it can't hurt to have a few friends over for a quiet party. Neither of them can have friends over at home, so it's tempting. The quiet party grows into a huge, rowdy, loud, and drunken revel, with about forty teenagers. Norton Kelly, a delinquent, steals an electrical apparatus from the house, and other kids, including Lorraine, get dressed in Conchetta's clothes. John goes after Norton for stealing, and in revenge, Norton smashes Mr. Pignati's precious collection of pigs, which belonged to his wife.

In the midst of this chaos, Mr. Pignati comes home and finds his house in a shambles and the people he loved and trusted, John and Lorraine, at the center of the chaos. They feel horrible, apologize, and try to make amends by asking him to go to the zoo with them to see Bobo. However, when they get there, the cage is empty, and a bored attendant tells them Bobo is dead.

The accumulated shocks and losses prove to be too much for Mr. Pignati, and he suffers a second heart attack and dies immediately. The two young people are left with the realization that his death may be their fault, and with an awareness of the sadness of his life and death, and life and human mortality in general. They realize that time is passing, that someday they, too, will die, that they may spend their later years alone and lonely, and they better grow up and get moving. As John says at the end of the book, "Our life would be what we made of it—nothing more, nothing less."

Characters

The Bore

See Mr. Conlan

John Conlan

John Conlan is a fifteen-year-old high-school sophomore who lives in Staten Island, New York, and is best friends with Lorraine Jensen, another student. He is good-looking, charming, and highly intelligent, but is bored with school and with life in general, and his humorless, joyless family life doesn't help. His father, known as "The Bore" to John, is a broker on the coffee exchange. The Bore is interested only in money and stocks, and urges John to get a similar job on the exchange as soon as he's able. John says, "I've been over to the Exchange and seen all the screaming and barking the Bore has to do just to earn a few bucks, and if he thought I was going to have any part of that madhouse, he had another thing coming."

John is also dismayed by his father's stressful lifestyle, and comments, "He's almost sixty years old, and I know he's not going to be around much longer. All the guys on the Exchange drop dead of heart attacks." John's father is oblivious to his son's lack of interest in finance, or to his creative talent, and responds with "Don't be a jackass" when John tells him he wants to be an actor. John's mother is an anxious, obsessively clean woman whose perfectionism fills up her whole life. Both of his parents constantly extol the virtues of his older brother, Kenneth, who is eleven years older than John and who works on the Exchange, just like John's father. John's life at home is hedged in by rules: his mother tells him what to eat and drink and cautions him not to make a mess and not to disturb his father, and his father urges him to become a responsible citizen, to get off the phone, cut his hair, and not disturb his mother, among many other things.

In response to their colorless style of living, John makes his own life more colorful. He exaggerates, lies, and invents dramatic pranks to amuse himself and others. He sets off firecrackers in the boys' bathroom, organizes his whole class to roll rotten apples across the classroom floor whenever there's a substitute teacher and, when his father puts a lock on the family phone to prevent John from using it, John fills the lock with glue so that the Bore can't use it either. Then John figures out a way to dial it anyway, so he's the only one who can use it. With Lorraine Jensen and some other friends, he begins a campaign of telephone games, culminating in one game in which the teenagers tell outlandish lies and try to keep a stranger talking for as long as possible.

In addition, John drinks and smokes more than any other boy Lorraine has ever known. His drinking is a habit started by his father, who used to give John beer when he was a boy and then praise him and laugh at him. He knows drinking and smoking are bad for him, but persists because his life is so oppressive that he feels there's no point in living a long life anyway.

Underneath his colorful exterior, John is sensitive and compassionate. Lorraine suspects that this is why he became her friend, because he had compassion for her loneliness. They are allies because both of them are lonely and alienated from their families.

Mr. Conlan

John Conlan's father, whom John calls "the Bore," works on the Coffee Exchange on Wall Street, and his life is totally subsumed in his job. His son says, "If he sells more than two hundred lots in a day, he's in a good mood. Anything less than that, and there's trouble." He is bothered by his son's apparent flightiness and his creative and disobedient streak, and notices only his superficial qualities, such as his long hair and his constant wisecracking humor. He doesn't see his son as he is—creative, intelligent, and talented—but wants to force him into a mold and remake him as a carbon copy of himself. He tells John, "At your age I was working hard, not floundering around in a fool's dream world."

Mr. Conlan was a compulsive drinker for most of John's childhood, and encouraged John to drink, too. When John was a toddler and young boy, his father would give him sips of beer at parties, and everyone present would laugh as he downed them. "A chip off the old block," Mr. Conlan said proudly, making it seem like drinking was a sign of manhood. Mr. Conlan was eventually diagnosed with cirrhosis of the liver and had to quit drinking, but by that time his son was used to alcohol and kept drinking. Of course, ironically, Mr. Conlan still doesn't think of him as a man.

Mrs. Conlan

John Conlan's mother, whom John calls "hyper" and "the old lady," is terrified of conflict, dust, dirt, and disorder of any kind, and spends her time dashing around cleaning, polishing silverware, monitoring her husband's and John's moods, and trying to smooth over the clashes between them. Her perfectionism makes it impossible for her to really listen to or converse with her son or her husband; the family's house, which she keeps as neat as a museum, is impossible to relax in because everything is either covered with plastic or is off-limits.

Hyper

See Mrs. Conlan

Lorraine Jensen

Lorraine Jensen is a fifteen-year-old high-school sophomore who lives in the same Staten Island neighborhood as John Conlan, her best friend. She is intelligent and thoughtful, is interested in psychology, and wants to be a writer. She moved into John's neighborhood at the beginning of freshman year, and the first few weeks were torture for her. She was depressed and isolated because she didn't know anyone, and she was shy and insecure about her looks. She met John on the bus, when he sat next to her one day and started laughing. At first she was offended, thinking he was laughing at her, but then she began laughing, too, and from that day on, they were friends.

Lorraine calls herself "paranoid," because she's worried that others don't think much of her, but this is clearly a response to the way her mother has always treated her. Her mother has always told her how ugly and clumsy she is, and at the same time, repeatedly warns her about the evil intentions of men and boys and tells her never to be alone with them. Perhaps because of her sensitivity, she is very compassionate toward others, particularly people she perceives as underdogs. Her compassion is unusual among teenagers; for example, she writes movingly of a poor teacher who keeps her elderly and ill mother in the living room of her apartment, and about Mr. Pignati, whose wife has died.

Mrs. Jensen

Lorraine's mother, a private-duty nurse, has raised Lorraine by herself. Lorraine's father left when she was pregnant with Lorraine, after cheating on her. He has since died, and the burden of single parenthood has fallen heavily on Mrs. Jensen. Since then, she has been fixated on how terrible her husband was, and how terrible men are, in general. This bitterness has soured her life, as well as her relationship with her daughter.

She's constantly making negative comments about Lorraine's hair, clothes, weight, and behavior, and Lorraine says, "If I made a list of every comment she's made about me, you'd think I was a monstrosity." Mrs. Jensen is very pretty when she lets her hair down and relaxes, but this seldom happens; she carries a weight of sadness and depression with her, and has a cynical attitude toward the terminally ill patients she takes care of. Because she believes she's not being paid enough, she steals things from them to even up the score: light bulbs, cleaning supplies, food. She has no shame about this, and no shame about the fact that when a patient dies, she refers their family to a funeral home that pays her ten dollars whenever she sends them some business. Money, or the lack of it, is constantly on her mind, and overtakes all other values. Instead of encouraging Lorraine to stay in school and get good grades so she can do well in the future, she asks her to stay home and clean the kitchen—with cleanser stolen from a dying patient. "I think you could take a year off from that school and not miss anything," she says, and Lorraine knows that if she told her mother she wants to be a writer, she'd never hear the end of it.

Norton Kelly

Norton Kelly is a student in Lorraine's and John's class, and John describes him as "a social outcast." He was once caught stealing a bag of marshmallows from a supermarket, and ever since then he's been taunted as "The Marshmallow Kid." He has a mean streak, and when he finds out that John and Lorraine have access to Mr. Pignati's apartment, he asks if Pignati has anything worth stealing. His mean streak started in childhood, when he got caught playing with dolls and all the other kids harassed him about it; after that, he went berserk and "turned tough guy all the way," according to John. From then on, he spent his time picking fights, throwing stones, beating up people, and calling all the other boys sissies. Since then, Norton has become a thief, shoplifting and stealing whenever he can. John says, "Then he got even worse, until now his eyes even drift out of focus when you're talking to him. He's the kind of guy who could grow up to be a killer." At a party in The Pigman's house, Norton steals an oscilloscope and breaks the old man's precious pig figurines, which were one of the few reminders of The Pigman's dead wife Mr. Pignati had left.

The Old Lady

See Mrs. Conlan

The Pigman

See Angelo Pignati

Angelo Pignati

Angelo Pignati, called "The Pigman" by Lorraine and John, is an Italian man in his late fifties. Trusting and good-natured, he offers to give them ten dollars when they call him up and pretend to be with a charity. The first impression they have of him is that he has a "jolly voice," and when Lorraine, who's making the call, starts laughing out of nervousness, he asks what the joke is, so he can laugh at it, too, and then tells her a joke. He tells her his wife, who's in California visiting his sister, loves his jokes, and then he talks on and on, telling joke after joke. Lorraine realizes that he's "terribly nice . . . but also lonely."

He is both, and he's also poor; his house is rundown and messy, but when they go over to his house, he meets them with a huge smile. Unlike their families, he's filled with a sense of enjoyment of life despite his problems. He plays games with them, invites them to go to the zoo with him, and shows them his wife's collection of pig figurines, which she began when she married him and changed her name to Pignati.

Mr. Pignati's wife is actually dead, and he has few friends, but he goes to the zoo frequently to visit and feed his "best friend," Bobo, a vicious baboon. The zookeeper dislikes Bobo because he's mean-tempered, but Mr. Pignati is so pure of heart that he can see no evil in anyone or anything, and believes Bobo is filled with all the love and kindness he himself feels.

Unlike the joyless families of John and Lorraine, Mr. Pignati knows how to have fun. Instead of filling their conversation with rules, he offers them wine and other delicacies, takes them on a shopping spree for luxury foods, buys them (and himself) roller skates, and the three of them roller skate throughout his house and have impromptu parties whenever the teenagers visit. With him, they can be children in a way that they never could with their parents.

Conchetta Pignati

Conchetta is Angelo's wife, and at the time of the story, she has been dead for several months. She is present in the story, however, through his memories of good times with her and through the pleasant habits he has continued: cherishing his collection of pigs, shopping for gourmet foods, and visiting the zoo. She was a sweet woman who always laughed at his jokes, and her possessions are still in his house.

Themes

Relationships with Parents

Both John and Lorraine have poor relationships with their parents, who regard them as disturbing burdens. Lorraine's father is dead, and her mother makes ends meet by working as a private-duty nurse. Mrs. Jensen's ethics and values are questionable: she steals from her patients, gets kickbacks from the undertakers she refers patients' families to, and urges Lorraine to stay home from school so she can clean the apartment. Lorraine feels sorry for her mother, but it's evident that these issues make her deeply uncomfortable. In addition, Mrs. Jensen projects her fears about men into Lorraine's life, hassling her about any contact she might have with boys, how dangerous boys are, and how men only have one thing in mind. These comments are not conducive to helping Lorraine develop a healthy understanding of adult relationships, so she must rely on her own instincts and on her friendship with John and Mr. Pignati to learn about what men are really like.

John's parents regard him as a disturbance that must be controlled, molded, and shaped into a carbon copy of his father, who leads an emotionally restricted and stressful life as a trader on the Coffee Exchange. They view John's energy, desire for fun, and dramatic talent as liabilities rather than gifts. Their household, like Mrs. Jensen's, is cold and not nurturing; he is constantly compared to his brother, who according to his parents is an ideal son. This coldness and comparison to an ideal he does not want to emulate foster a sense of alienation and rebellion in John, and this alienation and rebellion in turn prevent him from focusing his energy on anything productive.

Consequences

John and Lorraine, like many teenagers, have little sense of the consequences of their actions, and they learn that their acts have consequences only when it's too late to change anything. At first, they tell themselves that they're just having fun—just going over to Mr. Pignati's, just having a little party, just having a good time. The party, of course, gets way out of hand, and the shock eventually leads to Mr. Pignati's death. They both realize that they were involved to some degree in his death, but differ in the amount of responsibility they're willing to take. John doesn't take full responsibility, but Lorraine does, as she says, "We murdered him."

Near the end of the book, however, John says after Mr. Pignati's death, "We had trespassed too—been where we didn't belong, and we were being punished for it. Mr. Pignati had paid with his life. But when he died something in us had died as well." This is not an explicit claiming of responsibility on John's part, but the reader senses that he isn't go-

Topics for Further Study

- In the book, Mr. Pignati has a major effect on John and Lorraine. Write about an older person who affected your life in a way you'll never forget, and how they influenced you.

- John does not believe that he and Lorraine are totally responsible for Mr. Pignati's death, but Lorraine does. In your opinion, who is right, and why? If John and Lorraine were put on trial for killing him, what would the verdict be? Why?

- Mr. Pignati has lived a very lonely life since his wife died; he has no real friends until John and Lorraine come into his life by accident. Do some research to find out how most elderly people live. Is Mr. Pignati's isolation unusual, or typical? How does the American treatment of elderly people differ from the way they are treated in other cultures?

- John and Lorraine's parents don't talk to their children, and they often act as though the children are a disturbing burden. Do you think this is typical, or are most parents effective? Write a short essay about what it takes to be a good parent.

- John smokes and drinks, even though his father became ill from alcohol and he knows both habits are bad for his health. Why would he do these things if he knows they may eventually kill him?

ing to be throwing any more wild parties. As he says, "There was no one else to blame anymore.... And there was no place to hide." He has realized that his actions will have consequences, sometimes dire, and he will have to answer for them.

Life and Death

The book is filled with images and questions about life and death. Lorraine's father is dead, and her mother comes home daily with gripes and callous words about her dying patients; for example, of one old man, she says, "I wish this one would hurry up and die." She compares different funeral homes, considering which one will offer her a bigger kickback if she refers clients to them. Her callous attitude toward death is balanced by Lorraine's extreme sensitivity to suffering and death. This sensitivity leads her to feel sympathy for Mr. Pignati, who still suffers from the loss of his wife.

In Mr. Pignati's house, John and Lorraine find documents from Conchetta Pignati's funeral and read them with mingled sadness, horror, and fascination. Zindel reproduces some of these documents verbatim in the book, perhaps because most young people would be as interested in this glimpse of the adult world as Lorraine and John are.

Before Mr. Pignati's death, John has been unaffected by death, although several of his relatives have died. He didn't feel close to them, so the body in the casket looked "just like a doll." He says, "It gave me a feeling like being in Beekman's toy department to tell the truth—everything elaborately displayed." Because he was emotionally unconnected to the deceased, he is remote from the situation, viewing it in a superficial, childish manner. However, he is aware that he does this to avoid dealing with his fear of death: "Anything to get away from what was really happening." All this changes, of course, when Mr. Pignati dies and John is personally touched by the loss. He can't hide anymore, can't disconnect like he has in the past.

In addition, John, who feels dispossessed and alienated by his family, has picked up a number of self-destructive habits, such as smoking and drinking, and at one point Lorraine tells him, "You must want to die." He doesn't really have an answer for this, and near the end of the book he says, "Maybe I would rather be dead than to turn into the kind of grown-up people I knew." However, he realizes that this is not the answer either, and says with a new resolve, "Our life would be what we made of it—nothing more, nothing less."

Style

Point of View

Zindel's *The Pigman* is told from the point of view of its two main protagonists, who claim they are typing the story in the school library as the librarian, who thinks they're working on a book report, looks on. Chapters written by Lorraine alternate with chapters written by John; both tell the story in the breezy but honest and irreverent style

of adolescents, focusing on action more than on internal feelings, motivation, or consequences, although these do sometimes appear in the narrative.

By using two narrators with slightly different points of view to relate the story, Zindel gives the reader a more complete picture of the narrative. In many cases, John or Lorraine will go back and comment on something the other one has written, giving their own version of the events.

Extracts from "Real Life"

An interesting feature of the book is the occasional insertion of handwritten elements, such as John and Lorraine's signatures on an "Oath" to tell the truth about the incidents described in the book; some graffiti John writes on a desk; and some pencil-and-paper games Mr. Pignati plays with them. The book also has a page from a booklet on funeral planning, a bill for a funeral, and a piece torn out from an advice column. These elements add realism and immediacy to the story, making it even more believable.

Foreshadowing

In keeping with teenagers' tendency toward drama, Lorraine frequently notes "omens" that, in hindsight, she believes should have warned her that something terrible was going to happen. This foreshadowing is not subtle; for example, she describes her visit to the zoo with John and Mr. Pignati, where a woman selling peanuts is rude to her. "That was the first omen," she writes. "I should have left right on the spot." The second omen occurs when a peacock, seeing that she has a bag of peanuts in her hand, chases her, and a third one occurs in the Mammal Building, where she sees a child who is watching the people who've come to watch the vampire bats. "He made me feel as though I was a bat in a cage and he was on the outside looking at me. It all made me very nervous," she writes. In another omen, when she and John go downtown with Mr. Pignati, she sees a mentally ill woman who keeps repeating "Death is coming. God told me death is coming." In another scene, Lorraine dreams that she finds a long black coffin in Mr. Pignati's house. Although these "omens" might seem like ordinary occurrences to many readers, or in some cases, logical consequences of her fears about Mr. Pignati's survival after his heart attack, Lorraine's willingness to read a more global and deeper meaning into them is typical of the teenage point of view, and also warns readers that some as-yet-unidentified disaster will occur in the course of the book.

Dialogue

Zindel's style is heavily dependent on dialogue, perhaps because of his background as a playwright. The dialogue is skillfully written and extremely natural; Zindel has a true ear for the way teenagers, and adults, talk to each other. In addition, because the book is "written" by John and Lorraine in alternating chapters, even the narrative or descriptive parts of the book have a unique teenage flavor. The book begins:

> Now, I don't like school, which you might say is one of the factors that got us involved with this old guy we nicknamed the Pigman. Actually, I hate school, but then again most of the time I hate everything.

Artfully, Zindel kept the book from becoming dated by using language that sounds like slang, but has a minimum of slang terms, which can quickly become stale for readers. In chapter 3, John explains this principle, which Zindel seems to have adopted: "I really hate it when a teacher has to show she isn't behind the times by using some expression which sounds so up-to-date you know for sure she's behind the times." Instead of using slang current at the time the book was written, Zindel has his teenage characters use language that suggests slang, with words such as "dimwit," "nutty," and "crazy," and phrases such as "five-finger discount," "putrid brand of beer," and "these two amoebae" (referring to two delinquent boys). John calls his mom "The Hyper" or "The Old Lady" and he calls his dad "The Bore."

Instead of using curse words, he tells the reader that he will use the symbol "@#$%" for "a mild curse—like the kind you hear in the movies"—and "3@#$%" for a "revolting curse," "the raunchiest curse you can think of." This use of symbols has two benefits for Zindel and the reader: readers can insert whatever curses they are familiar with, thus keeping the book current, and because Zindel doesn't spell out the offending words, adult readers will have no objection to his use of them in a young adult novel.

Historical Context

The Pigman was written in the late 1960s, a time when American society was in an uproar. Protests against the Vietnam War, the growth of the Civil Rights and feminist movements, and a vigorous celebration of teenagers and young adults as the new, free generation were set against those who wanted to preserve the status quo and traditional values. Zindel's book was groundbreaking in its truthful depiction of teenagers who were not respectful to their teachers, whose parents had failed them, and who engaged in actions adults would disapprove of—such as minor vandalism, drinking alcohol, and smoking. Before the publication of *The Pigman*, few books for young adults were so open and truthful; instead, books tended to portray an ideal world in which adults wished teens would live.

Although Lorraine and John love their parents, they are open in their criticism of how their parents have failed them, a common complaint of the younger generation during the 1960s and early 1970s. "Never trust anyone over 35" was a commonly heard phrase among rebellious youths, who believed there was more to life than wearing a suit and making a living. As John tells his father, "I just don't want to wear a suit every day and carry an attaché case and ride a subway. I want to be *me*. Not a phony in the crowd." This celebration of creativity and individualism, which when taken to an extreme led the '60s generation to be labeled "The Me Generation," is typical of young people of that time. John's father, uncomprehending and scornful, insists that John's ambition to be an actor is "a fool's dream world," a comment typical of the older generation of that time. Interestingly, John's brother Kenneth, who is eleven years older, has remained on the older generation's side of the divide: he has accepted his father's values and works on Wall Street.

Another feature typical of the younger generation of that time is a pervasive distrust of anyone in authority, such as teachers, police officers, and parents. Both John and Lorraine have vast areas of their lives their parents know nothing about. Although Lorraine is less scornful of her mother than John is of his parents, she realizes that her mother is too wounded to help her or to understand what she's involved in, and she lies to her mother about what she's up to. John is more bitterly disappointed by his parents, and shows it by blatant disobedience and backtalk. When the police show up after Mr. Pignati's heart attack, John calls them "snotty" and "dumb," and both he and Lorraine lie to the police about being Mr. Pignati's children. He also says, after they leave, "They were probably anxious to get along on the rounds of the local bars and collect their graft for the week." Lorraine, who is not as cynical, is angered by this comment and

Compare & Contrast

- **1960s:** Teen smoking, drinking, and drug use become prevalent in the 1960s, when knowledge of the ill effects of drugs is still not widespread, and when a widespread sense of experimentation and rebellion is part of popular culture.

  Today: Teen smoking and drinking have increased since the 1960s, and every day, about 3,000 young people begin smoking. Nearly 1,000 of that number (1 in 3) will eventually die as a result of smoking-related disease. Use of cigarettes, alcohol, and drugs is more common among teens who do not feel emotionally connected to their parents.

- **1960s:** Not everyone can afford a telephone, and instead of using touch-tones, phones use a rotary dial system. Phone numbers have two letters and five numbers, like "Sa7-7295," the number for the hospital Mr. Pignati is in. The two letters are an abbreviation of the name of the "exchange," usually a neighborhood. Faxes, personal computers, and the Internet are unknown.

  Today: Phone companies have dropped the letter-and-number system in favor of all-numeric phone numbers, and the old rotary phones are considered obsolete; many telephone services cannot be accessed unless the caller has a touch-tone phone. The number of people needing phone numbers has continued to increase, so that every year, phone companies must create new area codes. In addition, cellular phones, fax machines, pagers, and the Internet allow people to be constantly connected to each other, even if they are on the other side of the world.

- **1960s:** In the 1960s, AIDS is unknown, and people don't worry about many of the consequences of sexual activity. Rates of teen pregnancy, divorce, and single-parent families are higher than those of earlier decades, and people regard these issues as shameful.

  Today: AIDS has forced many people to reassess their sexual activity and to take precautions against this and other diseases. However, divorce rates continue to increase, and teen pregnancies and single-parent families are now common. Attitudes toward divorce, teen pregnancy, and single parenting have changed, so that many people now regard these issues as painful, but without the sense of shame and blame that was still prevalent in the 1960s.

- **1960s–1970s:** The Vietnam War rages throughout the 1960s and early 1970s, sparking widespread anti-war protests in the United States. Throughout the war, in which 3 million Americans serve, 58,000 Americans die, 1,000 are declared missing, and 150,000 are wounded.

  Today: The United States has been involved in several smaller wars since the 1960s, most notably the Gulf War in the Middle East, but none have incited such widespread commentary and rebellion as the Vietnam War has. However, the hijacking of three planes on September 11, 2001, and the attacks on the World Trade Center Towers in New York and on the Pentagon in Washington D.C. are the largest terrorist attacks to date.

---

tells John she hopes he needs the police someday but can't find an officer to help him.

It's interesting that Zindel chose not to mention any of the political and social events, such as widespread protests, riots, and rallies, as well as the Vietnam War, which were taking place at the time that he wrote the book. Perhaps he did this in order to avoid making the book seem dated; more likely, he chose to do this because it's true to life. Many teenagers are unaware of political and social events, or only peripherally affected. For many teens, life at school, interactions with parents, and activities with friends take center stage in their lives.

An anti-Vietnam War protest

Critical Overview

The Pigman is widely acknowledged as a turning point in young adult literature. According to Jack Davis Forman in *Presenting Paul Zindel*, Zindel's "commitment to write realistically about the concerns of teenagers" set his books apart from "the previous genre of teen fiction calcified in the gender and age stereotypes of the 1950s." Forman quoted Kenneth Donelson and Alleen Nilssen, whose survey, *Literature for Today's Young Adults*, noted that *The Pigman* "established a new type of adolescent fiction in which teenagers dealing with

interpersonal or societal problems were depicted with candor and seriousness."

As Forman noted, previous books had portrayed teenagers as adults wished they were, or thought they should be, and were "pedestrian, predictable, and formulaic." Zindel was one of the first writers to show teenagers from a teenage point of view, unfiltered by adult notions of right, wrong, or what their behavior should be. According to Forman, a reviewer in *Horn Book* called *The Pigman* "a now book," and commented that few books were "as cruelly truthful about the human condition." Forman also noted that a *New York Times* reviewer wrote that the book had "the right combination of the preposterous and the sensible," but commented that Zindel's overt explanation of the book's "moral" was patronizing to readers. Forman also quoted *Publishers Weekly* reviewer Lavinia Russ, who remarked on her excitement at discovering such a skilled new writer by saying she felt "like the watcher of the skies when a new planet swam into its ken."

In *English Journal*, Loretta Clarke praised the book, except for the ending; like the *New York Times* reviewer, she felt that the last three lines were weak:

> Baboons.
>
> Baboons.
>
> They build their own cages, we could almost hear the Pigman whisper, as he took his children with him.

"These three lines intrude upon the story," Clarke wrote, but commented that otherwise, Zindel "has reflected through his adolescent writers an adolescent view of life."

In *Teacher Librarian*, Teri Lesesne wrote that the book was "one of those touchstone books that set apart novels for adolescents," that it "set the standard for writers to follow," and that it "is considered by many to be the first truly YA [young adult] book."

The book was listed as one of the Child Study Association of America's Children's Books of the Year for 1968, and won the Boston Globe-Horn Book Award in 1969. It was also listed as one of the American Library Association's Best Young Adult Books in 1975.

Criticism

Kelly Winters

Winters is a freelance writer and has written for a wide variety of educational publishers. In this essay, she considers themes of aging and death in Paul Zindel's The Pigman.

Throughout *The Pigman*, all of the characters reveal their attitudes toward aging and, particularly, death. Death is frequently mentioned throughout the story, and one of the main themes of the book is how awareness of death and its finality eventually leads John and Lorraine to mature and take responsibility for their lives. This is not a lesson they could have learned from their families, or at school. As the book shows, most of the adults they en-counter are not supportive, are unhelpful, and are too caught up in their own problems to help the teenagers sort out the answers to the deep questions they carry in their hearts. It takes the Pigman's life, and his death, to make them realize that they need to change their attitudes and their behavior toward both life and death.

Lorraine's mother, Mrs. Jensen, who ironically works as a private nurse for elderly and terminally ill people, has a callous attitude towards death. She steals things from her patients, calls them names like "old fossil," and is unmoved by their death, as shown by one of her conversations with Lorraine. Lorraine, who is far more sensitive, asks about the patient, "Did he die?" Her mother replies, "Of course he died. I told his daughter two days ago he wasn't going to last the week. Put some coffee water on." When referring to another patient, Lorraine's mother remarks, "I wish this one would go ahead and croak because her husband is getting a little too friendly lately." She's so consumed by her own past problems with her husband that she has no thought for the suffering of the sick woman she's taking care of.

Similarly, Mrs. Jensen is so wrapped up in her need for money that even a patient's death becomes a financial opportunity to look forward to. She gloats over the fact that the undertaker gives her ten dollars for every customer she refers to him, and she notes that she may switch to referring patients' families to another funeral home "when the next one croaks," because she's heard that they will give twenty dollars for the same favor.

John's father developed liver disease from excessive drinking, and although he quit drinking, his diagnosis evidently didn't make him reflect very deeply about his life. He lives a circumscribed, joyless, almost mechanical life; his mood is determined by how many lots he sells in a day, and he considers anything other than work to be "a waste of time." His job is extremely stressful, so stressful that John can't imagine doing it: "I've been over to the Exchange and seen all the screaming and barking he has to do just to earn a few bucks," he writes. Mr. Conlan is aware that eventually, all this "screaming and barking" and accumulated stress of his job will probably kill him, and he uses the threat of his own death as leverage to try and get John to agree to take over his business: "The business will be half yours, and you know it. I can't take the strain much longer." Mr. Conlan also reminds John, "Your mother isn't going to be around forever either, you know. When she's dead, you're going to wish to God you'd been nicer to her." This use of death as a tool to try and control his son's behavior is ineffective; although John is secretly disturbed by the fact that his parents will die someday, he's angered by his father's manipulation and negative attitude toward John's true dreams.

Mrs. Conlan never mentions death, just as she never mentions anything "unpleasant." Her days are spent in a whirl of anxious cleaning, smoothing things over, hovering between her husband and son. Whenever anything unpleasant arises, she either leaves the room, begins cleaning, or offers falsely cheery distractions, such as asking "Do you both want whipped cream and nuts on your strawberry whirl?" during an argument between John and his father.

Lorraine is more sensitive than either her mother or John about sickness, aging, and death. She tries to get John to stop smoking, she's bothered by her mother's crass attitudes towards the patients, and she is sympathetic to the situation of a teacher at her school whose aging and ill mother lives in the teacher's living room. "Who would want to marry a woman that keeps her sick mother in a bed right in the living room?" she wonders, thinking about how it must feel to be that teacher. As the story progresses, she notes morbid "omens" that, in hindsight, seem to indicate that something bad was going to happen, but also comments that she didn't see their meaning at the time they occurred. Unlike John, she accepts full responsibility for Mr. Pignati's death.

When Lorraine hears that Mr. Pignati's wife is dead, she realizes for the first time what a loss it must have been for him. All the things they shared—interests, activities, eating meals together, conversation—are gone. Of all the characters in the book, she's the only one who has any comprehension of the depth of his loss.

Despite the fact that Mr. Pignati can't even admit that his wife is dead, he is actually the only person in the book who is really confronting the depth of sadness and grief that death elicits in those left behind. He tries as hard as he can to believe that she's really only visiting his sister in California, not gone forever, because the pain of her loss is so great. Through his friendship with John and Lorraine, however, he comes to feel safe enough to begin dealing with his loss, and invites them to celebrate her personality and enjoyment in life by shopping for delicacies and visiting the zoo, things she loved. This enjoyment of life is the gift that he gives John and Lorraine—a gift they never received from their own families.

> In the last analysis, John realizes that an awareness of death sharpens one's sense of responsibility and meaning. As he puts it in one of the last sentences of the book, 'Our life would be what we made of it—nothing more, nothing less.'

When Bobo the baboon dies, the zoo attendant who has looked after him has the same attitude toward his death that Mrs. Jensen has toward her patients. He says, "Can't say I feel particularly sorry about it because that baboon had the nastiest disposition around here." He is oblivious to the fact that Mr. Pignati loved the baboon and that his death is a devastating loss, just as Mrs. Jensen is oblivious to the fact that her patients' families may love them and grieve them deeply.

John, Lorraine, and some of the other kids from school like to hang out at the local cemetery, which they see mainly as a quiet place where they can drink and smoke in peace, since adults rarely go there. They reflect briefly on the people who are buried there, but it's in a distant, almost amused way—they use the presence of the dead as a sort of prop to scare each other, but they never think that someday, they, too, will be buried there. John lies on the grass and imagines that a buried corpse will stick its hands up through the earth and grab him, but then reflects that he would actually love to see a ghost, because he has no faith that there's any sort of life after this one, which is dreary enough. He writes, "I'm looking for anything to prove that when I drop dead there's a chance I'll be doing something a little more exciting than decaying." He envisions death as quick and immediate, not preceded by the years or months of suffering and loneliness experienced by Mrs. Jensen's patients, or, later in the book, by Mr. Pignati. And he doesn't reflect on what death really means—that life is fundamentally short, eventually it will end, and that ultimately, only he is responsible for what he does with his life.

What Do I Read Next?

- *The Effect of Gamma Rays on Man-in-the-Moon Marigolds*, published in 1964, was Zindel's first play, and won the Pulitzer Prize for Drama in 1971. The play stars Tillie, a brilliant girl who lives with her epileptic sister and her overbearing mother; through her success in science, Tillie is able to break free from her stifling family.

- *I Never Loved Your Mind* (1970), Zindel's third novel, stars high school dropout Dewey Daniels and his true love, fellow dropout Yvette Goethals.

- In Zindel's *My Darling, My Hamburger* (1969), a high school girl discovers she is pregnant, but her abusive parents are no help, so she decides to visit an illegal abortionist.

- Zindel's *Pardon Me, You're Stepping on My Eyeball!* (1976) tells the story of two misfits who head out for adventure.

- In Zindel's *The Pigman's Legacy* (1980), a sequel to *The Pigman*, John and Lorraine visit the Pigman's empty house and find an old man who's hiding from the tax authorities. They see him as their chance to make up for how they treated the Pigman, and launch into new adventures.

- S. E. Hinton's *The Outsiders* tells the story of a high school "greaser," or delinquent, who hates the rich, popular kids—until his friend murders one of them, and he must come to terms with his beliefs about people and life.

John is aware that his father was once ill with liver disease and that he will probably die at a relatively young age because of the stress of his job, but he still half-jokes about it, not considering how the loss may affect him: "All the guys at the Exchange drop dead of heart attacks. They gather around this circle and bellow out bids all day long . . . " He is cynical about his parents' death and is unmoved when his father mentions that his mother will die someday, because death is not yet real to him. He responds, "Oh Dad, can't you see all I want

to do is be individualistic?" Because John has never experienced the loss of a truly loved one through death, his father's words are just an empty threat, a game parents play to manipulate their kids and make their kids feel guilty, and this game makes John feel frustrated and angry.

John has seen dead people before, when he attended funerals of distant relatives. Because he is so alienated from his family, the deaths didn't mean much to him, and he was unmoved at the funerals, where even seeing the dead people didn't bother him. He viewed them as if they were large stuffed dolls, and said, "So many things to look at. Anything to get away from what was really happening." In saying this, he has found one source of his unhappiness: alienation, detachment, disconnection, which is fostered by the emotional disconnection of his family.

When John finds a pamphlet on funeral planning while snooping around Mr. Pignati's house, death starts becoming more real, and this proximity gives him "the creeps." For the first time, he reflects on how the various adults in his life, and his teachers at school, are really not preparing him, or any of the other kids, for life. They may learn about literature, for example, but, he notes, "I don't think there's a single kid in that whole joint who would know what to do if somebody dropped dead." These words, of course, turn out to be prophetic, because not long after, Mr. Pignati has his first heart attack, and he and Lorraine are stunned. John does know what to do—he calls the police—but emotionally, both John and Lorraine are stunned, frightened, and angry, and for the rest of the book, they're desperately trying to make sense of their pain, or escape from it.

When they visit Mr. Pignati in the hospital, his roommate is a very old, very ill man, and John remarks flippantly, "He looked like he wasn't long for this world . . . a guy [who looked like he was 193 years old] with some kind of oxygen-tent thing nearby that looked like a malaria net." The patient, like the corpses moldering underground in the cemetery, is not seen as a real person, but as a sort of horror-movie prop, something to make the story more dramatic, and his suffering is not even considered.

However, secretly, John is affected by seeing Mr. Pignati so sick. He is frightened by how weak Mr. Pignati has become, and comments, "The smell of hospitals always makes me think of death."

When Mr. Pignati dies from a second heart attack, which is brought on by the news of Bobo the baboon's death, John finally realizes that it does matter to him that "I live in a world where you can grow old and be alone and have to get down on your hands and knees and beg for friends," and that he's now sharply aware that if he and Lorraine hadn't come along, "the Pigman would've just lived like a vegetable until he died alone in that dump of a house." He asks, "Didn't [Lorraine] know how sick to my stomach it made me feel to know it's possible to end your life with only a baboon to talk to?"

He realizes that everyone he knows—he, Lorraine, his parents, and Lorraine's mother—are all spending their lives concentrating on the wrong things: money, career, bad relationships in the past. No one in the book, except Mr. Pignati, is truly "awake" in daily life, living fully, living now.

By the end of the book, John knows that death does have a deep effect on the survivors, and that although he wants to pursue his own dream, his fun, and his individuality, as he tells his father, he knows now that he can't just pursue his own interests without considering their effects on others. Rollerskating with Mr. Pignati was just a game, but it had disastrous consequences when Mr. Pignati had his heart attack. Holding a party seemed like harmless fun, but it too got out of hand, and in the end, led to Mr. Pignati's second heart attack at the zoo—after the culminating event, the baboon Bobo's death. In the last analysis, John realizes that an awareness of death sharpens one's sense of responsibility and meaning. As he puts it in one of the last sentences of the book, "Our life would be what we made of it—nothing more, nothing less."

Source: Kelly Winters, Critical Essay on *The Pigman*, in *Novels for Students*, The Gale Group, 2002.

Paul Zindel and Teri Lesesne

In the following interview, Zindel discusses his works and his status as a writer for young adults.

Though there is some disagreement as to the exact date that young adult literature emerged as a separate and distinct genre from that for children and adults, scholars agree that a handful of novels led the way, broke new ground, and prepared the soil for what was to grow into a blooming genre. *The Pigman* by Paul Zindel is one of those touchstone books that set apart novels for adolescents. It did more than that, however. Zindel's remarkable novel set the standard for writers to follow. Mr. Zindel (or, as I address him, Paulissimus) recently found time to share his thoughts and feelings about writing for the YA audience.

[TL:] Your first novel for young adults, The Pigman, *broke such new ground. It is considered by many in the field to be the first truly YA book. What is your reaction to all of this?*

[PZ:] I'm glad someone noticed. When Charlotte Zolotow, then an editor and author at Harper-Collins, asked if I had any stories for teenagers in me, I went into classrooms and interviewed kids. I found out that in a group of a hundred boys, only two or three had read a single book. That book was always *Catcher in the Rye*. Sometimes one of the boys had read a second book. That was always *Lord of the Flies*. I asked the boys why they read those books and they told me it was because their girlfriends made them read it. I realized fairly quickly that there weren't many books around that showed teenage protagonists in a modern reality concerned with realistic problems—so I gave it a shot.

Did you think you were writing for a younger audience?

I knew I was writing for high school students. My first audiences were juniors and seniors, and as the years went by, the audiences got younger and younger. Most kids who read the book today are in the seventh or eighth grades.

Had you any suspicions that this book would be considered a "classic" in the field more than 25 years after publication?

I had made a wise choice long ago not to use slang or curses, because those are things that really date a book. I was also fortunate that my writing and speaking voice uses hyperbole and bathos naturally—something that had to do with the strong defenses I had to mount to survive growing up. I was lucky that these elements give the illusion of slang and oxymorons, without my being trapped by the changing language of youth.

Many of your books seem to explore the life and times of the misfit, the adolescent who does not seem to fit in. Is that a fair characterization?

Yes. I write about misfits, because I was a misfit growing up. I had no father at a time when that was considered freakish. I couldn't catch a baseball. I acted out and got involved in crazy, though relatively harmless, capers. I didn't know who I was or who I could be or what my career should be. I desperately wanted friends and to be liked, but my family moved around so much 1 never had the chance to keep very many friends. Most of my friends were misfits, too. I think being a misfit is a terrific requisite for becoming an author—becoming creative. When you're not doing so hot

> " I write about misfits, because I was a misfit growing up. . . . Most of my friends were misfits, too. I think being a misfit is a terrific requisite for becoming an author—becoming creative."

in the real world, you invent fictional worlds in which you can have a really spectacular and estimable life.

I know that asking an author to name a favorite book is like asking them to name a favorite child. However, of which book are you the most proud and why?

Pride is not a quality I allow myself to feel. It takes time. Awards take time. Patting oneself on the back takes time. I'm too busy writing about oddballs and rats and cruel cheerleaders and phantasmagoric teachers to sit around evaluating or dreaming of reviews or looking back. Were I to do that, I would probably have to say that stories I think I could continue to live with, either in sequel or movie or other forms, would be *The Pigman and I, The Effect of Gamma Rays on Man-in-the-Moon Marigolds* (a play), *The Doom Stone*, and several of the horror books. Oh, yes, I just remembered, I think the best book I've ever written may becoming out next year (2000). At the moment it's called *The Gadget* and it's my first historical novel— about the son of a physicist who lives at Los Alamos at the time when the first atomic bomb was being made. I think all the books that I'm really going to be proud of are still coming down the pike. With the benefit of history, I think I'm going to write some hot stuff.

You maintain a successful career writing for teens and for adults. Is it difficult to move between these two audiences?

Yes. I'm in a teen phase now. I talk, live and eat teens. I'm about 15 years old and I do very childish things and worry about extraordinary problems. I get jilted, go to movies, eat pizza and ice cream, hang out with my kids and lots of young people, and I don't notice that I'm three times their age. I am such a kid inside I can't imagine realizing that I'm almost old enough to die. I'm certain that death, when it comes, will take me by enormous surprise. I'll probably be getting ready to go on a roller coaster or attend a prom.

*Your recent books (*Loch, Reef of Death, Raptor, The Doom Stone*) focus on teens facing incredible danger in the form of prehistoric life forms. How did the transition from misfit to monster occur?*

I got tired of teenagers having problems. I felt the problems had all been written about for too long, and that kids were fed up with that posture. It also became somewhat disingenuous for adults to be writing about teenage problems when it's clear how mad and bizarre and foolish and dangerous and stupefying adult life has become. I wrote a one act play called *"Every 17 Minutes the Crowd Goes Crazy."* It's about the ultimate abandonment of parental interest by a mother and father who flee their five children to spend the rest of their selfish, frightened lives going to trotter race tracks and Native American Casinos. I wish it were a joke.

You seem to have a firm grip on what scares readers. What frightens you?

What frightens me is the thought that I might have a painful, massive heart attack, be shot in a home invasion, or have a rare and barbed tiny Amazon catfish swim into my urethra. I'm also frightened of my children being injured or shot at in a mini-market, being struck by lightning or a meteor, and being devoured feet first by, in order of horror, a crocodile, a great white shark, or a tiger in the swamps of Bengal, and dying of rabies.

I know you travel quite a bit. Are you inspired to write after you have visited a certain location? Or does the idea come first and mandate a trip to the locale?

Yes! I came back from Indonesia and wrote a book about giant bats in the jungle canopy. I got to hold a giant fruit bat that opened its five-foot wing span. I came back from India and wanted to write about rats taking over Staten Island by coming up through the toilets in chic middle-class housing. My stories come from my life. Ideas emerge from where I am living, where I am visiting—and most powerfully, from people I meet. I love people. I love kids. The right kid or the right adult will set my mind spinning into an adventure that mesmerizes me for years. Next year I'm planning on growing up and I'm going to write about love and divorce. There are so many things I should have been told about love, and now that I know all the secrets, I want to share them. I think I could write some startling stuff about the urge to merge.

What do you hear from readers?

My readers are fabulous and send me great fan mail and stuffed bears and prehistoric alligator teeth. I'm starting to give out my email address all over the place now because that's the easiest way for me to have a maddening career but keep in touch with the great kids and librarians and teachers. My e-mail is PaulZindel@AOL.com. I want to hear from the kids of the world, and this year I'm going to have a web site that will make my competition drool from its graphics and hilarity and emotional depth and truth and all kinds of things.

If you had to select a scene or chapter from one of your works to be placed in an anthology for the year 2000 literature books, which would that be and why?

It would be a scene from my play "Marigolds"—a scene where the mother is yapping at her daughter about the half life of the seeds the daughter has planted, and the mother's own half life as a human being. I would pick that scene because I think it is a dram of the true elixir. The writing soars because the literary metaphor of atomic radiation and the heartbreaking universal emotion of the mother melds with an extraordinary balance of irony and humor—and proof in spades that I have vision and talent, originality and compassion. It puts my best foot forward. I know it.

Source: Teri Lesesne, "Humor, Bathos, and Fear: An Interview with Paul Zindel," in *Teacher Librarian*, Vol. 27, No. 2, December 1999, pp. 60–62.

Sources

Clarke, Loretta, "The Pigman: A Novel of Adolescence," in *English Journal*, Vol. 61, No. 8, November 1972.

Forman, Jack Davis, *Presenting Paul Zindel*, Twayne Publishers, 1988, pp. 12–17, 57–59.

Lesesne, Teri, "Humor, Bathos, and Fear: An Interview with Paul Zindel," in *Teacher Librarian*, Vol. 27, No. 2, December 1999, p. 60.

Zindel, Paul, "Paul Zindel: Interview Transcript," *Scholastic*, http://teacher.scholastic.com (June 14, 2001).

———, "Paul Zindel's Booklist," *Scholastic*, http://teacher. scholastic.com (June 14, 2001).

For Further Reading

National Council of Teachers of English, *Speaking for Ourselves: Autobiographical Sketches by Notable Authors of Books for Young Adults*, National Council of Teachers of English, 1990.
    This compendium of autobiographies features Zindel and many other writers for young adults, who discuss their lives and works.

Raymond, Gerard, "The Effects of Staten Island on a Pulitzer Prize–Winning Playwright," in *Theater Week*, Vol. 2, No. 37, April 24, 1989, p. 16–21.
    The article discusses Zindel's difficult upbringing and its ramifications for his writing.

Rees, David, *The Marble in the Water: Essays on Contemporary Writers of Fiction for Children and Young Adults*, Horn Book, Inc., 1980.
    This collection of essays provides critical insight on the works of contemporary novelists who write for children and young adults.

Zindel, Paul, *The Pigman and Me*, HarperCollins, 1992.
    Zindel's autobiography discusses his painful childhood, his career as a writer, and the inspiration for his work.

A Prayer for Owen Meany

John Irving

1989

John Irving's *A Prayer for Owen Meany*, published by Ballantine in 1989, is a long, sprawling
novel in the tradition of Charles Dickens and other
nineteenth-century novelists. John Wheelwright, a
former American who is now a Canadian citizen
living in Toronto, tells the story. John recalls
growing up in a small town in New Hampshire
with a very unusual best friend, a tiny boy with a
high voice named Owen Meany. Despite his
strange appearance and voice, Owen is a boy with
a strong personality, intellectual gifts, and an air
of authority that enables him to take charge of a
situation. Owen also possesses a strong religious
faith and an uncanny knowledge of future events
in his life—including the exact time and circumstances of his own tragic but heroic death. It is
through Owen Meany that John becomes a religious believer.

A Prayer for Owen Meany is Irving's seventh
novel. Compellingly readable, it contains a large
cast of idiosyncratic small-town characters and has
many hilarious scenes and episodes. It also contains serious political and religious themes, exploring issues such as faith and doubt, predestination, the Vietnam War, and the wider issue of
American foreign policy from the 1960s to the
1980s. The book is also a mine of information
about American social history, from the advent of
television in the 1950s to the rock videos of the
1980s.

Author Biography

John Winslow Irving was born on March 2, 1942, in Exeter, New Hampshire, the son of Colin F. N. (a teacher) and Frances (Winslow) Irving. In 1961, he graduated from Phillips Exeter Academy, where he excelled at wrestling, and decided to become a writer. From 1961 to 1962, Irving was at the University of Pittsburgh because of its wrestling program, and from 1963 to 1964 he attended the Institute of European Studies, University of Vienna.

In 1965, Irving graduated with a bachelor of arts degree from the University of New Hampshire, and in 1967, he received a masters in fine arts from the University of Iowa. The following year, he became assistant professor of English at Windham College and published his first novel, *Setting Free the Bears*. More novels soon followed: *The Water-Method Man* (1972) and *The 158-Pound Marriage* (1974).

During the 1970s, Irving taught at Mount Holyoke College, South Hadley, Massachusetts, and Brandeis University and was a writer in residence at the University of Iowa, Iowa City. In 1978, he published a family saga, *The World According to Garp*, which was his first big commercial success. The book sold 120,000 hardback copies and received critical acclaim. It won the American Book Award in 1980 as the best paperback novel of 1979 and was made into a movie in 1982.

Irving continued his success with another family saga, *The Hotel New Hampshire* (1981), in which he explored, with his characteristic dark humor, issues such as incest, terrorism, and suicide. The book sold 150,000 copies and was made into a movie in 1984. *The Cider House Rules*, set in an orphanage and dealing with abortion, followed in 1985. Irving wrote an Oscar Award-winning screenplay based on the novel, and a movie was made in 1999 starring Michael Caine. *A Prayer for Owen Meany* (1989) was the third Irving novel to find its way to the movie screen, being freely adapted to produce *Simon Birch* in 1998.

During the 1990s, Irving continued his literary output. The novel *Son of the Circus* (1994), about an orthopedist who conducts genetic research on circus dwarfs in India, was followed by *Trying to Save Piggy Sneed* (1996), a collection of memoirs, short stories, and essays. A concise autobiography, *The Imaginary Girlfriend: A Memoir* (1997), was followed by Irving's eighth novel, *A Widow for One Year*, in 1998. Irving's most recent novel is *The Fourth Hand* (2001), which includes his cus-

John Irving

tomary mix of bizarre characters and situations, centering on a man who has a hand transplant.

Irving married Shyla Leary in 1964. They had two children and were divorced in 1981. In 1987, Irving married Janet Turnbull, who is also his literary agent; they have one son.

Plot Summary

Chapter 1: The Foul Ball

A Prayer for Owen Meany begins with the narrator, John Wheelwright, commenting that he believes in God because of his boyhood friend Owen Meany. John flashes back nearly forty years and recalls Owen. Not only was Owen tiny, but his vocal cords did not develop properly, giving him a high, strange-sounding, nasal voice. Then John explains his family background. He is from Gravesend, New Hampshire, and he can trace his family back to the Mayflower. However, John does not know who his father is, his birth being the result of an encounter between his mother, Tabitha, and a man she met on the Boston & Maine Railroad. John's mother is killed when he is eleven. Owen hits a foul ball, which strikes John's mother on the head, while he's playing Little League baseball.

Media Adaptations

- The movie *Simon Birch* (1998) was very loosely based on *A Prayer for Owen Meany*, although the story was altered and Irving refused to allow the name Owen Meany to be used.

Chapter 2: The Armadillo

The narrative jumps back and forth to different events and times in John's childhood. John recalls when his mother met her future husband, Dan Needham, a drama teacher. Dan gives John a stuffed armadillo. John recalls staying at Sawyer Depot during summer vacations with his boisterous older cousins Noah, Simon, and Hester. Owen meets the cousins at Thanksgiving at John's home. They are startled by his strange appearance, but they accede to his wishes about what games to play. After the fatal accident, as a way of apologizing to John, Owen gives him his precious collection of baseball cards. Dan and John realize that Owen also wants the cards back, so they return them. In exchange, John gives Owen his armadillo. Owen returns it but with the front claws removed. The chapter returns to the present, with an extract from John's diary entry for January 30, 1987. John now lives in Toronto, and he is angry about the policies of President Ronald Reagan. The moving back and forth between past and present happens in almost all the chapters.

Chapter 3: The Angel

John describes two important motifs in the novel, the dressmaker's dummy that his mother always kept in her bedroom and the red dress that she bought in one of her trips to Boston for singing lessons. Then he describes a night when Owen has a fever and goes to John's mother's bedroom, where he thinks he sees an angel. After Tabitha's death, Owen believes this was the angel of death, and because he had interrupted it, the angel reassigned its task to him. John then returns to describing the four-year courtship between Dan and his mother and their wedding in 1952. Then he describes the funeral service at some length. That evening, John discovers Owen at the cemetery reading from *The Book of Common Prayer*. He notices that Owen seems to take charge of things—for example, Owen insists on taking the dressmaker's dummy and putting it in his own room.

Chapter 4: The Little Lord Jesus

Owen talks the Reverend Dudley Wiggins into allowing him to play the infant Jesus in the upcoming Christmas pageant. Owen seems to take over the whole production, assigning many of the parts, rearranging the order of music, and generally annoying the rector's wife, Barb, who is in charge of the production. Tiny Owen takes charge in any situation, even presiding over the funeral of a neighbor's dog. He also lands another non-speaking part in the Gravesend Players' production of *A Christmas Carol*, playing the Ghost of Christmas Yet to Come. At rehearsals, Owen impresses the cast with his stage presence.

Chapter 5: The Ghost of the Future

As the Ghost of Christmas Yet to Come, Owen is a sensation; his eerie authority seems to frighten everyone. At the pageant, everything goes wrong, but Owen emerges as a mighty figure: he prompts the forgetful Announcing Angel, commands the stage, demands to be worshiped, and finally brings the show to an end as he banishes his parents from the congregation and instructs Joseph (played by John) to get him out of the church. The pageant ends in farce, but Owen has established himself as a formidable Christ child. The same thing happens on the last night of *A Christmas Carol*. Owen's performance is electrifying and also disturbing because he sees his own name and the date of his death on the gravestone, rather than that of Scrooge.

Chapter 6: The Voice

In the fall of 1958, Owen, who is academically gifted, and John, who is not, attend Gravesend Academy, a private school. Before that, their education came largely through movies and television. Owen soon makes a name for himself, writing witty, opinionated editorials in the school paper that earn him the nickname, the Voice. He is admired by students and listened to by the faculty, and even gets to interview applicants for faculty positions. Owen helps John with his academic work, and they also practice basketball together: John lifts Owen up in order for him to make a slam-dunk shot. Then a new headmaster, Randy White, is appointed at the school; he and Owen dislike each other. In

1961, Owen is inspired by the inauguration of President John F. Kennedy.

Chapter 7: The Dream

At Owen's prompting, John steps up the search for his father. They visit the store in Boston where his mother bought the red dress. They also discover that she sang at a supper club as The Red Lady, and they visit her voice teacher, Graham Mc-Swiney. Owen's outspokenness makes him enemies at the academy. After insulting Mrs. Mitzy Lish, the glamorous mother of one of the students (after she insulted him), he is put on probation and sent to see Dr. Dolder, a psychiatrist. Owen plays a prank, getting some basketball players to move Dolder's car to the stage of the Great Hall where the school's morning meeting is held. No one can prove that Owen was involved. But then it is discovered that he has forged draft cards and sold them to students so they can purchase alcohol. Owen is expelled from the academy, although he has the last laugh when the headmaster loses his job as a result of the incident. Finally, Owen has a dream that tells him how he is going to die.

Chapter 8: The Finger

John has little success with women, unlike Owen, who takes up with John's cousin Hester. Owen and John become freshmen at the University of New Hampshire. Owen has won a scholarship from the army. They discuss current events such as the Cuban Missile Crisis, the death of Kennedy, and the build-up in Vietnam. They still practice the basketball shot, accomplishing it in under three seconds. Owen believes he must go to Vietnam and become a hero by saving many Vietnamese children. After graduation, Owen gets assigned to an army desk job in Arizona, while John enters graduate school. Owen severs John's index finger so that John will not be drafted into the army.

Chapter 9: The Shot

The narrative skips back and forth between the present and the late-1960s. John describes how his cousin Hester became a famous rock star. He also describes an incident in which Owen helped him after Owen's death. John also recalls the time when Mr. Meany, Owen's father, told him that he and his wife never had sexual intercourse and therefore Owen was born of a virgin. However, the Catholic Church did not believe him, and neither does John. Meanwhile, Owen engraves his own tombstone, even including the date of his death, and John discovers that his father is the Reverend Merrill. He

also finds out that Merrill has lost his religious faith and arranges a bogus miracle involving the dressmaker's dummy to restore it; the ruse works. John then describes Owen's funeral. Only at the end of the book does he describe Owen's death. He is killed at an airport in Arizona, saving some Vietnamese refugee children from a grenade tossed by Dick Jarvits, an angry fifteen-year-old boy.

Characters

Mary Beth Baird

Mary Beth Baird is the girl who plays Mary in the Christmas pageant. She is very fond of Owen and tends to overplay her part. John meets her again at Owen's funeral.

Ginger Brinker-Smith

Ginger Brinker-Smith is the wife of one of the faculty members at Gravesend Academy. The recent mother of twins, she is a voluptuous strawberry-blonde and the object of the sexual fantasies of the boys at the academy.

Mr. Chickering

Mr. Chickering is the fat, good-hearted Little League coach who tells Owen to bat for John in their final game. This results in the hit that kills John's mother. Mr. Chickering feels he is partly responsible and weeps at the funeral.

Harold Crosby

Harold Crosby is the fat, self-conscious boy who plays the angel in the Christmas pageant. He is so overawed by the occasion that he forgets his lines.

Dr. Dolder

Dr. Dolder is the Swiss psychiatrist at Gravesend Academy to whom Owen is sent for psychiatric evaluation. Owen finds him lacking in insight.

Alfred Eastman

Alfred Eastman is John's friendly, manly uncle. When John is a boy, Alfred owns a lumber business in rural Sawyer Depot.

Hester Eastman

Hester Eastman is John's cousin. Not as attractive as her brothers, she has thick dark hair, broad shoulders, and big hands. But she is also intelligent and athletic, with an earthy kind of sex appeal. As a girl, she resents the fact that her brothers seem to get preferential treatment from their parents, and she becomes an emotionally and sexually aggressive young woman. Hester and Owen develop a close romantic relationship, punctuated by Hester's violent outbursts. Hester becomes an antiwar protester in the 1960s, and she is deeply affected by Owen's death. She cannot bring herself to attend his funeral. Always interested in music, by the 1980s Hester becomes a famous rock star performing under the name of Hester the Molester, the nickname her brother Simon gave her when they were children. Her lyrics reflect the pain she suffered as a result of Owen's death.

Martha Eastman

Martha Eastman is John's aunt, Tabitha Wheelwright's sister. Martha is less attractive than her sister and does not have Tabitha's talent for singing. John thinks she may have been jealous of Tabitha, even though Martha had a college education and Tabitha did not. Martha marries Alfred Eastman and they have three children.

Noah Eastman

Noah Eastman is John's eldest cousin. Like the others, he is boisterous and active, enjoying outdoor pursuits, like water-skiing, as well as indoor games. He takes particular pleasure in beating up his younger brother, Simon, who does not seem to mind much. He attends Gravesend Academy and later goes to college on the West Coast.

Simon Eastman

Simon Eastman, like his brother, is blond and handsome and a bit of a daredevil. Always the victim of his older brother, he takes it all in stride. He and Noah later attend Gravesend Academy and go to colleges on the West Coast.

Ethel

Ethel is the slow-witted maid who replaces Lydia at 80 Front Street after Lydia has her leg amputated.

Mr. Fish

Mr. Fish is the Wheelwrights' neighbor when John is growing up. He owns a dog called Sagamore, who is killed by a diaper truck. Mr. Fish develops an enthusiasm for amateur dramatics and plays roles in the productions of the Gravesend Players, including Scrooge in *A Christmas Carol*.

Germaine

Germaine is the maid who is hired to look after Lydia at 80 Front Street. She is young, shy, nervous, and clumsy.

Dick Jarvits

Dick Jarvits is the rude, aggressive, pot-smoking fifteen-year-old boy from a disreputable family in Phoenix, Arizona, who throws the grenade that kills Owen Meany. He is obsessed with violence and cannot wait until he is old enough to go to Vietnam and kill the enemy. Dick is killed by Major Rawls immediately after he throws the grenade.

Katherine Keeling

Katherine Keeling is the headmistress of Bishop Strachen School in Toronto and a close friend of John's, who also teaches at the school.

Larry Lish

Larry Lish is a rich student at Gravesend Academy. John calls him a "charming sociopath," and students and faculty dislike him. He tells the police that Owen has been forging ID cards, and this leads to Owen's expulsion.

Mitzy Lish

Mitzy Lish is the mother of Larry Lish. She is a beautiful, vain divorcée who spends her days in luxurious leisure in New York. When Owen meets her, she confirms what her son had told him, that President Kennedy has had an affair with Marilyn Monroe. Mrs. Lish also insults Owen, and he insults her in return. She then reports him to Randy White, the headmaster.

Lydia

Lydia is Harriet Wheelwright's cook and housekeeper. She loses a leg to cancer and is confined to a wheelchair but still lives in the family home at 80 Front Street. Lydia is about the same age as Harriet Wheelwright, and she develops the habit of imitating her in word and deed. As the years go by, she increasingly resembles her former employer. She dies at home on the last night of the performance of *A Christmas Carol*.

Graham McSwiney

Graham McSwiney is Tabitha's former voice teacher in Boston. When John and Owen visit him, he tells them about John's mother's singing career as The Red Lady.

Mr. Meany

Mr. Meany is Owen Meany's father. He is a man of few words, but he has a pleasant disposition. He owns a granite business. When Owen is eleven, Mr. Meany tells him that he and his wife never had sexual intercourse, so he believes Owen is the product of a virgin birth.

Mrs. Meany

Mrs. Meany is Owen Meany's mother. She rarely speaks to anyone, spending her days sitting by the window or staring at the fire. She is so melancholy and withdrawn that she appears to be mentally disturbed.

Owen Meany

Owen Meany is John Wheelwright's closest friend from boyhood. Owen is tiny, never growing taller than five feet, and he speaks in a high, nasal voice that never changes. His family is descended from Boston Irish, and Owen's father owns a granite quarry in Gravesend. When he is a teenager, Owen learns to work with granite like an expert. Owen is highly intelligent and has a charismatic presence that is hard to ignore. Even as a child, he seems able to take charge in any situation, and he ends up as the star of both the Christmas pageant and the play *A Christmas Carol*. Owen also has an unshakable belief in God. He is certain that everything happens for a purpose. He believes he is God's instrument, and he also has foreknowledge of his own death.

Unlike his friend John, Owen excels at Gravesend Academy, where he is known as the Voice because of the forceful and influential opinions he expresses as editor of the school paper. He wins scholarships to Harvard and Yale, but complications result when he is expelled from the academy for forging ID cards and selling them to students. He eventually accepts a scholarship from the U.S. Army and ends up going to the University of New Hampshire with his friend John. Owen is disillusioned about the American government after he learns that his hero John F. Kennedy is not the moral paragon Owen believed him to be. Owen can see many of the dangers inherent in the Vietnam War from an early stage, but he still fervently wants to go there because he believes that his destiny is to die in the act of saving many Vietnamese children as was foretold to him in a dream. The dream does come true, although the Vietnamese children Owen saves are refugees who happen to arrive at the airport in Phoenix, Arizona, while Owen is performing his duties as an army lieutenant, waiting to escort the body of a dead U.S. soldier. By his selfless act of saving the children, who are the intended victims of a grenade thrown by Dick Jarvits, Owen dies a hero's death. His death has lasting effects on John and on Hester Eastman, with whom Owen had a long and sometimes stormy relationships.

Reverend Louis Merrill

Reverend Louis Merrill is pastor at the Congregational church in Gravesend. He is an eloquent preacher, despite his stutter, and his religious faith is founded on the necessity of doubt. John finds this appealing. It later transpires that Merrill is John's father and that he has completely lost his religious faith. When John fools him by dressing up the dressmaker's dummy so that it looks like Tabitha, Merrill thinks that Tabitha has returned to forgive him. With this fake miracle, Merrill recovers his faith and preaches at Owen's funeral with renewed confidence.

Dan Needham

Dan Needham is a drama teacher at Gravesend Academy who marries Tabitha Wheelwright after a four-year courtship. After Tabitha is killed, Dan legally adopts John and raises him as if he were his own son. The two of them form an affectionate and loving relationship, which still continues at the time of John's life in Toronto in the 1980s. As a teacher, Dan is outstanding. He is dedicated to the task of providing a well-rounded education for the boys in his charge. He has an understanding of the problems of young people and a willingness to help, and he also has sympathy for the elderly. Dan revitalizes the Gravesend Players, getting half of the faculty and many of the townspeople involved in the productions.

Major Rawls

Major Rawls is a nineteen-year veteran of the U.S. Army and has served in Korea and Vietnam. He accompanies Owen Meany to Phoenix on his assignment of bringing the dead U.S. soldier home to his family. After the attack that kills Owen, Rawls kills the culprit, Dick Jarvits, with a machete blow.

Mrs. Walker

Mrs. Walker is the stern Sunday school teacher at the Episcopal church in Gravesend. John has little affection for her, in part because she always unfairly blamed Owen when the other children lifted him up into the air. Mrs. Walker also acts in productions put on by the Gravesend Players.

Harriet Wheelwright

Harriet Wheelwright is John's aristocratic grandmother. She is descended from John Adams, and she married into a wealthy family in Gravesend. The local people regard her with a kind of awe, almost as a figure of royalty. Harriet presides in authoritarian but loving fashion over the family home at 80 Front Street. Her passion is for reading, but later she installs a television set in the home and watches it constantly.

John Wheelwright

John Wheelwright, the narrator of the novel, is the son of Tabitha Wheelwright. Tabitha is killed by a baseball struck by Owen Meany when John is eleven. John's father is the Reverend Louis Merrill, although John does not discover this until he is in his twenties. John is raised in the aristocratic home of his grandmother, Harriet Wheelwright. His best friend, from a very early age, is Owen Meany. John deeply admires Owen, and as a middle-aged man, he declares that it is because of Owen that he believes in God. As they grow up, John always plays a supporting role to Owen; Owen is the leader, whereas John is a follower without much initiative of his own. This is typified when John plays the silent Joseph in the Christmas pageant while Owen steals the limelight as the infant Jesus. When they both attend Gravesend Academy, John is a poor student until Owen shows him how to write about literature. And, unlike Owen, John has no success with girls. After graduating from the University of New Hampshire, John goes to graduate school, and he allows Owen to amputate his index finger so that he can avoid being drafted and sent to Vietnam. After Owen's death, John decides to leave America for Canada. He becomes a Canadian citizen and teaches literature at a high school for girls. He never marries and remains without sexual experience. Deeply affected by the political upheavals in America in the 1960s, as well as by what happened to Owen, John retains an almost obsessive interest in American political affairs. He frequently denounces at length the policies of President Ronald Reagan.

Tabitha Wheelwright

Tabitha Wheelwright is John's mother. Known as Tabby, she is beautiful and has a talent for singing. She doesn't have to work since her mother provides for her, and she shows no interest in getting a higher education. She makes her own clothes, copying them from clothes she brings home from expensive stores in Boston, which she then returns to the stores. She gets pregnant with John after a brief affair with a man she met on the train to Boston, where she went for singing lessons. She sang in a club under the name The Red Lady, because of the red dress she wore. Tabitha marries Dan Needham, but after only a year of marriage, she is killed when a foul ball struck by Owen Meany hits her on the head.

Randy White

Randy White is appointed headmaster of Gravesend Academy while John and Owen are students there. White prides himself on being an effective decision-maker, and he makes many changes and reforms. He and Owen take a dislike to each other, and White eventually arranges for Owen to be expelled from the academy; however, his rash actions cost him his job.

Barb Wiggin

Barb Wiggin, the wife of the Reverend Dudley Wiggin, is a former flight attendant. John dislikes her, describing her as a "brash, backslapping redhead." Barb aggressively assists her husband in directing the Christmas pageant and reacts in a negative way when her authority is challenged by Owen's many suggestions about how the event should be staged.

Reverend Dudley Wiggin

The Reverend Dudley Wiggin is the rector of the Episcopalian church in Gravesend. He is a former airline pilot, whom John describes as a "pulpit thumper." Unlike the Reverend Merrill, Wiggin has no doubts about his faith, and he preaches with great zeal. John says that Wiggin's sermons "were about as entertaining and convincing as a pilot's voice on the intercom, explaining technical difficulties while the plane plummets toward the earth and the stewardesses are screaming." The Reverend Wiggin also directs the Christmas pageant in which Owen plays the infant Jesus.

Themes

Faith and Doubt

The theme of religious faith versus doubt is prominent throughout the novel. Owen Meany has an absolute faith in God and seems to have possessed it from a very early age. When he is eleven, for example, he tells John that God knows who John's father is and will eventually identify him. Owen never doubts that there is a purpose to everything, and his faith in his own destiny as decreed by God never wavers.

In contrast, John, as a child, has no particular religious beliefs or faith. He learns to believe in God mostly through his knowledge of Owen's seemingly miraculous life and death—particularly the fact that Owen possessed foreknowledge of the exact date and circumstances of his own death. However, John is never without his doubts. After Owen's death and his own move to Canada, John joins the Anglican Church, but it takes him years to accept the church's doctrines. Although he calls himself a believer, he admits that he wavers constantly: "Doubt one minute, faith the next—sometimes inspired, sometimes in despair." His faith is "a church rummage faith—the kind that needs patching up every weekend." It does not have the shining intensity and certainty of Owen Meany's faith.

A key figure in the theme of religious faith is the Reverend Merrill. Although he is a clergyman, he approaches faith only through doubt. For him, doubt is the essence of faith. He argues that it is natural to doubt, because the world presents so little evidence of the existence of God. Therefore, in the absence of proof, faith is necessary. John finds this an attractive position, but Owen does not. He comments that if the reverend is so full of doubt, he is, as a clergyman, in the wrong business.

The irony is that the Reverend Merrill's position becomes untenable, even for him. Just before John discovers that Merrill is his father, he realizes that Merrill no longer has any faith at all in the religious truths he preaches. Doubt has eaten him up and left nothing else. In another irony, Merrill's faith is restored by what he believes is a miracle—the very thing that he has spent his whole life saying is unnecessary. And in a crowning irony, the miracle that Merrill witnesses is completely bogus. It is in reality a trick played on him by John, who clothes the dressmaker's dummy so that it resembles his mother and fools the Reverend into believing that it is a vision of the dead Tabitha. This one fake miracle is all it takes to restore Merrill's faith, and even his stutter disappears as he preaches with new confidence.

The conclusion seems to be that, for most people, some kind of supernatural event, something that cannot be rationally explained, is necessary for religious faith to flourish. Even Owen Meany may not

Topics for Further Study

- Can religious faith exist alongside doubt, or are the two mutually exclusive? Explain your viewpoint.

- Why is John so anti-American? Is his contempt for America justified? Does he make any valid criticisms of Americans or American government policies?

- Can miracles happen? How would you define a miracle, and how might it be verified?

- Is there a purposeful pattern to everything in life, as Owen Meany believes, or are the events of life merely random? If there is a pattern and God orchestrates it, how does one know this? Is it a matter of faith, or can it be rationally demonstrated?

- Was the war in Vietnam an unjust war—a very costly mistake—or was it a justified war against communist aggression? Has your reading of the novel, including the references to the peace movement and the draft evaders as well as Owen's experience in the U.S. Army, altered your view of the war? Explain your answer.

- John expresses a wish that Americans might see themselves the way people from other countries see them. How do other countries perceive America today? Does John's status as an American who became a Canadian citizen make him better able to understand American politics? Explain your answer.

be an exception in this respect. After Owen's death, John learns that he believed his father's story that his parents never had sexual intercourse and that he was the result of a miraculous birth. This belief in a very personal miracle—his own existence—may have helped to buttress the religious faith that sustained Owen throughout his life.

Fate and Destiny

The theme of fate and destiny is connected to the theme of religious faith. The core of it lies in the belief that events in human life are all part of a pattern orchestrated by God. Everything that happens has a purpose; every event, every circumstance, contributes to the unfolding of a divine plan. People act, whether knowingly or not, as instruments of God. A consequence of this belief is that there are no coincidences, as Owen Meany says more than once. For example, John recalls how Owen used to refer to "THAT FATED BASEBALL" in connection with the accident that killed John's mother. When John insists that it was merely an accident, Owen corrects him by saying that nothing is an accident.

Owen believes that there is a reason for everything, including such strange things as his peculiar, high-pitched voice. (He is later proved right—it is because his voice resembles a child's that the Vietnamese children are so ready to trust him and follow his instructions.)

This belief that everything exists for a purpose, as part of a preordained pattern, raises the question of free will. If everything is predetermined, can humans exercise any free choices? Can fate be altered, or is it unalterably fixed? John asks himself this question in connection with the performance of *A Christmas Carol* when Owen sees the gravestone marked with his own name and date of death. John quotes the question that Scrooge asks in Dickens's story: "Are these the shadows of the things that Will be or are they shadows of the things that May be, only?"

From the evidence of the novel, the answer appears to be the former: these are things that will be, and nothing anyone can do can alter them. Certainly this is what Owen believes. He never feels that he has any choice, or free will. He tells John, "IT'S NOT THAT I *WANT* TO GO TO VIETNAM—IT'S WHERE I *HAVE* TO GO. IT'S WHERE I'M A HERO. I'VE GOT TO BE THERE."

He is wrong about the place, of course, but everything else works out exactly as he foresaw it.

Although this evidence of a predetermined pattern to life (at least to Owen Meany's life) contributes greatly to John's discovery of religious faith, he is also ready to admit that it leaves some questions unanswered: "If God had a hand in what Owen 'knew,' what a horrible question *that* poses! For how could God have let that happen to Owen Meany?"

The question of how a loving God can permit evil things to happen is a perennial and difficult one for religious believers. In *A Prayer for Owen Meany*, Irving is content to raise the question and leave it unanswered.

Style

Symbols

There is a recurring motif of armlessness and amputation. It is first mentioned early in the novel, in the figure of Watahantowet, the seventeenth-century Indian chief in John's hometown of Gravesend, whose totem was an armless man. John explains that, to some, the totem symbolized how Watahantowet felt powerless after the white settlers had taken his land. Sometimes the totem was shown with a tomahawk in its mouth, which some identified, according to John, as a sign of peace: the Indian literally would not take arms against his enemies.

Another armless symbol is the dressmaker's dummy. Since the dummy is used in the novel as a reminder of Tabitha—almost as her silent double—it perhaps also suggests powerlessness or helplessness. Tabitha is powerless to resist or alter her fate.

A third example of the symbol of armlessness is when Owen removes the statue of Mary Magdalene and places it in the great hall in the academy. He cuts off the statue's arms above the elbows. John comments on this, saying that "her gesture of beseeching the assembled audience would seem all the more an act of supplication—and all the more helpless."

A fourth example is the stuffed armadillo, but this carries a very different meaning than the other examples. Owen returns the armadillo to John with its front claws removed so it can no longer stand upright. Even at the age of eleven, Owen has a symbolic purpose in mind, although it is not until he and John are students at Gravesend Academy that he explains what he meant by his actions: "GOD HAS TAKEN YOUR MOTHER. MY HANDS WERE THE INSTRUMENT. GOD HAS TAKEN MY HANDS. I AM GOD'S INSTRUMENT." In other words, Owen does not believe that he has an individual will; he cannot act simply to please himself. He was used by God as the instrument of Tabitha's death—it was not his arms but God's arms that were swinging the bat that resulted in her death. Armlessness thus becomes a symbol of the submission of an individual person to the will of God. The symbol takes on a gruesome reality when Owen, meeting his destined death, obeying the will of God, literally has his arms blown off by the grenade that kills him.

Foreshadowing

Foreshadowing is a literary technique in which a future event is hinted at, often symbolically or obliquely, before it happens. An example is the symbol of armlessness explained above, which foreshadows the moment Owen literally loses his arms. Irving hints at this moment as early as chapter 2, when John sees Owen with his hands clasped behind his back and thinks he looks as armless as Watahantowet.

Another example of foreshadowing is when Tabitha is hit on the head by a hailstone at her wedding, which foreshadows the incident with the baseball that kills her. Just to make sure the reader gets the point, Irving has John squeeze a hailstone in his hand, and John finds that it is as "hard as a baseball." (Because of the nonlinear structure of the narrative, particularly in the early part of the book, this incident is placed *after* rather than before the description of the fatal accident.)

A third example is the way John and Owen practice their basketball slam-dunk shot. John's lifting of Owen and the need to accomplish the shot in three seconds both foreshadow the scene of Owen's death when the basketball move is repeated in a different context.

Owen's vision of the gravestone with his name on it and his dream of his own death are other examples of foreshadowing.

Suspense

A technique similar to foreshadowing is the storyteller's art of creating suspense. Irving accomplishes this often, simply by using the phrase "as you shall see" to hint at future plot twists. For example, at the end of chapter 3, John comments in his diary entry that he has in the past "been moved to do evil—as you shall see"; the reader is eager to discover what this evil might have been, which is only revealed near the end of the novel. (It is his deception of the Reverend Merrill with a bogus miracle.)

Another example of creating suspense is when Owen refers to the "UNSPEAKABLE OUTRAGE" that his father and mother suffered at the hands of the Catholic Church. This is mentioned in the first chapter and repeated several times during the course of the novel. What it refers to (Owen's supposed virgin birth) is not revealed until well into the last chapter. Similarly, at the end of chapter 2,

John says it was Owen who kept him out of Vietnam with "a trick that only Owen could have managed." It is another 350 pages before the reader finds out what this trick was.

Point of View and Structure

The story is told by a first-person narrator, John Wheelwright. Although John is an important character and events are seen through his eyes, he usually plays a supporting role to Owen Meany. In most scenes, he is the more passive character. In the Christmas pageant, for example, John plays Joseph and has little to do but stand and watch. As observer and interpreter, John reflects on the events that have so deeply affected him, and he does this from a double perspective. The first standpoint is that of his own thoughts and experiences as a child growing up with Owen as his best friend. John does not always follow chronological order in his relating of these events. The early chapters in particular jump back and forth in time between different incidents in his childhood.

The second perspective, interspersed with the first, is that of John as a man in his forties, now living in Toronto in 1987. He looks back at a distance of over twenty years at those same events of his childhood and early manhood, and he also comments on contemporary events.

The advantage of this two-level structure is that it enables John to link his anger and distrust of American foreign policy in the 1980s with events in the 1960s, particularly the Vietnam War. It also gives the reader deeper insight into the key events in John's and Owen's lives and shows how those events shaped the man John has become.

Historical Context

Vietnam War

The Vietnam War forms a constant backdrop in the novel, both in John's diary entries for 1987 and in the story of his and Owen's lives in the 1960s. Irving includes many statistics culled from the *Vietnam War Almanac* that show the stages by which the war escalated.

America's involvement in Vietnam began in the early 1960s, when the Kennedy administration sent military advisers to aid the South Vietnamese government in its confrontation with North Vietnam. In 1962, there were over 11,000 military advisers in

Compare
&
Contrast

- **1960s:** The United States is engaged in a war in Vietnam that bitterly divides the nation. It does not end until 1973. Many veterans encounter hostility toward them on their return to the United States.

  1980s: Vietnam veterans, once scorned, are accorded more respect. The Vietnam Memorial Wall is built in Washington, D.C., and dedicated in 1982. It soon becomes one of the most visited sites in the city.

  Today: The United States enjoys full diplomatic relations with Vietnam, which is one of the few remaining communist countries in the world. Many veterans still suffer from post-traumatic stress syndrome.

- **1960s:** In a decade of violent unrest, young people are in rebellion on college campuses. Many are deeply concerned with issues of social justice and America's role in the world. Liberalism is the dominant political ideology.

  1980s: During the 1980s, dubbed by some the "decade of greed," the nation moves to the political right under the administration of President Ronald Reagan (1981–1989).

  Today: On college campuses, there is a decline in liberal arts majors and a corresponding increase in business majors. Many students are more interested in acquiring business degrees and profiting from rapidly growing electronic technologies in an expanding global economy than in protesting social issues. Liberalism is on the defensive.

- **1950s:** The advent of rock 'n roll gives young people a music of their own. Elvis Presley begins his career and makes successful appearances on the Ed Sullivan Show, a popular television show. Some of the older generation are shocked by Elvis's music and his sexy style. Television becomes the preferred form of entertainment for millions of Americans.

  1980s: MTV is created and becomes hugely popular among young people. Sales of the new rock music videos soar. Madonna becomes a pop culture icon. Tipper Gore, wife of Senator Al Gore, leads a campaign against violent and sexually explicit song lyrics.

  Today: Some groups continue to show concern about the violent, racist, and sexist tone of some popular song lyrics, particularly those of rap. The Parents' Music Resource Center, cofounded by Tipper Gore in the 1980s, continues to label some commercially sold music with 'explicit lyric' warnings.

Vietnam, and President John F. Kennedy said that they would fire if fired upon.

In 1964, after attacks on U.S. destroyers by North Vietnamese patrol boats, the U.S. Congress passed the Tonkin Gulf Resolution, authorizing presidential action in Vietnam. By the end of that year, there were over 23,000 U.S. military personnel in South Vietnam, and in March 1965, the first U.S. combat troops arrived. In the novel, John and Owen follow the news about Vietnam, and at this point Owen presciently remarks, "THERE'S NO END TO THIS. THERE'S NO GOOD WAY TO END IT."

From this point on, American involvement in Vietnam escalated rapidly, as did American casualties. By the end of 1966, there were 385,300 American troops in South Vietnam, and 6,644 U.S. military personnel had been killed. (The number would rise to 56,000 dead by the end of the war.) By the end of the following year, the number of troops had risen to almost half a million. Troop numbers would peak at 543,000 in April 1969.

The Vietnam War quickly became unpopular at home. In 1967, large antiwar demonstrations took place in many American cities and on college campuses. In October, 50,000 antiwar protesters assembled at the Lincoln Memorial in Washington, D.C., and some participated in a "March on the Pentagon." In the novel, John Wheelwright is one of them. His cousin Hester is also a regular at antiwar rallies. The peace movement reached its peak in November 1969, when 250,000 antiwar demonstrators marched in Washington, D.C.

Another aspect of the peace movement was draft resistance. Many men burned or turned in their draft cards in public. More than 25,000 men were indicted for draft evasion, and 4,000 of them were sentenced to prison. Many others fled to Canada (where they formed the Union of American Exiles) and elsewhere. In the novel, John Wheelwright moves to Toronto, Canada (although not as a draft evader), where he meets many American army deserters and "draft dodgers." In 1977, President Jimmy Carter pardoned most Vietnam War draft evaders.

Iran-contra Scandal

In the present-day narrative, John is angered by the foreign policies of the Reagan administration. In particular, he is vexed about the Iran-contra scandal. This was a breaking scandal in 1987, the time of his diary entries. The heart of the affair was the discovery that the United States had sold arms to Iran in exchange for the release of hostages held in Lebanon. This was against stated U.S. policy of not negotiating with terrorists. Profits from the arms sales were then diverted to support the contras in Nicaragua. The contras were U.S.-backed rebels against the left-wing Sandinista government of Nicaragua. In 1984, Congress had voted to cut off aid to the contras, so financing them was illegal.

President Ronald Reagan defended his administration. He denied that arms were exchanged for hostages and claimed he did not know that profits were being channeled to the contras. There was skepticism in many quarters about Reagan's professed ignorance, as he was a passionate supporter of the contras. But Reagan survived the scandal; there was no enthusiasm among legislators for impeaching a popular president.

Critical Overview

Critical reaction to *A Prayer for Owen Meany* was decidedly mixed. R. Z. Sheppard's assessment in *Time* was almost entirely positive. Describing the

novel as "a fable of political predestination," he commented that Irving "delivers a boisterous cast, a spirited story line and a quality of prose that is frequently underestimated, even by his admirers." On the other hand, Peter S. Prescott in *Newsweek* expressed a strong dislike for the novel, deriding its hero's "prep-school capers and comments on American foreign policy" and advising any potential reader to "run while you can." Prescott complained that "this grossly long book lacks charm precisely because it works so hard to be sweet."

William Pritchard, in a generally positive review in the *New Republic*, picked out Irving's quality of readability as a virtue, arguing that "the best and funniest things in the new novel are its superbly narrated sequences of comic action." But Pritchard had doubts about how effectively the novel's larger themes were handled. In particular, he found the narrator's present life in Canada uninteresting; without Owen Meany, John is not a compelling character. But Pritchard concluded that there were enough excellent moments in the book to allow Irving to be compared to authors such as Mark Twain or to Booth Tarkington or J. D. Salinger.

Robert Towers, in the *New York Review of Books*, argued that the book did not merit a comparison with Charles Dickens, with whom Irving's name is often linked, because it lacked Dickens's "power, vision, or humor." Towers also commented, as other reviewers did, that the narrator, John Wheelwright, does not fully come to life as a character. He added that some of the other characters, such as John's grandmother, failed to transcend stereotypes. Towers also had reservations about the Christian aspects in the novel:

> It is hard to give imaginative credence to Owen's bizarre conviction without more to go on than the narrator's reporting of his words and actions, especially since the narrator himself does not inspire total confidence. Too often the Christian elements seem merely another aspect of the novel's sensationalism.

Towers conceded, however, that Irving had strong gifts as a storyteller: "The story of Owen and his fate has a lurid power, especially in the novel's final pages. Once he surrenders to the headlong rush of events, Irving shows himself a master of narrated action."

Lieutenant Colonel Oliver North of the U.S. Marine Corps, testifying at the Congressional trial investigating the Iran-Contra affair

Criticism

Bryan Aubrey

Aubrey holds a Ph.D. in English and has published many articles on twentieth-century literature. In this essay, he discusses Owen Meany as a Christ-figure and shows how Irving connects this to a larger network of symbolism to buttress his critique of American politics and society.

Hunting for Christ-figures in literature is a popular pastime amongst students searching for a thesis to carry them through a term paper assignment. Although Western literature can yield many examples of such figures (Melville's *Billy Budd* is perhaps the best example), identifying Christ-figures in modern literature is often a more problematic enterprise. Many have been proposed, ranging from Frodo or Gandalf in Tolkien's *Lord of the Rings* trilogy (1954–1956) to R. P. McMurphy in Ken Kesey's *One Flew Over the Cuckoo's Nest* (1962), although none of these examples is highly convincing. But such is not the case with Owen Meany in *A Prayer for Owen Meany*. Owen is clearly and unambiguously a Christ-figure on many levels, from the obvious to the subtle. Irving uses the more es-

oteric aspects of the Christ symbol to add depth to his portrayal of the significance of Owen's life, as well as to buttress his critique of American politics and society.

It is obvious from the beginning of the novel that Owen Meany is special. John, the narrator, comments that he used to think Owen's strange falsetto voice came from another planet; now he believes that "it was a voice not entirely of this world." When, as a child, John sees Owen framed by a shaft of sunlight in the attic as they are playing, his appearance is so striking that "he looked like a descending angel—a tiny but fiery god, sent to adjudicate the errors of our ways."

From then on, Irving gives broad hints that Owen is neither alien nor angel but a Christ-figure. There is nothing ambiguous or ironic about the religious allusions. Irving wields his symbolism like a heavy blunt instrument; he wants to make sure readers get the point. For example, in chapter 4, when Owen, Dan, and John return home after Owen has secured the part of the Christ child in the Christmas pageant, the chapter ends with a quotation from the well-known Christmas carol:

As Owen finished knocking the snow off his boots—as the little Lord Jesus stepped inside our house—Dan half-sang, half-mumbled the refrain we knew so well: 'Hark! the her-ald an-gels sing, 'Glo-ry to the new-born King!'

Readers are meant to make the connection and not to doubt or question it. Irving wants readers to believe that Owen is following in Christ's footsteps in a way that is more than human. When Owen plays the Christ child with great authority—even his parents obey him—Mr. Fish says it is clear that Owen's Christ is no ordinary baby: "You know, he's the *Lord*! Jesus—from Day One."

There are clear thematic parallels between the life of Owen and the life of Christ. Like Christ, Owen must sacrifice his own life to save others. Like Christ, he is aware of his fate in advance. (In the Gospel of Matthew, Jesus tells his disciples that he will be killed.) And just as Christ rises from the dead and appears to his disciples, so Owen "appears" to his friend John twice after his death. The first occasion is when John learns that the Reverend Merrill is his father and Merrill speaks in Owen's voice; the second time is when John believes that Owen's hand literally reaches out and keeps him from falling down the cellar stairs at his home. At the same time, he hears Owen's voice telling him that nothing bad is going to happen to him.

There is also the fact that Owen believes his parents' story that he, like Christ, is the product of a virgin birth. Although Irving cannot quite bring himself to present this without skepticism—John vehemently expresses his disbelief in such a notion—Irving very deliberately puts this extreme parallel to Christ in the reader's mind.

Owen is Christ-like in other ways as well. Everyone likes to touch him, which recalls how in the Gospel of Luke the crowd presses upon Jesus, wanting to touch him because of his healing power (Luke 6:19). And just as Christ describes himself in John's Gospel as "the light of the world," Owen is also consistently associated with light. The quality of his skin is such that it absorbs and reflects light, "as with a pearl, so that he appeared translucent at times." As a child playing in the attic, "The powerful morning sun struck Owen's head from above, and from a little behind him, so the light itself seemed to be presenting him." Owen brings light to the cemetery on the night John's mother is buried, arranging his flashlight so that it illuminates her grave. Then, at his own funeral, sunlight plays upon the medal that is pinned to the flag that covers his coffin. Irving regards this moment as so significant that he draws attention to it no less than

> "Owen is presented as a being who straddles two worlds and unites within himself opposite values. He is the bridge between the divine and the human realms, uniting matter and spirit."

four times in six pages. And just in case the reader has missed all these allusions to light, Irving sums it up, as if he is anxious to explain the symbolism of his own novel. The moment comes near the end of the book, as John waits at the airport in Arizona for Owen's plane to arrive:

> Although the sun had set, vivid streaks of vermilion-colored light traced the enormous sky, and through one of these streaks of light I saw Owen's plane descending—as if, wherever Owen Meany went, some kind of light always attended him.

Even the typographical technique of printing Owen's words in all capital letters suggests Christ; there are Bibles in existence that print the words of Jesus in this way.

In addition to these straightforward parallels between Owen and Christ, Irving mines the Christ symbolism for deeper, more mystical resonances. Owen is presented as a being who straddles two worlds and unites within himself opposite values. He is the bridge between the divine and the human realms, uniting matter and spirit. It is no coincidence that Owen learns to work with granite. Granite is a hard, dense, unyielding stone. It represents the opposite of spiritual transparency and lightness. Owen develops great skill in working in this dense medium, carving and engraving gravestones. This hints at a parallel with the actions of the Christian God, who reaches down into the human world of death and has the will and the power to refashion even the most opaque, recalcitrant aspects of the material world (including people like John, who eventually discovers religious faith). And yet Owen himself is physically light, the very opposite of the granite he works with. When Owen is very young, the children at school love to lift him up and pass him around over their heads. His physical lightness

What Do I Read Next?

- Charles Dickens's *Great Expectations* (1982, Bantam Classic edition with an introduction by Irving), which tells the story of the village boy Pip and his "great expectations," is one of the novels that inspired Irving to become a writer.

- The family saga *The World according to Garp* (1976) was Irving's first best-selling novel, achieving cult status as well as critical acclaim.

- Neil Sheehen's *A Bright Shining Lie: John Paul Vann and America in Vietnam* (1989) is a harsh critique of the war as exemplified in the career of John Paul Vann, who was an American military adviser in Vietnam. Sheehen is a journalist who covered the Vietnam War, and this book won a Pulitzer Prize.

- In *Miracles* (reprint, 2001), C. S. Lewis argues in his accessible, conversational style that miracles really do happen, even in everyday life, and are an essential element in the life of Christian faith.

- In *The Problem of Pain* (reprint, 2001), C. S. Lewis tackles the question of why a loving God would allow people to experience pain and suffering. He concludes that suffering is necessary to perfect a person and make him or her ready for heaven.

is a symbol for his spiritual status. Once more, Irving cannot resist pointing this out himself. Having near the end of the novel twice referred back to the childhood entertainment of passing Owen around, John reflects in the final paragraph that the reason Owen felt light—the children even regarded him as weightless—was simply that some other, spiritual force was holding him up:

> We did not realize that there were forces beyond our play. Now I know they were the forces that contributed to our illusion of Owen's weightlessness; they were the forces we didn't have the faith to feel, they were the forces we failed to believe in—and they

were also lifting up Owen Meany, taking him out of our hands.

Another way in which Owen Meany unites opposites is in that he is a curiously androgynous figure. As a child he is tiny, and even as an adult he is only five feet tall. He speaks in a falsetto voice, both as child and man. So although he is muscular and strong for his size, there is something very feminine about him, too. This represents yet another parallel with Christ. There is a long tradition on the fringes of mainstream Christianity that regards Christ as an androgynous figure, a savior who embodies both the male and female aspects of life. Depictions of an androgynous Christ can be found in medieval Christian art and in the writings of Protestant mystics such as the seventeenth-century German seer, Jacob Boehme.

The notion of an androgynous Christ points to a larger symbolic framework in *A Prayer for Owen Meany*. In this framework, American society is shown as being out of balance due to a preponderance of an aggressive, destructive male energy that rides roughshod over the feminine aspects of life. This is made clear in the analogy that Owen carefully draws when he hears about the death of Marilyn Monroe, the glamorous actress and icon of femininity in America in the 1950s and early 1960s. Owen believes that Monroe was the victim of powerful men who used her for their own ends, and he compares her to America itself: "SHE WAS JUST LIKE OUR WHOLE COUNTRY—NOT QUITE YOUNG ANYMORE, BUT NOT OLD EITHER; A LITTLE BREATHLESS, VERY BEAUTIFUL, MAYBE A LITTLE STUPID, LOOKING FOR SOMETHING—I THINK SHE WANTED TO BE GOOD."

Just as Marilyn Monroe was "used," so, in Owen's eyes, America is used by powerful men, including his former hero, President John F. Kennedy. These are men who say they love their country but in reality merely use it for their own selfish and immoral ends. In terms of the male-female analogy, this amounts to the rape of the country, in which the innocence of a people who crave a savior and want to do good is betrayed. As far as John, the narrator, is concerned, this deceitfulness manifests in America's aggressive war in Vietnam, and from there it is a direct line to the lies and political chicanery that he sees in American foreign policy in the 1980s.

Given his comments about the exploitation of the country by powerful men and his siding with the victim, it is not surprising that Owen Meany is symbolically linked to the armless totem of the Indian chief Watahantowet. (John makes the comparison explicit when as a child he sees Owen with his arms clasped behind his back.) Owen accepts the Indian belief in the sacredness of the land and repudiates the vanity of the white man who thinks that only humans have souls and spirits. As he does with Marilyn Monroe, Owen takes the side of the victim—in this case the Indians who were robbed of their lands by the ruthless trickery of the white man. And of course, eventually, Owen becomes a victim of a similar kind of male aggression. He meets his death at the hands of Dick Jarvits, an adolescent male who embodies the violence-prone, testosterone-driven, doped-up, male-dominant society that looms up in the book as the defining nature of America in the 1960s. The surly, threatening, weapons-loving Dick cannot wait to attain legal age so that he can commit government-approved mayhem in Vietnam. And Irving is not above making a crude double entendre when he names this young man "Dick," as if to force home the idea of a link between aggressive male sexuality and the destructive instincts that give rise to war. Stacked against all these forces of destruction, Owen Meany is destined to become, like his role model Christ, at once hero and victim. All Owen can do, like Jesus in the Garden of Gethsemane, is submit to the will of God, however difficult the consequences may be, and hope that that is sufficient.

Source: Bryan Aubrey, Critical Essay on *A Prayer for Owen Meany*, in *Novels for Students*, The Gale Group, 2002.

Debra Shostak

In the following essay excerpt, Shostak explores Irving's use of repetition to "confirm Owen Meany's conviction . . . that he has been ordained an instrument of God."

The structure of *A Prayer for Owen Meany* is likewise circular, but in this novel, the determination of plot takes on a vastly different emphasis. Whereas *The World According to Garp* posits design as psychological entrapment, *A Prayer for Owen Meany* presents patterns of repetition as elements in a providential plan. Determinism can be teased out of the plot of *Garp*, as I have tried to show, by looking at the patterns of repetition and their relation to the thematic plan and psychological energies depicted in the novel; *Owen Meany*, however, has an inherently deterministic premise. That is, Irving means the repetitions in the novel to confirm Owen Meany's conviction, prompted by

A Prayer for Owen Meany, however, maintains 'material reality' except in the distinctive way it repeats the signs of Owen's prophecy as they both defer meaning and develop toward their fulfillment in the climactic scene."

precognitive knowledge of his own future, that he has been ordained an instrument of God. Owen's "election" is, as it were, proven in the novel's climactic closing scene, where the major repeated elements—amputation, voice, the slam dunk shot, and allusions to Jesus—are brought together and "explained" by Owen's heroic rescue of a group of Vietnamese children from a grenade tossed into an airport bathroom. In this way, then, the whole of the plot may be seen to unwind, backward, from the requirements of its violent ending.

In many ways, it is this predestination plot that caused the novel to receive such mixed reviews. Alfred Kazin, for one, questions the depth of Irving's theology:

> There is something much too cute about Owen's conviction that since he can foretell so much he must be God's instrument. It never seems to occur to John Wheelwright [the narrator] . . . that his prophet Owen is caricaturing Calvinist predestination in the role of fortuneteller. To believe that everything is in God's hands hardly entitles anyone to believe that everything is determined in advance and that he knows exactly what will happen. This is astrology and denies the principle of free will.

Without taking up the theological debate, one can see the point in Kazin's assertion—Irving wishes in the novel to deny the principle of free will as it is represented by the development of plot. Irving asks a lot. His novel seems to suggest that spiritual meaning is discoverable only in the human recognition of a miracle that portends providential design—a divine plot—and that necessarily erases the possibility of fully autonomous choice. *A Prayer for Owen Meany* is, in a sense, a prayer for meaning, for events to add up into a purposeful design. The yearning for religiosity, for an intuition of meaningfulness, is epitomized in the novel by a mute object, a statue in a schoolyard:

> In all of Gravesend, the object that most attracted Owen's contempt was the stone statue of Mary Magdalene, the reformed prostitute who guarded the playground of St. Michael's—the parochial school. The life-sized statue stood in a meaningless cement archway—"meaningless" because the archway led nowhere; it was a gate without a place to be admitted to; it was an entrance without a house.

Irving's novel attempts to find where the archway leads, to be admitted to a place, to restore the meaning that has been stripped from this icon, and though perhaps lacking theological sophistication (or, as Kazin charges, irony), it is, like *Garp*, an earnest plea for a vision that will make sense of a world of otherwise random violence. By this token, the pun in the title implies that the novel is not just, in the conventional sense, a prayer said for the soul of a dead young man, but it is a prayer to discover the "meaning" that Owen Meany's name—and life—limn.

The miracle that Irving chooses to supply meaning—Owen's foreknowledge of events—is also peculiarly apt for testing the workings of narrative desire, because plot is a temporal phenomenon. First, foreknowledge is, in narrative terms, the mirror image of memory, because both involve a linear relationship between knowledge and time, one relating knowledge to the past, the other to the future. The temporality of narrative is therefore another reason that the plotting of *A Prayer for Owen Meany* reverses that of *The World According to Garp*. As Irving's novels imply, then, the compulsion to repeat derives either from what has happened or what must happen. Second, plot necessitates both the suppression and revelation of knowledge. Because Owen is prophetic, Irving's calculations involve what and how much knowledge to reveal as well as when to reveal it, so as to sustain the possibility of Owen's precognitions until their fulfillment. In this regard, Irving's remark to Michael Anderson is telling: he noted that it was "the element of precognition in the Gospels that appealed to his artistic imagination." That is, *A Prayer for Owen Meany* is perhaps driven as much by an aesthetic as by a spiritual conviction—by a desire to contrive a "miracle" that would seem to justify deterministic plotting. The book raises the question: what happens to narrative form if a character knows his own ending?

One of the risks Irving takes, as I suggested earlier, is that the "miraculous" repetition of event

from foreknowledge and symbolic motif into a narrative's "actuality," which so obviously counters commonsense expectations of verisimilitude, will cause readers to displace the uncanny feeling that arises with a judgment against the narrative's contrivances. Recurrence is, of course, at the center of Freud's insights about the source of the uncanny, and it may be useful to summarize part of his argument in order to see how it explains the uneven reception of *A Prayer for Owen Meany*. Freud observes that the uncanny is the result of "involuntary repetition" ("The 'Uncanny'" [1919]); having postulated the principle of the repetition compulsion, he concludes that "whatever reminds us of this inner 'compulsion to repeat' is perceived as uncanny." More specifically, he asserts that "this uncanny is in reality nothing new or alien, but something which is familiar and old-established in the mind and which has become alienated from it only through the process of repression." Finally, in trying to explain why "in the realm of fiction many things are not uncanny which would be so if they happened in real life", Freud concludes that "The uncanny . . . retains its character not only in experience but in fiction as well, so long as the setting is one of material reality; but where it is given an arbitrary and artificial setting in fiction [as in fairy tales], it is apt to lose that character." When Irving created uncanny effects in *The World According to Garp*, he did so, for example, in "The Pension Grillparzer," where we encounter the meaningful recurrences of Johanna's dream and the dream man's "unspeakable" ability to tell it; but this story is clearly, in Freud's terms, "artificial," and so the effects are simultaneously preserved and tamed in such a way that we absorb among the narrative's conventions what is potentially uncanny. Likewise, in the narrative of Garp's life, the self-fulfilling repetitions of violence, whose visitations conform to the novel's originating episode, are conventionalized by both the eccentricities of the novel's cast and the context of the pervasively violent world.

A Prayer for Owen Meany, however, maintains "material reality" except in the distinctive way it repeats the signs of Owen's prophecy as they both defer meaning and develop toward their fulfillment in the climactic scene. The novel thus retains its uncanny effect, resisting our efforts to naturalize its anomalies. The compulsive repetitions cannot be fully understood except in retrospect, once we have reached the end of the narrative—that is, once the repressed "memory-trace," which in this context is the knowledge of the future, has been restored by being enacted in present time. This uncanny effect must surely have been Irving's intention, because what is at stake in the novel is faith, and Irving's conception of faith, he has intimated, relies on the miraculous: "I've always asked myself what would be the magnitude of the miracle that could convince me of religious faith." How then to represent miracle within his customary mode of comic realism provides Irving with his primary challenge in the novel. As Owen Meany himself says, disparaging Cecil B. DeMille's *The Ten Commandments*, and in the capital letters that signify his "wrecked voice", "YOU CAN'T TAKE A MIRACLE AND JUST SHOW IT! . . . YOU CAN'T PROVE A MIRACLE—YOU JUST HAVE TO BELIEVE IT! IF THE RED SEA ACTUALLY PARTED, IT DIDN'T LOOK LIKE THAT . . . IT DIDN'T LOOK LIKE ANYTHING—IT'S NOT A PICTURE ANYONE CAN EVEN IMAGINE."

Irving's answer to his aesthetic problem of how to imagine the unimaginable is end-determined plotting, wherein secular coincidences reach toward saintly enactment. Repeated elements can be readily explained within their immediate contexts, but when they drive more and more obviously toward the end, they gather uncanny force, which strips them of their limited resonances until we are inclined to read them only in terms of their anticipated realization. In this sense the novel might be said to begin at its ending. The most encompassing example occurs in the link between the first and last chapters. The central event of chapter 1 is the death of Tabby Wheelwright, the narrator's mother, when a foul ball hit by Owen during a Little League game strikes her in the temple. This death, which anyone might term an accident, is what first seems to provoke Owen toward seeing a divine plan at work in his life, causing him to refer to it as "THAT FATED BASEBALL" and to become furious when John, the book's narrator, "suggested that anything was an 'accident.'" One could reasonably argue that psychological necessity alone lies behind Owen's search for the sacred—that he is, naturally enough, impelled by guilt over killing his best friend's mother—and Irving leaves that possibility open through much of the novel. In this respect, the novel might be seen to resemble Garp in evolving from an initiatory act of violence. Following that "accident," Owen's precognitions can be explained plausibly without appealing to providential design. The gravestone on which he sees his date of death during a theatrical performance of Dickens's *A Christmas Carol*; his compulsion to practice "the shot"; his diary entries

in which he records what he "knows," including "THAT I AM GOD'S INSTRUMENT"; and, most specifically, the dream he relates to John that includes most of the details of his heroic death—all of these might be determined by his guilt, which causes him to desire both punishment and exoneration. By its last chapter, however, the book narrows the range of interpretation. Here, the final "foul ball" in Owen's life—the tossed grenade, which he slam dunks onto a high window ledge—legitimates, at least for John Wheelwright, Owen's conviction that he has been chosen as an instrument of God, and that he has been given the gift of foresight into his own instrumentality. It is this last shot that bestows meaning on all that has gone before.

In narrative terms, then, the repetitions have been required—or, perhaps, foreseen—by the ending, and one of Irving's main concerns has been how to weave them in so as to ensure the uncanny effect that will justify the narrator's subsequent conviction of faith. Irving has said that his "major preoccupation, his most time-consuming task . . . is fashioning his characters and devising his plots, making sure that what appear to be throwaway details early on in the book pop up again as crucial elements of the story later on"; but his task, in this case, is also to build the case for foreknowledge gradually, so that readers will find the miracle at the end—the confirmation of Owen's precognition—convincing. The result is a series of motifs, some of them apparently random or for local comic effect, others more noticeably cumulative. In each case, the figure, symbol, or event is realized in the novel's closing scene, so that the revealed "divine plot" explains the compulsiveness of the repetitions. In a sense, the narrative's repressed "memory" may appropriately be said to comprise both violence and the meaningful context for violence found in the Christian conventions of martyrdom. For it is in hagiographic narrative, and particularly in prefigurative readings of biblical texts, that one finds the end directing the interpretation of the beginning and middle, investing isolated details with spiritual significance.

A Prayer for Owen Meany, however, more specifically represents repression in the narrator himself. In the opening sentence of the novel, John writes:

> I am doomed to remember a boy with a wrecked voice—not because of his voice, or because he was the smallest person I ever knew, or even because he was the instrument of my mother's death, but because he is the reason I believe in God.

This first sentence steers quickly away from the weight of the elegiac opening clause, which implies that this narrative is a memory of someone who has been lost. The paragraph continues in a rush of details so that the opening note of grief is easily forgotten, an account of its cause evaded. In fact, the essential piece of the puzzle—John's witness of the miracle, which also necessitates Owen's death—is suppressed in the narrative until its close. The narrative's suppression indicates the narrator's, and it continues even when he reaches the point at which the scene must be narrated. John tells the aftermath of Owen's death first, putting the epilogue before the climax, so that the event of the death is known long before its facts. Just before he narrates the climactic scene, John's language reveals his contradictory response to the trauma:

> Let's see: there's not much else—there's almost nothing to add. Only this: that it took years for me to face my memory of how Owen Meany died—and once I forced myself to remember the details, I could never forget how he died; I will never forget it. I am doomed to remember this.

The closing echo of John's introductory statement—his doom—placed against the casual disclaimer of the first sentence ("there's not much else") reinforces that this suppressed narrative is the source of all the compulsive repetitions in *A Prayer for Owen Meany*. The "mind" of both text and narrator struggle to bring it forth, as both horribly painful and necessary origin of all plot.

One telling sequence of repetitions begins early in the first chapter of *A Prayer for Owen Meany*. When John provides historical information about the New Hampshire town in which much of the action takes place, he includes a description of the local Indian sagamore, Watahantowet, whose totem was an armless man. Later, after John's mother has been killed by the foul ball, he and Owen negotiate their guilt and forgiveness by an exchange of prized property; when Owen returns John's stuffed armadillo, the front claws have been removed. After Tabby Wheelwright's death, Owen becomes attached to her dressmaker's dummy—similarly armless—and keeps it with him while he grows up, as a totemic reminder of his fate and of one of his earliest visions, when he thought he saw the angel of death hovering across Tabby's bed from the dummy. Even the above-mentioned statue of Mary Magdalene appears with her arms removed, when Owen wreaks his revenge against the unjust headmaster of his prep school. Each of these references makes secular sense in its context. Watahantowet provides ironic historical commentary on the arrival of Europeans among the peaceful Indians, as preparation for John's tirades against the violence and exploitations of contemporary American culture. The armadillo, as John's stepfather suggests, represents Owen's feeling that he has lost a part of himself with Tabby's death, and that he wishes he might obliterate his own hands, the agents of that death. The dummy connects him with his surrogate mother. And the statue of Mary Magdalene provides an appropriate stab at the headmaster's hypocrisy. All of these armless figures, however, prefigure Owen's fate. The repetitions prepare for the miraculous effects of his last act, when he traps the grenade against the very high window ledge with both hands and forearms so that it will not fall back into the room; when the grenade explodes, it amputates both of Owen's arms. He bleeds to death, but not before seeing that his action has saved the children and others gathered in the makeshift men's room.

Part of the power of the final repetition, and what makes it more convincingly miraculous, is that up until the end, even Owen cannot feel absolutely certain of the truth of his foreknowledge. For while he has had precognitive knowledge of his heroic action, it has been incomplete. He knows the date of his death and a number of its circumstances, but, like any text, his visions of the future have gaps, leaving room for interpretation—and, as it happens, for misinterpretation. Because his visions involve Vietnamese children, he assumes that the event must occur in Vietnam; when he finds himself on his foreseen date of death in Phoenix, he loses some of his certainty. Because this room for doubt matches and maintains the reader's uncertainty about the direction of the novel, it works to legitimize the final miraculousness of Owen's foresight.

Irving gathers up a number of other motifs in the final scene as well—these are obvious enough to need little explication. Owen's unchanging, "wrecked voice," which results because his Adam's apple is positioned in a "permanent scream", is explained when he must speak to the Vietnamese children in their language; they trust and obey him, because "it was a voice like their voice." Owen has been "afraid of nuns"; nuns are escorting the Vietnamese orphans through the airport, and a nun embraces Owen as he dies. Similarly, Owen and John have for many years made a game of practicing "the shot," the slam dunk maneuver enabling Owen, who is preternaturally small, to shoot a basket; they have worked to make it as fast and efficient as possible. "The shot" requires John to toss the ball to Owen, who leaps into John's arms and is propelled upward toward the basket; when a young homicidal maniac throws a grenade at John in the Arizona men's room, he and Owen do the maneuver in order to protect the room's inhabitants. Irving has emphasized each of these elements in the text—possibly drawing too much attention to them—so that their realization in the climactic scene will not be missed. But perhaps the most obvious web of motifs—and the one most difficult for many readers to accept—comprises the references, both overt and covert, to the life of Jesus.

In a sense, these repetitions provide a clue to how to read the novel. Some are local metaphors, and only in retrospect suggest Owen's saintly predestination, such as when John writes that solely by "some miracle" did Owen manage as a young child to catch a baseball; or when Owen, having played a trick on John while they swim in a granite quarry, becomes angry and says "REMEMBER THAT: YOU LET ME DIE"; or when at his first meeting with John's cousins, Owen looks like "a descending angel—a tiny but fiery god, sent to adjudicate the errors of our ways." But these references begin both to gather force and to strain credibility by the time that Owen appears, at the age of eleven (during the year of the fatal foul ball), as the baby Jesus in the Sunday school Christmas pageant or when, in describing Owen's expulsion from prep school, John writes that "they crucified him." Our incredulity is probably greatest when Mr. Meany assures John after Owen's death that Owen was immaculately conceived—like Garp, the issue of a virgin birth. Irving accomplishes several things in these accumulating allusions, however. First, with repetition they become self-conscious references, and so move toward ironizing their content, even as they tend, in the voice of the narrator, to retain their innocence enough to be suggestive of "truth." This doubling of the interpretive possibilities underscores the difficulty of faith—and the need for accepting the miraculous—because there is always the opportunity to discount miracle by an ironic interpretation. Our incredulity here is the point. Irving must encourage us to disbelieve in order to urge us to believe. Second, the repeated allusions contribute to the comedy in A Prayer for Owen Meany. By the time we read the late discussion of Owen's virgin birth, the references have become predictable; the writer who builds in the expectation of a repeated event or line is using one of the key conventions of the comic. Most important, however, is that Irving shows us the way John, as narrator, casts the plot in terms of his own religious

conversion. It is John's linguistic choices and emphases that connect Owen to sainthood—it is he who has "learned to view the present with a forward-looking eye"—and his narrative decisions serve the novel's ending by confirming Owen's precognitions.

John Wheelwright's teleological sense of how to govern the "dilatory space" of the narrative's middle is revealed in numerous comments that seem obvious or coy foreshadowings. About the coach who told Owen Meany to "Swing away" at the fateful baseball, he notes that "Had he known everything that would follow, he would have bathed his chubby face in even more tears." At the end of a chapter, he claims that "I have been 'moved to do evil,' too—as you shall soon see." He observes of the summer when he and Owen turned eighteen that "nothing seemed dangerous. That was the summer we registered for the draft, too; it was no big deal." In each case, Irving reminds us, as he had in the dream man's narrations of "The Pension Grillparzer," of the status of narration as a retrospective act. That is, from the privileged position of the end of events, a narrator can shape the plot toward his or her interpretation of the whole. As with the references to Jesus, then, Irving tries to have it both ways—to remind us of the mechanics of plotting the novel, that plotting is a self-conscious activity, and to prepare for the uncanny effects of the final scene. This is his answer to the question of what happens to narrative form if a character knows his own ending: the plot must be deterministic.

There are, of course, important differences between already-known meaning—ordained by God or, simply, invented by an author—and that which is forecast overtly to a reader rather than unfolding fully only by narrative's end, or, for that matter, that which is never fully revealed. Irving's decision to foreground these differences signifies his interest in exploring how narrative creates meaning. But he chooses to do his experiments within the context of realist conventions, and that qualification is significant. Even as he experiments, Irving stands in opposition to the postmodern literary culture that has questioned the referential meaning of language and, in turn, the connection between representation and human value. At this point, Robert Caserio's opening insight in Plot, Story, and the Novel is useful. He writes:

Walter Benjamin thought that when we lose interest in stories and storytelling we lose the ability to exchange experiences. It is perhaps more significant that when writers and readers of novels lose interest

Joseph Mazzello as Joe Wenteworth and Ian Michael Smith as Simon Birch in Simon Birch, *the 1998 film loosely based on the novel*

in plot and story, they appear to lose faith in the meaning and the moral value of acts.

Irving's concentration on some of the features of narrative desire suggest that he is committed to restoring "faith in the meaning and the moral value of acts." In the world according to Irving, acts mean because they form larger patterns of intentional design. In both *Garp* and *Owen Meany*, the compulsive repetitions open the door to understanding how acts are meaningful for Irving, because these repetitions are functioning within a closed scheme, directed either toward the origins or the end of the narrative. In this respect, his plotting of the fiction uncovers its ethical dimension. But Irving also exposes the epistemological dimension of narrative when he demonstrates the way plot itself constructs knowledge and belief. Garp's fictions purport to imagine a world and John Wheelwright's tale aims to represent one transparently, but each of them can only narrate the world that is "according" to him. For both, the point of view is inevitably limited to compulsive repetitions of traumas. The "last shot" is the last plot in the narratives John and Garp write and in those they live. Irving represents in this the way fictional narrative constructs its meanings deterministically. More generally, his novels define a circle in the way we structure the stories of our lives: our knowledge and experience always shape and are shaped by our already known patterns of meaning.

Source: Debra Shostak, "Plot as Repetition: John Irving's Narrative Experiments," in *Critique*, Vol. 37, No. 1, Fall 1995, pp. 51–70.

Edward C. Reilly

In the following essay excerpt, Reilly examines the overriding theme in Owen Meany—*religious faith and miracles—and how it informs every aspect of Irving's novel.*

Irving's *A Prayer for Owen Meany* contains no bears, no Vienna, no World War II, and no rapes. However, it does contain a boy's school, Gravesend Academy; a sports metaphor, slam-dunking basketballs; a war, the Vietnam War; dual settings in the United States and Canada; and violence. The major difference, however, between this novel and Irving's preceding ones is that it is ultimately about religious faith and miracles, a theme absent in the other novels. In commenting about *Owen Meany*, Irving emphasizes, "I've always asked myself what would be the magnitude of the miracle that could convince me of religious faith." This idea is the novel's core and controls the settings, characters, themes, and literary techniques.

Like *Cider House*, the setting is not expansive, and except for sporadic scene shifts to Sawyer's Depot in northern New Hampshire, the University of New Hampshire at Durham, and Phoenix and Fort Huachuca in Arizona, the primary setting is Gravesend, New Hampshire, where protagonists John Wheelwright and Owen Meany experience their rites of passage. Gravesend's history is linked with the novel's religious theme since Reverend John Wheelwright, the protagonist's ancestor, founded the town when he was banished from the Massachusetts Bay Colony because he proposed radical religious beliefs. Indeed, John claims that "his own religious confusion, and stubbornness, owe much to my ancestor." In Gravesend is the Wheelwrights' "grand, brick, Federal monster of a house", the scene for major portions of the novel's actions. While the home suggests permanency amid change, John will eventually forsake home and country when he emigrates to Canada after Owen Meany's tragic death. Dan Needham, John's stepfather, often asks him to return, but John says, "Although I enjoy my visits, not even the tempting nostalgia of the house at 80 Front Street could entice me to return to the United States." John thus becomes Irving's only protagonist who abandons his ancestral home for a self-imposed isolation in a foreign country. In this sense, too, Gravesend is important because it represents small-town life that is forever changed because of the Vietnam War.

Whereas in the other novels a foreign place, usually Vienna, suggests the *Anschluss*-spawned violence, in *Owen Meany* Canada represents a relatively calm refuge that contrasts with the violent anti-Vietnam War demonstrations and protests that are racking the United States. John Wheelwright even says that the Canadians calmly welcomed the American draft dodgers and war resisters. For example, even though he often apologizes, "I'm not really a draft dodger," he quickly realizes that "most Canadians didn't care *what* I was [and] didn't care *why* I'd come; they didn't ask any questions. It was 1968, probably the midpoint of Vietnam 'resisters' coming to Canada; most Canadians were sympathetic—they thought the war in Vietnam was stupid and wrong, too." Canada's relatively calm attitude is also evident when John notes that even the most militant American resisters in Canada, the Union of American Exiles, are a "pretty tame lot" when "compared to Hester—and her SDS friends."

> Owen writes and speaks in capital letters, an idea Irving adopted from 'editions of the New Testament in which Jesus' utterances appear in red letters.'

Partly to protest the Vietnam War but mainly in anger because of Owen's death, John crosses the New Hampshire-Canadian border in 1968, the year Owen is killed. Although his defection to Canada is supposed to be a "very forceful political statement," John admits that he "never had to suffer" because with his teaching experience at Gravesend Academy, his graduate degree, and his sound recommendations, he becomes "instantly respectable and almost immediately employed." John's expatriate life in Canada also heightens his alienation and isolation, especially since he teaches at Bishop Strachan School for Girls, where he is often the only male teacher.

Regarding John's self-imposed isolation and alienation in Canada, Dan Needham, his foster father, counsels: "Let bygones be bygones—not even Owen would *still* be angry. Do you think Owen Meany would have blamed the whole country for what happened to him? That was madness; this is madness, too." Canada thus becomes the setting in which John assuages his anger by rekindling his faith. He says that he is different from most Americans who fled to Canada because he has "the church; don't underestimate the church— its healing power, and the comforting way it can set you apart. . . And so the first Canadians I knew were churchgoers—an almost universally helpful lot, and much less confused and troubled than the few Americans I'd met in Toronto (and *most* Americans I had known at home)." Although he wrestles with his faith for the twenty years he lives in Canada, John's "*oral*" history" concludes with his renewed faith as he prays for himself and for Owen Meany. Metaphorically, just as Vienna teaches Irving's other characters about the world's ways, Canada teaches John about the ways of faith.

Irving says that in *Owen Meany* he wanted "to create two victims of the Vietnam period in our history," and one is John Wheelwright, the narrator-protagonist. Unlike Irving's other protagonists, John is mainly an observer and reporter instead of a principal actor in the plot, and various plot details emphasize his neutral role. During the Christmas pageant at Christ Church, for example, John plays Saint Joseph, a role requiring neither words nor actions. Even when he and Owen practice the slam-dunk shot, John says that "my part in this exercise was extremely limited." In addition, John never has a girl friend, is never sexually initiated, and he sadly admits, "I was twenty-one and I was still a Joseph; I was a Joseph then, and I'm just a Joseph now." When Owen cuts off John's right index finger to keep him out of the draft, John becomes even more isolated and alienated from his own generation. During a Vietnam War demonstration in Washington, for instance, John carries no placard and admits:"

> But I tried to feel I was part of the demonstration; sadly, I *didn't* feel I was part of it—I didn't feel I was part of anything. I had a 4-F deferment; I would never have to go to war, or to Canada. By the simple act of removing the first two joints of my right index finger, Owen Meany had enabled me to feel completely detached from my generation.

His further detachment and alienation also result when he moves to Canada but still craves news about the United States. As Canon Mackie gently reminds him, "You're a Canadian citizen, but what are you always talking about? You talk about America more than any American I know."

Indirectly, John becomes a Vietnam War victim. In 1968, the year Owen will die, John has completed his master's degree, will enter the Ph.D. program at the University of Massachusetts in the fall, and his student deferment plus his missing index finger will keep him out of the service. Moreover, because his grandmother finances his education, John confesses: "If I was thinking anything—if I was thinking at all—I was considering that my life had become a kind of doorstep-sitting, watching the parades pass by ... I wasn't doing anything; there wasn't anything I had to do." Finally, Owen Meany's death affects John the most. He says that both he and Hester were "damaged by what happened to Owen," and adds, "What has happened to me has simply *neutered* me. I just don't feel like 'practicing'."

Besides being an integral part of the novel's bildungsroman motif, John Wheelwright is necessary for the novel's religious theme. The narrative is not only John's prayer for Owen Meany, but the plot also analyzes various aspects of faith in the contemporary world. Whereas in *Cider House* Larch and Homer believed in private religious views and prayers, in *Owen Meany* the dramatic opening sentence announces the theme, "I am doomed to remember a boy with a wrecked voice—not because of his voice, or because he was the smallest person I ever knew, or even because he was the instrument of my mother's death, but because he is the reason I believe in God; I am a Christian because of Owen Meany."

Recounted twenty years after his emigration to Canada and Owen's death, John Wheelwright's narration traces the development of his own confused faith. He was baptized as a Congregationalist, confirmed as an Episcopalian, and finally becomes an Anglican with a "church-rummage faith—the kind that needs patching up every weekend." Significantly, too, as in most hagiographies, John's faith has often been tested by adversities that include his mother's death, the Vietnam War, and especially Owen Meany's tragic death. However, not only is the last chapter, "The Shot," a typical Irving epilogue that details the characters' fates but also the chapter's last five sections become both John's catharsis and the novel's main thrust. After *almost* concluding his story, John adds:

> Let's see: there's not much else—there's almost nothing to add. Only this: that it took years for me to face my memory of how Owen Meany died—and once I forced myself to remember the details, I could never forget how he died; I will never forget it. I am doomed to remember this.

How Owen died explains all that preceded it—the novel's armless symbols, Owen's prophecies and life's mission, and the reason for practicing "the shot." Besides becoming the novel's affirmative vision, the chapter's closing paragraphs are John's prayer for Owen Meany as well as John's testimony about his own faith that has been rekindled and strengthened because Owen "had been a hero" and a "miracle too." After admitting that he is "always saying prayers" for Owen, John confirms that Owen symbolized those "forces we didn't have the faith to feel, they were the forces we failed to believe in—and they were also lifting Owen Meany, taking him out of our hands. O God—please give him back! I shall keep asking You." John's quiet, reverent prayer not only assuages the novel's general chaos and confusion, but it explains his opening comments that what faith he has in God he owes to Owen Meany.

In contrast with John's observer-reporter role, Owen Meany is the novel's central focus because he is the principal actor. He hits the foul ball that kills John's mother, and this act convinces Owen that he is God's instrument. He also suggests and directs the games that he, John, Hester, Noah, and Simon play. Owen also directs the Christmas pageant at Christ Church when he suggests dynamic changes in staging and the actors' roles; similarly, he is instrumental in changing Dan Needham's ideas about staging and roles in *A Christmas Carol*. At Gravesend Academy where he edits *The Grave*, the campus newspaper, he is nicknamed "the Voice" for his outspoken editorials that criticize school policies and headmasters, especially the ingratiating Randy White. In addition, Owen is directly responsible for the fiascoes involving Dr. Dolder's Volkswagen and Mary Magdalene's statue, both of which appear on the Main Academy Building's stage. Finally, Owen subtly severs his relationship with Hester, decides that he must cut John's finger off to save him from the war, and he always insists that he and John practice "the shot."

Owen becomes, furthermore, a victim of the Vietnam War, and Irving tells Phyllis Robinson that he "wanted to create two markedly dissimilar victims of the war, one a hero, the other a defector." That Owen will be a hero is evident, first of all, in his desire to serve in Vietnam. As he tells John, "IT'S NOT THAT I *WANT* TO GO TO VIETNAM—IT'S WHERE I HAVE TO GO. IT'S WHERE I'M A HERO. I'VE GOT TO BE THERE" When John thinks Owen is joking, Owen ominously emphasizes:

I'M NOT PLAYING AROUND. . . WOULD I REQUEST A COMBAT ASSIGNMENT IF I WERE PLAYING AROUND? . . . I SAVE LOTS OF CHILDREN. . . THAT'S HOW I KNOW WHERE I AM—THEY'RE DEFINITELY VIETNAMESE CHILDREN, AND I SAVE THEM.

Owen's prophecies come true when, in an ironic plot twist, Owen saves John and the Vietnamese children, not in Vietnam, but rather in a temporary rest room at the Phoenix airport.

In terms of the novel's religious theme, Irving says, "Jesus has always struck me as the perfect victim and perfect hero," and loose parallels exist between Christ and Owen Meany. When Owen first meets the Eastman children while they play in the Wheelwrights' attic, John emphasizes Owen's divine appearance, halo and all:

The powerful morning sun struck Owen's head from above, and from a little behind him, so that the light itself seemed to be presenting him . . . there is no doubt that, in the dazzling configurations of the sun that poured through the attic skylight, he looked like a descending angel—a tiny but fiery god, sent to adjudicate the errors of our ways.

More specifically, Owen plays the Christ child in the Christmas pageant, and in *A Christmas Carol*, he is the Ghost of Christmas Future and, instead of Scrooge's name and dates on the tombstone, Owen sees his name and the date of his own death. As "the Voice" of Gravesend Academy, Owen makes enemies with his tirades against hypocrisy, injustice, and Philistinism. Old Thorny, the retired, benign headmaster, warns Owen: "You've made more enemies in less than two years than I've made in twenty! Be careful you don't give your enemies a way to get you." When his enemies find a way "to get" him, John emphasizes a Christlike fate, "the Executive Committee crucified Owen Meany—they axed him; they gave him the boot; they threw him out."

In addition to Owen's unique voice—John says Owen's voice is "not entirely of this world"—Owen writes and speaks in capital letters, an idea Irving adopted from "editions of the New Testament in which Jesus' utterances appear in red letters." Owen, of course, occasionally quotes biblical passages: "FATHER, FORGIVE THEM; FOR THEY KNOW NOT WHAT THEY DO"; "WOE UNTO THEM THAT CALL EVIL GOOD AND GOOD EVIL"; "WHOSOEVER LIVETH AND BELIEVETH IN ME SHALL NEVER DIE." Another loose parallel is that Owen's life and actions strengthen Dan Needham's faith and restore John's and Reverend Lewis Merrill's faiths. Not only does Owen selflessly sacrifice his own life for John and the Vietnamese refugees, but Owen's preknowledge about his own death is similar to Christ's knowledge. As Phyllis Robinson notes: "The part of Jesus himself that most impresses Irving, 'the biggest miracle of them all,' is that Christ knows what is going to happen to him. 'That is truly a heroic burden to carry.'"

Like Susie in *Hotel New Hampshire* and Melony in *Cider House*, Hester Eastman is big-boned and big-bosomed—"her body belonged in the jungle"—but unlike these other heroines, she is very attractive and sings beautifully. Because she is older than John or Owen, she is more worldly wise, especially in sexual matters, earning her the nickname "Hester the Molester." Although John is attracted to Hester, she is attracted to Owen and sexually initiates him, and they eventually fall in love. Because she believes that women should have equal rights, her alienation from her family inexorably begins when the Eastmans plan to send Noah and Simon to Gravesend Academy but make no plans for Hester's future: "Hester was in as much need of rescuing from the wildness within *her*—and from the rural north country rituals of her sex—as Noah and Simon were in need of saving." As Owen foretells, "THAT'S WHEN HESTER WENT ON THE WARPATH." Hester's warpaths include various affairs—all designed "to educate her parents regarding the error of their ways." Hester's wild rebelliousness will also spur her to join the decade's demonstrations protesting the Vietnam War.

If *Owen Meany* "grew out of Irving's conviction that the Vietnam War made victims of us all, not just those who were killed or who left their country," then Hester is just as much a victim as are John and Owen. Although Hester and Owen love each other, the Vietnam War thwarts their potential for forming a solid family basis when he decides to become an Army officer, and she becomes a war protester. In addition, even though she wants to marry Owen, he refuses because he has foreseen his fate. His refusal actually proves just how much he loves her, and John says, "I think I know what he was doing; he was helping her to fall out of love with him before he died." Even so, Owen's death affects her: "Hester was damaged by what happened to Owen Meany; I'm sure she thinks she was damaged even more than I was damaged. . . We were both damaged by what happened to Owen." After Owen's death, Hester never becomes "seriously involved" again because he had been the "love of her life."

When she becomes a hard-rock singer—she adopts her childhood nickname Hester the Molester—her voice is "equivalent to an abused woman crying for help from the bottom of an iron barrel." Her "truly ugly" videos depict:

> carnal encounters with unidentified young boys intercut with black-and-white, documentary footage from the Vietnam War. Napalm victims, mothers cradling their murdered children, helicopters landing and taking off and crashing in the midst of perilous ground fire, emergency surgeries in the field, countless GI's with their heads in their hands—and Hester herself entering and leaving different but similar hotel rooms, wherein a sheepish young boy is always putting on or just taking off his clothes.

Even her song titles reflect her life's circumstances, especially as they refer to Owen's life and death: "Gone to Arizona" (where Owen is stationed); "You Won't See Me at His Funeral" (Hester's words to Owen); "Drivin' with No Hands" (Owen's arms are blown off below the elbows);

"There's No Forgettin' Nineteen Sixty-eight" (the year Owen died); "Just Another Dead Hero" (the futility of Owen's and other Americans' deaths during the Vietnam War). As John also points out, the irony is that "out of Owen's suffering, and her own, Hester has made a mindless muddle of sex and protest, which young girls who have *never* suffered feel they can 'relate to'." Significantly, however, as do Irving's other strong heroines, Hester confronts life's forces and survives: "I admire her—she's certainly been a more heroic survivor that I've been, and her kind of survival is admirable."

Tabitha Wheelwright, John's mother, typifies Irving's strong motherly figures. When she becomes pregnant, for example, she easily transcends her "little fling," gets "over Lewis Merrill rather quickly," and bears "up better than stoically to the task of bearing his illegitimate child." She is also a loving person who, to quote John, wants "nothing from life but a child and a loving husband; it is important to note these *singulars*—she did not want children, she wanted . . . *just* me and she got me; she did not want men in her life, she wanted a man, the *right* man, and shortly before she died, she found him." Not only does she become a "perfect mother" for John, but she becomes a surrogate mother for Owen Meany and thus emphasizes the less-than-motherly image cast by Mrs. Meany. Tabitha loves Owen as if he were her son, often drives him home, promises that she will see that he is admitted to Gravesend Academy, and will even buy him the proper school clothes. Her death is significant for the novel's religious theme because Owen believes that he has become God's instrument through the foul ball that struck Tabitha down. In addition, when John recalls his mother's death, he realizes: "That was when I first began to think about certain events or specific things being 'important' and having 'special purposes' . . . I was not what was commonly called a believer then, and I am a believer now: I believe in God, and I believe in the 'special purpose' of certain events or special things." Finally, not only do memories of her have a healing effect on those whom she cherished and loved, but the dressmaker's dummy clad in her red dress soothes Lewis Merrill's tormented conscience and then restores his dead faith.

In referring to his stepfather, John says, "Dan Needham is the best father a boy could have." Although Dan is a loving, caring stepfather, he does not become overly protective as were Bogus Trumper, Severin Winter, or Garp. Instead, Dan Needham is more of John's best friend and counsellor. For example, while his mother's other suitors are all handsome and bring ridiculous gifts ranging from "rubber ducks for the bath" to Fowler's *Modern English Usage*, Dan is "tall and gawky" and brings John a stuffed armadillo—"the first present any of my mother's 'beaus' gave me that I kept." John then adds, "But he knew very well what a six-year-old was like; to his credit, Dan Needham was always a little bit of a six-year-old himself." When John's mother is killed, Dan also helps John understand why Owen gives him the baseball card collection: "to show me how sorry he was about the accident, and how much he was hurting, too—because Owen had loved my mother almost as much as I did."

Within the plot, Dan Needham proposes a positive alternative despite life's inexplicable forces. When Owen returns the armadillo *sans* claws, Dan explains that the clawless animal represents all of them—"We've lost part of ourselves"—but he then concludes: "There was no way any of this *was* acceptable! What had happened was unacceptable. Yet we still had to live with it." Dan's positive approach to the injustice of Tabitha's death is to devote himself to teaching, "Like many dedicated educators, Dan Needham had made education his religion." He becomes a "good, spirited" teacher who believes it is "more difficult to be a teenager than a grownup" but who also is more compassionate toward the elderly who are "suffering a second adolescence and . . . required special care." Dan's admirable fatherly virtues and his positive approach to life and faith contrast with Reverend Lewis Merrill, John Wheelwright's natural father.

While necessary for the novel's suspense regarding the identity of John's real father, Reverend Lewis Merrill is more significant for the novel's religious theme. While John's mother stoically transcends their affair, Merrill wallows in self-guilt and pity. However, when he sees her at the baseball game and realizes that he is still attracted to her, Merrill is ashamed and wishes that she would "drop dead." At that moment, Owen hits the fatal foul ball, and Merrill believes that "God had punished him; God had taught Pastor Merrill not to trifle with prayer." Merrill believes that he is now outside God's mercy and grace, and his faith dies. As John reminds him: "You're always talking about 'doubt as the essence and not the opposite of faith'—but it seems to me that *your* doubt has taken control of you. I think that's what Owen thought about you, too." Merrill's stutter symbolizes his lack of religious conviction and courage, and his stutter is especially evident as he talks to John about faith and

miracles: "You want to call Owen, and everything that happened to him, a m-m-*miracle*. . . You sound positively *converted*. . . I would be careful not to confuse your g-g-g-grief with genuine, religious belief."

Even as they talk, Merrill does not understand the miracle that occurs when he speaks "in the exact falsetto, the 'permanent scream'" of Owen's voice, which reveals the exact location of the fatal foul ball. However, John recognizes the miracle, "That was the first time that Owen Meany let me hear from him—after he was gone . . . Owen promised me that God would tell me who my father was." After learning from Dan that Merrill had "once tried to be brave and honorable" regarding his affair with John's mother, John decides that he could teach Merrill "how to pray again" and "have a little faith." John takes his mother's dressmaker's dummy, places it under the chancel windows, and throws the fated baseball through one of the stained-glass windows. Merrill rushes out, sees the dummy, imagines it is John's mother, and says: "God—forgive me! Tabby—I didn't tell him! I promised you I wouldn't and I didn't . . . Tabby— forgive me, please!." He falls on his side, draws his knees up, and babbles incoherently. Symbolically, Merrill's confession and repentance become his catharsis, and his faith is restored as evident when he begins the prayers at Owen Meany's funeral:

> "'I am the resurrection and the life, saith the Lord . . .'" my father began. There was something newly powerful and confident in his voice, and the mourners heard it; the congregation gave him their complete attention. Of course, I knew what it was that had changed him; he had found his lost faith— he spoke with absolute belief in every word he uttered; therefore, he never stuttered.

Source: Edward C. Reilly, "'The Magnitude of a Miracle': *A Prayer for Owen Meany*," in *Understanding John Irving*, University of South Carolina Press, 1991, pp. 121–35.

Sources

Campbell, Josie P., *John Irving: A Critical Companion*, Greenwood Press, 1998, pp. 125–41.

Prescott, Peter S., "Here They Come Again," in *Newsweek*, April 10, 1989, p. 64.

Pritchard, William, "Small Town Saint," in *New Republic*, May 22, 1989, p. 36.

Sheppard, R. Z., "The Message Is the Message," in *Time*, April 3, 1989, p. 80.

Summers, Harry G., Jr., *Vietnam War Almanac*, Facts on File Publications, 1985.

Towers, Robert, "The Raw and the Cooked," in *New York Review of Books*, July 20, 1989, pp. 30–31.

For Further Reading

Bloom, Harold, ed., *John Irving*, Modern Critical Views series, Chelsea House, 2001.

> This is a collection of some of the best recent critical essays on Irving's work.

Harter, Carol C., and James R. Thompson, *John Irving*, Twayne, 1986.

> This is a concise survey of Irving's work up to *The Cider House Rules*.

Irving, John, "In Defense of Sentimentality," in *New York Times Book Review*, November 25, 1979, pp. 3, 96.

> Irving writes in praise of Dickens's *A Christmas Carol* and *Great Expectations* and argues that writers should not shy away from the attempt to move their readers emotionally.

Reilly, Edward C., *Understanding John Irving*, University of South Carolina Press, 1991.

> Reilly writes for the general reader and includes chapters on all of Irving's novels up to *A Prayer for Owen Meany*, as well as an annotated bibliography.

Ship of Fools

Katherine Anne Porter
1962

The idea for *Ship of Fools* (Little, Brown and Company, 1962) originated in a voyage that Katherine Anne Porter took from Mexico to Europe in 1931. Some of the passengers she encountered on the ship became the models for the characters in *Ship of Fools*. Porter began work on the novel in 1941 and it took her twenty years to complete.

The title is taken from a moral allegory published in Latin in the fifteenth century. Porter wrote that the title of her novel symbolizes "the ship of this world on its voyage to eternity." The wide cast of characters includes German, Swiss, Spanish, Cuban, Mexican, Swedish, and American first-class travelers. In steerage, there are 876 Spanish workers who are being deported from the sugar fields of Cuba.

Ship of Fools is notable for its pessimistic view of the human condition. In particular, the Germans are portrayed in a harshly negative light. They are mostly anti-Semitic and contemptuous of races other than their own, with an arrogant sense of their own superiority. Critics have remarked on how accurately Porter conveyed the German mentality on the eve of the rise of Nazism. However, the other characters, with few exceptions, are unsavory also. The one Jew on the ship is filled with hatred for all Gentiles; the Spanish, who are members of a dancing troupe, are presented as amoral thieves, pimps and prostitutes. There is little genuine human love present in the novel, although there is much comedy and satire.

Katherine Anne Porter

Ship of Fools is the only novel Porter wrote. It was an immediate bestseller and was made into a movie in 1965. Critical judgment, however, was sharply divided over the merits of the novel, a debate that continues today.

Author Biography

Katherine Anne Porter was born Callie Russell Porter on May 15, 1890, in Indian Creek, Texas, the daughter of Harrison and Mary Alice Jones Porter. Porter's mother died in 1892, and the family moved to Kyle, Texas, to live with Porter's grandmother. In 1901, the grandmother died and the family moved to San Antonio.

Porter married John Henry Koontz, a railway clerk, at the age of sixteen; she left him after seven years and was divorced in 1915. Also in that year, she was diagnosed with tuberculosis and spent two years in sanatoriums. In 1917, Porter began her journalism career, writing for the *Critic*, a weekly newspaper in Fort Wayne, Texas. The following year she wrote for *Rocky Mountain News* in Denver. She also caught influenza and was dangerously ill.

In 1919, Porter moved to New York, where she worked for a motion picture magazine and wrote children's stories. In the early 1920s, she traveled twice to Mexico, where she studied Mexican art. Returning to New York in 1922, she wrote her first mature story, "Maria Concepción." In 1930, her first book, *Flowering Judas and Other Stories*, which included the well-known story, "The Jilting of Granny Weatherall," was published.

From 1931 to 1932, Porter sailed from Mexico to Europe, where she lived in Berlin and traveled around Europe. In 1939, her volume of stories, *Pale Horse, Pale Rider*, was published; *The Leaning Tower and Other Stories* followed in 1944.

From 1949 to 1962, Porter lectured at various institutions, including Stanford University, the University of Michigan, and the University of Virginia. Her unorthodox teaching style made her popular with the students. In 1952, she published a collection of essays, *The Days Before*, and her only novel, *Ship of Fools*, which she had been working on for twenty years, followed in 1962.

In 1966, Porter received a Pulitzer Prize and a National Book Award for her *Collected Stories*, which had been published the previous year. Her final publication was *The Never-Ending Wrong* (1977), a reminiscence of the Sacco and Vanzetti case of the 1920s.

Porter married Ernest Stock in 1926, but they were divorced within a few years. In 1933, she married for the third time, to Eugene Pressly, and that marriage also ended in divorce, in 1938. In the same year, Porter married Albert Erskine Jr.; they were divorced in 1942.

Porter died on September 18, 1980, in Silver Springs, Maryland.

Plot Summary

Part 1

Ship of Fools begins in the Mexican port town of Veracruz, where a group of travelers is about to embark on a twenty-six day voyage to Europe. The August weather is hot, and the local people, who dislike the travelers who pass through their town, try to exact as much money from them as possible. The travelers are hot, tired and frustrated at the bureaucratic delays that are put in their way. All they want is to get on the German ship *Vera* that waits in the dock and hurry away from the unpleasant town where there is labor unrest and the threat of social revolution.

The travelers are introduced at first as a collective, anonymous group, and then gradually they are individualized, but still nameless, described only in terms of their physical appearances. The exception to this is Dr. Schumann.

The passengers are a mixture of Germans, Swiss, Spaniards, Mexicans, Americans, and one Swede. As they embark and the ship sets off, they discover who their cabin mates are, and most of them are ill-matched. Almost everyone reacts negatively to everyone else, and it becomes clear that there are sharp racial divisions among the passengers; the northern Europeans despise the southern Europeans as well as the Latin Americans. The smug, nationalistic Germans, who all dine together at the Captain's table, are presented in a particularly negative light.

On the third day of the voyage, the ship puts into port in Havana, Cuba. A half-dozen Cuban students join first class, and nearly nine hundred Spanish unemployed sugar workers who are being returned home squeeze onto the steerage deck.

Part II

The ship heads for the high seas, and the travelers begin to live out their frustrations, animosities, and small adventures. On the first day or so, for example, Ric and Rac plot mayhem; Johann insults his uncle; David and Jenny quarrel; the Spanish dancing troupe mock the other travelers; Frau Hutten expresses her sentimental feelings over her dog; Jenny strikes up a friendship with Freytag; and Hansen pursues the dancer, Amparo. Each incident reveals something of the character of the participants, and often the narrator provides information about how the character's attitudes and motivation have been shaped by their experiences of life up to this point. Gradually, the reader learns more about this heterogeneous band of not very appealing travelers.

Soon the passengers' routine gets established. They spend their time strolling around the deck, lolling in deck chairs or hiding out in their cabins. They drink, gossip at gala dinners, and dance. In the evening, they play cards and chess and occasionally attend movies ("moving pictures"). On Sunday, there are church services. On the first Sunday, after Father Carillo has given morning mass on the steerage deck, a fight breaks out between one worshiper and a fat man who insults him. Amongst the first-class passengers, who have their

Media Adaptations

- *Ship of Fools* was made into a movie in 1965. It was directed by Stanley Kramer, and starred Vivien Leigh as Mrs. Treadwell, Simone Signoret as La Condesa, José Ferrer as Siegfried Rieber, and Lee Marvin as Denny.

own services, wild rumors spread about the fight, until the little scuffle has become magnified into a free-for-all between dangerous criminals.

During the early part of the voyage, Dr. Schumann becomes acquainted with La Condesa, who flirts with him and then declares that she loves him. Dr. Schumann gives in to her desire for drugs, and keeps her well supplied with them, even though there is no medical reason for him to do so. He is disturbed by his own amorous feelings towards La Condesa. Rumors spread on the ship about the nature of their relationship.

The more educated among the travelers often have discussions about worldly affairs. The Germans' contempt for other races is never far from the surface, and anti-Semitic views are rampant, particularly those expressed by Siegfried Rieber. The Captain hears a rumor that there is a Jew dining at his table. This is in fact Freytag, who is not Jewish, although his wife is. Freytag has confided this information to Mrs. Treadwell who foolishly passes it on to Lizzi, her cabin mate. At the Captain's dinner table, there is a nasty discussion about the Jews, and Lizzi blurts out what she knows about Freytag. Freytag immediately leaves the table. He is not allowed to return. Instead, he is allocated a small table near the service entrance, facing a blank wall. This also happens to be the table of Löwenthal, the only Jew on the voyage. He and Freytag quarrel, after which Freytag always tries to dine alone. He also confronts Mrs. Treadwell about her betrayal of him, and they manage to achieve some kind of a reconciliation.

The chain of petty incidents continues. David and Jenny continue to squabble; the Spanish dancers plan a festive dinner in honor of the captain, and even sell tickets for it, in spite of Frau Rittersdorf's careful explanation that this is a serious breach of ship etiquette. Denny pursues a dancer named Amparo, but is put off by the fee she tries to charge him. Little Hans reports that Ric and Rac threatened to throw him overboard. Rieber continues his lustful flirtation with Lizzi. At dinner at the Captain's table, Frau Hutten dares for once in her life to express opinions that are directly opposite to those of her husband.

The most dramatic moment comes when Ric and Rac toss Bébé, the bulldog, overboard. A man from steerage jumps into the water to try to save him, but he is drowned. The dog survives. Ric and Rac get their comeuppance when they are caught after stealing La Condesa's pearls. They are severely punished by their parents.

Part III

In September, the ship docks for a day at Santa Cruz de Tenerife, one of the Canary islands. For many of the steerage passengers, as well as La Condesa, this is the end of their journey. Dr. Schumann bids La Condesa a fond farewell. Some of the other passengers go ashore for sightseeing. The group of Spaniards busy themselves shoplifting; David, Jenny, Frau Otto Schmidt, Professor and Frau Hutten know what is going on but can do nothing to stop it.

The voyage resumes, and the gala evening in honor of the Captain takes place, with dinner, music, and dancing. The Spanish company take their seats at the Captain's table and offer effusive tributes to him, much to his embarrassment and displeasure, since he despises them.

The evening produces a lot of drunkenness and violence. Hansen breaks a beer bottle over Rieber's head and there is a scuffle. Lizzi, whom Rieber has been trying to seduce, runs away screaming. The drunken Denny pursues Amparo the dancer to give her a beating, while David discovers Jenny in an embrace with Freytag. The Baumgartners have a vicious quarrel that drives him to suicidal despair. Then Herr Baumgartner strikes his wife across the face, and this is followed by reconciliation. Mrs. Treadwell, who has also had too much to drink, encounters Denny and beats him about the face with the heel of her shoe.

The ship reaches Vigo, where the Spanish dancers disembark, and then heads for Gijón, Spain, and then to Boulougne, where Mrs. Treadwell and the Cuban students disembark. After stopping at Southampton, the *Vera* finally arrives in Bremerhaven, Germany, where all the Germans, as well as the Americans Denny, Jenny, and David, disembark.

Characters

Amparo

Amparo is one of the group of Spanish dancers on the ship. She is beautiful but often ungracious. She has sex with men for money, which she then hands over to her lover, Pepe.

Frau Greta Baumgartner

Frau Greta Baumgartner is Karl Baumgartner's wife. She is unable to halt her husband's decline and watches disapprovingly as he sinks further. Sometimes, she takes out her frustrations on their helpless son.

Hans Baumgartner

Hans Baumgartner is the timid and delicate-looking eight-year-old son of Karl and Greta Baumgartner.

Herr Karl Baumgartner

Herr Karl Baumgartner is a sickly looking German lawyer, who practiced law in Mexico City. For some years, his practice flourished, but then he developed a drinking problem; he could not resist his longing for brandy. His career went into a decline, and he lost three important cases in the Mexican courts. The stress of failure gave him stomach pains, and this is the situation as he and his long-suffering wife board the ship. He continues to drink to assuage the stomach pains.

Jenny Brown

Jenny Brown is a young American artist, the girlfriend of David Scott. She is black haired and attractive, with a bold manner, but she is also restless, dissatisfied, and superficial. Jenny enjoys getting involved with radical political causes, such as joining strikers on a picket line, but for her this is just a lark. She and David have a love-hate relationship, and she enjoys tormenting him, although she also believes that, in spite of everything, she loves him. However, she knows in her heart that their relationship is doomed. Jenny shares a cabin with Elsa Lutz and is pleased to share her views about love with the naive young girl.

Father Carillo

Father Carillo is one of the two Mexican Catholic priests on the ship. He has a hatred for atheism and political radicalism, which he believes lead the lower classes astray, and he regards the poor travelers in steerage with suspicion. However, he is a gentler man than Father Garza.

La Condesa

La Condesa is a fifty-year-old Spanish noblewoman who has lived many years in Cuba. She became involved in revolutionary politics and is now being deported from Cuba to Tenerife. Slender, with short, reddish hair, she wears expensive-looking clothes and exudes a kind of faded glamour. She is addicted to drugs. The Captain is informed that she is a dangerous revolutionary, but he thinks she is just an idle rich lady who likes excitement. La Condesa flirts with the young sailors and also with Dr. Schumann, who falls in love with her and accedes to her desire for drugs.

William Denny

William Denny is a young American chemical engineer from Texas, who is on his way to Berlin to work for a manufacturing firm. Tall and shambling, he is a bigoted man, who regards people from a class, nation, or race other than his own as inferior and refers to them by insulting names. According to David Scott, who shares a cabin with him, Denny thinks only of three things: sex, money (largely his determination not to be cheated by anyone), and his health.

Herr Wilhelm Freytag

Herr Wilhelm Freytag is connected with an oil company in Mexico and is returning to Germany to fetch his Jewish wife, Mary, and her mother. The thirty-year-old Freytag is good-looking and well dressed, and he comes from a solid Lutheran family. He is self-confident and feels that there is no barrier to his future success. However, he dreads introducing his Jewish wife to the German community in Mexico City, where he is emigrating because of the growing anti-Semitism in Germany. When it is discovered that Freytag has a Jewish wife, he is removed from the Captain's table for meals and instead is given a table with Herr Löwenthal, the only Jew on the voyage. Freytag forms a friendship with Jenny Brown, but he regards her as a flirt.

Father Garza

Father Garza is one of two Mexican Catholic priests on the ship. He has a cynical view of human nature (he doubts the genuineness of the expressions of pity at the funeral of the drowned man), and he can be argumentative and outspoken.

Herr Karl Glocken

Herr Karl Glocken is a hunchback who has sold his tobacco and newspaper stand in Mexico and is returning to Germany. He is only four feet tall and has a long, sad face, but he has a pleasant, good-humored nature.

Herr Wilibald Graf

Herr Wilibald Graf is a dying man who is pushed around in a wheelchair by his nephew, Johann. Graf is a former teacher of philosophy who has become a religious fanatic. He believes that God has given him the power to heal others by touching them. He is also a miser and refuses to give his nephew any money before he dies.

Arne Hansen

Arne Hansen is a big and clumsy Swede, with huge hands and feet, who was in the dairy business in Mexico. He is morose and argumentative, with strong opinions about religion and politics. He is often mistaken for a Dane, much to his annoyance. Hansen spends much of the voyage having sex with Amparo, for a fee. He also feuds with Herr Rieber, and they get into a scuffle at the final dinner.

Frau Professor Hutten

Frau Professor Hutten is Professor Hutten's wife. Like her husband, she is overweight. She is overly fond of their seasick white bulldog, Bébé, and spends an inordinate amount of time cleaning up after him. Frau Hutten has spent her marriage obeying her husband and being attentive to his needs. This has involved giving up her teaching career, but she did so because her husband told her that a woman's sacred mission was to create a happy home. Once at the dinner table during the voyage, Frau Hutten expresses her disagreement with her husband's views, and he rebukes her fiercely.

Herr Professor Hutten

Herr Professor Hutten is the former head of a German school in Mexico. He is a pedantic scholar, who is utterly convinced of the rightness of his views, which he expounds at length to anyone who will listen. He dominates his wife and expects her total and unwavering support. When Professor Hutten speaks in a group, it is not to make conversation but simply to announce his own thoughts and opinions. He struggles to uphold a view of the basic goodness of man, but there are strong hints that this opinion is at odds with what he really feels.

Johann

Johann is the nephew of Wilibald Graf. He takes care of his uncle, pushing him around in his wheelchair, but he does it with bad grace, believing his uncle to be a pious old hypocrite. Tall, with glittering golden hair, Johann is waiting for his uncle to die so that he can receive his inheritance. Eventually, he persuades his uncle to give him some money, and he uses it to pay Concha, one of the Spanish dancers, for sex.

Herr Julius Löwenthal

Herr Julius Löwenthal is a Jewish manufacturer and salesman; he is returning to his home in Düsseldorf to visit his cousin Sarah. His business takes him to all parts of Europe, South America, and Mexico, where he sells rosaries and plaster and wooden saint statues to Roman Catholics. Wherever there is a Catholic church, he can make money. Even though he hates Catholics, he is happy to do business with them. Löwenthal is conscious of being persecuted because he is a Jew, and he frequently expresses his distaste for all Gentiles. For meals, he is put at a table by himsel until Wilhelm Freytag is forced to join him.

Elsa Lutz

Elsa Lutz is the eighteen-year-old daughter of the Lutzes. She is a big, ungainly girl, who fears that she may never fall in love or be loved. She conceives a romantic fantasy about a tall, dark-haired, handsome student on the ship, just because he once happened to smile at her. But when he finally asks her to dance at the final gala dinner, she is so frightened she says she cannot dance.

Frau Lutz

Frau Lutz is Heinrich Lutz's wife. She is plain and dumpy and more serious than her husband. According to her daughter, Frau Lutz is unable to laugh. She is fond of giving motherly talks to her daughter about how she should conduct herself towards men, and she unsuccessfully tries to set Elsa up with Hansen.

Herr Heinrich Lutz

Herr Heinrich Lutz is a Swiss hotelkeeper from Mexico, who is returning with his family to Switzerland after fifteen years to start their own hotel business. He has an extremely limited outlook on life and is interested only in the narrowest of practicalities. According to his daughter, he is happy by nature and loves to have a good time.

Rac

Rac is one of the six-year-old twins of the Spanish dancer, Lola. Rac, and her twin brother Ric, are continually up to no good. They deliberately pour ink onto the carpet in the writing room, toss Frau Rittersdorf's pillow overboard, and try to do the same to the ship's cat. They do succeed in throwing the Huttens' bulldog, Bébé, overboard. They also steal La Condesa's pearl necklace and throw it overboard. The other passengers refer to them as little devils.

Ric

Ric is the twin brother of Rac. He and his sister enjoy pulling pranks on the passengers and are always getting into trouble.

Herr Siegfried Rieber

Herr Siegfried Rieber is the publisher of a ladies' garments trade magazine. He is small and fat, with a crude manner, and is of a lower class than the other Germans on the voyage. He is violently anti-Semitic and includes anti-Semitic propaganda in his magazine. At one point, he demands that he should not have to share a cabin with Löwenthal the Jew, whom he loathes because he is Jewish, but he cannot find anyone else who is willing to share with him. Rieber flirts throughout the voyage with Lizzi Spockenkieker, but on the night he plans to seduce her, he is thwarted by Hansen, who breaks a beer bottle over his head at the gala dinner.

Frau Rittersdorf

Frau Rittersdorf is a widow whose husband Otto was killed in the First World War. She comes from an humble background. Her father was a shoemaker and her mother a seamstress, and she lives on a modest inheritance passed to her by her husband's parents. However, she is vain and has become a snob. While in Mexico, she was expecting a Spanish nobleman to ask her to marry him. Since he did not, she convinces herself that a German woman should not marry outside her race. Frau Rittersdorf has a poor memory, so she writes every detail of her daily life in a diary, which is full of her jaundiced observations about life. On observing Glocken the hunchback, for example, she writes that she is in favor of euthanizing defective children, as soon as it is clear they are "unfit."

Frau Otto Schmidt

Frau Otto Schmidt was widowed in Mexico only six weeks before the voyage began. Her husband's coffin is traveling in the ship. Frau Schmidt was a teacher in the German school in Guadalajara in Mexico, and she is returning to Nuremberg. She is a timid woman, full of self-pity, and she often feels snubbed, ignored, or neglected.

Dr. Schumann

Dr. Schumann, one of the few admirable characters in the novel, is the ship's sixty-year-old doctor. He is amiable, well bred, dignified and handsome, with two dark dueling scars on his left cheek—a mark of distinction. He also has a heart condition that could kill him at any time. Dr. Schumann is a Catholic and a religious man, with a developed sense of his moral responsibilities. He is the only one of the Germans at the Captain's table who does not express anti-Semitic views. He has also thought deeply about the destiny of man and concludes that it is a mystery known only by God. However, against his will, Schumann allows himself to succumb to the charms of La Condesa, with whom he falls in love. He feels guilty about this, first because he is a married man and second because he prescribes for her the drugs she craves, although she has no medical need for them. After she disembarks at Tenerife, Schumann sends her a respectful note, but she declines to reply. This leaves him despondent at the end of the voyage.

David Scott

David Scott is a young American artist who lives with Jenny Scott. They are on their first trip to Europe, but they do not much enjoy each other's company. They are perpetually quarreling and seem to take delight in saying cruel things to each other. David does not trust Jenny and does not like or trust anyone else either, reacting very coolly to Denny, his cabin mate. He is also jealous of the friendship Jenny forms with Freytag. David thinks of himself as an outsider, and he does not seem to know how to enjoy himself—he refuses to dance, for example. He blames his morally strict Quaker upbringing for ensuring that he never really enjoys his life. Always restless, he habitually wants to be somewhere other than where he is.

Fraulein Lizzi Spockenkieker

Fraulein Lizzi Spockenkieker comes from Hanover and is in the ladies' garment business. In Mexico, she has been visiting her aunt and uncle. Tall and thin with close-cropped hair and a shrill voice, she carries on a constant flirtation with Siegfried Rieber. According to Mrs. Treadwell, with whom she shares a cabin, Lizzi's topics of conversation consist entirely of perfume, clothes, shops, and men.

Captain Thiele

Captain Thiele is the ship's captain. He is an arrogant man, completely sure of his own authority and superiority. He regards the poor people traveling in steerage as little more than cattle and threatens to lay in irons anyone who causes a disturbance. Captain Thiele believes that as captain he is the representative of a higher law that he must enforce to prevent a moral breakdown. He is fascinated by American gangster films and has violent fantasies in which he acts like a hero in putting down rebellions by lawless mobs. Thiele always feels somewhat disgruntled, and his general state of anger and ill-humor causes him to suffer often from digestive problems.

Mary Treadwell

Mary Treadwell is a divorced American of forty-five who is returning from Mexico to Paris. Mrs. Treadwell had a privileged upbringing and went to the best schools, but she married a man who had fits of jealousy and beat her. She tends to blame herself for the failure of the marriage, which lasted ten years. She has now been divorced for ten years and is bored with her life, which she thinks of as "shady, shabby, lonely, transient, sitting in cafes and hotels with others transient as herself," although she tries to shut this unpleasant truth out of her mind. On the ship, she drinks too much wine and spends a lot of time playing solitaire or dancing with a handsome young officer. (Mrs. Treadwell is still slender and pretty.) One of her faults is that she is too emotionally detached. She refuses to get close to people, in part because she feels their troubles too keenly.

Themes

Anti-Semitism and Nationalism

The voyage takes place in 1931, only two years before Hitler and the Nazis came to power in Germany, and in the novel, the Germans display a deep-seated anti-Semitism. The worst offender is Herr Rieber, the proto-Nazi. He uses the journal he publishes to disseminate anti-Semitic propaganda and proudly tells Lizzi that one the topics discussed

Topics for Further Study

- Investigate the causes of anti-Semitism. Why were the Jews so persecuted in Europe for hundreds of years?

- Why have Jews fared better in the United States than in Europe, as far as persecution is concerned? Is there anti-Semitism in the United States? If so, what form does it take?

- In the novel, Denny, the American, expresses contempt for other races and classes—for everyone who is not like him. Are attitudes like Denny's still common in America? Why do people so often despise people who are different than they are? What are the results often produced by this kind of thinking? What can be done to combat these seeds of racism?

- Are the passengers on the *Vera* representative of the whole range of humanity? If not, what is missing? Is the author too pessimistic about human nature, or is she merely being realistic?

- Which character in the novel repels you the most, and why? Which character or characters do you feel sympathetic towards, and why?

---

is the idea that "if we can find some means to drive all the Jews out of Germany, our national greatness will then assert itself and tomorrow we shall have a free world." Rieber warms to the subject of the Jews over dinner at the Captain's table, talking (in the way Nazis did) about cleansing the blood of Germany from the Jewish poison. No one dissents from this except Dr. Schumann, who represents a moral sensibility well above that of the others.

Rieber may be alarming, but fanatics with extreme racist views exist in many societies. What is most disturbing in the novel is how so many of the others go along with him. The empty-headed Lizzi, for example, absorbs Rieber's opinions and finds them congruent with her own. She says the Jews in her business are "trying to control everything and everybody"; they are unscrupulous and will try any

trick. When Mrs. Treadwell suggests mildly that all business is like that, Lizzi counters firmly that no, it is only the Jews.

A similar acquiescence occurs when Freytag is expelled from the Captain's table because he has a Jewish wife. None of the Germans protest this petty act of injustice—quite the reverse, they praise and justify it. Frau Rittersdorf congratulates the Captain on how tactfully the deed was done; Professor Hutten praises the Captain for his decisive leadership, which helped to remind them all of their principles. Hutten's anti-Semitism is of the intellectual type. He is the sort who would within a few years be justifying Nazi anti-Semitism under a veneer of scholarly objectivity.

Even Freytag, the victim in this situation, is not free of the assumptions of his fellow Germans. Thinking of Mary, his Jewish wife, he shows that he too has absorbed German ideas about the superiority of their race, musing that "our children's blood will flow pure as mine, your tainted stream will be cleansed in their German veins."

Anti-Semitism is only one manifestation of the Germans' nationalistic belief in the sacredness of their "mystic Fatherland" and their racial superiority. They despise all races other than the Nordic, and all classes other than their own. Freytag, for example, regards the poor as spawning "like maggots in filth, befouling the air around them," and Captain Thiele holds a similarly contemptuous view of the steerage passengers. Herr Rieber would prefer it if the low-life traveling in steerage were put in a gas oven instead. The Spanish are also despised as being of a lesser breed, and so are the Americans, whom the Germans regard for the most part as a coarse, vulgar, racially "impure" people. Frau Rittersdorf gives expression to this view when she complains of "The gradual mongrelization of that dismaying country by the mingling of the steerage sweepings of Europe and the blacks [which] had resulted only in a mediocracy of feature and mind impossible to describe."

The Germans are not the only ones to express intolerant, racist views. One of the Americans, Denny, is equally dismissive of anyone from another country, and of certain categories of people within his own. David Scott observes Denny's "vulgar habit of calling all nationalities but his own by short ugly names."

Love

The portrayal of love in *Ship of Fools* is a pessimistic one. Many of the characters are involved in relationships that should embody love, but almost none of them have been able to attain a mutually satisfying intimate relationship. There is only one example of a love that appears happy and full of promise, and that is between the unnamed Mexican bride and groom. This couple are given no dialogue of their own; they are simply viewed from time to time strolling around the deck, obviously deeply in love. But there is a hint that their idyllic private world will not last. After Jenny observes how lovely they look together, Freytag comments that the look on the bride's face is like "Eden just after the Fall. That little interval between the Fall and the driving out by that tricky jealous vengeful old God." What he means is that such love can last only for a short while; soon the couple will be exposed to the harsh realities of the world, which have distorted the love of many of the couples depicted on the *Vera*.

The love between Jenny and David, such as it is, is of quite another kind, and it is hard to imagine them ever attaining the serenity of the Mexican bride and groom. They are constantly quarreling. Jenny gets a clear insight into the essence of their relationship when she dreams of a vicious fight to the death between a Mexican man and woman that she once caught sight of from a passing bus. Gradually in the dream the faces of the man and woman change to those of David and herself. She holds a bloody stone in her hand; he has a knife poised to stab her already bleeding breast. Jenny then realizes that, metaphorically speaking, that is what David and Jenny are doing to each other in the name of love.

In her better moments, Jenny does in fact possess a higher, more idealistic vision of love: "She believed the thought of love as tenderness and faithfulness and gaiety and a true goodness of the heart to the loved one." But she has little idea of how to realize this love with David. As for David, he has a similar romantic idealism but like Jenny no practical skill in making it work in daily life.

The other couples on the ship are for the most part a sorry bunch. The Baumgartners, for example, are driven apart by the husband's alcoholism. He and his resentful wife experience only one moment of reconciliation, and that is when they make love after a vicious quarrel. But even this is not presented in a positive light, because it is shown through the frightened eyes of their little son Hans, who has just witnessed their quarrel. The best explanation that Frau Baumgartner can manage is to tell Hans that "Sometimes we are crossest with the ones we love best."

If the Baumgartners are mostly hostile to each other, the Huttens are complacent. They made a bargain long ago that the price of love was the wife's complete submission and obedience to her husband.

Of the other characters, Mrs. Treadwell is too damaged by her abusive marriage that ended ten years ago to allow herself to get close to anyone; Frau Rittersdorf lives, as far as love is concerned, in the past with her dead husband Otto, whom she lauds as a war hero but also resents for dying prematurely. Dr. Schumann, for all his worldly wisdom and moral rectitude, sinks into a sentimental, hopeless affair with La Condesa even as he reproaches himself for doing so. Freytag might seem a more promising example since he clearly loves his absent wife, but when he fully realizes how difficult their life will be because she is Jewish, the seeds of resentment are sown.

At the lowest level of the scale are Denny, Hansen, and Rieber, and even young Johann, for whom love has no meaning at all; their pursuit of women is entirely for the purpose of sex.

Style

Animal Imagery

Porter frequently uses animal and bird imagery to refer to the passengers on the ship. Much of this occurs in Part 1, as the travelers are first introduced. The implication is that this particular group of humans lacks some essential quality that would make them fully human, an implication that is often confirmed as their characters unfold during the course of the voyage.

Some examples of the imagery include Lizzi, who is likened to a "peahen"; Rieber, who is both "pig-snouted" and a "little short-legged strutting cock"; and Jenny, who is likened by some of the hostile local people to a mule or a monkey. The locals also observe that poor little Hans has been made into a "monkey" by the leather riding costume his parents force him to wear even in the hot weather. The Spanish girls are as "noisy as a flock of quarreling birds"; David Scott is like "a willful, cold-blooded horse."

The point is amusingly brought home by the fact that Bébé, the white bulldog that belongs to the Huttens, is presented in a more flattering light than his overweight, self-indulgent owners. Although Bébé has just spent an uncomfortable night tied up on a kitchen patio, it is clear from the following description that as far as human and animal qualities are concerned, the roles of Bébé and his owners have been reversed:

> Bébé the bulldog had borne his ordeal with the mournful silence of his heroic breed, and held no grudges against anybody. His owners now began at once to explore the depths of the large food basket they carried everywhere with them.

Point of View

The story is told by a third-person omniscient narrator. This means that the narrator has total knowledge of the actions of all the characters and also knows their thoughts and motivations. This applies to minor as well as major characters. The fact that there is an omniscient narrator also enables the author to constantly shift the point of view. A scene will be described from the point of view of one character, and then after a few pages, another scene takes place and another point of view takes over.

Sometimes this technique produces interesting contrasts in perception between different characters. For example, when the reader is first introduced to Mrs. Treadwell, it is explained that the bruise on her arm was the result of being hit by a beggar woman for refusing to give alms. But several pages later, when the point of view has switched to that of Dr. Schumann, he makes the assumption that the bruise was caused by a lover's pinch.

Structure

The novel is split into three parts of unequal length; there are no chapters. Instead, there are multiple small sections, or scenes. Each scene shows two or more characters interacting, or focuses on the inner life of one character. The scene unfolds for a few pages, and then another scene, involving different characters, takes its place. There is little plot in the traditional sense of the word, in which a series of interrelated actions leads to conflict and complications before reaching a climax and a resolution. Nor is there much in the way of character development; at the end of the voyage, the characters are much the same as they were when they embarked. This is unlike many novels, in which the main characters are changed in some meaningful way by the end of the story.

Irony and Satire

The grimness of the novel is relieved by the satirical approach of the author, who is always ready to poke fun at her characters, and allow them to reveal how small-minded and prejudiced they are. Porter's stance is one of ironic distance. As the lofty authorial voice, she manages to find a way of passing negative judgment on her characters through her careful choice of words and details. The effect is often humorous. The obnoxious Herr Rieber, for example, as he encounters some obstacles to his goal of seducing Lizzi Spockenkieker, decides that he must not be discouraged:

> After all, this was only another woman—there *must* be a way, and he would find it. He thought with some envy of the ancient custom of hitting them over the head as a preliminary—not enough to cause injury, of course, just a good firm tap to stun the little spirit of contradiction in them.

Porter also has some fun with Lizzi, the object of Rieber's desire. Early in the novel, she accidentally bumps into the Captain, almost knocking him over: "He threw an arm about her stiffly, his face a dark furious red; and Lizzi, blushing, whinnying, cackling, scrambling, embraced him wildly around the neck as if she were drowning."

At other times, the irony takes the form not of humor but of icy condemnation, as when at the dinner table the subject of Jews comes up:

> They then exchanged a few customary remarks about the Jews and their incomprehensible habits, a sort of small change of opinion which established them once and for all as of the same kind of people without any irreconcilable differences.

Historical Context

Germany in the 1930s

The Germany that the travelers in *Ship of Fools* were bound for was a nation on the brink of accepting the rule of Adolf Hitler's National Socialist Party. In September 1930, a year before the *Vera* arrives, six and a half million Germans had voted for the Nazi Party. This was an increase from 810,000 two years earlier.

The increasing strength of the Nazis was a consequence of Germany's desperate economic straits. In 1931, there were five million unemployed, the middle classes were facing financial ruin, and the unpopular government was unable to find a way out of the morass.

In March, 1932, Hitler won over eleven million votes—30 percent of the total—in the presidential election, denying President Hindenberg an absolute majority. In a second election, Hitler in-

Compare
&
Contrast

- **1930s:** Hitler's Nazi party takes over in Germany; Mussolini's Fascists rule Italy, and the world is plunged into war.

  1960s: The world is divided into two power blocs, the United States and the Soviet Union, and the cold war is at its height. Germany remains divided into East Germany, which is communist, and West Germany, which is a member of NATO.

  Today: A reunited Germany is at the heart of the European Union; the Soviet Union is a thing of the past, and the United States is the sole remaining superpower.

- **1930s:** A voyage from Mexico to Europe in a passenger/freight ship like the *Vera* takes twenty-six days. Ocean liners are the most common form of long-distance transportation across the ocean.

  1960s: The bulk of long-distance travel is by jet aircraft. Many of the large ocean liners are re-

tired; new passenger ships are built for the purpose of luxury cruises rather than essential transportation.

  Today: A flight from Mexico to Germany takes approximately twelve to thirteen hours.

- **1930s:** In America, particularly in the south, African Americans, as well as other people of color such as Mexican Americans, face hardship and discrimination at the hands of the white, Anglo majority. Public facilities are often designated for the use of whites only.

  1960s: The civil rights movement, which began in the south in 1955, produces concrete results, including the Civil Rights Act of 1964 and the Voting Rights Act of 1965.

  Today: America is still troubled by issues of race and racism. Overt discrimination is less than it was thirty or forty years ago, but subtler forms of discrimination, including corporate "glass ceilings," still exist.

---

creased his vote by two million. In July, 1932, the Nazis became the largest party in the Reichstag, the German parliament. Following months of political intrigue in the wake of another round of elections in November 1932, Hitler was appointed chancellor in January, 1933.

Hitler immediately set about reconstructing the German state in accordance with Nazi ideology. All other political parties were banned, and economic and cultural life was brought under the control of the central government and maintained by sophisticated propaganda. Hitler assumed the presidency on the death of Hindenberg in August, 1934.

The persecution of the Jews, along with other minority groups, was not long in coming. The Nuremberg Laws of 1935 deprived Jews of their German citizenship and forbade marriage between Jews and Aryans. More anti-Semitic laws were passed over the next few years, enough to satisfy

the many Herr Riebers (the proto-Nazi in *Ship of Fools*) who were now occupying government positions and promoting anti-Semitic propaganda, as well as others in the novel, like Frau Rittersdorf and Lizzi Spockenkieker, who believe firmly in the inferiority and corrupting influence of the Jews. In Nazi Germany, Jews were banned from professions such as medicine, law, the civil service, journalism, and teaching. They were not allowed to trade on the stock exchange. By 1936, it is estimated that about one half of German Jews were without a means of livelihood.

It was then only a few steps to the concentration camps and the extermination of six million Jews in the Holocaust during World War II.

During the 1930s, the rest of the world was slow in waking up to the threat to Western civilization that the Nazis represented. When the Olympic Games were held in Berlin in 1936, many of the worst aspects of Nazism were hidden from the world. Even David Lloyd-George, an astute statesman who had led Britain during World War I, was fooled. He visited Hitler in 1936 and declared him to be a great man. This ignorance is reflected in the novel, in which the Americans and some of the Europeans mildly disapprove of the anti-Semitism they observe on the ship, but have no inkling of the depth of the evil that is brewing in Germany. Mrs. Treadwell in particular has no knowledge of international politics and no desire to acquire any.

Critical Overview

When it was first published, *Ship of Fools* received near universal acclaim from reviewers. Leading the admiring chorus was Mark Schorer, in the *New York Times Book Review* (reprinted in *Katherine Anne Porter: A Collection of Critical Essays*), who called the book "a unique imaginative achievement." He praised Porter's "perfectly poised ironical intelligence" and "the brilliance and variety of characterization." Louis Auchincloss, in the *New York Herald Tribune* (reprinted in *Critical Essays on Katherine Anne Porter*) was equally enthusiastic, commenting that Porter was able to sustain the reader's interest in a collection of unattractive characters such as the Germans "because this vivid, beautifully written story is bathed in intelligence and humor," and the reader is able to "feel how easy it would be for anyone to turn into even the most repellent of these incipient Nazis." For Moss Hart in *New Republic* (quoted in Givner's *The Life of Katherine Anne Porter*), "[The novel's] intelligence lies not in the profundity of its ideas but in the clarity of its viewpoint; we are impressed not by what Miss Porter says but by what she knows."

There were a few dissenting voices, including Granville Hicks, in *Saturday Review* (quoted in the Hendricks' *Katherine Anne Porter*), who thought that although Porter

> is one of the finest writers of prose in America . . . the novel, for all its lucidity and all its insights, leaves the reader a little cold. There is in it . . . no sense of human possibility.

Commercially, the novel was a huge success. It was number one on the best-seller list within weeks of its publication in April, 1962.

However, after a few months, there was a backlash from critics who regarded the novel in a less than favorable light. Chief of these was Theodore

Solotaroff, in *Commentary* (reprinted in *Critical Essays on Katherine Anne Porter*), who wrote of crucial weaknesses in the novel:

> The main such weakness is that no effective principle of change operates on the action or on the main characters or on the ideas, and hence the book has virtually no power to sustain, complicate, and intensify either our intellectual interests or emotional attachments.

Solotaroff concluded that *Ship of Fools* revealed "little more than misanthropy and clever technique."

This emphasis on the lack of development in plot or character was the basis of much subsequent criticism. Porter was also attacked for presenting only the darker side of human nature, a charge she denied.

In spite of these criticisms, however, the novel has many defenders. It occupies an important place in post-World War II American literature, even though today it attracts fewer readers than Porter's short stories and short novels.

Criticism

Bryan Aubrey

Aubrey holds a Ph.D. in English and has published many articles on twentieth-century literature. In this essay, he discusses Porter's novel in terms of the self-deceit of many of the characters.

Perhaps it is not too obvious to remark that *Ship of Fools* is aptly titled. The sum total of human wisdom assembled on the *Vera* is heavily outweighed by the accumulation of folly, ignorance, vice, and sheer evil. If this novel is a portrait of the human condition, as some critics take it to be, it gives little cause for comfort.

The human failings presented in the novel are varied and numerous: the hateful rantings of Herr Rieber, the contemptuous authoritarianism of the Captain, the alcoholism of Herr Baumgartner, and the cheating and thieving of the Spanish dancing troupe, to name only a few. One fault that afflicts many of the characters is self-deceit. Perhaps because the truth is unpalatable, these are characters who tell themselves stories about their own lives and then convince themselves the stories are true.

For example, it is likely that Herr Graf is only able to come to terms with the fact that he is dying by inventing the notion that God has given him power to heal others. Professor Hutten, the intel-

Adolf Hitler

lectual, thinks he believes in the innate goodness of man, but later it transpires that this is a sham, a cover he has invented to hide his real, less acceptable beliefs. The stability of the Huttens' marriage also rests on a lie that they both conspire to believe, that Frau Hutten is the perfect, devoted wife, completely fulfilled by serving her husband.

Another example is Frau Rittersdorf, for whom small deceits have become a way of life. This is conveyed early in the novel, when she sends flowers to herself, with accompanying cards supposedly from two of her friends, both of whom happen to be dead. She convinces herself that this is not deceitful because they would have sent the flowers had they been alive. Frau Rittersdorf is so thoroughly mired in false appearances that she makes the Catholic gesture of crossing herself, even though she is Lutheran, simply because she thinks the gesture becomes her. Sometimes her self-deceit reaches comic proportions, as when she mistakenly writes in her diary that David Scott's last name is Darling and Jenny's is Angel (because that is how they always address each other) and congratulates herself on her own cleverness in analyzing the derivation of the names. Most seriously, her inflated idea of her own social standing makes her one of

the most intolerant and snobbish of the German passengers.

Lizzi Spockenkieker is another shining example of self-deceit—the lack of an accurate perception of oneself. She thinks she is beautiful, despite much evidence to the contrary, and she also believes that she has legions of male admirers who are just waiting to marry her, which sounds highly unlikely, to say the least, for a woman whose shrill laugh sounds like "a long cascade of falling tinware."

Sometimes the self-deceit takes on more subtle forms, as with the character of Mrs. Treadwell. She is an interesting character because she is one of the few who is not subject to the author's scathing irony. Mrs. Treadwell does not share the ignorant prejudices of many of the others: they are bigoted and unhappy; she is merely unhappy. And yet in spite of the sympathetic manner in which she is presented, Mrs. Treadwell's capacity for self-deceit may be the most thoroughgoing of all. If anything bad happens to her, she refuses to believe in it, as if it is only a bad dream. When she is attacked by the beggar woman who bruises her arm, Mrs. Treadwell convinces herself that this is not a thing that really happens to anyone, least of

> Even the most admirable character in the novel, the dignified, humane Dr. Schumann, falls victim, at least temporarily, to the vice of self-deceit."

all her. Because her life has been full of emotional pain, she tries to turn her back on it and deny it. The voyage itself is just another thing to flee from, and her desire is to disappear entirely from view: "moment by moment she would find a split second of relief from boredom in the very act of flight which gave her the fleeting illusion of invisibility." For Mrs. Treadwell, who is forty-five years old and has a birthday while she is on the ship, even her age is something temporary that she can somehow put off.

Mrs. Treadwell's great fantasy is that she can be happy in Paris, her destination, but the reader suspects that this is just another illusion. Paris is her Shangri-La, her mythical paradise that always beckons in the distance but is never found. There is also an irony in her choice of Paris because the reader knows what Mrs. Treadwell does not—that within a decade, Paris will be occupied by the Nazis. The horror that is in incipient form all around her on the voyage, and to which she is largely oblivious, will eventually envelop her in her hiding place.

Even the most admirable character in the novel, the dignified, humane Dr. Schumann, falls victim, at least temporarily, to the vice of self-deceit. The doctor clearly represents a higher form of morality, as can be seen in the very first description of him, in which his eyes have an "abstract goodness and even sweetness in them." He is dignified and well bred and is recognized as such by the other Germans, and he has the gift of making others think that he will understand them. Deeply religious, he is constantly measuring his conduct against a moral law that he knows from his Catholic faith, and he does not share the prevailing anti-Semitism.

But even Dr. Schumann cannot avoid sinking into behavior that is not worthy of him. His undoing lies in his relationship with La Condesa, the flighty, drug-addicted noblewoman. When he first meets her, he recoils in moral disgust at her addiction, but he is drawn in by her shamelessly intimate manner. Although he repeatedly tries to put what he regards as an "unruly relationship" back in order, something passes between them that he is unable to resist. Eventually, he gives way to her desire and supplies her with the drugs she craves. Although he has fallen from his high professional standards and betrayed his role as a doctor, for a while he convinces himself that he has done nothing wrong, that he was merely being merciful to her. He even gets Father Garza to agree that he was only doing what he could with a difficult patient.

But Dr. Schumann cannot sustain this lie for long. He soon feels shame and humiliation at having fallen in love with La Condesa—he, a married man. He realizes that he has abused his power and has used against her the vice that harms her most. The experience seems to unnerve him completely, and for a while he blames her, giving way to a bout of anger against women, which is uncharacteristic of him although common in virtually all the other male characters. The language he uses to himself about her is vitriolic:

> He had a savage impulse to strike her from him, this diabolical possession, this incubus fastened upon him like a bat, this evil spirit come out of her hell to accuse him falsely, to seduce his mind, to charge him with fraudulent obligations to her, to burden his life to the end of his days, to bring him to despair.

The violence of this suggests that underneath the even, calm temperament that usually characterizes the doctor, there may be much darker impulses. But at least he finally has the insight to recognize this, and he is horrified by what he regards as the presence of evil in his own nature. He even believes that he has ruined his own life because of her and that she will always be a burden on his conscience. For a man of his deep religious and moral convictions, the upset in his world has cosmic implications:

> The whole great structure built upon the twin pillars of justice and love, which reached from earth to eternity, by which the human soul rose step by step from the most rudimentary concepts of good and evil, of simple daily conduct between fellow men, to the most exquisite hairline discriminations and choices between one or another shade of faith and feeling, of doctrinal and mystical perceptions—this tower was now crumbling and falling around him.

It might seem to the reader that Dr. Schumann punishes himself more than is necessary, but the point the author wishes to make is surely that even the man who has the highest level of moral and spiritual development on the ship is not immune to bouts of immoral, selfish, self-deceiving behavior. If Dr. Schumann can fall, Porter seems to say, what hope is there for any of the others, or for us?

The sad truth is that there is only one noble, selfless act in the entire novel, and only one moment of true beauty. The selfless act is when one of the passengers from steerage, a man named Etchegaray, jumps overboard in an effort to save the Huttens' bulldog, Bébé, who has been thrown into the water by Ric and Rac. Bébé survives, but Etchegaray drowns. The Huttens wonder what prompted Etchegaray's actions. As might be expected, they look for some self-serving motive. The man must have expected a reward, says Frau Hutten, while Professor Hutten thinks he must have wanted to attract attention to himself, or to become a hero. The more likely explanation, as the reader well knows, is that Etchegaray, who was an artist who carved little figures of animals in wood, loved animals and wanted to save the dog's life simply because it needed saving.

The moment of beauty comes immediately after the fight that breaks out in steerage in the aftermath of Etchegaray's funeral at sea. Three whales are spotted, and all the passengers stop what they are doing and stare at them:

> [T]hree enormous whales, seeming to swim almost out of the water, flashing white silver in the sunlight, spouting tall white fountains, traveling with the power and drive of speedboats, going south—not one person could take his eyes from the beautiful spectacle until it was over, and their minds were cleansed of death and violence.

Unfortunately for the travelers, the beauty of the whales is quite alien to the human world, which sails on regardless, a ship of self-deceiving, small-minded fools heading for Germany, to its historic appointment with Nazism and a world plunged into war and evil.

Source: Bryan Aubrey, Critical Essay on *Ship of Fools*, in *Novels for Students*, The Gale Group, 2002.

Smith Kirkpatrick

In the following essay, Kirkpatrick explores the common link among the characters in Ship of Fools—*the various social masks they wear to cover their base natures.*

When you read Katherine Anne Porter's novel, you will find yourself already aboard her *Ship of Fools*, not overtly, not through the usual identification with one of the characters, but through a more subtle involvement with a familiar action.

What Do I Read Next?

- *The Collected Stories of Katherine Anne Porter* (1965), which won for Porter the formal awards that had eluded *Ship of Fools*: a Pulitzer Prize, the National Book Award, and the Gold Medal for Fiction awarded by the National Institute of Arts and Letters.

- *Letters of Katherine Anne Porter* (reprint edition, 1991) edited by her friend Isabel Bayley, contains many of the thousands of letters Porter wrote during the period 1930 to 1963.

- *Hitler's Willing Executioners: Ordinary Germans and the Holocaust* (1997), by Daniel Jonah Goldhagen, is an extremely controversial book. Using extensive research, Goldhagen argues that Hitler was able to carry out the Holocaust because vast numbers of ordinary Germans, not just the Nazis, supported it.

- *The Rise and Fall of the Third Reich* (1960), by William L. Shirer, is a classic account of Germany during the Hitler years, by an American journalist who lived and worked there during the 1930s.

Miss Porter's ship is a real, not purely symbolic, ship traveling from Vera Cruz to Bremerhaven during the early thirties and is peopled with passengers talking and traveling in that troubled time, but as the journey aboard the *Vera*, truth, continues the passengers tend to develop more towards caricature than characterization. And this is very close to Miss Porter's point. She has no clearly identifiable protagonist or antagonist. Her subject is too large to be shown through a central character; for as the ship progresses from the "true cross" to the "broken haven" she shows us how each passenger journeys not only to Bremerhaven but through life. In so doing she shows us the common manner in which we make the voyage, and she shows us the necessarily concomitant subject of what she views life to be.

"

The novel comes to no
conclusions, answers no
questions; its ending is the end
of the journey. But these masks
are our masks; this is the way
we cover our naked selves for
the swift passage . . ."

Since the reader cannot identify himself with one of Miss Porter's characters, just how does she involve his heart? She has chosen to locate the novel aboard a ship, to limit her action within the confines of a sea voyage where the characters for the most part are strangers to one another. With the ship-board opportunity for new friendships and fresh self-appraisals it is important to look at what the passengers bring with them on their journey. As the title says, the voyagers are all fools. The nature of their foolery is what the passengers bring aboard with them, and Miss Porter reduces the foolery to the oldest mark of the fool, the one thing that all fools in all time have had in common: the mask. She shows how intricately contrived are the masks. Each man wears not one but many. He peers at his existence from behind the various masks of nationality, age, sex, creeds, social rank, race, wealth, politics, and all other existential distinctions made by both the elemental and civilized man.

At times the masks are as pathetically simple as that of Frau Baumgartner, who in the tropic heat is momentarily too angry with her small son to heed his pleas to remove the buckskin suit in which she has wrongly encased him. She taunts him over his inability to endure the riding costume meant for mountain coldness and even begins to enjoy her cruelty and the pleasant feeling of hurting the pride of the boy sitting on the divan ". . . yearning for kindness, hoping his beautiful good mother would come back soon. She vanished in the frowning scolding stranger, who blazed out at him when he least expected it, struck him on the hand, threatened him, seemed to hate him." But in the next moment she "sees him clearly" and is filled with pity and remorse and tenderness.

At other times the intricacy of the masks is nearly as confusing as it is to Denny the Texan, whose bible is *Recreational Aspects of Sex as Mental Prophylaxis—A True Guide to Happiness* and whose consuming passion on the voyage is to buy, at *his* price, the wares of Amparo, a dancer in the zarzuela company. Sitting in the ship's bar Denny has an atheist on one side speaking like a bolshevik and over here a Jew, criticizing Christians and meaning Catholics. He didn't like Jews *or* Catholics and knew if he said, "I think Jews are heathens," he would be accused of persecuting Jews. He wished himself home in Brownsville ". . . where a man knew who was who and what was what, and niggers, crazy Swedes, Jews, greasers, bone-headed micks, polacks, wops, Guineas and damn Yankees knew their place and stayed in it."

Denny wants the mask simple and set and Miss Porter shows the results of a mask settling into reality through Mrs. Treadwell, an American divorcee, to whom the past is so bad, as compared to a future full of love she had expected as a child, it seems something she has read in newspapers. Denny in his final determination to conquer Amparo confuses the door and drunkenly mistakes for the face Amparo the face of "unsurpassed savagery and sensuality" which Mrs. Treadwell in drunken idleness painted on herself following the failure of the young ship's officer to arouse any feeling in her. She shoves Denny to the deck, and using her metal capped high heel beats in the face of the fallen and stuporous man with "furious pleasure" and is afterwards delighted at the sight of her "hideous wicked face" in her mirror. When worn as a reality, the mask comes close to covering insanity, which becomes a terrifying comment on all the Brownsvilles in the world.

Usually, though, the masks shift and change like the postures of a dance. Jenny and David, the American painters who have been living together but are now traveling in separate cabins, approach each other with feelings of love only to have their feelings turn suddenly into hatred and the hatred as it shows itself on their faces evokes the love again. They can no more decide their emotional destiny than they can decide their physical destination. One wants to visit Spain; the other, France. In the course of their constant argument they even swap positions but always the change is in reaction to an action or reaction in the other. And here Miss Porter takes the breath away with her absolute genius. Never, not once in the seemingly unending continuum of emotional and rational action and reaction, whether between total strangers operating behind the complicated masks of their civilized pasts or whether between selves almost submerged in old marriages, never, no matter how abrupt may be the reversal of a position or of a thought pattern, is there anything but complete belief that, yes, this is the way it would really be.

This constant change is the reason the passengers tend towards caricature. Exactly when is the passenger undergoing the final unveiling to his ultimate truth? Amparo and her pimp, Pepe, steal, swindle, and blackmail behind a flurry of costumery and poses and when at last they are left together, away from their victims, Amparo still full of the strange smells and heats of the recently departed liberal Swede, Arne Hanson, the final truth of these two seems about to be revealed. And the truth is beautifully revealed of them as pimp, whore, and lovers; but the scene ends with the revelation that both parties have long before planned, and even now are working towards, their mutual betrayals.

Perhaps the truth of the characters lies not in revealing the total man facing an action as large as life itself (perhaps no man can) but in the manner or the method with which the characters face life. If in this or that situation they wear this or that ready-made mask and in the next situation wear yet another of the thousand faces molded by the forms of civilization and elemental men, then perhaps we really are caricatures with our true selves forever unrealized. Certainly the passengers behind their masks hide from each other their love. Mrs. Treadwell says the passengers are all saying to each other, *"Love me, love me in spite of all! Whether or not I love you, whether I am fit to love, whether you are able to love, even if there is no such thing as love, love me!"*

The Germanic mask of discipline and family is so stolid on the face of Dr. Schumann, the ship's doctor, that even though he loves the beautiful Cuban Condesa, who has forsaken herself to ether and self-caresses, he degrades her and wants rid of her. In horror of himself he renounces all human kinship and in his own drugged sleep the Condesa's death-like, bodiless head danced before him still smiling but shedding tears. "Oh, Why, Why?" the head asked him not in complaint but wonder. Tenderly he kissed it silent. This was probably the last opportunity for love in his life.

The one unmasked act of love aboard the ship, an act nearly performed earlier by Dr. Schumann when he risked overtaxing a weak heart by stepping forward to save a cat, was performed by a man

in steerage, a wood carver who cries like a child when his knife is taken from him and who, when the white dog is thrown overboard into the night sea, leaps after the white object without hesitation or knowledge of whether it is a man or a dog and is drowned saving it. In the lean raggedness of this "worn but perhaps young" wood carver, who cannot but bring to mind another worker in wood, and in his unselfish act, is an opportunity for the passengers to see behind man's facade. But even the parent-like owners of the dog want only to forget the wood carver's name, and they lose themselves in the carnal interest the act has rediscovered for them.

The wood carver's burial ends with the priests turning their backs while their Catholic flock in steerage nearly kills a taunting atheist. The final results of the wood carver's act are that the dog is saved and fun is had by Ric and Rac, the twin children who threw the dog overboard in the first place.

If La Condesa can say of the Cuban students, "They are just their parents' bad dreams," then certainly this can be said of Ric and Rac even though their parents are in the zarzuela company and are almost bad dreams themselves. Ric and Rac have named themselves for two comic cartoon terriers who "made life a raging curse for everyone near them, got their own way invariably by a wicked trick, and always escaped without a blow." And this is Ric and Rac. They steal, kill, destroy, and hurt not for gain but from some profound capacity for hatred which with the capacity and need for love lurks always behind the mask. It is almost as though this capacity for hatred is the reason of being for the masks of civilization, and Miss Porter is writing of civilized men. She is writing of the passengers living in the upper decks, and they are terrified of the masses of humans traveling in animal misery in steerage. All weapons are taken from the masses, even the wood carver's knife. The elemental man is too apparent. Jenny is haunted by the memory of two Mexican Indians, a man and woman locked in a swaying embrace, both covered with blood and killing each other with cutting weapons. "They were silent, and their faces had taken on a saintlike patience in suffering, abstract, purified of rage and hatred in their one holy dedicated purpose to kill each other." In her dreams she is horrified to see that this is she and David.

And no matter how tightly the passengers may be enclosed in their formalized attitudes the zarzuela company reveals how thinly surfaced they are. By subverting the masks the whores and pimps make the passengers pay them to usurp the Captain's table, toast confusion, send the pompous Captain fleeing, and in their hatred mock the passengers by parodying them on the dance floor. The dance itself being a formalization, the parody by the whores and pimps becomes not only a parody of the individual passenger but of everything he considers civilized.

And the parody is meaningful because the passengers themselves are parodies, fools. Fools because behind all the masks and the love and the hatred is a selfishness, and the most selfish of all is the old religious zealot. His final prayer is that he be remembered for one merciful moment and be let go, given eternal darkness, let die forever—be the one man in all time released from the human condition, which must be lived to whatever its ends may be.

The novel comes to no conclusions, answers no questions; its ending is the end of the journey. But these masks are our masks; this is the way we cover our naked selves for the swift passage; this life is our lives moving steadily into eternity, the familiar action in which we are all involved. And the novel is a lament for us all, a song artistically resolved, sung by a great artist of the insoluble condition of man.

Source: Smith Kirkpatrick, "*Ship of Fools,*" in *Critical Essays on Katherine Anne Porter*, edited by Darlene Harbour Unrue, G. K. Hall & Co., 1997, pp. 233–36.

Howard Moss

In the following essay, Moss provides an overview of Ship of Fools, *concluding that it "is basically about love, a human emotion that teeters helplessly between need and order."*

Katherine Anne Porter's *Ship of Fools* is the story of a voyage—a voyage that seems to take place in many dimensions. A novel of character rather than of action, it has as its main purpose a study of the German ethos shortly before Hitler's coming to power in Germany. That political fact hangs as a threat over the entire work, and the novel does not end so much as succumb to a historical truth. But it is more than a political novel. *Ship of Fools* is also a human comedy and a moral allegory. Since its author commits herself to nothing but its top layer, and yet allows for plunges into all sorts of undercurrents, it is disingenuous to read on its surface alone and dangerous to read for its depths. Miss Porter has written one of those fine but ambiguous books whose values and meanings

shift the way light changes as it passes through a turning prism.

Except for the embarkation at Veracruz and a few stopovers at ports, all the events occur aboard the *Vera*, a German passenger freighter, on its twenty-seven-day journey from Mexico to Germany in the summer of 1931. There is no lack of passengers; the cast is so immense that we are provided with not one but two keys at the beginning, so that we can keep the characters clearly in mind. The passenger list includes many Germans; a remarkable company of Spanish zarzuela singers and dancers—four men and four women—equally adept at performing, thieving, pimping, and whoring; the satanic six-year-old twins of two of the dancers, and four Americans: William Denny, a know-nothing chemical engineer from Texas; Mrs. Treadwell, a divorcée in her forties, who is constantly thwarted in her attempts to disengage herself from the rest of the human race; and David Scott and Jenny Brown, two young painters who have been having an unhappy love affair for years, have never married, and quarrel endlessly. There are also a Swede, some Mexicans, a Swiss innkeeper and his family, and some Cubans. The Germans are almost uniformly disagreeable—an arrogant widow, a windbag of a professor named Hutten, a violently anti-Semitic publisher named Rieber, a drunken lawyer, an Orthodox Jew who loathes Gentiles, a dying religious healer, and a hunchback, to name just a few. Each suffers from a mortal form of despair—spiritual, emotional, or religious. At Havana, La Condesa, a Spanish noblewoman who is being deported by the Cuban government, embarks, and so do eight hundred and seventy-six migrant workers, in steerage. They are being sent back to Spain because of the collapse of the Cuban sugar market.

In the little world of the *Vera*, plying across the ocean, the passengers become involved with one another not from choice but by proximity. Because of this, not very much happens, from the viewpoint of conventional drama. Miss Porter is interested in the interplay of character and not in the strategy of plotting. Her method is panoramic—cabin to cabin, deck to writing room, bridge to bar. She has helped herself to a device useful to a natural short-story writer: she manipulates one microcosm after another of her huge cast in short, swift scenes. Observed from the outside, analyzed from within, her characters are handled episodically. Place is her organizing element, time the propelling agent of her action. The *Vera* is a Hotel Universe always in motion.

Director Stanley Kramer with Elizabeth Ashley as Jenny, Vivien Leigh as Mary Treadwell, and Gertrude Hartley, Leigh's mother, on the set of the 1965 film version of the novel

As it proceeds, small crises blossom into odious flowers and expire. There are three major events. An oilman, Herr Freytag, a stainless Aryan, is refused the captain's table once it is learned that the wife he is going back to fetch from Germany is Jewish. A wood carver in steerage jumps overboard to save a dog thrown into the sea by the twins, and is drowned. And the zarzuela company arranges a costume-party "gala" whose expressed purpose is to honor the captain but whose real motive is the fleecing of the other passengers. The characters, seeking release or support in one an-

other, merely deepen each other's frustrations. Often these random associations end in violence—a violence always out of character and always revealing. Hansen, the Swede, who talks about a society in which the masses are not exploited, clubs the publisher with a beer bottle. The source of his immediate anger is his disappointed passion for one of the Spanish dancers. The funeral of the wood carver, the gentlest of men, becomes the occasion for a religious riot. Mrs. Treadwell, a carefully contained woman, well aware of the pointlessness and danger of meddling in other people's business,

> Miss Porter has written one of those fine but ambiguous books whose values and meanings shift the way light changes as it passes through a turning prism."

emerges from behind her bastion and beats up Denny in a drunken frenzy with the heel of a golden evening slipper.

If the relationships are not violent, they are damaging. Schumann, the ship's doctor, falling suddenly in love with the drug-addicted and possibly mad Condesa, risks his professional, spiritual, and emotional identity. The American painters hopelessly batter themselves in an affair they cannot resolve or leave alone. And the most solid of *Hausfraus*, Professor Hutten's wife, speaks up suddenly, as if against her will, to contradict her husband at the captain's table, an act doubly shameful for being public. Unable momentarily to put up with her husband's platitudes, to support a view of marriage she knows to be false, Frau Hutten, in her one moment of insight, undermines the only security she has. As character after character gives way to a compulsion he has been unware of, it becomes evident why Miss Porter's novel is open to many interpretations. Through sheer accuracy of observation rather than the desire to demonstrate abstract ideas, she has hit upon a major theme: order vs. need, a theme observable in the interchange of everyday life and susceptible of any number of readings—political, social, religious, and psychological. Every major character is magnetized in time by the opposing forces of need and order. Mexico is the incarnation of need, Germany the representative of an order based on need. At the beginning, in Veracruz, there is a hideously crippled Mexican beggar, "dumb, half blind," who walks like an animal "following the trail of a smell." And the very last character in the book is a German boy in the ship's band, "who looked as if he had never had enough to eat in his life, nor a kind word from anybody," who "did not know what he was going to do next" and who "stared with blinded eyes." As the *Vera* puts in to Bremerhaven,

he stands, "his mouth quivering while he shook the spit out of his trumpet, repeating to himself just above a whisper, '*Gruss Gott, Gruss Gott,*' as if the town were a human being, a good and dear trusted friend who had come a long way to welcome him." Aboard the *Vera*, there is, on the one hand, the captain's psychotic authoritarianism, with its absolute and rigid standards of behavior, menaced always by human complexity and squalor; on the other, the Condesa's drug addiction and compulsion to seduce young men. Both are terrifying forms of fanaticism, and they complement each other in their implicit violence.

Dr. Schumann is the mediating agent between these two kinds of fanaticism. Suffering from a weak heart, he is going back to Germany—a Germany that no longer exists—to die. He is the product of a noble Teutonic strain, the Germany of intellectual freedom, scientific dispassion, and religious piety. He is a healer equally at home in the chaos of the steerage and in the captain's stateroom. But the Condesa shatters his philosophic detachment. He goes to her cabin at night and kisses her while she is asleep; he orders six young Cuban medical students to stay away from her cabin because he is jealous. Both acts are symptoms of a progressive desperation. First he refuses to express his need openly, out of fear; then he masks it by a display of authority. He becomes, finally, a conspirator in the Condesa's addiction. Since he is not able to separate the woman from the patient, in Dr. Schumann need and order become muddled. Mrs. Treadwell, an essentially sympathetic character, is drawn into Freytag's dilemma the same way—casually, then desperately. It is she who innocently tells her anti-Semitic cabinmate that Freytag's wife is Jewish, not knowing the information is meant to be confidential. He is bitter, forgetting that he has already blurted out the fact at the captain's table in a fit of anger and pride. Mrs. Treadwell wisely points out that his secret should never have been one in the first place. This is odd wisdom; Mrs. Treadwell has a few secrets of her own.

It is from such moral complications that the texture of *Ship of Fools* evolves—a series of mishaps in which both intention and the lack of intention become disasters. The tragedy is that even the best motive is adulterated when translated into action. Need turns people into fools, order into monsters. The *Vera's* first-class passengers stroll on deck gazing down into the abysmal pit of the steerage—pure need—just as they watch in envy the frozen etiquette of the captain's table and its frieze of simulated order. Even dowdy Frau Schmitt, a timid ex-teacher who cannot bear suffering in others, finally accepts the cruelty of Freytag's dismissal from the captain's table. If she does not belong there herself, she thinks, then where does she belong? A victim, she thus becomes a party to victimization—a situation that is to receive its perfect demonstration in the world of Nazi Germany, which shadows Miss Porter's book like a bird of carrion. Through the need to belong, the whole damaging human complex of fear, pride, and greed, a governing idea emerges from *Ship of Fools* that is rooted in the Prussian mystique of "blood and iron." It is the manipulation of human needs to conform to a version of order.

The flow of events in *Ship of Fools* is based on addiction (sex, drugs, food, and drink) or obsession (envy, pride, covetousness, and the rest). Yet even the most despicable characters, such as the Jew-hating Herr Rieber, seem surprisingly innocent. It is the innocence of ignorance, not of moral goodness. The humbug and misinformation exchanged between the passengers on the *Vera* are voluminous. Each person is trapped in that tiny segment of reality he calls his own, which he thinks about, and talks about, and tries to project to a listener equally obsessed. Not knowing who they are, these marathon talkers do not know the world they are capable of generating. Love is the sacrificial lamb of their delusions, and though it is pursued without pause, it is always a semblance, never a reality. Though they are terribly in need of some human connection, their humanity itself is in question.

Only the Spanish dancers seem to escape this fate. They transform need into a kind of order by subordinating it for financial gain or sexual pleasure, without involvement. They are comically and tragically evil; they have arranged a universe of money around sex and fraud. Consciously malignant, they are outdone by the natural malice of the twins, who throw the Condesa's pearls overboard in a burst of demoniacal spirits. The pearls are a prize the Spanish dancers had planned to steal. The evil of design is defeated by natural evil—a neat point. Even in this closed, diabolical society, in which the emotions have been disciplined for profit, the irrational disturbs the arrangement of things.

At one point, Jenny Brown recalls something she saw from a bus window when she was passing through a small Indian village in Mexico:

Half a dozen Indians, men and women, were standing together quietly in the bare spot near one of the small houses, and they were watching something very intently. As the bus rolled by, Jenny saw a man and a woman, some distance from the group, locked in a death battle. They swayed and staggered together in a strange embrace, as if they supported each other; but in the man's raised hand was a long knife, and the woman's breast and stomach were pierced. The blood ran down her body and over her thighs, her skirts were sticking to her legs with her own blood. She was beating him on the head with a jagged stone, and his features were veiled in rivulets of blood. They were silent, and their faces had taken on a saintlike patience in suffering, abstract, purified of rage and hatred in their one holy dedicated purpose to kill each other. Their flesh swayed together and clung, their left arms were wound about each other's bodies as if in love. Their weapons were raised again, but their heads lowered little by little, until the woman's head rested upon his breast and his head was on her shoulder, and holding thus, they both struck again.

It was a mere flash of visions, but in Jenny's memory it lived in an ample eternal day illuminated by a cruel sun.

This passage could be the center from which everything in Miss Porter's novel radiates. The human relations in it are nearly all reenacted counterparts of this silent struggle. Inside and out, the battle rages—the devout against the blasphemous, the Jew against the Gentile, class against class, nation against nation. The seemingly safe bourgeois marriages—of solid Germans, of stolid Swiss—are secret hand-to-hand combats. It is no better with lovers, children, and dogs. The dog thrown into the sea by the evil twins is at least rescued by the good wood carver before he drowns. But on the human level the issues are obscure, the colors blurred; the saint is enmeshed with the devil. Struggling to get at the truth—*Vera* means "true" in Latin—the passengers in *Ship of Fools* justify its title. What truth is there for people who must lie in order to exist, Miss Porter seems to be asking. Against her insane captain and her mad Condesa, Miss Porter poses only the primitive and the remote—an enchanting Indian servant aboard ship, the appearance of three whales, a peasant woman nursing a baby. They are as affecting as a silence in nature.

Miss Porter is a moralist, but too good a writer to be one except by implication. Dogma in *Ship of Fools* is attached only to dogmatic characters. There is not an ounce of weighted sentiment in it. Its intelligence lies not in the profundity of its ideas but in the clarity of its viewpoint; we are impressed not by what Miss Porter says but by what she knows. Neither heartless nor merciful, she is tough. Her virtue is disinterestedness, her strength objectivity. Her style is free of displays of "sensitivity," musical effects, and interior decoration. Syntax is the only instrument she needs to construct an enviable prose. But the book differs from her extraordinary stories and novellas in that it lacks a particular magic she has attained so many times on a smaller scale. The missing ingredient is impulse. *Ship of Fools* was twenty years in the writing; the stories read as if they were composed at one sitting, and they have the spontaneity of a running stream. *Ship of Fools* is another kind of work—a summing up, not an overflowing—and it is devoid of one of the excitements of realistic fiction. The reader is never given that special satisfaction of the drama of design, in which the strings, having come unwound, are ultimately tied together in a knot. Miss Porter scorns patness and falseness, but by the very choice of her method she also lets go of suspense. She combines something of the intellectual strategy of Mann's *Magic Mountain* (in which the characters not only are themselves but represent ideas or human qualities) with the symbolic grandeur of *Moby Dick* (in which a predestined fate awaits the chief actors). Her goodbye to themes of Mexico and Germany (two subjects that have occupied her elsewhere) is a stunning farewell, but it lacks two components usually considered essential to masterpieces—a hero and a heroic extravagance.

Ship of Fools is basically about love, a human emotion that teeters helplessly between need and order. On the *Vera's* voyage there is precious little of it. The love that comes too late for the Condesa and Dr. Schumann is the most touching thing in it. But the Condesa is deranged, ill, and exiled; the dying Doctor is returning to a Germany that has vanished. The one true example of love—a pair of Mexican newlyweds—is never dwelt upon. We are left with this image of two people, hand in hand, who have hardly said a word in all the thousands that make up Miss Porter's novel. In *Ship of Fools*, every human need but one is exposed down to its nerve ends. Love alone remains silent, and abstract.

Source: Howard Moss, "No Safe Harbor," in *Katherine Anne Porter*, edited and with an introduction by Harold Bloom, Modern Critical Views series, G. K. Hall & Co., 1997, pp. 35–41.

Sources

Givner, Joan, *The Life of Katherine Anne Porter*, Jonathan Cape, 1983, p. 443.

Hendrik, Willene, and George Hendrick, *Katherine Anne Porter*, rev. ed., Twayne, 1988, pp. 99–100.

Unrue, Darlene Harbour, ed., *Critical Essays on Katherine Anne Porter*, G. K. Hall & Co., 1997, pp. 40–42.

Warren, Robert Penn, *Katherine Anne Porter: A Collection of Critical Essays*, Prentice-Hall, Inc., 1979, pp. 130–49.

For Further Reading

DeMouy, Jane Krause, *Katherine Anne Porter's Women: The Eye of Her Fiction*, University of Texas Press, 1983.
This work studies Porter's work from the viewpoint of feminine psychology. *Ship of Fools* is seen in terms of the physical and psychological separation of men and women.

Givner, Joan, ed., *Katherine Anne Porter: Conversations*, University Press of Mississippi, 1987.
This is a collection of interviews with and articles about Porter covering a period of sixty years.

Hartley, Lodwick, and George Core, eds., *Katherine Anne Porter: A Critical Symposium*, University of Georgia Press, 1969.
This work contains sixteen essays on Porter's work, including three on *Ship of Fools*.

Mooney, Harry J., Jr., *The Fiction and Criticism of Katherine Anne Porter*, University of Pittsburgh Press, rev.ed., 1962.
This concise overview seeks to understand the meaning of Porter's work and the particular kinds of experiences in which she is most interested.

Nance, William L., *Katherine Anne Porter and the Art of Rejection*, University of North Carolina Press, 1963.
Like Unrue, Nance attempts to find a thematic unity in Porter's work. He finds it in a pattern of behavior he calls rejection, which governs the emotional effect of the work.

Unrue, Darlene Harbour, *Truth and Vision in Katherine Anne Porter's Fiction*, University of Georgia Press, 1985.
This study emphasizes the underlying thematic unity of Porter's works, which reflect an arduous, always incomplete discovery of truth. Knowledge comes from apprehending universal laws in oneself and in nature.

Sula

Toni Morrison
1973

Sula, published in 1973 in New York, is Toni Morrison's second novel. Set in the early 1900s in a small Ohio town called Medallion, it tells the story of two African-American friends, Sula and Nel, from their childhood through their adulthood and Sula's death. Morrison drew on her own small-town, Midwestern childhood to create this tale of conformity and rebellion.

Morrison began writing *Sula* in 1969, a time of great activism among African Americans and others who were working toward equal civil rights and opportunities. The book addresses issues of racism, bigotry, and suppression of African Americans; it depicts the despair people feel when they can't get decent jobs, and the determination of some to survive. Eva, for example, cuts off her leg in order to get money to raise her family. Morrison shows how, faced with racist situations, some people had to grovel to whites simply to get by, as Helene does on a train heading through the South. Others, however, fought back, as Sula does when she threatens some white boys who are harassing her and Nel.

The novel was well received by critics, who particularly praised her vivid imagery, strong characterization, and poetic prose, as well as her terse, realistic dialogue. The book was nominated for a National Book Award in 1974

Toni Morrison

Author Biography

Nobel laureate Toni Morrison was born Chloe Anthony Wofford on February 18, 1931, in Lorain, Ohio. She was the second of four children of Ramah and George Wofford. She studied English at Howard University, and earned a master's degree in English literature from Cornell, where she wrote her thesis on William Faulkner. She then became a teacher of English at Texas Southern University, and later at Howard University, where she worked until 1964.

While teaching at Howard, Morrison began to write. She told an interviewer for Borders that her beginning was almost accidental; she joined a group of colleagues at Howard University who had formed a writer's group and because members couldn't come unless they had written something, she began writing a short story, which eventually became her first novel.

In 1958 the author married Harold Morrison, an architect, with whom she had two sons, but in 1964 they divorced. After the divorce, Morrison moved to Syracuse, New York, where she supported her family by working as a book editor at Random House. During her tenure there, she edited the work of many well-known African-American authors, including Toni Cade Bambara, Gayl Jones, and Angela Davis.

Her first book, *The Bluest Eye*, was completed in the mid-1960s, but Morrison received many rejections of the novel until 1969, when it was finally accepted by Holt, Rinehart, and Winston, and published in 1970. Like all of Morrison's work, it considers issues of race and the African-American experience. *Sula* was published in 1973 and was nominated for a National Book Award in 1974. *Song of Solomon* was published in 1977 and won the National Book Critics Circle Award for that year. *Tar Baby* was published in 1981, and made best-seller lists for four months. *Beloved* (1987), which tells the story of ex-slaves haunted by their past, was widely acclaimed, as was *Jazz* (1992).

In 1993, Morrison was awarded the Nobel Prize for literature, and thus became the first African American and only the eighth woman ever to win the award. According to Maureen O'Brien in *Publishers Weekly*, Morrison said, "What is most wonderful for me personally is to know that the Prize has at last been awarded to an African American. I thank God that my mother is alive to see this day." In 1996, she received the National Book Foundation Medal for Distinguished Contribution to American Letters.

Paradise, set in an all-black town in Oklahoma, was published in 1998. Morrison has also written and edited many works of literary criticism, as well as a play, *Dreaming Emmett*. Her essays and interviews have been widely published in both popular and scholarly periodicals.

Since 1988, Morrison has been a professor at Princeton University, where she holds the Robert F. Goheen Professorship of the Humanities and is the chair of the Creative Writing Program. According to an article on the Web site *Voices from the Gaps*, Morrison was giving a lecture at Princeton when a student asked her who she wrote for. Morrison said,

> I want to write for people like me, which is to say black people, curious people, demanding people— people who can't be faked, people who don't need to be patronized, people who have very, very high criteria.

Plot Summary

Introduction

Sula opens with a description of "The Bottom," the African-American section of a town called Medallion in Ohio, which has been bought by whites, who force out the remaining inhabitants and level the old buildings to create a golf course. The Bottom got its name from a joke played on a slave by a white farmer, who said he would give the slave his freedom, and a section of rich bottom land, in exchange for doing some difficult chores. The slave fulfilled his work and the farmer gave him his freedom, but was reluctant to give away fertile bottom land. Instead, he told the slave that a section of eroded land high in the hills was really bottom land, because from God's point of view, it was "the bottom of heaven." The slave, not knowing any better, accepted the land, which turned out to be worthless for farming, and thus the African-American settlement was founded. The Bottom subsequently has a rich history as a lively African-American community.

1919

Shadrack is a shell-shocked veteran of World War I who is returned to the Bottom by a sheriff who figures out that he was originally from there. He lives in a shack and becomes famous for his invented holiday, National Suicide Day, which he celebrates on January 3rd of each year, starting in 1920. On this holiday, people who don't want to continue living with the fear of death are invited to kill themselves, thus taking control of a normally uncontrollable event. Although this holiday initially frightens people in the Bottom, eventually they become used to it and it becomes a part of local culture.

1920

Helene, Nel's mother, is the daughter of a prostitute, but was raised by her grandmother in a strict and sheltered environment. Helene marries Wiley Wright and moves to Medallion, where she lives an upright and respectable life, and forces Nel to do the same. When she receives a letter saying her grandmother, Cecile, is very ill, she reluctantly decides to go to New Orleans to see her. Her reluctance comes from the widespread racism in the South, and on the train ride to New Orleans, her fears are realized. The African-American passengers must sit in segregated cars, and there are no bathrooms for them; they have to use fields near the train tracks. Helene also must grovel to a white train conductor who is harassing her.

Cecile dies before Helene's arrival, but Helene sees her mother, Rochelle, and introduces Nel to her. Nel is fascinated and shocked by her grandmother's exotic looks and behavior. All of these experiences change Nel; after the trip, for the first time, she realizes that she is a separate person, an individual. She meets another girl, Sula, who comes from a wild family but appears at first to be calm and quiet. Helene, swayed by this good behavior, allows Nel to be friends with Sula, and the friendship grows.

1921

This chapter describes Sula's family, particularly her grandmother Eva. When Eva and her three children are abandoned by her husband, she goes away, then returns eighteen months later with only one leg and ten thousand dollars. Rumors say that she cut off her leg in order to collect the insurance money. She builds a huge, rambling house, where she lives on the top floor and gets around in a wheelchair. She uses the rest of the space to house "her children, friends, strays, and a constant stream of boarders."

Eva's daughter, Pearl, marries and moves away; her daughter, Hannah, is a promiscuous widow, and she and her daughter, Sula, live in Eva's house; and a third child, Plum, fights in World War I and returns home a drug addict. When Eva finds out the extent of his addiction, she pours kerosene on him and burns him to death while he's in a drug-induced, euphoric haze.

1922

Sula and Nel are now twelve years old, and are just becoming interested in men. They are best

friends, and have a deep understanding, despite their different personalities. Nel is calm and reliable, while Sula is unpredictable and even violent. When they're harassed by some white boys, Sula cuts off the tip of her own finger to show them how tough she is, which scares them away.

Sula overhears her mother telling some friends that she loves Sula, but doesn't like her. Sula is deeply hurt, but says nothing. She and Nel go down to the river, seeking shade from the heat, and see Chicken Little, a little boy. They play with him, and Sula grabs his arms and swings him around; her grip slips, and he flies out into the river and drowns. Frightened, Sula runs to see if Shadrack—who is in the nearest dwelling—has seen the incident. Shadrack doesn't even give Sula a chance to ask her question, instead saying, "Always," which Sula takes as a threat. Terrified, she flees, and Nel tells her it's not her fault, it was just an accident. Neither of them confesses to the killing or goes for any more help.

Chicken Little's body is found by a white man, who fishes it out and is annoyed at the inconvenience of dealing with a dead black child. Three days later, Chicken Little's remains are returned to his mother, and his funeral is held. Nel and Sula both attend, but they say nothing.

1923

The Bottom is in the middle of a summer drought, and Hannah asks Eva if she ever loved her children. Eva is angered by this question, and says that the sacrifice of her leg to keep them alive proves that she loves them. Hannah asks why, if she loved her children, she burned Plum to death. Eva says that she had many hard times keeping Plum alive as a child, that the war and the addiction had turned him back into a child, and that this time, she didn't have the power to save him. She says she killed him out of love, wanting him to die as a man. She explains that she held Plum lovingly in her arms before she killed him.

Hannah tells Eva that she dreamed of a red wedding dress, an omen of violence. She also tells her that Sula has been acting up lately, which everybody assumes is because she is getting her period. Sula is not the only person in the Bottom who is acting strangely. The heat and the drought have everyone on edge. Eva's comb is missing, and the shape and color of Sula's birthmark seem to be changing.

Like everyone else in the Bottom, Hannah begins doing the summer canning of fruits and veg-etables. When she goes out in the yard and lights the canning fire, her dress catches fire and bursts into flame. Eva hurls herself out of her wheelchair and through the second-story window, hoping she can drag herself across the yard fast enough to save Hannah, but Hannah runs out of the yard and becomes severely burned when neighbors try to put out the fire. An ambulance arrives, but Hannah dies on the way to the hospital. Eva, who was injured in the fall, almost bleeds to death.

While she is in the hospital recovering, Eva remembers the dream of the red wedding dress and realizes the fire is the event it foretold. She also realizes that during the fire, Sula was on the porch, watching her own mother burn to death and doing nothing to help. She tells her friends about this, but they all say Sula was probably so shocked that she couldn't do anything to help. Eva, however, believes that Sula intentionally let her mother die.

1927

Four years have passed, and Nel begins a relationship with Jude Greene, a waiter who wants to get a job on a road-building crew. His dream comes to nothing, however, because the road crew will not hire African Americans even if, like Jude, they are better-equipped for the hard labor than the "thin-armed white boys." This makes Jude bitter, and he asks Nel to marry him, hoping marriage will make him feel more manly. Nel happily accepts. Helene, Nel's mother, is excited, too, and plans a big, extravagant wedding unlike any ever held in the Bottom before.

The wedding is a fine event, and Nel is her usual traditional, proper self, looking forward to a settled life as a good wife. After the wedding, she notices Sula slip away. Sula leaves town, and does not return for almost ten years.

1937

Sula comes back to the Bottom, wearing expensive clothes, on the same day that a huge flock of robins arrives. The townspeople link these two events, considering them both evil omens. Sula walks through streets full of bird excrement as the people stare at her. She finally gets to Eva's house, and the first thing Eva says is, "I might have knowed them birds meant something."

Their relationship is now cold. Eva tells Sula that she needs to find a man and settle down, but Sula responds that she only needs herself. Sula reminds Eva that she killed Plum, and Eva reminds Sula that she stood by and watched her mother die.

Sula threatens to set Eva on fire while she's sleeping, and Eva locks her out of her room. Later, Sula obtains guardianship over Eva and commits her to a shabby nursing home, shocking everyone in town.

Nel, on the other hand, is excited about Sula's return and hopes that they can rekindle their friendship; unlike everyone else, she believes that good will result from Sula's coming home. They do revive their friendship, and Nel discovers that Sula has traveled and has been to college. Sula tells Nell about her decision to put Eva in the nursing home, then asks for Nel's help, because Sula is not good at making big decisions like this.

Nel's husband Jude is interested in Sula, and she in him; one day, Nel finds them in bed together. Jude, ashamed, leaves Nel, destroying her safe little world; she has lost her husband and her best friend in the same day. She thinks of Chicken Little's funeral and how everyone released their grief in mourning for him, but she is not able to find that kind of release for her grief over the loss of her husband.

1939

Sula ends her relationship with Jude, and he moves to Detroit and never comes back. The townspeople are shocked at Sula's behavior and—after a rumor goes around that Sula has slept with white men, "the unforgivable thing"—they decide that she's nothing but evil and trouble, and ostracize her. She becomes the scapegoat of the town, blamed for every bad thing that happens, including accidents and deaths. Despite this, or because of it, she also has a paradoxical good effect on the town; women comfort their husbands, who have been cast off from Sula after she sleeps with them, and take better care of their aging parents and grandparents, because they don't want to mirror Sula's treatment of Eva.

Sula begins seeing a man named Albert Jacks, or Ajax, who delivers milk to her house. He believes she's not interested in commitment, and neither is he; from his point of view, the relationship is only sexual. However, she begins to love him, and when he finds out, he decides to end the relationship. She is heartbroken and miserable.

1940

Three years later, Nel and Sula are still avoiding each other, but when Nel hears that Sula is sick, she visits her. Nervously, she practices what she wants to say, but Sula only wants action, not words: she directs Nel to get her some medicine. When she returns, they have a combative conversation in which Nel is annoyed by what she sees as Sula's arrogance about life. Nel accuses her of simply not dealing with her own loneliness, but Sula retorts that at least it's loneliness that she has chosen, not loneliness that has been forced on her by someone else leaving her (as Jude left Nel).

Nel becomes angry, but asks Sula why she had an affair with Jude. Sula says that she didn't love Jude, he simply filled a space in her life. Nel is shocked by this, and asks Sula if she ever thought about how it would hurt Nel. Sula tells Nel that she doesn't think sleeping with Jude should have broken up their friendship. Nel leaves, but not before Sula asks Nel how she knows she's the good one and Sula's the bad one; Sula says it could be the other way around.

Sula reflects on her life, and decides that it was a sad, worthless, and meaningless one. As she reflects, she realizes that she is not breathing and that her heart has stopped. She is dead, and didn't even feel her death. "Wait'll I tell Nel," she thinks.

1941

The townspeople are thrilled that Sula is dead, and believe that good omens indicate that more good changes are coming. The road contractors, getting ready to work on a tunnel, have announced they will hire African Americans, and a new nursing home is being built. However, all these signs come to nothing when a frigid spell keeps people inside, sickness increases, and the tunnel contractors don't hire many people after all. And without the threat of Sula as a catalyst, the townspeople turn to their old ways. Spouses are ignored, old people are neglected and children are beaten.

On January 3, Shadrack heads out for his annual celebration of Suicide Day. He thinks of Sula, the little girl who once came into his shack, the only visitor of his life, who is now dead. He is not really interested in running the Suicide Day celebration, but sets out anyway, ringing his bell. The townspeople are so demoralized by the recent hard times that many of them actually join him in the parade, needing an escape, and the procession eventually includes almost everyone in town. They turn toward the white part of town, toward the tunnel, "the place where their hope had lain since 1927." The mob begins smashing things, destroying the new construction. The tunnel collapses and great numbers of people are killed. Shadrack stands on a hill above, ringing his bell and watching the tragic event.

1965

Over twenty years later, Nel is fifty-five years old. She has spent her life taking care of her children, who are now grown, and who have forgotten her. She is alone, and the community of the Bottom has fallen apart; neighbors no longer take care of each other.

Nel, who still disapproves of Sula's putting Eva in the nursing home, visits Eva and finds her very confused. Eva talks about Chicken Little's death and accuses Nel of taking part in it. Nel tries to convince Eva that Sula, not Nel, caused his death, but Eva says, "What's the difference?" She understands that Nel was there, and that she and Sula were so close that they were like a single person, so the guilt cannot be separated and portioned out.

Nel leaves, feeling frightened, thinking about the difference between "seeing" something and "watching" it. She saw the accident; she did not watch it. Watching implies some sort of implicit participation, some sort of acquiescence. She remembers how upset and miserable Sula was after the accident, while she, Nel, was calm. She thinks about Eva and how she used to think the old woman was so wonderful; now, she thinks, Eva was spiteful, and remembers that she didn't even go to Sula's funeral. Nel thinks about this spite, which has infected the entire town. She thinks back to the funeral, where she was the only African American in attendance. As she walks away from the gravesite, she senses something that makes her think of Sula, and realizes that she misses Sula deeply, and that when she thought she was missing her husband Jude after he left, she was really missing Sula. With this realization, she finally releases the grief that she has held pent up inside her for years.

Characters

BoyBoy

BoyBoy is Eva Peace's husband, who gives her three children, Hannah, Eva (called Pearl), and Ralph (who is called Plum), then disappears. During the time they are together, he is largely preoccupied with other women and drinking, and is rarely home. When he leaves, Eva has "$1.65, five eggs, three beets and no idea of what or how to feel." He returns three years later with a new woman, apparently having heard of Eva's new wealth and seemingly hoping for a handout, but Eva doesn't give him anything, and he disappears again.

Chicken Little

Chicken Little is a small boy who comes to play with Sula and Nel at the river. Sula picks him up and swings him around, and accidentally throws him in the river, where he drowns. His body is found downstream by a white man, who is annoyed at having to deal with it, and after the bargeman, the sheriff, and a ferryman bicker over whose responsibility it is to return to the body to the child's family, it is finally taken to the embalmer four days later.

The Deweys

The Deweys are three little boys whom Eva takes in. Regardless of their original names, she calls them all "Dewey," last name "King," and they're collectively known as "The deweys." Although they look different from each other and come from different families, their individuality is gradually subsumed in their collective identity as "deweys," to the point where they never really grow up, and Morrison writes, "The deweys remained a mystery not only during all of their lives in Medallion but after as well."

Albert Jacks

A. Jacks, or "Ajax" as he's known to everyone, is "a twenty-one-year-old pool haunt of sinister beauty." He is a favorite among women and an accomplished swearer and curser. He advises Jude about women, "All they want, man, is they own misery. Ax them to die for you and they yours for life." Later, when he's thirty-eight and Sula is twenty-nine, they become lovers. She falls in love with him, but Ajax, feeling trapped, leaves her.

Eva Peace

Although Eva is Sula's grandmother, she outlives her granddaughter, and is present during all the events of the novel. She leaves her mark on Sula, helping to shape her character.

Eva is abandoned by her husband while she is still a young mother, and, faced with the problem of supporting her family without resorting to charity, she leaves her children with a friend, saying she'll be gone overnight. She returns eighteen months later on crutches, with one leg missing, but then begins receiving a series of regular checks in the mail. Although she is mysterious about what happened to her leg, the other characters assume that she allowed a train to run over it and cut it off so that she could collect the insurance money. She doesn't let her lack of a leg interfere with her enjoyment of life, or her enjoyment of men; she is famed for her gentlemen callers—although she never makes love with them—and for the fact that her remaining leg, still shapely, is "stockinged and shod at all times." She lives in a huge, rambling house with many rooms and passageways, takes in boarders—some paying, some not—and spends most of her time high up in the house, watching over the assortment of people in it. These include three boys, all of whom she has named "Dewey."

Everyone in the community admires Eva, despite her nontraditional life. Sula is the one person who does not admire her, however, and when Eva jumps from the second story of the house in order to save Hannah, Sula's mother, who is burning to death, Sula doesn't help either her mother or her grandmother. Later, Sula puts Eva in a nursing home.

Eva is a tough woman, a survivor, who is often brutally honest. Near the end of the book, she is visited by Sula's friend Nel, and reminds Nel that Nel, like Sula, was involved in Chicken Little's death; in the end, she forces Nel to contemplate about her and Sula's likeness.

Eva Peace II

Eva, known as Pearl, is Hannah's sister and Sula's aunt. She marries at fourteen, moves to Flint, Michigan, and writes occasional sad letters to her mother about minor troubles.

Hannah Peace

Hannah is Sula's mother. She married "a laughing man named Rekus" who died when Sula was three; after this, Hannah moves back into Eva Peace's big house, "prepared to take care of it and her mother forever." Like Eva, Hannah loves men, and has a steady stream of lovers, most of whom are married to her friends or neighbors. However, despite her promiscuity, she is leery of trusting anyone or becoming committed to anyone. Hannah is disliked by the "good" women in town, who find her morally reprehensible; by the prostitutes, who resent her for cutting into their business by giving her services away; and also by the "middling women" who have both husbands and affairs, because her lack of passion about her affairs seems strange and alien to them. Hannah is similarly detached from her own daughter, Sula; she loves Sula, but says she doesn't like her.

Ralph Peace

Ralph, known as Plum, is Eva's youngest child, and the one "to whom she hoped to bequeath everything." He goes off to fight in World War I and, like Shadrack, comes home damaged; he has become a heroin addict. When he finally returns to Medallion, his hair is uncombed and uncut, his clothes are dirty, and he is not wearing socks. "But he did have a black bag, a paper sack, and a sweet, sweet smile." He moves back into Eva's house, where he seldom eats or talks to anyone. When Eva realizes that he is an addict, she pours kerosene over him, sets him on fire, and kills him. High on the drug, Plum is unaware of what she's doing.

Sula Peace

Toni Morrison wrote in the *Michigan Quarterly Review*,

> I always thought of Sula as quintessentially black, metaphysically black, if you will, which is not melanin and certainly not unquestioning fidelity to the tribe. She is new world black and new world woman extracting choice from choicelessness, responding intuitively to found things. Improvisational. Daring, disruptive, imaginative, modern, out-of-the-house, outlawed, unpolicing, uncontained and uncontainable. And dangerously female.

Sula, as Morrison notes, is a dark character, not simply because of the color of her skin, but in terms of her soul. She is a strange child, defiant and different from other children. Although this difference seems innate in her, it is exacerbated by two occurrences in her childhood: one when she overhears her mother saying she loves Sula, but doesn't like her, and another when she is inadvertently responsible for the death of a little boy called Chicken Little. As a result of these events, Sula feels unloved and burdened by guilt.

Sula's mother, Hannah, values her independence from others, and Sula follows in her footsteps. The two times that she has a relationship and violates her rule of separateness, she is devastated. She falls in love once, with Ajax, and becomes so obsessed with him that he's frightened away, leaving her miserable.

More long-lasting is Sula's relationship with her best friend, Nel, who is from a very different background and has a very different personality. The two balance each other, and Sula is deeply attached to Nel. After Nel's wedding to a man named Jude, she leaves her hometown of Medallion for ten years. When she comes back, she's changed: she now has a college education and wears expensive clothes. These changes only make the townspeople, who have always regarded her as strange, feel even more alienated from her, to the point where whenever anything bad happens in the town, Sula is blamed.

She also puts her grandmother, Eva, in a nursing home, leading the town to further reject her. A year later, she is very sick with an unspecified but very painful illness. On her deathbed, she thinks about her alienation from all the people she's known: "The deweys, Tar Baby, the newly married couples, Mr. Buckland Reed, Patsy, Valentine, and the beautiful Hannah Peace. Where were they?" She has lost track of them all, and now she lies alone, "upstairs in Eva's bed with a boarded-up window and an empty pocketbook on the dresser." Even Nel, who has visited her and gotten a painkiller for her, has left and closed the door. Sula thinks about Nel:

> So she will walk on down that road, her back so straight in that old green coat, the strap of her handbag pushed back all the way to the elbow, thinking how much I have cost her and never remember the days when we were two throats and one eye and we had no price.

She feels that their old, deep kinship is gone, like her connections to the other people she remembers.

She also thinks of life with a sense of futility: "Nothing was ever different. They were all the same. All of the words and all of the smiles, every tear and every gag just something to do." And in the end, just before she dies, she is comforted by the boarded-up window that Eva jumped out of: "The sealed window soothed her with its sturdy termination, its unassailable finality. It was as though for the first time she was completely alone—where she had always wanted to be—free of the possibility of distraction."

However, after she dies, the first thing she thinks is, "It didn't even hurt. Wait'll I tell Nel," showing that despite her feeling of alienation, their friendship is deeper than she realized, continuing on past death.

On her deathbed, she thinks about her mother's comments about her, and about Chicken Little's death, and decides that she has lived a meaningless life.

Later in the book, when her mother's dress catches on fire, Sula watches with calm detachment as her mother is fatally burned. Although some of Eva's friends later rationalize her calm watching as the result of being "struck dumb" with shock, Eva "remained convinced that Sula had watched Hannah burn not because she was paralyzed, but because she was interested."

Pearl
See Eva Peace II

Plum
See Ralph Peace

Cecile Sabat
Cecile is Helene Sabat Wright's grandmother. She takes Helene away from her prostitute mother and raises her in a strict Catholic household.

Rochelle Sabat
Rochelle is Helene's mother. She sees Helene for the first time in sixteen years when Helene's grandmother, Cecile, dies and Helene returns to New Orleans for the funeral. The two look at each other with no recognition or warmth, and similarly, Rochelle is not warm to Nel, her own granddaughter. She is still vibrant and young-looking, and wears a canary-yellow dress and fragrant perfume. Nel is fascinated by her, but Helene is only too eager to get back to Medallion; she has made a break with her past, and she refuses to speak Creole, as Rochelle does, or to teach it to Nel.

Shadrack
Shadrack is shell-shocked from his participation in World War I, and after being released from a veteran's hospital, is arrested by police who assume he's drunk, then released. He drinks to medicate his mental turmoil, and lives in a shack near the river. He is famous in the Bottom as the inventor of "National Suicide Day," which he celebrates every January 3rd, leading a parade through town that most people avoid. Despite this, the holiday becomes part of the town's consciousness, so that people will date events by whether they occurred after or before a particular Suicide Day.

The only person who ever enters Shadrack's cabin is Sula, who runs there to see if Shadrack has seen her accidentally throw Chicken Little into the river and drown him. Shadrack doesn't give her a chance to ask her question, and simply says "always," which Sula perceives as a threat. However, because she is the only person who has ever visited him, Shadrack views her as his friend for the rest of his life. She has no idea that her life has given a sense of love and meaning to Shadrack. After Sula dies, he loses interest in his invented holiday, "National Suicide Day," and has to force himself to go, but the townspeople, who are depressed from the sudden downward turn of events following Sula's death, eagerly join the parade. The ensuing mob heads toward a half-finished tunnel that is being built mostly by white people, and, filled with hatred for the whites, they begin destroying it. They do so much damage that the tunnel caves in, killing the people inside it, while Shadrack stands on a hill above this scene of mass destruction (and inadvertent mass suicide) ringing a bell.

Tar Baby

Tar Baby is one of the boarders in Eva's house, "a beautiful, slight, quiet man who never spoke above a whisper." Most people think he is half-white, but Eva thinks he is totally white, and calls him Tar Baby as a joke. He lives simply, and when he loses his job, he scrounges around for odd jobs, buys liquor, and comes home to drink, but he is no trouble to anyone. Eventually it becomes clear that he simply wants a place to die, privately, but not entirely alone.

Helene Wright

Helene Sabat, born in a brothel in New Orleans to a Creole prostitute, was taken away from her original home as a baby, and raised by her grandmother, who told her to be on guard for any evidence of her mother's "wild blood" and brought her up in a strict Catholic household. Helene marries Wiley Wright, and despite his frequent and long absences, is delighted when she has a daughter, Nel, whom she raises as strictly as her grandmother raised her; however, because there is no Catholic church in Medallion, she joins the most conservative black church instead. Helene is famed in Medallion as an impressive, upstanding woman, a pillar of her church. The only battle she loses is over her name; the townspeople, who refuse to say "Helene," simply call her "Helen."

Nel Wright

An only child, Nel is brought up in a strict, quiet, orderly house, but she longs for excitement, variety, and adventure. She finds them in the company of Sula, her best friend. Although Nel has been brought up in a strict and orderly household— or because of her upbringing there—she hates the "oppressive neatness" of her mother's house and loves "Sula's woolly house," where something is always cooking on the stove, Sula's mother never scolds or tells her what to do, there's a constant chaos of people stopping in, and where one-legged Eva presides, handing out peanuts and telling her dreams.

The two of them are inseparable, each finding something in the other to fill a hole in her own life. Morrison writes that Nel's parents "had succeeded

in rubbing down to a dull glow any sparkle or splutter she had." Only with Sula did that quality have free reign, but their friendship was so close, they themselves had difficulty distinguishing one's thoughts from the other's. They are also bound together at a young age by their shared knowledge of exactly how Chicken Little drowned.

Eva grows up to be a traditional, quiet, "good" woman; she has a big wedding, to her mother's delight, has three children, and plans to have a quiet, orderly life. This plan is destroyed when she finds her husband and Sula having an affair.

When Sula is dying, Nel visits her for the first time in three years, since Sula's affair with Jude. They are uneasy with each other but pick up the relationship where it left off. Nel tells Sula she should be with someone who can take care of her, but Sula refuses. Nel is also offended by Sula's arrogant talk about how she doesn't need any man, never would have worked for anyone else, and doesn't need anyone now. She asks Sula why she had an affair with Jude, and Sula says it was just because Jude filled up a space in her life; Nel is hurt that she, as Sula's friend, didn't count to fill up any space. She can't get a straight answer from Sula about what their friendship meant to Sula, and realizes, "She can't give a sensible answer because she didn't know." The last thing Sula asks her is, "About who was good. How did you know it was you?" calling into question her identity as a "good" girl and a "good" woman. After Sula dies, however, the first thing Sula thinks is "Wait'll I tell Nel," showing that their friendship has endured past these difficulties, past death.

Themes

Poverty and Hopelessness

Throughout the novel, the lives of the characters are shaped by poverty, as they have little or no money, unlike many of their white counterparts in the town. Although no one in the book is rich, the people of the Bottom are exceptionally poor. Eva has money only because she sacrificed her leg; others must make do as they can, with menial jobs or no jobs, because work for African Americans is limited by the racism of those who could hire them. When characters have dreams, like Jude, who dreams of doing a man's work on the road crew instead of spending a menial day as a waiter, they are crushed.

Topics for Further Study

- Research the Jim Crow laws and describe how they affected every area of life for African Americans.

- Find out about the Civil Rights movements of the 1960s and discuss their effectiveness. What issues do you think still need to be addressed to ensure equality among different groups of people?

- Research the contributions of African-American soldiers in World War I or World War II. Choose a particular soldier and write about his life before, during, and after the war.

- How do you feel racism affects you? Write an essay about your experiences.

- In the book, relationships between mothers and daughters are difficult and painful. Do you think this is the case for most mothers and daughters? Why or why not?

- Choose a character from the book and write a story about his or her experiences during a period that is not covered in the book. For example, write about Sula's life during her ten years away from Medallion, or Shadrack's life during the war.

Existence in the Bottom is precarious at best, and is easily disrupted. Near the end of the book, people's hopes are raised by rumors that the new tunnel construction would use African-American laborers, and by the fact that an old people's home that was being renovated would be open to African Americans. However, these hopes are forgotten when a freezing rain kills all the late crops, kills chickens, splits jugs of cider, and makes the "thin houses and thinner clothes" of the Bottom people seem even thinner. Housebound, they make do with what they have, since deliveries have stopped and the good food is all being saved for white customers anyway. Thanksgiving that year is a meal of "tiny tough birds, heavy pork cakes, and pithy sweet potatoes." By spring all the children are sick and the adults are suffering from a variety of ailments.

All this suffering and malaise is accompanied by "a falling away, a dislocation." Mothers slap their children and resent the old people they have to take care of, wives and husbands become alienated from each other, and people begin bickering about small things. Christmas that year is a misery because of the sickness, lack of good food, and absence of money for gifts. The only gifts they can get are bags of rock candy and old clothes, given away by white people.

This feeling of doom and hopelessness leads almost everyone in town to participate in that year's celebration of National Suicide Day, with a feeling of reckless abandon at the idea of "looking at death in the sunshine and being unafraid," as well as the feeling of "this respite from anxiety, from dignity, from gravity, from the weight of the very adult pain that had undergirded them all those years before ... as though there really was hope." This is the same hope that has kept them laboring in white men's beanfields in hopes of bettering themselves, fighting in other people's wars, kept them solicitous of white people's children, "kept them convinced that some magic 'government' was going to lift them up, out and away from that dirt, those beans, those wars." In other words, it's a futile and misguided hope.

Caught up in the energy of the moment, seeking release, the crowd of people pours on down the New River Road toward the tunnel, where they see "the place where their hope had lain since 1927. There was the promise: leaf-dead. The teeth unrepaired, the coal credit cut off, the chest pains unattended, the school shoes unbought, the rush-stuffed mattresses ... the slurred remarks and the staggering childish malevolence of their employers." They try to destroy the tunnel, but in their desire to destroy it, they enter it and ultimately destroy themselves when the tunnel collapses under their attack.

Good and Evil

A major theme running through the book is good versus evil, and the fact that what people think is evil may be good, and vice versa. Shadrack, who appears in the first chapter, is considered dangerous and evil by the townspeople, and when he says "Always" to Sula, she takes it as a threat. However, he is not evil, he is simply shell-shocked and misunderstood; throughout the book, he never harms anyone. Sula is also considered evil, especially in the second half of the book, and Nel is considered good, but by the end of the book, Nel realizes that she has evil thoughts and has done evil things, while Sula has inspired the most good acts that the town has ever seen.

Eva, Sula's grandmother, is considered good, respectable, and a pillar of the community, but actually has a darker side. Her ruthlessness is hinted at by the rumor that she arranged to have own her leg cut off, a scene that is reflected by Sula when she cuts off the tip of her own finger to frighten off some harassing white boys. If she's able to do that to herself, she tells them, they should just think about what she'd be able to do to them. Sula's minor act of self-mutilation pales in comparison with Eva's, and the unspoken question the book asks is, "If she's able to do that to herself, what would she be willing to do to someone else?" The answer is, "Anything and everything," including killing her own son by pouring kerosene over him and setting him on fire while he's in a drug-induced haze.

Racism

The novel explores the relationship between the races, which is marred by racism and bigotry. In the opening scene, the founding of the Bottom is described; according to local legend, the area became the property of African Americans when a white man deceived a slave into thinking the high, dry, and eroded land was good for farming because it was the "bottom" of heaven. When Chicken Little is drowned, his body is found by a white man, who has no compassion for the dead child or his family, but who is merely annoyed at having to deal with the mess. On the train south, Helene and Nel experience degrading treatment at the hands of the white conductor and the white-run train system, which does not provide restrooms for African Americans. When Jude tries to get a job with the road-building crew, he is denied one, although the company hires scrawny whites who obviously can't do as good a job as he can; he can only get a job as a waiter, which he feels is servile and degrading. When Sula returns to town after a ten-year absence, her erratic behavior causes the townspeople to spread rumors about her causing all of their misfortunes, and the most damning rumor about her is that she willingly sleeps with white men.

Mothers and Daughters

Throughout the book, the many mother-daughter pairs have strained, unhappy relationships, and the lack of love a mother has for her daughter is passed on through the generations. In Nel's family, her grandmother, Cecile, disapproved of Rochelle, her prostitute daughter, and took Helene, Rochelle's daughter, away from Rochelle. Rochelle and Helene don't even know each other and are as alienated as Rochelle was from her mother. Nel, Helene's daughter, who is similarly alienated from Nel, feels oppressed by her mother's strictness and propriety, and feels stifled in her quiet, orderly house.

Eva, Hannah's mother, is an outwardly upstanding and secretly ruthless woman, and it's clear that her daughter, Hannah, didn't feel loved by her. At one point, she even asks Eva if she loved her children, a question that makes Eva angry. Hannah is also ambivalent about her daughter, Sula; Sula overhears her telling some friends that although she loves Sula, she doesn't like her, a comment that deeply wounds Sula. Because of this, Sula grows up feeling unloved and left out.

Style

Point of View

The novel is told from the point of view of a wise, omniscient narrator, who sees into all the characters' hearts and minds with tolerance and acceptance. The use of such a narrator is interesting; the characters are all given equal time, and no one, even Sula—for whom the book is named—is more major than anyone else. In addition, the use of varied points of view allows the reader to see all the sides of any event and understand the complexity of what really happened. In the book, horrendous events are depicted, but the narrator avoids making judgments about them; they are simply presented, and the reader sees various characters respond to them and is allowed to come to an independent determination of what these things mean and whether they are good or evil.

Realistic Dialogue

The author frequently uses dialect speech, bringing the characters to life and letting the reader hear them talk, in a very natural way. For example, in the following dialogue between Eva and Hannah, Hannah has just asked Eva if she loved her children and played with them when they were little, and Eva deflects the question by telling her about the hard times she went through:

> "I'm talkin' 'bout 18 and 95 when I set in that house five days with you and Pearl and Plum and three beets, you snake-eyed ungrateful hussy. What would I look like leapin' 'round that little old room playin' with youngins with three beets to my name?"

"I know 'bout them beets, Mamma. You told us that a million times."

"Yeah? Well? Don't that count? Ain't that love? You want me to tinkle you under the jaw and forget 'bout them sores in your mouth?"

By using dialect speech, Morrison allows us to hear the characters as real people, and shows their social class, education, and attitudes without having to explicitly discuss these aspects. We know from their talk that the characters are African American, poor, and most likely rural. They express themselves directly, with no social posturing or pretension; their speech is vigorous and active, full of energy and passion.

Although white people rarely appear in the novel, when they do, they also speak in dialect. In the case of the conductor on the train to the south, it's southern: he asks Helene, "What was you doin' back in there? What was you doin' in that coach yonder?" When she tells him she made a mistake and got in the white car by accident, he says, "We don't 'low no mistakes on this train. Now git your butt on in there." His dialect talk makes him seem uneducated and harsh at the same time that it underlines his similarity to the African Americans he despises, since the things he says, and the way he says them, could easily have been said by anyone in the Bottom in the same way. This similarity provides a subtle commentary on the misguided nature of racism, which erects artificial boundaries between people. He thinks he's "better" than the people in the "colored" car, but he is not as different from them as he'd like to believe.

Use of a Prologue

Sula, like many other novels, but unlike any of Morrison's other works, has a prologue that describes the Bottom and its origin, and makes the reader aware that this is a book about African-American people, set in an African-American settlement. In a discussion about the book in the *Michigan Quarterly Review*, Morrison noted that her original beginning simply began, "Except for World War II nothing ever interfered with National Suicide Day." After getting some feedback about the book from others, she realized that this was too sudden a beginning, and that it didn't make clear to the reader where the book was set or what was going on. She thought of the prologue as a "safe, welcoming lobby," and believed it was necessary to make readers comfortable in her African-American world before they could move on with the story. She said that she would not need this "lobby" now, and indeed, none of her other books have this

"lobby"; they refuse, she said, "to cater to the diminished expectations of the reader or his or her alarm heightened by the emotional luggage one carries into the black-topic text." She also said, "I despise much of this beginning," and noted that her other books "refuse the 'presentation'; refuse the seductive safe harbor; the line of demarcation between . . . them and us."

Historical Context

The events in *Sula* span much of the twentieth century, during a time of great changes in civil rights for African Americans and other minority groups.

African Americans in World War I

When the events of the book open, in 1919, veterans like Shadrack and Plum are returning from service overseas. Like Shadrack and Plum, many of them were emotionally and physically scarred from the experience of war, but African-American veterans did not receive as much respect for their service as their white counterparts. In the book, Shadrack is discharged from the hospital because there's no more room, and when he hits the streets, whites assume he's drunk, and he's arrested and taken to jail. All he has to show for his service is "$217 in cash, a full suit of clothes and copies of very official-looking papers."

During the war, more than 350,000 African-American soldiers served in segregated units. When they returned, many began working for civil rights, reasoning that if they were considered good enough to fight and risk their lives for their country, they should be given full participation in society. Both African Americans and whites joined the newly formed NAACP to fight discrimination and segregation, but it would be many years before segregation laws would be overturned.

African Americans had only recently been given the right to vote in the United States. Although they had supposedly held this right for much longer, various loopholes in the law ensured that few did. One law stated that an African-American man could vote only if his grandfather had. Poll taxes, literacy tests, voting fraud, violence against those who voted, and intimidation also kept people away from the ballot box. The NAACP fought successfully against the "grandfather clause," and it was overturned in 1915, but some of the other blocks to voting remained for many years.

Compare
&
Contrast

- **1920s:** More than 350,000 African-American soldiers, who serve in segregated units, return home from World War I.

  Today: The United States armed forces include large numbers of African Americans, who serve in every capacity and are no longer segregated; some African Americans, such as General Colin Powell, U.S. Secretary of State during the administration of George W. Bush, achieve the highest rank.

- **1920s:** Overall, the unemployment rate is about 5.2%, but this figure is much higher for African Americans because of prejudice against them.

  Today: Unemployment ranges between 5 and 6 percent and African Americans are integrated into all sectors of society, thought they still experience a higher level of unemployment than whites.

- **1920s:** "Jim Crow" laws, which were implemented in the late nineteenth century, segregate the South, mandating separate spheres of existence for African Americans and whites. Restaurants, stores, buses, hotels, transportation, housing, and other areas of life are rigidly separated, and African Americans who cross the barriers can be arrested and imprisoned.

  Today: The widespread and growing civil rights movement brings increasing attention to the problems caused by discrimination and segregation. Although old laws restricting African Americans from voting and full participation in society were finally overturned in the 1960s, racism, bigotry, and other prejudices still exist and act to restrict full participation for many people.

The Great Depression

In 1929, the stock market crashed, leading to widespread depression and deep poverty. Skilled and unskilled, African-American and white, few people escaped the suffering involved. When Franklin Delano Roosevelt was elected in 1932, he presented "New Deal" programs that would help housing, agriculture, and economic interests. Although African Americans had fewer opportunities than whites to benefit from the New Deal programs, they did participate in some of them.

Segregation

Through laws known as "Jim Crow" laws, Southern states were forcefully segregated, with separate facilities for travel, overnight lodging, eating, drinking, school, church, housing, and other services for African Americans and whites. These facilities were separate, and many times not equal; those for African Americans were frequently substandard or nonexistent. If an African American failed to obey the segregation laws, he or she could be arrested and imprisoned.

World War II and the Civil Rights Movement

Many African Americans served in World War II, and like those who served in World War I, returned home and were outraged that they could serve their country but yet not have equal rights in it. The civil rights movement grew with protests, nonviolent resistance, boycotts, and rallies, which received increasing attention in the national media. In addition, activists challenged the segregation laws in court. In 1948, President Harry Truman eliminated segregation in the United States armed forces. Through other battles, segregation in other areas of life, such as on buses and in schools, was attacked and outlawed, although racist incidents continued to cause trouble for African Americans, and other areas of life were not yet integrated.

In 1963, more than 200,000 people joined the March on Washington, calling national attention to the problems of segregation and discrimination. Dr. Martin Luther King, Jr. delivered his famed "I Have a Dream" speech, calling for racial equality.

In 1965, the Voting Rights Act finally outlawed the use of literacy tests and other methods to exclude African Americans from voting. Before this law, only about twenty-three percent of African Americans were registered to vote, but after it, registration jumped to sixty-one percent.

The Civil Rights Act of 1968, known as the Fair Housing Act, more forcefully ensured that African Americans were legally entitled to all the rights that went with full citizenship in the United States.

Critical Overview

As Paul Gray noted in *Time*, some reviewers have found Morrison's work "overly deterministic, her characters pawns in the service of their creator's designs." He quoted essayist Stanley Crouch, who commented that Morrison was "immensely talented. I just think she needs a new subject matter, the world she lives in, not this world of endless black victims." However, Gray also noted: "For every pan, Morrison has received a surfeit of paeans: for her lyricism, for her ability to turn the mundane into the magical."

In the *New York Times Book Review*, Sara Blackburn commented that *Sula* was "a more precise yet somehow icy version of [Morrison's first novel] *The Bluest Eye*," and that "it refuses to invade our present in the way we want it to and stays, instead, confined to its time and place." Although, as Blackburn noted, Morrison's dialogue is "so compressed and lifelike that it sizzles" and her characterization is so skillful that the people in the book "seem almost mythologically strong and familiar," somehow "we can't imagine their surviving outside the tiny community where they carry on their separate lives." Because of this, she wrote, the novel's "long-range impact doesn't sustain the quality of its first reading." Blackburn also commented that Morrison was too talented to continue writing about "the black side of provincial American life" and that if she wanted to maintain a "large and serious audience," she would have to address a "riskier contemporary reality."

In addition, interestingly, Blackburn confessed that she, like other reviewers, might have given Morrison's first novel, *The Bluest Eye*, more attention than it might have deserved. "Socially conscious readers—including myself—were so pleased to see a new writer of Morrison's obvious talent that we tended to celebrate the book and ignore its flaws." Presumably, she did not do this for *Sula*.

In the *Journal of Black Studies*, Marie Nigro wrote that the book is "an unforgettable story of the friendship of two African-American woman and . . . graciously allowed us to enter the community of the Bottom." By writing the book, Morrison "has given us an understanding of social, psychological, and sociological issues that might have been evident only to African Americans."

Jane S. Bakerman, in *American Literature*, wrote that "Morrison has undertaken a difficult task in *Sula*. Unquestionably, she has succeeded." She also praised Morrison's use of the tale of Sula and Nel's maturation as a core for the many other stories in the book, and said that as the main unifying device of the novel, "It achieves its own unity, again, through the clever manipulation of the themes of sex, race, and love."

In *Black Women Writers: A Critical Evaluation*, Darwin T. Turner praised Morrison's "verbal descriptions that carry the reader deep into the soul of the character. . . . Equally effective, however, is her art of narrating action in a lean prose that uses adjectives cautiously while creating memorable vivid images."

Jonathan Yardley, in the *Washington Post Book World*, noted that a chief distinction of the novel is "the quality of Toni Morrison's prose . . . [The book's] real strength lies in Morrison's writing, which at times has the resonance of poetry and is precise, vivid and controlled throughout."

In the *Harvard Advocate*, Faith Davis wrote that a "beautiful and haunting atmosphere emerges out of the wreck of these folks' lives, a quality that is absolutely convincing and absolutely precise."

The novel was nominated for a National Book Award in 1974, but did not win.

Criticism

Kelly Winters

Winters is a freelance writer and has written for a wide variety of educational publishers. In the following essay, she discusses mother-and-daughter relationships, and their effect on Sula and Nel's relationship, in Sula.

A prevalent theme in *Sula* is the influence of family and friends on the characters. The book focuses on two friends, Sula and Nel, but both have

African-American soldiers returning home from Europe after World War I

been shaped, and continue to be shaped, by their experiences with their families, particularly their mothers. Their mothers, in turn, have been shaped by their own mothers, in a chain reaction passing through the generations.

Eva, who has endured desperate and lonely poverty, is a strong, tough woman. She is also proud; she thinks of going back to her family in Virginia for help when her man leaves and she has no food, but as the narrator notes, "To come home dragging three young ones would have to be a step one rung before death for Eva." Instead, she scrounges as best she can for several months, and then heads out, either selling her leg to science or having it cut off in an "accident," for which she receives $10,000 in insurance payments.

This act indicates a certain ruthlessness in her character, and Eva is ruthlessly controlling, adopting three boys and giving them the same name, "Dewey," and treating them as a unit. The emotionally stunting effect of this treatment is plain; the boys eventually become so unindividuated that even their own mothers can't tell them apart, and they never grow, physically or mentally, but remain under Eva's sway.

When her son Plum returns from the war with a drug addiction, Eva pours kerosene over him and kills him by setting him on fire. She rationalizes this by saying that he would have lived a pathetic life, not the life of a man, so it was better for him to be dead.

Hannah, perhaps because she witnesses this event, gets up the courage to ask Eva if she ever loved any of her children. She feels unloved because Eva never played with them or said kind words to them. Eva defends her actions by saying there wasn't time for play and soft talk, that she was so busy just trying to get them food to eat that the notion of "play" was ridiculous, but it's clear that she's defensive, and the fact that she never actually answers the question shows that she's unable to answer "Yes."

When Hannah's dress catches fire while she's canning, Eva jumps out the window in an attempt to save her, showing that deep down, she does love her daughter. But Hannah's questioning of her mother, and her lifelong feeling of being unloved, shows that a certain amount of warmth was lacking in their relationship.

Although Hannah loves to spend time with men and has many boyfriends, she is never emotionally close to any of them; this is a legacy from Eva, who has the same temperament. Hannah passes this lack of warmth on to her daughter, Sula.

> The book could easily be titled *Sula and Nel*, because it focuses on the lifelong relationship between the two women, the most important relationship either of them ever has, superseding those with their mothers and the men in their lives."

Sula overhears her mother's friend discussing her daughter: "Well, Hester grown now and I can't say love is exactly what I feel."

Hannah says, "Sure you do. You love her, like I love Sula. I just don't like her. That's the difference."

To a child, however, there is no difference, and this comment sears itself into Sula's consciousness, filling her with a sense of her own unlovable nature and destroying her sense of trust. She has become just like Hannah and Eva, hardened and wary, and throughout the book, she remains detached from other people, as her mother always has. Although she has many relationships with men, she refuses to commit to any of them or to become emotionally vulnerable. She believes she doesn't need anyone else to be happy, and when she finally does fall in love with Ajax, her need for commitment scares him away, hurting her deeply. When she dies, she talks bitterly about the lack of love in the world, and in her life, reflecting on her experience with her mother.

Cecile, who lives in New Orleans, took her daughter Rochelle's baby daughter away from her as soon as she was born. Cecile didn't approve of Rochelle because she was a prostitute, and brought up the girl, Helene, in a strict Catholic atmosphere:

> The grandmother took Helene away from the soft lights and flowered carpets of the Sundown House and raised her under the dolesome eyes of a multi-colored Virgin Mary, counseling her to be on guard for any sign of her mother's wild blood.

Morrison doesn't discuss Cecile's reaction to this, but it's evident that mother and daughter did not have a close relationship, and that the daughter has remained bitter and closed because of it.

This lack of closeness continues between Rochelle and Helene. When Helene goes back to New Orleans after her grandmother dies, she meets her mother for the first time in many years; although Morrison doesn't make this clear, it may be for the first time since Helene was an infant. "The two looked at each other," Morrison writes. "There was no recognition in the eyes of either." Then Helene said, "This is your ... grandmother, Nel." The only conversation between Rochelle and Helene occurs when Rochelle asks Helene about Nel: "That your only one?" They have a stiff, chilly conversation about what will be done with the house, and when Rochelle speaks Creole, Helene tells Nel severely, "I don't talk Creole. And neither do you," thus denying her past, and her connection to her mother. When Nel says of Rochelle, "She smelled so nice. And her skin was so soft." Helene says scornfully, "Much handled things are always soft," referring to her mother's life as a prostitute.

Helene brings up Nel in a strict, religious, and emotionally chilly home. "Under Helene's hand the girl became obedient and polite. Any enthusiasms that little Nel showed were calmed by the mother until she drove her daughter's imagination underground," the narrator states, and gives readers a picture of Nel's life: "Nel, an only child, sat on the steps of her back porch surrounded by the high silence of her mother's incredibly orderly house, feeling the neatness pointing at her back ..." Nel longs for excitement, variety, and passion, but her mother doesn't foster any of these.

Because of her strict upbringing, Nel is attracted to Sula's wild, disorderly house, and Sula is equally attracted to Nel's quiet, calm qualities. "Their friendship was as intense as it was sudden," Morrison writes. Throughout the book, she makes it clear that each girl finds completion in the other; they are opposites, but they fit together and make a whole. Each is only a partial person without the other, and as girls, they're inseparable, perhaps finding in each other the warmth, support, and reassurance they didn't get from their families.

The book could easily be titled *Sula and Nel*, because it focuses on the relationship between the two women, the most important relationship either of them ever has, superseding those with their mothers and the men in their lives. Although they are very close as children, when they grow up they each feel betrayal from the other—Sula has an affair with Nel's husband Jude, forcing the end of the marriage, and when Nel gets angry and possessive about her husband and the affair, Sula feels betrayed. She had counted on Nel. Morrison writes, "Nel was the one person who had wanted nothing from her, who had accepted all aspects of her. Now she wanted everything, and all because of *that*," meaning marriage. From being a free and accepting friend, Nel has become one of "them," the traditional, possessive, small-minded and limited women of the town, according to Sula's view. This "surprised her a little and saddened her a good deal," because she had thought Nel was different.

Throughout most of the book, Sula is viewed by the other characters as evil, and Nel is seen as good. However, by the time Sula dies, their positions have become reversed. Nel visits Sula on her deathbed out of a feeling of duty—not out of true friendship or love—and feels virtuous about doing so. Sula, however, tells Nel that she may not be as good as she thinks she is. She plants a small seed of doubt in Nel's mind when she asks Nel, "How you know?" Nel responds, "Know what?" Sula says, "About who was good. How you know it was you?" Nel asks, "What you mean?" Sula responds, "I mean maybe it wasn't you [who was good]. Maybe it was me."

Soon after Sula's death, Nel goes to visit Eve, who is in a nursing home. Perhaps senile, perhaps clairvoyant, Eve looks at her and says, "Tell me how you killed that little boy," asking about Chicken Little. Nel says Sula was the one who threw him in the water, and Eve says, "You, Sula. What's the difference? You was there. You watched."

Nel thinks about her response to the accident. She was calm; Sula was distraught. Sula had sought help; Nel had said, "Come on, let's go." She realizes, when Chicken Little's hands slipped and he flew out into the water, she had a "good feeling." "Why didn't I feel bad when it happened?" she wonders. "How come it felt so good to see him fall?" She realizes that she is far more evil than Sula, that what she had told herself was maturity and compassion was "only the tranquility that follows a joyful stimulation"—in this case, the thrill of his death.

Nel realizes that she was even closer to Sula than she thought, more like her than she ever thought, and that her relationship with Sula was more important than any other; that it was more

What Do I Read Next?

- Morrison's *Beloved* (1987), written in an episodic, experimental style, examines the heritage of slavery.

- Morrison's first novel, *The Bluest Eye* (1970), stars Pecola, who prays each night for blue eyes, hoping that if she gets them she will finally be noticed and loved.

- Morrison's *Jazz* (1992) tells the story of a triangle of passion, jealousy, murder, and redemption.

- In *Song of Solomon* (1977), Morrison tells the story of Macon Dead, an upper-middle-class African-American entrepreneur who tries to isolate his family from other African Americans in the neighborhood, and how this affects his son.

- *Tar Baby* (1981), by Morrison, describes a love affair between an African-American model and a white man.

- In *Playing in the Dark: Whiteness and the Literary Imagination* (1992), Morrison discusses the significance of African Americans in American literature.

- Alice Walker's *The Temple of My Familiar* (1989) intertwines the lives of many people from the United States, England, and Africa, and provides perspectives on the colonial African experience as well as the experiences of African Americans.

- In *The Color Purple* (1982), Alice Walker describes an abused woman's struggle for empowerment.

important than her marriage. At the end of the book, after Sula's funeral, she thinks about her feeling of sadness after her marriage broke up and says to herself, "All that time, all that time, I thought I was missing Jude," when in fact, she was missing Sula, and that now her life without her will be, as Morrison writes, "just circles and circles of sorrow." These circles reflect, and are an amplification of, her original sorrow over her relationship, or lack of a relationship, with her mother.

Source: Kelly Winters, Critical Essay on *Sula*, in *Novels for Students*, The Gale Group, 2002.

Patricia McKee

In the following essay, McKee discusses how Morrison uses physical space to represent "the placement of experience" within a context.

In *Sula*, spacing—that is, closing down or opening up distances between things and persons—has extraordinary urgency. Houses and bodies are the sites of hyperactive mechanisms of containment and expulsion working to effect identity and distinction: of inside and outside, of self and other. Spacing, moreover, becomes crucial to issues of representation and meaning in the Bottom, the place in Medallion, Ohio, in which most of the action of the novel occurs. Houston A. Baker Jr. has called attention to the importance of place in *Sula*: "What Morrison ultimately seeks in her coding of Afro-American PLACE is a writing of intimate, systematizing, and ordering black village values," he suggests. But although the manipulation of persons and things in space can produce a symbolic order, Morrison seems more concerned with the placement of experience that orderly representation misses.

Two places in the novel that indicate her concern to locate missing experience are "the place where Chicken Little sank" in the river and the place Eva Peace's missing leg once occupied, "the empty place on her left side." Neither of these is quite what one would expect a place to be, for neither is the present location of anything. Like the empty spaces in a symbolic order, these places mark an absence. But unlike the lacks and open spaces that in works of Faulkner and James are necessary to structures of meaning, the experience of missing in *Sula* is a particular, historical experience. Absence is not represented by the open spaces that characterize an expansive white consciousness; it is experienced in the preoccupations of a historical consciousness with what has been and might be.

Placing Absence

Missing takes time and takes place in *Sula*; particular persons and things are missed from particular places. Although "the closed place in the middle of the river" and the place where Eva's leg once was have nothing in them, they mark the absence of persons or parts of persons once present. Morrison thereby fills in spaces of a kind white culture identifies as empty. In *Sula*, this means converting such unoccupied spaces into places on the basis of previous occupants. Morrison locates missing persons and parts of persons in places they have formerly occupied.

Locating such occupants is one kind of preoccupation that occurs in the novel. A second kind of preoccupation, however, rather than locating missing occupants once present, places missing occupations, ones that never occurred at all. By this I mean that Morrison identifies both failed possessions of places and failed actions: various connections between occupants and their places that never took place. This second kind of preoccupation is a more absolute missing—that is, missing compounded by the prior as well as present absence of what is missed. It is nonetheless a historical experience, given characters whose past is one in which the overwhelming "meaning" of experience was negative.

Such a history is "missing" in that it is not composed of positive facts known and recorded. But it is a missing history in another sense too: as a history of missing, a history *made* by people's knowledge of what they would never become, places they would never hold, things they would never do. In the first kind of preoccupation, people are aware of something that once was present; in the second kind, people miss things that might have been but never were. Thus Morrison places both missed presences and missed absences in *Sula*.

If the experience of missing is historical and specific, it is not abstracted into a component of cultural experience, as was the case when James confronted what white Americans were missing in the nineteenth century. Rather than being abstracted, missing is embodied in *Sula*, as missing persons and missing parts of persons become the focus of meaning. Preoccupations with absence in *The Sound and the Fury*, partly because absence seems not to be experienced bodily, can be universalized into abstract elements of white male psychology. When Faulkner's Jason Compson misses the job he never had, that lack becomes a stable determinant of meaning in his life; it also becomes the means of identifying him with other white men. What the Compson men miss, repeated in form if not in content, becomes a means of relationship among them, providing consistency in their experience. Over time, the experience of missing, represented as lost causes, becomes a historical likeness too. Men make history by reproducing themselves in the imagery of lost causes.

But Morrison's characters in *Sula* are missing the means of production by which James's and Faulkner's white characters make history. Those characters can experience individual consciousness as a medium of cultural reproduction because they can assume the representative character of individual consciousness. Inner experience and cultural experience become exchangeable, through the projections and introjections by which cultural identity is produced and reproduced. Characters in *Sula* neither produce nor reproduce the kind of forms or the kind of spaces that give both consistency and diversity to white identity. What these characters recognize in themselves and in their community are inconsistencies: broken bodies, broken objects, broken relations between persons and between persons and things. This means that they are able to produce meaning and community only by keeping experience within strict bounds.

The experience of missing what never was in *Sula* is not only an experience of missed objects but an experience of missed relations, missed connections. Such missing is clearest near the end of the novel, in 1941, when many people die at the construction site of the proposed tunnel. What the people of the Bottom see when they look at this place is not only what is there but what might have been there and is not there: all the things denied or negated by the fact that black people were never hired to work there.

> Their hooded eyes swept over the place where their hope had lain since 1927. There was the promise: leaf-dead. The teeth unrepaired, the coal credit cut off, the chest pains unattended, the school shoes unbought, the rush-stuffed mattresses, the broken toilets, the leaning porches, the slurred remarks and the staggering childish malevolence of their employers. . . .
>
> Like antelopes they leaped over the little gate . . . and smashed the bricks they would never fire in yawning kilns, split the sacks of limestone they had not mixed or even been allowed to haul; tore the wire mesh, tipped over wheelbarrows and rolled forepoles down the bank.

The first "thing" located in this place is hope; the second is promise. Both these relations to things were once alive and are now dead. The construction site seems preoccupied by them, and with their deaths numerous other losses are remembered. The losses recalled are things that these people did not do, things that they lost, things that broke or fell apart, but things that might have been done, kept, and changed for the better. What is missed here are hope and promise and the changes in things which they represent but which never happened.

... although the manipulation of persons and things in space can produce a symbolic order, Morrison seems more concerned with the placement of experience that orderly representation misses."

When people turn to look at the objects actually present, these too are seen in terms of failed relations. The bricks, limestone, and wheelbarrows have been denied to the people of the Bottom as objects of their labor. What these people see, therefore, is not only the objects but also their own missing occupation with these objects: bricks not fired, limestone not mixed, wheelbarrows not used to haul. Characters' realization of what they are missing is a recognition both of lost objects and of missed relations to objects: the loss of hope, promise, repair, credit, attention, occupation. These relations are attachments of people and things that function as meaningful connections by occupying one with another. With neither their minds nor their bodies occupied in labor as a creative relation to the world, labor in which they might become means of production and change, these people are unable to use objects or themselves to form and reform the world around them.

The tunnel site, then, is preoccupied with absences. Missing absent attachments means a massive "displacement": people tear things apart, throw things around, and start a landslide that carries some of them to their deaths in the river and buries others in the tunnel. For most of their lives, therefore, these people do not allow themselves to recognize what they miss in this scene. The role of Sula in the Bottom is to take the place of the absences that preoccupy these people at the tunnel in 1941. What circulates through the community at the tunnel site are not images of self that reassure the self of consistency in and with others but losses that individuals recognize in their own and others' experience. This awareness of loss cannot enter into circulation except with destructive effects. To contain that circulation, missing is projected onto one person, whose identification with loss will keep it within bounds.

By identifying Sula as evil and rejecting her categorically, characters are able to keep their distance from absences they cannot afford to acknowledge. In this case, keeping order depends not on emptying space of occupants but on filling in spaces whose emptiness is unbearable. Sula, occupied with loss, takes the place of absences people cannot afford to miss. Morrison has said that she "wanted Sula to be missed by the reader. That's why she dies early." To miss Sula is to recognize her occupation in and of the Bottom: what she did there and how she was a necessary part of the place, not only as a presence but because she took the place of absence.

Placing Experience

Various characters in Sula create order through spacing practices that allow them to control loss. The first personal perspective Morrison narrates, however, is not the perspective of any character but instead an outsider's view of the Bottom. Not really even personal, this perspective belongs to a seemingly generic "valley man."

> If a valley man happened to have business up in those hills—collecting rent or insurance payments—he might see a dark woman in a flowered dress doing a bit of cakewalk, a bit of black bottom, a bit of "messing around" to the lively notes of a mouth organ.... The black people watching her would laugh and rub their knees, and it would be easy for the valley man to hear the laughter and not notice the adult pain that rested somewhere under the eyelids, somewhere under their head rags and soft felt hats, somewhere in the palm of the hand, somewhere behind the frayed lapels, somewhere in the sinew's curve. He'd have to stand in the back of Greater Saint Matthew's and let the tenor's voice dress him in silk, or touch the hands of the spoon carvers (who had not worked in eight years) and let the fingers that danced on wood kiss his skin. Otherwise the pain would escape him even though the laughter was part of the pain.

A valley man is a European American, but he is identified in *Sula* not by race but by where he comes from: "white people lived on the rich valley floor in that little river town in Ohio, and the blacks populated the hills above it." The identification of this man by his place begins a scene in which Morrison places experience where it cannot be seen and in which the watching man misses it. Because he does not see and does not go to certain places that are parts of the black people's experience, he perceives spaces as empty that for them are occupied by pain.

Seeing no sign of pain, the white man sees the people's laughter as excluding pain, whereas for them "the laughter was part of the pain." This difference in perception is located as Morrison identifies places that pain resides, such as "somewhere under their head rags." Preoccupied by pain, the bodies of these people are locations of both laughter and pain, which the white man cannot recognize because he is ignorant of certain other places too. There are places he could go—to the back of Greater Saint Matthew's or up close enough to touch the hands of the carvers—where the pain of the black people's experience would not escape him.

The white man stands at a distance from the black people in this scene, excluded and exclusive. But rather than being separated by an empty space of necessary detachment, a distance built into knowledge or representation, the white man could move into places in which he could feel what he is missing. It is not only in the experience observed, then, that something is missed in this scene, for the white man both fails to recognize certain preoccupations in the people he watches and has never been in the places occupied by their pain. His distances from the people he watches depend on excluding certain occupations—and certain missed occupations such as spoon carving—from knowledge and thereby converting places of occupation into empty spaces of separation.

Patterns of Containment

In the histories of the Bottom's inhabitants, Morrison goes on to redefine space as place. The occupants of the Bottom whose histories are first given in the novel include Shadrack, who was a soldier in the First World War, and Helene Wright, who came to the Bottom from New Orleans when she married. These are the first of the characters who practice strict containments and limitations of experience that keep things in their places.

Morrison first charts the need for such constraints in the story of Shadrack. Having seen a soldier's head blown off on a battlefield of the First World War, Shadrack reacted with a terror of things out of place.

> Before him on a tray was a large tin plate divided into three triangles. In one triangle was rice, in another meat, and in the third stewed tomatoes.... Shadrack stared at the soft colors that filled these triangles.... All their repugnance was contained in the neat balance of the triangles—a balance that soothed him, transferred some of its equilibrium to him. Thus reassured that the white, the red and the brown would stay where they were—would not explode or burst

forth from their restricted zones—he suddenly felt hungry and looked around for his hands.... Slowly he directed one hand toward the cup and, just as he was about to spread his fingers, they began to grow in higgledy-piggledy fashion like Jack's beanstalk all over the tray and the bed.

Shadrack is able to put a limit on the size of his hands as well as the dimensions of death by "making a place for fear as a way of controlling it". He finds a place in the Bottom, founding National Suicide Day, in 1920, as a place for death: "If one day a year were devoted to it, everybody could get it out of the way and the rest of the year would be safe and free." Having focused his fears on this containment, Shadrack himself can be focused and contained. "Once the people understood the boundaries and nature of his madness, they could fit him, so to speak, into the scheme of things."

Like Shadrack, Helene experienced psychic chaos once when she left Medallion. With one slip, when she mistakenly gets into the "white" car on the train going south, she begins to lose control of her existence and slide back into an identity with her mother, "a Creole whore", from whom Helene has spent her life trying to separate herself. Morrison traces this slide in a series of displacements:

"What you think you doin', gal?"

... So soon. She hadn't even begun the trip back. Back to her grandmother's house in the city where the red shutters glowed, and already she had been called "gal." All the old vulnerabilities, all the old fears of being somehow flawed gathered in her stomach and made her hands tremble. She had heard only that one word; it dangled above her wide-brimmed hat, which had slipped, in her exertion, from its carefully leveled placement and was now tilted in a bit of a jaunt over her eye.

Watching Helene, two black soldiers observe her exchange with the conductor. Then, as Nel, Helene's daughter, watches them all, "for no earthly reason" her mother "smiled dazzlingly and coquettishly at the salmon-colored face of the conductor," and the two soldiers suddenly "looked stricken." "She saw the muscles of their faces tighten, a movement under the skin from blood to marble" and "she resolved to be on guard—always. She wanted to make certain that no man ever looked at her that way. That no midnight eyes or marbled flesh would ever accost her and turn her into jelly." Like Shadrack glaring at his rice and tomatoes, Nel watches the "custard" and "jelly" of her mother; she then resolves to resist their spread and slippage. Never again to leave Medallion, Nel

returns home to be her own self: "I'm me. I'm not their daughter. I'm not Nel. I'm me. Me."

The stories of Shadrack and of Helene and Nel's trip to New Orleans offer different experiences of a need for containment. Both characters set limits to preoccupations. These are memories that occupy their minds, but as memories of bodily disintegration they are, specifically, recollections of a loss of place. Shadrack, after seeing another body come apart, fears that his own body cannot be kept within bounds. Initiating National Suicide Day, he puts a limit to his fears, to death, and to bodily disintegration by limiting suicide to one day of the year and then "keeping" the holiday. Helene contains her fears by keeping house and keeping up standards of propriety, both in her house and in the Bottom.

But Helene's fears, and Nel's too, are apparently driven less by what they see than by what others, particularly men, see in Helene. Whereas Shadrack's body loses consistency in his own eyes, Helene is watched by others who see her body as that of a "loose" woman, "custard." Therefore Helene must contain not only her own slips but the way she spreads into someone else when men look at her. On the train south, she feels herself losing her place as Helene Wright and slipping into an identity with her mother, the whore. Then she sees herself losing her place in the men's eyes. They reflect not Helene Wright or her mother but just another black woman in sexual complicity with a white man. Once she begins to "slip," she spreads into this generalized identity because of history, memory, and fears of the men's own, preoccupations over which she has no control.

In the hospital, Shadrack is "relieved and grateful" when he is put into a straitjacket, "for his hands were at last hidden and confined to whatever size they had attained." He is further relieved when he is able to see his reflection. "There in the toilet water he saw a grave black face. A black so definite, so unequivocal, it astonished him. He had been harboring a skittish apprehension that he was not real—that he didn't exist at all. But when the blackness greeted him with its indisputable presence, he wanted nothing more." Helene, unable "to relieve herself" on the trip south because she is allowed no access to toilets, is perhaps without access either to the sense of presence that relieves Shadrack of his fears of nonexistence. As she sees herself reflected in men's eyes, she does not experience reflection as a means of bodily containment but as one other dimension in which she has difficulty keeping her place. Helene finds bodily relief in the grass but also in another "accomplishment": by the time she has reached Slidell, Louisiana, "she never felt a stir as she passed the muddy eyes of the men who stood like wrecked Dorics under the station roofs of those towns." She is relieved here not by bodily containment but by getting rid of something in her body: the urine she expels, as well as the feelings usually stirred by men watching her.

Patterns of Expulsion

Other women in the novel enforce more violent expulsions from their houses and their bodies, intent on getting rid of things and keeping their distance rather than keeping order. Whereas Helene Wright maintains strict standards and "the oppressive neatness of her home", the Peace women inhabit a "household of throbbing disorder constantly awry with things, people, voices and the slamming of doors." Their messy existence may not result from an indifference to limits, however; it seems instead one effect of a history of ejections and rejections by means of which the Peace women find relief in discharging fears rather than containing them. Walking out, throwing out, cutting off, sending things flying—these women affirm boundaries and their power over boundaries by getting rid of things.

Sula will walk out of Medallion on the day of Nel's wedding, as her grandmother Eva once walked out on her three children, to return "eighteen months later . . . with two crutches, a new black pocketbook, and one leg." Eva's lost leg becomes the subject of various stories. "Somebody said Eva stuck it under a train and made them pay off." But the stories Eva herself tells are of two kinds: "How the leg got up by itself one day and walked on off. How she hobbled after it but it ran too fast. Or how she had a corn on her toe and it just grew and grew and grew until her whole foot was a corn and then it travelled on up her leg and wouldn't stop growing until she put a red rag at the top but by that time it was already at her knee." According to these two versions, Eva's body is subject to both excursions and incursions of parts.

On her trip south, Helene Wright defends against the inconsistency of "custard" with "the best protection: her manner and her bearing, to which she would add a beautiful dress." Eva Peace deals with the inconsistency of her body not by means of consistent and beautiful forms but by making visible, even decorative, the difference between her absent and her present parts. "Nor did she wear overlong dresses to disguise the empty place on her left side. Her dresses were mid-calf so that her one glamorous leg was always in view as well as the long fall of space below her left thigh." Rendering her inconsistency itself a consistent expression of her distinction, Eva in her refusals to standardize her identity nevertheless places it by securing the difference between self and other, opening to others' scrutiny the space of the missing leg.

Eva's interest in boundaries and spaces is as evident in her house as in her body. "Sula Peace lived in a house of many rooms that had been built over a period of five years to the specifications of its owner, who kept on adding things: more stairwars—there were three sets to the second floor— more rooms, doors and stoops. There were rooms that had three doors, . . . others that you could get to only by going through somebody's bedroom." This house does not seem primarily a container so much as an excrescence. Eva keeps building, repeatedly pushing out and throwing up forms in additions whose messiness lies in the irregularity of access to them. Both over- and underaccessed, the parts of the house confirm Eva's control over ingress and egress. Spaces between are of more concern here than spaces per se, with an unusual amount of space given over to access. Even rooms are reduced to ways in and out of other rooms, so that any space may become itself a spacing, a distance between: not so much a room, as room to get in and out.

It is not that Eva and her house are open and free whereas Helene Wright and her house are constrained and closed. In terms of intent, the difference between the two is less than such oppositions suggest, because the primary concern of each woman seems her capacity to control and manipulate boundaries. Helene tries to preclude things slipping out of place; Eva lets things slip, even fly out of places in what may be an equally obsessive insistence on the permeability of boundaries. Hurling herself out a window of her bedroom to try to save her daughter Hannah, who has caught fire in the yard, Eva at another time burns up her son in his room because "there wasn't space for him in my womb" and "he wanted to crawl back in".

Both women are primarily occupied, then, with controlling, or even patrolling, boundaries so as to control the definition of their own selves. Both mark off the self through representations that rule out certain parts of their experience. Helene with her good form—her beautiful manner, bearing, and clothes—represents herself with a consistency that she lacks in her body and in her history. Eva's equally careful representation of her body presents an absence that also sets limits to her bodily and historical inconsistency. One woman places her past out of bounds to maintain consistency. The other maintains and thereby controls inconsistency by putting her past into a space defined by what is missing from it yet emptied of history as well as the leg. Eva's past can "take shape" only as something missing: an inconsistent, unknown, and mysterious gap in her existence.

Sula's Perspectives

There are at least three distances at which characters in the novel experience the representations that provide their identity, two of which I have already discussed. In the water in a toilet, Shadrack sees his definite identity as a black man reflected back at him. As in Lacan's "mirror stage," this experience of reflection defines the self as other. If Shadrack sees his ideal self reflected in a toilet, that reflection is both ideal and abject. Yet he is nevertheless reassured that he is "real" by the reflected image. Helene Wright and Eva Peace, I have argued, produce for themselves, by manipulations of things and bodies in space, definitive representations such as Shadrack finds in reflected images. For these women, definition is not provided by reflections. But they nonetheless, as they fill in and empty spaces, provide definite forms of and limits to meaning.

Eva's daughter and granddaughter both, like her, get rid or get out of things by increasing distances between one thing and another. As a child, Sula understands the defensive value of cutting off parts of her body; she scares away the white boys who chase her by chopping off the end of her finger. Later she lets fly a whole body when Chicken Little "slipped from her hands and sailed away out over the water" to his death. This is just after she herself has been "sent . . . flying up the stairs" by her mother's announcement that she does not like her. Sula, however, seems not to experience her manipulations of space as representative. Whereas Eva is characterized in stories as having cut off her leg, Sula actually cuts off part of her finger. And whereas her mother sends her flying figuratively, she sends Chicken Little's body through the air and kills him. Yet Sula does not control such acts; she does not mean them, and they effect no meaningful forms of experience for her. It is as if Sula does not have the distance from such events necessary to experience control of them.

On the one hand, Sula, like her mother and grandmother, is identified with breaks and separations. On the other, she does not use breaks and separations to give form or consistency to her experience. Unlike Eva, Sula does not place or contain inconsistency so as to limit it; she simply allows a place for losses, breaks, and separations that occur. She does not attempt to repair or reform or connect things that break or exercise any other control over them; she lets things go. Morrison says that Sula is "like any artist with no art form", and Sula does not use form to control experience. Nevertheless, she experiences definition, which occurs through the location of absence rather than in the re-presentation of forms. Because she does not use form to provide definition, Sula realizes the form and definition given to experience by absence. It is her recognition of the definitive power of missing that makes Sula's perspective extraordinary.

The ways in which Sula breaks meaning apart are to some extent familial. The Peace women enforce emotional distances, for example, with their tendency to throw things around. Because of such distances Sula can be identified, as Hortense J. Spillers argues, as "a figure of the rejected and vain part of the self—ourselves—who in its thorough corruption and selfishness cannot utter, believe in, nor prepare for, love." Sula's emotional detachment is evident in certain physical distances she maintains, such as "standing on the back porch just looking" as her mother burns to death. With this perspective, Sula goes beyond the bounds even of her family's sense of proper distance. She repeatedly opens up what Spillers calls "subperspectives, or *angles onto* a larger seeing" because she disconnects elements of meaning that other people connect.

Sula's capacity, to "just look" depends on experiencing no emotions or intentions that connect her to objects and no meaningful links, either, between one experience and another. She can look at things without presuming anything about them, holding to no assumptions that would affect the "clarity" of her perception. She thereby calls into question assumptions other characters hold. When Jude comes home from work expecting commiseration from Nel, for example, Sula looks at his experience another way.

[He] told them a brief tale of some personal insult done him by a customer and his boss—a whiney tale that peaked somewhere between anger and a lapping desire for comfort. He ended it with the observation that a Negro man had a hard row to hoe in this

A civil rights demonstration

world. . . . Sula said she didn't know about that—it looked like a pretty good life to her. . . .

". . . White men love you. They spend so much time worrying about your penis they forget their own. . . . And white women? They chase you all to every corner of the earth, feel for you under every bed. . . . Now ain't that love?"

Sula's insistence on looking at things another way provides Jude the relief of laughter rather than the comfort of monotonous sympathy. But this relief depends on disconnection and detachment.

What occurs in such scenes is similar to what occurs when Henry James's Adam and Maggie Verver produce new views of persons and situations in *The Golden Bowl*. Yet although James identifies those views as occurring in clear or open space, Sula's way of looking at things suggests that the Ververs do not merely look. Compared with Sula, the Ververs look at things with many assumptions, with what might be called a "backing": made up, for example, of the belief that they can change situations, if not persons, by viewing them differently. Adam Verver's consciousness is one other open space that Morrison might view as preoccupied. Backed by such beliefs, the Ververs view objects in relations. Backed by no belief in relations, "just looking," Sula makes clear that Jude's

experience is invisible. To look at it, it could be anything.

Source: Patricia McKee, "Black Spaces in *Sula*," in *Producing American Races*, Duke University Press, 1999, pp. 146–59.

Sources

Bakerman, Jane S., Review of *Sula*, in *American Literature*, March 1980, pp. 87–100.

Blackburn, Sara, "You Still Can't Go Home Again," in *New York Times Book Review*, December 30, 1973.

Davis, Faith, Review of *Sula*, in *Harvard Advocate*, Vol. 107, No. 4, 1974.

Gray, Paul, "Paradise Found," in *Time*, January 19, 1998.

Morrison, Toni, "The Salon Interview: Toni Morrison," in *Salon*, http://www.salon.com/ (July 23, 2001).

———, "Unspeakable Things Spoken: The Afro-American Presence in American Literature," in *Michigan Quarterly Review*, Vol. 28, Winter 1989, pp. 1–34.

———, *Voices from the Gaps: Women Writers of Color*, http://voices.cla.umn.edu/authors/ToniMorrison.html (July 23, 2001).

Nigro, Marie, "In Search of Self: Frustration and Denial in Toni Morrison's *Sula*," in *Journal of Black Studies*, Vol. 28, No. 6, July 1998, p. 724.

O'Brien, Maureen, "Novelist Toni Morrison Wins Nobel Prize for Literature," in *Publishers Weekly*, October 11, 1993, p. 7.

Turner, Darwin T., *Black Women Writers (1950–1980): A Critical Evaluation*, edited by Mari Evans, Doubleday, 1984.

Yardley, Jonathan, Review of *Sula*, in *Washington Post Book World*," February 3, 1974.

For Further Reading

Angelo, Bonnie, "The Pain of Being Black," in *Time*, May 22, 1989.
> In this interview, Morrison discusses racism in society and in her novels.

Basu, Biman, "The Black Voice and the Language of the Text: Toni Morrison's *Sula*," in *College Literature*, October 1996, p. 88.
> This article discusses Morrison's use of African-American vernacular in the novel.

Bloom, Harold, ed., *Toni Morrison's "Sula,"* Modern Critical Interpretations series, Chelsea House, 1999.
> This is a compendium of critical essays on *Sula*.

Carabi, Angels, "Toni Morrison," in *Belles Lettres: A Review of Books by Women*, Spring 1995, p. 40.
> In this interview, Morrison discusses her novel, *Jazz*, and race in American society during the middle of the twentieth century.

Grewal, Gurleen, *Circles of Sorrow, Lives of Struggle: The Novels of Toni Morrison*, Louisiana State University Press, 1998.
> This critical text examines Morrison's novels and the African-American experience.

Rice, Herbert William, ed., *Toni Morrison: A Rhetorical Reading*, Peter Lang Publishers, 1996.
> This collection of critical works on Morrison examines her work and its place in American literature.

Ryan, Katy, "Revolutionary Suicide in Toni Morrison's Fiction," in *African American Review*, Fall 2000.
> This scholarly article discusses the theme of suicide in Morrison's works.

Samuels, Wilfred D., and Clenora Hudson-Weems, *Toni Morrison*, Twayne Publishers, 1990.
> This critical volume describes Morrison's life and work.

The Three Musketeers

Alexandre Dumas

1844

The Three Musketeers, published in 1844–1845, is typical of Dumas's works: quick-witted heroes who fight and love unceasingly, fast-paced narrative, and entertaining dialogue. In its romantic subject matter, the book is typical of its time; what is not typical is the fact that it has survived and remains entertaining and accessible for modern readers.

The novel has been adapted for over sixty films and spin-offs and has sold millions of copies in hundreds of languages all over the world. Despite the fact that it is very long and is filled with improbable events, larger-than-life characters, and exaggerated dialogue—or because of these traits—it is a fast, exciting read and still feels fresh and entertaining despite the long time that has elapsed since it was first written.

The story was drawn from a number of original historical sources, including *Les Memoires de M. d'Artagnan* by Sandraz de Courtils and *Intrigues Politiques et Galantes de la Coeur de France*, memoirs of events from the period in which the novel takes place. Dumas's collaborator, Auguste Maquet, brought him a rough scenario for a book set during the reign of King Louis XIII and starring the King, Queen Anne, Cardinal Richelieu, and the Duke of Buckingham. This scenario, drawn from events in the original sources, would be fleshed out by Dumas to become *The Three Musketeers*. According to records kept by the Marseille library, Dumas checked out *Les Memoires de M. d'Artagnan* and never returned it.

Because Dumas's works have been so wildly popular, for a long time he was not considered a "serious" writer. However, in recent years, more attention has been given to him because his work laid the foundations for bourgeois drama as he brought history alive for a broad segment of the population who otherwise would have had no interest in it and as he created a new kind of Romantic novel.

Author Biography

Alexandre Dumas was born on July 24, 1802, in Villers-Coterêts, north of Paris. His father was a soldier in Napoleon's army and his mother was the daughter of a local innkeeper. However, his grandfather was a marquis, and his grandmother was a slave in what is now Haiti. Throughout his life, his part-African ancestry would fascinate Parisians, who found it exotic; some made racist comments about him but were usually charmed by his witty responses.

Dumas's father died when he was four years old and left the family penniless. Dumas learned to read and write from his mother, his sister, and a neighbor but spent most of his time hunting and fishing in the forest near his home instead of studying. When he was sixteen, he met two friends, Vicomte Adolphe Ribbing de Leuven and Amedee de La Ponce, both highly educated, who encouraged Dumas to read widely. In addition, de Leuven, who wanted to be a playwright, soon convinced Dumas to collaborate with him on writing a play. Dumas, who had very elegant handwriting, found work as a clerk and in his spare time continued to read and to write. He attended plays and made friends in the theater world.

His first success came with his play *Henri III et sa cour* (Henry III and His Court), which was performed by the prestigious Comedie Francaise and, through his acquaintance with the duc d'Orleans, Dumas was attended by princes and princesses who happened to be visiting the duc at the time. Overnight he had fame and fortune and was the toast of Paris. He became friends with all the leading literary figures of the time, spent his money generously, traveled widely, and wrote prolifically.

In 1836, he signed a contract to retell various events in French history in the Sunday edition of the newspaper *La Presse*. These pieces, enthusiastically awaited by the public, led him to begin writ-

Alexandre Dumas

ing historical novels. During the course of one year, 1844, he wrote *The Three Musketeers*, its sequels *Twenty Years After*, *Le Comte de Bragelonne*, and *The Count of Monte Cristo*. All of these works are still in print in France.

Dumas wrote an astonishing number of novels and plays, some of them hundreds of pages long; he usually worked with collaborators who did the historical research and often came up with plots. Then Dumas would flesh out the bare bones of the structure and bring the story vividly to life. One collaborator, Auguste Maquet, eventually sued for what he felt was his literary due. During the trial, his version of a chapter from *The Three Musketeers* was compared to Dumas's, and the court found in favor of Dumas because of the greater quality of his writing. None of Maquet's independent writing ever succeeded.

Although Dumas was hugely successful, he spent money as fast as he made it and had to keep writing to pay off his debts; however, it is likely that he would have written whether he was paid to or not. Although he had robust health throughout his life, at age 68 he went to his son Alexandre's house and told him he had come there to die. His son, like him, was a successful writer but led a more quiet life than Dumas had.

Dumas died in Puy, near Dieppe on the coast of France, on December 5, 1870. Before he died, he told his son that of all his works, his favorite was *The Three Musketeers*. In 1883, a statue in his memory was erected at the Places Malsherbes on the Right Bank in Paris.

Plot Summary

Part I: Chapters One through Ten

Young, ambitious d'Artagnan goes to Paris to seek his fortune, bearing a letter of introduction to Monsieur de Treville, captain of the King's Musketeers. He is impetuous and proud, and at his first stop at an inn, he gets into a fight with a nobleman who makes fun of his horse. The man's henchmen beat up d'Artagnan, but when he returns to consciousness, he sees the man talking to a beautiful woman in a carriage, calling her "Milady," before they set off. When he checks his belongings, he finds out that the man has stolen his letter of introduction.

He goes to see de Treville anyway and is impressed by the dash and swagger of all the Musketeers he sees at de Treville's headquarters. De Treville says he will help d'Artagnan but that he can't be a Musketeer before proving his worth, so he makes d'Artagnan a member of the King's Guards, a position that will allow him to prove himself worthy. D'Artagnan sees his enemy from the inn, "The Man from Meung," and runs out to attack him. On the way, he inadvertently insults Athos, Porthos, and Aramis, three Musketeers, and they each challenge him to a duel later that day.

When he arrives at the dueling ground, the Musketeers are surprised that they are all scheduled to fight the same man. However, d'Artagnan is a man of his word and is determined to fight even though he knows they will probably kill him. This courage and honor impresses them. When the fight is about to start, the Cardinal's guards show up to arrest the Musketeers because dueling is against the law. D'Artagnan joins the Musketeers, and they all beat the guards. The Musketeers are impressed with this and adopt him into their circle.

King Louis XIII hears about the fight and asks to meet d'Artagnan, but he is not home when they come to see him. They head off to the tennis court, where d'Artagnan gets in a fight with one of the Cardinal's guards. He wins again. They meet the King the next day, and he praises their loyalty and bravery and gives d'Artagnan a reward.

They spend the money on a lavish dinner and on a servant for d'Artagnan. Planchet is a loyal, intelligent man, the ideal servant. The others have servants too: Athos has Grimaud, a totally silent man; Porthos has Mousqueton, who shares his taste for luxury; and Aramis has Bazin, who is devout and who wants Aramis to quit the Musketeers and become a priest.

A stranger, Monsieur Bonacieux, shows up at d'Artagnan's house and asks him for help. His wife, who is a lady-in-waiting for Queen Anne, has been kidnapped, perhaps because she may know something about the Queen's affair with the Duke of Buckingham. Monsieur Bonacieux is d'Artagnan's landlord, so he agrees to help him in exchange for free rent. The kidnapper is the Man from Meung, d'Artagnan's enemy. D'Artagnan sees the man and runs after him, but loses him again.

The three other Musketeers agree that they should help Madame Bonacieux because helping her will help the Queen and annoy the Cardinal, who is their sworn enemy.

A group of the Cardinal's guards show up to arrest Monsieur Bonacieux, and d'Artagnan lets them take him. The Musketeers can't afford to be involved in this arrest—they have greater plans. The police then wait in Bonacieux's apartment and question everyone who shows up to visit him, while d'Artagnan eavesdrops from his apartment. When Madame Bonacieux arrives, however, he rescues her from their clutches and takes her to Athos's house. She says that the Cardinal's men kidnapped her and that she has escaped. She has important things to do for the Queen, so d'Artagnan takes her back to the palace. Meanwhile, he's fallen in love with her. He is aware that he may be questioned about what he did that evening, so he goes to visit Monsieur de Treville so that he will have an alibi. He changes de Treville's clock so de Treville will think d'Artagnan was with him at the time when he was really fighting the Cardinal's guards.

Part I: Chapters Eleven through Twenty

D'Artagnan goes to see Aramis and finds a woman knocking on Aramis's door. This surprises him, and so does the fact that a woman, not Aramis, answers. The women give each other handkerchiefs, and the woman in Aramis's house leaves. He is shocked to see that she is Madame Bonacieux.

He asks her what she's doing, and she doesn't tell him, but she allows him to walk with her to another house, where she's carrying out some secret mission. When he goes home, he finds that Athos has been arrested because the police thought he was d'Artagnan. He goes to the Louvre to tell de Treville about the arrest. On the way, he sees Madame Bonacieux, who is walking with Aramis. He's angered that she lied to him about being on a special mission, but when he confronts the man, he sees that it's not Aramis at all, but the Duke of Buckingham, the Queen's secret lover. Courteously, he agrees to guard them as they walk to the Louvre.

At the Louvre, the Queen and the Duke have a secret and emotional meeting. The Duke knows that the Cardinalists have summoned him to France and have made it look like the Queen summoned him. He's not fooled. But he wanted to see her so much that he came anyway. He adores the Queen, and she loves him, but she's more reluctant to admit it because she is married and he is loyal to the King of England, historically an enemy of the French. Buckingham says he will declare war on France if it will give him an excuse to make diplomatic missions to Paris and see her. She gives him a love-token—a set of twelve diamond tags that the King gave her for her birthday.

Meanwhile, Monsieur Bonacieux has endured imprisonment in the Louvre. He's petrified and broken down by fear. He is interrogated and brought to Cardinal Richelieu. Frightened and impressed by the Cardinal, he tells all about his wife's intrigues on behalf of the Queen and the Duke and swears that he will remain loyal to the Cardinal and tell him all about his wife's activities.

The following day, de Treville hears that Athos has been arrested. He goes to ask the King to release him, but the Cardinal arrives first and tells the King that Athos should remain in prison. However, de Treville does convince him that he can't arrest a Musketeer without a good reason. He tells the King that d'Artagnan was with him at the time in question, not knowing that d'Artagnan reset the clocks so he would have this alibi. The Cardinal is suspicious but can't do anything to prove his suspicions, so the King agrees to free Athos.

As soon as de Treville leaves, the Cardinal tells the King that the Duke of Buckingham has secretly visited the Queen. The King is furious, and the Cardinal slyly acts like he's defending the Queen's honor against scandal. He mentions that the Queen is apparently involved in a conspiracy with Buckingham and therefore England, as well as with Spain and Austria. This angers the King, but he is

Media Adaptations

- Over sixty films and spin-offs have been made based on the novel. The most notable were filmed in 1933, directed by Colbert Clark and Armand Schaefer and starring John Wayne; in 1948, directed by George Sidney and starring Lana Turner and Gene Kelly; in 1973, directed by Richard Lester and starring Raquel Welch and Oliver Reed; and in 1993, directed by Stephen Herek and starring Charlie Sheen and Kiefer Sutherland.

made even more furious by suspicions that the Queen is having an affair with Buckingham.

A search proves that the Queen does have incriminating letters, which show that she is involved in a conspiracy against the Cardinal but which don't mention any affair with the Duke. The King is relieved. He doesn't care about the plot against the Cardinal, since it doesn't affect him, and he decides to apologize to his wife by holding a ball in her honor. The Cardinal is the mastermind behind all of this and suggests that the King ask the Queen to wear all twelve of her diamond tags. Since she gave them to Buckingham, this will expose her when she shows up without them. The King has no idea that the tags are missing and is pleased with the idea of asking her to wear his gift.

Secretly, the Cardinal has had Milady, who is one of his spies, steal two of the tags from Buckingham so that if he tries to return the set to the Queen, her treachery will be revealed when she shows up with only ten.

The King asks the Queen about the tags, and she realizes that the Cardinal knows Buckingham has them. She arranges for Madame Bonacieux to send someone to England with a letter for Buckingham asking him to return the tags before the ball. Monsieur Bonacieux refuses to go and leaves to tell the Cardinal that his wife is planning this. D'Artagnan has overheard their fight and offers to go to England to get the tags, saying he is doing it because he is desperately in love with her and because he wants to serve the Queen. De Treville agrees to let all four of the Musketeers go on this mission.

On the way to England, Porthos, Aramis, and Athos are all waylaid, and d'Artagnan has to leave them behind. He duels with and almost kills the Comte de Wardes, an agent of the Cardinal who is trying to prevent him from getting to England, but finally he makes it and gets the Queen's letter to Buckingham.

Part I: Chapters Twenty-One through Twenty-Nine

Buckingham realizes that two of the tags are missing and that Lady de Winter has stolen them. He prevents all ships from leaving England so that Lady de Winter won't be able to get back to France to give the stolen tags to the Cardinal. This blockade is actually an act of war against France. Meanwhile, he has two other tags made, and d'Artagnan heads back to France with the now-complete set.

The Cardinal is confused when the Queen shows up with twelve diamond tags and his plan to expose her is foiled. He offers her the two missing tags, and the Queen acts surprised and thanks him for adding two more to her set of diamonds. In exchange for saving her, the Queen gives d'Artagnan a ring.

D'Artagnan gets a letter asking him to meet Madame Bonacieux the next night. He goes to visit de Treville, who asks him to be cautious in his involvement in royal intrigues. He advises d'Artagnan to sell the ring because if he is seen wearing it, enemies will have proof that he has helped the Queen. D'Artagnan refuses.

At the meeting spot, he waits for Madame Bonacieux. After an hour, he looks around and finds evidence of a struggle, and a man tells him a group of men came and kidnapped her.

De Treville believes the kidnapping was done by Cardinalist agents and tells d'Artagnan he will look into the matter. Meanwhile, he advises d'Artagnan to go find out what has happened to the other Musketeers. Before leaving, he finds that the Cardinal's guards are looking for him and that Monsieur Bonacieux was involved in the kidnapping.

D'Artagnan finds Porthos wounded but safe at an inn. Aramis is at a different inn, also wounded but safe, and Athos is at yet another inn, where he has locked himself in the basement and has been eating and drinking all the inn's supplies. He is very

drunk, and he tells d'Artagnan the reason for his secret sorrow: he is actually a nobleman and once married a beautiful young common woman because he was so in love with her. After the marriage, he found that she was a thief, branded with the fleur-de-lis, the mark of a terrible criminal, and that she and her lover had planned the marriage just so they could get Athos's money. Betrayed and angered, Athos hanged her.

D'Artagnan is horrified by this, and they agree not to talk about it again. All four friends go back to Paris, where they are informed that France is now at war with Britain and they need to find their own fighting equipment. Since they're all broke, this is a problem. Porthos is the first to get equipped, when he gets money from his mistress.

D'Artagnan sees the "Woman from Meung," who is actually Lady de Winter. He fights with the man accompanying her and finds that he is Lord de Winter, her brother. They agree to duel the next day.

Part I: Chapters Thirty through Thirty-Seven

The Musketeers meet Lord de Winter and three of his friends for the duel. The Englishmen are defeated, and although d'Artagnan disarms de Winter, he spares his life. De Winter is grateful and agrees to introduce d'Artagnan to Lady de Winter.

D'Artagnan begins visiting Lady de Winter, who is the woman known as "Milady." He falls in love with her, even though he knows she's evil. Milady's maid, Kitty, falls in love with d'Artagnan, but he ignores her until he realizes she can be useful; then he flirts with her and tells her he loves her. She tells him Milady loves the Comte de Wardes, and while he is with Kitty, he overhears Milady saying how much she hates d'Artagnan because he spared Lord de Winter's life. If Lord de Winter had died, Milady would have inherited all his money. She also mentions that she was involved in Madame Bonacieux's kidnapping and that the Cardinal wants her to be careful with d'Artagnan.

D'Artagnan is horrified and hurt. He steals a letter she wrote to the Comte and answers it himself, pretending to be the Comte and arranging a meeting at her house. When he arrives, the house is totally dark, and they have sex. She believes he is the Comte and gives him a ring.

Athos has seen the ring before—it is a family heirloom—and he once gave it away to a woman. D'Artagnan, still pretending to be the Comte, writes Milady a letter saying he can't see her any more. Milady is angered and decides to have revenge on the Comte by seducing d'Artagnan and getting him to kill the Comte. She invites him to her house, and after they have sex, he tells her there never was any Comte, that he was the one who visited her before. Enraged, she attacks him, and he tears her nightdress, revealing a fleur-de-lis, the mark of a criminal, branded on her left shoulder. Horrified, he escapes.

Part II: Chapters One through Twenty

D'Artagnan and Athos both realize Milady is Athos's wife, whom he thought was dead. Kitty comes to the Musketeers for help: they have to hide her from Milady, who is enraged at her complicity with d'Artagnan. She also tells them Milady was involved in Madame Bonacieux's kidnapping.

They pawn Milady's ring and buy equipment with it. D'Artagnan receives a letter from Madame Bonacieux asking him to meet her that evening and another letter from the Cardinal demanding his presence later on that same night.

Madame Bonacieux rides past the meeting spot in a carriage. The Musketeers can't tell if she's safe or a prisoner of the people she's with. They go to the Cardinal, who tells d'Artagnan that he wants d'Artagnan to be an officer in his guards. D'Artagnan politely declines, and the Cardinal warns him that now he will be unsafe from the Cardinal's attacks.

La Rochelle, a port town populated by Protestants, has been taken by British forces and is now under siege by the French. D'Artagnan's guard regiment is sent there to do battle, but the Musketeers remain behind. While he's alone there, he's shot at by two men, and the next day, on a spy mission, they try to kill him again. He kills one and captures the other, who tells him Milady was behind the assassination attempt. This other man is deeply grateful to d'Artagnan for not killing him, but he is later accidentally killed when d'Artagnan opens some poisoned wine that Milady has sent, and he drinks it. The four friends realize they need to stop Milady and rescue Madame Bonacieux.

The three Musketeers run into the Cardinal at an inn, and he tells them to act as his personal bodyguards while he has an important meeting. Milady shows up and they eavesdrop on the meeting. The Cardinal sends Milady to England with a message for the Duke of Buckingham, telling him he must stop the war against France or the Cardinal will tell about his affair with the Queen. He will also have him assassinated. In exchange, Milady asks the

Cardinal to put d'Artagnan in the Bastille and to find out where Madame Bonacieux is. Milady wants to kill Madame Bonacieux to get revenge on d'Artagnan.

Athos leaves the inn by himself. The other two Musketeers ride with the Cardinal to the army camp. Athos has been hiding in the woods, and he goes back to the inn and confronts Milady, who is shocked to see her old enemy and husband, whom she thought was dead. Athos tells her that if she does anything to d'Artagnan, he'll kill her. He also steals a safe-conduct pass the Cardinal has given her. This document says that whoever has the pass can do whatever he wants, in the Cardinal's name.

The four friends meet, and at an inn they brag and make bets with some soldiers that they can enter and hold the St. Gervais fort against attackers, all by themselves, for an hour. At the fort, they eat breakfast, make plans, and easily defeat all attackers for more than an hour, winning the bet. They decide to send a letter to Lord de Winter, warning him of Milady's evil history and her plans to kill him, and another letter to Madame de Chevreuse, who is Aramis's mistress and a close friend of the Queen, to warn the Queen that there's a plot to kill Buckingham.

Their gutsy defense of the fort comes to the Cardinal's attention, and he authorizes the captain of the guards to make d'Artagnan a Musketeer. He does, and now the four friends are even more closely united.

Milady arrives in England and is arrested. John Felton, a Protestant soldier, is her guard. She immediately begins plotting her escape.

The siege is still at a deadlock. The people inside the city walls are getting hungry and beginning to protest against the siege, which the Cardinal is happy about, but Buckingham sends word that in a week, English, Austrian, and Spanish forces will come to help them. This foils the Cardinal's plans.

The Cardinal catches the Musketeers reading a letter, and they taunt him and refuse to let him see it. The letter is from Madame de Chevreuse. The Queen has told her that Madame Bonacieux is safe in a convent in the small town of Bethune. The four friends decide that when the siege is over, they'll go rescue her.

Milady lies and tells Felton, who is a religious fanatic, that she is also a Protestant and that she is ill and the victim of the abusive Duke of Buckingham, who branded her with the fleur-de-lis because she fought against his supposed attempts to rape her. The brand would make people think she was a liar and a thief so that they wouldn't believe her story of being raped. She says Buckingham killed her husband, Lord de Winter's brother, and that Lord de Winter, who believed Buckingham's story that she was a thief, captured her. To prove her willingness to die for her religious beliefs, when Lord de Winter walks in on their conversation, she grabs a knife and pretends to stab herself. Felton now believes she's a religious martyr, who would rather die than be defiled, and he falls in love with her.

Part II: Chapters Twenty-One through Epilogue

Lord de Winter suspects that Felton is on Milady's side and sends him away. Felton comes back and helps her escape. Felton plans to kill Buckingham and go to France with Milady. He does kill Buckingham, but not before Buckingham receives a letter from the Queen saying she loves him and will forever love him and that she knows he has declared war on France because he loves her. He dies happy in the knowledge of her love.

Monsieur de Treville gives the four Musketeers permission to leave the siege and go get Madame Bonacieux. This is urgent because Milady is going to go to the same convent when she comes back from England, and if she sees Madame Bonacieux, she will kill her.

Meanwhile, she's already gotten there and has made friends with Madame Bonacieux, pretending to be a friend of d'Artagnan's, who is being persecuted by the Cardinal. Madame Bonacieux tells her that d'Artagnan is coming, which delights Milady, who plans to use Madame Bonacieux to hurt d'Artagnan.

The Man from Meung comes to see Milady. He is the Comte de Rochefort, the personal spy of the Cardinal. Milady tells him to have a carriage come and take her and Madame Bonacieux to Amentieres as soon as possible. She tells Madame Bonacieux that Cardinalist agents are coming to kidnap Madame Bonacieux and that she must come with Milady.

The Musketeers arrive first, foiling Milady's plan. She tries to get Madame Bonacieux, who has not seen them and thinks the Cardinalists have arrived, to run away with her, but Madame Bonacieux is paralyzed with fright. Disgusted, Milady poisons some wine and gives it to Madame Bonacieux to drink and then escapes by herself.

D'Artagnan comes in, and Madame Bonacieux dies in his arms. Lord de Winter arrives, looking for Milady. Athos tells de Winter that Milady is his wife, and they all join forces to chase her.

Athos sends the Musketeers' servants out to find out where in Amentieres Milady is, and then he and the others go to Madame Bonacieux's funeral. Athos then makes a mysterious visit to an unnamed stranger, whom he convinces to help them. When the servants return with Milady's whereabouts, the men all chase her and catch her just as she's about to leave France. They try her for all her crimes of murder and attempted murder and for inciting others to murder. When Athos mentions the fleur-de-lis on her shoulder, she challenges them to find the court that branded her.

The mysterious stranger speaks up now. He is the headsman, or executioner, of the town of Lille, and he knows her whole story. She was a nun who seduced a young priest, who was the headsman's brother. They stole the Communion plate and the priest was caught, but Milady escaped. The headsman had to brand his own brother with the mark of a thief, and he was so enraged that he hunted Milady down and branded her himself. After that, she and the priest went away to Athos's lands, where Athos met and married her. The priest killed himself in mad jealousy and grief after she married Athos.

They sentence her to death for her crimes, and the headsman drags her outside to execute her by cutting off her head. He then throws her head and body into the river.

The Musketeers head back to the siege, but on the way, de Rochefort arrests d'Artagnan in the Cardinal's name. In a private encounter with the Cardinal, d'Artagnan tells the Cardinal that the woman who made all the accusations against him was a murderer and thief and that she's now dead. He tells the Cardinal the whole story of her life and hands the Cardinal the safe-conduct pass that Athos stole from her, which says that the person holding it is free to do as he pleases, in the Cardinal's name. This letter frees him from being punished for anything he's done. The Cardinal, of course, could ignore this since he didn't issue the letter to d'Artagnan, but he admires d'Artagnan's cleverness and writes out a promotion to lieutenant in the Musketeers. The promotion has a blank space for the name, so that, like the letter, it can be used by anyone.

D'Artagnan tries to convince each of his three friends to take the promotion, but they insist that he take it. He does not like losing his friends, but he has no choice but to take the promotion.

The siege ends after about a year, d'Artagnan has a great career in the Musketeers, and he and de Rochefort eventually duel three times and then become friends. Athos retires to the provinces, Porthos marries his mistress after her husband dies, and Aramis becomes a monk.

Characters

Queen Anne

Queen Anne is married to King Louis XIII. She is originally from Spain, and is unhappy and unsettled as queen of France. She is still loyal to her Spanish origins, but wants to feel secure as queen; and she is in love with an Englishman, the Duke of Buckingham. The King knows she doesn't love him and he doesn't trust her. The Cardinal hates her.

Aramis

Aramis is handsome to the point of being almost beautiful. He claims that he's only in the Musketeers for a short term and that soon he will become a priest, his true calling, but he makes no attempt to leave the Musketeers' ranks. He is described as having "a demure and innocent expression, dark, gentle eyes and downy pink cheeks like an autumn peach." He spoke very little and when he spoke he drawled. Despite his effete mannerisms, he is a skilled fighter, and has great inner strength; when he is wounded, he says little, but keeps on fighting until he collapses. He never uses injury as an excuse to escape his duty, or a good fight. He has a mistress, Madame de Chevreuse, but he is private about his personal life and does not usually discuss her, or her identity, with the other Musketeers.

Athos

Athos is the leader of the Musketeers, partly because he is older than the others, but also because he is highly intelligent and brave and is a phenomenal fighter. He carries a secret sorrow and is usually melancholy. Later in the book he reveals that he was born a noble lord and once fell in love with a beautiful girl of sixteen, who seemed pure and devoted, who had moved to the area with her brother, a priest. Deeply in love, Athos flouted tradition, which said that noble men should only marry noble women, and married the girl. Only after the marriage did he discover that she was branded with a fleur-de-lis on one shoulder—the

mark of a thief. She had stolen a gold communion plate from a church. The "brother" was her first lover and her accomplice; they had conspired to marry her to Athos to get Athos's money. When Athos discovered that his beautiful love had betrayed him, he used his title as ruler and justice of the region to tie her hands behind her back and hang her from a tree until she apparently died. He tells d'Artagnan, "That cured me for ever of women, of enchanting creatures lovely as the dawn, and with the souls of poets. God grant you the same experience!" This cynicism masks a bitter pain and loneliness, which has marked Athos for life.

Bazin

Bazin is Aramis's personal servant. He is eager for Aramis to quit being a Musketeer and enter the Church.

Madame Bonacieux

Madame Bonacieux is the wife of Monsieur Bonacieux. She is lady-in-waiting to Queen Anne and is completely loyal to her. She's also beautiful and not above flirting behind her husband's back, and when d'Artagnan falls in love with her, he's drawn into a web of intrigue involving the King, the Queen, Cardinal Richelieu, Milady, and other noble and dangerous players.

Monsieur Bonacieux

Monsieur Bonacieux is d'Artagnan's landlord and the husband of Madame Bonacieux. He is weak willed and cowardly. When his wife is kidnapped, he first goes to d'Artagnan for help in finding her but then turns against his wife after the Cardinal flatters and threatens him. After this, he is loyal to the Cardinal.

Duke of Buckingham

The Duke of Buckingham, whose real name is George Villiers, is hopelessly in love with Queen Anne and will do anything to see her and to make her happy. Back in England, he is Minister of War for King Charles I, a position that makes it necessary for him to travel to France on diplomatic missions. During these trips, he always tries to see the Queen or send her loving messages. He is a true nobleman and is good-looking, rich, powerful, loyal, and brave.

d'Artagnan

D'Artagnan is the hero of the novel. He is a young man from a noble but impoverished family, who leaves his home province of Gascony and goes to Paris, hoping to make his fortune. He is ambitious, proud, brave, clever, and insightful, but he is also impetuous and, because of his rural upbringing, not very wise about the ways of the world. Soon after he arrives in Paris, he inadvertently offends Athos, Porthos, and Aramis, three of the King's Musketeers and ends up scheduled to fight three duels, one after the other, against these master swordsmen. The fight is interrupted by the arrival of Cardinal Richelieu's guards, and in the ensuing battle against them, d'Artagnan impresses the Musketeers so much that they all become friends, showing how d'Artagnan's personal charm, quick thinking, and gentlemanly conduct affect those around him. He also has a zest for love and romance, and he generally follows the chivalrous ideals of his class, although like many energetic young men, he sometimes tosses these ideals aside when he sees a pretty face.

Madame d'Artagnan

D'Artagnan's mother is filled with sorrow when he leaves home. Unlike her husband, who feels the same way but hides it, she cries openly. She gives him a parting gift of the recipe for a miraculous herbal salve that will heal all wounds, except heart wounds.

Monsieur d'Artagnan

Monsieur d'Artagnan, d'Artagnan's father, is an impoverished nobleman who clings to courtly ideals despite his financial ruin. He has taught sword fighting to d'Artagnan, a skill that will hold him in good stead. He is loyal to friends and family, aware of both the rights and responsibilities of his rank, and a staunch upholder of tradition. When d'Artagnan leaves home, he tells him, "Be honest and above board with everyone. Always remember your rank and carry on the tradition of good behaviour which your family has been true to for the past five hundred years." He also tells him, "Stand no nonsense from anyone but the King and the Cardinal. Remember, nowadays it's only by personal courage that a man can get by in the world," and he warns him to take opportunity without thinking and to take risks, live adventurously, and never shy from danger. All of these are ideals that d'Artagnan carries within him, and he lives them throughout the book.

Madame de Chevreuse

Madame de Chevreuse is Aramis's mistress. Because she is a friend of the Queen, the King sends her out of Paris because the Cardinal convinces him that she is helping the Queen conspire against the King.

Madame de Coquenard

Madame de Coquenard is married to a rich attorney, but she is Porthos's mistress. She adores him, and his visits are the high point of her life.

Comte de Rochefort

The Comte, the Cardinal's personal spy, is called "The Man from Meung" through most of the book because no one knows who he really is. He is d'Artagnan's personal nemesis and a mysterious figure who always appears when things are going wrong.

Monsieur de Treville

Monsieur de Treville is tough, strong, intelligent, and shrewd. He is the captain of the King's Musketeers. He is originally from the same province as d'Artagnan, and he and d'Artagnan's father are old friends. When de Treville was a child, he was a playmate of King Louis XIII, and like all children, they often wrestled and fought; often, de Treville gave the King a royal trouncing, leading the King to respect him for the rest of his life. This early exposure to royalty opened doors for him, but he has not earned his position only through royal favor. As d'Artagnan's father tells d'Artagnan, "Between this King's accession to power and the present day he's fought at least a hundred other duels, perhaps more. He's defied edicts, ordinance and decrees and see where he's got to! He's head of . . . a band of dare-devil heros who terrify the Cardinal, the great Cardinal, and it takes a good deal to frighten him." As his position shows, he is utterly loyal to the King.

Comte de Wardes

Comte de Wardes is loyal to the Cardinal and is one of his spies. Lady de Winter is in love with him.

Lady de Winter

Called "Milady" by many of the characters, she is beautiful, with a heart as evil as her face is lovely. She is sly, cunning, and loyal to Cardinal Richelieu, and she and the Musketeers are sworn enemies. She has a mysterious past; she claims to be from England but speaks French perfectly. (How did she become connected with the Cardinal?) And when d'Artagnan gets involved in a scuffle with her and tears her nightdress, he finds that she has a fleur-de-lis branded on her left shoulder. (What horrible crime did she commit to earn it?) Ultimately, the reader finds that she is the same woman who once married Athos. D'Artagnan is fascinated with her; she is unutterably beautiful, but when she thinks no one is watching, he sees her face change to that of a murdering animal.

Lord de Winter

Lord de Winter is Lady de Winter's brother-in-law. He is fastidious about his personal appearance and doesn't like to become involved in action, but later in the book, he becomes involved in Lady de Winter's intrigues.

John Felton

John Felton is an officer in the British navy. He is the ward of Lord de Winter and is a Protestant.

Grimaud

Grimaud is Athos's servant. Athos has taught him hand signals so he can communicate without speaking, and he is totally silent.

Kitty

Kitty is Lady de Winter's personal maid. She falls in love with d'Artagnan and, hoping to please him, allows him access to Lady de Winter's private chambers. She is sweet but easily led and becomes jealous when d'Artagnan seems more interested in Lady de Winter than in her.

King Louis XIII

King Louis XIII is weak, insecure, easily confused and led astray, and petty. He is manipulated by his various advisors, particularly Cardinal Richelieu, who use his petty obsessions against him; for example, the Cardinal uses his insecurity about his wife's affection for him to set a trap for the Queen. The King is oblivious of this and thinks those who manipulate him most are those who are most loyal.

The Man from Meung

See Comte de Rochefort

Milady

See Lady de Winter

Mousqueton

Mousqueton is Porthos's personal servant. He is similar to Porthos in that he has a taste for luxury.

Planchet

Planchet is d'Artagnan's personal servant. He is loyal, smart, and brave, and he will follow d'Artagnan anywhere.

Porthos

Porthos is loud and vain, and he likes to brag and to appear wealthier than he is. For example, he wears a gold-embroidered sash, but the gold is only where people can see it; where the sash can't be seen, under his cloak, it is plain. However, these flaws of vanity and self-importance are largely superficial; when it counts, he's brave and loyal, always ready to fight to the death for his honor or his friends' safety. He is the lover of Madame Coquenard, who is married to a rich attorney.

Cardinal Richelieu

Cardinal Richelieu, not the King, is the strongest man in the Kingdom and the true leader of France. He is egotistical, controlling, manipulative, and sly, but he understands people and their motives and thus is extremely effective at getting things done; if he were not evil, he would be a phenomenal leader. Although he hates the King and is secretly his rival, he publicly promotes loyalty to the King and privately acts as his advisor because he knows that his power and position are based on those of the King. Although he is a Cardinal, a high religious office, he is the least devout person in the book and the most evil; his character thus provides a commentary on Dumas's views of the corrupt nature of the Catholic Church during this period.

Themes

The Quest

The book begins with a quest: young d'Artagnan sets out for Paris to seek his fortune. Like many heroes of quests, he is of noble birth but humble circumstance and must rely on his own wits and talent to rise to the level of his destiny. He yearns to be a Musketeer but must first prove himself worthy of the position. Aided by his father's friend, de Treville, he becomes a guard, and because of his curiosity, initiative, and pride, he is drawn into the center of a web of intrigue that eventually allows him to prove his worth and gain success as a Musketeer.

The book also contains another quest: the Musketeers join forces to protect the honor of the Queen, to help her conceal her affair with Buckingham, and to help her to arrange meetings with him. This may seem like a relatively trivial matter to most modern readers when compared to the urgencies of the political situation of the time, but according to the code of chivalry and honor that the Musketeers be-

Topics for Further Study

- Research the code of chivalry and the ideals it upholds. How do the Musketeers advocate this code? Find several events in which their actions may be chivalrous but on another level are amoral or inhumane.

- The Musketeers' loyalty to each other, and their enthusiastic killing of enemies, is similar in some ways to how modern gangs operate. Read about modern gangs and write about the similarities and differences between them and the Musketeers.

- How accurately did Dumas portray Cardinal Richelieu? Read about the Cardinal's life and compare his real life to the life portrayed in *The Three Musketeers*.

- Dumas presents the siege of La Rochelle as an amusing picnic for the Musketeers. What was war really like in the seventeenth century?

lieve in, fostering true love is of the highest importance.

Love

All of the Musketeers view love as an exalted state and revere chivalry and honor. For example, their main mission in the book is to help Queen Anne in her affair with the Duke of Buckingham because they recognize that she and Buckingham share true love. D'Artagnan falls in love with Madame Bonacieux and gets into any number of dangerous situations when he tries to protect her from their mutual enemies. Athos, who once loved a woman, was forever scarred when she turned out to be a thief and liar who betrayed him.

Amorality

Despite their interest in true love, the characters are curiously amoral. If a woman is married, this is no obstacle to true love; they will happily have an affair with her if she's attractive enough. Although they defend each other to the death, they cheerfully kill any and all enemies and never give the dead another thought. And although they value honor and integrity, this does not extend to their enemies; d'Artagnan would defend Madame Bonacieux with his life, but he deceives Milady into making love with him in order to get revenge on her and lies to her maid Kitty, telling her he loves her to get information and help in his campaign against Milady.

Style

Complicated Story Line

The Three Musketeers, like other romances originally published in serial form, does not have the type of plot structure that modern readers recognize and approve of. There is no slow development of events, no building to a major climax. Instead, the action starts explosively and then simply continues, with new threads of action being woven in as the novel moves along. At some points, readers may feel that the book isn't getting anywhere but soon forget this as they become caught up in the action again. Although the chapters often end on "cliffhanger" notes, the plot is so complicated, with so many characters and events, that the overall story line of the book is difficult to sum up or describe.

Vivid Characters

Dumas's characters are vividly drawn and easily recognizable: d'Artagnan, with his youthful optimism, country-bumpkin naivete, and belief in his own self-worth; Athos, who is melancholy and carries a secret sorrow; Porthos, who is loud, grandiose, and flamboyant; and Aramis, who is somewhat effeminate and who longs to enter the Church. They are not "deep" characters, and the reader learns little about their inner feelings and motivations and even less about their pasts, but they are drawn vividly enough to become memorable people who remain in readers' minds and engage their interest.

Most of the supporting cast are "stock" characters who do not change or grow over the course of the novel: the evil Cardinal, the bumbling King, the beautiful Madame Bonacieux. These simple characters are a typical feature of the novels of Dumas's time.

Swashbuckling Action

Although Athos, Porthos, Aramis, and d'Artagnan are all very different characters, they have one thing in common: they are men of action who don't spend a lot of time considering the deeper meaning of life or of their actions. If someone is an enemy, they kill him and don't waste time wondering if they did the right thing or if his wife and children will grieve. They're ruthless with their swords, moving from one fight to the next with dispatch and energy. In the same way, if a woman is pretty, they flirt with her, whether she's married or not, and d'Artagnan is not above pretending to love a woman if she has valuable information he can use. They are careless about money, spending it if they have it and never worrying about tomorrow if they don't. Loyal to the death to each other, they have no compunctions about lying to others if the others are enemies or if it will get them what they need.

In all these traits, they are classic action heroes, similar to heroes of modern films, comic books, and novels. Dumas's style emphasizes action, and from his point of view, it had better be fast and entertaining.

Short, Fast-Moving Lines

La Presse, the newspaper in which the novel first appeared in serial form, paid authors by the line, so that a one-word line of dialogue, such as "Yes" paid as much as a whole sentence. Dumas invented the character of Grimaud, a servant, who had the habit of answering questions with a single word. This allowed Dumas to make a great deal of money without much work, until the paper changed the rule so that a "line" had to cover at least half the column. Dumas promptly killed off Grimaud, and according to Andre Maurois in *The Titans: A Three-Generation Biography of the Dumas*, told a friend who asked why, "I only invented him as a fill-up. He's no good to me now." Although Grimaud became a totally silent character in the novel version, Dumas's technique of using short, quick stretches of rapid repartee remained so that his work seems remarkably modern. He doesn't waste time or space on "he said" or "she said," when it isn't necessary, but simply presents the dialogue and trusts the reader to figure out who is speaking, as in the following excerpt:

> They've been seeing each other.
> Who? asked the Cardinal.
> She and he.
> The Queen and the Duke?
> Yes.
> Where?

> At the Louvre.
> You're sure of that?
> Positive.
> Who told you?
> Madame de Lannoy, who's absolutely trustworthy.

In *World and I*, Cynthia Grenier remarked, "Dumas's special talents were ahead of their time. His gift for creating dialogue and character and action plus his way of working with collaborators would have made him ideally suited for working for motion pictures."

Historical Context

Many of the characters who appear in *The Three Musketeers* were real people who are depicted reasonably accurately in the novel, although Dumas did take fictional liberties with their actions. King Louis XIII, Anne of Austria, and Cardinal Richelieu were important people during the period of the novel. Monsieur de Treville and Richelieu really were enemies—in fact, in 1642, de Treville was part of a plot to assassinate the Cardinal. Richelieu did have his own personal company of guards, who did have a fierce rivalry with the Musketeers. The tension between France and England, and the ensuing war in which the Guards and Musketeers fought, was an historical fact.

Louis XIII (1601–1643) ruled France from 1610 until his death, but the real ruler for much of that time was his domineering mother, Marie de' Medici. In 1617, he arranged the assassination of her minister, Concino Concini, forcing her into retirement. In 1622, he and she were reconciled, however, and in 1624, he allowed her protégé, Cardinal Richelieu, to run the government as chief minister. When his mother urged him to remove Richelieu from power in 1630, Louis, who believed Richelieu was on his side, sent his mother into exile instead. As in Dumas's book, Louis was melancholy and not very bright when it came to dealing with people, and he was happy to have the Cardinal do the work of ruling for him.

Richelieu strengthened the authority of the king and centralized government control. He also lessened the power of the nobility in favor of the king and suppressed the Huguenots, a Protestant faction, who were humbled by the siege of La Rochelle, which is described (albeit unrealistically) in the book.

D'Artagnan's character was based on Charles de Batz-Castelmore, who was from Gascony and

Compare
&
Contrast

- **1600s:** Medicine is in its infancy and still consists mostly of the use of herbs and other traditional medicines, many of which are more harmful than no treatment at all. No one knows that germs and viruses exist, and antibiotics, vaccines, and painkillers are unknown. People who are injured in duels, wars, or other combats often die from infections.

  1800s: Although doctors still use bleeding, purging, and some dangerous substances that have no therapeutic value, they have discovered morphine, digitalis, and other drugs, as well as the importance of cleanliness in preventing disease.

  Today: Medicine has rapidly advanced, with new treatments being invented every year. The most striking advance is the recent decoding of the entire human genome, which may allow treatment of previously incurable diseases.

- **1600s:** King Louis XIII and Cardinal Richelieu consolidate royal power, decrease the power of the nobles, and begin suppression of Protestants.

  1800s: King Louis Philippe promotes a rapprochement with England (although this ended in 1846). His unpopularity eventually leads to the French Revolution of 1848, after which he abdicates.

  Today: France is a democracy, with religious freedom for all, and both France and England are members of the European Union.

- **1600s:** Flintlock firearms are developed in the early 1600s, but swords are still important in combat.

  1800s: Percussion cap firearms, more reliable than flintlocks, are invented in the early 1800s, and guns become more common weapons than swords. However, swords are still used in hand-to-hand fighting.

  Today: With the development and widespread use of very accurate guns, swords are obsolete except for ceremonial uses.

---

had the title Sieur d'Artagnan through his mother's family. He left his home province in 1640 (the novel has him leaving home in 1625). He served as a Musketeer under Cardinal Mazarin and King Louis XIV (not, as in the book, their predecessors Cardinal Richelieu and King Louis XIII) and had a distinguished career. He died in 1673 while fighting at the siege of Maestricht.

In addition, Porthos, Aramis, and Athos were based on real people. Porthos was really Isaac de Porthos, who was a member of Captain des Essart's company of the King's Guards until 1643. After 1643, he served as a Musketeer with d'Artagnan. Aramis's character was based on Henry d'Aramitz, who was a relative of Monsieur de Treville, and became a Musketeer in 1640. Athos was really Seigner d'Athos et d'Auteville and was also a relative of de Treville's. He was a Musketeer and died in 1643, apparently as the result of a duel.

The main exception to Dumas's use of real people as bases for his characters is "Milady," or Lady de Winter. She was a creation of Dumas's, and it is interesting that she dominates the second half of the book, more than any of the "real" historical characters do.

Critical Overview

Dumas has been criticized largely because of his use of collaborators to produce his fiction and because his books have more action than emotional depth. Authors of his day were jealous of his phenomenal success; as Andre Maurois wrote in *The Titans: A Three-Generation Biography of the Dumas*, "It was a scandal that a single writer should produce all the serials in all the papers; offensive that he should employ a team of anonymous col-

Charlie Sheen as Aramis, Kiefer Sutherland as Athos, and Oliver Platt as Porthos in the 1993 film version of the novel

laborators." However, it must be remembered that at the time, it was considered perfectly acceptable for most writers to work with collaborators; what his detractors really objected to was his sheer volume and the success that emanated from it. One, Eugene de Mirecourt, went so far as to publish a pamphlet attacking Dumas, but it was so tastelessly written and so filled with offensive attacks on Dumas's African heritage and personal life that it was ignored.

His contemporaries also objected to Dumas's use of history for his own ends and his not being completely true to the facts. In *Smithsonian*, Victoria Foote-Greenwell wrote that when Dumas was accused of raping history, he replied, "Yes, but look how beautiful the children are."

According to J. Lucas-Dubreton in *The Fourth Musketeer: The Life of Alexandre Dumas*, Balzac actually could not stop reading the book once he got it, and although he scoffed at Dumas's use of history, he admitted that Dumas was a master storyteller.

Despite his use of collaborators, Dumas's talent for creating characters, dialogue, and interesting turns of events was the spark that could ignite even the dullest of plot frameworks. Maurois wrote,

"Dumas had genius of a certain kind—the genius that comes of vigour and a sense of the dramatic." Maurois also noted that the book's charm comes from the fact that Dumas conveys "a living spirit of France. . . . an epitome of that gracious, courageous, light-hearted France which we still like to recover through the imagination." In addition, he remarked that the lasting popularity of the book through the centuries and throughout the world is the surest mark of its value.

Lucas-Dubreton called the book a "masterpiece which remains as fresh and living as if it were written yesterday." Foote-Greenwell remarked that despite its length, improbable plot, and exaggerated events, "the book, awash with derring-do and sly comedy, is also great fun to read," and that this was the secret of its success. She also remarked that the book's fast action, adventure, and vivid characters "make Dumas's books a treasure trove for celluloid."

In *Great Foreign Language Writers*, Barnett Shaw wrote, "Two hundred years from now, you can be sure that at any given moment, someone, in some far-off place, will be reading *The Three Musketeers* or *The Count of Monte Cristo* in one of the dozens of languages into which Dumas has been translated."

Criticism

Kelly Winters

Winters is a freelance writer and has written for a wide variety of educational publishers. In this essay, she considers modern elements of Dumas's writing style in The Three Musketeers.

The Three Musketeers is still read and loved today, despite the fact that it was written over 150 years ago. Most work from that time has been forgotten, but Dumas's style, largely shaped by his originally publishing the story as a serial, is remarkably fresh and modern.

The style and structure of the novel were shaped by Dumas's need to write it as a serial, or, as the French called it, a *feuilleton*. Each week, a chapter would appear in the newspaper, ending on a suspenseful event, with the note, "To be continued in our next edition." This kept readers hooked, and it kept them buying papers.

Unlike some other writers of his time, Dumas could not afford to begin his story with a lengthy description of his characters' family background and personal history. A more traditional novel might explore d'Artagnan's family's past and explain why his father, a nobleman, had fallen on hard times, but Dumas doesn't bother. He dives right in. In the first pages of the novel, d'Artagnan has already left home and his bizarre-looking horse is already creating a ruckus in the market of the town of Meung. Readers find out later why he has left home and who his family is, but this is secondary to the action: he meets the man who will be his nemesis throughout the novel, the mysterious "Man from Meung."

Knowing that readers might not remember from week to week where he had last left off the story, Dumas recapitulates at the beginning of each chapter, telling readers the time, date, and place of the action.

Another aspect of the serial structure that affects the telling of the story derives from the fact that readers did not have the concentrated span of time necessary to delve into the psyches of complex characters. Thus, the characters don't change or grow much over the course of the novel. Although their fate may change, as when d'Artagnan is made a Musketeer and then a lieutenant, their personalities do not: they remain as they were when they were introduced in the first chapter. D'Artagnan remains quick-witted, energetic, and proud; Athos remains melancholy; Porthos remains strong and flamboyant; and Aramis retains his almost effeminate looks and his desire to join the Church. The Cardinal is evil through and through, although he does come to a truce with the Musketeers, and Milady similarly begins evil and stays that way, never learning from the consequences of her actions. These types of "flat" characters are a necessary part of serial fiction; their unchanging traits and appearance help readers remember them when picking up the story after some time has lapsed.

In addition to his strikingly modern technique of beginning the tale in the middle of the action, leaving out slow-moving background information, and ending each chapter on a cliffhanger, Dumas's style of dialogue also seems remarkably fresh to the modern ear. His dialogue is fast paced and often witty, despite the fact that it was written over 150 years ago by a man who lived in a society very different from modern times.

For example d'Artagnan gets in trouble with Porthos when he runs into him, gets entangled in his cloak, and notices what no one else has seen: Porthos's magnificent gold shoulder-belt is only gold in front, where it's visible. Under his cloak, it's plain fabric, revealing that he's a showoff and a braggart but is not really as well off as he would like others to think. Porthos asks d'Artagnan what he's doing, and d'Artagnan replies, "I'm very sorry, but I'm in a great hurry. I'm running after someone." Porthos angrily demands, "Do you always leave your eyes at home when you run?" D'Artagnan replies, "No, and my eyes are so good that they sometimes see things other people don't see," a sly dig to the embarrassing plainness of the back half of Porthos's shoulder belt. This of course angers Porthos, and the two schedule a duel.

In another amusing bit of dialogue, d'Artagnan gets in trouble with Aramis when he picks up a handkerchief Aramis has dropped. The handkerchief belongs to Aramis's mistress, and since one of her husband's friends is standing by, Aramis is not anxious to admit that she gave it to him. D'Artagnan insists that it belongs to Aramis, prompting Aramis to challenge him to a duel for embarrassing him. At the duel, Aramis doesn't want to tell the other Musketeers what the fight is about, so he says, "I'm fighting him on theological grounds," and the quick-witted d'Artagnan agrees, "Yes, we had a little dispute about a certain passage in St. Augustine."

In other cases, the dialogue sounds remarkably similar to conversations in modern movies, as when d'Artagnan bullies a stranger, asking for his travel permit:

> I want your travel permit. I haven't got one and I must have one.
> Are you mad?
> Not at all. I simply want your travel permit.
> Let me pass at once!
> No, Sir, said d'Artagnan.
> And he stood barring the stranger's way.
> In that case, Sir, I shall have to blow your brains out!

Another aspect of Dumas's style that gives it a modern feel is his use of short paragraphs, often only one or two lines long. This is in striking contrast to many other nineteenth-century works. A glance at the literature of the period usually shows lengthy paragraphs, sometimes a page long, with little dialogue. Dumas broke up his scenes into short, quick actions and stretches of fast dialogue, which makes the book read very quickly, like any modern "page-turner."

Part of the reason he did this may have been that he was not paid by the word, like many other writers (such as Dickens), but by the line. Thus, he would be paid three francs for the sentence, "Yes, I did see the Queen, at the Louvre," which would have covered one line. However, he could break up that line into six, for example:

> Have you seen her?
> Whom?
> The Queen!
> Yes.
> Where?
> At the Louvre!

By doing this, he could make eighteen francs, or six times as much, for the same amount of work. His characters frequently interrupt each other and ask short questions, which are replied to with one-word answers that require more questions to get the full information. They then interrupt the answers, making for even more lines.

Although Dumas may have hit on this technique in order to make more money, it had the side effect of making the story read very rapidly. Modern writers use the same technique, not because they're paid more—even in Dumas's time, editors wised up to this trick and refused to pay for one-word lines—but because they know it keeps readers in the story. Pick up any modern detective story, suspense thriller, or bestseller, and the same pattern of short paragraphs, a great deal of dialogue, and short lines will most likely appear on the pages.

His style of dialogue also appears realistic. In real life, people do interrupt each other, and they

> " His dialogue is fast paced and often witty, despite the fact that it was written over 150 years ago by a man who lived in a society very different from modern times."

rarely give a full explanation of anything when asked a question. A fatal flaw of much nineteenth-century fiction, and bad modern fiction, is dialogue in which people explain too much:

> As you know, Robert, my father has held this land since the late 1600s, when his ancestor came over from Ireland with only a few pennies in his pocket, married a rich Virginia girl, and used her fortune to begin raising horses.

This sort of thing is deadly for most readers, who will close the book in boredom.

It's impossible to know now how much of *The Three Musketeers* was the work of Auguste Maquet, Dumas's collaborator, and what exactly Dumas did for the work, but it's easy to guess. Typically, Maquet would draw up an outline of events, characters, and scenes, which Dumas would bring to life with dialogue, humor, vivid description, and breakneck action. This method of working is common today in television and film production, where a writer's original work is often drastically rewritten to cut out any slow parts and fill it with action and intrigue.

Dumas, who used collaborators for most of his work, was very open about the practice; in fact, he wanted to have Maquet's name printed along with his as the author of the serials, but the newspaper editors objected, saying that Dumas's name alone would sell far more copies than those of Maquet and Dumas together. They refused to print Maquet's name, leaving Dumas open to accusations that he abused his collaborators, making money off their work and doing little of his own. However, even in his own time, these accusations didn't go far. At a trial aimed at determining who was the true author of *The Three Musketeers*, Maquet presented his version along with Dumas's, hoping that

What Do I Read Next?

- Dumas's *The Man in the Iron Mask* (1848–1850) tells the tale of a mysterious political prisoner in the late 1600s.

- Dumas's *Twenty Years After* (1845) is a sequel to *The Three Musketeers* and continues the story of d'Artagnan, Athos, Porthos, and Aramis.

- In Dumas's *The Count of Monte Cristo* (1844–1845), Edmond Dantes is falsely accused of treason and arrested on his wedding day. He escapes to seek revenge.

- Victor Hugo's *The Hunchback of Notre Dame* (1831), set in fifteenth-century Paris, tells the story of a deformed bell-ringer who falls in love with a beautiful woman.

- Gaston Leroux's *The Phantom of the Opera* (1910) is the tale of a disfigured man who falls in love with a beautiful singer.

---

it would convince the judge that he was the real author. Instead, his version was so colorless and lifeless compared to Dumas's that the case went nowhere. All of Dumas's collaborators have been forgotten, and none of their own work is still read, proving that Dumas's talent was the spark that brought the stories to life.

Source: Kelly Winters, Critical Essay on *The Three Musketeers*, in *Novels for Students*, The Gale Group, 2002.

R. S. Garnett

In the following essay, Garnett discusses the question of authorship of The Three Muskateers.

On the evening of 27th October 1845, an unrehearsed scene took place on the stage of the Ambigu Theatre, Paris. On the final fall of the curtain, while the applause still thundered, a man precipitated himself on the stage, where, shedding tears of mingled joy and gratitude, he embraced another man.

The first man was Auguste Maquet.

The man whom he embraced was Alexandre Dumas.

The play that had been performed was *The Musketeers*.

Dumas *fils*, who narrates the incident, says that he was in a box, Maquet and his family being in the next one as ordinary spectators, they having no expectation of the occurrence of anything unusual; that the piece was nearing the end when his father summoned him by means of an attendant, and said, "If the play continues to go like this, I promise you some pleasure. I want to give Maquet the surprise of hearing himself named with me. No warning. And you will see how he takes it. But be careful to say nothing."

The Three Musketeers is one of those rare books which have a universal popularity. The man hardly exists who can read of the adventures of Athos, Porthos, Aramis, and d'Artagnan unmoved. Perhaps he could find a score of critical objections to the story if he tried; but he will not care to try, and he will never forget the pleasure he experienced. From Flaubert and Stevenson to the man in the street, admirers of the book are numberless. The romance on its publication in 1844 won instant fame; in Paris copies disappeared like snowflakes in sunshine, and almost at once translators were at work. In recent years a statue of d'Artagnan has been unveiled, archives have been ransacked for facts about his family and those of his companions in arms, and books and articles have been published about them. Today the cinematograph is showing the Musketeers all the world over, and they are the subject of an opera. D'Artagnan had by far the most distinguished career of the four; it is said that his master, Louis XIV., wrote a verse to commemorate him when he was killed at the siege of Maëstricht. Furthermore, a prolific author of the time, Gatien Courtilz de Sandras, wrote three thick volumes entitled *Mémoires de Monsieur d'Artagnan*. Much read in its day, this book passed into oblivion. After its use as the idea or foundation for the romance called *The Three Musketeers*, copies were sought for. Thackeray tells us that he chanced to pick up the first volume in Gray's Inn Road, London, for 5d., and that he liked d'Artagnan in that book best. Victor Hugo bitterly regretted Dumas' use of it, he himself wanting to utilise one of its episodes. A partial version in English has appeared. As for *The Three Musketeers* it is read as much as or more than ever, and the few who do not like it are resigned to its selling for aye with its sequels *Vingt ans après* and *Le Vicomte de Bragelonne*.

In the month of January 1919 the European bookshops began to display a volume encircled by a band bearing the conundrum

WHO WROTE *THE THREE MUSKETEERS*—DUMAS OR MAQUET?

The text within the covers gave as the answer—Maquet.

The author, M. Gustave Simon, wrote on behalf of the Maquet family. He held all the Maquet papers, and claimed to be fulfilling a duty imposed by Maquet on his heirs. The book was the forerunner of the *cause-célèbre*, echoes of which reverberate throughout the world of letters even today. The lawsuit, which turned chiefly on the interpretation of a contract between Dumas and Maquet and the application thereto of the copyright law in respect of the author's royalties, has been decided. The books written by Dumas and Maquet in collaboration still bear the name of Dumas only; but nearly all those who have read M. Simon's book, and thousands who have not read it, but have read the almost unanimous verdict of the French Press in Maquet's favour, consider that he was the author of *The Three Musketeers*. M. Simon's thunderbolt first fell from the *Revue de Paris*, for it was there that the most striking portion of his book appeared. In his book he complacently refers to the anguish of men of letters, who, after reading the *Revue*, asked themselves what had Dumas to do with *The Musketeers*, seeing that Maquet had found the subject of the romance and then written it. M. Simon, in effect, answers: "I cannot help it. It is the documents that are in Maquet's favour." Well, I ask no better than to be allowed to prove by reference to documents that M. Simon is in error. The anguish of the men of letters will then be relieved, and it is hardly too much to say that even unlettered men will breathe more freely. If Maquet really and truly were the author of *The Three Musketeers*, ought they not to read the many volumes signed 'Auguste Maquet'?

As M. Simon's book preceded the lawsuit, he had not the pleasure of recording there that, in the absence of any evidence to the contrary, his conclusions were adopted by M. *le Substitut* Tronche-Macaire in a speech which has become famous. M. *le Substitut* would be astonished to find that his speech must now be corrected.

Alexandre Dumas, who was born in 1802, and was the despair of his would-be instructors, after living in dire poverty, educated himself and

> That Dumas was immensely assisted by Maquet, I feel sure, for Dumas had most of the failings commonly attributed to men of genius, while Maquet had the valuable qualities of the all-round man of ability."

achieved fame in 1829, when his play *Henri III. et sa cour* gained a triumphant success. On that eventful night, his collar, cut by himself, was of paper, but this passed unobserved, so dazzling was the triumph which was applauded by a score of princes and princesses blazing with diamonds. Before Maquet made his acquaintance, early in 1839, Dumas had successively produced *Christine*, *Antony*, *Richard Darlington*, *Le Mari de la Veuve*, *La Tour de Nesle*, and other equally remarkable plays besides fresh and charming volumes of *Impressions de Voyage*, and many novels and romances, chief among which, perhaps, was *Acté*, a tale of the days of Nero, which had placed him in the front rank of historical novelists. Everything that he produced was the subject of violent controversies, and yet looking back, we see that in 1839, in France, Dumas' works ranked in popular esteem only after Lamartine's and Victor Hugo's. In England his name was scarcely known. His personality was more than attractive—magnetic; his conversational powers unforgettable.

Auguste Maquet, who was born in 1813, was a model student, and at an early age turned a good education to account, for he earned his living as a school teacher, while he wrote plays in collaboration with his young friends Théophile Gautier and Gérard de Nerval—plays which were not performed, however. The school management, rightly suspecting him of being at heart a Romantic, treated him too hardly; he handed in his resignation. In his desk were some five or six MS. plays. One of them, entitled *Un Soir de Carnaval*, was judged worth the offer to a manager. On its refusal, Gérard de Nerval took it to his friend Dumas. Dumas, wholly to oblige Nerval, rewrote it, called it *Bathilde*, and sent it to the same manager who had refused *Un Soir de Carnaval*. It was accepted, and successfully performed as Maquet's work.

It was in this way, then, that Maquet, whose personality was reserved, a little unsympathetic, made Dumas' acquaintance. Maquet next wrote a novel in two volumes called *Paresse*, which relied on analysis of character rather than on action for its interest, but he failed to place it with a publisher. Not allowing himself to be discouraged, he resolved to follow Dumas' example, and weave an episode from history into a story, a story of (it is said) sixty pages called *Le Bonhomme Buvat, ou Le Conspiration de Cellamare*, and offered it to the *Presse*. The editor declined it. The dispirited author, happening to meet Dumas, briefly told him the subject of the story, which Dumas, after paying for it, took to Florence, where, utilising it, he wrote the celebrated romance in four volumes known as *Le Chevalier d'Harmental* (1843). With another somewhat similar and equally popular historical romance, *Ascanio*, published by Dumas at about the same time, Maquet had nothing whatever to do. But we know that Maquet received payment from Dumas for the idea, communicated verbally, of a third story called *Sylvandire*, and that Dumas dedicated the book to Maquet.

So far, Maquet had not collaborated with Dumas, for he had not written a book with him, but it was known that Dumas was indebted to him for ideas. Now he began to find publishers for various stories, which met with some little success. Dumas, in a letter dated 17th February 1845, addressed to the Society of Men of Letters, says that in the preceding two years Maquet had put to his individual credit *Le Beau d'Angennes*, *Les Deux Trahisons*, *Cinq mots sur un mur*, *Bathilde*, *Vincennes*, *Bicêtre*.

Although the first-named work—a romance—is the only one that is in the least remembered today, Maquet must not be thought, as many have considered him, a man who could not stand on his own feet. With a certain modesty and great uprightness of character, he had great facility in composition, ingenuity, a wide fund of information, and an unflagging capacity for work. His education was altogether superior to Dumas', whose knowledge of the world and absolute confidence in himself were then so lacking in his young friend.

We come now to 1844, the year of the publication of *The Three Musketeers*, which M. Simon calls the most celebrated romance of that period. As a matter of fact, *The Count of Monte-Cristo*, a large part of which was published in the same year, had an even greater vogue. Ignoring *Monte-Cristo* for the time being, M. Simon writes:—

> In 1844 a great event occurred. It was spoken of everywhere and in all ranks of Society. Announcements were displayed in all the bookshops. It was the publication of *The Three Musketeers*, a romance! But what a romance! It enraptured the public. . . . Maquet had until then worked alone. There had been no collaboration properly so called until then. He confined himself to taking his "copy" to Dumas, who manipulated it as he chose, without mutual understanding, without exchange of ideas; he was so full of respect and admiration for the Master, he was so happy to see each of his works favourably received. Was it not for him a kind of warrant of capacity which could create for him rights for the future? And what a stimulant for him, what an exhortation to perseverance. What an eager desire to discover a new subject! What joy to exercise his industry as discoverer! And, above all, what a happy good fortune if he could, without consulting Dumas, bring him some important work. A popular work! He had hunted out the *Mémoires d'Artagnan*, which were almost unknown at that time. What a windfall! He immediately became enraptured with his subject, his heroes. He wrote, full of ardour, without rest, the sheets accumulated, he was already in possession of several volumes, and he carried his trophy to Dumas.

All this is absorbingly interesting, or would be so, if we were sure that it was a statement derived from documentary evidence, and not the result of M. Simon's imaginative talents. M. Simon naturally foresaw the question: what had Dumas to do with the book? He writes:—

> Oh, let us have the indulgence and generosity of Maquet; let us not deprive Dumas of what belongs to him. He had an active part in the collaboration, he modified the order of some chapters, he added some developments, but it was Maquet himself who conceived and conducted the romance. Maquet had handed Dumas his work ("the several volumes"). They discussed it together. Such a splendid subject, with such a scope, necessarily inspired Dumas with new episodes. But the plan and the intrigue were so well contrived, the sheets of "copy" were so numerous that the work of revision was relatively easy. It was not more than the dotting of the i's.

M. Simon does not refer his readers to any documents whatsoever in support of all this, but tells us that Maquet expressly declares in his notes that he wrote the first volumes. "In a list of manuscripts," adds M. Simon, "there are these lines— 'Manuscript of the end of The Musketeers. My first work—*à moi seul*.'"

As against Maquet's private notes, M. Simon cites, however, in the note at the end of his book, a passage from a carefully written letter which was communicated to him as his work was going to press. It was addressed to M. Paul Lacroix with the object of rectifying certain erroneous statements made by a biographer. Maquet wrote:—

> All the execution of *The Musketeers* is wrongly attributed to me. I had, together with Dumas, arranged to write an important work to be drawn from the first volume of the *Mémoires d'Artagnan*. I had even, with the ardour of youth, begun the first volumes without an agreed plan. Dumas happily intervened with his experience and his talent. We finished it together.

M. Simon cannot explain away this passage, but his final words are, "The author is Maquet."

This letter, especially in the circumstances in which it was written, must altogether outweigh a note which its writer never printed.

So far, in his relations with Maquet, Dumas, as we have seen, had done more than the lion's share; he had adopted ideas and developed them entirely at his ease in his own manner. With what result? That these works, when published, fitted in with and resembled his other works (written by himself alone or in collaboration with others). In fact, *La Comtesse de Salisbury, Le Capitaine Paul, Acté, Georges, Gabriel Lambert, Le Capitaine Pamphile, Le Maître d'Armes, Pauline, Les Frères Corses, Amaury, Ascanio, Maître Adam le Calabrais, Isabeau de Bavière, Souvenirs d'Antony*, all resemble one another in the same sense that *Ivanhoe, The Talisman, Quentin Durward, Anne of Geierstein*, widely different though they are, resemble each other. The books bear the stamp of their respective authors.

We turn now to M. Simon on the subject of *Monte-Cristo*. "*It happens that Dumas to set idle gossip at rest wrote an account of the genesis and composition of this book*." M. Simon, having found the account, utilised and adopted it. There being no dispute in the matter, I will only say that the idea of the book and the first plan were Dumas'; that in the course of a conversation after Dumas had written a volume and a half, Maquet made a remark of the utmost value about the plan; that Dumas adopted Maquet's view; and that the two men then wrote the rest of the book together. It is clear, therefore, that either M. Simon trusts Dumas to give a correct account of the literary history of *Monte-Cristo*, or he considers it binding on him because Maquet did not dispute its accuracy.

What would M. Simon not have given to have found a *Causerie* by Dumas on the subject of *The Musketeers*? What a drain on his imagination would it not have saved him! Unfortunately, in re-

sorting to his imagination, he completely overlooked the clues given by Dumas both in his Preface to the romance and again in his letter of 1845 to the Society of Men of Letters, wherein, as M. Simon shows, he enumerates his own publications without Maquet's collaboration. This enumeration included his *Louis XIV. et son siècle* in nine volumes. (Dumas erroneously says ten volumes.) Let us first of all turn to the Preface, and extract a few sentences:—

[PREFACE TO *THE THREE MUSKETEERS*.]

Wherein it is proved that, in spite of their names in os *and* is, *the heroes of the history which we shall have the honour of relating to our readers are not mythological.*

> About a year since, while making researches in the Bibliothèque royale for my *History of Louis XIV.*, I lighted by chance on the *Mémoires de M. d'Artagnan*, printed, like so very many of the works of that period whose authors wanted to write the truth without risking a more or less lengthy enforced stay in the Bastille, at Amsterdam, and issued by Pierre Rouge. The very title was seductive; I carried it off, by permission of the Librarian, if you please, and I devoured it.

And then Dumas, after referring his readers to the *Memoirs*, adds:—

> But, as is well known, what strikes the poet's capricious fancy is not always what fixes the attention of the Multitude. So while admiring, as others will doubtless do, the details we have mentioned, what struck us was something to which certainly no one else had paid the slightest attention.

> D'Artagnan relates how, on his first visit to M. de Tréville, Captain of the King's Musketeers, he encountered in the ante-room three young men serving in the illustrious Corps to which he solicited the honour of admission, and named Athos, Porthos, and Aramis.

> We admit it, these three strange names struck us, &c., &c., &c.

As for the *History of Louis XIV.* (with which Maquet had nothing to do), it was there naturally that Dumas had written the name *d'Artagnan* for the first time. Its readers, moreover, have the pleasure of comparing Dumas, the historian, with Dumas, the romancer; for one of the most exciting episodes in the history—that of the diamond studs given by Anne of Austria to the Duke of Buckingham—is developed in the romance. All who have studied their Dumas know that a mine once found was never relinquished until every ounce of ore had been extracted from it. Did he write a history, it was sure to provide him with a romance or two, and perhaps a play as well; did he write a romance, it would suggest a play, a history, or a volume of memoirs, so-called; and it is astonishing how fresh and delightful each successive work invariably is. Dumas made little use of the *Mémoires d'Artagnan* for his *History of Louis XIV.*, but the hour or so spent over the first volume was to bear good fruit in due season. How is it that M. Simon neglected both Dumas' Preface and his *History of Louis XIV.?*

But in all probability M. Simon would say: "I admit that I did not notice these clues, as you call them, but they prove but little. Dumas says that he found the *Mémoires* at the Bibliothèque royale, but later in his Preface he says that he also found there a manuscript written by the Comte de la Fère, which we know never to have existed. The Preface was a piece of *blague*. It is of no importance. And as for the *History of Louis XIV.*, I admit that to write it Dumas had to read some volumes of history and memoirs in which the name d'Artagnan occurred, but what then? How do we know that Maquet did not read similar books, including, as I have said in my book, the *Mémoires de M. d'Artagnan*, which inspired him to write several volumes of *The Musketeers*. It was a coincidence only that the two friends happened to pursue a similar course of reading. But I confess that if Dumas had devoted a *Causerie* to *The Musketeers*, which we know he never did, his volumes of *Causeries* not having a word about it, if, I say, he had done so—well, then, it would be different. . . ."

I could not quarrel with such remarks as these, and am glad to be able to invite M. Simon to read a *Causerie* written by Dumas about *The Musketeers*, with a similar object to his famous *Causerie* about *Monte-Cristo*. It is to be found in one of his own journals, in one appropriately named 'D'Artagnan.'

Here it is:—

LES MOUSQUETAIRES.

It was in 1844, as near as I can remember, that there fell into my hands a volume entitled *Les Mémoires de Monsieur d'Artagnan*, by Courtilz de Sandras.

The book was given to me as a sufficiently correct picture of manners of the Seventeenth Century.

In fact, the *Les Mémoires de Monsieur d'Artagnan*, published at La Haye in 1689—that is to say, in the most fatal and reactionary period of Louis XIV.,—have preserved a certain cavalier air which was not then the mode, and which, indeed, belongs entirely to the first part of the Seventeenth Century.

I read it without remarking anything more than the three names of Athos, Porthos, and Aramis. These three strange names belonged to three Musketeers, friends of d'Artagnan. But in the whole book, to which we refer those who are interested, nothing is explained respecting the characters of those gentlemen.

One episode only struck me—that of the love affair of d'Artagnan with an English woman called Milady, who tries to have him killed by her lover, one de Wardes. But in the book of this romancer, sitting astride on the times of Louis XIV. and Louis XV., everything is glanced at, nothing is really examined, and the style, a really surprising thing at that period which lay between the days of Mme. de Sévigné and those of the Duke de Saint-Simon, style and composition are alike mediocre.

Nevertheless, the names of Athos, Porthos, and Aramis remained in my memory. The episode of Milady, whom I kept on thinking of, in spite of myself, led me to sketch a first outline, altogether a shapeless one, which I submitted for Maquet's appreciation.

Maquet, without caring much for the subject which, besides, was not then found, set himself to work. I retook the book from his hands, and succeeded in communicating to him a certain enthusiasm for the task.

When the book was finished, I, having a contract with the *Siècle*, sent it to Desnoyers, who at that time superintended the *feuilleton*, with the title *Athos, Porthos, and Aramis.*

Desnoyers read, or did not read, the four volumes deposited by me in his hands. In any case, he did not much care for them. Nevertheless, as the acceptance of my romance by the *Journal* had nothing to do with him, he was notified by the Management to send it to the Printer. It was then that I received from him a letter to the following effect:—

"MY DEAR DUMAS,—Many of our subscribers jib at the title, *Athos, Porthos, and Aramis*. Some of them believe that it is the history of the three Fates which you have undertaken to write, and as, unless you have new sources of information about these three goddesses, the story does not promise to be gay, I propose the less ambitious but much more popular title of *Trois Mousquetaires.*

"An answer if you please."

I replied by return of post,

"I am all the more of your opinion to call the romance the *Trois Mousquetaires*, since, as they are four, the title will be absurd, which promises for the book the greatest success."

The romance was called *Les Trois Mousquetaires.*

No one remarked that there were four.

It is strange, no doubt, to have to realise that the famous title *The Three Musketeers* was imposed on Dumas by a man who did not care for the volumes of MS., but we have no choice.—A search of the files of the *Siècle* has elicited the fact that on 29th December 1843 the *feuilleton* section contained the following announcement: "Athos, Porthos, et Aramis, roman historique en 5 parties par M. Alexandre Dumas," and that on 14th March of the following year the romance began to appear under the title, *Les Trois Mousquetaires*.

By the side of Dumas' illuminating *Causerie* I would place some remarks culled from a book which was published in 1848—that is to say, only four years after the publication of *The Three Musketeers*. The work in question is *Galerie des Gens de Lettres au XIX siècle*, by Charles Robin. It contains two long and deeply interesting studies on Dumas and Maquet respectively. The latter abounds with intimate personal details, which must have been supplied by Maquet himself or his family, and it is astonishing that it should have been unknown to M. Simon. Respecting *Les Trois Mousquetaires*, Robin wrote:—

Dumas had sent to Maquet the first volume of the *Mémoires de Monsieur d'Artagnan* with these few words:—

"My dear friend, tell me whether you think that two men of ability can make an interesting book out of this?" "Certainly," Maquet answered, after having run through the volume in half an hour; and, without even opening the remaining volumes, he took his pen and dashed three or four chapters on the paper. A good beginning was made, and the peculiar character of the book indicated. To what purpose servilely to follow the steps of Courtilz de Sandras? Why not be original, dramatic, and much more amusing than the author of the *Mémoires* themselves had managed to be?

Alexandre Dumas was not, however, quite of Maquet's opinion. He wished that there should be brought into action in the romance of *The Three Musketeers* the great historical figures of the time—for instance, Buckingham, Anne of Austria, and many others of minor importance. As for Maquet, he dared to pronounce a contrary opinion; according to him, the action of the romance would gain much and develop much more easily merely with the picturesque element, new characters, and the few well-drawn personages delineated by Sandraz. The success of the book amply justified Dumas.

Nevertheless both opinions combined, both brains and both pens worked together, and this romance of *The Three Musketeers*, which is simply a masterpiece of its kind, amused the whole of Paris, the whole world, during fifteen months.

It would be interesting, would it not, to ascertain whether Maquet was in agreement with Robin's presentment of the details which he had gleaned, for it is always possible that the writer submitted his notice to Dumas and that Dumas added something. So might M. Simon say, though I think he would agree that certainly it would be

totally unlike Dumas to have added anything to his own advantage. Still, we would like to be able to show that Maquet approved of the notice. Well, we are able to do so, thanks this time to M. Simon, for it is from his own book that we quote from a letter written by Maquet in 1857 to a journalist who had asked him for biographical information:—

SIR,—The biography which I have the honour to send you will give you a sufficiently precise idea of my younger days and of my works. The author addressed himself to my family in 1847 to obtain his information.

It remains to fill the gap which separates 1848 from 1857.

The biography was naturally that written by Robin for his *Galerie* in 1847, and published in 1848. M. Simon cites Maquet's letter without realising at all to what biography Maquet referred. He little dreamt that in so doing he destroyed his own case.

Maquet being satisfied with Robin's statement respecting the matter, there is no longer any need to explain why he (Maquet) failed to challenge the accuracy of Dumas' *Causerie*, which gives substantially the same account. The fantastic narration of M. Simon—where is it? M. Simon pictured Maquet finding the *Mémoires de Monsieur d'Artagnan*, pictured his enthusiasm for the subject, for his heroes, his writing several volumes without rest and taking them to Dumas. Why? M. Simon did not know that it was Dumas who had found the *Mémoires*, Dumas who had supplied the title *Athos, Porthos, and Aramis* to the *Siècle*, Dumas who pressed to fulfil his contract, sent the book to Maquet, Dumas who insisted on the story being a *roman historique*, Dumas who took up the work from Maquet, and completed it with him.

And here is yet another link in the chain of evidence which will interest M. Simon:—

Fiorentino, another of Dumas' "ghosts," records that Dumas, being accustomed to fill his twenty sheets a day, finished *Monte-Cristo* in his presence on the fifteenth. But not wishing to depart from his rule, the romancer took more paper and completed the first five sheets of the new story— *The Musketeers*—before finishing for the day.

Here is indisputable evidence that Dumas who, I concede, had received Maquet's "copy," treated it as a draft only. It is only the MS. of Maquet's "copy" of the end of *The Musketeers* that is forthcoming. That "copy," as M. Simon shows, is but a

Illustration by Norman Price and E. C. Van Swearingen, from a 1953 version of the novel

draft. We have proved that Maquet wrote a few chapters, and not a few volumes, before taking the "copy" to Dumas. That Dumas rewrote it is obvious to any one familiar with the works of Dumas and those of Maquet. I can picture Maquet's justifiable annoyance when, on reading his copy of the *Siècle*, he found that Dumas, in his tenth chapter, forgetful or regardless of the latter portion of his Preface (in which, as has been said, he attributes the authorship of the book to the Comte de la Fère), had written as follows:—

> As perhaps our readers may not be familiar with the slang of the rue de Jerusalem, and as during our life as an author, which is fifteen years long, it is the first time that we have had to employ the word in the sense in which we now use it, let us explain what a mouse-trap is.

We know that at that time—1844—Dumas' life as an author was fifteen years long, for *Henri III. et sa cour*—his first success—was performed just fifteen years before *The Musketeers* was written. Moreover, it was a foible of Dumas' to refer to himself in his works, and certainly Maquet would not have the least idea of writing such a sentence.

It is clear from the foregoing that, as in the case of *Monte-Cristo*, the idea and the plan of *The Musketeers* belong to Dumas. Not only did he refuse to alter it, as he and Robin recorded, but we may affirm also that Dumas either wrote the MS. or revised Maquet's drafts. M. Simon's claim that Maquet conceived and conducted the romance, and that Dumas did little more than dot the i's, is inadmissible. Oddly enough, M. Simon considers that by printing a chapter of Maquet's manuscript of the end of the romance—a chapter carefully selected by him,—he adduces a final "proof." Maquet's draft was a good one, and suitable for the Master to deal with, and, indeed, he let most of it stand. But his deletion of inept passages, his interpolations and alterations, are marvellously effective, such, indeed, as only he could have made. What was merely a situation becomes a reality. Maquet ought, I think, to have done even better work, near the end of the book especially, when it is remembered what lessons his Master had given him throughout seven volumes, not to speak of *Monte-Cristo*, *Sylvandire*, and the *Chevalier d'Harmental*. That the "copy" was better than what Maquet could write when he was without Dumas' inspired encouragement it is easy to understand. In truth, one has only to read Maquet's romance *Beau d'Angennes* (1842) to see what a difference there is between his unaided work and his work as Dumas' "ghost." Then he had no intimacy with the Master, none of those wonderful conversations with him. That Dumas was immensely assisted by Maquet, I feel sure, for Dumas had most of the failings commonly attributed to men of genius, while Maquet had the valuable qualities of the all-round man of ability.

I am sure that, if Maquet had not assisted Dumas with his real devotion, unflagging toil, and undoubted talent, many of the latter's best romances would not be in existence, for no one man could have written nearly so many unaided. Maquet, though by no means a profound scholar, must often have saved the time of Dumas, whose general knowledge then was weak in comparison. Moreover, the two friends, so opposite in temperament, remedied each other's defects. Dumas was too gay and brilliant, too volatile, too much in the air; Maquet too sentimental and sombre, wanting in humour and in dramatic power, too much on the ground. When Dumas insisted on having his way, we get such characters as Chicot and Gorenflot (the former of whom Maquet failed badly with, when, years later, he transplanted the immortal jester into his romance *La Belle Gabrielle*); when Maquet had the better of the friendly contest of ideas, we get a hero such as the worthy but rather dull Vicomte de Bragelonne. I have a vivid recollection of one of Maquet's heroes—a lovesick young man who spends the night leaning on a balustrade, which in the morning is wet with his tears. Dumas would not have suffered that youth. Maquet's Travels and *Memoirs* would have been as widely different from Dumas' *Memoirs* and Travels as can be imagined, and these works are assuredly most suggestive of the most popular of the Dumas romances. Hence my conviction that Dumas was the genius in the collaboration and Maquet the ghost. This I contend, while duly acknowledging that the ghost was more widely read than the genius. If any one considers that Maquet was the Master, the genius, let him read the books which Maquet wrote after his rupture with Dumas, such as *La Belle Gabrielle*, and others. If any one wishes to know what Dumas could accomplish in the field of historical romance without Maquet, let him read *La Comtesse de Charny*, *Le Page du Duc de Savoie*, *Les Compagnons de Jéhu*, *La San-Felice*, *Les Blancs et les Bleus*, *Acté*, and others. I have much respect for Maquet—a man, in his private character, worthy of great esteem, and had he been the author of *Les Trois Mousquetaires*, I should have been among the first to acknowledge the fact. As it is, I must think that his chief claim to a niche in the temple of fame rests on the fact that Dumas considered him by far the best of his many collaborators, and one of the best of his friends. That he did so is strikingly and pathetically shown in the following passage, which I have pleasure in citing.

Dumas concludes a *Causerie*, written in 1859, with a summary of his new dramatic undertakings by saying:—

> Now I must express regret that, except for *La Dame de Monsoreau*, which was written six or eight years ago, I am not bringing myself before you with my customary collaborator Auguste Maquet.
>
> As a man of talent and good feeling who has been my companion in my travels in Spain and Africa, and who never failed me in my arduous undertaking of the Théâtre Historique, he would never have the idea of severing our friendship. I ascribe the same to jealous feelings on the part of his family.
>
> I have regretted, I do regret, and I shall always regret our severance by which both our works suffered, by which I lose the most, since I loved him, and he apparently did not love me.

Whether Dumas was right in his conjecture about "the family" I cannot say, but it would have rejoiced him to know that accompanying Maquet's papers was found a note in which this passage occurs:—

> I will never try to disparage this great writer (Dumas), my master, and during a long time my friend. I proclaim him one of the most brilliant among the illustrious, and the best perhaps among men of goodwill—*bonæ voluntatis*—I have said among men.

Maquet knew better than did any one Dumas' compelling reason for needing a collaborator—it was pressure of time.

The Three Musketeers, like *Don Quixote*, will, I fancy, some day be annotated. Before this is done, it is well to settle the question of its authorship. Such is the purpose of this paper.

Source: R. S. Garnett, "The Genius and the Ghost, or, 'Athos, Porthos, and Aramis'," in *Blackwood's Magazine*, Vol. 226, No. 1365, July 1929, pp. 129–42.

Sources

Foote-Greenwell, Victoria, "The Life and Resurrection of Alexandre Dumas," in *Smithsonian*, July 1996, p. 110.

Grenier, Cynthia, "Dumas, the Prodigious: A Profile of Alexandre Dumas," in *World and I*, June 1998, p. 284.

Lucas-Dubreton, J., *The Fourth Musketeer: The Life of Alexandre Dumas*, Coward McCain, 1928, pp. 126–49.

Maurois, Andre, *The Titans: A Three-Generation Biography of the Dumas*, translated by Gerard Hopkins, Harper and Brothers, 1957, pp. 171–87.

Shaw, Barnett, "Dumas, Alexandre," in *Great Foreign-Language Writers*, edited by James Vinson and Daniel Kirkpatrick, St. Martin's Press, 1984, pp. 165–72.

For Further Reading

Cooper, Barbara T., "Alexandre Dumas, père," in *Dictionary of Literary Biography*, Vol. 119: *Nineteenth-Century French Fiction Writers: Romanticism and Realism, 1800–1860*, edited by Catharine Savage Brosman, Gale Research, 1992, pp. 98–119.

  This biography provides a list of selected works by the author and a detailed list of sources for further reading.

Hemmings, F. W. J., "Alexandre Dumas Père," in *European Writers: The Romantic Century*, Vol. 6, edited by Jacques Barzun and George Stade, Charles Scribner's Sons, 1985, pp. 719–43.

  This biographical chapter emphasizes Dumas's development as a playwright and his subsequent career as a novelist.

———, *Alexandre Dumas: The King of Romance*, Charles Scribner's Sons, 1979.

This biography traces Dumas's life, from his African heritage to his death as a famous writer.

Ross, Michael, *Alexandre Dumas*, David and Charles, 1981.

This biography traces the writer's life and career.

Whitlock, James, "Alexandre Dumas, père," in *Cyclopedia of World Authors*, rev. 3d ed., edited by Frank Magill. Salem Press, 1997, pp. 582–84.

This brief biographical entry provides a complete list of all of Dumas's works.

U.S.A.

John Dos Passos
1938

John Dos Passos wrote the three novels that make up the trilogy *U.S.A.* between 1927 and 1936, drawing on his own childhood and education, his service in the ambulance corps during World War I, and his left-wing political views of current events. The trilogy was first published as a whole in 1938. Dos Passos aimed to produce a satire on American life, permeated with popular songs, current events, and headlines, that would truly portray the whole of American culture and events. The trilogy spans the years from the opening of the twentieth century through the dawn of the Great Depression and expresses Dos Passos's view of the ill effects of capitalism on the American people.

The trilogy is notable for Dos Passos's use of various experimental techniques, such as the "Camera Eye," a series of stream-of-consciousness monologues that are inserted throughout the chapters; the "Newsreels," collages of headlines, lines from popular songs and pieces of current events; and twenty-seven biographies of typical or important people of the time. He had first developed some of these techniques in his earlier work, *Manhattan Transfer*, his first novel to receive widespread readership and critical attention. In using them, he was inspired by such disparate sources as the poems of Walt Whitman, the fragmented images of postimpressionist painting, James Joyce's *Ulysses*, and silent filmmakers D. W. Griffith and Sergei Eisenstein, who used montage, or contrasting scenes, to portray the busy and often ironic contrasts of the real world.

John Dos Passos

fied, romanticized images other writers had provided.

He followed this with *Manhattan Transfer* (1925) and then began writing the massive *U.S.A.*, a trilogy intended to give readers a comprehensive, realistic view of American society from the turn of the twentieth century to the stock market crash and the beginnings of the Great Depression. The trilogy, which Dos Passos viewed as an indictment of American society, was made up of the novels *42nd Parallel* (1930), *1919* (1932), and *The Big Money* (1936) and was first published as a whole in 1938.

He also wrote several other novels, plays, poetry, and many volumes of nonfiction, emphasizing historical and political topics.

Dos Passos's novels are typically long and populated by a huge number of characters. Some appear only for a page, while others are focused on and followed through decades of their lives. For Dos Passos, society and setting were as important as characterization or plot—if not more so—and he typically spent a great deal of energy in describing them. He also used several experimental techniques: the "Camera Eye," which was an impressionistic collection of details specific to a particular time and place; the "Newsreel," which was a collection of popular songs, newspaper headlines, and scraps of news stories; and biographical sketches of important people of the time. These experimental techniques and his deeply detailed portraits of American society earned Dos Passos a great deal of critical praise.

These techniques brought praise from critics of the time. Dos Passos's style of emphasizing history and current events in his narrative and his striving to produce an all-encompassing portrait of the America of his time influenced many later writers of the twentieth century, including Jean-Paul Sartre, Norman Mailer, and E. L. Doctorow.

Author Biography

John Dos Passos was born on January 14, 1896, in Chicago, Illinois, the son of John Randolph Dos Passos, a wealthy attorney, and Lucy Spriggs Madison. His parents were not married, and Dos Passos spent most of his youth traveling throughout Europe and the United States with his mother; he later recalled having "a hotel childhood." He graduated from Harvard University in 1916 and served in the ambulance corps during World War I. His first novel, *One Man's Initiation: 1917*, was published in 1917, but his writing didn't receive widespread attention until the publication of his second novel, *Three Soldiers* (1921), which was based on his war experiences and intended to present a truthful portrayal of the horrors of war rather than the glori-

During his early career, Dos Passos was politically leftist and radical and was once even jailed for his views; his early novels showed his great sympathy with workers and other underdogs, and he helped to shape other "proletarian novels" that depicted the exploitation of workers by the American capitalist system. However, the events of the Spanish Civil War did much to disillusion Dos Passos, and when he grew older, he leaned toward the political right. He altered the focus in his writing, emphasizing democracy and American history. This shift did not please many of his readers and critics, who preferred his earlier work.

Dos Passos died in Baltimore, Maryland, on September 28, 1970.

Plot Summary

U.S.A. does not have a conventional plot. Dos Passos follows twelve major characters and hundreds of minor ones through the first three decades of the twentieth century. Sometimes his characters' lives intersect; sometimes they do not. Major characters in one chapter are often only fleetingly mentioned in other chapters, and not all characters are followed to what most readers would consider a satisfying end to their stories. Their tales simply leave off, as Dos Passos takes up another life and another thread in the American tapestry. As the narrative progresses, the characters do not learn and grow, but remain static, hapless representatives of their times and their particular obsessions.

The sixty-eight Newsreels, each a few pages long, are mosaics of headlines, popular song lyrics, headlines, and news of the time. They are artifacts of their times, often satirical, mysterious, or sad and are often obliquely related to incidents in the lives of the main characters. Because they focus on incongruous, trivial, or grotesque events, they give the reader a sense of the seamy, meaningless, or dangerous side of American life, a sense of moral decay or social ill, and because they're fragmented, the reader never learns the whole story behind them, adding to this sense of unease.

The fifty-one Camera Eye monologues also relate to events in the characters' lives and those described in the Newsreels and short biographies. They are written in a stream-of-consciousness style, with little punctuation or capitalization, and are typically filled with vivid, dreamlike imagery. The narrator of the monologues, never identified, is apparently Dos Passos himself, and over the course of the novel, the narrator learns and grows as a human being, unlike the characters whose lives are described in the more traditional chapters.

In the twenty-seven biographies, Dos Passos presents short sketches of the lives of people who were famous or who somehow personified the events of their time. Their stories accentuate or contrast with the lives of the fictional characters. The biographies tend to star people who were rebels against the majority during their time, who took risks, who were inventors, or who promoted new political or entrepreneurial ideas. For example, they include Frank Lloyd Wright, Thorstein Veblen, Henry Ford, John Reed, and Eugene Debs. He also presents portraits of men he did not admire but who were highly influential, such as J. P. Morgan,

Woodrow Wilson, Andrew Carnegie, and William Randolph Hearst.

The stories in the book emphasize society and history over individuality, and they provide commentaries on corporate finance, labor-management disputes, left-wing politics, union agitators, public relations, World War I, the stock market, profiteering, and their effect on American society. The author's depiction of American society is not all-encompassing; for example, Dos Passos emphasizes characters who live in the Northeast and Midwest, and all of his main characters are white.

U.S.A. opens at the beginning of the twentieth century, as industry is gaining a hold on society and the old agriculturally based culture is passing away. People feel hopeful and optimistic, until the nation enters World War I. During the war, industrialists make a great deal of money, while others lose it and class divisions become more hardened. Workers begin protesting against exploitative policies and are violently put down by the authorities. Fear of labor uprisings is fed by fears of socialism, anarchism, or Bolshevism, and workers and immigrants, who are often involved in the labor disputes, are stigmatized.

By the 1920s, America is entering a period of prosperity and glamour, despite the presence of Prohibition. Organized crime, Hollywood spectacles, and wild profits on the stock market spiral higher and higher; the rich are widely admired, and everyone else wants to get in on the money train. Middle-class and lower-class people emulate the rich and give up their souls to move in their sphere and be just like them, and any concern for the poor and downtrodden is utterly lost. Old values of respectability, hard work, and thrift have disappeared, replaced by joking familiarity, meaningless sex, moneymaking schemes, and flamboyance.

All of this ends, of course, with the crash of the stock market in 1929 and the collapse of the airy balloon of wealth that had buoyed up the nation. President Hoover's feeble reassurances do nothing to convince people that they'll be all right, and the nation sinks into the depths of the Great Depression.

Characters

Charley Anderson

Anderson grows up in Fargo, North Dakota, where his mother runs a boarding house. His father left the family about the time he was born. He is "a chunky little boy with untidy towhair and gray eyes." He has a knack for mechanical things and works as a machinist. He is politically leftist and on the side of the workers, serves as a pilot during war, and after the war goes into manufacturing with a friend. They produce airplane starter motors. At first, the business world is over his head, but he wants to make big money and be a wheeler and dealer, and eventually he learns to discuss stocks and move in the world of high finance. He loses touch with his origins, with the radical sympathies of his younger days, and with his own high standards for mechanical work. In the end, he argues with his friend, who doesn't want the production line in the factory speeded up; Charley, who was formerly so proud of his skilled work, says that competition in the business means they have to speed up, even if it means the parts aren't perfect. The two of them go on a test flight and the plane fails, leading to his friend's death. This is, of course, Charley's fault, and as a result of his failure and his increasing alcoholism, his life falls apart. He eventually dies of peritonitis.

Ben Compton

Ben Compton is a member of the Industrial Workers of the World, or "Wobblies," and works to unite workers against the bosses. He is caught and savagely beaten by authorities in Seattle, who view him as a subversive. He is a conscientious objector to the war and, as such, refuses to be conscripted. In the end, he is sentenced to jail for his beliefs. He never gives in when others attack him for his principles, no matter what the punishment they hand out and no matter how many people are against him.

He and Mary French have an affair. She wants to have a child, but he tells her it's not the time; they should save their time and energy for the movement. Later, he realizes sadly that time has passed them by and that they should have had the child. Ironically, he is expelled from the Communist Party because of internal dissents, crushing his ability to do the work for which he lives.

Concha

Concha is the woman Fenian O'Hara McCreary begins seeing after he flees his marriage with Maisie and moves to Mexico.

Daughter

See Anne Elizabeth Trent

Dick

See Richard Ellsworth Savage

Margo Dowling

Margo's mother died when she was young, and she was raised by her father and her stepmother, Agnes. Her father, an alcoholic, deserts them, and eventually Agnes remarries and takes Margo to live with her and her new husband, Frank Mandeville. He's a vaudeville performer, and through him Margo is introduced to the stage as a child. Her given name, Margery, is changed to Margo, and she learns to sing and dance. Frank sexually abuses her, a secret shame she keeps tight inside her and which makes her grow up too soon. She becomes involved with many other men, including a Cuban, Tony Garrido. Eventually, she marries him and moves to Cuba, which at first seems exotic and exciting, but she soon feels imprisoned by the slow life and repressive attitudes toward women there and flees back to the States and has an abortion; she was pregnant with Tony's child but doesn't want it.

Back in the States, she returns to the theater, sleeps with various men who might help her career, and uses her Cuban experience by telling people that she grew up on a Cuban sugar plantation and that she's descended from Spanish nobility. She meets a rich college boy, but Tony squashes that romance by showing up and saying he's her husband. He also steals the jewelry and money she's accumulated.

She moves to New York and takes up with Charley Anderson, who spends a great deal of the money he's earned in the airplane market on her. She's mercenary, chiefly interested in a man for his money, and Charley is no exception; Dos Passos notes that although Agnes talked a lot about true love, "Margo liked better to hear Mr. Anderson blowing about his killings on the stock market and the planes he'd designed, and how he was going to organize a set of airways."

Despite her lack of education, she's a shrewd self-promoter and has a good mind for business. She and Agnes head for California, and she gets jobs as a silent-film extra and impresses people with her story of being from a very wealthy family of Spanish nobles. Realizing that Hollywood is all about surface appearances, she takes a risk, buys an expensive car, and shows up for filming, with Tony dressed as her chauffeur. She looks like a star, acts like a star, and this of course convinces people that she is a star. She becomes a phenomenally wealthy and successful star of silent films. However, her career eventually ends when speaking movies come in because although she's beautiful, her voice "sounds like the croaking of an old crow over the loudspeaker."

Fainy

See Fenian O'Hara McCreary

Mary French

Mary French is an idealistic young girl, the daughter of a doctor who works in a rough mill town, and his ambitious wife. Her father wants to serve the poor, and her mother wants him to move the family to a better place and only care for rich patients. Mary inherits her father's idealistic streak. She goes to college, planning to do social work, and then quits college because she can't wait to get started. She gets a job as a reporter and is assigned to cover a story about some striking steelworkers. The editor believes they are all agitators, anarchists, and revolutionaries, paid by Russian Communists with stolen jewels. She goes to talk to the workers and finds that they're ordinary people who are being misled and exploited, and of course she's fired for writing about these atrocities.

Getting fired shocks her and galvanizes her to work for the rights of the people. She becomes a labor activist, working with Wobblies and other labor groups. During this time, she becomes pregnant and has an abortion. Then she gets back to work, this time in New York, where she takes in Ben Compton. He is a labor agitator on the run, and she lets him hide at her place. They have an affair, and although she asks him for a baby, he says they should spend their energy on the cause, not deflect their energy with a child. Reluctantly, she agrees. She spends all her time working for the cause of Sacco and Vanzetti, Italian anarchists who were accused of murder. Most people believe they are innocent but that they are accused and later declared guilty because of their radical politics. Mary throws herself into the cause of drumming up public feeling for their cause and working on appeals. She and Ben break up, and she becomes involved with another activist, who disappears to Russia and later returns married to another woman. Mary has devoted her life to causes she believed in but at the expense of her personal life. She has not had time for anything but work, and her personal relationships have suffered.

Eveline Hutchins

Eveline, the daughter of a minister, shows talent in art as a child, and as she grows up, she continues this interest. She and Eleanor Stoddard start a decorating business, and although it doesn't make much money, they meet interesting and influential people, and are "in the vanguard of things in Chicago socially." They go to New York to design costumes and scenery for a show, which closes after two weeks, but while there they meet more influential people.

Eveline is a fundamentally discontented person who has romantic and dreamy views of the world, is impressed by wealth, and wants to attach herself to it. As her interest in art indicates, she is influenced by beauty and expense. She moves from relationship to relationship, seeking something but never finding it. She and Eleanor have an uneasy friendship, nice on the surface but marred by deeper jealousies and rivalries.

By the end of the trilogy, she has become "coolly bitter" but still has hopes for her life. When Dick Savage flirts with her, she says, "There's somebody I like very much. . . . I've decided to make some sense out of my life." The man she's referring to is a columnist, someone she idolizes as "the real poet of modern New York," but who is obviously a pompous phony. The reader has the sense that nothing will really change for her.

J. W.

See John Ward Moorehouse

J. Ward

See John Ward Moorehouse

Johnny

See John Ward Moorehouse

Mac

See Fenian O'Hara McCreary

Maisie

Maisie is the young woman Fenian O'Hara McCreary dates and eventually marries, after she is pregnant with his child.

Fenian O'Hara McCreary

Known as "Fainy" to his family and "Mac" to his friends, he is born in Middletown, Connecticut, to Irish immigrant parents. His mother is a washerwoman, and his father is a night watchman at a textile mill. After his mother dies and his father loses his job because of a strike, he moves to Chicago with his family. Seeking work, he ends up as assistant to an itinerant con man and pornography salesman, rides the rails, takes various odd

jobs, and eventually becomes part of the young labor movement, which thrills him with a sense of
camaraderie among "working stiffs." He joins the
Industrial Workers of the World, or "Wobblies."
He falls in love with a girl named Maisie, who
isn't interested in his socialist ideas because they
are "too deep for her." The contrast between her
desire for a staid life and his new Wobbly acquaintances, who urge him to go to Nevada and
take part in a labor action there, galls him, but she
pressures him, and he gives in and agrees to marry
her, depressed because he's "selling out" to the
mainstream life. However, at the last minute, he
ditches her and goes to Nevada anyway.

In Nevada, he runs into trouble, as the authorities of the town are on the lookout for agitators.
He also gets a letter from Maisie, telling him she's
two months pregnant. Excited by the labor movement, he ignores her letters for months but eventually hops a freight to San Francisco, marries her,
gets a job at a printer's shop, and starts making pay-
ments on a little bungalow. They have a second
child. He wants to help out any labor agitators who
come to town, but is afraid she will find out, so he
can't do much. Her brother Bill owns a lot of real
estate and offers to set them up in an expensive
house in a rich area of Los Angeles. This puts Mac
in an uncomfortable situation of living beyond his
means. Everything goes to various debts and the
mortgage. He still goes to IWW meetings but is
afraid to do much for fear of losing his job as a
linotype operator. The other Wobblies "thought he
was pretty yellow but put up with him because they
thought of him as an old timer."

When he takes money out of their bank account to pay for his Uncle Tim's funeral, Maisie
finds out about it, accuses him of being a worthless bum who can't take care of his own family,
and says she wants a divorce. Fed up, he leaves and
goes to Mexico, where the Mexican Revolution is
underway, and links up with other socialists. He
gets a job at the *Mexican Herald* and settles down
with a girl named Concha and eventually buys a
bookstore. By the time the United States enters
World War I and the revolution is fully heated up,
he considers leaving, but in the end he goes back
to the bookstore and Concha.

John Ward Moorehouse

Moorehouse is called "Johnny" as a child but
later changes his first name to the more distinguished J. Ward, and eventually to the enigmatic
J. W. Born on the Fourth of July in Wilmington,
Delaware, Moorehouse becomes, during high

school, the head of the debating team, class orator,
and winner of a patriotic essay contest. He gets a
job for a real estate company that isn't doing very
well, but then the firm sends him to Ocean City,
where he gets a job with a company that is selling
land. He meets a charming girl, falls in love with
her, and decides to marry her because her father is
wealthy and she is pregnant. They marry and go to
Europe so that people back home won't find out
about the pregnancy, and while there, she has an
abortion. He is horrified, and from then on they
lead separate lives and eventually divorce. He returns to the United States, where he eventually gets
a job working in advertising and promotion for the
Bessemer Steel Company. He becomes devoted to
advertising, learning all about the industry, thinking up different ways to manipulate the customers
into buying. In this, he has a kind of genius. He
meets a rich girl, and when he becomes prosperous
and her father dies, apparently leaving her a lot of
money, he marries her. However, later he finds out
that the money was all left in trust to her mother
and she will only get fifteen thousand a year until
her mother dies.

He convinces his mother-in-law to invest fifty
thousand dollars into his new public relations business. He keeps filing cards on everyone he meets,
such as judges, senators, and industrialists. He fills
out the cards with every scrap of information that
will help him influence them. He views World War
I as "America's great opportunity" to make money
from "Europe's ruin" because there will be no competition from European manufacturers. He also
campaigns for industry to stand together against the
growing labor movement, exhorting that it is time
for "an educational campaign and an oral crusade
that will drive home to the rank and file of the
mighty colossus of American uptodate industry
right now, today." Pompously, he offers his services to the government "to serve in whatever capacity they see fit for the duration of the war." He
becomes involved in the negotiations of the peace
conference at Versailles and uses his influence to
see that the corporate interests are served. By serving them, he serves himself. His public relations
business prospers. His personal life, however, is a
mess; his wife assumes he's having an affair with
his companion, Eleanor Stoddard (in truth, their relationship is sexless), and his mother-in-law sues
him to force him to return the money she invested.
By the end of the trilogy, he's become a complete
phony, utterly superficial, like the worst sort of
politician. Janey, his secretary, is completely impressed by him. However, he has no true depth or

substance despite all his success, and he is not happy.

Late in the trilogy, Moorehouse has a heart attack and makes Richard Savage a partner in his firm, perhaps because he knows he won't live long.

Richard Ellsworth Savage

Known as Dick to his friends, he attends Harvard, where he writes poetry and dreams of the literary life. However, toward the end of his college years, he enlists in the volunteer ambulance service and ships out to France. Seeing the war shocks him out of his rather effete, sheltered world view, and he writes a letter to friends that expresses his true feelings: the war is "a dirty gold-brick game put over by governments and politicians for their own selfish interests, it's crooked from A to Z." As a result, he's collared by the American authorities and sent back to the States, where, through an influential friend, he gets a military commission and winds up back in Europe as a captain in the Post Dispatch Service. Colonel Edgecombe, head of the Service, offers him a position as a courier for the upcoming Peace Conference in Paris. Through this job, he moves in wealthy and diplomatic circles and meets J. Ward Moorehouse and Eleanor Stoddard, who is Moorehouse's companion. When he is sent to Rome on an errand, he meets Anne Elizabeth Trent, who has just joined the Near East Relief. They have an affair, and she gets pregnant and expects him to marry her, but he won't; he's not in love with her at all.

He's alarmed by her pregnancy, which may embarrass him or affect his career, and urges her to have an abortion, saying he'll pay for it. He has some small regret at the trouble he's caused her, but not much; shallowly, he "wished he had a great many lives so he might have spent one of them with Anne Elizabeth."

Savage admires J. Ward Moorehouse and aspires to be just like him. He becomes his protege and probable successor, working on advertising campaigns, coming up with ways to manipulate people into buying products by appealing to their vanity or other failings. He becomes wrapped up in this world, although he's not happy there. When Moorehouse has a heart attack and makes him a partner in the firm, his fate is sealed. Stressed, he goes out drinking and becomes embroiled in a sexual scandal that may cost him his career.

Eleanor Stoddard

Eleanor's father is a coarse, crude man who works as a butcher. She hates him and can't wait to get away from home. When she's thirteen, her mother dies, and she moves out of her father's house at the age of eighteen. She is interested in art and opens an interior decorating shop with her friend Eveline Hutchins. She eventually becomes a theatrical designer for a play in New York, but it fails after two weeks, and she never gets paid. She stays in New York, though, and through a friend gets a job decorating J. Ward Moorehouse's new house. Thus begins a long, nonsexual relationship with Moorehouse. She loves him, and everyone, including his wife, assumes they're having an affair, but their relationship remains platonic.

When the United States enters the war, she decides to go to France to join the Red Cross. Moorehouse comes too, claiming he's offered his services to the U.S. government. She remains his inseparable companion. When Dick Savage meets her in Europe, he notices, from the way she walks into the room and from the way Moorehouse greets her, "that she was used to running the show in that room."

Eleanor has a confusing and disappointing love life, and she ends up marrying a Russian prince, not for love, but for the title and money involved.

Anne Elizabeth Trent

Called "Daughter" by her family, Anne Elizabeth Trent grew up in Dallas, the darling of a well-to-do Southern family. She is a tomboy, quirky and energetic, and though she's somewhat tamed and taught to act like a lady, underneath her dressed-up exterior she's still a wild child. She goes to Europe to work with the Near East Relief near the end of the war and is bored by the staid, conservative, and proper women with whom she works. She falls in love with Dick Savage; they have an affair, and she gets pregnant. She wants to keep the baby and to marry Savage, but he's not interested and urges her to have an abortion. Heartbroken, she decides to die. She meets an airman, gets drunk with him, and talks him into taking her flying and doing loop-the-loops. Of course, he's not sober enough to do this safely, and the plane crashes, killing them both.

Janey Williams

Janey Williams and her brother Joe grow up in the Georgetown area of Washington, D. C., then an area of working-class families. When her brother Joe enlists in the navy and leaves town, Janey gets a job as a stenographer, despite her mother's objections that it isn't ladylike for girls to work. Janey doesn't care; she feels that there is "a great throbbing arclighted world somewhere outside" and she wants to be part of it. She moves up to working at Dreyfus and Carroll, patent lawyers, and becomes worldlier, "kidding" with men and being proud of being a "bachelor girl." After her father dies, her mother takes in boarders, giving Janey the chance to move out on her own. She's proud of being educated and making good pay and feels embarrassed about her brother, who is "so rough and uneducated." She learns to bleach her hair, use makeup, and play bridge, all marks of the "smart set" she wants to be part of.

As World War I progresses, Janey becomes uncomfortable working for Dreyfus, who according to rumor is a German spy, so she quits. After being out of work for several months, she ends up working for J. Ward Moorehouse, who impresses her with his obvious wealth and smooth style: "Everything had a well-polished silvery gleam." He talks importantly of "powerful interests in manufacturing and financial circles" who are "watching these developments with the deepest interest" and mentions the president among them. She's thrilled to be so close to such an obviously powerful man, and she develops a crush on him; in her mind, he can do no wrong. She spends the rest of the trilogy as his faithful secretary. She never marries or has a full life. Dick Savage sees her as "a tiredlooking sharpfaced blonde." Eleanor Stoddard remarks, "She's a treasure. Does more work than anybody in the whole place," but this has a patronizing air. Most people who meet her feel vaguely sorry for her.

Joe Williams

Joe is a wandering seaman who can't keep a job and who always seems to be on the outs with authorities. He is emotionally flat and limited, not educated, not imaginative, and doesn't think about his life much. He loves his sister Janey, but they are separated by her ambition and her growing embarrassment at his uneducated, low-class speech and behavior and by his lack of desire to better himself.

As a child, Joe is "an untalkative sandyhaired boy who could pitch a mean outcurve when he was still little." He is active, swimming and diving in the C & O Canal, and wants to be a streetcar motorman when he grows up. His father, who works in the Patent Office, often beats him for being too noisy, leading both Joe and his sister Janey to hate their father. When their mutual best friend, Alec, is killed in a motorcycle accident, Joe escapes his pain by enlisting in the Navy. However, he deserts in Buenos Aires after punching out a petty officer. He's traveled all over the world but has little ap-preciation for the things he's seen; his lack of education prevents him from understanding them.

He gets a counterfeit certificate saying he's an "Ablebodied Seaman" and eventually winds up in England, where he's arrested for not having a passport or other documents, which he lost when he skipped out on the Navy. They send him back to the States, and after more bumming around and more hapless adventures, he visits Janey, who is embarrassed to be seen with him. She asks him why he doesn't get a different job. She means an office job, but he says, "You mean, in a shipyard? They're making big money in shipyards, but hell, Janey, I'd rather knock around ... It's all for the experience, as the feller said when they blew his block off." He also tells her, "All my future's behind me," and "The whole world's crooked from start to finish." As an example, he notes that the Germans don't torpedo any of the French Line boats because if they do, the French won't secretly sell them munitions, which they use to blow up other French people. "All those babies are makin' big money ... while their own kin are shootin' daylight into each other at the front," he says.

He gets a legal third mate's license and marries a girl named Del but immediately ships out to France. On the way home, his ship is torpedoed, but he survives, only to find he won't get paid because of "some monkeydoodle business" about the ship's owners changing while the ship was en route. He gets on to a fruit ship and bums around the world some more. When he comes to New York again, this time he can't even reach Janey. She is J. Ward Moorehouse's secretary and is "out West on business." He bounces around some more, in and out of work, to Europe and back, and on one visit finds his wife with another man. Eventually, he heads back to Europe on yet another ship, and in a bar on Armistice Day, he gets into a fight over a woman. Someone smashes a bottle on his head, killing him.

Themes

Materialism

As Dos Passos writes in a Newsreel toward the end of the book, "America our nation has been beaten by strangers who have turned our language inside out who have taken the clean words our fathers spoke and made them slimy and foul." Moorehouse, as a supreme practitioner of bending words to his will and manipulating people with them for his own profit, is a supreme example of this statement. He has taken the vast opportunities America once offered and made a great success out of phoniness, selfishness, corruption, and greed.

Throughout the trilogy, characters comment on materialism. Behind the scenes, the wealthy wheel and deal, making arrangements to make more money even as the hapless recruits die at the front. The Peace Conference is marred by corporate interests, which make sure their interests are served. The characters who are the most financially successful and respected by others—Moorehouse, Margo Dowling, and Eleanor Stoddard—are those who are the most greedy, superficial, and materialistic. Those few who are altruistic, such as Ben Compton and Mary French, live in poverty.

Exploitation of the Working Class

The plight of the working class is frequently discussed in the book. Mac McCreary, Joe Williams, and even Janey Williams (despite her exalted position as Moorehouse's secretary) are working people, eaten up by the system. Janey is a particularly sad example of this since she thinks it's a great honor merely to serve Moorehouse. She's completely indoctrinated into the capitalist system and, in the end, gets little from it. J. Ward Moorehouse and Margo Dowling profit from the gullibility and lack of sophistication of the working class—Moorehouse because they produce and buy the products he advertises and Margo because they go to see her films. Ben Compton and Mary French try to improve things for the workers but don't succeed. Charley Anderson and Dick Savage try to become profiteers but don't survive the Darwinian winnowing of the system. In addition, the lengthy exploration of the workers' cause in the "Mary French" chapters and the depiction of the Sacco-Vanzetti trial in *The Big Money* further show how the system is arranged to crush the workers.

The disparity between the owners and the workers is also dramatized in many of the biographies, particularly those that deal with wealthy and powerful men—Carnegie, Keith, Morgan, Wilson, Hearst, Taylor, and Ford—and those that describe the opponents of capitalism—Haywood, Debs, La Follette, Reed, Hibben, Everest, and Veblen.

Just as the workers are corrupted and limited by capitalism, in the end, so are the wealthy. To be sure, they may have lives of ease and pleasure, but they are no happier than the poorest poor and, in some cases, more miserable. No one is served by

Topics for Further Study

- The trilogy ends on the eve of the Great Depression. Find a person who lived through the Great Depression and ask what life was like during that time. Ask about food, jobs, shelter, the general mood of the population, and how people coped with the poverty of that time. Write a short description of the person you interviewed and describe his or her life during the Great Depression.

- The power of advertising is a recurrent theme in the trilogy, and this industry has only grown since the time of the book's publication. Count the number of advertisements you see or hear in one day. Don't forget to include billboards, posters on trucks and in shop windows, television and radio advertisements, newspaper and magazine advertisements, and ads on the Internet. Look for ads in sneaky places, such as company logos on T-shirts and other clothing. Are you surprised by what you find? Do you think the spread of advertising in our culture is good or bad? Explain why or why not.

- Research a workers' rights group, such as the Wobblies. Write a speech from the point of view of a Wobbly and another one from the point of view of a factory owner who is against the labor movement.

- Research the Treaty of Versailles, which redefined the borders of several European countries and created some new nations—some of which no longer exist. Explain how the provisions of this treaty contributed to the tensions that led to World War II.

the system in the end. The book's wealthy and powerful characters do not come to any better ends than its most downtrodden workers.

Decay of Traditional Values

Although most of the characters in the novel come from traditional families, none of them end up with healthy families, or even healthy relationships, of their own. "Free love" is a fashionable concept, and the story line is filled with one-night stands, visits to prostitutes, unplanned pregnancies, abortions, divorces, and sexual scandals. The male characters use sex as they use alcohol, to numb the senses and the mind rather than to awaken them, and many of the female characters use sex in the same way, as well as to feel better about themselves: finally, someone wants them. Once a liaison occurs, they share an undefined and inarticulate longing for marriage, fueled not by love for the man, but out of some sense that this is what they "should" do. In many cases, the women end up pregnant, and, urged on by their male partner, have an illegal abortion. Many of the men contract sexually transmitted diseases, as do some of the women. Dos Passos never portrays sex as mediating an emotional, spiritual, or intellectual connection between people; it's always mindless, mechanical, repetitive, and unsatisfying, like the lives of his characters as a whole. Even Ben Compton and Mary French, his two most sympathetic characters, miss their chance to have a healthy family and realize too late what they've missed.

In addition, most people in the novel are impressed by money, flashiness, phoniness, and greed—all aspects of J. Ward Moorehouse's character. It's no surprise that he is the most financially successful and widely respected individual in the book: he embodies the flaws of his age, which people saw as desirable and impressive traits.

Drunkenness appears frequently in the book, often occurring along with sexual encounters, and it's never depicted as simple social drinking but as a wish for oblivion, for a dullness of the senses, for a total loss of thought, a blotting out of the senses. Often, during drunken sex, children are conceived, but they are not wanted, another symptom of what Dos Passos viewed as the emotional shallowness and corruption of the times.

Style

Experimental Techniques

A notable feature of *U.S.A.* is its experimental sections, the "Camera Eye," "Newsreel," and biography sections. The Camera Eye sections offer a disjointed collage of headlines, story fragments, song lyrics, and other scraps, almost like what one would have heard while walking down the street in a busy town during the period. The scraps are carefully chosen to reflect, amplify, or comment on the material in the fictional chapters; for example, an early chapter about Mac McCreary portrays his realization that the fine traveling sales in publishing jobs he's found is a scam and his boss is a con artist and a crook. The chapter ends with Mac running for his life from a farmer with a shotgun, followed by a Newsreel that begins "IT TAKES NERVE TO LIVE IN THIS WORLD." After this comes a piece of a story about an anarchist plot and the lyrics of a song about the simple rural life—ironic since Mac has just fled from a farm. More fragments portray the difficulties of workers, a commentary on his situation, since he is now out of a job.

In another example, a chapter about Joe Williams describes his ship being torpedoed, and this is followed by a Camera Eye piece about the author swimming in the Marne River while serving during World War I, "with that hammering to the north pounding the thought of death into our ears," and notes, "the winey thought of death stings in the spring blood." Joe is too blunted and inarticulate to be moved by thoughts of war and death when his ship goes down. This fragment offers an oblique reflection on his experience, and on the author's.

Narrative Voice

Dos Passos's style in *U.S.A.* is deliberately rambling, repetitive, and unselective, as he meant to give the effect of real people talking, real people thinking about their lives. The text is cluttered with one event after another, some leading to other things, some not relevant at all in the long run.

In addition, in each chapter, Dos Passos adapts the voice to that of the character whose story he's telling. For example, chapters about Joe Williams are told in the rough, down-to-earth voice of a sailor: "In the afternoon, Joe's watch got off, though it wasn't much use going ashore because nobody had gotten any pay. . . . Joe was thirsty for a beer but he didn't have a red cent." Joe's chapters contain very little reflection, no commentary on thoughts, hopes, or feelings; he is usually reacting to things outside himself, rarely making conscious decisions or planning for his future.

In the first chapter about Anne Elizabeth Trent, known as "Daughter," Dos Passos adopts the breathless, bragging voice of a child who has been told her state and her people are the best:

> The Trents lived in a house on Pleasant avenue that was the finest street in Dallas that was the biggest and fastest growing town in Texas that was the

biggest state in the Union and had the blackest soil and the whitest people and America was the greatest country in the world and Daughter was Dad's onlyest sweetest little girl.

Chapters about J. Ward Moorehouse, who is skilled with words and in using them to flatter and influence people, are written in a puffed-up, euphemistic style similar to his speech: "But the financial situation of his family was none too good, his father said, shaking his head." This is in great contrast to chapters about Joe, who is commonly "flat broke" or "without a red cent" but who would never be described as having a "financial situation" that is "none too good."

The people seem recognizable, the voices familiar, ones that readers might hear on any street corner, in any bar. Because the style is personalized for each character, the stories work their way into the reader's psyche. The familiar voices and seemingly endless proliferation of details about these characters' daily lives make them seem like people one has always known: friends, relatives, coworkers.

Emotionally Flat Characters

The characters in the trilogy rarely reflect on their fate, and when they do, they seem helpless to change it. Their understanding of their own lives is fragmented, and they seem like sleepwalkers, never questioning what they value or why they value it. The exceptions to this are the activists, Mary French, Ben Compton, and, in the early part of his life, Mac McCreary, who don't like what they see and work to change it. However, their work is ineffectual and ultimately they don't succeed.

All of the characters are alienated to some degree from their families, from their wives or husbands, boyfriends or girlfriends. No one in the book ultimately has a lasting or satisfying relationship with anyone else.

This alienation reflects the alienation Dos Passos saw in society: contemplation was not valued, but action, however mindless, was. In addition, he saw society as superficial, interested in money and power and flash, not in any inner qualities of the individual; esteeming people for their morals, education, or character had become out of style, allowing people like the unctuous Moorehouse and the flashy Margo Dowling to succeed.

Historical Context

The Wobblies

The Industrial Workers of the World was founded in 1905 in Chicago at a convention of two hundred socialists, anarchists, radicals, and trade unionists from all over the United States. Its purpose, according to Bill Haywood, who opened the convention, was:

> the emancipation of the working-class from the slave bondage of capitalism. . . . to put the working-class in possession of the economic power, the means of life, in control of the machinery of production and distribution, without regard to the capitalist masters.

The members of the IWW, or "Wobblies," as they came to be known, believed that workers and employers had nothing in common and were fundamentally enemies. The Wobblies aimed to organize all workers in every industry into one big union, which would not be divided by gender, race, or skills. They also believed that negotiating with the owners was a mistake because it often sidetracked workers from their goals. They advocated direct action by the workers themselves, rather than negotiation by "labor misleaders" or "scheming politicians." An IWW pamphlet explained "direct action" as "the worker on the job shall tell the boss when and where he shall work, how long and for what wages and under what conditions."

Naturally, this militant attitude was powerfully attractive to some workers and powerfully frightening to industry owners. Although the IWW never had more than five thousand to ten thousand members at any one time, it was feared, detested, and attacked by various authorities: newspapers, courts, police, military, and ordinary people. Workers were often arrested simply on suspicion of being Wobblies, and when the Wobblies demonstrated or went on strike, they were frequently the targets of police brutality and illegal arrests. Some were shot, and at least one, Frank Little, was tortured and hanged.

Wobblies spread their ideas by writing, speaking, and singing about them. A well-known song was "The Preacher and the Church," also known as "Pie in the Sky," in which a poor man asks a preacher what he can eat. The preacher offers no help but says, "You'll get pie in the sky when you die."

The Versailles Peace Conference

By the end of the First World War, there were endless new fields of gravestones across Europe. Nine million people had died in the war, and those

Compare & Contrast

- **1938:** German dictator Adolf Hitler begins his expansion throughout Europe with his occupation of Austria. In November, 191 synagogues are set on fire, 7,500 Jewish businesses are looted, and thirty thousand Jews are rounded up and sent to concentration camps. Eventually, over 6 million Jews will be killed before World War II and Germany's domination of Europe are brought to an end.

    Today: With attacks on the World Trade Center Towers in New York and on the Pentagon in Washington, D.C., and with increasing fears about conventional, biological, and nuclear terrorism, the United States may be poised on the brink of yet another war.

- **1938:** Advertisers begin to tap the vast power of radio. More than one-third of the billings at top advertising agencies are for radio ads; other ads are posted in newspapers, magazines, and billboards. Advertisers are beginning to realize that understanding the psychology of consumers is key in successful advertising.

    Today: Advertising pervades every aspect of American culture. Advertisers use the Internet, television, and other media to get their message across, and they collect detailed information on consumers to help target their ads more effectively. Some of this information-gathering borders on invasion of privacy; for example, some pharmacies have sold information on what medicines their customers are taking to drug companies, who then mail targeted ads to these individuals.

- **1938:** The Great Depression, which began with the crash of the stock market on October 29, 1929, continues, and only ends when the United States joins the fight in World War II.

    Today: After the financial growth of the 1990s, the United States again borders on recession in 2001, which is later worsened by the September 11 terrorist attacks and subsequent drops in the value of stocks in transportation, travel, hospitality, and insurance industries, as well as widespread job layoffs in those industries.

---

who survived swore it would never happen again—it had been "the war to end all wars."

At the Versailles Peace Conference, held in 1919 at the French palace of Versailles, President Woodrow Wilson promised that that new peace would be held securely by the new League of Nations and by disarmament of the aggressors in the war. The League of Nations was supposed to allow nations to discuss their disagreements and resolve them through negotiation so that international conflicts would no longer escalate to war.

The Treaty also required that Germany pay reparations to the countries it had attacked, and it set out borders for new nations: Czechoslovakia, Yugoslavia, and Poland, carved out of the old Germany. This, of course, left Germans bitter, and their bitterness increased as the burden of paying reparations affected their economy. Inflation skyrocketed, spreading poverty throughout the country.

The United States did not join the League of Nations; Congress refused to ratify it. Most Americans believed that America was far away from Europe and that Americans didn't need to become involved in European problems or negotiations. This isolationism, of course, would not last. By the Second World War, it would become apparent to Americans that they could not separate themselves from the rest of the world.

The Trial of Sacco and Vanzetti

In 1920, Italian anarchists Nicola Sacco and Bartolomeo Vanzetti were arrested in South Braintree, Massachusetts, near Boston and were charged with killing a shoe factory paymaster and his guard. Vanzetti was also charged with a previous attempt at robbery, and this lesser crime, in which no one was hurt, was tried first. Although Vanzetti had a strong alibi, many of the witnesses in his defense did not speak English well. At the time, prejudice against Italians and other immigrants was strong, and the Italian witnesses' testimony failed to convince the American jury that Vanzetti was innocent. In addition, Vanzetti did not take the stand in his own defense because he was afraid of revealing his anarchist activities. His silence hurt his case, and he was found guilty. He was sentenced to ten to fifteen years, a much harsher sentence than usual.

The harshness of this sentence made the two men think that the authorities might have a political or hostile bias against them. They hired Fred H. Moore, a socialist lawyer. He agreed that they were known to the authorities as anarchist militants who were involved in labor strikes, political agitation, and antiwar protests. At the time, the authorities were deeply afraid of any socialists, anarchists, or activists and punished them severely.

In the trial for the Braintree robbery, both men initially lied about their involvement in radical politics. This only raised the authorities' suspicion that they were guilty. Moore's defense focused on exposing the prosecution's prejudice against their politics and establishing that they had been arrested because they were known radicals, not because they were guilty. Moore enlisted the help of labor unions, international groups, and the Italian government and distributed thousands of pamphlets about the case throughout the United States. All this publicity made the trial into an international workers' cause. After a six-week trial, however, the two men were found guilty of robbery and murder, on July 14, 1921. The defense continued to struggle for a new trial until 1927, when the two men were sentenced to death. By this time, they had come to represent social justice and freedom of speech to many people who believed they were innocent.

To this day, their actual guilt or innocence is still in question, and the case is still of interest because of what it reveals about how political and social attitudes may potentially pervert the purity of American justice.

Critical Overview

According to Daniel Aaron in *American Heritage*, the publication of *U.S.A.* "secured John Dos Passos's place in American literary history." However, Aaron remarked, eventually his reputation "faded, and his rowdy, acrid masterpiece petrified into a 'classic.'" Despite this, Aaron noted, "no other

novelist of his times had so ingeniously evoked the scope and variety of the United States."

Many critics have commented on the book's pessimistic nature, but most have found this pessimism a necessary part of Dos Passos's style and message. Perry D. Westbrook wrote in the *Reference Guide to American Literature* that the book is "disheartening," remarking that:

[The book] inevitably leaves the reader with the sense of profound loss, a feeling of ideals and values betrayed. Yet the fervor with which Dos Passos wrote indicates that he believes the loss might not be irretrievable. He wrote from imagination and outrage perhaps, but not total despair.

In *John Dos Passos: Politics and the Writer*, Robert C. Rosen wrote that the book may appear to be "a self-defeating novel of protest: characters are so degraded they seem incapable of full human development in any social order; there is nothing to be saved." However, he noted, some of the characters do have personal will and determination, and their choices, as well as "the tension between naturalism and the intense moral indignation" that pervade the novel, provide much of the novel's energy. He commented, "Its bleak vision of nearly universal defeat demands radical social change."

Joseph Warren Beach, in the *Sewanee Review*, noted that although some readers might be repelled by "the inconclusiveness of the story, and by the little meaning and little value in the lives presented," this is exactly Dos Passos's point: "his main impression of contemporary life is of ordinary people caught in the mechanism of a soulless society, and exceptional cases would be irrelevant to the point he is making." In the end, he noted, Dos Passos "has given us the most comprehensive and convincing picture of American life in certain highly characteristic phases that is anywhere to be found."

George J. Becker remarked in *John Dos Passos* that because of Dos Passos's skill as a writer, the novel "comes close to being the great American novel which had been the aspiration of writers since the turn of the century" and commented that it's ironic that "when the great American novel did arrive, it turned out to be condemnatory and pessimistic rather than a celebration of the American way."

Some critics have remarked on Dos Passos's use of the Camera Eye and Newsreel pieces, as well as on his insertion of biographies of real people into the text. Although the Camera Eye and Newsreel pieces were praised when the book first came out, some readers since then have found them difficult to get through. For example, in *Commonweal*, Edward T. Wheeler wrote that as a younger man he found the book's experimental passages impenetrable. However, he wrote, "the passage of time has cleared up the nature of Dos Passos's masterpiece. I wish the book had been longer!"

Jean-Paul Sartre wrote about the experimental techniques in *Literary and Philosophical Essays* saying, "Dos Passos has invented only one thing, an art of story-telling. But that is enough to create a universe."

Criticism

Kelly Winters

Winters is a freelance writer and has written for a wide variety of educational publishers. In this essay, she considers Dos Passos's depiction of women in his novel.

At first glance, it might seem that Dos Passos's depiction of women is sexist or negative—after all, most of the women in *U.S.A.* are superficial examples of various stereotypes of women: the devoted secretary, the coarse but successful show-business woman, the jealous wife, the career girl, the dedicated social worker, as well as countless one-night-stands, prostitutes, and simple girls who think a man will marry them if they get pregnant but are proved wrong. Most of the main female characters become pregnant one or more times and, when they don't have a miscarriage, opt for abortion; in fact, sexual liaisons, inevitably followed by pregnancy, occur frequently throughout the trilogy. At times, this pattern is varied when characters become ill with venereal disease, making the sex seem even more distasteful.

Dos Passos's depictions of women characters are all flat, but what must be remembered is that Dos Passos's depictions of *all* his characters—male or female—are flat. There is no love in the book, no humor, nothing light or flighty, and nothing religious or spiritual. His characters do not dream, wish, or hope. They live solely and solidly on the physical plane, and any emotions they do have are simple reactions to physical events around them: fear, greed, lust, triumph, anger, frustration, jealousy. Confusion is perhaps the prime emotion many of them feel, as the world seems to be moving too fast for them, leaving them no time to reflect.

This somewhat shallow presentation of characters may seem to be a flaw, but this was simply Dos Passos's point: he believed that American culture was becoming increasingly shallow, materialistic, and crass, leading either to shallow, materialistic, and crass people, or to the destruction of those who did not fit into this mold or who were used or abused by the materialists. The most successful people in the book are the most greedy and self-serving, such as Margo Dowling and J. Ward Moorehouse. Significantly, both have mastered the art of manipulation, giving people what they think they want, using appearances to impress. Both act important, respected, and wealthy, and because people believe in this false front, they succeed.

Dos Passos's characters are not individualists; most of them want to belong to a group or be admired by a group. Even those who buck the system by becoming labor activists are buoyed up by their sense of being part of a sweeping movement. Joe, perhaps the biggest loner among them, is also the biggest loser; and he is not a loner by choice but simply because he is out of step with the times. Trusting, clever with his hands but not his head or heart, he is being left behind in the new America, where "working stiffs" like him are bound to fail. Another loser is Janey, who desperately wants to belong to the "smart set" and feels deeply honored simply to be Moorehouse's secretary; she never dreams of rising farther but is relieved to have a place where she belongs.

Although Dos Passos vigorously describes the oppression of working people, he offers no overt comment on the oppression of women in society in the fictional portions of the trilogy. In addition, of the twenty-seven short biographies appearing in between the chapters, only one, that of dancer Isadora Duncan, describes the life of a woman.

However, perhaps Dos Passos is not as sexist as these facts might at first imply. His presentation of only one women in twenty-seven influential people could just as easily be seen as a commentary on the fact that women were not allowed to hold influential positions during the time span covered by the trilogy.

In addition, in the fictional part of the trilogy, half of the main characters are female, and of all of them, the one who is most admirable is Mary French, the social activist. Although many of the other women characters are presented as shallow and limited, the presentation of their stories suggests that Dos Passos was indeed aware of their oppression. For example, he shows how Anne Elizabeth Trent, who begins as such a bright, tough tomboy, is brought low by the limited opportunities available to her and by the continual social pressure on her to "behave" and attach herself to a man. When she finally does, she chooses Richard Savage, who uses her and then dumps her, and she eventually commits suicide by flying with a drunk pilot and urging him to do loop-the-loops. If she had lived in a more open society, where she was able to use her energy and drive productively, it's doubtful that such a strong woman would have resorted to this desperate measure.

In addition, Dos Passos shows, through his depictions of women characters through the course of the trilogy, how women's roles were changing as the decades progressed. In *The 42nd Parallel*, Eleanor and Janey are both leery of men, vaguely frightened of them and their power, believing they're "out for one thing." Both eventually develop careers of their own, but these are fueled by the career of a man who has power: Janey is J. W. Moorehouse's secretary, and Eleanor is his quasi-mistress. Without J. W., or some other man, they could not succeed, and even with him, they're limited: it's unthinkable that they could be wheeling and dealing like he is, running a company, or bossing anyone, because they are women.

Later, in *The Big Money*, women are still not free but have made some strides. Mary and Margo are both strong women who are able to have careers of their own, independent from the careers of men, and influence large numbers of other people.

Perhaps Dos Passos's most obvious commentary on the status of women occurs in the Newsreel portions of the trilogy, where women are frequently degraded or depicted as occupied with trivial matters; for example, in between fragments about the sinking of the *Titanic* is a frivolous description of a bride's dress; and in between a series of fragments describing the ominous and violent events leading to World War I are pieces of romantic songs, fashion columns, and commentaries on debutantes. This juxtaposition continues throughout the trilogy, emphasizing the difference between the dreamy, childish world occupied by women and the real world occupied by men, where people were killed in labor riots and wars.

In *1919*, fragments of accounts of women being raped, harassed, killed, and committing suicide increase in the Newsreels. These are juxtaposed with pieces about military conquest and comments that, because of the war, marriages and births have declined. The few mentions of women in the News-

> " His presentation of only one women in twenty-seven influential people could just as easily be seen as a commentary on the fact that women were not allowed to hold influential positions during the time span covered by the trilogy."

reels become increasingly bizarre: "Tattooed Woman Sought by Police in Trunk Murder," "Army Wife Slashed by Admirer," "Piteous Plaint of Wife Tells of Rival's Wiles." In the last Newsreel of the book, a woman tells how her first husband, second husband, and son were all killed while crossing train tracks. These all add up to provide a sense of futility and loss for women of the time.

In *The Big Money*, more stories of suicide appear in the Newsreels. A headline about a Russian baroness committing suicide is followed by a song line: "the kind of girl that men forget / Just a toy to enjoy for a while." This echoes the earlier story of Anne Elizabeth Trent, who committed suicide when Richard Savage abandons her. However, along with the violent pieces, the fragments also show women becoming active in labor disputes, voting, and being involved in military events, reflecting their changing role in society. Newsreel LI presents a long list of jobs for women, available because so many men were killed in World War I. However, along with this, it also presents less savory job offers and symbolically includes stanzas from "St. James Infirmary," a song about a dead, cold woman lying on a hospital table. This implies that even while women were enjoying increased economic freedom and opportunity, there was a dark side to this, and their economic freedom did not necessarily mean that they were socially equal to men. The job ads reflect this, noting "a good opportunity for stylish young ladies," echoing the obsession with style and fashion even in the face of horror that was presented in the Newsreels of *The 42nd Parallel*.

What Do I Read Next?

- *One Man's Initiation* (1917), Dos Passos's first novel, tells about his experiences on the Western Front during World War I.

- Dos Passos's *Manhattan Transfer* (1925), set in New York City, shows his experimentation with some of the same fictional techniques he later used in *U.S.A.*

- Dos Passos's *Three Soldiers* (1921) was considered the best war novel written up to that time.

- Upton Sinclair's *The Jungle* (1906), a depiction of the horrors and abuses in the turn-of-the-century American meat packing industry, was so influential that it led to the establishment of the Food and Drug Administration, as well as Pure Food Laws.

- John O'Hara's *Appointment in Samarra* (1934) portrays the effects of the coming depression and the increased diversity of America on characters from various parts of society.

- *Babbitt* by Sinclair Lewis (1922) tells the story of a vulgar real-estate man, the total conformist, in this commentary on American commercial culture.

Because Dos Passos selected these fragments from the wealth of headlines, news clippings, songs, and advertisements of the era, it's clear that he's shaping a pattern and presenting a message about the times. He provides commentaries on war, on fads of the time, on politics, and on the fate of working people. Along with these commentaries, the continuing thread of pieces about women in the Newsreels makes clear that he is aware that women are abused, that their talents are wasted and their energies misdirected, that they are overlooked and exploited just as workers are. The Newsreels invoke a variety of mixed emotions: anger, sadness, a sense of incongruity, and a feeling of bewilderment and despair.

Source: Kelly Winters, Critical Essay on *U.S.A.*, in *Novels for Students*, The Gale Group, 2002.

John H. Wrenn

In the following essay excerpt, Wrenn explores the themes of memory, language, tragedy, and doubt and affirmation in U.S.A.

I. A Book of Memories

U.S.A. is first of all a book of memories. These memories, all relating to the United States during the first third of the twentieth century, are presented and developed contrapuntally in autobiography, history, biography, and fiction. The form is that of the associational process of memory itself, by which perceptions are established in the mind and later recalled. And the purpose of the work is equivalent to the function of the memory: to establish in the mind perceptions which, in association with other perceptions from experience such as those of pleasure or pain, develop into attitudes toward certain kinds of experience, frames of reference, or standards by which we judge today.

Dos Passos' intent was to establish for himself and his audience a broad and pertinent framework of memory. This required a maximum selective recall of his own experience, supplemented by the general experience and that of other individuals recorded in documents of the times. It also required an imaginative organization of these materials into a mnemonic unity which could suggest appropriate attitudes toward related kinds of past, present, and future experience.

If he could get a sequence of enough memories, or even a characteristic segment of them, into focus in his camera's eye, he could develop it, edit it, and give it artistic form. Then he could run it through again, stop the motion for a moment if he wished, and present a close-up or a flash-back: "Now who was that, could that have been me in that funny hat?" He could also give a tune or a speech on the sound track. The viewer might even leave the theater wiser than when he went in; at any rate, a few people might risk a nickel to see it. It would probably be misleadingly advertised as one of the "exclusive presentations of the Mesmer Agency" containing comments on "the great and near great" and "a fund of racy anecdotes"—as Dos Passos later satirized the bally-hooing of his books in *The Prospect Before Us* (1950). But for himself, he would present it only as one man's attempt to "add his nickel's worth."

When it was ready, some risked their nickels; and almost the first thing they saw was the producer-director as a little child flitting across the screen, like Alfred Hitchcock sneaking into his own films. As autobiography Dos Passos presented his own story directly in the Camera Eye sequences, in stream-of-consciousness—or more accurately, stream-of-memory—narration. His story in *The 42nd Parallel* is almost entirely separate from the rest of his history of the country in the early years of the century; but, as the novel progresses through the three volumes, there is a continuous tightening in the relationship of its several parts—narrative, Camera Eyes, Newsreels, biographies—as the narrator becomes one with his subject.

In *1919* the autobiography of the Camera Eyes begins to merge with the fictional story of Dick Savage, especially at Harvard and in the war. Toward the end of the final volume, *The Big Money*, Camera Eyes Forty-nine and Fifty include indirect biography of Sacco and Vanzetti; and in between those two sequences Dos Passos' story merges with the fictional story of Mary French in her work for the Sacco-Vanzetti defense and with the history of the time as outlined in Newsreel LXVI. Finally, within the last twenty-five pages of the trilogy, the fictional Ben Compton (the prototype of Glenn Spotswood in his next novel, *Adventures* and of Jay Pignatelli in *Chosen Country*), expresses, peering "through his thick glasses," Dos Passos' relationship to the Communist Party: "oppositionist . . . exceptionalism . . . a lot of nonsense." And in the final sketch, "Vag," of the last two and a half pages, the Camera Eye has become the biography o the depression vagrant, a distinctive phenomenon of the times. It is also very nearly the picture of Jimmy Herf hitchhiking west out of Manhattan.

In *U.S.A.* Dos Passos placed himself securely within the history of his country in his time. But he emphasized the history above the importance of his relation to it. As an historian, he did not need to be told that his country's own brand of idealism was "democracy"; the problem was to discover what the word meant. It seemed to have pretty much lost its meaning at about the time the United States had fought a war to make the world safe for it. Taking the word at its pre-war value, Dos Passos devoted his trilogy to a history of the struggle for industrial democracy in America.

As a critic Dos Passos has always been principally interested in the effects of phenomena upon individual men and women. This interest helped to make him a novelist; and it—and not simply his

> The focus of *U.S.A.*, therefore, is upon the twenty-six *actual* persons engaged in the struggle and the twelve principal *fictional* persons also engaged in it and affected by it."

training as a novelist—focuses all of his histories upon personalities and traits of character. The focus of *U.S.A.*, therefore, is upon the twenty-six *actual* persons engaged in the struggle and the twelve principal *fictional* persons also engaged in it and affected by it. The actual people of the biographies are those who influenced the pattern of the struggle—labor leaders, politicians, artists, journalists, scientists, and business leaders. The fictional characters represent average men and women molded by the complex of forces about them.

The fictional characters illustrate more than anything else the dissolution of the once central cohesive institution in American society (the one Dos Passos first achieved with his marriage in 1929, as he began *U.S.A.*), the family. Although most of them come from fairly secure family units, they are unable to form them for themselves. The fictional narrative is filled with pathetic promiscuity, perversion, vague temporary alliances, divorces, abortions. Ben Compton, again, sums up the need at the end of *The Big Money*. Speaking to Mary French, who is one of the most sympathetically portrayed of the principal characters and whose maternal instincts have made her a devoted worker for the oppressed, Ben says, "You know if we hadn't been fools we'd have had that baby that time . . . we'd still love each other."

In Dos Passos' picture of the U.S.A., it was essential to reinstitute the family; but neither of the two larger institutions in which the forces of the times had become polarized—*laissez-faire* capitalism and Stalinist communism—appeared to permit its free growth. Until people achieved a social system which would give the average man a sense of participation—of responsibility for and pride in his work—the smaller more vital social units would be ineffective. To achieve that system, the meaning of the old mercantile-agrarian democracy and its libertarian phraseology—liberty, equality, pursuit of happiness—must somehow be restored in the scientific, urban-industrial present.

The makers of that present and those who hoped to remake it are the subjects of the biographies. Toward each of the principal fictional characters, each of whom is seen as a child, the reader shares Dos Passos' affection, which turns to scorn or pity as they become mere cogs or pulp in the capitalist or communist machines, or to indignation as their individualism leaves them crushed and dead—like Joe Williams and Daughter, both killed by accident in France in the aftermath of the war—or stranded and alone like Ben Compton. Toward the biographies, however the reader's reaction is principally a sharing of the burning indignation with which most of them were written. Of the twenty-six, not counting the two portraits of the anonymous Unknown Soldier and "Vag," fourteen are sympathetic and twelve are not.

The criterion of judgment of them as of the fictional characters is the courage or will of the individual to maintain the faith that most of them were born to in the untarnished meanings of the democratic creed. By this criterion we recognize them as friends or strangers whatever their births or origins or ends. If their work is intended to uphold the dignity of the individual man and woman and the integrity of their language as Americans, they are friends. If they are scornful or even like Edison and Henry Ford merely "unconcerned with the results of [their] work in human terms," they are "strangers" of Camera Eye Fifty, "who have turned our language inside out who have taken the clean words our fathers spoke and made them slimy and foul."

Dos Passos is not at all mysterious as to his purposes; he even states them directly in Camera Eyes Forty-seven and Forty-nine of *The Big Money:* ". . . shape words remembered light and dark straining to rebuild yesterday to clip out paper figures to stimulate growth Warp newsprint into faces smoothing and wrinkling in the various barelyfelt velocities of time." Or again, reporting his reporting of the Sacco-Vanzetti case: "pencil scrawls in my notebook the scraps of recollection the broken halfphrases the effort to intersect word with word to dovetail clause with clause to rebuild out of mangled memories unshakably (Oh Pontius Pilate) the truth." Here is the meaning of the terms "straight writing" and "architect of history."

Yet the architect of history works not only "to rebuild yesterday" as the foundation of today, but to build of today a sound foundation for tomorrow. By straight writing and with the materials of contemporary speech, the writer provides contexts of meaning for today's speech, which will be the basis of tomorrow's memories. Dos Passos achieves his contexts through the use of dialogue and even of direct narration phrased in the colloquial language appropriate to the character he is treating. The reader sees and hears the speech in conjunction with actions and through the consciousness of the character concerned. We participate in the individual's attitudes toward events.

Further than this, Dos Passos has the reader share, at least for the moment, the attitudes of quite different individuals toward the same or similar events. We see the affair between Dick Savage and Daughter (Anne Elizabeth Trent), for instance, through the eyes and feelings of each of them. To Dick it is simply an affair which becomes awkward and threatens to embarrass him in his career when Daughter expects him to feel some responsibility for her pregnancy. To her it is a tremendous event which results in tragedy. The reader also sees and experiences a variety of attitudes toward business, labor, government, the war, the Sacco-Vanzetti case, and many other institutions and particular events. Since he cannot sympathetically entertain at the same time two opposing attitudes toward a single phenomenon, he is forced to choose, to criticize, to formulate standards.

As a realist Dos Passos reveals his characters in the historical framework of time, place, and social milieu which help to form them. These backgrounds, usually presented through the memories of the characters themselves, are various enough to provide a representative cross-section, geographically and socially, of American society. In the "Introduction" to *Three Soldiers*, Dos Passos remarked that "our beds have made us and the acutest action we can take is to sit up on the edge of them and look around and think." In describing his characters' beds, Dos Passos is an objective reporter of existing phenomena. But in portraying the individuals themselves and their attempts to sit up and look around and think, he is a selective critic. He controls our choice of attitude by creating characters with whom we must at first sympathize, for their beds and their wants are ours. We continue to sympathize as they struggle to express themselves and to satisfy their needs; but we become indignant at the Procrustean forces that chain them prone in their beds or at the individuals as they lose the courage to struggle, refuse to think, or prefer to crawl back under the sheets within the security of the familiar narrow limits of their bedsteads.

II. *Tools of Language*

Half of the fictional characters of *U.S.A.* and nearly half of the subjects of the biographies have a special facility with the tools of language, the means with which to build or to restrict human freedom. Of the fictional ones, most are poor or careless keepers of their talents. J. Ward Moorehouse becomes a public-relations executive—a propagandist for big business who exploits language for profit; Janey becomes his expert private secretary and an efficient, warped old maid; Dick Savage degenerates from a young poet to Moorehouse's administrative assistant and contact-man—a sort of commercial pimp. Mac surrenders his principles as an itinerant printer for the labor movement and succumbs to the security offered by a girl and a little bookstore of his own in Mexico; Mary French and Ben Compton become pawns of communist politics. Only Ben emerges at the end, though rejected and alone, still looking around him and thinking.

In contrast, only three of roughly a dozen subjects of the biographies seem to misuse their gifts of language: Bryan, "a silver tongue in a big mouth"; Woodrow Wilson, "talking to save his faith in words, talking . . . talking"; Hearst, whose "empire of the printed word . . . this power over the dreams of the adolescents of the world grows and poisons like a cancer." Most of the heroes of Dos Passos' biographies are chosen from among the heroes and martyrs of the working-class movement: men who looked around, thought critically, and developed their abilities in an effort to restore the meanings rather than to exploit the phraseology of American democracy. They were men like Eugene Debs, Bill Haywood, La Follette, Jack Reed, Randolph Bourne, Paxton Hibben, Joe Hill, Thorstein Veblen.

Dos Passos' own handling of the language can be demonstrated in an example from his fictional narrative in *1919*. Dick Savage at the end of the war is still in Paris; Daughter, spurned by her "Dickyboy" and carrying his child, goes off alone in a taxi Dick, now captain but angling for a public relations job after the war, goes to bed with a hangover; but he cannot get to sleep:

> Gradually he got warmer. Tomorrow. Seventhirty: shave, buckle puttees . . . Day dragged out in khaki. . . Dragged out khaki days until after the signing of the peace. Dun, drab, khaki. Poor Dick got to go to work after the signing of the peace. Poor Tom's cold. Poor Dickyboy . . . Richard . . . He brought his feet up to where he could rub them. Poor Richard's feet. After the signing of the Peace.

Dick is a Harvard graduate; he had intended to become a writer. He has nearly lost our sympathy because of his attitude toward Daughter. Here he gives up the struggle to sit up and think as he climbs literally and figuratively into bed, self-indulgent, self-pitying. "Poor Tom" suggests his subconscious awareness of his disguise—in part the uniform of an officer and a gentleman, in part his role of a dedicated poet; and it also suggests the contrast of his character with that of Edgar in *King Lear*. "Poor Dickyboy" reveals the transfer of his pangs of conscience into self-sympathy. "Poor Richard" indicates his falling from critical awareness into the thoughtless selfishness of the old American cliché of success (Franklin's Poor Richard and Horatio Alger's Ragged Dick), as he resumes the foetal position because he lacks the courage to think and to doubt; he has, in the vernacular, cold feet: "By the time his feet were warm he'd fallen asleep."

The picture is at once comic and pathetic and somewhat revolting. Up to about this point we have been sympathizing with Dick as another struggling, wanting human; suffering with him; and enjoying his occasional successes as our own. In this passage, Dos Passos' method prevents our suddenly ceasing to participate. We must share Dick's experience—after all a rather ordinary one, already familiar to us—at the same time that we reject it. We share from within his consciousness; we observe and reject from outside it. By the multiplication of such experiences Dos Passos attempts to establish in the reader something like what T. S. Eliot called the objective correlative of the work of art; but another name for it is a critical standard or part of a frame of reference. Once established, it exists outside of, even independent of, its original source. If Dick Savage's retreat from responsibility, for example, is established as symbolic of all retreat from responsibility, and if we are made to reject it here, then we must reject it whenever we encounter it.

This process Dos Passos once explained in a little-known "Introductory Note" to the first Modern Library edition of his *42nd Parallel* as the destruction and reconstruction of stereotypes. He was aware that it would probably lose him readers "People feel pain when the stereotype is broken, at least at first." But it was the necessary method of the architect of history. The reaction from the reader is similar to the "grin of pain" that Dos Passos described as the essential response to satire in his essay about George Grosz in 1936.

Yet the reader's reaction to Dos Passos' novels is only remotely and occasionally one of mirth. To *U.S.A.* it is more nearly a grim realization of the sores and weaknesses of our culture which cry out for repair. To some readers, doubtless, it is too bad that Dos Passos is not more nearly the satirist than he is. Perhaps a leavening of humor that could change a grimace to a grin would make him more palatable to both readers and critics and, therefore, presumably more effective because more widely read. But Dos Passos' intent is vitally serious. He does not write to entertain but to communicate, to inform—in brief, to educate. He has always been too close to his materials, too involved personally, to be able to attain the special kind of detachment demanded of the satirist. Like Swift indeed, he heartily loves John, Peter, Thomas, and so forth; but he can by no means manage a principal hate and detestation for that animal called man.

III. Method of Tragedy

Rather than satire—or rather including the satire and including also his naturalism—Dos Passos' method in *U.S.A.* is that of tragedy, a method based on an ironic attitude toward the past. *U.S.A.* is a great agglomerate tragic history. The protagonist, obviously enough, is the real U.S.A. in the first third of the twentieth century. Its tragic characters are the real subjects of the biographies: Debs, Luther Burbank, Bill Haywood, Bryan, Minor Keith, Carnegie, Edison, Steinmetz, La Follette, Jack Reed, Randolph Bourne, T. R., Paxton Hibben, Woodrow Wilson, and the rest. Merely to read their names is to sense the tragedy of their era: so much talent, ambition, love—all frustrated or misdirected or drained away into war, profits prohibitions, intolerances, and oppressions.

In the background of the novel, democractic individualism and reliance on the future (pursuit of happiness) are the characteristics which gave the U.S.A. its greatness. A too narrow individualism, a too great reliance on the future—a loss of memory—and a warped interpretation of happiness in purely material terms: these are the characteristics which brought on its apparent downfall in the years Dos Passos wrote of. They are the tragic flaws of the society which rejects its best men. But its failures and its worst men have their own equivalent flaws—Bryan's "silver tongue in a big mouth," Wilson's "faith in words," and the overweening ambition of the Morgans, Insull, and others.

The fictional characters—like the anonymous "Vag" and the Unknown Soldier and the narrator—

have not the stature of tragic characters. They are the extras, the *demos* or ordinary citizens like ourselves, or the members of the chorus with whom we can participate as they work and suffer in the shadow of the struggle for industrial democracy. Yet, while we participate, we also watch; and for our capacity as objective audience, there is the more formal chorus of the Newsreels, in which the past provides its own ironic commentary about the past and reveals our recent idiocies to ourselves.

Many Americans in the audience have been unwilling to sit through Dos Passos' documentary tragedy. If they have come to it for entertainment or escape, they have been disappointed. But those who have stayed to see and hear have been exposed to a unique dramatic experience. This experience is one of participating satire; for, as Dos Passos said of the painter Grosz, he "makes you identify yourself with the sordid and pitiful object." This identification, in turn, provides the catharsis, "a release from hatred"—in part because the reader or spectator cannot wholly hate himself and in part because the hatred is already expressed more adequately than most could express it through vitriolic portraits of the villains, real and fictional. The uniqueness, however, is in the partial nature of the catharsis: it might be said to be both catharsis and anti-catharsis. The reader is purged only of the self-indulgent emotions of hatred and self-love, which allow him to forget. He is denied complacency and forced to remember. The tragedy he has witnessed is that of the unfulfilled potential of the individual, including himself, in a society dedicated, ironically, to the possibilities of its fulfillment. He is left with a feeling of incompleteness.

Part of the reason for Dos Passos' unpopularity is probably his lack of sufficient self-esteem for the reader to share. His contemporary, Hemingway, for example, had it both in himself and in his characters. Even in Swift the reader can climb to the heights of satire with the author—Gulliver being only an alter ego, the equivalent of some of the fictional characters of *U.S.A.*—and look down on the puny mass of men with the possibility of self-gratulation that he is not among them. But in Dos Passos' participating satire even the author is satirized; if the reader indulges in any identification (which he can scarcely avoid), he must lose not only his self-esteem but also his complacency.

Dos Passos' self-esteem is almost wholly of the abstract "self," the essential *I, you, me, he, she* of the tragically unfulfilled individual potential. In fact, it is almost the sole object of his esteem. So where another writer—and particularly another autobiographical writer such as Hemingway—might appear to caress his characters, possibly because they contain so much of the author, Dos Passos scorns his, partly for the same reason. He scorns them also because they are not true individuals and because it is not his fault, but theirs. He cannot help them; for, if they are to achieve their individuality, to fulfill their potentials, they must do it themselves. The most he can do is to help define the problem and some of the conditions of its solution. Yet Dos Passos is thoroughly sympathetic, especially towards the fictional men and women who give their names to the narrative sections of *U.S.A.* He shows a pervading pity for his characters, real and fictional, which is evident even in his most acidulous biographical portraits; an example is his quoting from the pathetically presumptuous will of the first J. P. Morgan in his biography of "The House of Morgan" in *1919.*

Both the scorn and the pity come through to the reader. Since one can properly scorn only inevitable weakness or meanness, the reader is left at the end of the tragedy with a sense of awe not so much at the power and authority of the destructive or restricting external forces as at the potential beauty and unity of the thing destroyed, the free personality. Bernard De Voto felt it in "the gusto and delight of American living" whose absence in *U.S.A.* he so deplored.

Yet this sense of incompleteness in the reader—the feeling of having been cheated of some of the ideal goods of life and that something should be done about it—is precisely the reaction that Dos Passos, the architect of history, desired. Unfortunately for his purposes, many readers have felt only the incompleteness and have missed the further implications of his criticism that something can be done about it, but that each individual must do it himself.

IV. Doubt and Affirmation

Perhaps one reason for the failure of his message is related to the fact that he has had one. As a novelist his chief concern has been, as he wrote in "The Business of a Novelist" for the *New Republic* in April, 1934, "to create characters first and foremost, and then to set them in the snarl of the human currents of his time, so that there results an accurate permanent record of a phase of history." Yet as a man with a message, his chief concern has been with its recipients; and his characters, despite the sympathy of his portrayal, he has left deliber-

ately underdeveloped. Similarly, he has always aimed at discomforting his readers—at stirring them into fresh thought and action by destroying the stereotypes from which they viewed the world. The great antagonist of *U.S.A.* is complacency. Probably most of the adverse criticism of the novel could be traced, like De Voto's, to the critics' protests against Dos Passos' attack on one or another of their complacencies. "When complacency goes," Dos Passos concluded his critical appreciation of Grosz, "young intelligence begins."

The essential first step to the freedom of intelligent action was to doubt. Yet some compromise between doubt and acceptance must be made before real action can begin. Until the early thirties Dos Passos' compromise was in the acceptance of immediate goals: in broadening the range of his own experience and in satisfying chiefly through travel his eager curiosity about the world around him; in participating directly in behalf of the obviously oppressed such as Sacco and Vanzetti, the Scottsboro boys, and, later, refugees from Europe; and in endeavoring to stimulate doubt in others. Then sometime before the fall elections of 1936 he reached the climax of his own doubting: his doubt turned inward upon itself.

The struggle of this moral crisis can be read in Camera Eye Forty-six early in *The Big Money:* "if not why not? walking the streets rolling on your bed eyes sting from peeling the speculative onion of doubt if somebody in your head topdog? underdog? didn't (and on Union Square) say liar to you." From this point on, the reader can trace the development of his Everlasting Yea, which begins with his condemnation of both the capitalistic and communistic viewpoints in *The Big Money* and his enthusiastic vote for Roosevelt in 1936 and which culminates in his novel *Chosen Country,* in his appreciative study of Jefferson, and in his two recent histories of the founders of the republic, *The Men Who Made The Nation* (1957) and *Prospects of a Golden Age* (1959).

In his probing into the meanings of the democratic phraseology and their bearings on his country in his time, Dos Passos found what he sought in an appreciation of the dynamics of his society. From his study of the history of his country and his awareness of the forces of history in action—particularly in the increase of despotism abroad—he came to realize that, for him, the U.S.A. *was* the last, best hope of men.

"The shape of a piece of work should be imposed, and in a good piece of work always is imposed, by the matter," Dos Passos wrote in his "Introductory Note" to the first Modern Library edition of *The 42nd Parallel*. The conscious, organized incompleteness of *U.S.A.* was not merely a device to stimulate the reader; it was the artistic form imposed by the organic necessity of the artist's materials. His study of his matter, American history, had finally revealed to him the secret of form in his society: that the pattern of American society lay where he had intuitively recognized it in the individual—in its potential and incompleteness. Sometime during the composition of his trilogy, Dos Passos became aware of a resurgence of what must have been a still-existing fluidity and dynamic potential in the American social structure. In such a society a man, if he would, could give meaning to his life.

Having intellectually grasped the pattern—or at least one which was satisfying and meaningful to him—and realized its form in his art in *U.S.A.*, Dos Passos had accomplished his major task as an artist. His materials for *U.S.A.* were all historical—the products of his study of the nation's past, his awareness of significant events acting about him, and a mass of painfully remembered detail from his own life. By the effort of his imagination, he constructed from these materials an organic unity which revealed the nation which he had made his own. By his own efforts he had carved out his niche and made himself a citizen.

Believing above all in the responsible and purposeful action of the free individual, Dos Passos was not a man to waste in inaction the freedom he had taken forty years to acquire, or to take lightly the duties of citizenship. However, having achieved the form he sought in his life and in his art, his energies could now take a slightly different direction. History in the service of art had completed the pattern. Henceforth Dos Passos' efforts would be more nearly historical than artistic. Art in the service of history should confirm the pattern and maintain the flexibility of the form.

Source: John H. Wrenn, "*U.S.A.*," in *John Dos Passos*, Twayne, 1999.

George J. Becker

In the following essay, Becker examines the pessimistic tone of U.S.A. *and Dos Passos's use of "newsreels" and "biographies" to provide supplementary background information.*

By its intricacy and by its comprehensive sweep the trilogy *U.S.A.* comes close to being the great American novel which had been the aspiration of writers since the turn of the century. It is one of the ironies of our times that when the great American novel did arrive, it turned out to be condemnatory and pessimistic rather than a celebration of the American way. Yet there is an underlying affirmation in Dos Passos' denial. The American dream, battered and corrupted by men of ill will, or little will, still manifests itself—though in anguish—not completely stifled by the trappings of empire and the machinations of self-interest that the author describes.

What first aroused the enthusiasm of readers and critics was the technical virtuosity of the work. Dos Passos was clearly the heir of Balzac, Zola, and Galdós in his attempt to mirror contemporary society—as he was the competitor of Jules Romains, whose *Hommes de bonne volonté* was appearing during the same span of years. It is equally evident that the idea of multiple perspectives is something he owed to *Ulysses*. But the techniques he employed and the balance of elements he achieved are his own and stamp him as the last of the great inventors in the field of the social novel. He welded together four separate, even disparate, types of material, each of which is necessary to the statement the novel ultimately makes. He spoke of this as his "four way conveyer system," which is apt enough, since four kinds of ore are being mined simultaneously.

One of the problems of the novelist attempting to mirror social actuality is how to include a sufficient body of data to give the basic tone or temper of the times as background to the necessarily particular experience of fictional characters. Balzac, Zola, and Galdós did this largely by repetition; that is, within the loosely associated novels of their series they subjected characters from various walks of life to the same basic determining and limiting forces. They were generally content with only a brief suggestive notation of public events. Even though change was their subject, there was something relatively static about their social backdrop. Later novelists, like James T. Farrell and John Steinbeck, attempted to remedy this deficiency. Steinbeck, in *The Grapes of Wrath*, by means of intercalated chapters which are poetic or rhetorical rather than directly documentary, both sets the social background and incorporates change as one of the dimensions of that background.

Dos Passos meets the problem by an invention that he calls the "Newsreel." There are sixty-eight such sections fairly evenly distributed among the three novels of the trilogy. These sections are a mixture of newspaper headlines, fragments of news stories, and bits and pieces of popular songs. They rarely run over two pages; a few are very short. They are typographically arresting with their headline type and their inset lines of verse. Their function is threefold: they precisely date the narrative action; they arouse a feeling for the time in question; and they frequently have a thematic or ironic impact.

In each volume of the trilogy the first and last Newsreels are of particular importance for all of the reasons just stated. *The 42nd Parallel* (1930) opens with a proclamation by way of headlines that the new century has begun. The repetitive banality of these statements becomes ludicrous, a tone that carries over to Senator Albert J. Beveridge's claim that "The twentieth century will be American. American thought will dominate it. American progress will give it color and direction. American deeds will make it illustrious." In counterpoint there is obvious triviality: "Society Girls Shocked: Danced with Detectives," and venality: "Officials Know Nothing of Vice." Then follows an ominous note of prophecy with mention of the disastrous Boer War and the nascent American empire: a jingle from the Cuban campaign; a headline: "Claims Islands for All Time"; and finally a song from the Philippine campaign, bits of which appear throughout the section, culminating with a warning of the cost of empire:

> There's been many a good man murdered in the Philippines Lies sleeping in some lonesome grave.

The final Newsreel of the volume is shorter and less complex. The declaration of war in April 1917 is announced in headlines; there are lines from the popular song "Over There," reference to the fact that the Colt Firearms Company has increased profits by 259 per cent, and two headlines: "Plan Legislation to Keep Colored People from White Areas" and "Abusing Flag to Be Punished." The long-range implications of war are set down without comment.

The opening theme of *1919* (1932) is one of a capitalistic system both intoxicated by opportunity and frightened by lurking dangers: the New York Stock Exchange is now the only free market in the world; vast quantities of money are pouring in from abroad; but "Europe [is] reeking with murder and the lust of rapine, aflame with the fires of revolution." The concluding Newsreel is savage: "the placards borne by the radicals were taken away from them, their clothing torn and eyes blackened before the service and ex-service men had finished

> ❝ The reader is brought to see the hollowness, the sterility of many men of popular reputation and is forced, often painfully, to reassess unpopular personalities whom he had assumed to be beyond the pale."

with them." "Machineguns Mow Down Mobs in Knoxville." Juxtaposed to this violence is the phrase "America I love you." The war is over. Its fruits are becoming known.

In *The Big Money* (1936) the first Newsreel comes after a narrative section. It contains much less detonative material than the foregoing: a line from "The St. Louis Blues," headlines about a daylight robbery, observations about automobiles and social status. Though the word is not used, this is President Harding's "normalcy." The contrast provided by the final Newsreel is dramatic: "Wall Street Stunned" (the stock market crash); "Police Turn Machine Guns on Colorado Mine Strikers Kill 5 Wound 40;" "Rescue Crews Try to Upend Illfated Craft While Waiting for Pontoons." All this is interspersed with lines from the saga of the illfated Casey Jones, whose locomotive is hell-bent for destruction. Finally there are the hollow soothing words of the President at the dedication of the Bok carillon in Florida, a scene of peace and promise already denied by the headlines: "Steamroller in Action against Militants," "Miners Battle Scabs."

Some of the content of the Newsreels is just plain fun. Advertising slogans such as "Itching Gone in One Night," the whole fulsome sequence of headlines about Queen Marie of Romania's visit, saccharine songs juxtaposed with serious events, all of these give a sense of the human comedy and also bring a powerful evocation of the past to the reader who has lived through it. Intellectually he may be aware of triviality and folly, of stultifying forces that controlled his life, but his emotions discount all that. It is his past, a poor thing but his own.

The present-day reader has to ask himself what is the enduring value of these sections, what kind of impact do they have on people who have not lived through the time portrayed? In general, popular songs wear themselves out by repetition; they rarely reappear to stir the emotions of another generation, though certain ballads like "Casey Jones," certain fighting chants of the IWW and other leftist groups, and hardcore revolutionary anthems like "The Marseillaise" and "The Internationale" do have long-term currency. The problem is even more evident when it comes to headlines and excerpts of news stories, many of which are extremely hard to pin down with the passage of time. It takes an effort of will, and some luck, to be able to recall that "Peaches" was Peaches Browning, that "The Sheik" was Rudolph Valentino, or to be able to piece together the details of the Hall-Mills murder case. Perhaps the relative inaccessibility of these materials does not matter. The author operates on the scattershot principle: some of the shots are sure to hit.

The second of Dos Passos' conveyor belts, the short biographies of actual persons, is also highly original. Living people have been used before as touchstones in novels, as objects of glorification or as objects of scorn. What is unusual here is the number and variety of the biographies and the encapsulated way in which they are presented. There are twenty-seven of them equally distributed among the three novels. They direct attention to both success and failure in the first third of the century and to major social currents of that period. By the selectivity evident in their choice it is clear that the author has here cast aside his role of objective observer and has actively intervened to influence the reader's judgment. A completely different statement would emerge if the cast of living persons were different.

There is no easy formula for classifying these figures, though, as has been indicated, they fall broadly into groupings of good guys and bad guys, heroes and villains, constructive and destructive human beings. But the sketches are so imbued with irony that the reader does not know what to expect in advance. He is obliged to examine each sketch in its context and to be ready for an ironic twist which will upset his expectation. The initial biography, "Lover of Mankind," is of Eugene V. Debs, the first nationally celebrated labor leader. This choice, and the tone in which the biography is written, constitutes an unambiguous manifesto. Debs' aspiration is for "a world brothers might own where everybody would split even." The section ends with the ringing quotation: "While there is a lower class I am of it, while there is a criminal class I am of it, while there is a soul in prison I am not free." The authorial voice betrays partisanship when it asks where were Debs' brothers in 1918 "when Woodrow Wilson had him locked up in Atlanta for speaking against war." The central issue which is gradually to become clear in the course of the novel is implicit in this biography: there are two nations, men with a sense of brotherhood like Debs and "the frockcoats and the tophats and diamonded hostesses," the wielders of power who "were afraid of him as if he had contracted a social disease, syphilis or leprosy."

Two other biographies in the first volume reinforce this statement. "Big Bill," that is, Big Bill Haywood the IWW leader, dreamed of "building a new society in the shell of the old"; he was the victim of the mentality of the men who "went over with the A.E.F. to save the Morgan loans" and "lynched the pacifists and the pro-Germans and the wobblies and the reds and the bolsheviks." Another idealist and victim is "Fighting Bob" La Follette, the reformer who made Wisconsin a model state, who fought corruption and big business and "the miasmic lethargy of Washington." He was "an orator haranguing from the capitol of a lost republic."

The Luther Burbank sketch raises important questions. America is a hybrid, promising a brave new social organism, but it is threatened by intolerance of ideas, something which did not destroy Burbank but left him "puzzled." Edison's fame is undercut by the fact that he worked with men like Henry Ford and Harvey Firestone, "who never worried about mathematics or the social system or generalized philosophical concepts," and put his inventions at the service of these analphabetic masters of the capitalist system. Likewise Steinmetz, a hunchback and a genius and a socialist whose mathematical discoveries are the basis of all electrical transformers everywhere, was merely "a piece of apparatus belonging to General Electric," which indulged him in his socialist dreams but did not allow him to interfere with the stockholders' money or the directors' salaries.

Alongside these men manipulated by the system we see three of the manipulators. The most openly attacked is Minor C. Keith, builder of railroads in Central America and creator of the United Fruit Company. Andrew Carnegie, like Steinmetz an immigrant, worked hard, saved his money, and "whenever he had a million dollars he invested it . . . whenever he made a billion dollars he endowed an institution to promote universal peace always except in time of war." The most ironic sketch of all is that of William Jennings Bryan, "the boy orator of the Platte," whose silver tongue chanted indiscriminately of pacifism, prohibition, and fundamentalism; the leader of the people's crusade who became the clown in the courtroom at the monkey trial in Dayton, Tennessee, who became a barker selling real estate in Coral Gables, Florida.

This pattern is repeated in *1919* but in *The Big Money* the biographies have a different orientation. They are illustrative of the anti-human, anti-cultural wasteland of the Twenties: Frederick W. Taylor, the inventor of the system of industrial management that reduces workmen to the status of machines (to the point of emasculation, one of the fictional characters observes); Henry Ford, chief architect of the new society produced by the automobile, whose social outlook belonged to the horse-and-buggy age; and William Randolph Hearst, a manipulator of men's minds and a vulgarizer of ideas. In Isadora Duncan and Rudolph Valentino are summed up both the inanity of pseudo-art and the vacuous enthusiasms of a vulgar public. Three biographies only are touchstones of what is useful and admirable: Thorstein Veblen, who saw through the glittering facade of conspicuous consumption and became an academic pariah for his pains; the Wright Brothers, who with single-minded devotion pioneered man's entry into the space age; and Frank Lloyd Wright, whose vision of a humane functional architecture was one of the few creative achievements of the age.

These twenty-seven portraits are in general a cruel and unsparing debunking, less cantankerous than H. L. Mencken's parallel effort but more deadly. They demand a reassessment of reputations in terms of a constant vision of a good society; they strip away the window-dressing of factitious public image. Underlying all of them is a basic question: Who were the great men of the new century? This question cannot in fact be answered until valid criteria of greatness are established. Dos Passos leads us to those criteria in a negative manner for the most part. The reader is brought to see the hollowness, the sterility of many men of popular reputation and is forced, often painfully, to reassess unpopular personalities whom he had assumed to be beyond the pale. For all the cool, precise succinctness of these biographies there is nothing impersonal about them. They constitute the most brilliant writing Dos Passos ever did, but that brilliance is one of polemic thrust under the cloak of objectivity. Not only do they set up a general value sys-

tem for the novel; they act as reflectors for the fictional personages, as in the case where the narrative of Margo Dowling is interrupted by a biography of Valentino.

The third device invented by Dos Passos, the "Camera Eye," is the most interesting because the most difficult to pin down as to its function. There are fifty-one of these sections, over half of them appearing in the first novel. Whereas the approach of all the other elements in the work is public and ostensibly objective, the Camera Eyes are private and subjective. Their style is lyrical in contrast to the dry factual presentation of the rest. Through them an unexpected persona appears on scene, a poetic speaker who is different from the impersonal narrator and who for practical purposes must be identified with that unique individual John Dos Passos. This individual is both representative and unique. He is the sensitive protected being who must emerge from the safety of childhood and come to an understanding of the harsh realities of adult life. There is a strict parallel between his experience and that of the United Skates in the twentieth century. Youth undergoes crisis when it discovers that the maxims—the official verbal formulas—on which it has been nurtured do not square with reality. Two courses are open to meet this crisis: a cynical capitulation to the way things are, or a radical reassessment of traditional values and a determination to sweep away all that is not valid at whatever cost. In other words, the Camera Eyes provide a core of belief and value in the midst of apparent disintegration of value. In simplistic terms they chart the making of a radical.

Dos Passos here mines his own experience with virtually no resort to invention. The twenty-seven Camera Eyes in *The 42nd Parallel* carry the speaker through childhood and adolescence to his post-Harvard trip to France in 1916. Curiously enough, the definitive end to childhood is deferred to the beginning of *1919*, when the deaths of mother and father (separated in fact by several years) are brought together in the opening section, along with the experience of a soldier's life (largely imaginary). These experiences are described as the closing of one book and the beginning of another, a *Vita Nuova*, "the first day of the first month of the first year" of a new existence.

The first Camera Eye describes insecurity in a foreign city. The second is doubly thematic, expressing a patronizing attitude toward Negroes and windy patriotic hyperbole. The third section echoes this class consciousness: "workingmen and people like that laborers travailleurs greasers." This theme comes up again in the seventh: in reference to muckers, Bohunks and Polack kids who "put stones in their snowballs write dirty words up on walls do dirty things up alleys their folks work in the mills," an attitude that is undercut in the next Camera Eye by the intolerance, cruelty, and dirty words at the speaker's own select school. As the novel continues, sex, patriotism, social consciousness (the Lawrence, Massachusetts, street car strike), an account of a New York radical meeting where "everybody talked machineguns revolution civil liberty freedom of speech but occasionally somebody got in the way of a cop and was beaten up and shoved into a patrol wagon," and growing awareness of the evil of war—"up north they were dying in the mud and the trenches but business was good in Bordeaux"—chart the sensitivity of the speaker.

With this persona established, it is possible to limit the range of the Camera Eye sections in the other two novels. Those in *1919* parallel Dos Passos' experiences of war and differ very little from the passages in his war novels and in his autobiography. They are not soapbox oratory against war—rather they are poetic epiphanies—but they do raise uncomfortable questions about the waste of lives and the denial of free speech to those who dissent. Commentary on the May Day 1919 celebration in Paris is less a paean to revolution than to the utopia that it promises. In *The Big Money* the emphasis is on the promise and denial of basic freedom in the United States. The speaker ruminates about wealth and poverty: "why not tell these men stamping in the wind that we stand on a quicksand?"; he is ashamed of himself for dreaming and not acting; he wonders "what leverage might pry the owners loose from power and bring back (I too Walt Whitman) our storybook democracy." Protest rises to a peak with the Sacco-Vanzetti case, contrasting the fate of these immigrants in Plymouth with the original settlers, who were "kingkillers haters of oppression." Number 50, which states "they have clubbed us off the streets they are stronger they are rich," reaches the anguished conclusion, "all right we are two nations."

If we ask the question, What makes a man of gentle rearing, artistic and intellectual taste, and abhorrence of violence turn to the revolutionary left? the answer has been chronicled in the Camera Eyes. We see his development through experience of war, of capitalistic dehumanization, and of repression of dissent. The Sacco-Vanzetti case is the catalyst which purifies him of uncertainty and commits him to the cause of the downtrodden and the dispos-

sessed. The Camera Eyes suggest, without arrogance, that this is the path a man of good will must follow through the iron labyrinth of the twentieth century, and they provide a standard by which to measure the twelve fictional characters who are the major exhibits of the novel.

U.S.A. in the jargon of some critics has been called a "collective" novel. The term is unfortunate in its ideological implications and fails to convey the central fact that this is a novel without a protagonist, one in which no single life provides a center of interest and meaning. This work exhibits multiple parallel lives on a scale never before attempted. Its form is radial; that is, each spoke has the same importance as the others, all converging on a common center. If the reader's mind could, indeed, focus on all these characters at once he would perceive that unity. But since the experience of the novel is temporal, not spatial, simultaneity is not possible, except in brief passages, and the reader must keep the various characters in suspension until he can weigh them as a group.

These fictional personages fall into three categories: the twelve exemplary characters who are given major billing by having narrative sections bear their names; a limited number who turn up at various points in the work as they relate to some of the above but for whom no substantial background is provided; and incidental ones who, however prominent, relate to only one of the major figures, fleshing out his life, acting as foils on occasion, but in themselves not under examination for their own sake.

The way the narratives of the twelve major characters are woven into the novel is varied, though they can be counted on not to appear as a block. The story of Mac, the first one we meet, is told in seven episodes uninterrupted by other narratives. Then three other characters appear and 167 pages later there is a final Mac section, after which he disappears from the novel. Janey Williams, J. Ward Moorehouse, and Eleanor Stoddard have name sections only in the first novel, though they reappear in the other two. In *1919*, five characters have name sections, three of them completely new. Two of them appear only in this volume. Joe Williams' career comes to an end in a barroom brawl; Daughter dies in an airplane accident. The other, Dick Savage, continues to be important in *The Big Money* along with Charley Anderson, who appeared in the first but not the second novel. Finally, in *The Big Money* two characters, Mary French and Margo Dowling, occupy much of the narrative. This lack of pattern lends an air of random verisimilitude, though with the exception of Mac all twelve are interconnected and nine of them do proceed to the end.

It is important to note that when name sections for a given character cease, he is not necessarily downgraded. J. Ward Moorehouse and Janey Williams are ubiquitous in *1919*. Eleanor Stoddard and Eveline Hutchins are in view through all three novels. Ben Compton, who has only one name section (in *1919*), is occasionally on scene in the following work. Sometimes the same events are told from two points of view, especially in the case of Janey and Joe Williams and of Eleanor Stoddard and Eveline Hutchins. Sometimes the interconnections of the major figures seem forced, and indeed unnecessary. Nothing is gained by having Mac encounter J. Ward Moorehouse (and George H. Barrow, a continuing secondary character) in Mexico. It is amusing but of no importance that Joe Williams is the sailor whom Savage and his friends meet in a bar outside of Genoa. At the very end there is irritating contrivance when at Eveline Hutchins' party Mary French, Margo Dowling, Dick Savage, and G. H. Barrow are all brought under the same roof. Indeed if one is to fault Dos Passos' handling of the intricate counterpoint of so many lives it is in respect to the unnecessary tightness of relationships, which casts doubt on the randomness of his sampling.

The actual narrative, while more conventional than the other dimensions of the novel, does not lack technical interest. In comparison with *Manhattan Transfer*, *U.S.A.* makes very little use of dialogue and dramatic scene. What gives the various life histories impact is the use of summary stream of consciousness in language appropriate to the character. Within the limits permitted, Janey Williams or Dick Savage or Mary French comes alive because we are aware of how each perceives experience through the very language he uses. This may degenerate into formula: Eveline Hutchins' catchphrase "It's all so tiresome;" but usually the language is flexible, employing slang, profanity, simple or mannered vocabulary as they are appropriate. Because of Dos Passos' acute ear for nuances of speech, language is a refined instrument of characterization. We hear his people better than we see them, and we hear them not only in regular dialogue but in so-called narrative passages as well.

When we consider whether this cast of characters is representative, we must concede at once

that it does not present an adequate cross section and that the selection is clearly and deliberately slanted in the direction of vacuity and failure. These lives may be exemplary, but most readers agree that they are exemplary of only one aspect of human endeavor. The very fact that these are hollow men and women whose course is downward constitutes an inescapable indictment of American life and institutions in their time.

If we apply criteria for success and failure in simplified terms, we must see Mac as a radical who settles complacently into the comfort of middle-class existence, Joe Williams a working stiff incapable of living beyond the moment, Janey Williams a person who achieves identity only in symbiotic relationship with the boss, Daughter an unruly youngster who flees responsibility, and Margo Dowling the synthetic product of a synthetic industry. Ben Compton exists more as horrible example, a pathetic and feckless victim of the repressive forces of society as he goes off to a twenty-year prison term at the age of twenty-two. Five of the remaining six fail even more egregiously: J. Ward Moorehouse peddling words as a public relations expert and selling himself with words as empty as his own character; Eleanor Stoddard taking refuge in a sterile elegance; Eveline Hutchins, a pursuer of pleasure who finds it all so boring that she commits suicide; Charley Anderson, a simple man who is good with engines but is destroyed by high living and high finance; Dick Savage, potentially a man of sensibility, who pursues the main chance and loses his own soul. Only Mary French, who has genuine compassion for the underdog, plods resolutely ahead to a worthy goal. She will not reach it because she has no defense against being used by others, but we admire her for her ability to subordinate herself to the needs of others.

These major characters nearly all come from homes that are in some way broken, without normal security and love, and none of them is capable of achieving a satisfactory marital existence. Over and over we see sex drives as a source of exploitation and enslavement. The two working stiffs, Mac and Joe, are trapped by nice girls who use sex first as a means to marriage, then as coercion to insure a materially safe existence. Janey sublimates sex in adoration of J. Ward Moorehouse. Eleanor Stoddard, a potential lesbian, has an occasional meaningless affair. Eveline Hutchins sleeps around, marries Paul Johnson and soon divorces him. Daughter is seduced by the sexually ambivalent Dick Savage, who refuses to marry her when she becomes pregnant. Mary French accepts the free-love doctrines of her radical friends and is let down by Don Stevens, her communist lover. Whoring comes naturally to Margo Dowling; she uses her body first to escape poverty, then to rise to stardom. J. Ward Moorehouse enters into two marriages for money, sleeps with Eleanor Stoddard and Eveline Hutchins, and is happiest submitting to the ministrations of call girls. Charley Anderson can leave neither women nor booze alone and is taken for all he has by his calculating wife in Bloomfield Hills, as he would have been a second time by Margo Dowling if he had lived. Dick Savage sleeps with girls without much enthusiasm; at the end we see him prey to blackmailing homosexuals in Harlem. For these people sex is Robert Penn Warren's "great twitch" with a vengeance and a major strand of the determinism of the novel. Their unsatisfactory sexual lives are damning evidence of a basic sterility in human relations.

Another curious limitation of the group chosen is what we may call a vocational inertia. They are all untrained (except Janey Williams) and drift into jobs rather than coming to adulthood with definite purpose. To be sure, Dick Savage finishes Harvard, emerging as a promising minor poet, vintage 1915, and Mary French has a couple of years at Vassar before she drops out, while Eveline Hutchins and Eleanor Stoddard have desultory interludes at the Chicago Art Institute. It must be admitted that Moorehouse teaches himself French and that Joe Williams studies to get a succession of licenses. Even though lack of advanced schooling is the norm for the generation Dos Passos is portraying, these people strike us as undisciplined, opportunistic, and drifting. A more representative cross section would show some people at least setting up and achieving goals, using their minds in a disciplined way and subordinating their egos to the demands of some profession.

Still another aspect of their lives, so prominent as to constitute a major theme, is an ineradicable inhumanity, an intolerance toward people and ideas in any way offbeat. There is snide disparagement of all who do not belong to the category of nice people. Pejorative terms like "bohunk," "guinea," "shine," "greaser," and the host of others vulgarly used to refer to the non-white Anglo-Saxons are always on the lips of Dos Passos' characters. This is but one of the ways in which he accurately, and painfully, records the speech of the people. There are more developed instances of discriminatory attitude and action. Even Mary French is disturbed because her friend Ada Cohen is so Jewish. Margo

Dowling takes pleasure in humiliating her Cuban husband by making him wear a uniform and act as her chauffeur. This class- and race-consciousness separates officers from men, manual workers from white-collar workers, "muckers" of any stamp from the distinguished people in the rotogravure section.

When the chips are down, this automatic consigning of aliens and oddballs to coventry leads to exploitation and violence. Since such people have been tagged as less than human, they are fair game. If a man is a Wobbly, he may legitimately be beaten, castrated, crucified. It is this denial of freedom of speech and action that Dos Passos returns to again and again. He can make fun of social snobbery—witness Eveline Hutchins' party for refugee Russian noblemen; what he cannot abide is persecution of dissenters. The stories of Mac, of Ben Compton, of Joe Williams, of Mary French, and of Charley Anderson in his early years are central to this theme. It is significant that Mac begins and Mary ends the novel. Mac as a boy is arrested for distributing union handbills during a strike; his uncle, a socialist, is bankrupted. Mary at the end is steadfastly trying to break down barriers, pathetically trying to convince her capitalist stepfather that the striking Appalachian miners are human beings. The three novels use the full gamut of their techniques to emphasize this theme. We see a man being run in in San Francisco for reading the Declaration of Independence to a crowd. We are present with Ben Compton at a riot in Everett, Washington. We are told of the hounding of Thorstein Veblen. The examples are legion. The weakest part of this is the attempt to show in Ben Compton how a revolutionary is made. The lack of psychological depth characteristic of Dos Passos' people is fatal here. It is not enough to see Ben pushed and broken by external forces. We need to feel the generation of internal resolution and an anguished perception that the system is out of joint. The interlarded quotations from Marx that attend Ben's development are not enough, unless indeed the author is already being ironic about the claims of socialist doctrine.

Parallel to the theme of repression of dissent is a second theme, the aggressive and soulless power of wealth. This, as we have already seen, is carried chiefly by the Newsreels and the short biographies. In the narrative proper there are sinister background figures, like a man named Rasmussen, who is present at the Paris peace conference to guard the interests of Standard Oil. The war itself is repeatedly presented as an effort to safeguard the Morgan loans to the Allies. Since of the major figures only J. Ward Moorehouse represents big business—and that in a parasitic way—this part of the novel's statement is weak, suggestive rather than convincingly documentary.

There is a unified progression of ideas as we move through the three parts of *U.S.A.* The first presents a fairly kindly, innocent America, where the ordinary man's aspirations are usually blocked but where he can dream of controlling his own destiny and throwing off the shackles which he feels but does not analyze. The war brings an end to innocence. It is in part a diversionary action to stifle dissent at home. President Wilson becomes the villain of the piece: *1919* is an ironic contrast between the idealistic promises he made to make the world safe for democracy and the actualities of power politics as they are revealed at the peace conference. The third novel shows the fruits of this deception, of the moral and social debacle that the war is seen to have brought. The opportunities for the average man narrow. As he resists, coercion is more and more overt. The hysteria of war years becomes an habitual state of mind directed at exaggerated or imaginary dangers. The Sacco-Vanzetti case is used as the prime example, but the final scenes showing the destitution of the miners and their harsh repression by the police and courts are actually more effective. As Archibald MacLeish wrote, "America was promises." *U.S.A.* is a chronicle of promises betrayed or forgotten, of a diminution of human dignity and liberty, of a basic disregard for human worth.

The overall statement is a pessimistic one. The "American Century" proudly announced in the opening Newsreel turns out to be a fatal misadventure. The swelling imperial theme of the opening leads to military adventures in Mexico and on a grand scale in Europe, where a tremendous expenditure of blood and treasure made the world safe—for international oil. The whole of American might was turned against the aspirations of the common man as expressed in the Mexican and Russian revolutions and the abortive attempts at revolution in war-torn Europe. The novel does not examine the implications of those revolutions; it takes them on trust as consonant with the traditional American belief in freedom. Thus abroad as well as at home, the American dream has become a nightmare.

U.S.A. is not a depression novel. It lacks the shrill immediacy and ideological confusion of such works as Jack Conroy's *The Disinherited* or Robert Cantwell's *The Land of Plenty.* But it was written

during the depression, and the mounting anguish of the last volume certainly derives from the author's awareness of the havoc that a third of a century of misdirection has wrought. The reader, moreover, can supply his own scenario of economic and social decay, breadlines, foreclosures, evictions, and riots as they flow from the breakdown of the system. It was inevitable that Dos Passos should become the darling of the left during those years. None of the adherents of the socialist or communist parties could write with anything like his power. None of them grasped the fatal perspective of history, even though they were provided with a ready-made perspective by Marx. Because Dos Passos shared their passion, they allowed themselves to believe that he shared their formula for the eradication of the evils that aroused their passion. They needed his eloquence to communicate their cause. As it turned out, he was forced by his integrity to a decision that he did not need them. Theirs was, in his opinion, a tunnel vision; his compassion had a much wider temporal and spatial sweep.

This disavowal of left-wing orthodoxy is already evident in *The Big Money.* Mary French, the embodiment of radical aspiration, explicitly states that she is not a member of the Communist Party. There is enough evidence of a narrowing concern for humanity on the part of the Russian regime supplied by the Newsreels to enable us to evaluate Don Stevens' opportunism for what it is and to see Ben Compton's expulsion from the Party as a portent of its oppressive practices. Both sides are hardening. The future of genuine freedom is dark because it is threatened from left and right. The novel is in fact even more pessimistic than its critical acclaimers were willing to perceive.

Source: George J. Becker, "Visions . . .," in *John Dos Passos*, Frederick Ungar, 1974, pp. 58–79.

Sources

Aaron, Daniel, "U.S.A.," in *American Heritage*, July–August, 1996, p. 63.

Beach, Joseph Warren, "Dos Passos 1947," in *Sewanee Review*, Summer, 1947, pp. 406–18.

Becker, George J., *John Dos Passos*, Ungar, 1974.

Rosen, Robert C., *John Dos Passos: Politics and the Writer*, University of Nebraska Press, 1981.

Sartre, Jean-Paul, "Literary and Philosophical Essays," translated by Annette Michelson Rider, 1955, in *John Dos*

Passos: A Collection of Critical Essays, edited by Andrew Hook, Prentice Hall, Inc., 1974, pp. 61–69.

Westbook, Perry D., "U.S.A.: Overview," in *Reference Guide to American Literature*, 3d ed., edited by Jim Kamp, St. James Press, 1994.

Wheeler, Edward T., "Book Review: USA," in *Commonweal*, April 11, 1997, p. 24.

For Further Reading

Casey, Janet Galligani, "Historicizing the Female in *U.S.A.*: Re-Visions of Dos Passos's Trilogy," in *Twentieth Century Literature*, Fall 1995, p. 249.

    This article considers Dos Passos's depiction of the relations between men and women, as well as the effects of capitalism on women.

Dow, William, "John Dos Passos, Blaise Cendrars, and the 'Other' Modernism," in *Twentieth Century Literature*, Fall 1996, p. 396.

    This article explores the influence of other authors on Dos Passos, particularly that of the French author Blaise Cendrars.

Ludington, Townsend, "Dos Passos, John," *Reference Guide to American Literature*, 3d ed., edited by Jim Kamp, St. James Press, 1994.

    This article provides a short discussion of Dos Passos's life and work.

Magny, Claude-Edmonde, "Time in Dos Passos," in *The Age of the American Novel: The Film Aesthetic of Fiction between the Two Wars*, translated by Eleanor Hochman, Ungar, 1972, reprinted in *John Dos Passos: A Collection of Critical Essays*, edited by Andrew Hook, Prentice-Hall, 1974, pp 128–44.

    This article examines Dos Passos's portrayal of time in *The Big Money*, the third book of the *U.S.A.* trilogy.

Tate, J. O., "John Dos Passos: One Man, One Life," in *National Review*, December 31, 1985, p. 68.

    This article describes Dos Passos's personality, life, and career.

Trombold, John, "From the Future to the Past: The Disillusion of John Dos Passos," in *Studies in American Fiction*, Autumn 1998, p. 237.

    This article explores changes in Dos Passos's political views over the course of his life and career.

Wrenn, John H., *John Dos Passos*, Twayne, 1961.

    This book provides a detailed biography of Dos Passos as well as a critical analysis of his works.

The Wrestling Match

Buchi Emecheta
1983

Buchi Emecheta's *The Wrestling Match* was first published in 1983 in Great Britain by Oxford University Press, in conjunction with University Press Ltd. of Nigeria. The story is a deceptively simple tale of a boy coming of age in a Nigerian village, but Emecheta uses the tale as a commentary on war, as well as on relationships between generations and the need for everyone to have productive work.

Emecheta retains the strong storytelling tradition of her Nigerian homeland; *The Wrestling Match* is told in simple yet vivid language, and makes readers feel as if they're in "an open clearing in which children and old people sat, telling stories and singing by the moonlight," as the narrator of the book notes.

Many of Emecheta's works deal with poverty and the oppression of women, both in Nigeria and in England; in this sense, *The Wrestling Match* is a departure, as it tells the story of a young man and his uncle, and the women in it are marginal characters who retain their traditional roles as wives or wives-to-be.

In an interview with Julie Holmes in *The Voice*, Emecheta told Holmes that writing is the "release for all my anger, all my bitterness, my disappointments, my questions and my joy."

Buchi Emecheta

and Emecheta worked to support them all while her husband studied. By the time she was twenty-two, they were divorced, and Emecheta supported all the children and continued her own education. She eventually earned a degree in sociology, and began writing fiction. She completed a novel, *The Bride Price*, but her husband burned the manuscript; later, she would rewrite it from memory.

In 1972, her work began to be published in the journal *New Statesman*, and in that same year, her autobiographical story collection *In the Ditch* was published. This began her career as a novelist and, since then, she has supported herself and her family from writing; M. Keith Booker noted in *The African Novel in English* that she may be the first full-time professional African writer.

Emecheta has written numerous novels and short stories, as well as poems, television plays, and essays, most of which explore the position of women in both African and European society. She has also written young adult fiction, including *The Wrestling Match*. She has remained in England since 1962, and has won worldwide recognition as a chronicler of women's experience.

Author Biography

Buchi Emecheta was born as Florence Onye Buchi Emecheta on July 21, 1944, near Lagos, Nigeria. Her parents were from the Igbo village of Ibuza in southeastern Nigeria, and although they were nominally Christian, they also retained traditional Igbo beliefs, so that Emecheta grew up with a multiplicity of cultures. Her parents made sure that she spent time in their village so that she would know her original culture, but she grew up in Lagos, where another ethnic group, the Yoruba, was dominant.

Emecheta became aware early that not only was she a member of a minority in Lagos, but also that her own culture, the Igbo, valued boys more than girls. These experiences gave her a feeling of being an outsider that continued throughout her life, and was often expressed in her writing.

As a girl, she dreamed of becoming a writer someday, but this dream was discouraged by her teachers. When she was sixteen, she left school to marry, and two years later her husband traveled to London to study. Emecheta and their two young children went with him.

In London, they experienced deep poverty and intense prejudice. They had three more children,

Plot Summary

Chapter 1

The Wrestling Match opens with a conflict that disrupts a quiet evening in the compound of Obi Agiliga, when his senior wife, Nne Ojo, yells at his sixteen-year-old nephew, Okei, for Okei's sullen bad manners. Okei has been adopted by his uncle because his family was killed in the Biafran War, or Nigerian Civil War, and the event has left him confused and rootless. Also, like some of his age-mates, he has had some education, which makes him reluctant to labor on his uncle's farm, work he sees as demeaning, exhausting, and fruitless, since every year they end up going hungry no matter how hard they work. Like teenagers everywhere, he is fed up with being nagged and told, "When I was your age" by his uncle and others.

His uncle tells him that some of his age-mates have been stealing from old people. Okei discusses this with his friends Nduka and Uche, who are shocked, and also annoyed at the fact that because they are all in the same age-group, they will all be blamed. Like Okei, Nduka and Uche are fed up with being told they have to grow up, with being nagged to work on their parents' farms, and with being compared to the "good" boys of their age-group, who did not go to school and who are content to work on the farms.

Chapter 2

Okei and his friends head toward the neighboring village, Akpei, to meet girls from their own village who are coming home from selling plantains there. The girls walk the distance instead of selling in their own village because they can make a little more money at the other market. The boys overhear the girls bathing in a stream and gossiping, saying that maybe the boys did rob someone, since everyone in the other village is talking about it and "there's no smoke without fire." They also comment on the fact that because the boys have been to school, they are "bigheaded." Unlike the girls, who have to work all the time, the boys have plenty of free time to get into trouble, and the girls complain about the way the people in the other village are saying bad things about their boys. The main gossiper is Kwutelu, a seventeen-year-old who is the leader of her age-mates. She is known for her sense of style and her sharp tongue. Her friend is Josephine, a quieter girl.

Okei is upset by their gossip. He tells his friends that they must go around the village the next day and make announcements that all the members of their age group will meet for a discussion, but he doesn't say what for.

Chapter 3

Obi Agiliga is working on his farm, and takes a rest in the heat of the day. He wishes he could have more help on the farm, and his youngest son, Onuoha, asks him why Okei won't join them. Onuoha admires Okei's strength, and Obi Agiliga worries that when he is older, he will turn into a shirker like Okei. However, he understands that Okei is confused and troubled, both by the violence in his past and by his education, which is at odds with traditional culture.

Obi Uwechue, a man from the neighboring village of Akpei, visits him and explains that the boys of his village are also restless and bored, starting fights and making trouble. He suggests that the village elders give the boys of both villages something to worry about. "I think we will have to create a big worry for our young men," Obi Uwechue says. "By the time they have finished solving that problem they will be wiser."

Obi Agiliga agrees, saying that the girls of the villages will be useful, since they tend to gossip and they can be useful in the plan. "Leave the rest to me," he says.

Chapter 4

The next morning, Uche and Nduka meet each other at the stream and discuss how to make the announcement of their age-group meeting. Uche wants to show off by making the announcement in English, but Nduka scoffs at this, saying it will exclude people who don't know English, and is inherently wrong anyway, because if everyone used education to exclude someone else, Uche would be left out by the people who are already in college. Uche decides to use the traditional method of beating a gong and yelling out the announcement, and Nduka writes the message on notebook paper and hands the sheets out to people.

At the meeting, Okei is elected the leader of his age group. The group decides that the insults the other village has heaped on them will be settled by a wrestling match. The best wrestler from each village will be involved. They will not invite the village elders to judge the match; it will be strictly judged by young people.

Obi Agiliga comes home from a long day at the farm, and tells them all, "Clear out, you lazy, good-for-nothing pilferers of fishes and muggers of the old." He knows very well that they are not bad boys; he's just egging them on to prove their worth. "These boys thought they were the only people who have ever been young," he chuckles to himself. "They will learn, sure they will learn."

Chapter 5

Okei begins practicing wrestling, getting up early, running, and toughening himself. He and Nduka wrestle on the path to the stream, and Kwutelu and the girls come by and tease them, telling them they've heard the boys steal fish and steal from old people. Okei says he doesn't know who the thieves are, but if he did, he'd tell them to go to Kwutelu's house and rob it. She tells him time will tell if he's guilty or not, because tradition says the innocent will win at a wrestling match.

Chapter 6

Kwutelu goes home and tells Josephine that Okei threatened her. They discuss the situation, and Josephine says she thinks the elders from both villages have stirred up the trouble on purpose.

Kwutelu's father, Obi Uju, comes home from his farm. He lives apart from Kwutelu's mother, and she is so close to him that she often sleeps in his house, not her mother's. Kwutelu tells him about Okei's threats, exaggerating and saying that he threatened her personally. This angers him, and he goes to bed early that night.

Later, when Kwutelu comes in to sleep, he hears her opening the door and assumes it's Okei, come in to rob and make trouble. He grabs a knife and, in the dark, attacks the robber. It's not Okei, it's Kwutelu, but before he realizes it, he cuts off her ear.

Chapter 7

Okei was home sleeping when this occurred, so he is exonerated; still, it's a tragedy that this happened to Kwutelu. The accident has a chastening effect on her, however; she's now more quiet, less teasing, less forward. It also changes Okei, who begins to trust his uncle and aunt because they spoke up for him and protected him from the charges of robbery. "He is sleeping now," Obi Agiliga's wife tells him. "I think he is beginning to trust us at last. He knew that you would take care of everything."

Chapter 8

Okei wakes up and wonders what really happened the night before. He gets up early and resumes his wrestling training. Uche shows up and tells him about Kwutelu's ear, and also mentions that God will be on their village's side during the wrestling match, because they are in the right. Okei wisely says that the other side will be praying just as hard, and "God will not come down and wrestle with the Akpei boys for us."

Obi Agiliga and Obi Uwechue talk and discuss the knifing. They are sorry because they know that through their encouragement of the girls to gossip, they are indirectly responsible. However, they agree that the situation could have been much worse; Kwutelu could have been killed. They also note that the boys are all busy, and don't have time to harass anyone in the footpath, steal fish, or make any other trouble. Obi Agiliga notes that they are beginning to act and think a little more like adults, and says, "even my nephew is beginning to look at me as if I am somebody at last. Before, I was just an old man to be shouted at."

Chapter 9

On the next market day, the girls go to the neighboring town as usual to sell plantains, but the tensions over the intervillage wrestling match have risen to the point where no one will buy from them. An old woman tells them they may as well give their plantains to her for free, because otherwise they will have to carry them home. This turns out to be true. Empty-handed, they go home and have to throw their plantains away because the plantains will spoil anyway. They are upset by this, because they were planning to use the money they earned to buy fine new clothes to show off at the wrestling match. When the male elders hear about this, they "smile with a conspiratorial wink," because it's all a part of their plan.

Chapter 10

The boys' age group meets again. They choose Okei and Nduka to wrestle for their village. A farmer's son tells Okei that his uncle was a master wrestler, and he should go to him for advice to learn the proper wrestling dance. Okei reluctantly agrees.

Chapter 11

Okei is shocked to think that he and his age-mates could ever make any mistakes, and dismayed that he will have to get advice from his uncle. But he goes to his uncle, who teaches him a host of master moves and agile dances. Through this, the two become closer.

Chapter 12

In the preparations for the wrestling match and the yam festival, even Kwutelu joins in the singing to praise Okei, the village wrestler. Okei's uncle tells him that even if he loses, it's important for him to do his best.

Chapter 13

On the day of the match, the villagers beat their drums to announce the event. The rival villagers arrive, and the match begins. The young people in charge vow that the match will be friendly and will solve the problems between the two villages, and the old men chuckle and wink knowingly at each other.

Chapter 14

The match begins as a friendly contest, but soon degenerates into a brawl, in which every boy is fighting another boy from the opposite village. At the height of the fight, the elders from the two villages wade into the melee and beat the drums and shout. Eventually, everyone calms down. Obi Agiliga announces that the fight has been very successful, and that now everyone has learned that "in all good fights, just like wars, nobody wins. You were all hurt and humiliated. I am sure you will always remember this day."

Characters

Obi Agiliga

Obi Agilaga is the uncle of Okei, who took the boy in when his parents were killed in the Biafran War in Nigeria. Like most of the people in his village, he is a farmer, and grows yams, which the family subsists on. He is well-off enough to hire helpers, but watches them carefully, because he knows they may take any opportunity to sneak off and shirk doing work; however, he is also fair, and when he takes a rest from the hard work and midday heat, he insists that they do so, too. He wishes he had more help, because he is worried about harvesting all the yams before the village's yam festival. When he was an adolescent, he was the leader of the wrestling group of his age, and when Okei is elected to wrestle in a match with the neighboring village, he teaches Okei all he knows about wrestling. "I have to teach it all to this young man here. It is his turn now. My turn has come and gone." He also wisely tells Okei, "Even if you lost, it won't be a complete loss because you would have added a new art to the game of wrestling, and then you would have taken part and done your best."

Josephine

A girl in Okei's age group, she, like her friends, walks many miles to the rival village of Akpei to sell plantains, because they can get a little more money for them there.

Kwutelu

A seventeen-year-old girl, she also sells plantains in the neighboring village's market. She is the oldest in her age group, the most sophisticated, and the leader; the others all model their behavior after hers. She has a sharp, mocking tongue, and likes to tease. She is engaged to someone from another village, and soon will leave her home to marry and live with him. When she comes quietly into her father's house at night, he attacks her, thinking she is Okei, and cuts off her ear. After the accident, she is more quiet and less mocking of others.

Mbekwu

See Uche

Nduka

One of Okei's friends, he is also sixteen, but unlike Okei he is short and stocky. He also has a very sharp tongue, and loses his temper easily. Nduka, like Okei, is cynical about older people and their supposed wisdom; he remarks, "trouble with these old men is that they say things simply to hurt, without any proof."

Nne Ojo

Senior wife of Obi Agiliga, she is exasperated with Okei's adolescent bad manners, and his reluctance to contribute to the family welfare by working on their farm. She is quick-tempered, and threatens to get other boys to beat up Okei if he doesn't behave.

Okei

A thin, lanky sixteen-year-old boy, he has gone to school, which sets him apart from his uncle and many of the other young people in his village. He doesn't want to work on a farm, as his ancestors have always done; he complains that the work is endless, and every year they run out of food. However, he doesn't know what he does want to do, and is restless and bored. He's also fed up with his uncle's telling him "when I was your age," and telling him what to do. In addition, he is still troubled by the deaths of his family; he was spared only because he went out into the backyard while the soldiers killed them. He is regarded as intelligent by others in his village, and his friends admire him because he is taller, more polished, and originally came from a wealthier family, which, in their opinion, makes him a natural leader for his age group. The girls of his age, however, mock him as being a little too bigheaded. He is actually modest, and when he is elected leader, is doubtful of whether they have made the best choice.

When he is elected leader, he's assigned to wrestle a boy from the neighboring village to settle a rivalry between the two. He takes this seriously, and immediately begins toughening himself up, running and wrestling with his friends to improve his chances of winning. This shows that he is not inherently lazy, as his reluctance to work on the farm might make him seem; he simply needs a focus for his energies.

Onuoha Obi

Agiliga's twelve-year-old son, who works on the farm and is obedient and well-behaved. He wishes Okei would come to the farm and help.

Uche

Uche, whose nickname is "Mbekwu," or "Tortoise," is easy-going and laughs often, at everything and everyone, a habit that others find annoying. He is an age-mate of Okei and Nduka. They, and others their same age, are all known as "Umu aya Biafra," or "Babies born around the [Nigerian] civil war." Like Okei and Nduka, he is tired of being told to prove his manhood by going and laboring on the family farm. He likes Josephine, but tells others she is just a friend. He inadvertently gets into trouble when he goes to the neighboring village to fish in the river, and unintentionally muddies some cassava pulp that the women of that village have left in the river to soak.

Obi Uju

Kwutelu's father; she is his favorite daughter, and often sleeps at his house instead of her mother's, because it's more relaxing. He is very protective of her, and when he hears rumors that girls are being harassed, he is determined to prevent anyone from hurting her. Like Obi Agiliga, he is a farmer, and is worried because he doesn't have enough workers to harvest all his yams before the yam festival. He hears a rumor that Okei threatened Kwutelu, and goes to sleep with a well-sharpened knife; when he hears someone coming into his house after dark, he gets the knife and goes after them, cutting off an ear. The person turns out to be Kwutelu, coming in to sleep.

Obi Uwechue

A man from Akpei, the neighboring village, who comes to see Obi Agiliga to discuss the problems both villages are having with their adolescent boys. He explains that the young men are restless and bored, have too much education and too much time on their hands, and that they are picking fights with girls and making minor trouble for the adults. He tells Obi Agiliga that they should create a diversion for the young men, some kind of "minor worry" or problem that they will have to solve. "By the time they have finished solving that problem they will be wiser," he says.

Themes

Generational Conflict

The novel opens with a conflict between Okei and his uncle, Obi Agiliga, which continues throughout the book, but is resolved by the end of the story. At the beginning, Okei is restless, bored, tired of his uncle's nagging, and thinks he can solve his own problems and that his uncle is hopelessly out of touch. He also thinks his uncle has nothing to teach him, since he has been educated. This attitude is common among his age-mates who have been to school; none of them want to work on their parents' farms, although they are happy to eat the food their parents provide. The girls of their same age, who unlike the boys are expected and required to do productive work for their families, think the boys are "bigheaded" and lazy.

Obi Agiliga, however, does remember what it was like to be a young man, and he secretly sympathizes with and understands Okei's problems, although he can't convince Okei of that. Their relationship is complicated by the fact that Okei is an orphan and believes his uncle took him in out of duty, so he is reluctant to trust Obi Agiliga. As the story progresses and Obi Agiliga comes up with a scheme to keep all the boys busy and teach them a lesson, Okei gradually learns that his uncle is trustworthy, that he does know more than Okei thinks he does, and that it might be wise to ask his advice every now and then.

One turning point in their relationship comes when Okei is wrongly accused of being in Obi Uju's house, and his uncle and aunt protect him. Okei realizes for the first time that his uncle will truly stand behind him, and that despite his "nagging," he really believes Okei is a good person.

A second turning point occurs when another boy, a farmer's son, tells Okei that his uncle was once the best wrestler in the village. This is news to Okei, who has never bothered to listen or to ask about his uncle's past, because he just assumed he was a boring old man. Obi Agiliga teaches him the traditional songs and wrestling moves, the old way, and also shows him some special techniques to attack the opponent when he is unprepared. While teaching, he regains some of his old skill and youth, and Okei is fascinated. Obi Agiliga says, "I have to teach it all to this young man here. It is his turn now. My turn has come and gone." He also praises Okei for being not only the leader of the wrestling group, but also the leader of his age group. This true praise helps Okei to trust him even more, and they are finally close; a bond of trust has been created.

Tradition versus Change

Much of the conflict in the book stems from the fact that times have changed, even within Okei's lifetime. He began life in a stable family, but that was quickly destroyed during the Biafran War, when his family was killed and he had to go live with his uncle. He lives with the pain of this past history.

Things are also different for his generation because some (though not all) of them have been educated. In the past, young men simply farmed, like their fathers. It has also made the educated boys reluctant to work on their fathers' farms, and leads them to look down on other boys who have not been to school. These other boys, dutiful and traditional, seem dull to the educated boys, but in the end may be wiser; one of them advises Okei to go learn from his uncle, an act which makes him a much better wrestler and which he would not have thought of on his own.

The schooling has opened up new possibilities, but as one of the gossiping girls points out, not great ones; in her opinion, Okei is educated enough to be a houseboy, but has too high an opinion of himself to succeed even at that lowly job.

Because of the schooling, Okei and the other boys are in a kind of limbo—they don't want to work on the farms, and they are not educated enough to do anything else. This leaves them restless and bored, with a lot of energy but nothing productive to do with it, leading to trouble. Kwutelu observes, "They are so proud about being partly educated. They are like bats, neither birds nor animals."

Futility of War

The book ends with the sentence, "In a good war, nobody wins," and this theme is brought up early, when the narrator describes how Okei lost his family in the Biafran War. "It was a civil war that did cost Nigeria dear. Almost a million lives were lost, and not just on the losing side; those who won the war lost thousands of people too—showing that in any war, however justified its cause, nobody wins."

At the end of the wrestling match, which turns into a mass brawl, Obi Agiliga tells everyone that the fight has ended "well." By this, he doesn't mean that anyone has won, or that any real good came from the actual fight. What he means is that it ended

Topics for Further Study

- Research the Biafran War, also known as the Nigerian Civil War. How did the conflict start? What kept it going, and what was the ultimate result? How is this similar to, or different from, the conflict between the young men in the villages in *The Wrestling Match*?

- In the book, Okei's uncle and a man from the neighboring village invent a diversion to give the teenagers a positive outlet for their energy. If you could invent a similar diversion for young people in American society, what would it be? What do you think would happen as a result?

- Okei is reluctant to go to his uncle and ask him for help, because he is afraid his uncle will say, "I knew you would have to ask me," and "I told you so." Do you think these feelings are universal in young people in all cultures? Why?

- In the book, the characters often comment on how things have changed: some of the young people are now educated, and instead of doing traditional dances at the yam festival, they are wrestling—perhaps because they have lived through a war. Research Nigerian society in the 1970s and today, and discuss how it has changed in the last few decades.

- For the characters in the book, yams are a staple food. Find out what other foods are important in Nigerian society and culture. Research a Nigerian recipe, then cook a Nigerian dish.

as the elders expected it to. "You were all hurt and humiliated," he tells them. "I am sure you will remember this day."

One would hope that the young people would remember the lesson they've learned, but the book itself makes it clear that although they may remember it, their offspring may not. Memory is short when it comes to avoiding conflict; the young people, themselves the offspring of a war, are all too ready to start another one, perpetuating a futile cycle.

Style

Storytelling

The most notable feature of *The Wrestling Match* is the style in which it is told. Readers may feel as if they're in "an open clearing in which children and old people sat, telling stories and singing in the moonlight." Emecheta adopts an intimate tone, taking the reader in and telling the story as if the reader is sitting right there and knows all the people involved. In addition, she uses rhythm and repetition, as in the opening paragraph:

> It was the time for the swishes of the fronds of the coconut-palms to be heard; it was the time for the fire-insects of the night to hiss through the still air. It was the time for the frogs in the nearby ponds to croak to their mates, as if to say that they should now seek shelter because night was fast approaching.

The language of the book is deceptively simple and clear, but at the same time, vividly poetic, particularly in the descriptions of the natural world, which is ever-present. Birds, animals, the seasons, night, day, and other aspects of nature are as important as the characters, and help to ground the story and add to its traditional flavor.

The narrator of the story adopts a wise, omniscient persona, that of an elder who has seen the foibles of every generation, who understands both Obi Agiliga's frustration with Okei and his compassion with him, and also his wounded pride because his nephew won't listen to him. She also has sympathy for Okei's haunted past, his ambition, and his restlessness. She shows every character in an affirming, positive light, despite their individual flaws, and presents hope for everyone to improve their lives and work together.

Setting and Culture

Another notable feature of the novel is its setting in a small Nigerian village of farming people. On every page, the reader is treated to the sounds, scents, textures, and customs of village life, made vividly real. Emecheta presents this culture as the story progresses, not stopping to explain, but simply dropping it into the text; characters eat pounded yam for dinner, wear "abada cloth," live in compounds of thatched huts, bathe in the river, and have large, polygamous, extended families. Emecheta

presents village life in a larger context of cultural change, as the younger generation becomes more educated, and the girls become interested in making money so they can buy themselves better clothes.

An important part of village culture is the "age group," in which young people born around the same time are expected to socialize together and support each other. The members of a particular age group all wear the same distinctive hairstyle and go through coming-of-age ceremonies together; they elect a leader and conduct their business largely outside adult view, although they are expected to consult their elders when necessary. The leader of the age group is expected to defend their reputation, to speak for them, and to represent them to the larger world.

In this culture, girls marry young; Kwutelu is only seventeen, but is already engaged and soon will marry. Boys apparently wait until they are older, because although Okei and his age-mates are sixteen, they are still only a little interested in girls, and not interested in becoming able to support a family.

Historical Context

The Biafran War

Nigeria was a British colony until 1963, when it became a republic with four regional governments. The ruling party, made up largely of people from the north, dominated the government. Like other African nations, Nigeria is made up of many different ethnic groups, which coexist within boundaries that have no connection with traditional lands, but were drawn up by the European powers that controlled Africa in the past.

In 1964, people boycotted the first general election, leading to a crisis, and in 1965, this escalated to general rebellion when the leading political party rigged elections in the western region.

In January, 1966, army officers of the Igbo ethnic group led a coup to overthrow the government. They killed the prime minister and the premiers of the northern and western region. After this coup, Major General Johnson T. U. Aguiyi-Aronsi took control with a military government, and ruled the country until he was ousted by another coup, this time led by officers who were members of the Hausa ethnic group. During this coup, Igbo people living in the north were killed, which led great num-

Compare & Contrast

- **1970:** The Nigerian Civil War ends, leaving a total of over 1 million people dead from war, starvation, and disease.

  Today: In 1999 and 2000, under the rule of President Olusegon Obasanjo (elected in 1999), rival religious and tribal groups continue centuries-old conflicts with violent rioting; in one riot, over 300 people are killed in hand-to-hand fighting. Shortages of food and fuel, as well as power blackouts, exacerbate the situation, and the country teeters on the brink of another civil war.

- **1970:** The illiteracy rate in Nigeria is 86% for females and 65% for males.

  Today: The illiteracy rate in Nigeria has decreased to 48% for females and 30% for males.

- **1970:** Nigeria experiences one of the world's worst famines in the wake of the Civil War.

  Today: The country of Nigeria remains today in the condition of massive debt, poverty, and inflation into which it plunged in the 1980s, following a period of unprecedented prosperity (brought on by soaring oil prices) during the middle and late 1970s.

- **1970:** Within Nigeria, ancient rivalries between ethnic and religious groups simmer to the boiling point and are not lessened by the ending of the Nigerian Civil War.

  Today: Conflicts which began hundreds of years ago remain today, and, as in the 1960s and 1970s, continue to fuel social, political, and economic problems in Nigeria.

---

bers of Igbo people to flee to their ancestral eastern region. However, even in this region, Igbo people were killed.

Between September and November of 1966, the four regions tried to come to a truce, but failed, partly because representatives of the eastern region refused to participate in the negotiations after the first meeting. More meetings occurred in 1967, but led to nothing, and on May 27, 1967, Lieutenant Colonel C. O. Ojukwu declared that the eastern region was a sovereign and independent republic. In response, the federal government declared a state of emergency and officially divided Nigeria into twelve states.

Three days later, Ojukwu proclaimed that the eastern region was seceding from Nigeria and was now the Republic of Biafra. Biafran and federal forces soon clashed. The Biafrans did well initially, but by October, the Biafran capital of Enugu was captured by federal troops. The war continued until 1970, when the Biafrans were so starved they were unable to continue fighting.

Ojukwu left Nigeria in 1970, and a Biafran delegation formally surrendered to the Nigerian federal government on January 15.

As Emecheta explains in the book, "it was a civil war, which started among the politicians; the army stepped in to keep the peace, then the military leaders started to quarrel among themselves, and one created a new state, taking his followers with him." Almost a million people died in the war, not just military people but also civilians; as Emecheta notes, this shows that "in any war, however justified its cause, nobody wins."

Diversity in Nigeria

Nigeria is roughly the size of Texas, but unlike Texas, contains more than 300 different ethnic groups who speak 300 different languages. When Nigeria was defined as a nation by the European colonialists, the borders of the nation were drawn up without regard to natural divisions between ethnic or regional groups. Thus, there are now a great number of ethnic groups within Nigeria, and divisions among them have led to frequent conflicts. "Ethnic group" is defined as a group of people who

Soldier in the Biafran War. In the novel, Okei's family was killed in this war

share a common language and cultural values; as Simon A. Rakov noted in the Brown University *Postcolonial Web*, there is as much difference between these groups "as there is between Germans, English, Russians, and Turks."

Most of the 300 ethnic groups are in the minority, and thus do not have political clout, or the resources needed to take advantage of development or modernization. The three "majority" groups are the Hausa-Fulani in the north, the Igbo (or Ibo) in the southeast, and the Yoruba in the southwest. These groups together make up fifty-seven percent of the Nigerian population, with the rest belonging to "minority" groups.

Critical Overview

According to M. Keith Booker in *The African Novel in English: An Introduction*, Emecheta "is probably Africa's best-known and most widely read woman novelist." She has been supporting herself and her family with her writing since 1972, when she published her first book *In the Ditch*. Her work has been widely translated and read all over the world, and indeed, she told interviewer Reed

Way Dasenbrock in *Interviews with Writers of the Post-Colonial World*, "I try to write for the world."

However, she has occasionally been criticized by Nigerian writers, who feel that in some of her books, she writes about topics that, as a woman, she should not consider. Of her book *Destination Biafra*, about the Nigerian civil war, she told Dasenbrock, "Nigerian critics feel that the language I use . . . is not appropriate. They would like me to use big military words, because I'm writing about what happened at Biafra." She also commented that some are offended by her simply because she is a woman. She quoted Chinweizu, a Nigerian critic, who remarked "Buchi, I am going to ruin you." When she asked why, he said, "Why should you be writing about what men are doing? Did you go to the warfield?"

Emecheta also commented in her interview with Dasenbrock that criticism in Nigeria is heavily weighted, depending on what ethnic group the reviewer and the author are from; if they are from the same group, the reviewer usually praises; if they are from different groups, the reviewer harshly criticizes "according to who you are, your people, and the people you know."

In Europe and North America, however, she noted that "people will just artificially boost a black person. I find that a most hurtful attitude—more patronizing than supportive."

According to Chikwenye Okonso Ogunyemi in *African Wo/Man Palava: The Nigerian Novel by Women*, Emecheta's greatest achievement "lies in internationalizing the Nigerian novel by women," and her work is enriched by the contrast between two cultures, and her outlook as a woman who has lived outside Nigeria.

Ogunyemi points out that although Emecheta is considered a feminist writer by many critics, she does not consider herself to be a feminist. According to Ogunyemi, Emecheta said, "I think we women of African background still have a very very long way before we can really rub shoulders with such women." In an interview with Julie Holmes in *The Voice*, she said, "I work toward the liberation of women, but I'm not feminist. I'm just a woman."

Ogunyemi noted that "her novels reveal a paradox: a dual vision, one insistently feminist, the other consistently denying or punishing feminism," and commented that "The subsequent tension in her works results in a mixed reception, particularly in Nigeria, where she is less popular than she is in Europe . . . and in America."

Holmes quoted African-American writer Alice Walker, who said that Emecheta "integrates the profession of writer into the cultural concept of mother/worker, because she is both." Emecheta has integrated her life and her work through her writing, since much of her work is autobiographical. She told Holmes, "I'm not really very creative. I have to experience something or know someone who has seen something in order to write convincingly."

Ogunyemi praised Emecheta for using her personal story to bring wider attention to the situation of women in Nigeria: "She has shifted what was a strictly domestic agenda into the international sphere, thus situating the [discussion] in the court of world opinion."

Criticism

Kelly Winters

Winters is a freelance writer and has written for a wide variety of educational publishers. In the following essay, she discusses themes of intergenerational understanding, the nature of war, and the place of women in this novel.

Buchi Emecheta's *The Wrestling Match* is notable for its clear, simple language and vivid sensory and cultural details, which bring this tale set in a Nigerian village to life. However, behind its deceptively simple façade, the novel considers deeper questions about intergenerational understanding and the nature of war.

One prevalent theme, running throughout the story, is that of intergenerational conflict versus intergenerational understanding. Okei believes that his uncle and aunt, as well as other adults, are hopelessly out of touch, have no idea what he's going through, and have no sympathy for his problems. He has suffered the loss of his family, and is further confused because he and his friends, unlike previous generations and unlike many of the other people in the village, have experienced a few years of schooling. Thus, he is unsure of what he will do in the future, unlike his uneducated and more traditional counterparts, who run their lives according to well-worn customs and are secure about their place in the world.

Although Okei believes his uncle has no idea what he's thinking or going through, the narrative reveals that his uncle does understand him, and has compassion both for his loss and for his confusion

> **If the book has a flaw, it is how well-adjusted and 'normal' Okei seems to be, despite the horrifying things he's seen."**

about his role in life. As he explains to his younger son Onuoha:

> He is troubled about something, Onuoha. We don't know what it is. And he did not dream that he would ever be asked to come and work on the farm. That Awolowo free education has given him and his age-group airs. They will grow, never mind. They will all grow.

Although he is sometimes exasperated with Okei's adolescent disrespect and apparent laziness, he realizes that what Okei and his friends need is something productive to do—some cause into which they can hurl their considerable energy and ability. Thus, he and Obi Uwechue come up with a scheme to provoke a conflict between their two villages. Because his scheme involves conflict, both within and between the two villages, in some sense, Obi Agiliga could be viewed as a troublemaker. However, he believes that the conflict is in the service of a higher goal: teaching a lesson and helping the young men to grow up.

Interestingly, the adults don't seem bothered by potential trouble they could cause if the mass brawl gets out of control. It does get out of control, and everyone in it gets soundly thrashed and humiliated, but the elders are able to restore control by beating drums and yelling. No one is seriously injured in the fight, which seems somewhat unrealistic, and the elders never consider what they would have done if someone had been injured or if they were unable to stop the fighting. In addition, when Kwutelu's ear is cut off when her father mistakes her for a robber, the two elder men, Obi Agiliga and Obi Uwechue, simply shrug and remark that it could have been worse—she could have been killed. They have no apparent compassion for her disfigurement, and the narrator also seems to approve of it because it has stilled Kwutelu's "sharp tongue."

The two elders don't let anyone know that they're ultimately responsible for starting the hys-

What Do I Read Next?

- Emecheta's *Joys of Motherhood* (1980) tells the story of a young village woman who grows up and endures the trials of life in colonial Nigeria.

- An autobiographical novel, Emecheta's *Second-Class Citizen* (1973) tells the story of an intelligent, resourceful Nigerian girl who emigrates to Great Britain.

- In *Bride Price* (1980), Emecheta insightfully depicts the life of an Ibo girl in Nigeria.

- Emecheta's *Double Yoke* (1995) is an unusual novel about university life in modern Africa.

- *Efuru* (1966), by Flora Nwapa, one of Emecheta's favorite authors, explores Nigerian village life.

- In *So Long a Letter* (1991), Mariama Ba exposes the double standard between men and women in Africa.

---

teria that made Kwutelu's father think Okei was going to rob him. They are sorry, but they keep their regret to themselves, an act that seems surprisingly irresponsible. They are more interested in the successful continuation of their plan, and a few paragraphs later, they "chuckle knowingly at their cleverness" in creating problems for the "know-all" adolescents.

It's also interesting that instead of creating a positive cause for the young men to become involved in, the elders create a negative diversion—spiteful gossip and conflict between the two neighboring villages. One might think that Obi Agiliga, knowing the pointlessness of conflict, would shy away from creating it, but perhaps he knows that each generation only learns from its own experiences, not from the philosophical talk of those who are older. Thus, the boys must be allowed to experience conflict for themselves—hopefully on a small scale, rather than the full-scale war Okei has already witnessed—in order to learn that war is ultimately futile.

Despite these flaws in his character, Obi Agiliga is generally depicted as wise and kind, and so is his senior wife, Nne Ojo. The story reinforces traditional Nigerian beliefs that elders do know what's best for the young, and that younger people should both attend to their example and learn from their philosophical wisdom. For example, Okei, at the urging of a more traditional youth, reluctantly goes to his uncle to learn some wrestling moves. To his surprise, he finds that Obi Agiliga was the best wrestler in his own age group, and he also learns to take defeat philosophically. Obi Agiliga tells him, "Even if you lost, it wouldn't be a complete loss because you would have added a new art to the game of wrestling, and you would have taken your part and done your best." Okei and his friends are chastened by the lesson they learn. As Nduka, another "big-headed" youth who formerly mocked the stodgy beliefs of the elders, "prayerfully" says near the end of the book, "A village that has no elders has no future. I hope we will always have elders."

Early in the book, the narrator describes the Nigerian civil war, or Biafran War, in which the new, and short-lived, nation of Biafra was created in 1967. The war, which Emecheta notes killed almost a million people, marked more than one generation, but particularly *Umu aya Biafra*: "babies born around the civil war." However, Okei must have been more than a baby, because the narrator notes that when his family was killed by federal soldiers, he ran out into the back yard and thus escaped death. The narrator never discusses his reaction to this event, but other characters note that "Something is troubling him, we don't know what." In addition, Obi Agiliga comments that Okei was born to a more wealthy family and never expected to have to work on a farm. This indicates that he was old enough to remember his parents and his life before the war, and to remember their presumably horrific deaths.

Okei is depicted as sullen, wary of his elders, and as having a cockiness that is rooted in an inner insecurity and rootlessness, as well as in his small amount of education. Although some of these traits may result from the traumatic loss of his family during his childhood, they are also typical of many teenagers who are beginning to separate themselves from their parents and find their own role in the world; his friends, Uche and Nduka, whose families were not slain, share them. If the book has a flaw, it is how well-adjusted and "normal" Okei seems to be, despite the horrifying things he's seen. It would seem that he, of all people, does

not need a lesson in the futility of war; he has presumably seen, first hand, the waste of lives and
dreams, and it would seem that he should be more
obviously marked by his tragic past. In fact, the
events he's been through would probably have one
of two effects: they would either mark him with a
burning desire to revenge himself on his family's
killers, or with a more mature awareness that "in
war, nobody wins," the lesson he seemingly learns
only after the relatively trivial conflict of the
wrestling match.

Although most of Emecheta's work examines
the roles of women in Nigerian and western society and protests against the limited roles they have
been assigned, *The Wrestling Match* takes a thoroughly traditional view of girls and women and
their roles, perhaps because it is set in a traditional
village where these roles have remained unchanged
for many years.

In the story, the adolescent girls of the village
don't need conflicts invented for them, because
they are already dealing with adult concerns. They
work hard for their families, assisting with household chores such as "claying" the huts; they walk
many miles with heavy burdens on their heads to
sell plantains and other produce; and at least one
of them, Kwutelu, is engaged (at age seventeen)
and will soon marry. They don't have time to waste,
unlike the boys, who have so much time on their
hands that they begin to make trouble for everyone
else. Nor do they have the education that gives the
boys such a high opinion of themselves. They are
destined to be wives and mothers, and to take care
of men, as the multiple wives of the elders do
throughout the book: cooking, cleaning, nurturing.

These depictions of girls and women are natural, since the story takes place in a traditional culture where these roles are the norm, but interestingly enough, the narrator seems to approve of this
situation, and is undisturbed about the girls' lack
of education or the disparity in expectations between the girls and boys. In addition, the narrator
presents Kwutelu's loss of an ear in a "positive"
light: it has finally stilled her sharp tongue, and now
she may be more modest and better-behaved, because she's afraid of people making fun of her.

However, these presentations of girls and
women are surprising, considering that Emecheta
is the author, and in her other books, she protests
bitterly against her culture, in which men are valued more than women. In her other books, she presents women as equals of men, and encourages

*Women in an Ibo village like the one in which
the story is set*

them to become educated and find roles beyond
simply being wives and mothers.

Source: Kelly Winters, Critical Essay on *The Wrestling
Match*, in *Novels for Students*, The Gale Group, 2002.

Sources

Booker, M. Keith, *The African Novel in English: An Introduction*, Heinemann, 1998.

Holmes, Julie, " 'Just' an Igbo Woman," in *The Voice*, July
9, 1996.

Jussawalla, Feroza, and Reed Way Dasenbrock, *Interviews
with Writers of the Post-Colonial World*, University Press
of Mississippi, 1992.

Motherland Nigeria, http://www.motherlandnigeria.com
(July 25, 2001).

Ogunyemi, Chikwenye Okonso, *African Wo/Man Palava:
The Nigerian Novel by Women*, University of Chicago Press,
1996.

Rakov, Simon A., *The Postcolonial Web*, http://landow.stg.
brown.edu/ (July 25, 2001).

United Nations Web site, http://www.un.org (July 25, 2001).

For Further Reading

Arndt, Susan, *African Women's Literature, Orature, and Intertextuality: Igbo Oral Narratives as Nigerian Women Writers' Models and Objects of Writing Back*, Bayreuth University Press, 1998.

This volume examines Igbo oral tradition and its influence on the work of Nigerian women writers.

Fishburn, Katherine, *Reading Buchi Emecheta*, Greenwood Publishing Co., 1995.

This book provides a critical analysis of Emecheta's life and work.

Umeh, Marie, ed., *Emerging Perspectives on Buchi Emecheta*, Africa World Press, 1995.

This is a collection of critical essays on Emecheta's work.

Uraizee, Joya F., *This Is No Place for a Woman: Nadine Gordimer, Nayantera Sahgal, Buchi Emecheta, and the Politics of Gender*, Africa World Press, 2000.

This is an analytical survey of three post-colonial African women writers.

Glossary of Literary Terms

A

Abstract: As an adjective applied to writing or literary works, abstract refers to words or phrases that name things not knowable through the five senses.

Aestheticism: A literary and artistic movement of the nineteenth century. Followers of the movement believed that art should not be mixed with social, political, or moral teaching. The statement "art for art's sake" is a good summary of aestheticism. The movement had its roots in France, but it gained widespread importance in England in the last half of the nineteenth century, where it helped change the Victorian practice of including moral lessons in literature.

Allegory: A narrative technique in which characters representing things or abstract ideas are used to convey a message or teach a lesson. Allegory is typically used to teach moral, ethical, or religious lessons but is sometimes used for satiric or political purposes.

Allusion: A reference to a familiar literary or historical person or event, used to make an idea more easily understood.

Analogy: A comparison of two things made to explain something unfamiliar through its similarities to something familiar, or to prove one point based on the acceptedness of another. Similes and metaphors are types of analogies.

Antagonist: The major character in a narrative or drama who works against the hero or protagonist.

Anthropomorphism: The presentation of animals or objects in human shape or with human characteristics. The term is derived from the Greek word for "human form."

Antihero: A central character in a work of literature who lacks traditional heroic qualities such as courage, physical prowess, and fortitude. Antiheroes typically distrust conventional values and are unable to commit themselves to any ideals. They generally feel helpless in a world over which they have no control. Antiheroes usually accept, and often celebrate, their positions as social outcasts.

Apprenticeship Novel: See *Bildungsroman*

Archetype: The word archetype is commonly used to describe an original pattern or model from which all other things of the same kind are made. This term was introduced to literary criticism from the psychology of Carl Jung. It expresses Jung's theory that behind every person's "unconscious," or repressed memories of the past, lies the "collective unconscious" of the human race: memories of the countless typical experiences of our ancestors. These memories are said to prompt illogical associations that trigger powerful emotions in the reader. Often, the emotional process is primitive, even primordial. Archetypes are the literary images that grow out of the "collective unconscious." They appear in literature as incidents and plots that repeat basic patterns of life. They may also appear as stereotyped characters.

Avant-garde: French term meaning "vanguard." It is used in literary criticism to describe new writing that rejects traditional approaches to literature in favor of innovations in style or content.

B

Beat Movement: A period featuring a group of American poets and novelists of the 1950s and 1960s—including Jack Kerouac, Allen Ginsberg, Gregory Corso, William S. Burroughs, and Lawrence Ferlinghetti—who rejected established social and literary values. Using such techniques as stream of consciousness writing and jazz-influenced free verse and focusing on unusual or abnormal states of mind—generated by religious ecstasy or the use of drugs—the Beat writers aimed to create works that were unconventional in both form and subject matter.

Bildungsroman: A German word meaning "novel of development." The *bildungsroman* is a study of the maturation of a youthful character, typically brought about through a series of social or sexual encounters that lead to self-awareness. *Bildungsroman* is used interchangeably with *erziehungsroman,* a novel of initiation and education. When a *bildungsroman* is concerned with the development of an artist (as in James Joyce's *A Portrait of the Artist as a Young Man*), it is often termed a *kunstlerroman.* Also known as Apprenticeship Novel, Coming of Age Novel, *Erziehungsroman,* or *Kunstlerroman.*

Black Aesthetic Movement: A period of artistic and literary development among African Americans in the 1960s and early 1970s. This was the first major African-American artistic movement since the Harlem Renaissance and was closely paralleled by the civil rights and black power movements. The black aesthetic writers attempted to produce works of art that would be meaningful to the black masses. Key figures in black aesthetics included one of its founders, poet and playwright Amiri Baraka, formerly known as LeRoi Jones; poet and essayist Haki R. Madhubuti, formerly Don L. Lee; poet and playwright Sonia Sanchez; and dramatist Ed Bullins. Also known as Black Arts Movement.

Black Humor: Writing that places grotesque elements side by side with humorous ones in an attempt to shock the reader, forcing him or her to laugh at the horrifying reality of a disordered world. Also known as Black Comedy.

Burlesque: Any literary work that uses exaggeration to make its subject appear ridiculous, either by treating a trivial subject with profound seriousness or by treating a dignified subject frivolously. The word "burlesque" may also be used as an adjective, as in "burlesque show," to mean "striptease act."

C

Character: Broadly speaking, a person in a literary work. The actions of characters are what constitute the plot of a story, novel, or poem. There are numerous types of characters, ranging from simple, stereotypical figures to intricate, multifaceted ones. In the techniques of anthropomorphism and personification, animals—and even places or things—can assume aspects of character. "Characterization" is the process by which an author creates vivid, believable characters in a work of art. This may be done in a variety of ways, including (1) direct description of the character by the narrator; (2) the direct presentation of the speech, thoughts, or actions of the character; and (3) the responses of other characters to the character. The term "character" also refers to a form originated by the ancient Greek writer Theophrastus that later became popular in the seventeenth and eighteenth centuries. It is a short essay or sketch of a person who prominently displays a specific attribute or quality, such as miserliness or ambition.

Climax: The turning point in a narrative, the moment when the conflict is at its most intense. Typically, the structure of stories, novels, and plays is one of rising action, in which tension builds to the climax, followed by falling action, in which tension lessens as the story moves to its conclusion.

Colloquialism: A word, phrase, or form of pronunciation that is acceptable in casual conversation but not in formal, written communication. It is considered more acceptable than slang.

Coming of Age Novel: See *Bildungsroman*

Concrete: Concrete is the opposite of abstract, and refers to a thing that actually exists or a description that allows the reader to experience an object or concept with the senses.

Connotation: The impression that a word gives beyond its defined meaning. Connotations may be universally understood or may be significant only to a certain group.

Convention: Any widely accepted literary device, style, or form.

D

Denotation: The definition of a word, apart from the impressions or feelings it creates (connotations) in the reader.

Denouement: A French word meaning "the unknotting." In literary criticism, it denotes the resolution of conflict in fiction or drama. The *denouement* follows the climax and provides an outcome to the primary plot situation as well as an explanation of secondary plot complications. The *denouement* often involves a character's recognition of his or her state of mind or moral condition. Also known as Falling Action.

Description: Descriptive writing is intended to allow a reader to picture the scene or setting in which the action of a story takes place. The form this description takes often evokes an intended emotional response—a dark, spooky graveyard will evoke fear, and a peaceful, sunny meadow will evoke calmness.

Dialogue: In its widest sense, dialogue is simply conversation between people in a literary work; in its most restricted sense, it refers specifically to the speech of characters in a drama. As a specific literary genre, a "dialogue" is a composition in which characters debate an issue or idea.

Diction: The selection and arrangement of words in a literary work. Either or both may vary depending on the desired effect. There are four general types of diction: "formal," used in scholarly or lofty writing; "informal," used in relaxed but educated conversation; "colloquial," used in everyday speech; and "slang," containing newly coined words and other terms not accepted in formal usage.

Didactic: A term used to describe works of literature that aim to teach some moral, religious, political, or practical lesson. Although didactic elements are often found in artistically pleasing works, the term "didactic" usually refers to literature in which the message is more important than the form. The term may also be used to criticize a work that the critic finds "overly didactic," that is, heavy-handed in its delivery of a lesson.

Doppelganger: A literary technique by which a character is duplicated (usually in the form of an alter ego, though sometimes as a ghostly counterpart) or divided into two distinct, usually opposite personalities. The use of this character device is widespread in nineteenth- and twentieth-century literature, and indicates a growing awareness among authors that the "self" is really a composite of many "selves." Also known as The Double.

Double Entendre: A corruption of a French phrase meaning "double meaning." The term is used to indicate a word or phrase that is deliberately ambiguous, especially when one of the meanings is risqué or improper.

Dramatic Irony: Occurs when the audience of a play or the reader of a work of literature knows something that a character in the work itself does not know. The irony is in the contrast between the intended meaning of the statements or actions of a character and the additional information understood by the audience.

Dystopia: An imaginary place in a work of fiction where the characters lead dehumanized, fearful lives.

E

Edwardian: Describes cultural conventions identified with the period of the reign of Edward VII of England (1901-1910). Writers of the Edwardian Age typically displayed a strong reaction against the propriety and conservatism of the Victorian Age. Their work often exhibits distrust of authority in religion, politics, and art and expresses strong doubts about the soundness of conventional values.

Empathy: A sense of shared experience, including emotional and physical feelings, with someone or something other than oneself. Empathy is often used to describe the response of a reader to a literary character.

Enlightenment, The: An eighteenth-century philosophical movement. It began in France but had a wide impact throughout Europe and America. Thinkers of the Enlightenment valued reason and believed that both the individual and society could achieve a state of perfection. Corresponding to this essentially humanist vision was a resistance to religious authority.

Epigram: A saying that makes the speaker's point quickly and concisely. Often used to preface a novel.

Epilogue: A concluding statement or section of a literary work. In dramas, particularly those of the seventeenth and eighteenth centuries, the epilogue is a closing speech, often in verse, delivered by an actor at the end of a play and spoken directly to the audience.

Epiphany: A sudden revelation of truth inspired by a seemingly trivial incident.

Episode: An incident that forms part of a story and is significantly related to it. Episodes may be either self-contained narratives or events that depend on a larger context for their sense and importance.

Epistolary Novel: A novel in the form of letters. The form was particularly popular in the eighteenth century.

Epithet: A word or phrase, often disparaging or abusive, that expresses a character trait of someone or something.

Existentialism: A predominantly twentieth-century philosophy concerned with the nature and perception of human existence. There are two major strains of existentialist thought: atheistic and Christian. Followers of atheistic existentialism believe that the individual is alone in a godless universe and that the basic human condition is one of suffering and loneliness. Nevertheless, because there are no fixed values, individuals can create their own characters—indeed, they can shape themselves—through the exercise of free will. The atheistic strain culminates in and is popularly associated with the works of Jean-Paul Sartre. The Christian existentialists, on the other hand, believe that only in God may people find freedom from life's anguish. The two strains hold certain beliefs in common: that existence cannot be fully understood or described through empirical effort; that anguish is a universal element of life; that individuals must bear responsibility for their actions; and that there is no common standard of behavior or perception for religious and ethical matters.

Expatriates: See *Expatriatism*

Expatriatism: The practice of leaving one's country to live for an extended period in another country.

Exposition: Writing intended to explain the nature of an idea, thing, or theme. Expository writing is often combined with description, narration, or argument. In dramatic writing, the exposition is the introductory material which presents the characters, setting, and tone of the play.

Expressionism: An indistinct literary term, originally used to describe an early twentieth-century school of German painting. The term applies to almost any mode of unconventional, highly subjective writing that distorts reality in some way.

F

Fable: A prose or verse narrative intended to convey a moral. Animals or inanimate objects with human characteristics often serve as characters in fables.

Falling Action: See *Denouement*

Fantasy: A literary form related to mythology and folklore. Fantasy literature is typically set in non-existent realms and features supernatural beings.

Farce: A type of comedy characterized by broad humor, outlandish incidents, and often vulgar subject matter.

Femme fatale: A French phrase with the literal translation "fatal woman." A *femme fatale* is a sensuous, alluring woman who often leads men into danger or trouble.

Fiction: Any story that is the product of imagination rather than a documentation of fact. Characters and events in such narratives may be based in real life but their ultimate form and configuration is a creation of the author.

Figurative Language: A technique in writing in which the author temporarily interrupts the order, construction, or meaning of the writing for a particular effect. This interruption takes the form of one or more figures of speech such as hyperbole, irony, or simile. Figurative language is the opposite of literal language, in which every word is truthful, accurate, and free of exaggeration or embellishment.

Figures of Speech: Writing that differs from customary conventions for construction, meaning, order, or significance for the purpose of a special meaning or effect. There are two major types of figures of speech: rhetorical figures, which do not make changes in the meaning of the words, and tropes, which do.

Fin de siecle: A French term meaning "end of the century." The term is used to denote the last decade of the nineteenth century, a transition period when writers and other artists abandoned old conventions and looked for new techniques and objectives.

First Person: See *Point of View*

Flashback: A device used in literature to present action that occurred before the beginning of the story. Flashbacks are often introduced as the dreams or recollections of one or more characters.

Foil: A character in a work of literature whose physical or psychological qualities contrast strongly with, and therefore highlight, the corresponding qualities of another character.

Folklore: Traditions and myths preserved in a culture or group of people. Typically, these are passed on by word of mouth in various forms—such as legends, songs, and proverbs—or preserved in customs and ceremonies. This term was first used by W. J. Thoms in 1846.

Folktale: A story originating in oral tradition. Folktales fall into a variety of categories, including legends, ghost stories, fairy tales, fables, and anecdotes based on historical figures and events.

Foreshadowing: A device used in literature to create expectation or to set up an explanation of later developments.

Form: The pattern or construction of a work which identifies its genre and distinguishes it from other genres.

G

Genre: A category of literary work. In critical theory, genre may refer to both the content of a given work—tragedy, comedy, pastoral—and to its form, such as poetry, novel, or drama.

Gilded Age: A period in American history during the 1870s characterized by political corruption and materialism. A number of important novels of social and political criticism were written during this time.

Gothicism: In literary criticism, works characterized by a taste for the medieval or morbidly attractive. A gothic novel prominently features elements of horror, the supernatural, gloom, and violence: clanking chains, terror, charnel houses, ghosts, medieval castles, and mysteriously slamming doors. The term "gothic novel" is also applied to novels that lack elements of the traditional Gothic setting but that create a similar atmosphere of terror or dread.

Grotesque: In literary criticism, the subject matter of a work or a style of expression characterized by exaggeration, deformity, freakishness, and disorder. The grotesque often includes an element of comic absurdity.

H

Harlem Renaissance: The Harlem Renaissance of the 1920s is generally considered the first significant movement of black writers and artists in the United States. During this period, new and established black writers published more fiction and poetry than ever before, the first influential black literary journals were established, and black authors and artists received their first widespread recognition and serious critical appraisal. Among the major writers associated with this period are Claude McKay, Jean Toomer, Countee Cullen, Langston Hughes, Arna Bontemps, Nella Larsen, and Zora Neale Hurston. Also known as Negro Renaissance and New Negro Movement.

Hero/Heroine: The principal sympathetic character (male or female) in a literary work. Heroes and heroines typically exhibit admirable traits: idealism, courage, and integrity, for example.

Holocaust Literature: Literature influenced by or written about the Holocaust of World War II. Such literature includes true stories of survival in concentration camps, escape, and life after the war, as well as fictional works and poetry.

Humanism: A philosophy that places faith in the dignity of humankind and rejects the medieval perception of the individual as a weak, fallen creature. "Humanists" typically believe in the perfectibility of human nature and view reason and education as the means to that end.

Hyperbole: In literary criticism, deliberate exaggeration used to achieve an effect.

I

Idiom: A word construction or verbal expression closely associated with a given language.

Image: A concrete representation of an object or sensory experience. Typically, such a representation helps evoke the feelings associated with the object or experience itself. Images are either "literal" or "figurative." Literal images are especially concrete and involve little or no extension of the obvious meaning of the words used to express them. Figurative images do not follow the literal meaning of the words exactly. Images in literature are usually visual, but the term "image" can also refer to the representation of any sensory experience.

Imagery: The array of images in a literary work. Also, figurative language.

In medias res: A Latin term meaning "in the middle of things." It refers to the technique of beginning a story at its midpoint and then using various flashback devices to reveal previous action.

Interior Monologue: A narrative technique in which characters' thoughts are revealed in a way that appears to be uncontrolled by the author. The interior monologue typically aims to reveal the inner self of a character. It portrays emotional experiences as they occur at both a conscious and unconscious level. Images are often used to represent sensations or emotions.

Irony: In literary criticism, the effect of language in which the intended meaning is the opposite of what is stated.

J

Jargon: Language that is used or understood only by a select group of people. Jargon may refer to terminology used in a certain profession, such as computer jargon, or it may refer to any nonsensical language that is not understood by most people.

L

Leitmotiv: See *Motif*

Literal Language: An author uses literal language when he or she writes without exaggerating or embellishing the subject matter and without any tools of figurative language.

Lost Generation: A term first used by Gertrude Stein to describe the post-World War I generation of American writers: men and women haunted by a sense of betrayal and emptiness brought about by the destructiveness of the war.

M

Mannerism: Exaggerated, artificial adherence to a literary manner or style. Also, a popular style of the visual arts of late sixteenth-century Europe that was marked by elongation of the human form and by intentional spatial distortion. Literary works that are self-consciously high-toned and artistic are often said to be "mannered."

Metaphor: A figure of speech that expresses an idea through the image of another object. Metaphors suggest the essence of the first object by identifying it with certain qualities of the second object.

Modernism: Modern literary practices. Also, the principles of a literary school that lasted from roughly the beginning of the twentieth century until the end of World War II. Modernism is defined by its rejection of the literary conventions of the nineteenth century and by its opposition to conventional morality, taste, traditions, and economic values.

Mood: The prevailing emotions of a work or of the author in his or her creation of the work. The mood of a work is not always what might be expected based on its subject matter.

Motif: A theme, character type, image, metaphor, or other verbal element that recurs throughout a single work of literature or occurs in a number of different works over a period of time. Also known as *Motiv* or *Leitmotiv.*

Myth: An anonymous tale emerging from the traditional beliefs of a culture or social unit. Myths use supernatural explanations for natural phenomena. They may also explain cosmic issues like creation and death. Collections of myths, known as mythologies, are common to all cultures and nations, but the best-known myths belong to the Norse, Roman, and Greek mythologies.

N

Narration: The telling of a series of events, real or invented. A narration may be either a simple narrative, in which the events are recounted chronologically, or a narrative with a plot, in which the account is given in a style reflecting the author's artistic concept of the story. Narration is sometimes used as a synonym for "storyline."

Narrative: A verse or prose accounting of an event or sequence of events, real or invented. The term is also used as an adjective in the sense "method of narration." For example, in literary criticism, the expression "narrative technique" usually refers to the way the author structures and presents his or her story.

Narrator: The teller of a story. The narrator may be the author or a character in the story through whom the author speaks.

Naturalism: A literary movement of the late nineteenth and early twentieth centuries. The movement's major theorist, French novelist Emile Zola, envisioned a type of fiction that would examine human life with the objectivity of scientific inquiry. The Naturalists typically viewed human beings as either the products of "biological determinism," ruled by hereditary instincts and engaged in an endless struggle for survival, or as the products of "socioeconomic determinism," ruled by social and economic forces beyond their control. In their works, the Naturalists generally ignored the highest levels of society and focused on degradation: poverty, alcoholism, prostitution, insanity, and disease.

Noble Savage: The idea that primitive man is noble and good but becomes evil and corrupted as he becomes civilized. The concept of the noble savage originated in the Renaissance period but is more closely identified with such later writers as

Jean-Jacques Rousseau and Aphra Behn. See also Primitivism.

Novel of Ideas: A novel in which the examination of intellectual issues and concepts takes precedence over characterization or a traditional storyline.

Novel of Manners: A novel that examines the customs and mores of a cultural group.

Novel: A long fictional narrative written in prose, which developed from the novella and other early forms of narrative. A novel is usually organized under a plot or theme with a focus on character development and action.

Novella: An Italian term meaning "story." This term has been especially used to describe fourteenth-century Italian tales, but it also refers to modern short novels.

O

Objective Correlative: An outward set of objects, a situation, or a chain of events corresponding to an inward experience and evoking this experience in the reader. The term frequently appears in modern criticism in discussions of authors' intended effects on the emotional responses of readers.

Objectivity: A quality in writing characterized by the absence of the author's opinion or feeling about the subject matter. Objectivity is an important factor in criticism.

Oedipus Complex: A son's amorous obsession with his mother. The phrase is derived from the story of the ancient Theban hero Oedipus, who unknowingly killed his father and married his mother.

Omniscience: See *Point of View*

Onomatopoeia: The use of words whose sounds express or suggest their meaning. In its simplest sense, onomatopoeia may be represented by words that mimic the sounds they denote such as "hiss" or "meow." At a more subtle level, the pattern and rhythm of sounds and rhymes of a line or poem may be onomatopoeic.

Oxymoron: A phrase combining two contradictory terms. Oxymorons may be intentional or unintentional.

P

Parable: A story intended to teach a moral lesson or answer an ethical question.

Paradox: A statement that appears illogical or contradictory at first, but may actually point to an underlying truth.

Parallelism: A method of comparison of two ideas in which each is developed in the same grammatical structure.

Parody: In literary criticism, this term refers to an imitation of a serious literary work or the signature style of a particular author in a ridiculous manner. A typical parody adopts the style of the original and applies it to an inappropriate subject for humorous effect. Parody is a form of satire and could be considered the literary equivalent of a caricature or cartoon.

Pastoral: A term derived from the Latin word "pastor," meaning shepherd. A pastoral is a literary composition on a rural theme. The conventions of the pastoral were originated by the third-century Greek poet Theocritus, who wrote about the experiences, love affairs, and pastimes of Sicilian shepherds. In a pastoral, characters and language of a courtly nature are often placed in a simple setting. The term pastoral is also used to classify dramas, elegies, and lyrics that exhibit the use of country settings and shepherd characters.

Pen Name: See *Pseudonym*

Persona: A Latin term meaning "mask." *Personae* are the characters in a fictional work of literature. The *persona* generally functions as a mask through which the author tells a story in a voice other than his or her own. A *persona* is usually either a character in a story who acts as a narrator or an "implied author," a voice created by the author to act as the narrator for himself or herself.

Personification: A figure of speech that gives human qualities to abstract ideas, animals, and inanimate objects. Also known as *Prosopopoeia*.

Picaresque Novel: Episodic fiction depicting the adventures of a roguish central character ("picaro" is Spanish for "rogue"). The picaresque hero is commonly a low-born but clever individual who wanders into and out of various affairs of love, danger, and farcical intrigue. These involvements may take place at all social levels and typically present a humorous and wide-ranging satire of a given society.

Plagiarism: Claiming another person's written material as one's own. Plagiarism can take the form of direct, word-for-word copying or the theft of the substance or idea of the work.

Plot: In literary criticism, this term refers to the pattern of events in a narrative or drama. In its simplest sense, the plot guides the author in composing the work and helps the reader follow the work. Typically, plots exhibit causality and unity and have a beginning, a middle, and an end. Sometimes, however, a plot may consist of a series of disconnected events, in which case it is known as an "episodic plot."

Poetic Justice: An outcome in a literary work, not necessarily a poem, in which the good are rewarded and the evil are punished, especially in ways that particularly fit their virtues or crimes.

Poetic License: Distortions of fact and literary convention made by a writer—not always a poet—for the sake of the effect gained. Poetic license is closely related to the concept of "artistic freedom."

Poetics: This term has two closely related meanings. It denotes (1) an aesthetic theory in literary criticism about the essence of poetry or (2) rules prescribing the proper methods, content, style, or diction of poetry. The term poetics may also refer to theories about literature in general, not just poetry.

Point of View: The narrative perspective from which a literary work is presented to the reader. There are four traditional points of view. The "third person omniscient" gives the reader a "godlike" perspective, unrestricted by time or place, from which to see actions and look into the minds of characters. This allows the author to comment openly on characters and events in the work. The "third person" point of view presents the events of the story from outside of any single character's perception, much like the omniscient point of view, but the reader must understand the action as it takes place and without any special insight into characters' minds or motivations. The "first person" or "personal" point of view relates events as they are perceived by a single character. The main character "tells" the story and may offer opinions about the action and characters which differ from those of the author. Much less common than omniscient, third person, and first person is the "second person" point of view, wherein the author tells the story as if it is happening to the reader.

Polemic: A work in which the author takes a stand on a controversial subject, such as abortion or religion. Such works are often extremely argumentative or provocative.

Pornography: Writing intended to provoke feelings of lust in the reader. Such works are often condemned by critics and teachers, but those which can be shown to have literary value are viewed less harshly.

Post-Aesthetic Movement: An artistic response made by African Americans to the black aesthetic movement of the 1960s and early '70s. Writers since that time have adopted a somewhat different tone in their work, with less emphasis placed on the disparity between black and white in the United States. In the words of post-aesthetic authors such as Toni Morrison, John Edgar Wideman, and Kristin Hunter, African Americans are portrayed as looking inward for answers to their own questions, rather than always looking to the outside world.

Postmodernism: Writing from the 1960s forward characterized by experimentation and continuing to apply some of the fundamentals of modernism, which included existentialism and alienation. Postmodernists have gone a step further in the rejection of tradition begun with the modernists by also rejecting traditional forms, preferring the anti-novel over the novel and the antihero over the hero.

Primitivism: The belief that primitive peoples were nobler and less flawed than civilized peoples because they had not been subjected to the tainting influence of society. See also Noble Savage.

Prologue: An introductory section of a literary work. It often contains information establishing the situation of the characters or presents information about the setting, time period, or action. In drama, the prologue is spoken by a chorus or by one of the principal characters.

Prose: A literary medium that attempts to mirror the language of everyday speech. It is distinguished from poetry by its use of unmetered, unrhymed language consisting of logically related sentences. Prose is usually grouped into paragraphs that form a cohesive whole such as an essay or a novel.

Prosopopoeia: See *Personification*

Protagonist: The central character of a story who serves as a focus for its themes and incidents and as the principal rationale for its development. The protagonist is sometimes referred to in discussions of modern literature as the hero or antihero.

Protest Fiction: Protest fiction has as its primary purpose the protesting of some social injustice, such as racism or discrimination.

Proverb: A brief, sage saying that expresses a truth about life in a striking manner.

Pseudonym: A name assumed by a writer, most often intended to prevent his or her identification as the author of a work. Two or more authors may work together under one pseudonym, or an author may use a different name for each genre he or she publishes in. Some publishing companies maintain "house pseudonyms," under which any number of authors may write installations in a series. Some authors also choose a pseudonym over their real names the way an actor may use a stage name.

Pun: A play on words that have similar sounds but different meanings.

R

Realism: A nineteenth-century European literary movement that sought to portray familiar characters, situations, and settings in a realistic manner. This was done primarily by using an objective narrative point of view and through the buildup of accurate detail. The standard for success of any realistic work depends on how faithfully it transfers common experience into fictional forms. The realistic method may be altered or extended, as in stream of consciousness writing, to record highly subjective experience.

Repartee: Conversation featuring snappy retorts and witticisms.

Resolution: The portion of a story following the climax, in which the conflict is resolved. See also *Denouement*.

Rhetoric: In literary criticism, this term denotes the art of ethical persuasion. In its strictest sense, rhetoric adheres to various principles developed since classical times for arranging facts and ideas in a clear, persuasive, appealing manner. The term is also used to refer to effective prose in general and theories of or methods for composing effective prose.

Rhetorical Question: A question intended to provoke thought, but not an expressed answer, in the reader. It is most commonly used in oratory and other persuasive genres.

Rising Action: The part of a drama where the plot becomes increasingly complicated. Rising action leads up to the climax, or turning point, of a drama.

Roman a clef: A French phrase meaning "novel with a key." It refers to a narrative in which real persons are portrayed under fictitious names.

Romance: A broad term, usually denoting a narrative with exotic, exaggerated, often idealized characters, scenes, and themes.

Romanticism: This term has two widely accepted meanings. In historical criticism, it refers to a European intellectual and artistic movement of the late eighteenth and early nineteenth centuries that sought greater freedom of personal expression than that allowed by the strict rules of literary form and logic of the eighteenth-century neoclassicists. The Romantics preferred emotional and imaginative expression to rational analysis. They considered the individual to be at the center of all experience and so placed him or her at the center of their art. The Romantics believed that the creative imagination reveals nobler truths—unique feelings and attitudes—than those that could be discovered by logic or by scientific examination. Both the natural world and the state of childhood were important sources for revelations of "eternal truths." "Romanticism" is also used as a general term to refer to a type of sensibility found in all periods of literary history and usually considered to be in opposition to the principles of classicism. In this sense, Romanticism signifies any work or philosophy in which the exotic or dreamlike figure strongly, or that is devoted to individualistic expression, self-analysis, or a pursuit of a higher realm of knowledge than can be discovered by human reason.

Romantics: See *Romanticism*

S

Satire: A work that uses ridicule, humor, and wit to criticize and provoke change in human nature and institutions. There are two major types of satire: "formal" or "direct" satire speaks directly to the reader or to a character in the work; "indirect" satire relies upon the ridiculous behavior of its characters to make its point. Formal satire is further divided into two manners: the "Horatian," which ridicules gently, and the "Juvenalian," which derides its subjects harshly and bitterly.

Science Fiction: A type of narrative about or based upon real or imagined scientific theories and technology. Science fiction is often peopled with alien creatures and set on other planets or in different dimensions.

Second Person: See *Point of View*

Setting: The time, place, and culture in which the action of a narrative takes place. The elements of setting may include geographic location, characters' physical and mental environments, prevailing cultural attitudes, or the historical time in which the action takes place.

Simile: A comparison, usually using "like" or "as", of two essentially dissimilar things, as in "coffee as cold as ice" or "He sounded like a broken record."

Slang: A type of informal verbal communication that is generally unacceptable for formal writing. Slang words and phrases are often colorful exaggerations used to emphasize the speaker's point; they may also be shortened versions of an often-used word or phrase.

Slave Narrative: Autobiographical accounts of American slave life as told by escaped slaves. These works first appeared during the abolition movement of the 1830s through the 1850s.

Socialist Realism: The Socialist Realism school of literary theory was proposed by Maxim Gorky and established as a dogma by the first Soviet Congress of Writers. It demanded adherence to a communist worldview in works of literature. Its doctrines required an objective viewpoint comprehensible to the working classes and themes of social struggle featuring strong proletarian heroes. Also known as Social Realism.

Stereotype: A stereotype was originally the name for a duplication made during the printing process; this led to its modern definition as a person or thing that is (or is assumed to be) the same as all others of its type.

Stream of Consciousness: A narrative technique for rendering the inward experience of a character. This technique is designed to give the impression of an ever-changing series of thoughts, emotions, images, and memories in the spontaneous and seemingly illogical order that they occur in life.

Structure: The form taken by a piece of literature. The structure may be made obvious for ease of understanding, as in nonfiction works, or may be obscured for artistic purposes, as in some poetry or seemingly "unstructured" prose.

***Sturm und Drang*:** A German term meaning "storm and stress." It refers to a German literary movement of the 1770s and 1780s that reacted against the order and rationalism of the enlightenment, focusing instead on the intense experience of extraordinary individuals.

Style: A writer's distinctive manner of arranging words to suit his or her ideas and purpose in writing. The unique imprint of the author's personality upon his or her writing, style is the product of an author's way of arranging ideas and his or her use of diction, different sentence structures, rhythm, figures of speech, rhetorical principles, and other elements of composition.

Subjectivity: Writing that expresses the author's personal feelings about his subject, and which may or may not include factual information about the subject.

Subplot: A secondary story in a narrative. A subplot may serve as a motivating or complicating force for the main plot of the work, or it may provide emphasis for, or relief from, the main plot.

Surrealism: A term introduced to criticism by Guillaume Apollinaire and later adopted by Andre Breton. It refers to a French literary and artistic movement founded in the 1920s. The Surrealists sought to express unconscious thoughts and feelings in their works. The best-known technique used for achieving this aim was automatic writing—transcriptions of spontaneous outpourings from the unconscious. The Surrealists proposed to unify the contrary levels of conscious and unconscious, dream and reality, objectivity and subjectivity into a new level of "super-realism."

Suspense: A literary device in which the author maintains the audience's attention through the buildup of events, the outcome of which will soon be revealed.

Symbol: Something that suggests or stands for something else without losing its original identity. In literature, symbols combine their literal meaning with the suggestion of an abstract concept. Literary symbols are of two types: those that carry complex associations of meaning no matter what their contexts, and those that derive their suggestive meaning from their functions in specific literary works.

Symbolism: This term has two widely accepted meanings. In historical criticism, it denotes an early modernist literary movement initiated in France during the nineteenth century that reacted against the prevailing standards of realism. Writers in this movement aimed to evoke, indirectly and symbolically, an order of being beyond the material world of the five senses. Poetic expression of personal emotion figured strongly in the movement, typically by means of a private set of symbols uniquely identifiable with the individual poet. The principal aim of the Symbolists was to express in words the highly complex feelings that grew out of everyday contact with the world. In a broader sense, the term "symbolism" refers to the use of one object to represent another.

T

Tall Tale: A humorous tale told in a straightforward, credible tone but relating absolutely impossible events or feats of the characters. Such tales were commonly told of frontier adventures during the settlement of the west in the United States.

Theme: The main point of a work of literature. The term is used interchangeably with thesis.

Thesis: A thesis is both an essay and the point argued in the essay. Thesis novels and thesis plays share the quality of containing a thesis which is supported through the action of the story.

Third Person: See *Point of View*

Tone: The author's attitude toward his or her audience may be deduced from the tone of the work. A formal tone may create distance or convey politeness, while an informal tone may encourage a friendly, intimate, or intrusive feeling in the reader. The author's attitude toward his or her subject matter may also be deduced from the tone of the words he or she uses in discussing it.

Transcendentalism: An American philosophical and religious movement, based in New England from around 1835 until the Civil War. Transcendentalism was a form of American romanticism that had its roots abroad in the works of Thomas Carlyle, Samuel Coleridge, and Johann Wolfgang von Goethe. The Transcendentalists stressed the importance of intuition and subjective experience in communication with God. They rejected religious dogma and texts in favor of mysticism and scientific naturalism. They pursued truths that lie beyond the "colorless" realms perceived by reason and the senses and were active social reformers in public education, women's rights, and the abolition of slavery.

U

Urban Realism: A branch of realist writing that attempts to accurately reflect the often harsh facts of modern urban existence.

Utopia: A fictional perfect place, such as "paradise" or "heaven."

V

Verisimilitude: Literally, the appearance of truth. In literary criticism, the term refers to aspects of a work of literature that seem true to the reader.

Victorian: Refers broadly to the reign of Queen Victoria of England (1837-1901) and to anything with qualities typical of that era. For example, the qualities of smug narrowmindedness, bourgeois materialism, faith in social progress, and priggish morality are often considered Victorian. This stereotype is contradicted by such dramatic intellectual developments as the theories of Charles Darwin, Karl Marx, and Sigmund Freud (which stirred strong debates in England) and the critical attitudes of serious Victorian writers like Charles Dickens and George Eliot. In literature, the Victorian Period was the great age of the English novel, and the latter part of the era saw the rise of movements such as decadence and symbolism. Also known as Victorian Age and Victorian Period.

W

Weltanschauung: A German term referring to a person's worldview or philosophy.

Weltschmerz: A German term meaning "world pain." It describes a sense of anguish about the nature of existence, usually associated with a melancholy, pessimistic attitude.

Z

Zeitgeist: A German term meaning "spirit of the time." It refers to the moral and intellectual trends of a given era.

Cumulative Author/Title Index

Numerical

1984 (Orwell): V7

A

Absalom, Absalom! (Faulkner): V13
The Accidental Tourist (Tyler): V7
Achebe, Chinua
    Things Fall Apart: V2
Adams, Douglas
    The Hitchhiker's Guide to the
        Galaxy: V7
Adams, Richard
    Watership Down: V11
The Adventures of Huckleberry Finn
    (Twain): V1
The Adventures of Tom Sawyer
    (Twain): V6
The Age of Innocence (Wharton): V11
Alcott, Louisa May
    Little Women: V12
Alice's Adventures in Wonderland
    (Carroll): V7
All the King's Men (Warren): V13
Allende, Isabel
    The House of the Spirits: V6
Allison, Dorothy
    Bastard Out of Carolina: V11
All Quiet on the Western Front
    (Remarque): V4
Alvarez, Julia
    How the García Girls Lost Their
        Accents: V5
    In the Time of the Butterflies: V9
Always Coming Home (Le Guin): V9
The Ambassadors (James): V12
Anaya, Rudolfo
    Bless Me, Ultima: V12

Anderson, Sherwood
    Winesburg, Ohio: V4
Angelou, Maya
    I Know Why the Caged Bird
        Sings: V2
Animal Dreams (Kingsolver): V12
Animal Farm (Orwell): V3
Annie John (Kincaid): V3
Appointment in Samarra (O'Hara):
    V11
As I Lay Dying (Faulkner): V8
Atlas Shrugged (Rand): V10
Atwood, Margaret
    Cat's Eye: V14
    The Handmaid's Tale: V4
    Surfacing: V13
Auel, Jean
    The Clan of the Cave Bear: V11
Austen, Jane
    Persuasion: V14
    Pride and Prejudice: V1
The Autobiography of Miss Jane
    Pittman (Gaines): V5
The Awakening (Chopin): V3

B

Baldwin, James
    Go Tell It on the Mountain: V4
Ballard, J. G.
    Empire of the Sun: V8
Banks, Russell
    The Sweet Hereafter: V13
Bastard Out of Carolina (Allison): V11
Baum, L. Frank
    The Wonderful Wizard of Oz: V13
The Bean Trees (Kingsolver): V5
The Bell Jar (Plath): V1

Bellow, Saul
    Herzog: V14
    Seize the Day: V4
Beloved (Morrison): V6
Betsey Brown (Shange): V11
Billy Budd, Sailor: An Inside
    Narrative (Melville): V9
Black Boy (Wright): V1
Blair, Eric Arthur
    Animal Farm: V3
Bless Me, Ultima (Anaya): V12
The Bluest Eye (Morrison): V1
Body and Soul (Conroy): V11
Bowen, Elizabeth Dorothea Cole
    The Death of the Heart: V13
Bradbury, Ray
    Fahrenheit 451: V1
Brave New World (Huxley): V6
Breathing Lessons (Tyler): V10
The Bride Price (Emecheta): V12
Brideshead Revisited (Waugh): V13
Brontë, Charlotte
    Jane Eyre: V4
Brontë, Emily
    Wuthering Heights: V2
The Brothers Karamazov
    (Dostoevsky): V8
Brown, Rita Mae
    Rubyfruit Jungle: V9
Bulgakov, Mikhail
    The Master and Margarita: V8
Butler, Octavia
    Kindred: V8

C

The Caine Mutiny: A Novel of World
    War II (Wouk): V7